Death on the Gallows
The Encyclopedia of Legal Hangings in Texas

By: West C. Gilbreath

www.WildHorsePress.com

Copyright © 2017
By West Gilbreath
Published By Wild Horse Press
An Imprint of Wild Horse Media Group
P.O. Box 331779
Fort Worth, Texas 76163
1-817-344-7036
www.WildHorseMedia.com
ALL RIGHTS RESERVED
1 2 3 4 5 6 7 8 9
ISBN-10: 1-68179-051-3
ISBN-13: 978-1-68179-051-0

Cover Design By

Flying Gorilla Studios

www.FlyingGorillaStudios.com

Table of Contents

Anderson 1	Gonzales 141	Nueces 277
Atascosa 3	Grayson 147	Orange 280
Austin 4	Gregg 154	Palo Pinto 282
Bastrop 7	Grimes 157	Parker 283
Bee 13	Guadalupe 158	Polk 285
Bell 15	Hardin 161	Presidio 288
Bexar 19	Harris 162	Rains 290
Bowie 32	Harrison 180	Red River 291
Brazoria 34	Hays 184	Reeves 296
Brazos 36	Henderson 185	Refugio 298
Brewster 39	Hidalgo 187	Robertson 299
Burleson 40	Hill 188	Rusk 303
Burnet 42	Hood 190	Sabine 305
Caldwell 43	Houston 192	San Augustine 306
Calhoun 44	Hunt 195	San Jacinto 308
Callahan 45	Jack 199	San Patricio 309
Cameron 46	Jasper 200	Shelby 310
Camp 50	Jefferson 201	Smith 312
Cass 51	Johnson 205	Tarrant 313
Castro 54	Karnes 212	Taylor 323
Chambers 55	Kaufman 214	Titus 325
Cherokee 56	Kinney 218	Travis 326
Coleman 60	Lamar 220	Trinity 337
Collin 62	La Salle 229	Tyler 338
Colorado 66	Lavaca 231	Uvalde 339
Cooke 73	Lee 233	Val Verde 340
Coryell 75	Liberty 237	Van Zandt 341
Dallas 77	Limestone 239	Victoria 342
Delta 90	Live Oak 242	Walker 344
Denton 91	Matagorda 244	Washington 349
DeWitt 94	Maverick 245	Webb 354
Donley 97	McLennan 247	Wharton 358
Duval 99	Medina 258	Wilbarger 363
Ellis 100	Menard 259	Williamson 365
El Paso 107	Midland 260	Wilson 370
Erath 113	Milam 262	Wise 373
Falls 115	Montague 263	Young 374
Fannin 122	Montgomery 266	Hangings by Alphabetical Order . 376
Fayette 127	Morris 267	Hangings in Chronological Order . 386
Fort Bend 130	Nacogdoches 268	Sources 396
Freestone 134	Navarro 271	Author Bio 407
Galveston 136	Newton 276	

*In dedication to the memory of my brother,
James A. Gilbreath (Oct. 31, 1959 – Jan. 11, 1975)
whose death guided me into a lifetime career in law enforcement.*

Preface

Texans, in general, have always been very proud of their state, western heritage, history, and the reputation of being the toughest state when it comes to punishing criminals. This reputation can easily be said to have started before Texas was a Republic when the first legal execution occurred in 1834 in Nacogdoches.

Many people today believe hangings were all conducted from tree limbs as featured in early western movies, or because various plaques in Texas town's identified a certain tree within the courthouse square as being the county's "hanging tree." When in fact, the plaque should have read that the tree had been used for the purpose of lynchings, as the law required that executions would be from a constructed gallows. Texas law later directed the sheriffs to conduct the hanging in private from within the walls of the jail when available. If not, the law limited the number of those who were allowed to be present. Several historic jails when constructed had chambers, towers or high ceilings for a gallows in anticipation of having to execute a person in their county.

At the same time, many believe that the hanging of a criminal was first developed in the Wild West as a form of western justice, when in all reality this form of punishment was brought to America with the arrival of pilgrims from England. The first execution in the New World took place at Jamestown, Virginia, in the fall of 1608. That execution, however, was not at the end of a rope, but rather by firing squad when Captain George Kendall was executed after he was tried and found guilty of being a spy for Spain. The first legal hanging took place on September 30, 1630, at Plymouth Colony, Massachusetts, when John Billington was tried for the shooting death of John Newcomer whom he viewed as his enemy.

After researching and publishing, *Death on the Gallows, The Story of the Legal Hangings in New Mexico*, I again became curious as to how many legal hangings had occurred in Texas before the state changed the method to electrocution in 1923. Because of the change in the law, Texas law removed the responsibility from the county sheriff to the state in order to electrocute the condemned. Many county sheriffs welcomed the change of not having to execute a person, whereas other sheriffs viewed the task as their duty along with the $30 fee each received for serving the court order.

At the same time, I was curious to know how many counties in Texas performed executions. I wanted to know what were the names of the people legally executed, how many of those were women, and what was the largest number of executions held at one time in Texas. I also wanted to know if the circumstances of crimes committed in Texas were similar to those in New Mexico. Crimes such as train robbery, saloon shootouts, raids by border bandits, assaults on women, and the murder of travelers crossing through the desert during their journey to the next town. The answer was yes and more. Those executed in Texas committed murders during land feuds or over politics. They shot and killed lawmen while making arrests or escapes from jails, murdered during train robberies, and raped of women. Mexican bandits crossed over into the U.S. to commit raids of towns, while others murdered travelers or their companions for the purpose of taking their possessions. At the same time, I was surprised at the number of murders committed against the person's spouse, loved ones or because a woman rejected his courtship or marriage proposal.

I also wondered if Texas law was similar to the laws that I had written about in New Mexico. The research for this book showed a vast difference from both. Texas being a Republic in 1836, enacted the death penalty by hanging those guilty of committing murder, arson, rape, robbery, burglary, slave stealing, escape from confinement or counterfeiting money. In pre-Civil War, death penalty crimes were enacted toward slaves for assaulting or murdering their owner or sexually assaulting women.

However, the laws for death penalty cases did differ. In New Mexico, if a defendant's case was moved to another county for trial on a change of venue and if he or she was found guilty, the defendant was returned back to the county where the crime was committed to await execution. In Texas, the prisoner was executed in the county where he was found guilty, regardless of the change of venue. For example, all three men executed jn Denton County were granted a change of venue from Cooke and Montague County.

Although, both states automatically provided the condemned a thirty-day stay to file an appeal to the higher court, Texas allowed the prisoner the option to waive the time period and to be executed immediately. Men such as Dick Garrett in Shelby County were tried, and hanged all in the span of four days after committing a murder. Henry Johnson of Kaufman County was captured, tried, and executed within five days of committing a rape.

During the Civil War, "citizen's courts" were held in Decatur, Wise County and Cooke whereby citizens were accused for being sympathizers of the Union. They were tried for treason and afterward hanged from tree limbs outside the county courthouse. Those instances are only noted here as the victims were not afforded the due process from a court, an appeal process, or charged with a state criminal offense.

Texas has 254 counties of which, 122 counties executed criminals for the crimes they were found guilty of. This is not to say this book has identified all people legally hanged. On December 28, 1850, Howard Slaughter was hanged in Cameron County for murder. Two Mexican men who were also hanged for murder with Slaughter have not been identified or the circumstances of the crime they committed for which they were executed. Court records and early newspapers that reported the execution are at times difficult to locate.

Many criminals, who were sentenced to death by the court, later escaped the noose by receiving commutation from the governor, committing suicide, or dying from other causes while incarcerated. Others escaped or were lynched by an angry town mob who wanted to ensure punishment was swift because of the heinous crime the offender was accused of committing. In Texas, it was not unusual for vigilante mobs to storm county jails and forcibly remove the prisoner for swift justice. At the same time, sheriffs used every precaution in an effort to protect the prisoner. Sheriffs often called upon the militia, Texas Rangers, and swore in trusted citizens as special deputies to protect the jail from being overtaken. Other times, sheriffs took extreme measures while placing themselves in danger to transport the prisoner to a larger and stronger jail for the prisoner's protection until trial. Many times, the last words spoken by the condemned before the spectators on the gallows was his appreciation to the sheriff, his deputies, and jailers for the kind treatment and protection given to him.

Of the 467 hanged, three of the condemned were women, and all of the women were accused of committing murder. Jane Elkins was hanged on May 27, 1853, in Dallas, Lucy Dougherty on March 5, 1858, in Galveston, and Josefa "Chipita" Rodriguez on November 13, 1863 in San Patricio.

Texas held the second largest single execution event in the country. The largest occurred on December 26, 1862, when thirty-eight Dakota people were convicted of rape and murder and were all executed at the same time from a four-sided platform in Mankato, Minnesota. In 1917, thirteen United States soldiers from the 24th Infantry Division were hanged in Bexar County for murder and mutiny when they took part in the Houston riot on August 23, 1917. All thirteen were hanged at the same time from a massive gallows that had been built in secret, overnight by the Army Corp of Engineers. After President Woodrow Wilson reviewed the case and the soldiers' involvement, he approved of another six infantrymen being executed by hanging.

As viewed from photographs and early newspaper accounts, sometimes thousands of men, women, and children traveled from surrounding counties by horseback, buggy, and train to attend an execution, while the town stores closed so they too could attend. Boys climbed trees or telephone poles, while homeowners sold space on their rooftops to spectators so they could have a bird's eye view of the gallows. Spectators expected the condemned to walk to the scaffold with a "firm step" and to "die game."

On the other hand, the crowd had expectations of the sheriff as to how he conducted the execution. Because women and children were among the spectators, those present did not want to visibly see the condemned suffer by strangulation or die from decapitation. They wanted the prisoner to die from a broken neck. For that reason, it was not uncommon for the sheriff to borrow a rope from another county sheriff who had used the rope in several previous hangings as his "lucky charm." In other instances, the sheriff built a "trap" around the base of the scaffold with wood planks or used canvas tarps to shield the body from view should the rope cut into the neck.

At the same time, those present took the opportunity to socialize with friends and family, but also expected to be entertained by speeches from politicians, religious services, and hoped the condemned person would provide a last statement and confess his or her guilt. An example of this was when a newspaper commented days prior to the execution of Lee Hughes in Washington County, that the execution would bring a larger crowd than the approaching circus arriving in town.

In closing, it was my intent to provide a more accurate and factual account than previously available of each person, date, location, and crime that was committed.

West C. Gilbreath

Anderson County
County Seat - Palestine

Charles Thomas

Alias: Chess Thomas
Offense: Murder
Execution: August 11, 1882
Race/Gender: Black Male
Offense Date: March 6, 1881
Age: 35
Weapon: Pistol

On Sunday morning, March 6, 1881, as the church bells rang, families dressed in their Sunday best rode into Palestine in their wagons, and buggies, to attend church.

Charles Thomas, better known as Chess was working at a saloon on Spring Street where he was employed. On that morning, Houston McMeans arrived at the saloon drunk as he had been drinking throughout the night. Thomas and Houston were not on friendly terms because Henry Micheaux and Thomas had swore to written affidavits, and later each testified as witness against McMeans on a complaint of unlawful gambling. McMeans as a result was heavily fined and claimed that both Thomas and Micheaux had sworn a lie against him, and for that reason he intended to "cut their bowels out."

While at the saloon, McMeans asked Thomas to join him in a drink, which he refused. McMeans then asked for Thomas to assist him in hitching up a horse at the stable so that he could to do some hauling. Thomas at this point began pushing McMeans towards the front door and telling him to get out. Once McMeans was outside and standing on the street, Thomas drew his pistol and shot him in the back.

McMeans took off running into an adjoining alley in an attempt to escape. Thomas pursued after him and fired two more shots as he chased McMeans. After McMeans collapsed on the steps of the Advocate Building, Thomas raised his pistol to fire a final shot, but he city marshal arrived just in time and knocked the pistol away. McMeans then begged for someone to bring his wife to him so he could see her one last time before he died. He then gave a dying declaration and died at 3 p.m. that afternoon.

After the Court of Appeals affirmed the conviction, the gallows was erected within the jail corridor making the execution private, except for the 300 witnesses invited. On the scaffold, Thomas said the killing of Houston McMeans was in self-defense, but that he had no regrets, and was resigned to his fate. Thomas then turned to Sheriff Henry Davis and said, "Hang me high and let me die easily."

After the legs were bound and hands tied, Sheriff Davis asked, "Are you ready?"

From under the black cap, Thomas answered, "yes." The rope holding the trap was cut with an ax, dropping Charles "Chess" Thomas to his death. After hanging for fifteen minutes, he was pronounced dead.

Charles Thomas was born into slavery and took the last name of Thomas from his master. Thomas was believed to be thirty-five years-old and was said to have killed four men in Palestine, but was acquitted in each case as he was justified while in defense of his own life.

The *Evening Light* (San Antonio), Saturday, August 12, 1882, provided their readers with details of the crime and execution.

George Kenny
(Also spelled as Kenney)

Race/Gender: Black Male
Execution: May 28, 1904
Offense: Rape
Offense Date: August 21, 1903

George Kenny was employed as a section hand for the International and Great Northern Railroad, when he raped the daughter of the section foreman. On the day of the crime, at the town of Elkhart, Kenny was recuperating from a gunshot wound, when he saw three-year-old Adelie Hawkins playing by herself in the yard. Kenny told the girl that he wanted to get the "ticks" off of her and carried the child into the house where he assaulted her. When the child's mother returned from her ironing, she quickly reported the crime. A posse was quickly organized and searched for the criminal. The following morning, the posse had tracked Kenny to Grapeland and after being wounded by the posse was captured and taken to Palestine and put in jail.

On March 9, 1904, the Texas Court of Appeals affirmed the conviction of Kenny, and returned the case back to the court for sentencing. On April 25, 1904, at 3 p.m. Deputy Barrett escorted George Kenny from the jail to the courthouse for sentencing. Judge Gooch directed Kenny to stand and he asked if Kenny had anything to say why sentence should not be passed upon him.

Photo of the Last Hanging to take place in Anderson County, Photograph, ca. 1904. *Courtesy of Anderson County Historical Commission, Palestine, Texas.*

Kenny replied, "Yes, I am innocent." Kenny then asked for his lawyers to write the Governor and request that his sentence be commuted to life in the penitentiary. Showing no signs of concern for the death sentence being passed upon him, he turned to Deputy Barrett and asked if he would give him money so that he could buy tobacco.

On May 23, 1904, Sheriff Henry Watts received a letter from the Governor informing him that he was declining to interfere with the execution. When told of this, Kenny requested that his execution be made public. The gallows was erected at the old Crawford Brickyard south of town near the railroad tracks within a deep depression. The location gave the appearance of an amphitheater and provided the 6,000 spectators with a good view of the execution.

From the gallows, Kenny spoke for three minutes protesting his innocence and warning the young men of his race to live good lives. Kenny said he was at peace with God and going straight to heaven. He then urged the black race to all vote for the re-election of Sheriff Henry Watts who had treated him good and who had saved him from being lynched by a mob. As the black cap was pulled over the head, Kenny bade all those present, "goodbye."

The *Palestine Daily Herald*, dated Saturday, May 28, 1904, provided their readers with details of the crime and execution.

Atascosa County
County Seat - Jourdanton

Porfirio Torres

Race/Gender: Hispanic Male **Offense:** Murder **Offense Date:** October 25, 1913
Weapon: .44 caliber Rifle **Execution:** August 14, 1914

Atascosa County's only legal execution was the result of a change of venue from La Salle County. On the night of October 25, 1913, rancher Ike Hill arrived at Brigida Potino's home to pick up his laundry he had dropped off earlier in the day to be washed. As the rancher spoke with the woman, Porfirio Torrez rode up on a grey mare. Ms. Potino expressed to Ike that she was afraid of Torrez and was concerned for her safety. When Torres approached, Ike and Torres exchanged words. Torres in response raised an old Springfield .44 caliber rifle and shot Ike dead.

At 11:30 a.m. on the morning of the execution, Torres was told the end was near as it was time for his execution. Torres asked the sheriff that the execution be delayed until 2 p.m. as he was expecting a reprieve from the governor. When the sheriff declined the request, Torres fought, struggled, bit and kicked the four deputies who were required to carry him out from the cell to the gallows. Torres' last words as the trap was sprung were screaming curses. His neck was broken by the fall, and left hanging for eleven minutes. The rope was the same rope that Lee Johnson in San Antonio was hanged with.

Alejandro Saril was jointly indicted with Torres for the murder, but was granted a severance in their case. District Attorney T. P. Morrison dismissed the case against Saril on November 22, 1913.

The *Galveston Daily News*, dated Saturday, August 15, 1914, provided their readers with details of the shooting and the execution at Pleasanton, Texas.

Austin County

County Seat - Bellville

Joseph Clayton

Race/Gender: White Male **Offense:** Murder **Offense Date:** June, 1834
Weapon: Knife **Execution:** July 1834

In June of 1834, at San Felipe, Joseph Clayton who was drunk at the time, stabbed fifty-seven-year-old Abner Kuykendall in the neck with a knife. The blade broke off, and Abner died a month later from tetanus, commonly referred to as lock jaw. Clayton was tried and found guilty of murder. Clayton was executed in July of 1834, and this was one of the earliest legal executions in Texas.

Miles Thompson

Race/Gender: Black Male **Age:** 21 **Offense:** Rape & Murder
Offense Date: July 19, 1880 **Weapon:** Ax **Execution:** February 17, 1882

Miles Thompson was convicted of the murder of a Mrs. Johnson at her home near Bellville. Thompson had arrived at her home at about 10 a.m. on the pretense of asking for work. When Mrs. Johnson informed him that she had no work for him, Thompson asked for food. As Mrs. Johnson turned to re-enter her home, Thompson jumped the yard fence and attacked her. Mrs. Thompson's elderly father tried to come to his daughter's rescue with an ax. Thompson took the ax away, and struck the old man in the head, fracturing his skull. Thompson afterwards raped the woman, and her father died as a result of his head wound two months later. Two days later Deputy Sheriff Glenn captured Thompson and put him in jail.

Thompson was tried and the conviction was affirmed by the court of appeals. Two days before the execution, the gallows was erected in the yard of the jail.

On the gallows, Thompson told the 2,500 witnesses that he was guilty of the crimes he had been charged with. After speaking for twenty minutes, he warned the coming generation to take heed from his example, and be obedient to their parents. Thompson bid the crowd farewell and told them that he was prepared, and ready to die and would meet them all in heaven.

At 1:36 p.m. the black cap was put over his head, and the noose was adjusted. The rope holding the trap door in place was then cut with a sharp hatchet. After hanging for fifteen minutes the body was cut down and lowered into a coffin.

The *Brenham Weekly Banner*, dated Thursday, February 23, 1882, printed a full account of the execution.

Andrew Chappell

Alias: Buck Chappell **Race/Gender:** Black Male **Age:** 18
Offense: Robbery & Murder **Offense Date:** December 18, 1895 **Weapon:** Shotgun
Execution: March 18, 1896

Clem Strawther

Race/Gender: Black Male **Age:** 23 **Offense:** Robbery & Murder
Offense Date: December 18, 1895 **Weapon:** Shotgun **Execution:** March 18, 1896

Andrew Chappell was hanged on March 18, 1896, for the robbery and murder of Dora Ernshoff. On the evening of December 18, 1895, Ernshoff was traveling home after selling her cotton crop. In the back of the wagon was Ernshoff's nine-year-old daughter Clara who was asleep in the bed of the wagon wrapped in a blanket. During the trip, a unknown man stepped out in the road and ordered Ernshoff to come to a stop. Clara woke up and peeked out from under the blanket and saw a man pointing a shotgun at her mother while demanding she turn over all of her money.

After Mrs. Ernshoff refused his demand, the robber fired the shotgun hitting her in the forehead and under the right eye. The impact from the shotgun blast knocked the woman's body onto the wagon bed. At the same time, the shotgun blast frightened the horses into a running gallop. Little Clara climbed out from under the blanket and over her mother's body to take control of the horse reins and drive the team for help.

Clem Steauther and Andrew Chappel on the gallows.
Courtesy of the Bellville Historical Society, Bellville, Texas.

The sheriff tracked the killer down with a bloodhound to Chappell's father's house and apprehended Andrew Chappell. On January 3, 1896, Chappell was found guilty and sentenced to hang on the same day as Clem Strawther.

Clem Strawther was hanged on March 18, 1896, for the murder of Alois Peters. Peters was shot to death with a shotgun while he was sleeping in his bed at his home in Wallis, Texas.

The shotgun Strawther used to shoot Peters had been loaded with various pieces of scrape iron. Taking the shotgun, Strawther crept up outside the bedroom Peters was sleeping in. Strawther stuck the barrel of the weapon through the open window and fired the weapon at what he believed was Peters' head. Peters, however was lying in the opposite direction. The wounds Peters received to his legs were filled with iron, bedding and feathers from the bed. In severe pain, Peters died the next day from loss of blood as the doctor was amputating his feet. Strawther dropped the shotgun which was recovered by the sheriff. The owner was identified and explained he had lent the weapon to Clem Strawther.

On January 18, 1896, Strawther was tried and took the stand in his own defense. While testifying, Strawther first attempted to blame the murder on a Roy Justice, but during cross-examination by the state, he confessed that he had shot and killed Peters. Strawther then changed his plea from not guilty to guilty, and begged for mercy before the court. The jury deliberated for two hours before returning a verdict of guilty and assessed the punishment of death. Strawther was then sentenced to hang on the same day as Andrew Chappell in Bellville.

On the day of the execution, both men ate their last meal which consisted of biscuits, chicken, ham, cakes and pies. On the gallows, Strawther spoke first and told the 3,000 witnesses, "They are not hanging me innocent, but for the deeds I have done. I committed the crimes."

He warned the young black men of the effect of bad company, saying it had brought him to his ruin. He told them to stay with their mothers, as they were the best friends they had. He thanked Sheriff Glenn for the many acts of kindness he had shown him, and finished by saying, "Oh Lord! I wonder where is _____." He then bade all good by.

Buck Chappell then addressed the crowd. Chappell said he was eighteen years-old and innocent of the crime for which he was about to die. He claimed that his mother and father had forsaken him, and that it was hard for one's father and mother to go back on them. He bade all goodbye and asked them to meet him in heaven.

At 1:10 p.m. the trap was sprang in the presence of 1,000 to 3,000 witnesses. The county was afterwards billed $22.30 for the building of the scaffold and $10 for the digging of two graves.

The *Galveston Daily News*, dated Thursday, March 19, 1899, provided a full account of the crimes committed by Clem Strauther and Andrew Chappell.

Augustus Davis

Alias: Gus Davis **Race/Gender:** Black Male **Age:** 29
Offense: Murder **Weapon:** Revolver **Offense Date:** December 22, 1900
Execution: March 14, 1901

On December 22, 1900, Herman Schluens who lived three miles from town, drove his wagon into Bellville to have dinner and visit with friends. At about 4:40 p.m., Herman was outside the True Blue Saloon talking with a friend when Davis shot him in the head from behind with a revolver. Davis was immediately arrested and told the officers, "I did what I came to town to do."

Sheriff William Palm fearing a mob would retaliate for the death of the respected farmer placed Davis on a horse and with an armed guard of deputies. The officers then traveled by horseback to Brenham and then to Cameron where Davis was held until trial at the January term of District Court. Davis was afterwards convicted of murder and Judge S. R. Blake sentenced Davis to hang on March 14.

On the afternoon of the execution, the hanging was privately held with only those admitted by invitation as witnesses. After Davis declined to make a final statement. Sheriff Palm stepped to the side, and said, "Goodbye, Gus," as he pulled the lever releasing the trap.

The *Galveston Daily News*, dated Friday, March 15, 1901, provided its readers with details of the murder and execution.

Bastrop County
County Seat - Bastrop

Smith Jackson

Race/Gender: Black Male **Offense:** Murder **Offense Date:** December 23, 1876
Weapon: Rope & Lynching **Execution:** December 14, 1878

Pryor Jones

Race/Gender: Black Male **Offense:** Murder **Offense Date:** December 23, 1876
Weapon: Rope & Lynching **Execution:** December 14, 1878

In November of 1876, cattleman Bob Olive left Bastrop for Nebraska when he came upon six-year-old John Henry Owens in the road. Instead of taking the child to his parents, Olive decided to take the child with him. When the child did not return home, and had last been seen with John Black's children, a search was immediately initiated. When the child was not located, the family called upon a hoodoo spiritualist by the name of Sam Squirrelhunter for his assistance in locating the child. Squirrelhunter told the group John Black's children had killed the child by striking him with a club. The spiritualist said John Black put the body in a sack and thrown the child into a nearby creek.

Three meetings where held, whereby it was decided that Black would be taken to a location and threatened with death until he gave the location of the boy. If he should refuse to talk, Black would be killed.

At about midnight on December 23, 1876, the door of John Black's house was battered down. Black was grabbed from his bed and carried out of the house. His hands were tied and he was dragged behind the mule that Pryor Jones was riding for a mile and a half. There, a noose was placed around his neck and the rope tossed over a tree limb.

The group demanded that Black divulge the location of John Owens. When Black said he did not know where the boy was and knew nothing of his death, Black was hoisted up and then let back down. After the second time, Tom Robinson said to hang Black, as he would be the ruin of them all if turned loose. Black was pulled up a third time and the rope tied off around the tree where the body was found the next day.

Jackson and Jones were the only two people tried and convicted for the murder after other people from the group testified as state witnesses.

The gallows was constructed from large cedar posts, and was erected on the courthouse square for the public execution. On the day of the execution, both men told the crowd of 3,000 witnesses that they were going to heaven and wanted to see all of them there.

Six weeks after the disappearance of John Henry Owens, the child was returned home to his parents.

The *Galveston Daily News*, dated Sunday, December 15, 1878, provided a full account of the murder and execution.

Samuel Sampson Howard

Race/Gender: White Male **Age:** 22 **Offense:** Murder
Offense Date: June 1, 1878 **Weapon:** Double Barrel Shotgun **Execution:** June 18, 1880

Sam Howard was accused and tried for the murder of his brother-in-law, Alexander "Alex" Farmer. Farmer had partnered with Ulysses Howard in operating a general store near the town of Paige with Farmer being the principle investor. The store was not profitable, and the partnership was in the process of being dissolved when the store was partially burned down in December of 1877.

On the day of the murder, Farmer was riding across the prairie to the town of Bastrop when someone rode up to him on horseback and shot him with a charge of double buck. It was speculated afterwards that Ulysses had his brother Samuel murder Farmer in order to keep all the money, store contents and property for himself.

A few days after the murder, Ulysses was found dead upon the prairie between his father's house and the railroad depot, riddled with bullets. No one was ever arrested or charged with this murder.

On October 23, 1878, Samuel Howard was tried and found guilty of murder with the death penalty being assessed. After the Court of Criminal Appeals affirmed the lower court's decision, Judge Moore called for Samuel Howard to be brought before his court for sentencing. On April 22, 1880, as Howard stood before Judge Moore, the judge asked Howard if he had anything to say as to why the sentence of death should not be pronounced upon him.

Howard replied, "If the officers had done their duty in summoning my witnesses, I would not be condemned to die." Howard had no further statement to make, and Judge Moore ordered his execution to take place on Friday, June 18, 1880.

At 1 p.m. on the day of the execution, Howard was taken from the jail and led to the gallows which had been erected on the courthouse lawn. In the presence of 2,500 witnesses, Howard declined to make any statement or have a spiritual advisor on the scaffold with him. George Farmer, a brother of the murdered man, ascended the scaffold and asked Howard why he killed his brother Alexander.

Howard replied, "I did not do it." At 1:15 p.m. the lever was pulled, and Howard fell seven and a half feet, breaking his neck instantly.

The *Galveston Daily News*, dated Saturday, June 19, 1880, provided Samuel Howard's family history, a full account of the court proceedings and testimony of witnesses.

Tobe Cook

Alias: Henderson Cook
Offense: Rape & Murder
Execution: June 10, 1892
Race/Gender: Black Male
Offense Date: June 17, 1891
Age: 37
Weapon: Strangulation

On June 17, 1891, at about 5 p.m., sixteen-year-old Ida Bella Moore left a neighbors home after her visit to make the half mile walk home. The young girl never made it home alive. When Ida failed to return home, the sheriff was notified and a search party was immediately organized. Soon, the nude body of the girl was found in the woods near the road she had been dragged from. At the time of the murder Moore wore a large metallic breast pin with sharp points and sharp edges to it. As the murderer choked her to death, the breast pin was pressed against her throat with such violence that the pin was bent, and pressed into her neck.

At the scene, the sheriff noticed the very unusual foot impression left by the murderer. The left impression had three holes within the track, and an unusual mark that extended to the front. The right track possessed an impression of a stitching seam. When Tobe Cook was apprehended, he was wearing moccasins which had been made from old leather boot tops. The left moccasin contained three holes and the right one had the seam. Both measured the same size as that found at the murder scene. When arrested Cook had four wounds upon his right thumb and forefinger that may have been made by the breast pin.

Cook further could not account for his whereabouts at the time of the murder, and this added to his conviction and sentence of death.

After his arrest, Governor James Hogg telegraphed Sheriff G. W. Davis to "protect the prisoner at all hazards," adding, "there is a standing reward of $1000 for the arrest of each and every man who assists or engages in mob law."

Tobe Cook was indicted and tried on one count each of rape and murder. Cook was declared guilty of murder and the death sentenced assessed. After the case was appealed and affirmed, Cook was taken before Judge Hans Teichmuller for sentencing. After he directed Tobe Cook to rise from the seat. Judge Teichmuller said:

Tobe Cook, at the last term of the district court, the grand jury returned an indictment against you for the murder of Miss Ida Belle Moore; you were arraigned and tried before a jury of your own selection; unable to employ counsel, the court appointed able counsel for you, in the person of two attorneys, Hons. R. L. Batts, and R. W. Siddall; the jury returned a verdict of guilty with the death penalty; through your attorneys, application was made for a new trial, which, after careful consideration of the argument, was overruled, when your case was appealed to the appellate court which court had affirmed the sentence of the court below, have you anything now to say why the sentence of death should not be passed upon you?

Cook replied:

Yes, Judge; I am perfectly innocent of the charge, I am as innocent, Judge as a strand of hair on your head. I was never, through thirty-seven-years-old, on that farm; I am innocent of the accusation.

Judge Teichmuller replied:

Your trial has been fair and impartial; after a patient investigation of your case, you have been found guilty; the evidence against you, through circumstantial, has been voluminous and very positive; if there had been any doubt in my mind of your guilt, the fact that your case, in all its enormity, has been carefully reviewed by the appellate court, a court where no influence of passion or prejudice can reach, has destroyed every shadow of doubt; your protestations of innocence are natural, and but to be expected. I will designate Friday, the 10th day of June, 1892, as the day of your execution, when, within the walls of the county jail of Bastrop County, the sheriff will proceed to execute the sentence of the court, by hanging you until you are dead.

As the prisoner left the courthouse, he bid the crowd:

Good-bye to you all, I'll see many of you and more, but I want you to remember there is one darkey as innocent as a stran of hair on your head, going to die for the crime of another." While in jail, Cook continued to protest his innocents and saying, "ain't it harrid; I have been dragged from the old jail to LaGrange, and with handcuffs my hands, shackles on my feet and a rope around my body, I have suffered from freezing cold, till my feet and legs are swollen from the effects of the frost bite. O-h-h-h-h ain't it ha-r-r-d?

The gallows used were erected inside the jail so that the execution could be conducted in privacy. The gallows were described as being a wooded structure, about sixty-eight feet in size, with the rope hanging from a large steeple fastened in the ceiling about seventeen feet from the floor. The drop being eight feet.

On the afternoon of the scheduled day, Sheriff G. W. Davis and Deputies H. N. Bell, James Fitzwilliams, and J. F. Nash started the march with Tobe Cook to the scaffold.

Cook cried out, "Here is an innocent man dressed up for the gallows." Passing up the steps of the gallows, he said, "Here we go, here we go."

Sheriff Davis then read to him the death warrant, after which Elder Sterling Warmer conducted religious services.

The sheriff asked Cook if he wished to make a statement. Cook stepped forward and spoke for twenty-five minutes and said:

Everyone of you that swore falsely against me, the innocent stands before you, dressed for the gallows, to suffer for the death of Ida Belle Moore; I am innocent, ignorant of her death! He asked, "Do you want to hear a lie?" Someone from the crowd, said, "I am satisfied of your guilt." At this he cried, "Don't you believe the truth? Don't you believe the truth, standing here with this rope in my hand, ready to die? Could I hold this rope and not tell the truth?

At 2:16 p.m. his hands were tied behind his back, the rope placed around his neck, and the black cap over his head. As the cap covered his face, he exclaimed: "Innocent blood." Two minutes later the trap was sprung with the fall breaking the neck.

The *Bastrop Advertisor* dated, Saturday, June 11, 1892, wrote, "His case having gone before All Earthly Tribunals, Now Goes Before the Great Bar of God."

Alexander Brown

Race/Gender: Black Male **Offense:** Murder **Offense Date:** October 15, 1892
Weapon: Ax **Execution:** July 28, 1893

On the night of October 15, 1892, Alexander Brown killed Jane Wilkins by striking her on the head with an ax on the front porch of her home. Alex Brown was married, but had been having an affair with the woman when the two argued at her home. Both the sheriff and city marshal were notified of the murder. They were aware of two previous incidents when Brown had assaulted the woman, and had threatened to kill her. With knowledge of his history, Alex Brown was arrested on the suspicion of murder. When arrested, Brown could not account for the fresh blood found on his hat, pants and shoes.

Brown was tried and found guilty and the jury assessed the death penalty. Three days prior to the execution, Alex Brown attempted to cheat the gallows by cutting his throat.

On the day of the execution, deputies led Brown to the gallows from his jail cell, and Brown appeared perfectly calm. Sheriff Davis asked him if he wanted to make a statement to the 100 witnesses that were present. Brown replied Elder Cole would talk in his place. Elder Cole told witnesses that he had talked with Brown, and that Alex hoped the merciful God had forgiven him.

Elder Cole then asked Brown, "What shall I tell your children?"
Brown replied, "Tell them to serve the God that I now serve, and I hope to meet them in heaven."
"What message have you for your fellows?"
"Tell them to be warned by my experience and meet me in Heaven."
"Do you believe that Christ is the Son of God, and that your sins have been forgiven?"
Brown replied, "Yes, I do."
Brown then confessed to the murder and said:

I went to Jane Wilkins' house on the night of the killing about 7:30 p.m. Holiday's boys went by, while I was at the fence on the outside talking with Jane, I didn't see Ben Holiday that night. Jane wanted me to give her some money. I told her I didn't have any, that I'd given it to my wife. She called me a liar two or three times. I then started off to Sam Fowler's church and I stood and listened to him preach a while. Then I started to go to town. Then I started home and met Jane. She grabbed me by the collar and said she'd been looking for me. I told her to go away. She said I'd been running after another woman. There were many people on the street and I didn't want to fuss with her and we walked up to her house. She holding me by the collar all the time and said before I should have another woman she'd kill me. We went through a gap in the fence. We went up to the house by the step, when she reached down under the house and grabbed the ax. I grabbed her, took the ax away and struck her on the left-side first and then on the right. She didn't scream but fell after the second blow. I got blood on my hand. I ran and jumped the fence and dropped my hat. I picked it up and got blood on my hand. I went home and went to bed and dozed off and was awakened by my wife when the alarm was given.

As Brown turned to have his arms tied he told the crowd, "Good-bye to all." At 1:39 p.m. the black cap and rope were adjusted, and the trap sprung. The fall broke his neck, and the body of Alex Brown remained suspended for fifteen minutes until the doctors pronounced the body dead.

The *Houston Daily Post*, dated Saturday, July 29, 1893, provided a full account of the execution that took place at Bastrop, Texas.

Elisha Swan

Race/Gender: Black Male **Age:** 20 **Offense:** Murder
Offense Date: June 25, 1898 **Weapon:** .45 caliber pistol **Execution:** March 31, 1899

On June 25, 1898, Elisha Swan asked his father for permission to attend a party, and to allow him to borrow his father's horse and buggy. His father, Cliff Swan refused both requests and went to bed. After Cliff had fallen asleep, Swan quietly entered his father's bedroom and removed his father's .45 caliber pistol and shot him to the head. Swan notified the authorities and attempted to convince the officers that an intruder had murdered his father. Swan was arrested and tried for murder on July 9, 1898, and found guilty. After the conviction, the case was appealed and affirmed on October 19, 1898.

Dressed in a new black suit on the day of the execution, Swan talked from the gallows for ten minutes. He told the witnesses that the whites had treated him better than the blacks. Swan confessed he had murdered his father, and hoped no one would ever commit the same crime. Swan said he was induced to kill his father by his stepmother for whom he loved. Swan said God had forgiven him, and he had the kindest feelings toward all the officers, especially Sheriff G. W. Davis and jailer Nash.

At 1:35 p.m. the sheriff sprang the trap dropping Swan to his death. After the physicians declared the body dead, the body was lowered and given to Doctor H. B. Combs to be used for scientific study.

The *Houston Daily Post*, dated Saturday, April 1, 1899, provided an account the crime and execution.

Enoch Moss

Race/Gender: Black Male **Age:** 21 **Offense:** Murder
Offense Date: July 19, 1899 **Weapon:** Shotgun **Execution:** September 3, 1900

On the morning of July 19, 1899, Enoch Moss and his employer, Neil Lane argued over Moss's lack of work. During the day, Lane was in the process of loading rails onto a wagon when Moss stopped plowing. Moss told Lane he needed to go back to the cabin and would return to resume his plowing. Moss armed himself at the cabin with Lane's shotgun and waited in the tree line for the opportunity to shoot him. When Lane came within range, Moss shot Lane twice with his own shotgun and killed him. Moss afterwards fled, but was captured about three weeks later four miles south of Devine, Texas.

Upon his capture, Moss said, "I killed Lane because he went for me with a knife. He wanted me to work on the road, whether I was old enough or not. Yes, I had owed Lane some money, and we had some words, and then Lane went after me with a knife."

On the gallows, Moss told the 100 people witness (mostly women) that he killed Lane in self-defense and said, "I have acknowledged my crime and I have God's forgiveness. Good bye, all. Farewell to the world."

Sherman Daily Register, dated Monday, September 3, 1900, printed details of the murder and execution at Bastrop, Texas.

Abe Washington

Race/Gender: Black Male **Age:** 28 - 30 **Offense:** Murder
Offense Date: June 19, 1906 **Weapon:** Pistol **Execution:** February 14, 1907

Abe Washington's Valentine gift was that of the hangman's noose for the murder he committed on June 19, 1906. On that day Washington murdered his lover, Jennie Moore at Pine Oak Creek about twenty miles southeast of Bastrop. Washington tried to persuade Jennie to leave with him, and when she refused, he drew a revolver and shot her. Jennie ran from Washington, but stumbled and fell dead after she was shot two more times. Washington fled afterwards, but was captured in Fayette County on July 2. In court, Washington pled guilty to the charge of murder, and the jury assessed his punishment as death.

From the gallows, Washington told the black witnesses who were present, "to stay away from bad company and whiskey." He said his own race had deserted him, but that Sheriff Townsend and deputies had treated him kindly.

At 1:53 p.m. the trap was sprung and eighteen minutes later he was pronounced dead.

The *Shiner Gazette*, dated Wednesday, February 20, 1907, provided its readers with details of the murder and execution.

Johnnie Green

Race/Gender: Black Male **Age:** 20 **Offense:** Robbery & Murder
Offense Date: January 30, 1908 **Weapon:** Ax **Execution:** February 25, 1909

W. P. Green was an old man who had served as a solider in the Confederacy during the War Between the States. The old soldier lived in a small hut near the mouth of Wilbarger Creek on the Colorado River, and supported himself with his small Confederate pension, and by selling fish that he would catch from the river.

On January 31, 1908, fisherman arriving at the camp discovered the old soldier dead near his fire with a gruesome wound to the back of the head. Sheriff Woody Townsend was told that nineteen-year-old Johnnie Green had been at the camp, and was seen on the day of the murder at Sandy Creek tearing a strip of clothing from his overalls that was blood stained.

The following day Green was arrested and he confessed to the murder. Green told officers he had killed the old man for the purpose of robbing him of his money. Green said he killed his victim by striking him to the back of the head while he sat by the camp fire and was putting on his shoes. After the murder, Green searched the clothing and only found forty cents in the pockets. Green's confession was further collaborated when he directed Sheriff Townsend to the location where he had hidden the murder weapon. Johnnie Green was tried for the murder on July 6, 1908, and found guilty of murder.

On the way to the gallows, Green stopped at a window and told the crowd outside, "You see where this has brought me, and now I am going to leave you in a few minutes, so good bye."

On the gallows, Johnnie Green made the following statement. "Hello, people; boys I want to warn you boys, be good; don't get into trouble; stay at home. You see where I am. I am going to heaven and I want to meet you all there."

The *Bastrop Advertiser*, dated Saturday, February 27, 1909, provided its readers with the details of the murder and execution. The paper ended the article with, "and thus we have had exemplified again that the wages of sin is death."

Bee County
County Seat - Beeville

Bartolo Guerra

Race/Gender: Hispanic Male **Offense:** Murder **Offense Date:** August, 1870
Execution: December 22, 1871

Bartolo Guerra murdered Alexander Reed in August 1870 over a $20.00 gold piece that Alexander was accused of stealing or losing.

The *San Antonio Daily Express*, dated Thursday, January 26, 1871, announced that the execution had taken place.

John Edward Singleton

Race/Gender: White Male **Age:** 22 **Offense:** Robbery & Murder
Offense Date: 1876 **Weapon:** Firearm & Knife **Execution:** April 27, 1877

Twenty-two-year-old John Singleton was tried and found guilty of the murder of John C. Dwyer, a merchant from Oakville in Live Oak County, Texas. Dwyer arrived at Beeville carrying money and a San Antonio bank draft for $600 which he intended to used toward the purchase of a wagonload of whiskey and other barroom supplies as he intended to open a saloon at Tilden, Texas. After arriving in Beeville, Dwyer met Singleton and invited him to go to Rockport with him. It was agreed that Dwyer would pay for all of Singleton's expenses. Singleton accepted the invitation and the two spent the entire day and late into the evening drinking whiskey, before they rode out together from Beeville on their way to Rockport.

The next morning, Dwyer's body was found lying in the roadway six miles from Beeville with a bullet to the head and his throat cut. At the town of Indianola, Singleton presented the bank note for payment and was arrested. In Singleton's possession were Dwyer's money and pocket watch. From the inside of the watch case, Singleton had attempted to scratch Dwyer's initials.

Singleton was tried and convicted of murder in the first degree and sentenced to death. The conviction was appealed to the Texas Court of Criminal Appeals who affirmed the verdict in January of 1877.

Two days prior to his execution, Singleton wrote the following letter to his mother, Mrs. J. A. Singleton.

Dear Mother – When you read this, I, your sinful, rebellious, neglectful son, will be no more on this earth. But, mother dear, I am not going to give these worthy people of Bee county the pleasure of publicly executing me. You will understand by this that I contemplate destroying my life. And such is the case. I am aware that you look upon it as an unpardonable sin, or almost as such, but I can not bear the idea of being hanged in public, before gaping magnitude of fools, and especially Bee county fools. I am compelled to lose my life, mother dear; there is no other alternative, and you will pardon me, I'm sure, for this act, for it is only shortening my existence a few hours at most.

As for the justice of my conviction, I will not speak or write falsely to you at this time, and I reckon the verdict of the jury was a just one. I did the murder, but not with malice aforethought, as everyone thinks, nor was I actuated by any hope of gain. It was for a quarrel about a trifle, and the provocation was not sufficient to warrant the killing, therefore, I don't fell justified.

It's hard, mother dear, for me to calmly contemplate death, and a great deal harder, when I think of your long suffering toil and privations for me. I know you are suffering and will suffer after my death. I would to God I could avert it from you, but I can not; but I think it's better to take my life, than to be executed by the minions of the law in this place. I will not ask you not to grieve for me, mother, for I know that would be useless; but try and bear up the best you can. I trust that we may meet again in the better world beyond the grave. I do not feel capable of saying anything that will strengthen or comfort you at this time, when I know how much you need comfort and strength. But one thing, mother, please for my sake, and for the sake of Lee and Mamie, do not despair nor give up, if you can help it. Think how you, and none but you, can instruct them how to be great and good men. Some would think that my career was contradiction of what I say, but God knows that the fact of my now being under sentence of death, and my name forever disgraced, is not the consequence of my home training. I was taught things that were right, but I was too weak and sinful to profit by your good teachings, but I do hope to God it will be different with the two younger ones. Teach them always to do right at all times, and for my sake teach them to think with pity and never with scorn of the disgraced and outcast murderer. For with all my faults, I always loved them; but I am not much afraid on that score, if they continue, as they are now, as I do not in the least doubt their love for me. I saw Mamie this evening. I am thankful that I was permitted to see him once more. I regret not having seen Lee very much, but as I did no, you must convey my loving farewell to him. I must close this, mother, for writing here, solitary and alone as I am, of our loved ones causes such a rush of old half-forgotten memories that I am almost overpowered. I am not as near cast-iron as I thought.

Well, dear, dear mother, farewell, and may God, in His infinite mercy, bless, comfort and console you is the prayer of your loving but unhappy son.

James Edward Singleton

While waiting for his execution to take place, Singleton wrote out his will where he requested that his corpse be skinned, and that the skin be stretched over a drumhead. Singleton wrote it was his wish for the drum to be given to the prosecuting attorney and on each anniversary of his hanging; the prosecutor could beat the drum to the tune of "Old Mollie Hare."

Singleton's last wish to be skinned after death was not granted.

The *Galveston Daily News*, dated Saturday, May 5, 1877, wrote there was a large number of spectators present to witness the execution. The only statement Singleton made from the scaffold was that he had no thought of killing Dwyer until a few moments before he committed the deed.

Bell County
County Seat - Belton

Joe Lewis

Race/Gender: Black Male **Age:** 37 **Offense:** Murder
Offense Date: August 28, 1889 **Weapon:** Razor Blade Knife **Execution:** March 27, 1891

Joe Lewis and his wife Mary Lewis lived until their separation in Washington County. The marriage was troubled and Joe was soon in jail on a misdemeanor complaint and after being convicted for making several threats directed at his mother-in-law, Francis Nora. Mary soon moved out of their home and back with her mother in Belton, Texas, to be safe from Lewis.

After release from jail, Lewis had been seen near his mother-in-law's home several times during the day before the murder. On the morning before the crime, Lewis had gone to the home where he dropped his razor blade knife. The next morning while the victim was washing clothes in the backyard, Lewis was seen by both Mrs. Kelly and Mrs. Cochran entering the yard and walking up to the home. Both ladies went to the back door and confronted Lewis to inform him that he was not welcome, and that he better leave. Lewis replied he was soon leaving Belton, and merely wanted to speak with his mother-in-law and with no intentions of hurting her. Lewis' mother-in-law then left the house and returned to the wash tub, while Mrs. Cochran walked back to the sitting room.

About ten minutes later, a scream was heard and Mrs. Cochran looked through the window and saw that Lewis had Francis Nora bent over backwards across his left arm. Lewis released the woman and walked across the street carrying a long razor blade knife. The woman screamed, "He has cut me all to pieces!"

She died two days later from three deep lacerations to her stomach. Lewis fled the scene and escaped by stealing a bridle, saddle, and horse. The owner of the horse followed Lewis into Brazos County where he was arrested.

On December 11, 1889, Lewis and a number of other prisoners made their escape from jail. Lewis again stole a horse from a stable near the jail and was closely pursued by a sheriff's posse. During the pursuit, Lewis was forced to abandon the horse a few miles from town and ran into the woods. Lewis was able to escape the posse and worked his way down to Mexico, where he remained for several months. On July 11, 1890, Lewis was arrested in Laredo, Mexico, and returned to Bell County.

On July 31, Lewis stood trial and testified that he had gone to the home the morning of the murder to ask for the return of a letter from his mother-in-law that was meant for his wife. During their conversation, the victim was to have said, "Joe, Mary does not care for you. Let's you and I get married, and go off and live. You can work and make a living for us."

Lewis was to have told her that she should be ashamed of herself and that if he could not live with Mary he still would not live with her. Lewis stated he then asked Francis if she had found the razor knife that he had lost. Francis replied she had and Lewis asked for her to return it.

Francis was to have said, "I will give it to you in a way you won't like it," and made a threatening gesture towards Lewis with it. Lewis described how they had struggled over the razor and Francis Nora was accidentally cut. He blamed Nora for causing her own death.

The jury did not accept his version of events and found Joe Lewis guilty and accessed the punishment of death. The case was appealed and the court of appeals affirmed the decision of November 8, 1890.

On the afternoon of the scheduled execution, Joe Lewis was brought to the scaffold where he spoke for half an hour to the 5,000 witnesses. Lewis told the crowd he had been unjustly convicted, and that witnesses had sworn falsely against him at his trial. Lewis asked for his friends in attendance to take charge of his body and to bury him next to his mother-in-law, who he had killed, and that their graves be fenced in together.

At the conclusion of his statement, the black cap was put over his head and Sheriff S. A. Sparks pulled the trigger. Lewis fell nine feet with the fall breaking his neck. After hanging for twenty minutes the attending physicians pronounced him dead.

The *Galveston Daily News*, dated Saturday, March 28, 1891, provided its readers with a full account of the crime, execution and Joe Lewis' background.

Buck Wilkerson

Alias: Will Wilkerson
Offense: Double Murder
Execution: October 14, 1892
Race/Gender: Black Male
Offense Date: July 21, 1891
Age: 24
Weapon: Double Barrel Shotgun

Susan Harrison was a widow who married Buck Wilkerson in 1887. On June 28, 1891, Buck Wilkerson left home with his fourteen-year-old stepdaughter Jenny Lind and sexually assaulted her. Upon their return home, Jenny told her mother what had happened. Susan Wilkerson immediately reported the assault to authorities. An arrest warrant for the crime of incest was issued, and on July 2, 1891, Wilkerson was located and arrested in the town of Lorena in McLennan County. Susan and Buck separated and Susan moved out of their home to stay with neighbors.

On July 21, 1891, Susan was sitting in a rocking chair in the gallery of the house when Buck Wilkerson entered the yard and shot his wife in the head with a shotgun. Wilkerson afterwards dragged his stepdaughter from the home as the girl resisted and screamed for help. About fifty yards from the house, a black church choir was practicing and heard the shotgun blast and the screams from Jenny Lind. Will Hamilton approached Buck Wilkerson who still had hold of the screaming girl.

When Will Hamilton was about ten yards from Wilkerson, the murderer raised his shotgun and shot Hamilton in the chest. The good Samaritan died hours later from his wounds. During his attempted escape, Wilkerson shot at several posse members, and killed one of them. Wilkerson escaped and worked his way to Laredo and into Mexico and later back to Laredo where he was arrested August 10, 1891.

Buck Wilkerson was tried for murder in the first degree and the case was affirmed by the court of appeals on June 29, 1892.

On October 14, 1892, Buck Wilkerson told a newspaperman:

_____ _____ is the cause of my death; he is the cause of my death, and nobody else. I went up on purpose to kill him, and I killed my wife, and intended to kill them both if I caught them together. He has been causing this trouble on me for the past two years; made threats to kill me, and swore he would kill me. That's enough, all I have to say.

On the gallows, Wilkerson told the crowd of 5,000 that although he intended to kill his wife, the killing of Will Hamilton was an accident. After the trap was sprang, Wilkerson was pronounced dead at 2:12 p.m. and left hanging until 2:23 p.m.

The *Dallas Morning News*, dated Saturday, October 15, 1892, provided readers with a full account of the crime and execution at Belton.

George F. Hornsby

Alias: George H. Scott
Offense: Murder & Robbery
Execution: April 14, 1922
Race/Gender: White Male
Offense Date: October 18, 1920
Age: 28
Weapon: Hammer

George Hornsby, was an army deserter who arrived at Brownwood, Texas, in August of 1920, using the alias of George H. Scott. Soon after his arrival, Hornsby began a relationship with Myrtle Chambers and quickly moved into the home she shared along with her sixteen-year-old brother, Willie Clark.

On October 18, 1920, Hornsby told Willie Clark to go to J. N. Weatherby's garage and tell Weatherby, that

Myrtle requested he come that evening to her home as she wished to see him. J. N. Weatherby had become a successful businessman by owning an automobile garage in Brownwood, and was known for his wealth by the $4,000 diamond ring he wore.

Hornsby told Clark that when Weatherby arrived, he intended to kill the man for the diamond ring. That evening Hornsby greeted Weatherby at the door and invited him inside the home to take a seat. After Weatherby sat down, Hornsby struck the man several times about the head and face with a nail hammer. Later the body was wrapped in a quilt and carried through a house window to keep anyone from seeing them carrying the body out the front door. In an attempt to conceal the murder, coal oil was poured on the house and set on fire. Weatherby's body was carried to his car and witnesses watched as both Hornby and Clark drove off while smoke was pouring from the house. Seven and a half miles out of town, the car broke down and both the body and car were abandoned until discovered the next day.

After Hornsby abandoned the car, he fled to Birmingham, Alabama, where he was apprehended on January 27. Not fighting extradition back to Texas, Hornsby was indicted on January 4, 1922 for murder in the first degree. The case was tried on March 15 before Judge M. B. Blair of Bell County on a change of venue from Brown County. Willie Clark turned State's witness for the prosecution. Four days later, the jury returned a verdict of guilty and assessed the death penalty. Hornsby's counsel, Judge Sam D. Snodgrass immediately filed an appeal to the Texas Court of Criminal Appeals and the court affirmed the conviction December 14, 1921.

On March 8, 1922, Hornsby once again stood before Judge Blair for sentencing. Judge Blair asked, "Is there anything before the bar of sentence being passed?"

Hornsby replied, "Yes sir, I am an innocent man. I have been tried without a chance. I haven't had a chance all the way through. I hope the good people of Bell County will pray for me because I am an innocent man." Judge Blair then set the date of execution to take place on April 14, 1922.

On March 21, 1922, a petition containing 6,548 signatures was presented to Governor Neff asking that George Hornsby's sentence be commuted to life imprisonment. Governor Neff called for Willie Clark and personally interviewed him. Afterwards, the Governor sent word that he was not going to intervene and to allow the law to take its course. Sheriff Albert Bonds and Captain Frank Hamer of the Texas Rangers then transported Hornsby by car, on April 13, from Austin where he had been held for safekeeping back to Belton.

On the morning of the execution, a reporter interviewed Hornsby. He said, "Tell the people of Bell County that I appreciate what they have done for me. I am going to my death an innocent man. I did not kill this man, so help me God!"

The reporter asked if he knew who had killed Weatherby: "I do not know who did. If I did I would tell the world and if I had done it I would tell it. I could not go to God with a lie upon my lips. If the truth could only be known about this case I would gladly die. I do not fear death and would not mind to lie down on this cot and die, but I hate to go to my death on the gallows."

The execution was held privately in the jail yard and was surrounded by a thirty-foot high fence. From the gallows Hornsby said:

> People, I don't know many of you but lots of you know me. People, I stand before you a saved man, I accepted Christ as my personal Savior, I am going to leave you people but I am going to a better land, I am going to where we will all be treated alike, we will all be charged alike, and I want to tell you people I am going as an innocent man. I have lived a sinful life but I have not committed any murder, so help me God. People, I don't hold it against these people here, they are doing their duty, but remember me in your prayers, I have no father and mother but remember my brother and sisters, tat they may know that their brother went to God an innocent man."

> People, I don't know what else to say. The officers here have treated me all right. I have been treated as well as could be expected, but I want to thank all of you for what you have done for me. I came here without friends and I understand that I got lots of friends here now, and you people that haven't got religion, please get it, please get it. I want to tell you people some people have made the remark about had anybody asked me to tell the people that I was innocent. People, there had been no one told me to say I was innocent. I have told people from the start that I was innocent because I was innocent. So you people will understand it, I came here without friends. I didn't have a chance, but the

people have been mighty nice to me and Judge Snodgrass, God bless him, God bless you, judge, you have done all you could judge.

Judge Snodgrass replied, "Yes, I have done all I could do. I have never told you to tell a lie either."

Hornsby answered, "No sir. I am going to leave you people. But I am going to a better land; I am going to where all will be treated alike. We will all be charged alike and I want to tell you people that I am going an innocent man."

At the conclusion with tears in his eyes, Sheriff A. W. Bonds said, "George, goodbye, God have mercy on your poor soul," as he sprang the trap.

The body of George Hornsby was afterwards buried at the Hillcrest Cemetery in Temple, Texas. His tombstone reads, "I am Innocent."

The *Bartlett Tribune and News*, dated Friday, April 21, 1922, provided its readers with a large article detailing the crime and execution.

Bexar County

County Seat - San Antonio

Francisco Quiroz and Lino Flores were jointly hanged on January 5, 1854. The details of their crime and execution are not currently available.

Edward Jenkins

Race/Gender: Black Male **Offense:** Murder **Offense Date:** April 23, 1873
Weapon: Pistol **Execution:** August 17, 1874

On the spring morning of April 23, 1873, Ed Jenkins was working in the rock blasting fields of the Kampmann's Rock Quarry near San Antonio when he engaged in a heated argument with a site foreman. Company foreman Schroeder arrived at Jenkins work site and began to remove blasting powder from a keg when Jenkins stopped the foreman and told Schroeder if he wanted powder, he had to submit a request order. The two men argued and words were exchanged between the two. At the conclusion of the argument, Jenkins stomped off towards his cabin to retrieve his handgun.

Jenkins returned to the site gunning for Schroeder, and was quickly disarmed, but in the process the pistol discharged without the bullet striking anyone. Jenkins then returned to his cabin to reload his weapon. This time, Jenkins climbed to the top of the quarry and waited until he saw Schroeder. Without warning, Jenkins shot Schroeder in the back, killing him instantly. At first Jenkins fled and hid from a posse, but later that evening he turned himself in.

The scaffold was erected in the southeast corner of the jail yard with a drop of four feet. On the morning of the execution, Jenkins walked out of the jail and bid all present with a goodbye. Jenkins afterwards sat down on a bench, closed his eyes, and appeared to everyone that he had fallen asleep. Sheriff H. D. Bonnett walked up and asked Jenkins if he wished to say anything. Jenkins replied, "I can't do any more."

Sheriff Bonnett and a deputy led him to the scaffold, which he ascended without much difficulty. Once on the scaffold, Jenkins suddenly collapsed. An attempt was made to seat him in the chair, but he sank from the chair to the floor. The sheriff consulted with the county physician who recommended that he hang Jenkins at once. Jenkins was partially lifted up and the trap was sprung without bounding the legs. When Jenkins failed to fall though the trap, officers had to kick both feet off the platform to drop him through the trap.

The *Galveston Daily News*, dated Saturday, August 22, 1874, provided a full account of the execution.

Jose Cordova Jr.

Race/Gender: Hispanic Male **Age:** 25 **Offense:** Robbery & Murder
Offense Date: July 7, 1877 **Weapon:** Knife **Execution:** July 7, 1879

Jose Cordova was tried and convicted for the murder of Robert Trimble and executed two years later on the anniversary of the murder. Trimble employed Cordova and the motive for the murder was the robbery of Trimble's wagon and supplies. On July 7, 1877, Cordova stabbed Trimble twice in the heart with a knife while he was riding in the wagon south of San Antonio near the river. Trimble's body was thrown from the wagon, and a rope was then tied around his legs and the body was dragged through the cactus and brush. The vest Trimble wore further showed evidence of him being shot, but the bullet did not penetrate the body.

The execution took place in the San Antonio jail behind the cells and in the presence of fifty witnesses. Cordova who dressed in a white shirt and white pants, walked firmly to the gallows. Turning to the sheriff, Cordova said, "You are hanging an innocent man."

Deputy Gleason approached carrying the black cap in his hand. Cordova told the officer, "You may do as you please about that."

After the noose and cap were adjusted, Deputy Bennett knocked the wedge away which held the trap door in place. When Cordova shot down through the trap opening, his toes scraped along the top of the rock floor. Deputies quickly threw another rope over the suspended rope holding Cordova, and pulled the rope back until the toes were suspended above the floor. The seven foot drop dislocated Cordova's neck, and he was declared dead fifteen minutes later.

The night before the execution, Cordova wrote the following statement:

I, Jose Cordova, knowing that tomorrow the 7th day of July, I have to die in consequence of the sentence of death passed upon me by the district judge for the murder of Robert Trimble, two years ago, and knowing that I have to give an account to God, to whom I give up my soul, I declare that I am not culpable of the death of said Robert Trimble. But I am resigned to die, and I further declare that my brother Feliciano, and my nephew Enriquez, knew nothing about the bargain of the wagon that I bought from Antonio Garcia. If they are condemned it is unjust, and I say so with the knowledge while on the point of death.

Signed, Jose Cordova

After Cordova had made claim that he had unknowingly purchased the stolen wagon from an Antonio Garcia, no such person by this name was known to anyone nor was he located. The story was disregarded as an attempt by Cordova to convince the prosecutor not to charge his brother and nephew or to shed some doubt upon the jury from convicting either. Jose Cordova's brother, seventeen-year-old Feliciano Cordova, was tried and convicted as being an accomplice to the robbery and murder, and he received a sentence of life in the penitentiary. It was believed the name Cordova provided was a fictitious person as no one in town knew of a person named Antonio Garcia.

The *New York Times*, dated Tuesday, July 8, 1879, printed details of the execution.

Jacob Hainline

Race/Gender: White Male **Age:** 35 **Offense:** Robbery & Murder
Offense Date: February 24, 1878 **Weapon:** Ax **Execution:** August 8, 1879

On February 26, 1876, two boys named Herman Patchusky and Herman Steppenbock were both fishing on the San Antonio River near Guenther's Mill below the lower iron bridge when they observed a floating object. Believing that the object was a tree log, the boys began throwing rocks in competition against one another as to who could hit it first. The waves created by the rocks splashing in the water slowly turned the log. It was then that the boys realized the log was actually a body floating by, and quickly ran to alert authorities.

An inquest of the body showed the forehead and right temple had been crushed with a club or an ax. The identity of the victim was unknown at the time, and the remains were buried in the poor house graveyard. The identity of the victim was soon questioned after William Patterson arrived in town and he heard the description of the murdered victim. Patterson reported to City Marshal Dobbin that he had last seen his friend, Peter Maddox on the Fort Concho road heading towards San Antonio. Patterson related to Marshal Dobbin that Peter was driving his ox-pulled wagon with a load of buffalo hides and buffalo meat with a man he did not know. Patterson said after arriving in town, he saw the same man selling buffalo meat from the wagon at the military plaza and asked him where Maddox was. The man looked around as if he expected to see him and replied, "Why, the old man is right around here somewhere."

Patterson afterwards went to the marshal and pointed to the man, who the marshal recognized. Marshal Dobbin went before Justice of the Peace Cotton on February 28, and obtained an arrest warrant for Jacob Hainline and placed him under arrest. Inside the bed of the wagon, the marshal located an ax with bloodstains. Justice of the Peace Cotton decided to have the remains exhumed in the presence of Hainline and Patterson for identification of the body.

Gravediggers were then employed to unearth the coffin. After the coffin was uncovered and the lid removed, the body was raised up into a sitting position. William identified the body as that of his friend, Peter Maddox and accused Hainline of the murder. Hainline showed no emotion and carelessly said, "I have never seen the man before."

When confronted that he had been seen riding in the wagon with him, Hainline commented by saying that he thought the remains might be old man Peter Maddox, but knew nothing of his death. Doctors reexamined the wounds and reported that the ax that was found in the bed of the wagon caused the head wounds.

The case was tried on December 12, 1878. Defense attorneys attempted to prove that someone other than Hainline had killed Maddox because Hainline had plenty of opportunities to kill him over the past two years while they hunted buffalo. After the attorneys closed their arguments, the jury returned a verdict of guilty and assessed the death penalty. Hainline wrote a public statement in which he accused William Patterson for the first time of committing the murder.

On August 8, 1879, Hainline became the first white man hanged in Bexar County. The execution took place inside the jail and on the same gallows that Jose Cordova was hanged from the previous month. After Hainline dressed himself wearing white pantaloons, white shirt, black alpaca coat and polished shoes, he was led to the scaffold where fifty witnesses attended the event.

On the gallows, Hainline was asked if he wished to make any last statement. Hainline replied he had no ill feelings against the officers as they all had treated him well, and took his place over the trap door. Hainline's arms and legs were tied and the noose adjusted. Deputy Bennett then sprang the trap, dropping Hainline seven feet, which broke the neck. After hanging for eighteen minutes, the body was cut down, placed in a coffin, and given to relatives to be taken back to Atascosa County for burial.

The *Galveston Daily News*, dated Friday, August 8, 1879, provided details of the execution.

Charles W. Ward

Race/Gender: Black Male **Age:** 35 **Offense:** Rape
Offense Date: August 21, 1881 **Weapon:** Physical Force **Execution:** August 21, 1882

Charles W. Ward was a discharged soldier who on August 21, 1881, attacked seventeen-year-old Dora Ellerman, and dragged her out into the brush where he raped her.

Convicted and sentenced to hang for the assault, Ward stood on the gallows as he leaned on a crutch for support as he had lost a leg. The execution was private, with only seventy-five people allowed admittance to witness the execution. An additional 500 people waited outside the jail in silence in hopes of hearing the trap fall or given the opportunity to see the remains after the body was cut down.

On the gallows Ward denied committing the rape. Turning to Sheriff Thomas McCall he said, "Are you in a hurry? I am ready whenever you are."

The ice factory whistle blew about this time and when the whistle stopped blowing he said, "That whistle annoyed me some, but this man-trap (referring to the scaffold) will annoy me more, I suppose." After the noose had been placed around his neck and before the black cap was adjusted, Ward shouted to the prisoners in their cells, "Goodbye, my friends."

The *Galveston Daily News*, dated Tuesday, August 22, 1882, provided its readers with details of the execution at San Antonio, Texas.

James Eli McCoy

Race/Gender: White Male **Age:** 32 **Offense:** Murder
Offense Date: December 26, 1886 **Weapon:** Rifle **Execution:** August 23, 1889

Charles B. McKinney, a former Captain of Texas Rangers ran for, and was elected to the office of La Salle County Sheriff on November 7, 1882. He was re-elected on November 4, 1884, and it was near the end of his second term when he was shot and killed which led to the execution of James McCoy. The case was given a change of venue from La Salle County to Bexar County

On December 26, 1886, Sheriff McKinney and Deputy Marshal S. V. Edwards traveled twelve miles south of Cotulla to Twohig. The lawmen had ridden late into the evening to get to the White ranch so they could arrest Jonathan "Dow" White who was accused of raping an eleven-year-old girl. When the sheriff and his deputy arrived at the White ranch house, Sheriff McKinney became separated from Deputy Edwards while speaking with Bud Crenshaw who was armed with a Winchester rifle.

Sheriff McKinney had one leg over the pommel of his saddle with his one hand resting on the knee.

Upon inquiring as to the whereabouts of Dow White, Bud Crenshaw without warning jammed the rifle barrel under the sheriff's chin and pulled the trigger. James McCoy then fired his pistol at Deputy Edwards striking him in the left shoulder. The shooting frightened the deputy's horse into a gallop, which aided him in his effort to escape death. Sheriff McKinney who began his law enforcement career at the age of sixteen as a private with the Texas Rangers was dead at the age of thirty.

Texas Rangers trailed the two fugitives to a water hole. When Bud Crenshaw was ordered to "throw up your hands," he fired at the lawmen and in response; he was shot and killed by six rangers. James McCoy escaped capture, but surrendered three days later making the comment, "I would rather be hanged than lead a dog's life any longer."

Two weeks prior to the murder, James McCoy made statements at Butler's Saloon in Cotulla that if Sheriff McKinney ever came to Twohig he had better get off the train and come shooting. This statement was presented during the appeal where the court of appeal affirmed the judgment of the lower court on February 20, 1889.

On the morning of August 23, 1889, McCoy walked unassisted on his crutch towards the gallows, only to stop to shake hands and bade those he recognized with a goodbye. After walking up the steps, he laid his crutch down and rested against one of the two beams. After a prayer was given, McCoy was asked if he wished to make a statement. With a slight quivering of the lips, McCoy said:

> McKinney had no business to persecute me. He was a good man to his friends, I reckon, but he treated me wrong. We never were good friends, and when he got to be sheriff he employed a lot of outlaws to fix up scheme to kill me, and they shot my leg off in Cotulla. While I was sick, he made his talks and called me a murderer, a thief, and a dead son of a bitch. I never was called a murderer until I got with McKinney and Edwards and the only cold-blooded murder I ever did commit was with them near Cotulla. I may be a hard man; I know I have been in some ways, but.

Father Maloney asked the prisoner to confess his sins and ask God to forgive them. The prisoner evaded the request and continued: "I know I am not a good man, but I've been good to my friends."

McCoy closed his remarks with a message to his wife for her to raise their boy right, and coolly stepped upon the trap.

The drop of seven feet broke his neck and he was pronounced dead nine minutes later.

After the body was cut down, an undertaker placed the body in a coffin. Later in the afternoon friends took the body so that McCoy's remain could be buried in Atascosa County.

The *Fort Worth Daily Gazette*, Saturday, August 24, 1889, edition provided its readers with a full account of the murder, trial, execution and James McCoy's background.

Austin Brown

Race/Gender: Black Male **Age:** 32 **Offense:** Murder
Offense Date: February 14, 1894 **Weapon:** Pistol **Execution:** May 25, 1894

Anderson "Andrew" Harris was an ex-San Antonio police officer who worked as a hackman and who was very popular among the black population of the city. Andrew lived with his wife and children at 306 Indianola Street in San Antonio. Sometime in 1892, Austin Brown became acquainted with Mrs. Harris and befriended her husband. The friendship between Mrs. Harris and Austin Brown led into an affair, which her husband did not suspect. A friend confided to Harris of his suspicions about Austin Brown and the frequent visits he was making to his home. Harris quickly confronted Brown, and told him that he was no longer welcomed at his home and further demanded that he stay away from his wife.

Having fell in love with Mrs. Harris, Brown pointed out Harris to Elois Vidal who was sitting in his hack at the Alamo Plaza. Brown told Vidal that he wanted him to hire Harris in four days to drive Vidal to a house near the first mission for the purpose of bringing back several women who would be spending the evening there. Brown paid Vidal in advance the money needed to hire the hack and driver.

On the scheduled night, Elois Vidal did as he was asked and hired Harris. Austin Brown then waited at a secluded hiding place at Goliad Lane, just east of South Predro Street where he could see the hack coming from a distance. While waiting for the hack, Brown wrapped his shoes in heavy cloth and prepared his pistol. Just as the hack arrived near him, Brown yelled for the driver to stop. Brown quickly jumped up onto the wheel of the vehicle and shot Harris in the face. The bullet entered just behind the left ear and lodged two inches under the skin behind the right ear. A second bullet was fired into Harris's upper chest. His body then slumped over and fell half way off the seat. After committing the murder, Brown gave Vidal the pistol and they both fled across an open field.

Brown was arrested the following afternoon by sheriff deputies and jailed. Brown confessed to the lawmen that he provided Vidal with a pistol and paid him $2.50 to do the killing because Harris had cut up a suit of clothes that belonged to him.

Austin Brown had initially made a plea of not guilty to the murder, but on the second day of the trial, Brown stood up and told the judge he wished to change his plea and make a full confession to the jury. During his confession, Brown insisted he only witnessed the murder and Vidal was the shooter. The jury retired and returned a few minutes later finding the defendant guilty of murder and assessed the death penalty. The case was affirmed by the Court of Appeals on March 24, 1894.

At 11:27 on the morning of May 25, 1895, the execution of Austin Brown took place in the Bexar County Jail. The drop of eight feet, six inches, broke his neck. Brown gave no last statement and only said, "Goodbye, everybody."

The *Waco Evening News*, dated Friday, May 25, 1894, edition provided details of the execution.

Juan Rocha

Race/Gender: Hispanic Male **Age:** 61 **Offense:** Murder
Offense Date: January 16, 1901 **Weapon:** Ax Handle **Execution:** August 2, 1901

On the afternoon of January 16, 1901, at about 5:30 p.m., John Grimsinger was asleep on a cot inside his house wearing only his underclothes and socks. While his wife Guadalupe waited in the next room, Juan Rocha took a three-foot piece of oak wood and sharpened one end with an ax. As John laid on his left side, Rocha approached the sleeping man, and then struck him with the wood club on the right side of his head. Rocha then struck Rocha three or four more times to the center of the head to ensure he had killed him.

Guadalupe then emerged from the room and began preparing their dinner while Rocha dressed the body. Rocha afterwards picked the body up and carried it over his shoulder through the house. The body was carried a short distance down the street from the house, and left on the sidewalk where the corpse was found the following morning. To conceal the murder, oil was trailed on the floor throughout the house, the doors locked, and the front gate wired shut, and then set on fire.

Firemen who responded to the alarm arrived quickly and were able to make entry into the home and extinguished the fire confined to two rooms. The firemen then observed a blood trail from where the victim had been carried through the house.

Juan Rocha was soon apprehended by Sheriff John Tobin, along with his Deputies Chas. Stevens, Green and Irvin. After Rocha was tied and placed on a horse to ride back to town, he related the events of the murder to Deputy Stevens. Rocha told the deputy he had known Guadalupe since she was a child, and always had a great affection for her. Rocha said he lived with the Grimsingers doing odd jobs and errands. Rocha said Grimsinger was cruel towards Guadalupe, often coming home drunk, and he knew Guadalupe was unhappy in her marriage. A month before the murder, Guadalupe asked him if he wouldn't put Grimsinger out of the way for her. He and Guadalupe then talked over their plan for two weeks preceding the murder.

Guadalupe and Juan Rocha were tried separately after their cases were severed. On February 13, 1901, Rocha was tried and found guilty of murder. The case was appealed, and on June 29, 1901, the Court of Criminal Appeals affirmed the sentence. A week prior to his execution, Rocha recanted his confession and attempted to save Guadalupe by saying she had nothing to do with the murder of her husband. Guadalupe Grimsinger was tried in San Antonio, and on April 26, 1901, she was found guilty and sentenced to serve the rest of her life in prison.

On the day of the execution, Rocha walked unassisted to the gallows wearing a new black suit. Once on the scaffold, Rocha pulled out a handkerchief and placed it on the floor to kneel upon to protect his pants from dirt while he prayed. After the prayer, Rocha picked up his handkerchief and placed it back in his pocket. Rocha did not address the 100 witnesses about his crime, but told Sheriff Tobin he had no grievance against Grimsinger, and only killed him because Guadalupe had told him to do so.

The *Dallas Morning News*, dated Saturday, August 3, 1901, provided its readers with details of the murder and execution at San Antonio.

Vicente E. Saucedo

Race/Gender: Hispanic Male **Age:** 27 **Offense:** Rape
Offense Date: April 1901 **Execution:** September 19, 1902

Vincent Saucedo was convicted in June of 1901 of the criminal assault on Gunecenga Morales, his ten-year-old stepdaughter. After assaulting the child, Saucedo threatened to kill her if she told her mother. That evening Gunecenga was suffering pain as a result of the assault and told her mother what Saucedo had done to her. When arrested, Saucedo confessed to committing the crime and said he hoped to have a speedy trial so that he could be hanged.

In June, Saucedo was tried and found guilty by the jury of criminal assault. When a motion for a new trial was denied, the case was appealed to the Court of Criminal Appeals, which affirmed the lower courts decision. Saucedo's attorney attemptedd an insanity plea and filed this motion before the court. An insanity trial was then ordered, but the jury found Saucedo to be sane.

On September 11, 1902, Governor Joseph Sayers addressed a letter to Sheriff John Tobin which read:

Austin, Tex., Sept. 11. – John W. Tobin, Sheriff Bexar County, San Antonio, Tex.-
Dear Sir: You will immediately inform Vicente Saucedo, now in jail under death sentence, that I have most carefully examined all the proceedings had in the District Court of Bexar County, Texas, as well those relating to his sanity as those to his guilt of the crime for which he had been convicted, also all the applications submitted to me for the commutation of his sentence, and that I have been unable to reach any conclusion other than that the sentence should be executed. His application for commutation is, therefore, denied.

Joseph S. Sayers,
Governor of Texas

Six days later, Governor Sayers received a handwritten letter addressed to him from Saucedo. In the letter, Saucedo blamed whiskey for all of his trouble, and wrote if he did the crime, it was while he was under the influence.

On the gallows, Saucedo told the witnesses to learn from his fate and begged for their forgiveness of the crime he committed. He then thanked the sheriff and jailers for the kindness given to him. Saucedo then stepped upon the trap door and said, "Adios, meet me in heaven." After the execution, Vicente Saucedo was buried at the San Fernando Cemetery in San Antonio.

The *San Antonio Express*, dated Saturday, September 20, 1902, provided their reader with details of the crime and execution.

George H. Turner

Race/Gender: White male **Age:** 43 **Offense:** Robbery & Murder
Offense Date: March 9, 1905 **Weapon:** Razor Blade **Execution:** December 22, 1905

With the motive being robbery, George Turner began making plans for what he believed would be an easy target without getting caught. Turner learned that sixty-five-year-old Elizabeth Lynch was home alone while her husband was away on a business trip in California, and wanted to take advantage of this opportunity to commit the robbery. Turner believed the Lynchs kept a large sum of money in their home. In preparation for the robbery, he first removed a doorknob from a door in his house in order to make a homemade club. The knob was then wrapped in cloth, twisted and tied with twine.

Taking a razor knife and his homemade club, Turner attacked the woman, but she escaped and ran into the backyard screaming. Catching his victim, Turner slashed her throat with the razor. Fearing the screams attracted the neighbors, Turner fled into the brush leaving evidence behind at the murder scene that was used to convict him at trial. Once arrested, Turner confessed to a room full of officers and newspapermen stating that he thought she had money and used a razor to cut Mrs. Lynch's throat

On the day of the execution, 250 witnesses, including twenty-five sheriffs gathered to watch the execution. As Turner was led from his cell to the scaffold, a quartet of black prisoners which included Monk Gibson (later executed), sang *God Be With You Till We Meet Again*. On the gallows, Turner was asked if he wished to make a final statement. Turner said, "I have nothing to say. I want to thank all the officers for their courtesy to me while in prison and want to say I forgive my enemies." As Sheriff Tobin placed the noose around the neck, Turner said, "John, place it carefully so it won't hurt me when I go through. I want to die instantly."

After the execution, a jailer found a note left in the cell. Turner wrote that he was asking to be forgiven by all, and wished everyone a Merry Christmas and Happy New Year. Turner's body was buried at St. Mary's Catholic Cemetery in San Antonio.

The *Galveston Daily News*, dated Saturday, December 23, 1905, provided its readers with details of the murder, evidence, and execution.

H. L. Mays

Race/Gender: Black Male **Age:** 34 **Offense:** Murder
Offense Date: July 29, 1905 **Weapon:** Pistol **Execution:** October 12, 1906

In 1905, H. L. Mays worked for the Southern Pacific Railroad as a hand in the rail yard. Leo Woods worked for the car inspector's office and upon seeing Mays would jokingly call him Irish. Mays who was not amused and did not care for the nickname of Irish, warned Woods to stop referring to him by that.

On July 28, 1905, while Mays was at work, Woods again saw Mays and called out to him by the name of Irish. Mays stopped and warned Woods for the second time to stop calling him Irish or that the third time would be the charm for him. The next morning, Leo was inside the rail office standing next to the window when he saw Mays walking past the office. Woods told the other workers in the office, "There goes Irish."

Mays hearing this statement stopped, pulled out a revolver he had taken with him to work and shot Woods through the window. Mays then fired a second bullet into Woods' body to ensure he had killed him. One bullet hit Woods in the arm and the other passed through both lungs and he died three hours later

Mays was tried and convicted of murder in the first degree and sentenced to death. The case was appealed and after the case was affirmed, Mays attempted to win an insanity claim, but was judged sane and hanged on October 12, 1906.

The *Dallas Morning News*, dated Saturday, October 13, 1906, provided details to its readers of the murder and execution.

James Williams

Alias: Doc **Race/Gender:** Black Male **Age:** 27
Offense: Robbery & Murder **Offense Date:** April 22, 1908 **Weapon:** Hatchet
Execution: July 31, 1908

Thomas J. Turner wanted to find a drier climate for his wife who was suffering from tuberculosis, and hoped the dryer Texas air would help cure his wife of her illness. Turner with his wife and eighteen-month daughter traveled from Covington, Kentucky, to San Antonio in early April, 1908. After locating a small house on Nacogdoches Street to rent, Turner searched for work, but was unable to locate any employment. With what little money he and his wife had, Turner believed he could support his family by traveling the countryside purchasing chickens and eggs from farmers, and then reselling them for a profit in San Antonio. Turner not having a wagon and horse team to start his business venture went to the Duke's Saloon on Bowie Street in search of a partner.

On the morning of April 20, Turner met James "Doc" Williams and entered into a partnership agreement.

In the agreement, Turner would supply the funds to purchase the chickens and eggs, while Williams would provide the wagon and horse. After a few drinks, the pair loaded the wagon with egg cases and boxes of oranges to peddle during their trip. After introducing Williams to his wife, Turner received $50 from his wife and then kissed her and his baby goodbye for the last time before climbing onto the wagon and riding off.

At the town of La Vernia, 25 miles to the east of San Antonio, Turner sold his oranges and purchased chickens and eggs from area farmers. With the wagon loaded, Turner and Williams left to make the trip home.

On April 23, Williams arrived back in San Antonio alone and sold Turner's pocket watch at the East Commerce Pawn Shop for $6. Williams then sold eighty dozen eggs to a poultry dealer for a $1.50 and loaned a Colt .45 pistol belonging to Turner to a friend by the name of Ed Hamilton. Williams now having money, spent his nights drinking at Duke's Saloon where he was arrested on suspicion of murder on April 26, after the body of Turner was found the previous day. When arrested, Williams was wearing Turner's black Stetson hat that was easily identified from the Cincinnati newspaper that Turner had placed in the hat band for a tighter fit.

On the afternoon of April 25, a passerby discovered Turner's body lying in the brush near the La Vernia road, after he noticed a dog gnawing on a leg. Seventeen miles from San Antonio, Turner and Williams had pitched a tent to camp for the night and prepared a campfire for their coffee. As Turner laid inside the tent sleeping, he was struck twice to the head with a hatchet. Either wound would have been fatal. The body was afterwards pulled from the tent and placed in the brush and set on fire. The badly burned and decomposed body was transported back to San Antonio, and Mrs. Turner identified her husband's remains by a scar on the forehead and portions of the clothing that had not been destroyed by the fire.

On May 18, Williams went to trial and testified in his own defense. Williams claimed that he went as far as La Vernia and left after Turner met and struck a deal with a Mexican man who had a two-horse wagon to transport the chicken and eggs. Williams claimed the Mexican had a larger wagon and Turner dismissed him after he received his share of the goods. There was no evidence to support the story, and the jury did not believe Williams, and found him guilty of murder on May 20, and assessed the punishment at death.

Before the execution, Williams wrote two letters. One letter written on July 11, 1908, he gave it to his attorney L. W. Greenley with instructions not to release it until after his execution as the letter contained his confession to the murder. The second letter was written to his wife Carrie Williams which he asked a jailer to deliver along with $1.20 which was all the money he had to give her. The letter read:

Dear wife: I wish you to pardon me for all the trouble I have caused you, and mother to forgive me as God's forgives me. All the pains I have given you and I would like for you to see Mr. Torres. He will prepare a place for you to stay when you have none. Believe me, I am happy in the faith I am dying in. I should like for you to join the Holy Catholic Church, so that we may meet in heaven. Good-bye, dear wife and parents, till we meet again in heaven.

Doc Williams.

On the day of the execution, six deputy sheriffs carried Williams to the gallows because he had a broken leg from attempting to escape from jail. While jumping from the jail to a shed, the left leg was broken in the process.

On the gallows, Sheriff Tobin encouraged Williams to make a confession by telling him, "Nothing can save you, and it would be in the interest of humanity for you to do so."

In a low voice, Williams said, "I am guilty. I killed Mr. Turner and want everybody to know it after I am dead. Mr. Tobin, I also want to tell you Mr. Weyel had nothing to do with my attempted escape. He did not assist me in any way. I planned that all by myself."

When the preparations were complete, Sheriff John Tobin pulled the lever and Williams dropped seven feet to his death, breaking his neck. After the body hung for twenty-three minutes, it was cut down and released to Zizik Undertaking. The following morning, Father Joseph Waring performed a few simple rites over the casket moments before the undertaker transported the remains to St. Peter Clavier's #3 African American section in the cemetery as no one else arrived to pay their last respects.

The gallows used to execute Williams were first built thirty years prior in preparation of executing six men for murder in DeWitt County, but the gallows were dismantled and stored after the condemned men were set free. The same scaffold was used for the execution of Jose Cordova, Jacob Haneline, Charles Ward, Jim McCoy Austin Brown, Juan Rocha, Vincente Saucedo, George Turner, and Henry Mays. The rope used to hang Mays, was the same rope that hanged Williams.

The *San Antonio Daily Express*, dated Saturday, August 1, 1908, provided its readers with a large article of the history of the crime, jail escape and execution.

Lee Johnson

Race/Gender: Black Male **Age:** 18 **Offense:** Murder
Offense Date: August 18, 1913 **Weapon:** .32 caliber Pistol **Execution:** September 26, 1913

Lee Johnson was an eighteen-year-old man who had been employed as a yardman for Doctor Augustus Maverick and his family where they lived at 822 West Magnolia Avenue in San Antonio. Because of threats Johnson had been making toward a servant girl after she had rejected him, Dr. Maverick had no choice but to discharge him.

Two nights later, on August 18, 1913, at about 10 p.m., Fena Outoine and Bertha Jahn were preparing for bed when Jahn reached to turn off the bedroom light. Just then Johnson, who was watching both women prepare for bed while standing on a ladder outside the window, told Jahn not to turn the light off. Outoine hearing Johnson's voice, jumped from bed screaming and ran out into the hallway. Johnson ripped the window screen away from the window and quickly entered the house in pursuit of Outoine.

While chasing after Outoine, Johnson fired two pistol shots at her with one bullet striking her to the back. Johnson then repeatedly kicked and beat Outoine in the face with his fist. Jahn in the meantime ran to the bedroom of William Maverick, while Augustus Maverick, who was downstairs in his library study, heard the screams and shots from the second floor and ran up the stairs. The doctor then saw Johnson standing over Outoine while striking her in the face.

Augustus seeing Johnson with the pistol wrestled and grappled for control of the weapon. During the struggle, Augustus was shot three times in the throat, but while collapsing had wrestled the handgun away from his murderer. Augustus's father, William H. Maverick rushed into the hall with his own gun. Johnson then struck Augustus's six-year-old daughter. William took aim and shot at Johnson. The bullet hit Johnson in the side, where he then turned and ran back to the bedroom through which he had entered and scrambled back down the ladder to the ground.

Minutes later mounted police officer Duke Carver who was responding to the Maverick home, came upon Johnson running away from the direction of the house. The officer ordered Johnson to stop, and seeing that Johnson was bleeding, handcuffed him to a telegraph pole so that he could continue on to the Maverick home and investigate the disturbance. Upon learning of the murder, Officer Carver returned to the telegraph pole and took Johnson to the city jail. Fearing an assault on the city jail by a mob, Johnson was dressed in a woman's dress and bonnet to disguise him for transport to a stronger and more secure county jail for safekeeping.

Johnson told detectives he had been infatuated with Outoine who cooked for the family and had gone to the doctor's home to see her. When Outoine rejected him, Johnson said he became enraged and shot Outoine in the back with a Hopkins and Allen .32 caliber pistol. The five shot pistol was recovered and the cylinder showed Johnson had fired all five bullets. The twenty-seven-year-old doctor is buried next to his wife at the Saint Mary's Cemetery in San Antonio.

The two-day trial began on August 22 before Judge W. S. Anderson of the 37th District Court. Johnson pled not guilty to the charge. The following day A. B. Story for the State told the jury during final arguments, "Taking of the life of that black brute would not be adequate punishment. I urge the jurymen by their verdict to send a pledge of security into every home in San Antonio, that such unlawful deeds shall not go unpunished here. May God go with you gentlemen into the jury room when you retire, and bless the hand that writes the verdict in this case." Forty-three minutes later the jury returned a verdict of guilty and assessed the death sentence.

From the gallows, Lee Johnson addressed the 300 witnesses and said:

Gentlemen, I have a little statement to make," he said, with a barely perceptible tremor of the voice. "I think the people and the police and sheriff for the kind treatment they gave me. I thank the jailers and all the people. I am sorry for the crime I committed, and the sorrow if brought to the family of Mr. Maverick. I ask their pardon as I ask the pardon of God for me. If I had it to do again I would never do it. I ask God to pardon me, that's all I have to say."

After Johnson had finished his statement, both his hands and legs were then bound. While Sheriff Tobin was adjusting the noose about his neck, he accidentally caught the rope on a St. Mary medallion Johnson had around his neck. Johnson told the sheriff, "wait a minute." After the rope was untangled, Johnson kissed the religious medal and said, "That's all right now, go ahead." As the black cap was being adjusted, Johnson told Sheriff Tobin, "I'll meet you all in heaven."

The body of Lee Johnson was released to Father Kane for burial at St. Peter Clavier's Cemetery.

The *San Antonio Light*, dated Friday, September 26, 1913, provided its readers with a large article detailing the murder and execution.

George McKinley Grace

Race/Gender: Black Male **Age:** 22 **Offense:** Rape
Offense Date: February 24, 1920 **Weapon:** Knife **Execution:** January 6, 1922

On the night of February 24, 1920, while a woman lay in her bed asleep, she was suddenly startled by a black man touching her. As she struggled to get away, the intruder first tried to restrain her by choking her. The woman desperately fought for her life and while doing so, her hand was severely cut by the open bladed pocket knife he was holding. The intruder, who had quietly entered the house through an open window, went to the crib next to the bed and threatened to cut her five-year-old daughter's throat if she did not comply with his demands.

After the intruder left, the assault was immediately reported to the police and the victim provided a description of her attacker. The following day, the police going on a tip from the description provided, went to the home of George Grace who lived at 605 Callahan Ave, just blocks away from the victim. The detectives placed Grace under arrest and he afterwards provided detectives a signed statement which read, "There was a scuffle and in the scuffle her hand was cut with the knife which I had in my hand, caused by her keeping on trying to shove me away."

At his trial on March 8, 1920, Grace was tried for criminal assault the first time in the 37th District Court. The victim took the witness stand and told the jury the details of her assault. Pointing to Grace, she then said, "That is the Negro, I could never forget that face in a thousand years."

Grace denied he had committed the assault and claimed he only provided a confession for fear of a lynch mob. On March 11, Grace was found guilty by the jury after deliberating one hour and twenty minutes, declaring Grace guilty and assessed his penalty at death.

On appeal, the case was sent back for retrial due to Judge W. S. Anderson having allowed clothing worn by Grace, which contained bloodstains, to have been allowed into evidence. Grace was retried on January 22, 1921 and found guilty with the punishment assessed at death for a second time. After the second appeal was affirmed, Judge Anderson on November 29 passed sentence upon Grace and ordered that he be hanged on Friday, January 6, 1922.

From the gallows, Grace said, "I am ready to meet my God, for I am not guilty. I am innocent."

The gallows were built within the San Antonio jail with the trap door having a push button release. Three deputies who were selected were assigned one button. Two of the buttons were not wired while a third button with an electric current was wired to the trap, which released the door when pushed. The three officers were never told which button was wired to the trap.

The *San Antonio Light*, dated Friday, January 6, 1922, provided readers with a large article detailing the crime and execution.

Clemente Apolinar

Race/Gender: Hispanic Male **Age:** 32 **Offense:** Murder
Weapon: Rock **Offense Date:** August 16, 1921 **Execution:** February 23, 1923

Clemente Apolinar, as a boy growing up in San Antonio, received a severe blow to the head. The head injury caused permanent damage to his brain, and he was committed to an asylum. Years later, Clemente escaped from the asylum, and lived on the streets.

In the summer of 1921, a group of boys that included fourteen-year-old Theodore Bernhard teased Clemente and threw rocks at him while he was drinking water from a spring. On August 16, 1921, Bernhard and his younger brother Kirby were herding cattle and stopped at a watering hole to allow the cattle to drink. While the cattle were watering, the boys entertained themselves by playing in the spring with hollowed out gourds made into boats.

Clemente Apolinar walked up to the spring to drink water and asked the boys what they were doing. The boys replied. "Muddying the water."

Apolinar told the boys to stop, as he wanted to drink. The boys laughed and continued playing. Apolinar then picked up large rocks and chased after Theodore and Kirby. Theodore who was not as fast as Kirby was overtaken by Apolinar and hit in the back of the head with a large rock. Apolinar used the large rock to crush the boy's skull and gouged out his eyes.

Keeping one of the eyes as a souvenir, Apolinar was said to have shown the eye to a farmer's wife and told her, "Doesn't it look like a dog's eye."

Kirby who had left his brother behind had continued running home to notify his mother of the attack. The police located Apolinar near the scene, and they discovered one of Theodore's eyes that Apolinar was still carrying in his vest pocket.

Apolinar was charged and tried for murder in the first degree. The jury found him guilty of murder and assessed the penalty for his crime at death. The case was appealed to the Court of Criminal Appeals which affirmed the decision of May 17, 1922. A petition claiming insanity was quickly filed which resulted in a nine-day trial where Apolinar was judged to be sane on December 21, 1922, and two days later sentenced to hang on February 23, 1923.

The day before Apolinar's scheduled execution, Apolinar wrote the following bio about himself:

There is not much for me to write about my life because there wasn't anything much happened until I got in this trouble, except a couple of times when I was sick and they sent me to the insane asylum.

I was born in San Antonio and have been here most of the time. When they break my neck tomorrow, I will be 32 years and 3 months old to the day. I was born in a house in the east end of town.

My father died when I was 13 years old, and I left school when I was 14 so that I could help my mother. When I was 16, something happened to make me sick and I always tried to run away from home. They caught me and took me to the County Jail and the doctor said he thought I should be brought to the insane asylum. They took me to the Southwestern Insane Asylum and kept me there a year. Then they let me go.

I went back home and a little while later I tried to run away again and they put me back in the asylum again. I don't remember how long they kept me there that time, but it was several months.

I made two trips out of San Antonio. One time I went to Alaska to help fish for salmon and another time I went to Tennessee to work in a powder plant. That was during the war. They would not take me in the army because they said I was sick.

I have five brothers, and one sister named Santos. My brother's names are Saosnao, Eneniencio, Yguacio, Jose and Jacobo.

On the morning of the execution, Clemente walked out of the holding cell wearing a new blue suit with a collar shirt and tie. At the gallows, Clemente kneeled for a final blessing while the sheriff fastened the rope to a large and heavy iron ring from the ceiling of the third floor. Apolinar requested that no blindfold or black cap be used which was granted. After the blessing, the noose was adjusted around his neck and the trap sprung at 11:07 a.m. At the end of the drop, the rope cut through the neck and almost severed the head from the body.

A prisoner watching the execution from his cell screamed out, "Cut him down, and hang the man that hung him."

After the body was cut down, the remains were carried outside to an awaiting hearse to be transported to Riebe's Undertaking Parlor.

Sheriff John W. Tobin had purchased the hemp rope for the hanging and it was also used to hang Harvey Hughes in Brewster County. After the state law changed the method of executing the condemned from hanging to the electric chair, the rope was used for many years by the Bexar County Sheriff's Department as a tow rope for vehicles.

The *San Antonio Evening News*, dated Friday, February 23, 1923, provided their readers with the details of the crime and execution.

Soldiers of the Twenty-Fourth Infantry

The Twenty-Fourth U.S. Army Infantry Division was one of the all black "Buffalo," regiments formed on November 1, 1869. The Twenty-Fourth fought in several campaigns over the years, and in 1916, the regiment was stationed at Camp Furlong at Columbus, New Mexico, as part of the border protection from Poncho Villa and his army. Then on July 27, 1917, the army ordered the Third Battalion of the Twenty-Fourth to travel by train to Houston, Texas, to guard the construction site of Camp Logan. Companies I, K, L, M, consisting of 645 enlisted men and seven officers were assigned to guard the construction site located five miles west of Houston.

Soon after their arrival racial tension began to grow to the point of exploding with deadly consequences. On August 23, 1917, Houston police officers Lee Sparks and Rufus Daniels pursued a black man whom they were attempting to arrest for participating in a dice game. The officers entered the home of Sara Travers after accusing her of hiding the man. They dragged her outside into the street, dressed in her bathrobe, and began beating her.

Private Alonso Edwards seeing the woman being assaulted by the two white officers approached and began questioning as to what they were doing. Sparks then turned on the private, pistol-whipped and placed him under arrest for interfering.

Once news of the arrest of Edwards was known at the infantry camp, Corporal Charles Baltimore of the military police was directed to obtain information of the charges and circumstances. Corporal Baltimore traveled to the Houston police station and confronted Officer Sparks. Sparks replied, "It was none of Baltimore's business, and that he did not have to tell a Negro anything."

Corporal Baltimore tried to explain that the private was on guard duty, and therefore he would have to report the matter to his commanding officers. Sparks then hit Baltimore twice over the head with his pistol and when Baltimore fled, Sparks fired three shots at him. It didn't take long before reports and wild rumors reached the infantry encampment of the beatings and the belief that Sgt. Baltimore had been shot and was dead. In response, 156 soldiers raided the armory tent for rifles and ammunition and began a march to the Houston Police Department.

The end result of the riot was twenty-two citizens killed, four of which were police officers with one of the four being Rufus Daniels. Of the 118 soldiers indicted for murder, mutiny, aggravated assault, and disobeying an order, sixty-three were found guilty. The verdicts were forty-one soldiers sentenced to imprisonment from two years to life; and nineteen soldiers were ordered to be executed. The first thirteen men to be executed were all found guilty on November 28, 1917, but were not given an execution date.

On December 9, 1917, the prisoners were told they were to be executed in two days, and the army made no further announcement of the pending executions. On the morning of December 11, 1917, just as the sun was about to rise, the men were hanged from a massive gallows that had been built throughout the night by the Engineer Corps two miles east of Camp Travis, near San Antonio. Standing on the gallows, their last words were, "Goodbye boys of Company C." After the thirteen men were pronounced dead and cut down, the remains were buried in unmarked graves near the site of the gallows that had been dismantled.

On September 17, 1918, five more soldiers were executed, and the final soldier on September 24. On each date of an execution, it was done in secrecy with no announcement to newspaper correspondents, family members or civilians other than Sheriff John Tobin who was the only civilian allowed to witness the executions.

On March 20, 1918, Camp Logan was closed. Between 1934 and 1937, all the remains were exhumed and reburied at Fort Sam Houston National Cemetery except for two. The other two remains were released to family members who chose to bury their loved ones elsewhere.

The *Dallas Morning News*, dated Wednesday, December 12, 1917, listed the following thirteen soldiers who were executed:

Sergeant William C. Nesbitt
Corporal Larnon J. Brown
Corporal James Wheatley
Corporal Jesse Moore
Corporal Charles W. Baltimore
Private William Brackenridge
Private Pat MacWhorter
Private Carlos Snodgrass
Private Ira B. Davis
Private James Divins
Private Frank Johnson
Private Thomas C. Hawkins
Private Risley W. Young

The *Dallas Morning News*, dated September 18, 1918, listed the following five soldiers who were executed on September 17, 1918:

Private Babe Collier
Private Thomas McDonald
Private Joseph Smith
Private James Robinson
Private Albert D. Wright

The *Tulsa World*, (Tulsa, OK), dated September 25, 1918, listed the last soldier of the 24th infantry who was hanged on September 24, 1918, as Private William D. Boone.

Bowie County
County Seat - Boston

James Jones

Race/Gender: Black Male **Age:** 25 **Offense:** Murder
Offense Date: August 6, 1886 **Weapon:** Pistol **Execution:** May 13, 1887

On August 6, 1886, James Jones worked during the day as a tie cutter, and at night gambled with the rail workers. Jones was considered a bully and a tough man among the men in the railroad camp and they usually stayed out of his way. On May 13, 1887, Jones was hanged in the presence of 5000 witnesses for the shooting death of Cate Hicks, the camp cook after the two argued over a cup of water.

On the day of the shooting, Hicks told Jones not to take water, as it was scarce. Jones replied that he didn't care either way, and he was going to take it anyhow. Some hard language followed and Jones left the kitchen, returning a few minutes later with a cocked revolver in his hand. Jones walked up to Hicks and commenced cursing him and asked if he didn't like his style. When Hicks replied he didn't, Jones knocked him down by striking him with his fist. Hicks retreated to the back part of the room, where he had an empty gun. Jones exclaimed, "Damn you, keep your hands off that gun," then fired his revolver hitting Cate to the head.

Tried and found guilty of murder, the case was affirmed on November 17, 1886. In rendering the opinion of the Court of Appeals, Judge Wilson, concluded by writing:

The conviction is amply sustained by the evidence. There is no room to doubt the defendant committed the murder and that he was actuated by express malice. It was a deliberate homicide, unprovoked and without mitigation. It is but justice that he should suffer the extreme penalty of the law and the judgment is affirmed, there being no reason appearing to us why it should be set aside.

The gallows were erected a half mile south of the jail. On the day of the execution, Jones was driven to the scene in an open hack. Upon arrival, Jones ascended the scaffold and listened to the reading of his death warrant. Afterwards Jones spoke for twenty minutes and told the crowd, to hunt him up when they got to heaven, and shouted, "Farewell, everybody; you will meet me close to the throne of my Lord!"

The noose was then adjusted and the black cap pulled over his head. A blow from the hatchet cut the rope and Jones shot straight downward six feet. His neck was broken, and he was pronounced dead in nine minutes. At the end of thirty minutes the body was taken down and given to his wife and her friends who carried the remains to the cemetery.

James Jones told a reporter of the *Fort Worth Daily Gazette*, during an interview the morning of the execution, that if the same thing had to be done over again he would do it, as he thought himself perfectly justifiable. He said he had made his peace with his Savior and was ready to meet his maker. The newspaper printed a full account in the Saturday, May 14, 1887, edition.

J. E. Shutt

Race/Gender: White Male **Age:** 63 **Offense:** Murder
Offense Date: May 1, 1902 **Weapon:** Pistol **Execution:** May 29, 1903

J. E. Shutt and his employer, J. C. Whitener, had been friends for twenty-five years. One night Shutt became angry with Whitener for refusing to advance him any additional loans. Shutt armed with a pistol located Whitener playing a game of dominos at a local saloon and whispered something in his ear. Shutt then took a couple steps back, drew his revolver and shot Whitener who died hours later.

At trial, Shutt alleged that he killed Whitener because Whitener had betrayed his honor. Shutt was convicted of murder in the first degree and sentenced to hang. After being sentenced to death, the conviction was appealed to the Court of Criminal Appeals and after review of the case affirmed the decision on December 11, 1902. Shutt's wife afterwards gathered 3,000 signatures to commute the sentence and delivered the petition herself to the Governor Samuel W. T. Lanham. Governor Lanham notified Sheriff T. C. Morris to proceed with the execution. When Shutt was told his petition had been denied, he replied his punishment was "just," and refused to eat, only asking for whiskey.

At 5 p.m. on the day of his execution, J. E. Shutt was led to the gallows in New Boston. Shutt did not make a statement about his crime at the suggestion of his advisors, but he asked God for mercy. Shutt told the witnesses he held no malice against anyone, and was ready to go. After the trap was sprung and Shutt was pronounced dead, the body was placed in a coffin. The remains were then transported by the Texas & Pacific train to Jefferson, Texas, for burial.

The *Shiner Gazette*, dated Wednesday, June 3, 1903, provided details of the murder and the execution at Texarkana, Texas.

Sol Johnson

Race/Gender: Black Male **Offense:** Robbery & Murder **Offense Date:** February 9, 1922
Weapon: Pistol **Execution:** July 20, 1923

On February 9, 1922, Sol Johnson and his nephew George Johnson entered G. W. Landers' general store with the intent to rob the elderly merchant. After the men made a small purchase, the robbers drew their handguns and demanded that the partially deaf store merchant hand over all of the money from the cash box. During the robbery, Landers was shot and killed. When his wife attempted to run to her husband aid, one of the men fired a shot at her.

Mrs. Johnson provided the sheriff with the description of both robbers which matched the description provided by other witnesses that had seen the pair near the store. Sol Johnson was captured near Mount Pleasant, but his nephew eluded arrest. While being held in the Bowie County Jail, Johnson escaped custody, but was recaptured three days later. On December 15, Johnson was tried for robbery and murder and convicted. After failed attempts on a motion for a new trial, an appeal to the Texas Court of Criminal Appeal was made. The higher court affirmed the conviction, and a plea to the governor to commute the sentence was also declined.

Johnson was sentenced on June 20, 1923, to be executed at the end of thirty days. Johnson made a second attempt for freedom, which was diverted after it was discovered the bars in his cell had been partially sawed through with a hacksaw and acid which were both found during the search of the cell. Johnson claimed he had received the acid and saw from Deputy Frank Luckett who he had paid $40 for both items. Deputy Luckett was tried for attempting to aid in the escape and sentenced to two years in the penitentiary. Luckett was later acquitted on appeal.

On July 20, 1923, while protesting his innocence, the trap was sprung at 11:15 a.m. dropping Sol Johnson to his death.

The *Galveston Daily News*, dated Saturday, July 21, 1923, reported that the execution had taken place at Texarkana, Texas.

Brazoria County
County Seat - Angleton

Frank Holland

Race/Gender: White Male **Age:** 25 **Offense:** Robbery & Triple Murder
Offense Date: March 6, 1892 **Weapon:** Ax & Pistol **Execution:** February 23, 1893

In March of 1892, a man known only by the last name of Smith, traveled to Brazoria County along with two brothers, James and Steve Cravey. Smith carried a large sum of cash as he was prospecting the coastal counties to purchase land for a ranch. Not knowing the area, Smith hired Frank Holland and his nephew Jerome Baker as guides.

Holland learned of the large sum of cash and conspired with Baker to kill Smith and the Cravey brothers for their money, guns, horses and personal effects. On the night of March 6, 1893, while the three men were asleep, Holland struck each man in the head with an ax, and then shot each of them with their own guns.

The bodies, which had been buried in the mud along the San Bernard River were discovered nine days later, after part of a wagon was found in the river. A letter found on one of the bodies addressed to Steve Cravey, provided the first clue as to the identity of the dead. This letter led to the arrest of Frank Holland and Jerome Baker.

On June 24, 1892, the grand jury indicted both Baker and Holland for the murder of Steve and Jim Cravey, and Smith. Jerome Baker was tried first and found guilty. After being sentenced to life in the penitentiary, Baker said Smith had foolishly displayed the large amount of money he was carrying to Frank Holland. Baker admitted to burning the wagon and robbing the victims of their property, but claimed Holland did all of the killing.

On July 10, 1892, Holland was tried for murder and he claimed self-defense as the reason he had killed the three victims. Holland said Smith insulted him by making fun of any women who chewed tobacco and used snuff. Holland said:

> We got into a fight and the two Craveys also jumping on me and I went to shooting and killing'em all. I'm the quickest hand on the trigger in Texas. After I had finished'em, me and Baker cut'em up and burned the wagon. We concluded it was a shame to throw good clothes and bed clothes, gun, horses and money away, so we took them along.

The jury did not believe his version and found him guilty of murder, and accessed the death penalty. On the day of the execution Holland stepped upon the gallows and thanked to the officers for their kindness. As the black cap was being drawn over his head Holland said, "Goodbye, God bless you." Sheriff R. M. Yerby then sprang the trap. The papers wrote, "Holland died game and expressed no regret for his crime."

The *Galveston Daily News*, dated Friday, February 24, 1893, provided its readers with a full account of the murders and discovery of the crime.

Caesar Harris

Race/Gender: Black Male **Age:** 28 **Offense:** Murder
Offense Date: June 13, 1898 **Weapon:** Shotgun **Execution:** March 16, 1899

Caesar Harris was tried and convicted for the shotgun murder of his wife Susan Jackson. The couple had separated on several occasions during their two-year marriage, but on June 13, 1898, Harris attempted to repair their differences and asked her for reconciliation. During the conversation, Susan asked Harris to buy her a new dress. When Harris refused, she replied if he would not, she knew a person who would. This comment angered Harris to the point that he shot her dead.

On March 16, 1899, Caesar Harris was executed at Angleton, Texas. On the gallows, Harris asked Sheriff Weems not to tie the noose down too tight around his neck, and said he had nothing further to say.

After the physicians declared Harris dead, the body was lowered into a pine coffin. The coffin was then slid into the bed of a wagon where a family friend was to drive the remains to Columbia for burial. Late that night, the friend arrived at Columbia on foot and declared that Caesar Harris had come back to life.

The friend refused to return to where the wagon was located at night, and related to the town folks that after he had crossed Oyster Creek, he heard a tapping coming from inside the coffin. The tapping became louder and louder until he stopped the wagon. Just after stopping, one of Caesar Harris' legs broke through the coffin lid. The friend jumped from the wagon and ran screaming in horror.

The following day, citizens from Columbia returned to the location to find the horses and wagon on the side of the road. In the wagon bed was the coffin with a leg protruding out from under the lid. After removing the lid, they found that Harris' body was warm and he had a faint heartbeat. By the time they arrived at Columbia, Harris was dead. Harris was buried two days later in Columbia. The story made national headlines, although the validity of the story has always been in question.

The *Houston Daily Post*, dated Friday, March 17, 1899, printed details of the crime and execution.

Nathan Lee

Race/Gender: Black Male **Age:** 34 **Offense:** Murder
Offense Date: September 7, 1922 **Weapon:** Shotgun **Execution:** August 31, 1923

Nathan Lee was a black farmer who entered into a lease agreement on a portion of land owned by a wealthy farmer by the name of John Spurgeon. Lee raised cotton, and as the cotton crop was coming in, he argued with Spurgeon as to their agreement that Spurgeon was to a receive a portion of the cotton, and money owed to him on the lease.

On September 7, 1922, soon after the disagreement, Lee and Spurgeon went rabbit hunting together. As Spurgeon walked through an opening in a fence, Lee shot him in the back of the neck with a shotgun. Two days later, Spurgeon's body was found lying in a ditch near his home and Nathan Lee was quickly arrested. Lee confessed to the murder and placed an X on the written statement as his signature.

At the trial, Lee attempted to convince the court that he had only confessed to the murder after he had been forced to do so. On July 30, 1923, the court did not believe Lee's story, and Judge Milim S. Munson sentenced him to hang for murder on August 31, 1923. The court of criminal appeals affirmed the lower court's decision on April 18, 1923.

Days before his execution, Lee again admitted to the murder of John Spurgeon, and retold the story of shooting him because of their disagreement over the lease of the land and cotton crop. On the day of the execution, Lee told the 100 witnesses from the scaffold erected on the courthouse lawn, "I did it, I am to blame, I am guilty, no one else had anything to do with it, and I don't want anyone else punished for it."

At 11:20 a.m. the trap was sprang dropping Nathan Lee, who made history as the last man to be legally hanged in the State of Texas. The state had enacted a new law which changed the method of execution from hanging to electrocution. The new law also removed the responsibility to execute those condemned by the court from the county sheriff to the State Penitentiary at Huntsville, Texas.

The *Galveston Daily News*, dated Saturday, September 1, 1923, reported to their readers that the execution of Nathan Lee had occurred at Angleton, Texas.

Brazos County

County Seat - Bryan

Ezekiel Bradley

Alias: Zeik
Offense: Murder
Execution: May 2, 1879

Race/Gender: Black Male
Offense Date: December 25, 1878

Age: 21 or 22
Weapon: Pistol

On Christmas day, 1878, a drunken Ezekiel Bradley and his friend Shep Wilson staggered to Steele's store located 15 miles west of Bryan, Texas, to purchase a bottle of whiskey. Once in front of the store, Shep Wilson began fighting with Buck Pollock and called Pollock "a goddamned son of a bitch!"

Pollock replied that he would not take that, and struck Wilson in the face with his fist. Wilson returned the blow and as Pollock drew back his arm to strike again, Zeik Bradley came up behind Wilson, pulled a concealed pistol, reached over his shoulder, and shot Pollock in the mouth, saying, "Damn you, take that!" and killing Pollock instantly. Bradley was arrested the following day for murder and maintained up until the trap was sprung that he did not recollect the shooting because of his intoxicated state.

On May 2, 1879, at 2:30 p.m. in the afternoon, Ezekiel Bradley, was placed in a hack by Sheriff William Forman and two deputies, and driven to the gallows. He was also escorted by the Bryan Rifles. The hack reached the gallows at 2:50 to an awaiting crowd of 4000 to 6000 people.

Bradley then ascended the scaffold, kneeled down before a Catholic priest who placed the crucifix to the prisoner's lips and prayed. Bradley afterwards stood up and said, "Friends, sister, and brothers, I have got to go home. All of us have got to die, and you will not see me again until the day of resurrection." Quoting a song, Bradley said, "On Jordan's stormy banks I stand. I am going home to eat sweet milk and honey, and feast at the table of our Jesus."

Dr. Hardewicke, a Baptist minister and spiritual advisor for Bradley gave the following speech:

This is most solemn occasion; one that some of you will never forget. In a few minutes a young man in perfect health will be executed in compliance with the sentence of a law modeled after the Mosaic code, which says, "Thou shalt do not murder. Whose sheddeth man's blood, by man shall his blood be shed!" We recognize the majesty and justice of this law, and bow to its decision,; we look with the deepest regard upon those who violate it, but with resolute wills and firm hands execute its sentence.

The law knows nothing of revenge; its officers are not influenced by any such spirit to-day. The duty is a sad one, but it must be discharged.

Why is Ezekiel Bradley not a free man today? A few months ago he was as free as any man here. Ah; a crime has been committed – a man has been murdered. Why did the prisoner murder Mr. Pollock? He shall answer himself: "I was drunk. I did not know that I had killed him until I was told of it by my mother."

See what drunkenness has done. It has robbed Mr. Pollock of a son, and it brings his slayer here to die at the hands of an officer. Bradley has a mother, a wife and a young child, and drink has robbed them of a son, husband and father. Beware of drunkenness! It dehumanizes man; makes him brutal in feeling, and untrue to his God, his fellow-man, his family and himself. It takes away his sense of justice, destroys his appreciation of the value and his reverence for the sacredness of human life. The blood of young Pollock cries from the ground against this sin. Here, with this platform on which I now stand, the beam above me, this drop upon which the doomed man will soon stand before you. I warn you all to beware of the sin of drunkenness.

If I had the power I would make it unlawful for any one to sell and impossible for any one to purchase liquor to be drank as a beverage. Drunkenness is lining this land with graves, filling our prisons, and preparing men for crimes that make such occasions this a necessity. Beware of drunkenness and the carrying of concealed weapons!

This custom is contrary to the code of Texas; the law makes it an offense, and fixes a heavy penalty for its violation. This law should be enforced. Grand juries and courts should do their duty. A drunken man with a loaded pistol endangers the peace and safety of a community. The custom of carrying concealed weapons is ordinarily unnecessary. If Ezekiel Bradley had not been drunk last Christmas, and if he had not been in possession of a loaded pistol he probably would not appear here today to die for the crime of murder.

Human life is from God. Man may destroy it, but he cannot restore it. It is so sacred that God has hedged it about with the wisest cautions, and guarded with the most solemn enactments. The malicious, wanton destruction of human life is the greatest crime that man commits against man—a crime so baneful that divine law requires "a life for a life; blood for blood." No man, except in self-defense or in obedience to the law of the land, had a right to deprive another of his life.

Since the late war the crime of murder has become common to all sections of our country. There is much in the current literature of the day—in the dime novels that make heroes of red-handed assassins; in the papers which abound with the details and pictorial illustrations of crime to produce this state of things. We find men who think it a brave thing to have it said. "He has killed his man!" "He will shoot!" "He is a man who will not hesitate to kill!" "He is brave!" It is not a brave thing to violate the law.

Men who commit murder are not brave when alone in the dark. They are not brave when confined in a felon's cell. They may appear brave when before the public; they may smile on friends while remorse is consuming their peace. To the man who with malice aforethought coolly plans to take the life of another that's is no peace. Juries may acquit him because of a reasonable doubt or for want of evidence; courts may discharge him, nature may smile, flowers may bloom, but the soul of such a man will never smile again. No flowers will ever grow in his heart—unless he is washed in the blood of Jesus, which cleanses from all sin.

In the name of the sorrowing love ones of the men who have been murdered in the game of law and order, in the name of God, the Maker of us all, do I on this solemn occasion warn you to beware of drunkenness and of the unlawful custom of carrying concealed weapons. And, again, do I warn you to beware of the slightest temptation to commit the fearful crime of murder.

At the conclusion, Bradley's feet and hands were then tied; and stepped upon the trap door with firmness; the black cap was put over his face and the noose adjusted. Just at the closure of the last prayer, Sheriff Forman pulled the lever, dropping Bradley six feet and launching him into eternity.

Prior to the execution, reporters from the *Galveston Daily News*, interviewed Ezekiel Bradley, the interview was printed along with details of the execution in the Saturday, May 3, 1879, edition:

I am twenty-one or two years old; have been raised in the Brazos bottom; have never had any moral training, and have been a drinking and quarrelsome boy all my life. On Christmas day two women had caught my Christmas gift, and I went to Steele's store to pay it. I had been drinking all that day and night before. I got five dollars changed and went over to Evan's Ton-Pie Alley and commenced betting and drinking again, and became very drunk. In some way (I do not know how) I learned that Ben Barbee had a pistol, and borrowed it. I did not tell him what I wanted with it, in fact, I had no use for it, not have had difficulty with any one. Up to that time I was entirely unarmed, not having even a pocket-knife. I stayed at Evan's store a good while after I got the pistol and until Shep Wilson asked me to treat him. I told him if he would go to Steele's store I would get a quart, and we went there. I got to the store and saw Ben Barbee there; and that is the last I remember of what occurred at the store. When I became conscious again I was at Col. Wilson's quarters, about a mile from there. My cousin came to me – told me what I had done; that white men were after me, and that I had better leave. I was surprised and could not remember anything they told me of. I never knew and had never seen Pollock before that day, and could not have had malice towards him; and my sorrow has been expressible and indescribable, and I have lain down and wept at the thought of having killed a man who had never done me harm or injury, and whom I had not known. I have no complaint to make of my treatment while in confinement; it has been good. I have had a fair and impartial trial. My punishment is just and the law ought to be enforced. Several ministers have been to see me and prayed with me. I have joined the catholic church and have been baptized by the priest, and feel ready and willing to die, and believe that I will be saved. I desire to warn my race against the use of whiskey and carrying concealed weapons, as they alone have brought upon me this great affliction.

Bob Ballard

Race/Gender: Black Male　　**Age:** 32　　**Offense:** Robbery & Murder
Offense Date: November 7, 1900　**Weapon:** Firearm　**Execution:** November 22, 1901

Bob Ballard was a man with a reputation for having a bad temper and proved over the years that he would not hesitate to shoot a man that he quarreled with. On November 7, 1900, Ballard argued over a glass of beer with the saloon bartender by the name of Jacob Schramek at the small town of Smetana, located twenty-one miles west of Bryan, Texas, and pulled his pistol. Without hesitation, Ballard shot the bartender, then mounted his horse and fled from the scene believing he had killed the man.

Riding towards Bryan, Ballard rode up on Frank Blazek and decided to rob him of his money. Ballard pulled his pistol and told Blazek to hand over his money. When he replied he had none, Ballard shot him twice.

Ballard was tried and found guilty of murder. The jury assessed the punishment at death. The case was appealed, and the Court of Criminal Appeals finding no error, affirmed the decision on May 8, 1901.

The execution was held privately and only those with invitations were admitted inside the jail. As Ballard walked out of the cell towards the gallows, he said, "God has saved my soul, I am ready and willing to go." After mounting the gallows, Ballard declined to make a final statement, but asked the preachers to pray for him. After the drop, the body was released to his father, Dennis Ballard for burial.

The *Dallas Morning News*, dated Saturday, November 23, 1901, provided readers with details of the shootings, past history of his criminal exploits, and the execution at Bryan, Texas.

Brewster County
County Seat - Alpine

Harvey Hughes

Race/Gender: White male **Age:** 22 **Offense:** Robbery & Murder
Offense Date: January 24, 1922 **Weapon:** Firearm **Execution:** April 7, 1923

Harvey Hughes was accused of shooting a traveling companion on a westbound train near Alpine, Texas. On the night of January 24, 1922, the brakeman heard the sound of a person groaning from inside one of the boxcars. Sliding the metal door back, the brakeman, using his lantern, saw a man lying on the floor with a handkerchief tied over his mouth. The brakeman notified the sheriff's office and they were called to the scene.

The injured man who had been shot and badly beaten told the officers his name was C. H. Rodgers, and he said he had been shot for the $20 he was carrying. Before dying, Rodgers provided a description of the man who robbed him and said, "It is hell to feed a man and then have him shoot you in the back for $20."

Six miles west of Alpine, a deputy sheriff apprehended a man matching the description. He was identified as being Harvey Hughes. On Hughes' person, officers located a fountain pen, watch and money that all belonged to the victim. At trial, Hughes testified that he shot Rodgers in self-defense which the jury did not believe and found him guilty of murder in the first degree and assessed his punishment at death.

While standing on the gallows, Sheriff Townsend sprang the trap while a prayer was being given.

The *San Antonio Express*, dated Sunday, April 8, 1923, announced the execution took place at Alpine, Texas.

Burleson County

County Seat - Caldwell

Cal Parks

Race/Gender: Black Male **Age:** 21 **Offense:** Rape & Double Murder
Offense Date: May 9, 1892 **Weapon:** Pick Handle **Execution:** July 15, 1892

About two miles north of the town of Lyons along the Gulf, Colorado and Santa Fe Railway, H. M. McDonough worked as a section foreman. As a section foreman, he and his family lived in the section house the railroad provided.

On May 9, 1892, after lunch, Josie McDonough's husband returned to work, leaving her alone with his six-year-old son and their five-month-old baby daughter. At around 5:30 in the evening, workers heard the baby crying and entered the home to investigate and found Josie lying dead on the bedroom. Her stepson was lying on his bed and he was gasping for his last breaths of air.

Evidence at the scene indicated Josie had been sitting in her chair sewing a dress for her daughter when she was struck on the head with a pick handle. Injuries on the body indicated she had been struck nine times with the wood handle and sexually assaulted afterwards. The boy never regained consciousness and died at 10:30 that night. The baby girl was left unharmed.

The murderer was identified as an ex-convict by the name of Cal Parks. Parks had worked for Mr. McDonough for five months before being terminated from employment. Upon his capture at a farm near Navasota, Parks confessed to the sheriff of committing the murders and placed an X as his signature on a written confession. Parks would later deny that he committed the murders or made any confession to the crime.

On June 7th, Parks stood before Judge John Bryan. Judge Bryan asked Parks if he had anything to say as to why the sentence should not be pronounced. Parks replied, "No sir, I have nothing to say." The following month, Parks stood on the gallows at Caldwell, in the presence of 3000 witnesses.

On July 11, 1892, Cal Parks signed a second confession from the jail which read:

One the Friday before the Monday of the killing as I was going to the section house I saw Frazier Davis going into the section house. I stopped and hid in the corner of the fence until Frazier left and committed the crime. There was nobody at the section house except the lady, boy and myself. I left immediately after the killing, went straight on to Clay station, where I camped that night and bought my breakfast the next morning. I went to Dave Hardy's place and went to work. I took the clothes I had stolen at the section house down to Ed Brown's, who lives about two miles from Hardy's, and left them there. I was arrested at Hardy's farm.

The killing was done somewhere about 4 o'clock in the evening of the 9th of May, 1892. The only reason I can give for the killing is that about a week before the commission of the crime I had a quarrel with Mr. McDonough, the foreman, who ran to get his shotgun, and after Mr. McDonough, Watson and myself had some words.

On the day that the killing was done I was in Lyon's drinking some thing I had never drank before. I was not drunk but just had enough to make me feel it, when the words of Mr. and Mrs. McDonough came back to me and made me mad, and I concluded to commit this awful crime. I know I had no right to do it. I did not do the killing with the intention of robbery.

After arriving at the section-house as stated above I went into the room of Mrs. McDonough twice before the killing took place. The first time I went in I told her that I had come to see the new foreman. She told me that he had gone out on the road with the hands. She asked me if a train that was passing was the local. I told her I did not know. I then went into the yard and stood around for a while. I went over to the car house across the railroad track and picked up a club that was in the tool house, but concluded that it was not heavy enough and left it there and went into the room of the section house where I had been sleeping and got the pick handle from under the head of the bunk. This was the pick handle that was found in the room and the one the killing was done with. I went to the door of the room that Mrs. McDonough was in to see what she was doing. I don't think that Mrs. McDonough saw me at the time. She was standing in the middle of the room and the boy was sitting on the bed playing with some bright looking tin trick that come over the tops of sealed bottles. The boy was nearest to me and I struck him the first blow.

Mrs. McDonald screamed and asked me what I had done that for. I never give her any answer. She grabbed me after I had struck the boy one blow. I jerked loose from her and struck her one blow, but she warded it off and it did not knock her down. I struck her again and she fell. She fell on her face and I turned her over on her back and struck her four times about the head. I then went back to the bed and struck the little boy several times, I don't know the exact number of times. I then went through the house to see if I could find any money, but I did not find any. I then bundled up the clothes that was afterwards found in my possession. Mrs. McDonough and the boy were both breathing when I left.

I went out of the north door by the cistern and through the wire fence, then up a cornrow to the railroad. I went into the tool house and pulled off my socks, which were muddy, and put on my shoes and went off as stated above. In her struggle Mrs. McDonough may have pulled up her dress up herself. I did not touch her with my hands nor was it my intention to commit rape. I stay in the tool house only long enough to pull off my socks and put on my shoes. Nobody was with me nor knew anything about the crime except myself. I was drinking some, but was not drunk as above stated. I had never drank any whisky before that day. I have been treated kindly by the officers. Mr. Womack has treated me like a gentleman.

his
Cal X Parks.
Mark.

The *Dallas Morning News*, dated Saturday, July 16, 1892, ended their article of the execution by writing, "He had previously made a full confession of the crime. He made a short talk from the gallows of the usual type—justly condemned, bad example, home to heaven."

Frank Mitchell

Race/Gender: Black Male **Offense:** Murder **Offense Date:** March 21, 1907
Weapon: Ax **Execution:** August 1, 1908

Frank Mitchell and his girlfriend, Charity Bradford argued on the evening of March 21, 1907. The heated argument was over another woman that Bradford had seen Mitchell give a sack of flour. The giving of the flour was not an act of kindness, but rather a gift from Mitchell as he was having an affair with the lady. It is unknown how much Charity knew of the relationship since Mitchell continued to live with Bradford up to this time.

After arriving home, Bradford prepared for bed, while Mitchell left to take a walk, not returning home until 10 p.m.. To end his relationship with Bradford, Mitchell picked up an ax that had been left by the door and walked into the bedroom. While sleeping in bed with her four-month-old baby, Mitchell struck Bradford on the head twice with the ax, killing her. Mitchell afterwards left the house with the ax and stayed the night with the other woman after he secretly hid the weapon under her house. The next morning Mitchell returned and told neighbors he had killed Bradford in her bed. The police were summoned and Frank Mitchell was arrested and charged with Bradford's murder.

At trial, Mitchell confessed and pled guilty to the murder and was sentenced to death. The case was appealed on new information that Mitchell was not of sound mind because of a head injury he had received as a child. The high court affirmed the sentence on December 4, 1907, and Frank Mitchell was executed eight months later.

During the walk to the gallows, a deputy asked Mitchell where he expected to go when dead. Mitchell said, "I don't talk like most Negroes and say I am going to heaven. I tell the truth. I have hopes, but I don't know where I am going."

The *Galveston Daily News*, Sunday, dated August 2, 1908, provided readers with the details of the crime and the execution at Caldwell, Texas.

Burnet County
County Seat - Burnet

Arthur Shelby

Race/Gender: Black Male
Weapon: Shotgun & Knife
Offense: Murder
Execution: January 15, 1873
Offense Date: August 1872

Ben Shelby

Race/Gender: Black Male
Weapon: Shotgun & Knife
Offense: Murder
Execution: January 15, 1873
Offense Date: August 1872

William Smith

Race/Gender: Black Male
Weapon: Shotgun & Knife
Offense: Murder
Execution: January 15, 1873
Offense Date: August 1872

Ball Woods

Race/Gender: Black Male
Weapon: Shotgun & Knife
Offense: Murder
Execution: January 15, 1873
Offense Date: August 1872

Ben Shelby, Arthur Shelby, Ball Woods and William Smith were all tried and convicted of murder in December of 1872 for the death of Benjamin McKeever. In August of that year, McKeever was riding his horse when he came up upon an ex-slave settlement on Double Horn Creek. Ben Shelby's dog ran out onto the road barking and snapping at the heels of McKeever's horse. McKeever drew his pistol and fired several shots at the dog. None of the bullets hit the dog, and McKeever pointed his pistol at Ben Shelby, as a warning before riding on to a friend's house.

Later that night, as McKeever was returning home and riding past the settlement, he was shot off his horse from a shotgun blast. While lying on his back injured, the four men moved in on their prey and cut his throat. The body was afterwards loaded on the back of a horse and carried three miles to a 150-foot deep sink hole known as "Dead Man's Hole," where the body was dumped. Because of the frequency of bodies being thrown into the hole, friends immediately went to Dead Man's Hole to conduct a search. Inside the sink hole the badly mangled body of Ben McKeever was found. In examining the body, they found the cut to the neck had almost decapitated the victim and the torso was riddled with shotgun pellets.

Officers searching for the crime scene, located the spot where the murder had occurred in the road, outside Ben Shelby's cabin. A large rock had purposely been placed over the blood where McKeever's neck had been cut. When the rock was removed, cloth from McKeever's coat was found, as well as a piece of the shotgun wading. The paper wading used was from the Chimney Garner advertisement. In continuing the search another piece of the wadding was found under the front porch of Shelby's home. In examining Shelby's shotgun, the same paper wadding was found. All three pieces were then placed together and matched to the store's advertisement.

All four men arrested were tried for murder in the first degree in December of 1873, and then sentenced to hang on January 15, 1873.

The *Galveston Daily News*, dated Tuesday, January 28, 1873, provided the details of the crime and execution of the four men.

Caldwell County
County Seat - Lockhart

Bill Davis

Race/Gender: Black Male **Age:** 29 **Offense:** Murder
Offense Date: October 20, 1878 **Weapon:** Shotgun **Execution:** November 6, 1879

On the night of October 20, 1878, Bill Davis decided to take out his revenge against Dolly Hudspeth, another African American. Hudspeth had provided testimony against Davis who was indicted for gambling. During the night, and while armed with a shotgun, Davis crept up to Hudspeth's shanty and fired through a crack in the wall, killing him.

Tried and found guilty, the case was appealed. The Court of Appeals found no error in the lower court decision and affirmed the sentence. Upon being asked at his sentencing if he had anything he wished to say. Davis simply requested that he be hanged on a Thursday. The judge granted the request, and sentenced Davis to hang on Thursday, November 6th, 1879.

On the scheduled day of the execution, Davis bid the 5,000 witnesses a good-bye and said, "Farewell, all. I feel worthy of death. Farewell, I am going home; I will meet you all again."

The *Galveston Daily News*, dated Friday, November 7, 1879, printed a full account of the murder and execution at Lockhart, Texas.

Jace Murphy

Race/Gender: Black Male **Offense:** Murder **Offense Date:** 1890
Execution: January 9, 1891

The *Galveston Daily News*, dated Saturday, January 10, 1891, printed the following short article:

HANGING AT CALDWELL

Jace Murphy Pays the Extreme Penalty for the Murder of His Wife.

Caldwell, Tex., Jan. 9.—Jace Murphy, colored, the wife murderer, was hung today inside of the jail building.

Murphy was convicted at the spring term, 1890, of murder and sentenced to be hung in June last. All preparations were made for the execution at that time and when about to be taken from the jail to the place of execution, a telegram was received from the governor ordering a respite until his sanity could be determined in accordance with law. His insanity having been suggested by some of the citizens.

At the last term of court these questions were tried before a jury and they pronounced him sane, and he was again sentenced to be hung. He hung about twenty two minutes before pronounced dead.

There were but a few persons in the jail who witnessed the hanging. Quite a number were outside hoping to hear something drop. An application was made to the governor to commute the punishment to life in the penitentiary, but the governor refused to further interfere with the course of the law.

Calhoun County
County Seat - Port Lavaca

W. J. O'Conner

Race/Gender: White Male **Offense Date:** 1869 **Offense:** Murder
Execution: March 9, 1857

W. L. O'Conner was tried and convicted of murdering a man named Vanzile in 1855 at Port Lavaca. Some sources list the execution as occurring either March 2 or 3.

The Texas State Gazette (Austin, Texas), dated Saturday 14, 1857, printed the following short announcement:

W. J. O'Conner was hung at Powderhorn on Monday last. He made no public confession of his murder.

Henry Wilson

Alias: Will Wilson **Race/Gender:** Black Male **Age:** 35
Offense: Robbery with a Deadly Weapon **Offense Date:** February 15, 1914
Weapon: Railroad Coupling Pin **Execution:** December 14, 1914

On February 15, 1915, Henry Wilson walked into the Johnson Grocery Store at Ann and Center streets in Port Lavaca, and asked the clerk, a Miss Jeffie Hedgepeth for some potatoes. While bent over to retrieve the potatoes, Wilson struck the retired schoolteacher and store clerk with a railroad-coupling pin to the back of the head. Wilson then stole a silver dollar and about $1.55 in change, and fled out the front door.

Witnesses who saw the lone robber fleeing the store provided a description to Sheriff J. D. O'Neil and Town Marshal A. Pennington. The lawmen organized a posse, and it didn't take long for Wilson to be captured in the marsh along Linn's Bayou. After Wilson was placed within a jail cell, Miss Hedgepeth identified Wilson as her attacker and robber. It was discovered Wilson was a transient and had used several aliases in the Port Lavaca area.

At trial, Wilson was found guilty of robbery with a deadly weapon and sentenced to hang. Wilson appealed to the Court of Criminal Appeals who affirmed the decision on October 21, 1914.

While waiting for the appointed day, Wilson confessed to his death watchman that he committed many murders including the murder of a woman in Brazoria County.

From the gallows, Wilson denied ever making the confession, and died protesting his innocence.

The *Victoria Daily Advocate*, dated Tuesday, December 15, 1914, provided details of the robbery and execution.

Callahan County
County Seat - Baird

Alberto Vargas

Race/Gender: Hispanic Male   **Age:** 18   **Offense:** Murder
Offense Date: October 19, 1905   **Weapon:** Butcher Knife   **Execution:** January 4, 1907

Emma Blakely was a waitress for the Sigal Hotel at Baird, Texas. A dishwasher for the hotel by the name of Alberto Vargas was secretly in love with the beautiful woman. Blakely had no interest in Vargas as she had accepted a marriage proposal from a railroad worker to marry the following month. Jealously overwhelmed Vargas once he learned of the engagement and he decided the only way he and Blakely could be together was to kill her and himself.

Vargas purchased a butcher knife at the general store and waited until October 19, 1905 to kill the woman he loved. On that day, as Blakely came out of the dinning room carrying dishes, Vargas grabbed her by the right arm and plunged the butcher knife deep into her chest. The knife had pierced the heart and killed her instantly as the dishes crashed to the floor. Vargus turned the knife towards himself to commit suicide when the owner of the hotel overpowered and held him until officers arrived. The self-inflicted wound was severe enough that the county physician was unsure if Vargas would survive.

When Vargas was searched at the time of his arrest, officers found a handwritten letter which read:

Oh, Emmaly, you will never know how much I love you. You were going to marry an American man and I could never consent for you to do that. We will be together and be one in the eternal church.

At about 8 p.m. that night a lynch mob appeared at the jail in Baird. Sheriff Irvin seeing the possibility of the jail being over run by the mob, quietly and quickly move Vargas out of the back of the jail to an awaiting hack without being seen and transported him to the jail in Abilene for safe keeping. At midnight the jail was opened to a selected few members of the lynch mob to search the jail until they were satisfied that Vargas was no longer in the building.

Vargas was tried and found guilty of murder and sentenced to hang on January 4, 1907. On the day of the execution, Vargas was escorted from the county jail to the scaffold by Sheriff T. A. Irvin, Jailer Felix Raines and Sheriff G. E. Bedford of Eastland County and mounted the scaffold at 1:50 p.m. Vargas said:

I can not talk English like Mexican, but I am ready to go. The road to crime is like a stairway of funnel shape, small in the beginning but expanding farther as one went (Vargas, for example used a paper and made a funnel), and when one is in the descending stairway or funnel it is impossible to break away, and that on account of the opening in the funnel being small, it is impossible for all to get in, and that every one that entered this funnel would find themselves in the midst of crime.

At 2:13 the black cap and hood were placed over his head. As the noose was being tightened around the neck, Vargas said, "Goodbye gentlemans and womens." Sheriff Irvin then pulled the trigger at 2:15 p.m. dropping Vargas eight feet to his death. At 3:10 Vargas was pronounced dead and later buried at the county cemetery.

The *Shiner Gazette*, dated Wednesday, April 9, 1907, provided readers with details of the murder and the execution at Baird, Texas.

Cameron County
County Seat - Brownsville

Howard Slaughter

Race/Gender: White Male **Offense:** Murder **Offense Date:** July 25, 1850
Weapon: Iron Bar **Executed:** December 28, 1850

On July 25, 1850, Howard Slaughter and Solomon Dubart were fist fighting on a water levee. During the fight, Slaughter picked up an iron bar from the ground and struck Solomon several times to the head. The blows fractured the skull in two places, and Solomon died at 11 p.m. that night.

Slaughter was tried in October for murder and sentenced to death. On December 28, 1850, Slaughter was hanged from the gallows with two Mexican men who had been convicted of a murder as well. Their names and the circumstance of their crimes are not currently available. Howard's last words were, "Beware of liquor, for it has brought me to this."

The *Mississippi Free Trader*, Natchez, Miss., dated Wednesday, March 5, 1851, reported on the execution at Brownsville, Texas.

Robert Rodgers

Race/Gender: White Male **Offense:** Murder **Offense Date:** 1866
Execution Date: June 11, 1866

Robert Rodgers was a private in the 77th Ohio Infantry Regiment, assigned at Fort Brown located near Brownsville. Pvt. Rogers was charged with murdering the regiment assistant surgeon, Dr. Gardner.

Rodgers was found guilty of murder, and sentenced to be hanged on April 27, 1866. After preparations for the execution were complete on the scheduled day, officers went to the cell to remove Rodgers and discovered he had escaped from the stockade. It was rumored that Rodgers had escaped into Mexico and joined the Contra Guerilla Battalion in Matamoras. Unknown to the officers, Rodgers who had been held on a second floor cell had chipped out a hole through the wall behind his bunk, and climbed down the wall each night with a rope. Once on the ground, Rodgers went into a side jail yard where there was no sentry posted, and dug a tunnel underground with the use of a canteen. Rodgers worked throughout the night, then would climb back up the rope before sunrise to be back in his cell to be accounted for.

After it was believed Rodgers had escaped and fled into Mexico, Rodgers would continue to return back to his cell during the night to receive food and water from the other prisoners who had rationed their meals for him. The tunnel Rodgers dug was three feet under the surface and traveled a distance of 90 feet. Four weeks later, Rodgers surfaced under a house and the residents notified authorities who took him into custody. Once the tunnel was completely searched for any other prisoners, soldiers filled in the escape tunnel for good.

With the recapture of Rodgers, the execution was carried out on June 11, 1866.

Juan Vela
Race/Gender: Hispanic Male
Offense: Murder
Offense Date: September 28, 1859
Execution: June 22, 1866

Florencio Garza
Race/Gender: Hispanic Male
Offense: Murder
Offense Date: September 28, 1859
Execution: June 22, 1866

Vicente Garcia
Race/Gender: Hispanic Male
Offense: Murder
Offense Date: September 28, 1859
Execution: June 22, 1866

Juan Vela, Florencio Garza, and Vicente Garza were all tried and convicted of the murders of Dr. Viviano Garcia and Robert Johnson, the town jailer. The murders occurred during the raid on Brownsville on September 28, 1859, by Juan N. Cortina and his army of seventy men who referred to themselves as Cortinistas.

The photograph of the three men moments before the execution is believed to be the earliest of such photographs. The photograph shows the three men standing at the edge of the platform being supported by a bar. Their legs are bound, the nooses adjusted, and the Calvary and crowd watching from a distance behind the gallows.

Texas' earliest known photograph of the legal hanging. (Left to right) Vicente Garcia, Juan Veal, and Florencio Garza. June 22, 1866. *Courtesy of Southern Methodist University, Degolyer Library.*

Quirino Gaitan
Race/Gender: Hispanic Male
Weapon: Knife
Offense: Murder
Execution: June 9, 1882
Offense Date: August 13, 1881

On the night of August 13, 1881, a Fandango (dancing ball) was taking place at the county fairgrounds in Brownsville, Texas. Special Policeman Juan Ruiz was working the ball when he observed Quirino Gaitan with Simon Delgado and Juan Medina causing a disturbance and annoying the families who were in attendance. Officer Ruiz seeing the commotion that Gaitan was causing warned him to stop annoying everyone and ordered him to leave the grounds outside the enclosure.

Gaitan walked in the direction of the benches where hack driver Luz Contreras was standing so that he could watch the ball and his horses at the same time. Gaitan walked over to Luz and purposely stepped on his foot.

Luz asked Gaitan, "Why, my friend, are you driving a cart?"

Gaitan said, "Why, don't you like it?"

Luz replied, "Why should I like it?"

Gaitan then said, "*Cabron*, how you like this then!"

Gaitan then plunged his bowie knife to the let side of Luz's abdomen. Officer Ruiz seeing people gathering, started in that direction when he heard someone from the crowd yell, "Quirino Gaitan has murdered Luz Contreras." The officer then saw Gaitan running through the crowd with his bowie knife in his hand, but dropped the knife while trying to return the blade to the sheave. The officer chased after Gaitan and ordered him to surrender.

Gaitan stopped and turned around and rushed at the officer saying, "I will show you how I surrender, you son of a bitch," and with the knife stabbed the officer before fleeing again. Luz in the meantime walked to his horses and stood leaning up against them and slowly slid down to the ground dead. Officer Ruiz's wound at first was considered fatal, but he survived the attack.

Gaitan was tried in December of 1881, and found guilty of murdering Luz Contreras in the first degree. The case was appealed and affirmed in March of 1882. On the day of the execution, troops from Fort Brown lined the bank of the river, while forty special deputies guarded the gallows to ensure there was no attempt to rescue Gaitan by any of the 7,000 spectators who had gathered at the scene.

The scaffold stood eight feet above the ground with the crossbeam six feet higher. After Gaitan arrived by wagon under heavy guard, he walked up to the gallows and stood beside Sheriff Santiago Breto who read the death warrant out loud both in English and Spanish. When the sheriff finished, Gaitan drew a sealed envelope from his pocket, tore it open, and handed it to the sheriff to read. The letter read that these were his last words. Gaitan acknowledged the justice of his sentence and said it was the lack of education that had brought him where he was. He said that he was a Catholic, and that he died in that faith. When the sheriff finished, Gaitan waved his hat and handkerchief, shouting; "*Adios, todos la gente,*!"(good-bye, all you folks) to which the crowd answered, "*Adios*!"

At 4:55 p.m., the executioner who was concealed in a box behind the gallows from public view pulled the lever dropping Gaitan five feet to his death.

The *Galveston Daily News*, dated Sunday, June 11, 1882, printed a full account of the crime and execution at Brownville, Texas.

Jose Buenrostro

Race/Gender: Hispanic Male **Age:** 23 **Offense:** Robbery & Murder
Offense Date: August 6, 1915 **Weapon:** Firearms **Execution:** May 19, 1916

Melquiades Chapa

Race/Gender: Hispanic Male **Age:** 25 **Offense:** Robbery & Murder
Offense Date: August 6, 1915 **Weapon:** Firearms **Execution:** May 19, 1916

On August 6, 1915, fourteen Mexican bandits raided the small town of Sebastian for food, clothing, money, guns and ammunition. The bandits then rode north where they came upon A. L. Austin, his son Charles and two other men who were operating a corn sheller. The Mexican bandits demanded that the Austins surrender all guns and ammunition which they owned at their ranch. Five bandits followed the Austins back to their home to retrieve the guns and ammunition. After all the guns were secured, the bandits escorted the Austins back to the sheller where the other bandits waited while guarding the other two men. Before riding off, the bandits gunned down, A. L. and Charles and left the other two unharmed. Austin was the president of the Sebastian Law and Order League and many citizens believed the killing was in revenge.

Jose Buenrostro and Melquiades Chapa who had been arrested for theft were later identified by witnesses as taking part in the raid on the town and the murder of the Austins. At the trial for murder, the testimony provided identified Buenrostro as the person who fired the fatal shots as Chapa stood guard.

On the morning of the appointed day, both of the condemned men wrote the following note.

On May 19, 1916, Jose Buenrostro and Melquiades Chapa. Senores: We give thanks to the public for what they have done for us.

Chapa wrote a second statement which read:

I Melquiades Chapa am innocent of the crime of which they accuse me, but we pardon all without exception as I hope for pardon from my God.

Signed, Melquiades Chapa.

At 2:13 p.m. the trap was sprung and both men paid the penalty for their crimes.

The *Brownsville Herald*, dated Friday, May 19, 1916, provided readers with details of the raid and murders committed by both men.

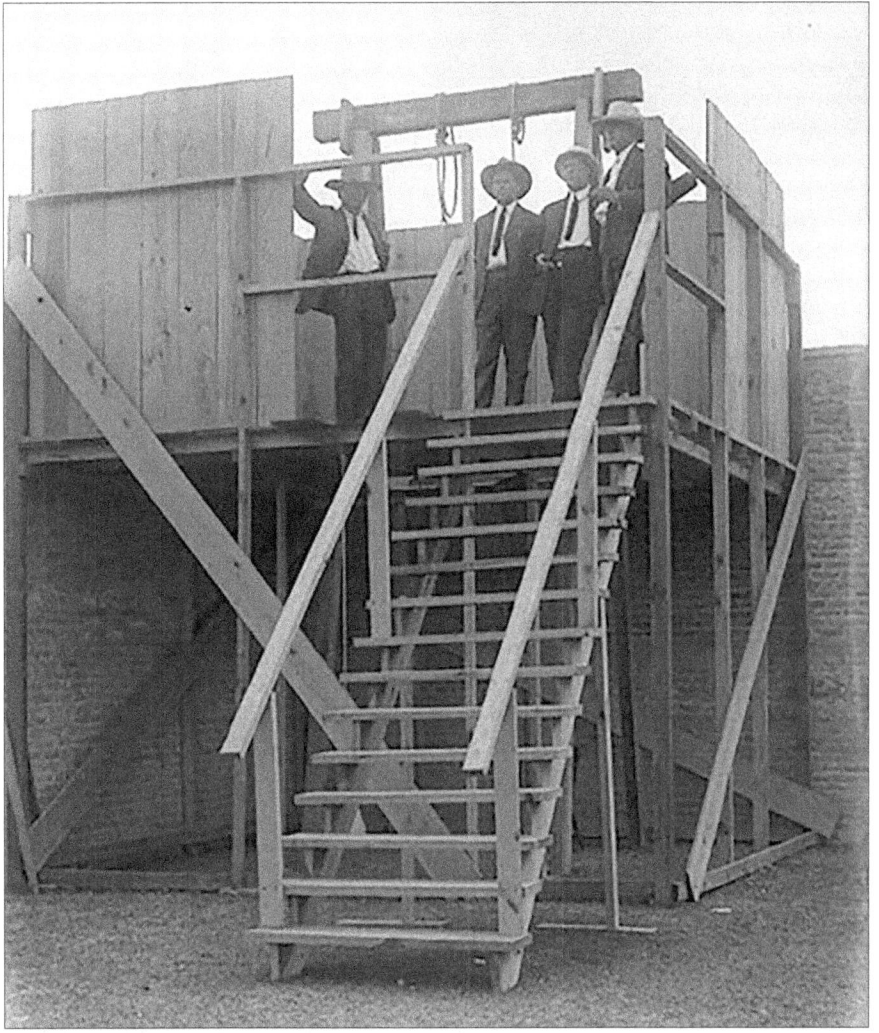

Officers standing on the gallows waiting for Melquiades Chapa and Jose Buenrostro, May 19, 1916.

Camp County
County Seat - Pittsburg

George Harkey

Race/Gender: Black Male   **Age**: 37   **Offense**: Murder
Offense Date: September 24, 1902   **Weapon**: Shotgun   **Execution**: June 30, 1903

George Harkey and Gip Wright were not only neighboring farmers in the small community of Myrtle Springs in Camp County, but each considered the other as a friend. In 1902 George Harkey in need of money to support his family, mortgaged his cotton crop to make ends meet until the cotton could be delivered and sold. But the cotton production of 1902 was at its lowest due to the boll weevil infestation.

When Harkey learned that the mortgage note on his cotton had been closed, he vowed to kill any man who hauled his cotton away from Turner's Gin. Gip Wright was soon hired to take the cotton from the gin and deliver the load to Winnsboro. Harkey kept his vow and went to Gip Wright's home.

Wright said, "Here I am, Harkey; what do you want?"

Harkey answered, "You are the man I am looking for," and instantly fired a load of shot into his body. Reloading the shotgun, Harkey fired a second load into the prostrate body; and afterwards gave a triumphant yell and went home.

Harkey was tried and convicted at Pittsburg, Texas, and sentenced to death. The sentence was then appealed to the court of criminal appeals who affirmed the lower court's decision on January 21, 1903. On June 27 the Governor sent word that he refused to interfere with the court's decision. The hanging was public with 7,000 spectators in attendance at the scaffold that had been built three quarters of a mile from the courthouse in an open field.

On the gallows, Harkey told the sea of people that God had pardoned his sins and he hoped to meet everybody in Heaven. Harkey asked, "The colored race to quit carrying pistols and guns and do the right thing at all times."

As the black cap was being adjusted he told the sheriff that it made little difference how it fit, as he would soon exchange this world for a better one. Once the preparation was final, the trap was sprung. Fifteen minutes later Harkey was pronounced dead, and the body was cut down and released to relatives to be buried at his home located twelve miles southwest of Pittsburg.

The next morning, Sheriff Stafford received reports that Harkey was alive and currently eating a breakfast of biscuits and milk at his family's home. Sheriff Stafford and Doctor Lacy rode out to the Harkey home to view the body. The doctor for the second time pronounced the body dead.

The *Galveston Daily News*, dated Wednesday, July 1, 1903, provided its readers with details of the murder and the execution at Pittsburg, Texas.

Cass County
County Seat - Linden

A slave by the name of Phillips was hanged on January 5, 1855, for murder. Information on the crime and execution are not currently available.

Tom Miles

Race/Gender: Black Male **Age:** 18 **Offense:** Robbery & Murder
Offense Date: December 8, 1889 **Weapon:** Railroad Car Coupling Pin
Execution: June 6, 1890

Henry Holden

Race/Gender: Black Male **Offense:** Robbery & Murder **Offense Date:** December 8, 1890
Weapon: Railroad Car Coupling Pin **Execution:** June 6, 1890

Fletcher Holden

Race/Gender: Black Male **Offense:** Robbery & Murder **Offense Date:** December 8, 1890
Weapon: Railroad Car Coupling Pin **Execution:** June 6, 1890

In early December of 1890, James McGregor had moved to Atlanta, Texas, and immediately befriended Tom Miles, Sam Jackson, Henry Holden and Fletcher Holden. McGregor having money, freely bought liquor for his new friends, and the four became drunk. McGregor was later lured out to the railroad roundhouse where Tom Miles struck him with a railroad coupling pin, killing him. His clothing was then searched for money, and the body was carried away about a mile, and left by the side of the roadway.

After the body was found the next morning, all four men were arrested on suspicion of murder as they were the last people seen with James. Fletcher Holden confessed and provided a written statement, which was used against the defendants at trial:

I was at Atlanta on Saturday, the 7th day of December, 1889, the day before McGregor was killed at night. I saw this man in town at 5 o'clock p. m. Sam Jackson came in town with him. When he came in a crowd of us were standing together on the street. He spoke and said he would give any man as much as he could drink to get him a woman. It was the white man said above. About fifteen or twenty minutes after this I saw McGregor and Tom Miles together. I never saw him any more till he and Tom went to the saloon and got some beer. I never saw them any more till about 8 o'clock that night. Tom Miles went to Queen City and got my brother and told me and Sam Jackson to stay there till he came back. Sam and myself met Tom Miles and my brother at the Texas and Pacific railroad crossing in Atlanta. Tom Miles asked us to go to a woman's house with him. Tom called Mr. McGregor out in the street and told him lets go down in town. We got nearly to town and Tom said lets go to the roundhouse of the Jefferson lumber company's railroad.

When we got there Tom said to the white man: I suppose you have been after my woman? The white man said: Yes, I have; and damn it I will get after her again. When he said this Tom struck him on the head with an iron car coupling pin, and the man fell. He then got up and started towards Tom, and Henry Holden grabbed him and started off with him. Tom then ran up and struck him with the same pin. He fell and my brother Henry said, " Now Tom, you have killed him."

After he fell Tom said, "Let's carry him home." We all four, Sam Jackson, Tom Miles, Henry Holden and myself picked him up and started home with him, and Tom said, "Lets wash the blood off of him." We carried him to the branch and all of us washed the blood off of him. We then picked him up and started homeward with him. We carried him about one-half a mile west from Atlanta. We asked Tom how far the man lived, and we carried him about one-fourth of a mile further and laid him down and Tom put his hat over his face. We then went back to town. He was not dead when we left him. We left Tom with him, but he caught up with us before we got to town. I saw Tom Miles with some money when we got back. I don't know where he got it. The money was greenback. Sam, my brother, and myself went to Queen City that night." (Signed) Fletcher Holden.

The four men were found guilty of murder, and the jury assessed the death penalty. One week prior to the execution, a newspaper reporter was granted permission to go into the jail to conduct an interview with the condemned prisoners and received the following statement:

Fletch, why do you maintain your innocence after you have confessed your guilt?

I was driven onto making that statement. Folks said it was the best thing I could do to get out of it.

And you say you never saw McGregor?

No, sir, I never saw him in my life. I don't know what sort of a man he was.

Are you ready to die?"

I hate to die for something I know nothing about, but I trust it all in the hands of God. I feel that the Lord has pardoned my sins and if it's his will that I should die this way I am ready to die. I expect to make a statement the day I am hung and want everybody to come and see how an innocent man can be drove into a trap as I have been.

Henry Holden was then asked:

How do you feel, Henry?

I feel all right.

Do you feel like you are ready to die?"

Yes, sir, if it is the Lord's will I am."

Do you feel that you will go to heaven?"

I couldn't go anywhere else."

Have you no doubts about getting to heaven?"

No, sir; I never done anything. The Lord knows my feelings. I have asked him to forgive my sins, and feel like he has done it."

Have you no doubts or fears; does nothing trouble you?"

No, sir, nothing troubles me but flies."

On the morning of June 6, 1890, a crowd of 4,000 gathered at the gallows to witness the triple execution.

Sam Jackson however escaped the noose when he was granted a new trial. On June 6, 1890, Jackson sat in the death cell as he watched his three friends being escorted one by one out of the cell and led to the gallows. Jackson was tried a second time on September 15, 1890. Jackson took the stand in his own defense and told the jury that he was present when Tom Miles struck James with the coupling pin, and that James McGregor was still alive when he left him. The jury returned a verdict of guilty of murder, but this time sentenced Jackson to life imprisonment. Satisfied he was not going to hang, Jackson raised no further appeal.

The *Fort Worth Daily Gazette*, dated Saturday, June 7, 1890, provided its readers with details of the murder, and trial.

Alamo McKee

Race/Gender: Black Male **Age:** 18 **Offense:** Robbery & Murder
Offense Date: May 5, 1895 **Weapon:** Shotgun **Execution:** October 25, 1895

On May 4, 1895, a jewelry peddler by the name of Staffian Rafial arrived at the town of Linden to stay the night and rest before he continued on with his fourteen mile journey to Atlanta, Texas. The next morning, Staffian was last seen alive going in the direction of Atlanta. Soon after his departure, Alamo McKee arrived in town showing a large amount of jewelry and money which caught the attention of Sheriff J. H. Lanier. McKee who was known never to have work or have any money was placed under arrest on suspicion of committing a robbery.

The arrest of McKee, and the search for his victim was the talk of the town for several days. A traveler from Atlanta arrived to town, and upon hearing the story, he wondered to himself if the foul odor he had smelled outside of town could be the victim of the robbery. In returning to the area, the traveler located the body of Staffian, and notified the sheriff. The body was returned to town and was identified. Personal effects that McKee was carrying when he was arrested were also identified as belonging to Staffian. McKee confessed to the robbery and murder and implicated two other men. The grand jury indicted McKee, but found no evidence to support charging anyone else.

On the afternoon of the execution, Sheriff J. H. Lanier and his prisoner ascended the scaffold. At 2:55 the trap was sprung and McKee died of strangulation eleven minutes later. After the body was cut down, the following statement was read to the witnesses at the request of McKee:

_____ and _____ come to my house after the peddler had passed and wanted me to get my gun and all my shells and begged me to go with them. _____ shot him and _____ carried him off. I stood on the side of the road and watched. They gave me the money to get changed for them and I kept it five days. They did not give me the money to keep. I kept the goods. After I gave them the money _____ went to Jefferson and _____ went to Holden. By the time _____ got back I was arrested.

The *Galveston Daily News*, dated Saturday, October 26, 1895, provided its readers with details of the murder, investigation and execution at Atlanta, Texas.

Castro County
County Seat - Dimmitt

Felix Powell

Race/Gender: Black Male **Age:** 30 **Offense:** Rape & Multiple Murders
Offense Date: September 28, 1905 **Weapon:** Adz Gripping Hoe, Iron Crow Bar & Knife
Execution: April 2, 1907

On December 6, 1906, Felix Powell was tried for his participation in the rape and murder of twelve-year-old Mildred Lee Conditt on September 28, 1905. On that terrible day, Felix Powell and Monk Gibson murdered Midred's mother and three brothers (ages three to ten) before turning their attention to her. Powell was indicted jointly with Monk Gipson, but their cases were severed. Monk was tried in DeWitt County and Powell was granted a change of venue from Jackson to Castro County, and was tried before Judge J. C. Wilson.

The most damaging testimony to Powell's innocent plea came from Augusta Diggs. Ms. Diggs testified she was born and raised in Jackson County and lived near the Conditt family. Ms. Diggs told the jury she had known both Felix Powell and Monk Gibson most of her life. Ms. Diggs said on the day of the murders she was out in the back yard washing clothes when she looked over towards the Conditt farm and saw Monk Gibson plowing the field with Felix Powell following behind him. Felix later returned back to her house, changed clothes, and approached Ms. Diggs telling her, "There has been something at the Conditt house which I had been wanting, and I got it," (the assault on Mildred Conditt). Felix went on to tell Ms. Diggs that while at the farm, Monk Gibson, Henry Howard and he had killed the Conditt family. Felix afterwards left, but not before warning Ms. Diggs that he would kill her if she told anyone what he had told her.

On December 12, 1906, the jury went into deliberation at 1:30 p.m. At 2:40 the jury announced they had made a decision. Powell was then escorted back to the courtroom by Texas Capt. Ranger William J. McDonald, Ranger J. W. McCauley, Ranger C. T. Ryan, Sheriff R. S. Weisinger, Deputy Louis Hudler, Constable R. S. Cocke and City Marshal H. Dether. Once Powell was seated, the court clerk having received the verdict from jury foreman, J. H. Marklin read. "We the jury find the defendant guilty of murder in the first degree and assess his punishment at death."

The gallows was built outside the county jail and on the day of the execution, there was a crowd over 3,000 witnesses. Once on the scaffold, Sheriff Albert Egg asked Powell if he had anything to say. Powell replied: "I know nothing I want to say. If it is the will of the master and the laws of the county that I should be punished in this way for this crime, I am willing to die. I am trusting in the Lord, Jesus Christ for life hereafter."

Monk Gibson was hanged with the same rope for his crimes in DeWitt County on June 28, 1908.

The *San Antonio Gazette*, dated Tuesday, April 2, 1907, provided their readers with details of the murders and the execution at Victoria, Texas.

Felix Powell Standing on the gallows, April 2, 1907 at Victoria, Texas. *Photograph, is by courtesy of the Victoria Regional History Center, Victoria College/University of Houston-Victoria Library.*

Chambers County

County Seat - Anahuac

Chillers Banks

Race/Gender: Black Male   **Age:** 28   **Offense:** Murder
Offense Date: June 10, 1887   **Pistol:** .32 caliber Pistol   **Execution:** April 13, 1888

On June 10, 1887, Chillers Banks and his brother went to the home of Martha Henderson to confront her over a rumor she supposedly had said about him. In approaching the door, Her sister told Banks that Martha was too busy to come to the door as she was in the kitchen preparing dinner. Banks pushed the woman out of the way and walked directly to the kitchen where he swung open the door leading into the kitchen and shot Martha Henderson once to the abdomen and once to the thigh with a .32 caliber pistol.

Mark Henderson, hearing the shooting, grabbed a shotgun that was loaded with birdshot and fired at Banks. The bird shot peppered Banks in the face and head, but did not cause any severe injury. Banks fled the home and swore he would never be arrested by the law without a fight. Sheriff G. C. Davis arrested Banks who was still carrying the weapon he used to kill Martha and still contained three bullets in the cylinder. Banks told the sheriff he had killed Martha because, "She had said bad things about me." Tried and convicted of murder, the jury sentenced Banks to hang. On April 13, 1888, Chillers Bank became the only person to be legally hanged in Chambers County.

The *Galveston Daily News*, dated Saturday, April 14, 1888, printed the following short article:

LAST WORD ON EARTH.

Chillers Banks Hanged at Wallisville for the Murder of a Colored Woman for Alleged Slander.

Liberty, Tex., April 13. – Chillers Banks, colored, was hanged at ten minutes past 1 o'clock to-day at Wallisville. The execution was public and was witnessed by hundreds of people.

Banks was game to the last, meeting his doom with stolid indifference up until his last word on earth. The crime for which he was punished was the murder of a colored woman named Martha Henderson. Banks claimed that the woman had slandered him, and on hearing this he went direct to her home, called her out and shot her without a word.

Cherokee County
County Seat - Rusk

John Felder

Race/Gender: Black Male **Offense:** Murder **Offense Date:** August 9, 1891
Weapon: Double Barrel Shotgun **Execution:** October 9, 1891

Wade Felder

Race/Gender: Black Male **Offense:** Murder **Offense Date:** August 9, 1891
Weapon: Double Barrel Shotgun **Execution:** October 9, 1891

On the night of August 9, 1891, Yance Thompson was asleep at Mack McBeasley's house when Wade Felder and his half brother John arrived shooting their shotguns into the home. Thompson who was in bed asleep was hit and died instantly. Both men were arrested and tried for murder. Wade who pled not guilty was first tried and found guilty. John was next tried and pled guilty to the charge and both men were sentenced to death and they both declined to appeal their sentence.

On the morning of October 9, 1891, John and Wade Felder after waking up began preparing for their execution. Both men were dressed in black shirts, black pants and white vests. A newsman visited the men in the cell where John Felder was heard warning colored visitors to, "leave off their sins and seek the Lord." John finished by saying, "Now I have said enough to save 10,000 souls. If you go in your sins I can't help it. I can dress for the grave; I dressed myself. I can walk to the gallows and ascend its heights without a tremor and without a fear."

At 12:20 that afternoon, all of the stores in town closed and the streets were deserted as everyone had gathered at the scaffold that had been erected on a hill east of town. The parade of sixty armed special officers arrived with the Felders, where upon both men walked to the gallows while smoking cigars.

Both Wade and John Felder were told they could make any statement they saw fit. Wade Felder stepped forward and spoke for fifteen minutes. In his address to the crowd, Wade said he was going to die as he had been found guilty, and said he was a wicked man when he was sentenced. But while he was incarcerated, Jailer McCord talked to him and told him of the awful consequences of dying in sin. Jailer McCord he said led him to repentance and believing in Christ. Wade said he was prepared and willing to die. At first he had thought of the governor in the start, but had sought the love of God, which "is shed around in my heart."

John Felder stepped forward and said Wade and he had agreed to buckshot the door in order to scare Mack McBeasley. John said he too had been a wicked man. John said he been a gambler with dice and implored the crowd never to touch dice, not to gamble, not to lie, but for them to seek the Lord; and that the love of God was strong in him because of the efforts of Jailer McCord who had sat by his cell reading the Bible. Wade then turned to a Mr. Thompson and said, "Mr. Thompson, you hired a lawyer to prosecute me and I hated you or it, but since I told the truth and the Lord has forgiven me, my feelings have entirely changed and I love you."

Sheriff John Reagan then read the death warrants. At the conclusion, Sheriff Reagan asked if either man had anything further to say. Wade arose from his seat and told the witnesses:

Well, my colored and white friends, I must depart this life. All who are sorry for me please hold up your hands. (About 6000 hands were raised.) I am not sorry for myself, but am sorry for you, for I have the love of God to back me, and you sinners, friends, ought to be sorry for yourselves. I am glad I am going to die, for I am the richest man in the world. I am here to tell you that the Savior was hung on he cross from the sixth to the ninth hour for me and I willing to hang on the gallows for him. I might make some of you mad if I were to talk to you about your sins. I don't care what the living think about me, my body dies on the 9th day of October, but my spirit ascends to heaven. Sinners you had better lay down everything and serve the Lord. I would not walk down from this scaffold for the world.

John then told his brother, "Don't take up so much time; let us leave this world." Wade continued by saying, "I wish I could talk to you longer, but my lungs are worn out. Now, the next time I stand up will be in the glory land. Farewell, lawyers; farewell, judges; farewell, friends; farewell, enemies."

After Wade returned to his seat, John stood up and said, "Well, I am prepared to die. I hope my friends and playmates will meet me in heaven. I wish each one in this vast assemblies to love God in his soul. Some of you say I have happened to bad luck, but I considered it good luck, for I have the love of God in my heart. I don't want to take up your time farewell, friends and enemies."

At 1:30, both men were bound, their nooses adjusted, and the traps were sprung. The rope with which John was being hanged from broke, and he fell to the ground. Officers rushed under the scaffold, picked John up and then carried him back up to the platform where they sat him on a chair while the officer prepared the noose. When the trap was reset and sprung again, the rope held this time and broke the neck. Both bodies were afterwards cut down and interred in the state prison cemetery.

The *Fort Worth Gazette* headlines dated Saturday, October 10, 1891, printed that the double execution "drew better than a circus."

George Charles King

Alias: Charles King **Race/Gender:** Black Male **Age:** 24
Offense: Robbery & Murder **Offense Date:** August 18, 1894 **Weapon:** .45 caliber Pistol
Execution Date: July 2, 1895

In 1888, George King Jr. who went by his middle name of Charles was seventeen-years-old, and the oldest of seven siblings. The family lived on a small farm three miles south of Cookville, in Titus County. Two miles east of the King home, was the home of John Shulze and with his family which consisted of his wife and their two sons, Will and George. In September of that year, George King Sr.'s oldest daughter eloped with Will Shulze after forging her father's signature on a consent to marry affidavit to obtain a marriage license. The news of the marriage was not accepted very well by George King and he vocally threatened to prosecute Will Shultz of forgery.

In December of the same year, George King rented another farm about a mile south of where they lived with the intention of moving his family. On the new farm was a smoke house for meat. After killing and quartering hogs, the meat was placed in a smoke house and Charles was told to stay on guard over night to protect the meat. The next morning, Charles walked into Cookville and reported to the sheriff that after he returned home that morning, he discovered his family's house burned to the ground and all of his family members were dead. It was determined that the King family had been murdered and Will Shulze quickly became the suspect. It was well known Shulze had made several threats directed towards his wife's father that if he was ever prosecuted of the forgery, George King would pay dearly.

Will Shulze was indicted for the murder and after being convicted, he received the death penalty. The conviction was appealed to the Court of Appeals on December 18, 1889, and the decision was reversed. The case was later dismissed against Shulze after it was learned that during the murder trial, two witnesses gave false testimony against him. Both witnesses were convicted of perjury and sentenced to five years in prison.

Charles King soon took employment with E. R. Nelson, east of Mount Pleasant as a laborer. Soon after hiring on, King stole a pair of mules owned by a Mr. Nelson. Suspecting that King may take the mules to Daingerfield to sell, Nelson went there and as he suspected, recovered his mules. King was indicted for horse theft and sentenced to six years to the penitentiary at Rusk.

While imprisoned at Rusk, inmate labor was used to cut timber which would than be used for charcoal for the iron furnaces located about fifteen miles away. The cut timber was moved to the furnaces by way of trains. King was part of the inmate labor and quickly recognized the routine of the prison paymaster always arriving by train to pay the guards and other employees in cash. King began fantasizing of the day he would be released from prison and then rob the paymaster of the entire payroll.

King was released from prison in May of 1894, and immediately began putting his plan into action. King first ordered a false beard with a mustache, and a .45 caliber pistol from Montgomery Ward and Mail Order Company. Once King received the items, he selected a location on the railroad near Wells, Texas, where he placed railroad cross-ties on the tracks to force the train engineer to bring the train to a stop. While wearing his disguise and hiding in the bushes near the tracks, King waited for the arrival of the train.

Riding on the train that day was a dentist, A. F. Drewry. The dentist was on the train to attend to the dental needs of the prison guards and inmates. Dr. Drewry had been riding in the switch engine when the train came to a stop, and he volunteered to assist in removing the ties from the track. After climbing down from the train, King came out from the hiding place wearing his disguise. Seeing the dentist, King mistakenly took him as being Captain N. M. Harrison, the financial officer. With a pistol in his hand, King ordered, "hands up, damn you, I want your money."

King removed from Dr. Drewry his pocket watch with a charm, five dollars in silver, three five dollar bills, with one of the bills having a missing corner, a pocket knife, and a twenty-three dollar check drawn from the First National Bank of Rusk. King shot Dr. Drewry several times, and Drewry died two days later from his wounds.

On August 22nd Deputy Dorrough apprehended King on a train between Dial and Jacksonville. Upon his arrest, King was carrying the five-dollar bill with the missing corner, the pocket watch and chain, and a pocket knife, which were all identified as belonging to Dr. Drewry. King was tried at Rusk on May 15, 1895 and received the death sentence. After the case was appealed and affirmed, King was taken before Judge James T. Polly. King was asked if he had anything to say as to why sentence should not be pronounced. King replied, "Nothing, except that I am not guilty in spite of what courts and juries might say." Judge Polly afterwards sentenced George Charles King Jr. to hang by the neck until his body be dead on Tuesday, July 2, 1895.

On July 2nd, 5,000 spectators gathered to watch the hanging of Charles King. King was taken to the gallows and given a pint of whiskey to drink. At 12:18 the trap was sprung and fourteen minutes later King was pronounced dead. Although never proven or charged, citizens of Cookville believed Charles King had sexually assaulted his sister on December 11, 1888, and afterwards murdered his entire family.

The *Galveston Daily News*, dated Wednesday, July 3, 1895, provided its readers with a full account of the crime and execution at Rusk, Texas.

Perry Waggoner

Race/Gender: Black Male **Offense Date:** July 10, 1899 **Offense:** Murder
Weapon: Wood Club **Execution:** July 6, 1900

Perry Waggoner while serving a life sentence for murder in the penitentiary in Rusk, Waggoner beat to death another inmate J.J. Davis with a wood stick. Waggoner exclaimed, "No white man can run over me."

Tried and found guilty of committing his second murder, Waggoner was sentenced to death. Attorneys in Waggoner's behalf requested Governor Joseph Sayers to commute the sentence to life. After an investigation into the matter, the governor issued the following statement.

In the case of Perry Waggoner the sentence of the court will be executed. Not a circumstance, wither in the life or character of the applicant or in the manner of the killing, is shown that would in the least justify an amelioration of the sentence imposed.

Joseph D. Sayers, Governor.

The *Dallas Morning News*, Dated July 9, 1900 provided their readers with the following headlines and story of Perry Waggoner's crime and execution:

DIED WITH A CURSE.

Perry Waggoner, A Convict, Hanged at Rusk for Murder.

Special to the News.
Rusk, Tex., July 6. – Perry Waggoner, colored, was executed here today for the murder of J. J. Davis, a white

man, on July 10, 1899. Waggoner, a life convict assaulted Davis, also a convict, with a bludgeon braining him while sitting picking his teeth after dinner. The tragedy occurred within the prison walls here. Waggoner was indicted and at the November term, 1899, of the District Court was tried, convicted and given the death penalty.

He was defended by able counsel appointed by the court. His case was appealed and affirmed. His counsel asked the Governor to commute his sentence to life imprisonment, which the Governor declined to do after giving the matter a thorough investigation.

Waggoner refused all religious consolation and died cursing on the gallows. He declined to say anything in regard to himself or his crime.

He was serving a life sentence for a murder committed in Van Zandt County. It is said his Van Zandt victim was indebted to him in the small sum of 50c, and had gone to the field where his debtor was at work and killed him because he did not pay him.

It is estimated that some 5,000 people, mostly colored, were here today to witness the execution. Everything passed off with out any disturbance. Waggoner's neck was broken, he dying without a struggle.

Henry Henderson

Race/Gender: Black Male **Age:** 25 **Offense:** Robbery & Murder
Offense Date: December 17, 1909 **Weapon:** Hammer **Execution:** July 8, 1910

E. C. Landrum was the storekeeper at Rusk, Texas, in Cherokee County. On the morning of December 17, 1909, Henry Henderson was seen walking into the store with the handle of a hammer protruding from his pocket. A short time later, at 8 a.m. in the morning, the body of E. C. Landrum was found lying on the floor in a pool of blood. Landrum died from the result of being struck seven times to the head with a hammer. The hammer broke every bone in his head except for one.

Boots covered in blood worn by the murderer were found hidden in some bushes a short distance from the store. Officers continued to search the area and found hidden under some wood bark close to where the boots were, the stolen money from the store. The hammer used to commit the murder was identified as belonging to Henderson's father-in-law, and Henry Henderson was placed under arrest.

On December 20th, Henderson was indicted on the charge of robbery and murder in the first degree. Ten days later on December 30, 1909, Henry Henderson was tried and found guilty of the crimes and sentenced to death. On March 30, 1910, the Court of Criminal Appeals affirmed the decision of the lower court.

On July 8, 1910 at 1:30 p.m., Sheriff C. K. Norwood and his deputies left the jail with Henderson and transported him to the gallows one-mile north of Rusk. On the gallows, Henderson said he wished to thank the jailer, Mr. Martin, for the kind treatment he had extended him while he was in jail. After the black cap was adjusted, Sheriff Norwood sprung the trap that dropped Henry Henderson seven and a half feet to his death.

The *Galveston Daily News*, dated Saturday, July 9, 1910, provided its readers with details of the crime and the execution at Rusk, Texas.

Coleman County
County Seat - Coleman

John A. Pearl

Race/Gender: White Male   **Age:** 25   **Offense:** Robbery & Murder
Offense Date: December 5, 1900   **Weapon:** .38 caliber Pistol   **Execution:** October 22, 1901

The only hanging to have taken place in Coleman County was not the result of a murder that occurred in that county, but rather was the result of a change of venue from Brown County.

John Pearl, a twenty-year-old farm laborer, decided on December 5, 1900, to kill his employer, Ed Tusker. Tusker had emigrated from Germany to Texas, and lived alone on his small cotton farm located near Clear Creek at Brownwood, Texas. Pearl murdered Tusker on that day so that he could lay claim to the cotton crop, livestock, wagon and team owned by Tusker.

On December 8th, Pearl drove Tusker's wagon team into Brownwood with a load of cottonseed. Sheriff M. H. Denman recognized the team as belonging to his friend, Ed Tusker. Sheriff Denman approached and questioned Pearl about how he came into possession of Tusker's property. Pearl explained to the Sheriff that he had bought Tusker's cotton crop as Tusker wanted to return to Germany for a visit.

The Sheriff realized that Pearl was inconsistent in his story as to how Tusker was traveling back to Germany. Sheriff Denman knowing his friend very well became suspicious of Pearl's story, and feared his friend may have been a victim of foul play. The next day, Sheriff Denman decided to investigate further by taking deputies to the Tusker farm. Once at the farmhouse, the Sheriff located a drag trail from the front gate to a water tank about a half-mile away. The fifteen foot deep water tank was dragged for two days with the use of trot lines until the body of Ed Tusker was recovered.

The body had been weighted down with large rocks weighing sixty to eighty pound and tied to the body with wire. The body was naked except for a shirt, which had been tied around his head. Tied to the feet was rope, which the Sheriff learned Pearl had recently purchased. An examination of Tusker's head revealed he had been shot with a .38 caliber bullet to the back of head. The same caliber pistol with one empty bullet casing was found in Tusker's home.

Sheriff Denman immediately arrested Pearl who then claimed that another person had murdered Ed Tusker. Pearl said he did help hide the body, and burn Tusker's clothing, and said that was the only thing he was guilty of. Pearl did not reveal the name of the person who was had supposedly killed Tusker.

Pearl was indicted by the Brown County Grand Jury on December 12, 1900. Following the indictment, Pearl was tried, convicted, and sentenced to death. A motion for a new trial and change of venue was granted with the second trial held at Coleman County. Pearl was again convicted of the murder, and given the death sentence. The Texas Court of Criminal Appeals affirmed the second conviction on June 12, 1901. The date of execution was reset to take place on October 22nd.

The gallows for the execution were built within the Coleman County Jail on the second floor. A cross beam was constructed in the jail attic and a hole was cut into the floor where a holding cell was located.

The *Dallas Morning News* reported that on the day of execution, it was estimated that 2,000 people from the surrounding communities gathered in the jail yard to hear Pearl make his last public statement. Pearl did address the crowd from a jail window for one hour and fifteen minutes during which time he gave a brief account of the killing of Ed Tusker, but said to the last that he was innocent of the killing. Pearl again made the claim he "had helped to secrete the body." After a prayer for the public and himself, Pearl bade all good-bye and walked towards the gallows with a firm step. He ascended the gallows and after shaking hands with the guard and witnesses called all to kneel and pray. He then prayed earnestly to God for forgiveness and called on Rev. Birdwell to lead a prayer for him. Pearl then called out to those present to see his execution to take note that he had "died game." With a firm stand he again bade all good-bye. When the black cap was adjusted and with a prayer on his lips, John Pearl was launched into eternity.

Sheriff Bob Goodfellow pulled the trap at 2:46 and Pearl's body remained hanging for fourteen minutes when the body was lowered at 3:15. Pearl was then lowered into a coffin and buried at the Coleman Cemetery.

The *Dallas Morning News*, dated Wednesday, October 23, 1901, provided their readers with details of the murder.

Collin County
County Seat - McKinney

Stephen Merris Ballew

Race/Gender: White Male **Age:** 28 **Offense:** Robbery & Murder
Offense Date: October 21, 1870 **Execution:** May 24, 1872

Stephen Ballew had traveled with James P. Golden from Illinois for the purpose of selling mules. On October 21, 1870, three miles from the town of McKinney, Texas, Ballew killed Golden and buried his body in a shallow grave. Ballew afterwards returned back to Illinois denying to Golden's family any knowledge as what had happened to him. Once the body was found, Sheriff William Nelson Bush traveled to Quincey, Illinois, to arrest Stephen Ballew, and brought him back to Texas on June 24, 1871, to stand trial for murder.

Because the Collin County Courthouse at the time was a log structure and too small to hold such a large trial, the trial was held inside the First Christian Church. After being convicted, Ballew was sentenced before Judge W. H. Andrews who pronounced the following sentence:

> Sir, at the last term of this court, you, after a protracted and impartial trial, were, by a jury of your own selection, found guilty of murder in the first degree, and your punishment assessed at death. For the highest crime known to the law you were adjudged to suffer the severest punishment known to human tribunals. From this judgment you prayed for an appeal to our Supreme Court, which reviewed for all possibility of prejudice, upon a full examination of your case, affirmed the judgment of this court. Therefore, in obedience to the mandate of our said Supreme Court, which is now upon file in this court, it becomes my solemn and painful duty to pronounce upon you the sentence of the law in pursuance of the verdict of the said jury by which you are to pass from Time into Eternity.
>
> Before doing so, I would recommend to you that you devolt the short time yet allowed to you by the law, to a preparation for your appearance before that Great Tribunal Whose Judge is Infallibler.
>
> Have you any lawful reason to offer why this awful sentence should not now be pronounced. It appearing to the court that you have no legal reason to differ, it is ordered by this court that you be remanded to the custody of the Sheriff of Collin County to be by him safely kept until Friday, the 24th of May next, 1872, when in pursuance of the judgment of this court, and obedience to the mandate of our said Supreme Court, you shall by said Sheriff, within the hours prescribed by the law, be hanged by the neck until you are dead. May you be enabled in the mean time to obtain pardon from your sins and salvation for your soul. Mr. Sheriff, the prisoner is yours.

On May 24, 1872, the day of the execution, Ballew stepped out from the jail wearing a new suit of clothes and a large white hat. The wagon carrying Ballew's coffin pulled up to the front of the jail to transported Ballew to the gallows. Seeing that he would have to walk a few steps through the wet mud to the wagon, Ballew requested the sheriff that wood planks be laid down over the mud to prevent getting mud on his new shoes. After entering the wagon, Ballew sat on top of his coffin while smoking a cigar.

At the gallows, Ballew walked up the stairs and stood directly over the trap door and asked Sheriff Bush if his feet were in the correct place. After the feet were strapped, Ballew took his white hat off and handed it to Sheriff Bush saying, "Here Captain, lay my hat over there." His hands were then tied and moments later the trap sprung.

The *Galveston Standard*, dated Monday, June 3, 1872, ended their account of the execution by writing, "Thus perished Ballew, the majesty of the law has been vindicated, and the lesson, it is hoped, will not be without its salutary effects.

Shadrack Meshack Abednego Caldwell

Alias: Shack Caldwell **Race/Gender:** Black Male **Age:** 20
Offense: Murder **Offense Date:** October 16, 1881 **Weapon:** Pistol
Execution: August 18, 1882

Shack Caldwell was eighteen-years-old when he killed W. R. Norvell, over a $3 labor dispute. Caldwell and his younger brother had worked on a small house that Norvell owned on his 160-acre farm. The argument between the two men ended on October 16, 1881, when Caldwell went to Norvell's home near Melissa, Texas, demanding the balance. When Norvell refused, Shack Caldwell drew a pistol and said, "I have come for that money; if you don't pay me, I'll blow your damned old brains out."

As Norvell attempted to rise from his chair, a shot was fired with the ball entering the abdomen and lodged near the spinal column. Caldwell then fled from the scene, stole a neighbor's horse and headed north.

Sheriff William Worden was notified of the shooting and Norvell gave a dying declaration. Eight days later, Norvell succumbed to his injury. Sheriff Worden searched for Caldwell for two weeks until he located him on a farm near Clinton, Missouri.

Shack Caldwell was returned to Texas and tried before Judge Joseph Bledsoe on February 20, 1882. The trial concluded on February 21, when Jury foreman W. T. Duer read, "We, the jury, find the defendant guilty of murder in the first degree, and assess his punishment at hanging by the neck until he is dead."

On June 7, 1882, the Court of Criminal Appeals affirmed the judgment of the lower court. Judge Bledsoe afterwards called for Shack Caldwell to be brought before him for sentencing. Judge Bledsoe ordered that the execution to take place on August 18, 1882. Judge Bledsoe continued with "He shall be taken by the said Sheriff (Wms. Warden) within the hours prescribed by law, and in the manner of the statutes of the State in such case made and provided that he be hanged by the neck until dead, Dead, DEAD: and may God have mercy upon his soul."

On the day of his execution, Caldwell was transported by wagon under heavy guard to the gallows that had been erected two miles north of town. While Caldwell sat on top of his awaiting coffin, he sang, "As I passed by the wicked crowd, I heard a woman cry" during the ride to the gallows. Once at the gallows, Prayers were read and religious songs were sang. Caldwell said, "The Negro race to take warning not to follow in my footsteps." Caldwell claimed he was going to heaven, felt no malice for any one, bid the crowd good-bye, asked all to meet him in heaven. He then turned to the officers and told them he was ready to die.

The trap was sprung and Caldwell fell nine feet. The fall failed to break his neck, and physicians did not pronounced the body dead for fifteen minutes. The remains were then lowered into a coffin. Caldwell had requested that he be laid to rest beside his sister, who was buried about five miles north of McKinney. In support of Caldwell's mother, a large number of souvenir photographs of Caldwell were sold for twenty-five cents with the money going to her.

The *Waco Daily Examiner*, dated Saturday, August 19, 1882, printed a full account of the execution and history of the murder. The newspaper printed the below interview Caldwell had with a reporter:

In regard to killing Norvell, he said the latter had wronged him badly in their business dealing, and had swindled him out of money that was honestly due him; that he went to his house the evening of the tragedy to again ask for it, as he needed some funds to take a short trip with a friend; that he found Norvell seated near the door, in a chair, whittling with a large, three-inch blade pocket knife; that when he asked for the money Norvell flew into a passion, and jumping up from the chair came toward the door menacing him with the knife and ordered him off the premises; that he ordered Norvell to halt, fir if he advanced with that knife he would kill him; that Norvell rushed toward him and that he retreated, running around the house, that Norvell pursued him, and as they ran he (Caldwell) drew a pistol from a small Sunday school satchel (he had been to church, and was returning, he said) and fired, that Norvell kept on around the house until he reached a chair and sank into it, and that he left the premises and concluded to leave the country as he knew he would be hung if captured, although his act was committed in self-defense. He said there was no use in lying about the matter now, that he had not the least hope of executive clemency, and that every word he had uttered was the truth. The testimony proved that a trail of blood around the house was such as to corroborate the doomed man's story, but the location and general features of the wound, as testified to by physicians, fully carried out the dying statement of Norvell. But some of the parties who visited the house shortly after the shooting testified to finding a large open pocket knife on the floor, which apparently corroborated Caldwell's tale and contradicted Norvell.

William Ezell Stepp

Race/Gender: White Male **Age:** 47 **Offense:** Murder
Offense Date: September 2, 1921 **Weapon:** Blunt Object – Eye Hoe
Execution: November 22, 1922

Hardy Mills was a day laborer who lived at the Ezell Stepp farm which was located about four miles northwest from the town of McKinney, Texas. Each morning, Hardy with his lunch in his hand, would leave his wife and five small children to go to work at the construction site at the Crouch building in McKinney. On his way Hardy Mills would pass by Ezell Stepp's home which was about a quarter of a mile away.

On September 2, 1921, Hardy left home as usual except that he did not report to work, failed to pick up his week's pay, or return back home. Two days later, the Sheriff was notified of Hardy Mills' disappearance and he began his investigation. On Monday, September 5, several officers went to Ezell Stepp's home and questioned him. Stepp provided no information as to the disappearance, and after the premises were searched, the officers left his home.

It wasn't until 4 p.m. on September 15, that Hardy Mills's body was discovered. On that afternoon, W. J. (Billy) Baxter was riding by an old well on his farm located seven miles northwest of McKinney, and three miles from Ezell Stepp's home. The old well had always been kept covered by a tub which had been removed, but lying near by. Baxter recovered the tub and while in the process of covering the well, he saw the body lying in the old abandoned well, and immediately notified the sheriff.

The body was badly decomposed and the head and shoulders were partially covered with an old automobile duster. The legs from the knees to the ankles had been wrapped in bailing wire and the legs weighted down by a heavy piece of a railroad iron tied to the feet. Wire had further been run through the mouth in a horse bridal, and the head tied down to his chest.

The body of Mills was taken to Sam J. Massie Undertaking to be examined by the undertaker and physicians. During the examination, it was found that the skull had a dent in the forehead, a hole on the ride side of the skull and a wound behind the left ear.

Sheriff Blakeman placed Ezell Stepp under arrest for the murder, while deputies arrested Stepp's nephew, Arlye Stepp, and placed him under arrest. On September 20, Arlye confessed to County Attorney A. M. Wolford at the county jail that his uncle had killed Hardy Mills with an eye hoe. Aryle told Wolford that on September 2, he had brought back cotton pickers from McKinney to his home. Afterwards he went to the Ezell home and stayed the night. It was during the night that his uncle told him he had killed Hardy and that the body was lying in the cornfield and he needed his help to dispose of the body. The next morning he and his uncle placed the body in a car and dropped the body in the old well. In exchange for his testimony as a state witness, Arlye was not tried.

Ezell Stepp always maintained his innocence throughout the trial and up until his execution. Friends would go to the jail and ask for Stepp to tell the truth so that "you won't hang with a lie on your lips."

A newspaper man asked Stepp, "Have you anything to say about the matter."

Stepp replied, "No, I guess not, only I will say I did not kill that man."

The reporter told Stepp if he had anything to say to the public through the newspaper that and he would print it.

Stepp was quoted saying, "Well, say this, it's unjust, I am innocent. I did not kill that man. But if it is necessary for an innocent man to suffer somebody else's crime, I can and am ready to do it. They can condemn me here on earth, but they can't condemn me hereafter."

On October 10, 1921, Ezell Stepp went to trial at the Fifty-Ninth District Court in Collin County, and was represented by A. S. Baskett of Dallas and local attorneys Jewell Abernathy, Martin Kindle and John D. Reese.

The sensational trial brought such a large crowd to the courtroom that many spectators brought their lunch to the courtroom so that they could watch the trial without losing their seats. Seven days later the trial concluded when the jury returned a verdict of guilty.

On June 14, the Court of Criminal Appeals affirmed the conviction of the lower court. A petition was then circulated with several hundred signatures to Governor Pat M. Neff asking that Stepp receive a commutation from the death sentence to life imprisonment.

Five days before the execution, local contractors constructed the gallows outside the Collin County Jail at McKinney. The gallows were erected on the south yard of the jail having a frame enclosure that was seventeen feet by fifty feet to allow the eighty-five to 100 witnesses to view the execution. The gallows itself was eight by sixteen feet in dimension. The west half of the gallows had a space of six by eight feet and consisted of the steel trap door. The height of the trap door above the ground was thirteen feet.

On the morning of the execution officers and jailers went to the cell to escort Stepp to the gallows. Stepp said, "I am going to leave here with a clear conscience."

Dallas County Sheriff Dan Harston said, "Well, within the next thirty minutes you are going to meet your maker."

Stepp answered with, "I am dying absolutely innocent."

Stepp dressed in a new suit, black tie, and new shoes, was then escorted from the death cell to the gallows by Deputy Harry White and Jailer Jim Kimbriel.

Upon arrival at the gallows Deputy White strapped Stepp's feet together and Sheriff Harston buckled his hands behind his back with a leather strap. Deputy Allen Seale of Dallas adjusted the black cap over his head and the noose about his neck. Before the 100 witnesses, Stepp said, "I want everybody to meet me in a better country, I am innocent, the hanging is unjust. Gentlemen, please don't choke me, Good-bye."

At 11:23 a.m., Sheriff Ed Blakeman sprang the trap and the body fell out of sight from the witnesses. Once the body was pronounced dead, undertaker Clarence C. Harris placed the remains in a grey metal casket with the words inscribed, "At Rest." The remains were buried the following day at Horn Cemetery, northwest of McKinney.

The *Daily Courier Gazette*, (McKinney, Texas) dated Friday, November 22, 1922, provided readers with a large article of the crime and execution.

Colorado County
County Seat - Columbus

James Stanley

Race/Gender: Black Male **Offense:** Robbery & Murder **Offense Date:** November 27, 1882
Weapon: Ax **Execution:** October 19, 1883

On November 25, 1882, Walter Strickland left the family store in the care of his younger brother, sixteen-year-old Robert Strickland. The small store was located on the Strickland farm about eight miles from the town of Eagle Lake, Texas. The store not only provided nearby farmers and laborers with a place to purchase their supplies, but a place to socialize.

Because of recent heavy rain, many of the farm workers were unable to work, as was the case on Monday morning, November 27, 1882. Harry Riggins, Lewis Brooks and Jim Stanley were all visiting with one another at the store when James Stanley commented that he did not know what he was going to do if it did not stop raining because he did not have any money to buy provisions.

Robert Strickland soon afterwards took out a sack from a drawer and said, "Look here, boys, how much money I have made in the past few days. I am going to take it to my mother. My brother will come after it."

Stanley then asked when his brother would arrive, and young Strickland replied today or tomorrow. Strickland then placed the sack in a trunk and locked it. The sack was half full and contained $64 in a combination of paper money and silver coins. Later that night, Jeff Lewis arrived at the store to visit. When Lewis left the store, James Stanley was the only person who remained in the kitchen and was cooking supper for Strickland and himself.

The next morning, Lewis Brooks arrived at the store to buy some meat and he discovered the front door to the store was locked. Thinking that Strickland had over slept, Brooks began banging on the front door while calling out Robert's name. When he did not answer, Brooks walked around the building and observed that all the window blinds had been lowered. Brooks then climbed on top of a barrel and looked through a wall crevice. He was able to see Strickland lying in bed, and appeared to be still asleep. When Strickland did not respond or move as he yelled and banged on the wall, Brooks then noticed that Strickland's head and clothing were bloody.

Brooks sent for Walter Strickland to come to the store as he believed the younger Strickland was hurt. When Walter arrived, they kicked in the front door. In going to the back bedroom, they found Robert was dead, having being murdered in his bed while asleep. It was determined that Robert had been struck twice to the head with an ax. Near the bed, the murderer had left his bloody shoes which were identified as belonging to James Strickland.

Sheriff J. L. Townsend at Columbus received word that night of the murder and quickly went to the train depot to catch the next east bound train to Eagle Lake. At the train depot, the sheriff saw James Stanley waiting for the west bound train for San Antonio, but at the time did not have Stanley's physical description. After the sheriff's arrival to Eagle Lake and while investigating the murder, he received a pair of bloody overalls from Doug Wilson who lived about a mile from the store. The sheriff learned that James Stanley lived with Wilson, but had left after the murder was discovered.

Wilson told the sheriff that on the morning of the 28th he was feeding stock and Strickland said, "Doug, how much money do I owe you? I want a settlement."

Wilson replied, "Jim, what is the matter."

Stanley said, " I am going to leave, and you may never see me again."

Stanley then went to the house and handed Doug Wilson's wife a silver dollar. Wilson told the sheriff that Stanley owed him $12 dollars. Because Stanley had no money to repay him, Stanley had previously given Wilson his pistol in exchange for payment.

During the investigation, Sheriff Townsend learned on the night he had seen James Stanley at the Columbus depot waiting for the train, Stanley had been at the town mercantile store. Sheriff Townsend was told Stanley had spent between $20 and $25 for a new overcoat, hat, a valise, and a pair of shoes.

Sheriff Townsend then boarded the next train for San Antonio and with the aid of a San Antonio police officer, the two lawmen quickly located Stanley and placed him under arrest. When Stanley asked why he was placed under arrest, the Sheriff replied, "There has been a murder committed below Eagle Lake, and you were in the neighborhood at the time."

Stanley replied, "Mr. Townsend, I am not the man that killed Robert L. Strickland, and I don't know anything about it."

When the sheriff searched Stanley he removed eleven silver dollars from his pocket. The next morning, Sheriff Townsend obtained a hack to transport his prisoner from the jail to the train depot. Strickland told the sheriff, "I want to tell you about the killing. Mr. Townsend, I did not kill the deceased, but I know who did and will tell you in time. There was a man who came to me the night the deceased was killed, and said to me: 'Jim, I know where we can get some money, and if you go with me I will go in and get the money and give you half.' I went with the man and stood about thirty yards from the store and watched while the other man went in and got the money and came out and gave me $30. The $11 you got from me last night is Robert L. Strickland's money; and I knew from the treatment he gave the deceased that the deceased could not live."

Stanley was tried and convicted of murder in the first degree. The jury afterwards assessed the penalty at death. The case was sent to the court of appeals and the court affirmed the conviction on June 2, 1883. On September 10, 1883 the date of the execution was set. After the appeal was affirmed, Stanley confessed that the motive for the murder was robbery. Stanley explained that his girlfriend, Sarah Walker, had persuaded him to raise some money quickly so they could go to Mexico.

On the day of the execution, 3000 spectators gathered around the gallows at the county farm one mile from town to witness the execution. On the gallows, Stanley said:

> I have found my way to glory. I have repented my sins and God will send angels from heaven to meet me. I am going straight to glory. Whiskey, cards, and women have brought me to this. I am going to heaven. Won't you meet me there? (Shouts from the colored crowd, Bliss God, he will.) My spirit will be flying around in glory and you sinners that drink and play cards and attend balls had better repent and pray or God will damn your souls. I forgive my enemies. God waits for me. Wave your lights. I shall have golden slippers and a golden ring.

After a couple of gospel hymns were sang and a prayer offered by the minister, the cap was adjusted. Stanley then cried out, "Let me see Sarah Walker." The woman was brought to the foot of the scaffold and Stanley exclaimed, "Oh, Sarah, see what you have brought me to. You did not fell me to commit this crime, but I did it for you. Pray Sarah, farewell, I'll meet you again in heaven."

The *Daily Gazette*, Colorado Springs, Colorado, dated Saturday, October 20, 1883, provided a full account of the crime and execution.

William Washington

Race/Gender: Black Male **Age:** 19 or 20 **Offense:** Rape, Robbery & Murder
Offense Date: December 27, 1887 **Weapon:** Knife **Execution:** October 20, 1888

John and Mary Miller along with their two daughters, ages two and four had been enjoying the Christmas season until on the morning of December 28, 1887, a horrible crime was discovered.

On the evening of December 27, John left home to play in a band at a wedding celebration at the Somerlotte home. The wedding party did not end until early the next morning, with Miller arriving home about sunrise. When he entered his home, Miller checked on his daughters and found both girls sound asleep in their bed, but could not locate his wife. While investigating her whereabouts, John noticed a trail of blood inside the house leading out the back door. The trail continued to the horse corral where he found Mary on the ground lying on her back and dead. Her night clothes had been pulled up above her waist, the right side of the mouth and right eye were bruised as were the left breast and arm. She had died as a result of her neck being slit.

Inside the house, a cuff button belonging to the murderer was found. The trunk inside the house was forced open and taken from inside the trunk was a $10 gold piece and $2 in silver. John Miller ran to his neighbor's house, which was Charles Aschenbeck and asked for his help to notify the sheriff of the murder. After the notification was made, William Washington was then seen running away from the Aschenbeck house into the field.

Sheriff J. L. Townsend after being notified of the murder responded to the scene along with Deputy George Crawford and Constable William Ordner. The lawmen searched the scene and located foot tracks and a button cuff. Hearing of Washington running away from the Ashenbeck's house lead the sheriff back that location. In the room where Washington stayed, a pair of bloody pants was found. Inside the pants pocket were two bloody pocket knifes. The lawmen picked up the fugitive's trail and tracked him for twenty miles to his aunt's house in Austin County. Upon arriving, Deputy Crawford and Constable Ordner then dismounted from their horses and walked up to the front door as Sheriff Townsend rode around to the back of the house. Just then, Washington ran out the back door and into the brush. The lawmen pursued after Washington and captured him. The sheriff observed the sleeve of the undershirt Washington was wearing possessed blood on it as well. Sheriff Townsend then warned Washington that any statement he made would be used against him at his trial.

Washington told the sheriff:

Miller owed me some money and his wife would not let him pay it, and I got mad and killed her for it. I went to Somerlotte's house and saw Miller there playing the accordion. I then went to Miller's house, stood on the galley, looked through the window and watched Mrs. Miller put the children to bed and undress herself. She then came to the door and looked out, and as she turned I caught her and asked for her to give me some. She refused and got away from me, and I cut her once in the house. She went to the back door and I went out at the front door and caught her in the lot. Then I threw her down and killed her and then I did what I wanted too. I then went into the house, opened the trunk and got the money out of a purse which was in the trunk.

Washington went on to explain he used the $10 gold piece to buy an accordion for $8 dollars. Deputy Crawford returned the accordion to the seller and received the $10 gold coin back to be used as evidence to corroborate Washington's confession.

In March of 1888, Washington went on trial for murder and was found guilty. The case was afterwards appealed to the Court of Criminal Appeals who affirmed the decision on May 2, 1888.

On the day of the execution, 3,000 spectators gathered at the scaffold erected a half-mile west of town. At the gallows, William Washington said he had nothing to say.

The *Dallas Morning News*, Friday, October 21, 1888, provided readers with a short article announcing the execution had taken place at Columbus, Texas.

James Morris

Alias: Henry Holmes, & Tally Guy **Race/Gender:** Black Male **Offense:** Robbery & Double Murder
Offense Date: December 29, 1903 **Weapon:** Iron Pipe **Execution:** November 25, 1904

On December 29, 1903, the horribly mangled body of Juan Bell (real name was Juan Ville) was found. At first the authorities believed the death was the result of a terrible accident and a passing train had hit him. When the body of three-year-old Emil was located lying near the tracks, and not showing any signs of being struck by the train, it was determined that both Bell and Emil had been struck to the head with an iron pipe and killed. After robbing the body of $17, the killer placed Bell's body on the railroad tracks to conceal the murder, and give the appearance of a horrible accident.

On March 28, 1904, James Morris was tried for the robbery and murders of Juan Bell and Emil. The jury deliberated twenty minutes then returned a verdict of guilty and assessed the death penalty. After the Court of Criminal Appeals had affirmed the case, District Court Judge Kennon on September 19, 1904, sentenced

Morris to hang by the neck until dead on November 25, 1904.

On the gallows, Morris who had been going by the name of Henry Holmes told the witnesses his real name was James Morris and that his home had been at Columbia in Brazoria County. Morris admitted to killing another person but refused to give the name or circumstances and believed God had forgiven him of his sins.

The *Galveston Daily News*, dated Saturday, November 26, 1904, provided its readers with details of the crime and the execution at Columbus, Texas.

Henry Bates

Race/Gender: Black Male **Age:** 24 **Offense:** Robbery with a Deadly Weapon
Offense Date: July 15, 1905 **Weapon:** Club **Execution:** December 8, 1905

Henry Bates worked as a laborer for Fred Kuhlee and his wife, Anna, on their farm located five miles southeast of Eagle Lake, Texas, in Colorado County. On July 12, 1905, Bates was dismissed from his job, but returned during the night of July 15 armed with a club. After entering the home, Bates beat Fred Kuhlee and his wife with the club until they were unconscious. Bates afterwards stole a small amount of money and a Colt .45 pistol from the home.

After Bates was arrested, he pled guilty to committing a robbery with a deadly weapon. Texas had created a new law making the offense of robbery with a deadly weapon a capital offense with punishment by death. On October 12, 1905, Walter Bates was brought before District Court Judge Mumford Kennon for sentencing which was published in the *Weimar Mercury* on October 21, 1905.

Judge Kennon: Stand up, Walter Bates. At a former day of this term you were tried upon an indictment which charged you with the robbery of Anna Kuhlee, and charging further that you committed the robbery by the use of deadly weapons. After being duly warned by the court of the consequences of your plea, and after having been informed what the penalty is for this offense, you pleaded guilty. The jury, after hearing you plead and the evidence, found you guilty, as charged in the indictment, and assessed your punishment at death. Have you anything to say why the sentence of the law should not be pronounced against you?

Bates: Yes sir.

Judge Kennon: What is it?

Bates: Me and another fellow was going to town, and we got to the lake and he goes on back home a piece – at least, he said he was going back home. He and another fellow, I disremember what his name was, went on back home, and I goes on down there by myself, and I done it by myself; but this woman I didn't intend to strike her. I struck her through mistake.

Judge Kennon: You struck her though mistake?

Bates: I just pleaded guilty to it, which I did do it by myself.

Judge Kennon: You want to let it be known that nobody had anything to do with it but yourself?

Bates: Yes sir. I done it by myself, and pleaded guilty to it. I didn't think I could be hung for the crime.

Judge Kennon: Well, that was a matter with the jury.
Bates: I ask for thirty days before hanging.

Judge Kennon: You are entitled to not less than thirty days, and I want to inform you also that you have the right to appeal this case and take it to a higher court, if you want to.

Bates: No sir, I done it by myself, and nobody didn't persuade me to do it and nobody didn't help me to do it.

Judge Kennon: Mr. Malsch, have you consulted with him in regard to appealing this case?

Edwin A. Malsch (Bates counsel): Yes sir.

Judge Kennon: Do you want to be sentenced now?

Bates: No sir

Malsch: He asked you if you wanted to be sentenced now.

Bates: Yes sir.

Judge Kennon: You understand, of course, that when this sentence is pronounced you can't go any further with it. I don't know that I exactly understand you in regard to the time. You say you want the shortest time?

Bates: Yes sir. I want the shortest time.

Judge Kennon: You understand fully what you are doing?

Bates: I am asking for thirty days if I can get it.

Judge Kennon: You can get thirty days or more.
Bates: Yes sir.

Judge Kennon: The sentence is that on Friday, December 8 of this year, the sheriff, in accordance with law and between the hours prescribed bylaw, shall carry out the sentence of the court by hanging you by the neck until you are dead.

Now, I don't think it is the place of the Judge whose duty it is to pronounce this sentence to deliver you a moral lecture. You seem to be a man of ordinary intelligence. You confessed before a jury in the perpetration of this crime, a very grave one, and in the exercise of their discretion, they saw fit to inflict the death penalty. Of course I appreciate the gravity of the situation. You will appreciate the fact, no doubt, that there is no prospect of this sentence being mitigated. I have no idea that the Governor would interfere in this case to commute your sentence to imprisonment for life, and I think it is my duty to tell you that there is not prospect of your being pardoned or your sentence being commuted, and it would be well, if you have any hopes of a future life to make preparation for it. So far as I am personally concerned, I don't believe that any time is too short for a man to sincerely repent and be forgiven. I know that it is fashionably to look at deathbed repentances and all that sort of thing with derision, but when it comes to looking at death face to face, I believe that even the evilest may, upon sincere repentance depend upon the mercy of God, which I now invoke in your behalf. Take your seat.

On the day of the execution, 1,000 people were present to witness the execution that included Mr. and Mrs. Kuhlee. Bates walked to the scaffold carrying a cigar in one hand and a bouquet of chrysanthemums in the other. On the gallows, Bates only said he had prayed for his sins and asked that they be forgiven. Bates then joined two clergymen in the singing of *Jesus, thou Art the Sinner's Friend*. As Bates was being bound, the preachers sang, *I will meet you in the City of the New Jerusalem*. While the noose was being adjusted, Bates laughed and asked the sheriff to adjust the knot so that he would not choke him to death. When the trap was sprung, Bates fell ten feet, with the fall breaking the neck.

The *Galveston Daily News*, dated Saturday, December 9, 1905, provided readers with an account of the crime, trial and execution.

John Armstrong

Race/Gender: Black Male   **Age:** 28   **Offense:** Murder
Offense Date: August 25, 1906   **Weapon:** Knife   **Execution:** April 26, 1907

John Armstrong met his future wife, Catherine Brown, when both were imprisoned at a convict farm working off their fines. After Catherine was released, Armstrong and Catherine were married. Within a short time, the newlyweds were experiencing marital problems because Catherine was paying to much attention to other men in the community of Eagle Lake.

On August 25, 1906, as Catherine was sitting at a restaurant table with another man, Armstrong approached and waited outside on the sidewalk for his wife. Catherine seeing her husband went outside and spoke with him briefly. During the conversation Armstrong asked Catherine to return home with him. Catherine laughed and cursed at Armstrong saying she had no intentions of returning back with him and she intended to stay the night at another man's house. Catherine turned away and walked back towards the restaurant.

Armstrong told a friend, "I am fixing to start something here. If I do, I am going to be at the head of it."

As Catherine was slipping through the restaurant door, Armstrong came up behind her while pulling out his knife and cut her throat. Catherine died a half hour later.

Armstrong fled the scene, but was located the next day at the town of East Bernard in Wharton County. After being found guilty of murder and sentenced to death, the case was appealed. The Court of Criminal Appeals affirmed the decision of December 5, 1906, and Armstrong was sentenced in February of 1907 to hang on April 26, 1907.

On the day of the execution, Armstrong was led out of the jail and transported to the permanent scaffold, which the county maintained on the county farm. On the gallows, Armstrong confessed to the murder and said other people would have committed his crime under the same circumstances. Armstrong said for the love of his wife he would not now tell why he killed her.

Once the preparation for the execution was complete, the sheriff sprung the trap. Armstrong fell through the trap, but his feet hit the ground. Officers standing above on the scaffold were alerted that Armstrong's feet were touching the ground. The officers took hold of the rope and pulled back until the feet were lifted from the ground. After hanging twelve minutes, the attending physicians declared the neck was broken and the body dead. The body was then lowered into a coffin and was afterwards loaded onto a Southern Pacific train to be delivered to a brother in Sealy, Texas, for burial.

Reports were later circulated from train passengers that John Armstrong was revived and was living quietly with family and friends. The rumors were publicized, but never investigated.

The *Galveston Daily News*, dated Saturday, April 27, 1907, provided their readers with details of the murder and execution.

Albert Woolridge, Jr.

Race/Gender: Black Male **Age:** 22 **Offense:** Murder
Offense Date: May 20, 1921 **Weapon:** Shotgun **Execution Date:** December 15, 1922

Albert and Emma Woolridge had been married less than two years, and their union was described as a troubled marriage from the beginning. Both Emma and her husband lived in a cabin on the farm they worked. On the night of May 20, 1921, the owner of the farm heard a gun blast, and ran to the cabin to find Albert standing in the room with blood on his clothing and shoes. He then looked over to see Emma sitting in a chair and barely alive from a wound to the face and mouth. Because her tongue had been torn off from the shotgun wound, Emma was unable to speak and she soon died. Emma was afterwards buried at Pleasant Hill in Columbus, Texas.

Woolridge told his employer that he had been out in the lot when he too heard the shotgun blast. Woolridge said he heard Emma say, "Oh, kid, I have shot myself." The case was investigated and on September 16, 1921, Albert Woolridge was arrested and charged with murder. At trial, Woolridge testified in his own defense. Woolridge testified that he first heard Emma make her last statement moments before the gunshot was heard, implying to the jury she had committed suicide. However, Woolridge could not explain why she did not have any powder burns on her body or why he had blood on his clothing and shoes. On October 5, 1921, the jury returned a verdict of guilty and on October 13, 1921, he was sentenced to hang.

On the day of the execution, 1000 people witnessed the hanging at the county poor farm. On the scaffold, Woolridge maintained his innocence, but said he was ready to die. Sheriff John Wegenhoft sprang the trap and Albert Woolridge was pronounced dead nine minutes later.

Ray Jones

Race/Gender: Black Male **Age:** 30 **Offense:** Rape
Offense Date: August 1921 **Execution:** March 9, 1923

Ray Jones was arrested on August 31, 1921, for the rape of a white woman near Pilgrim, Texas, in Gonzales County. On a change of venue, the case was transferred to Colorado County. Jones was tried on September 28, and the jury found him guilty of the crime and assessed the death penalty the following day. On May 31, 1922, the Court of Criminal Appeals affirmed the lower courts decision.

On March 9, 1923, at 1:50 p.m., Jones was driven to the county farm located one mile east of the town of Columbus where the gallows had been erected. Because the execution was made public an eager crowd of 2,000 spectators awaited his arrival. Once Jones reached the platform he told the witnesses:

"I have lived a fast life and have been a thief, a robber and perhaps a murderer together with the crime I was now charged with having committed. I have been saved and expected to see Jesus."

Jones who had maintained his innocence handed Sheriff Adam Burttschell an envelope that contained a letter from him confessing to the crime. After the trap was sprung, Deputy Wegenhoft announced that there would be no souvenirs given from the rope used in the execution, as any souvenirs would be given to the citizens of Guadalupe County. Jones was hanged from the same gallows as Albert Woolridge who was executed on December 22, 1922.

The *Eagle Lake Headlight*, dated Saturday, March 17, 1923, provided readers with a large article detailing the assault and execution.

Cooke County
County Seat - Gainesville

William Pitman
(Pittman)

Race/Gender: White Male **Offense:** Murder **Weapon:** Firearm
Execution: June 8, 1860

Henry F. Rour lived twelve miles southwest of Muenster at Rour Spring. During a dispute with William Pitman, Henry was shot and killed.

The *Ledger and Texan*, (San Antonio, TX), dated Saturday, June 30, 1860, provided the following short article:

Wm. Pitman, the murderer of Dr. Rowe, was hung on the 8th inst., at Sherman. He struggled but little, yet his neck was not broken, and his pulse continued to beat after he was cut down.

Note: The paper wrote that the execution occurred at Sherman in Grayson County and spelled Rour's last name differently. Other material shows the execution occurred at Gainesville in Cooke County.

Oscar Clark

Offense: Murder **Offense Date:** April 1870 **Execution:** June 20, 1871

The *Houston Telegraph*, dated Thursday, June 22, 1871, provided the following details of the execution:

THE EXECUTION. – On last Tuesday at 1 o'clock, p. m. in the presence of two or three thousand persons from this and adjoining counties – Oscar Clark, the murderer of young Wm. Jones, was hung and order of our last District Court.

The convict was conducted to the gallows by our sheriff and a strong guard of citizens, who were deployed around the gallows to preserve order. He was accompanied upon the scaffold by the sheriff and two of the guards. He was perfectly composed and rational and realized fully his situation, and made a full acknowledgement of his guilt, which is embraced substantially in his written confession which we give below. – He than sang the hymn – "Am I a soldier of the Cross" – and after asking forgiveness from all men, begged that all evil doers would take warning from him; after which the white cap was drawn over his face and while he continued repeating, good-bye," "farewell," the sheriff knocked the trigger and the platform fell breaking his neck, and he died without a struggle. — Gainesville Gazette.

Lucien M. Noftsinger

Race/Gender: White Male **Age:** 24 **Offense:** Murder
Offense Date: August 7, 1878 **Weapon:** Double Barrel Shotgun **Execution:** April 30, 1880

Lucien Noftsinger had arrived in Texas from Virginia in 1876, and settled in the small farming community of Dexter, in Cooke County. There he received employment as a clerk at W. F. Whittington's store. Soon Noftsinger began courting a beautiful young girl by the name of Helen, and later the two were engaged to be married in the fall of 1878.

The engagement ended in March of 1878, after Helen had danced with Willis Cline who Noftsinger disapproved of. Noftsinger told Helen that Cline was nothing more than a low-down pup, and he did not approve of her dancing with him. Helen ended the argument by breaking off the engagement and later married Willis Cline on July 4, 1878.

On August 1, 1878, Noftsinger borrowed a side-by-side double barrel shotgun on the pretense of shooting stray cats, and kept the weapon under the front counter of the store. Then on the night of August 7, 1878, Noftsinger asked W. S. Barnes to go with him as a witness saying, "He was going to get away with a man, and that the man had deprived him of his pleasure, and that he intended to deprive the man of his."

Barnes refused to go saying, "They will catch you, and break your damned neck." Noftsinger shrugged it off and afterwards had a drink with E. S. Garzer (Gardner) and asked Garzer to ride with him to be a witness.

Willis and Helen Cline lived four miles north of Dexter. On the hot summer night, the Clines placed their mattress on the front porch of their home and made their bedding on the porch in order to escape the heat from inside the house and sleep in the cooler night's breeze. While the couple was sound asleep, Helen was awaken by the shotgun explosion to see her husband dead from being shot to the head.

Lawmen suspecting Noftsinger of the crime went to the store and examined the shotgun. The weapon's left barrel showed to have recently been fired. Both Noftsinger and Garzer were arrested and jailed. Both men were tried and found guilty. The jury assessed the death penalty on Noftsinger, while Gardner received a sentence of ninety-nine years in the penitentiary, but he died of measles in the county jail while awaiting his appeal.

On the day of the execution, thirty-two heavily armed officers escorted the prisoner to the scaffold and kept the crowd away who were clamoring for his release. Many citizens believed Noftsinger should be released as the governor had commuted Benjamin Krebs and James Preston on their sentence of death for murder.

After mounting the gallows, and as the rope was about to be adjusted, the crowd of 10,000 made a rush from all four sides toward the scaffold, but guards pulled their pistols and held their ground, and kept the crowd back. Noftsinger then addressed the crowd and said, "Fellow citizens, if you think I ought to die, I am willing. I do not thank Governor Roberts in my case; through he was honest in his convictions. Judge Carroll promised to recommend my commutation. You all know how he used me. Krebs and Preston were released. I have to die. If Governor Roberts wants me to die, I am ready. Friends and all, goodbye. I hope to meet you all in a better world."

At 4:30 Lucian Noftsinger told Sheriff M. M. Ozment good-bye, and stepped upon the trap. Sheriff Ozment placed the noose around the neck and, the trap was sprung. After hanging twenty minutes Noftsinger was cut down and his remains turned over to his father, who returned the body to Virginia for burial.

The *Galveston Daily News*, dated Saturday, May 1, 1880, wrote, "The gallows was erected in the northeastern suburbs of the town, is within view of the celebrated "hangs-men tree," of Cooke County. Upon the low, outstretching limbs of this monarch of the woodland, forty men were gibbeted during the fifteen days of terrorism in 1862."

Coryell County
County Seat - Gatesville

Ed Powell

Race/Gender: White Male
Weapon: Pistol
Offense: Murder & Robbery
Execution: September 29, 1891
Offense Date: December 17, 1889

Jim Leeper

Race/Gender: White Male
Weapon: Pistol
Offense: Murder & Robbery
Execution: September 29, 1891
Offense Date: December 17, 1889

The only execution in Coryell County was the double execution of Ed Powell and Jim Leeper. Both men had been tried and found guilty of the murder and attempted robbery of John T. Mathis.

On December 17, 1889, Powell and Leeper waited for farmers leaving town to return home so that they could rob them of the money they had been paid for selling their cotton. One of those farmers was John Mathis. When Powell and Leeper attempted to stop Mathis, the farmer whipped his mules to outrun the robbers. In response, Powell and Leeper fired their revolvers at Mathis in order to stop him. As the frightened mules galloped on, one of the bullets hit Mathis in the back where upon he fell backwards into the bed of the wagon. The unmanned mules continued on until they reached the gates of Mathis's home.

Both Powell and Leeper were tried for robbery and murder and found guilty on February 13, 1890. The case was appealed and affirmed in May 24, 1890 and Judge C. K. Bell sentenced both to death on July 25, 1891.

The day before the execution the sheriff read to Powell and Leeper the governor's message to "let the law take its course."

Powell was silent, but Leeper said, "Let her go."

Powell's mother who was present when the message was read became enraged and told both "To die like men, and pay no attention to religion—if there was a God he was unjust."

When Powell and Leeper looked out their cell window into the jail yard to see a man standing on the scaffold, both cursed the man and said, "Get off that; that's ours."

The next day, Ed Powell and Jim Leeper were both dressed in new black suits with geranium button banquets on their lapels. Once escorted to the gallows, Leeper addressed the witnesses first by saying, "Gentlemen, I wish

Photograph of Ed Powell and Jim Leeper on the gallows at Gatesville in Coryell County. The photograph was afterwards printed on postcards and sold as souvenirs. *Courtesy of Southern Methodist University, Degolyer Library.*

to tell you of the respect I have for Sheriff Hammack for the uniform courtesy with which he has treated us. I'm perfectly willing to die and am not afraid to die. I'm innocent of the crime."

Ed Powell spoke next. "I do not know that I have anything to say. I agree with everything Mr. Leeper has said. I die innocent and I die game for the crime of someone else."

After the prayer, Powell spoke again and said: "I believe my sins are forgiven and I can die and believe I will go to heaven. I believe my sins are washed away. I wish every man here wealth, health and prosperity and then go to heaven when they do and meet me, as I believe I am going to heaven."

At 1:55 p.m., the black caps were pulled over their heads and the sheriff asked if Leeper and Powell were both ready. After the reply of, "Yes," the trap was sprung. The drop of eight feet did break Ed Powell's neck, and he was pronounced dead about twenty minutes later. Leeper's neck however was not broken, and he strangled for fourteen minutes. After both were pronounced dead, the bodies were cut down and released to relatives. Relatives of Powell transported the remains for burial to Memphis, Tennessee, and Leeper was to be buried in Callahan County.

The *Fort Worth Gazette*, dated Wednesday, September 30, 1891, provided its readers with a full account of the crime and execution at Gatesville, Texas.

Dallas County
County Seat - Dallas

Jane Elkins

Race/Gender: Black Female **Offense:** Murder **Weapon:** Ax
Execution: May 27, 1853

Jane Elkins earned the distinction of being the first woman to be legally executed by hanging in the State of Texas.. Elkins, a slave, was executed in Dallas County on May 27, 1853, for the murder of her owner, named John Windom. She was accused of killing her Windom with an ax while he was asleep in bed with his two small children at his home in Farmers Branch.

Elkins was tried and found guilty on May 16, 1853, when the verdict was read out loud by D. R. Cameron, jury foreman. "We the jury find the defendant guilty of murder in the first degree. We further find that the defendant is a slave of value of seven hundred dollars and that the owner of the defendant has done nothing to evade or defeat the execution of the law upon said defendant."

On May 17, Judge John H. Reagan asked Elkins if she had anything to say why judgment and sentence of death should not passed upon her. She stood silent. Judge Reagan said very well. "It is therefore ordered adjudged and decreed by the court that the Sheriff of Dallas County keep said Jane in close confinement in the common jail of Dallas County until Friday the 27th of the present month of May and that between the hours of 11 o'clock a.m. and 3 o'clock p.m., the Sheriff take said Jane from the common jail of said county and convey her to a gallows erected for the purpose and there hang Jane by the neck until she is dead."

Wesley Jones

Race/Gender: Black Male **Offense:** Rape **Offense Date:** November 1, 1875
Execution: August 11, 1876

Wesley Jones was convicted of raping a German woman by the last name of Benson on the muddy creek located twelve miles from Dallas. Mrs. Benson was home alone on the farm when Jones arrived and attacked the woman.

The *Galveston Daily News*, dated Saturday, August 12, 1876, reported that a band played songs as Jones was driven to the gallows that had been erected on the riverbank.

Jones' wife and children went to him on the platform, and after much weeping, they said their goodbyes. Jones then made a short speech, in which he confessed to the crime. Jones then told the 10,000 witnesses that he was prepared to die, and would be pardoned by the Savior. He hoped all present would take warning by his fate.

Allen Wright

Age: 21 **Race/Gender:** Black Male **Offense:** Murder
Offense Date: February 4, 1880 **Weapon:** Shotgun **Execution:** August 27, 1880

Allen Wright was hanged at Dallas for the shotgun murder of Jesse Wicks that occurred near Hutchins, on February 4, 1880. The murder of Wicks was over a rail-splitting dispute in which Wright provided the following confession:

> The killing grew out of a rail-splitting contract. Jesse Wicks and myself were partners. The contract was for clearing land and splitting 30,000 rails for Dr. J. C. Michner. The terras were payable weekly

or daily, as we saw fit to collect. My count of work done was taken by the doctor, after we had been working for him sometime, and settlements made accordingly, with the voluntary promise on my part to make good any shortage. During the job I was taken sick, and substituted in my stead a good working hand named Moses Perkins. It was understood, after deducting Wick's and Perkins's wages, the profits should be divided equally by the firm. When I was able to resume work, we concluded to keep Perkins as a hand. I could see, however, that Wicks and Perkins had cornered to oust me out of the contract. Being in feeble health, I availed myself one day of a job to clean out a well, and told my partner of it.

The next day I went back to work on the contract. Wicks and I had some words about my refusal to represent to the doctor that more work had been done than was actually done, to cover the loss of my absence, and he raised an ax on me, and would have killed me but for Perkins interference. The partnership was then and there dissolved between us, and we separated. The next day Wicks collected all that was coming to the firm from the doctor but .95 cents. Meeting him afterwards in company with Perkins, we quarreled about the matter. The only satisfaction he would give me was that he had already spent the money he had collected. Hot words followed and Wicks again attempted to brain me with the ax. Leaving them, I went to Dr. Stone's and borrowed the shotgun for the alleged purpose of going turkey-hunting. This was about dark. I went straight to the stock-pens in search of Wicks. On the way I halted and concluded not to kill him, and I turned homeward.

Brooding over my wrongs, I recalled all the acts of Wicks; how I secured the contract, took him in as a partner when I could have simply employed him; how I had worked myself into ill health to increase the profits; how I had been forced out of the partnership and swindled. All this, together with the fact that Wicks knew I was without money and about to be married to my sweetheart, Zuddy Williams, so angered me that I returned toward the pens, found Wicks and pulled down on him, killing him outright. The charge of buckshot took effect above the left hip, I believe. I gave myself up to Mr. Perry and Mr. Bledsoe, who pinioned my arms behind, and started to Dallas with me.

As the train stopped at Hutchins, they saw Sheriff Moon aboard, and turned me over to him. I have been well treated since I was placed in jail, and, since I have professed religion, I pray for the sheriff and his deputies. It is murder, I know, now, but how many under similar circumstances, would have done just as I did in the heat of passion! When I was tried, and the jury brought in the verdict of the death penalty, I was so sick and bewildered that I then preferred death, and refused to appeal my case. I am sorry now I did not, for it would give me more time to prepare for the hereafter. I believe in the old bible's hell of eternal fire. It is awful; and think of it – ministers of my own color have denied me consolation.

The scaffold was erected on the Trinity "bottom" northwest of the courthouse and the bridge of the Texas and Pacific Railroad. At noon Wright walked out of the jail wearing black pants, white shirt with imitation diamond studs, white vest with blue buttons, black coat with an arm gaiters on each. Wright was then placed in a wagon and driven to the gallows by the sheriff, deputies and two companies of state volunteers. At 1:35 p.m. Wright mounted the gallows where the death warrant was read in the presence of the 5,000 spectators who had assembled to witness the execution. At the conclusion of reading the warrant, Wright addressed the crowd and said, "Before you stands Allen Wright, who is to be executed. When I drop from this scaffold, I expect to drop into the arms of Jesus. Take warning by my fate, and don't let your temper lead you astray, as my had done to me. Endeavor always to walk in the path of righteousness. I have committed a great sin, for which I am to suffer to-day, though I believe I have been forgiven by God. I thank you for your kind attention."

After a prayer, the noose and black cap was adjusted. Wright then said, "Farewell to all," as the trap was sprung. The neck was not broken, and it took seven minutes for attending physicians to pronounce him dead. The body was then cut down and lowered into a coffin to be buried at the potter's field.

Adam Thompson

Alias: Adam Armstrong
Offense: Robbery & Murder
Execution: July 1, 1881

Age: 26
Offense Date: July 1, 1876

Race/Gender: Black Male
Weapon: Ax

Adam Thomson was executed for the murder of a German man named Joseph Schoemaker at Cedar Hill. Old man Schoemaker made his living by operating a small general store located six miles west of Dallas. The murder was not discovered until the following morning when a passersby noticed Schoemaker lying nude under a mattress in front of his store and notified the police. It was then discovered that Schoemaker had been killed from a blow to the head with an ax.

Tracks leading away from the store, led to the discovery of the broken and empty store cash box. Adam Thompson, Wesley Pollard and Jerry Gantt (or Grant) were quickly suspected as they were wanted for questioning by police for several other robberies that occurred earlier on Bryan Street in Dallas. When Thompson was arrested, officers searched his trunk inside his home and discovered a key, a counterfeit half-dollar, and a pen holder belonging to Schoemaker. Thompson at first told officers he did not participate in the robbery and murder, but watched the murder take place from two miles away on the prairie. Thompson maintained his innocence up to the moment the trap was released.

The execution was private with the gallows erected on the west side of the jail yard. As Thompson walked passed the other prisoners cells to the gallows, he told them, "Goodbye boys, Goodbye boys."

On the scaffold, Thompson was asked if he had anything to say. He replied, "Nothing, farewell vain world, farewell."

The drop of seven and a half feet did not break the neck and Thompson strangled to death. After hanging for twenty minutes, his body was cut down and turned over to the undertaker. Wesley Pollard who was an accomplice died in prison from consumption, and Jerry Gantt was never apprehended.

The gallows used were the same one which Allen Wright was hanged from. The newspaper wrote, "The job was neat, clean and expeditious, reflecting credit on the sheriff."

A reporter from the *Daily Democrat*, (Ft. Worth) interviewed Thompson which was printed in the Saturday, July 2, 1881, edition.

Adam, I am a representative of the Fort Worth Democrat, and would like to talk to you a little. Have you any objections?

Oh, no sir.

Do you feel any uneasiness or nervousness now that your time is so near at hand?

No, sir; I know it won't do any good, and so (smiling) I just have to go ahead and stand it.

Do you sleep any now?

Oh, yes, I sleep at night just as I always did. I never do sleep any in the day time.

Have you lost your appetite to any extent?

No, sir, I eat all I can get, or anyhow as much as I usually do.

Have you been treated kindly since your confinement?

Yes, sir, just as kindly I reckon as a man can be treated in jail. Mr. Moon, when he was a sheriff, was good to me, and Mr. Jones and all of them seem to do all they can, and are allowed to do to make me comfortable.

How long have you been in jail?

Nearly five years, I believe I was put in jail on July 13th, 1876.

Where were you born and raised?

I was born in Tennessee, and belonged to man whose name was Thompson. You see I was taken away from my father and mother when I was quite young and carried to Kansas, not having my father's name, I always carried my old master's name. From Kansas we came to Texas, and I have been principally raised in northwest Texas.

Are you married.

No sir, never was married.

Do the ministers of religion come to see you?

Yes they have all come to see me and tried to do all they could for me I reckon, but as I don't belong to any church and never professed any religion I don't know whether there has been any change in me or not.

Did you or have you tried for a commutation?

I have'nt tried yet, but my lawyer is carrying around a petition to-day. I did try to get the colored folks interested in the matter some time back and wanted them to get up a petition and use their influence for me, but I reckon, it was because I didn't belong to any church they didn't do it. I did have two lawyers, but one of them gave me up, and I have only had Mr. Clint for some time past. He is doing all he can for me, but I don't expect it will do any good.

Now Adam, it is pretty certain you will hang and it will do no good to deny it, nor will it do any harm to tell the truth about it, are you guilty or innocent?

Sir, I am innocent.

Henry Miller

Race/Gender: Black Male **Age:** 33 **Offense:** Murder
Offense Date: May 24, 1892 **Weapon:** Pistol **Execution:** July 28, 1893

On Tuesday evening, May 24, 1892, Dallas police officers Jim Beard, Brandenburg, and C. O. Brewer, arrested Henry Miller at the Union Depot train station in downtown Dallas on the charge of slander of a white woman.

Henry Miller had been drinking and singing earlier at Wiley Skelton's Saloon when he made statements to patrons that he had just returned from sleeping with a white section boss's wife. After the affidavits of slander were signed, sheriff deputies asked Dallas police officers to watch for Henry Miller, and arrest him.

Dallas police officers did locate Henry Miller and placed him under arrest. While Officer Beard had gone to call for a police wagon to transport the prisoner, Officer Brandenburg remained alone with Miller. Miller asked the officer several questions about his bond, and the officer replied that he did not know, because he did not know what his charge was.

Miller said, "Then damn you, I'll give you bond," and pulled out a hidden .44 caliber pistol. Both Miller and Officer Brandenburg exchanged gunshots, but both missed their mark. Miller ran off while firing his pistol at the pursuing officers.

Officer Cassee O. Brewer, a three-year veteran of the Dallas Police Department was hit by a bullet and died. Miller was overtaken on Hawkins Street after the pursuing officer jumped onto a city fire department wagon and captured him. Officer Cassee Brewer was buried in Dallas, Texas, at Greenwood Cemetery.

Once word spread that Officer Brewer had been killed and Miller was lodged in the Dallas Jail, a mob formed demanding that Miller be released to them for quick justice. At one point the Sheriff Ben Cabell had to address the crowd from an open window on an upper floor and said, "Ain't you all friends of mine?"

The reply was, "We are, but we want that Negro."

The sheriff said, "If you insist on doing this, I'm doing my duty will be bound to kill some of you and you may kill all of us. You see the situation I would rather give up every drop of my blood than hurt one of you if it were not for doing my duty, but I will be very firm with you, I'll shoot before I'll allow the prisoner to be taken out."

Seconds later men began using a battering ram against the jail's iron door. From within the jail, deputies fired shotguns and slightly injured three members of the mob. After members from the mob exchanged gunshots, the mob calmed down and cooler heads prevailed. This gave the opportunity for the sheriff to secretly take Miller out of the jail and transport him to Waco until his trial two weeks later.

At trial, Miller was tried and found guilty of murder in the first degree and sentenced to death. The case was then appealed to the Court of Criminal Appeals who affirmed the lower court decision. Miller was then sentenced to hang on July 28, 1893. Four days prior to the execution, Governor James Hogg sent word that he "found no warrant for interfering with the course of the law, but hoped the Lord would have mercy on the soul of the condemned."

On the morning of the execution, Henry Miller was dressed in a new black suit, with a black tie, leather shoes and white gloves. Sheriff Ben Cabell entered the cell and read the death warrant. When he finished reading the document the sheriff said, "You are the first man I ever read this kind of a warrant to Henry and I regret it very much. Henry now put on your white gloves."

While doing so Miller turned to Will Tanner and told him, "You have treated me kind and I want to meet you in heaven."

Then turning to a reporter he said, "You have been mighty fair with the ole darky an I hopes to meet you in the better land."

Miller then spoke to the ministers saying, "I want to meet my God. I want to talk to my God. I've not been locked up in here all this time for nothing, I'se been prayin to be saved. An' I is saved thank God."

After a song was sang, Miller said, "My God is gwine to call me d'rectly and I'm feelin good. Th' angels will be there to conduct my spirit to th' bar of God. I grew up under trials an' tribulations. I don't fear death because my God has promised me a place in his kingdom. What have I been in this jail all this time fur? I'se been on my knees prayin to my God." When he finished talking Miller lighted a cigar and leaned against an iron bar and smoked in silence.

At 1:40 p.m. deputies John Bolick and Dick Winfry came to Miller, told him it was time for them to walk to the gallows. As Miller smoked a cigar on the way to the gallows within the jail, Sheriff Cabell asked him if he had anything to say. Miller said, "Goodbye my friends. I wants you all to meet me in heaven. I'm glad Ise on this thing. I knows Ise goin to heaven. The officers has been as good to me as if I wuz a rich white man. I r'members one day my dinner didn't come an Sheriff Cabell come up an said that when my vituals didn't come up all right to jes let him know and he'd see that they did come up all right. Ise nothing against any man. Ise willa to die. If anybody here's got anything against this old nigger tell me an I'll fall at yo feet an ax yu furgiveness."

Miller replied that he was glad the end of his life was near, and that his mind was in Heaven. Thirty people including the press, Chief of Police Maddox, Sheriff Adam Euless of Fort Worth, Sheriff Tom Beall of Hill County and Joe L. Mars of Denton, witnessed the execution. As the black cap was placed over the head and the rope adjusted, Miller began to sing, "Yes, Jesus Yes, I am coming to you." The singing ceased when Sheriff Cabell pulled the cord to the trap.

The *Dallas Morning News*, dated Saturday, July 29, 1893, provided its readers with a full account of the murder, execution and description of the gallows used.

Joseph Malone

Alias: Doba Joe
Offense: Rape
Execution: September 2, 1898

Age: 23
Offense Date: July 15, 1898

Race/Gender: Black Male
Weapon: Heavy Shoe & Strangulation by Hands.

Joseph Malone was tried and executed in less than two months from the time he had committed the rape of a farmer's wife in Dallas County. On the morning of July 15, 1898, Joseph Malone was walking toward the Stein farm when he saw sixty-five-year-old Katherine Stein working in the garden. He then hid in the cornfield, and worked his way up as close as he could near the house where Mrs. Stein was working. Malone then sprang from the field where he grabbed his victim by the throat to prevent her from screaming and then dragged her back into the field where he assaulted her. Malone fled after he had chocked and beat the woman about the head with a heavy shoe leaving her for dead in the field.

Sheriff Ben Cabell was notified about a half hour later and organized a posse of deputies to ride to the farm and begin tracking the fugitive. For seven hours the officer trailed after their suspect through brush, river bottoms, cornfields, meadows, until late into the afternoon when Malone was shot several times and captured. Three days later Malone was indicted for rape and following his indictment he confessed to the crime.

At trial, Mrs. Stein identified Malone as her attacker, and Malone pled guilty to the charge. On July 28, 1898, Charles F. Clint sentenced Joe Malone to hang on September 2, just forty-eight days from the day he committed the crime.

In the early morning hours of the day of the execution, 2,000 people arrived at the Dallas County Jail. Although they all knew the execution was private within the walls of the jail, the crowd arrived in hopes of being chosen as a witness or to at least hear the release of the trap at the moment of the drop. At 11:30 a.m., Malone was baptized and then dressed himself in his new suit of clothes.

At 12:15, Malone was handcuffed and his elbows were bound to his sides with twine. Sheriff Cabell, Sheriff Sterling Clark of Tarrant County, Sheriff P. C. Moore of Wise County, and Dallas Police Chief G. E. Cornwall, then led Malone from his death cell to the gallows.

Waiting at the gallows was Rev. Z. T. Pardee. Rev. Pardee told Malone, "Don't forget those words I spoke to you just now, Joe."

Malone replied, "I won't forget."

As Sheriff Cabell placed the noose around Malone's neck, Rev. Pardee said, "I'll repeat them, Joe, I want you to listen . . . My faith looks up to thee Thou lamb of Calvary; Savior divine – O, hear me while I pray, take all my sins away."

When the Rev. Pardee finished, Malone asked Sheriff Cabell to loosen the knot so that he could speak a few words to his friends.

Malone said, "You see what way I am going, and I have left the history of my life out that so that you can read for yourself. I want you to take warning from me. Good-bye."

Sheriff Cabell then tightened the noose, placed the black cap over the head and pulled the trigger. After the body was declared dead, it was cut down and turned over to the undertaker for burial..

The *Dallas Morning News*, dated Saturday, September 3, 1898, provided its readers with a large account of the crime and execution at Dallas, Texas.

Holly Vann

Age: 30 **Race/Gender:** White Male **Offense:** Robbery & Murder
Offense Date: November 29, 1904 **Weapon:** Pistol **Execution:** May 12, 1905

At about 9 p.m., on the night of November 29, 1904, just as the small family store was about to close, two men entered the store of Sol Aronoff, located at 236 South Harwood Street in Dallas. One of the two men made a twenty-five cent purchase for a bag of tobacco. When Aronoff turned from the register to hand the change back, he was surprised to see a pistol pointed at his face with the demand for him to "hold up his hands."

Aronoff told the men, "Why, you can't shoot me, I'm in my own house."

Aronoff was pushed back towards the bedroom where his eleven-year-old son, Nathan was sleeping on a cot. Four shots were fired. Holly Vann fired the first two bullets from a .38 caliber pistol. One of the first bullets hit the dresser drawers next to where Nathan was lying, and the second bullet struck Aronoff above the left breast, causing him to fall dead across his bed.

A third bullet was fired by Burrell Oates, but a fourth bullet was fired by Mrs. Oronoff who fired a pistol at the robbers as she was running to the aid of her husband.

The next day twelve men were lined up inside the Dallas City Hall building so that Mrs. Aronoff could view them as possible suspects. Upon seeing Holly Vann, Mrs. Aronoff pointed at him and yelled, "That is the man! Give me a pistol and let me kill him as he killed my husband!"

Nathan Aronoff also identified Holly Vann as the killer of his father.

Chief of Police Knight then prepared two arrest warrant affidavits for the arrest of Holly Vann and Burrell Oates which read "did and with malice aforethought, kill and murder Sol Aronoff with a gun or pistol."

Both suspects were arrested that same afternoon. Vann gave his age as being twenty-eight and Burrell

Oates as thirty-one-years-old. A third person named Frank McCue had also been arrested and charged as an accomplice, but turned state's evidence against Vann and Oates to secure his release.

Frank McCue testified that he was with Vann and Oates riding in Vann's buggy from Oak Cliff in Dallas, when they passed by Aronoff's store. While passing the store, Vann made the comment that they should to rob the store. Vann then hid and parked the buggy. It was then decided between Oates and Vann as to who should carry the larger or smaller of the two pistols.

On December 22, 1904, the jury deliberated for two hours on Vann's future and returned a verdict of guilty and assessed the death penalty. Vann's attorney's then appealed the verdict to the Criminal Court of Appeals.

While waiting for the decision from the higher court, Vann escaped from the Dallas County Jail. On January 25, 1905, at 4 p.m. it was discovered Vann and other prisoners had sawed through the cell bars. Vann was accompanied by Burrell Oates, Albert Johnson, and Will Chamberlain. The next day, Vann returned to the Dallas County Jail and surrendered.

The following week Oates went on trial for his part in the murder and he was convicted and sentenced to death as well. His verdict was immediately appealed which started a long process to see the man hang. The Court of Appeals reversed three previous death sentences before on June 26, 1912, when the Court of Criminal Appeals finally affirmed the conviction. Attorneys then made a request for the Court of Appeals for a rehearing, which was refused on October 16, 1912. On October 21, Burrell Oates was sentenced to hang with the execution date being November 29, 1912; eight years after the robbery and murder had taken place.

Holly Vann photo from the *Fort Worth Record*, Saturday, November 30, 1912.

On the afternoon of the execution, sixty people with invitations were allowed into the jail yard as witnesses. Outside the jail another crowd of 4,000 gathered. On the gallows, he declared his innocence of the crimes he had been convicted of.

At noon of the day of the execution Sheriff Arthur Ledbetter arrived at the cell to read the death warrant. After the reading, Vann called his five brothers to him. He pleaded with them to be men of strong character and upright life. Holding in his left hand the Bible that has been his one book in his cell, he raised it high and said:

> Boys, read this book and follow all its teachings. In an hour when no friend on earth can aid you, the things that are in this old book will give you strength to bear what God has sent upon you. I am about to go away from you. I have confidence in the forgiveness that is promised here and shall expect you to try to meet me in heaven. It was keeping bad associates and using strong drink that has brought me to this and they will be the ruin of any man. Let them alone, my brothers, and be men.

When Vann finished Sheriff Ledbetter asked him if wished to make any statements.

Yes, I know I have a right make a statement, "but I hardly know what I can say more than I have said. I am not guilty of this crime; God knows that I am not. He and I are the only two who do know. He knows that I didn't have a gun and didn't fire the shot.

> Association with bad company got me into this trouble. I want you, Mr. Ledbetter to warn all young people, and especially my brothers, to keep out of bad company and leave strong drink alone.

> In olden times the law was made for the right; today it is made for the man with money. I have no money, and I am where I am. I am prepared to meet my doom. Mr. Ledbetter, and I won't be any more

nervous than you. I will stand up to it like a man. I have known you a long time; I helped elect you and I know that you are fulfilling the law. It is your sworn duty and I could have no hard feelings against you. I have no hard feelings against any one. I want to thank my counsel for what they have done; they have done all that could be done.

Vann was then instructed to dress for the execution and after several minutes in the death cell he came out dressed in a black suit, black tie and wearing a white chrysanthemum. After receiving a shot of whiskey, he then shook hands with the prisoners in the other cells and told them all good-bye.

The floor of the scaffold was on a level with the second story of the jail. As Vann stood on the platform he called out to several of his acquaintances and told them farewell. Vann told the sixty witnesses, "I have no ill feelings to any man. Every enemy I have forgiven. Officers of the law have done only the things that their oaths require and I harbor no ill to them. It is my final warning, avoid bad companions and strong drink."

As Sheriff Ledbetter was about to pull the cap over the head, Vann said: "Mr. Ledbetter, if a report gets out that I was not full of nerve to the last, please correct it for me, Will you?"

At 1:20 p.m. Sheriff Ledbetter sprang the trap and the crowd of 4,000 that had gathered outside the jail were informed that the execution had taken place and Holly Vann was dead.

The *Dallas Morning News*, dated Saturday, May 13, 1905, provided a large article to inform readers of the crime and execution.

Julius B. Robertson

Alias: Bubber Robinson
Offense: Robbery & Murder
Execution: May 14, 1910
Race/Gender: Black Male
Offense Date: November 11, 1908
Age: 28
Weapon: Pistol

Julius "Bubber" Robertson was one of three men who on Thursday, November 11, 1908, held up Frank Wolford at Dallas. Wolford who was a farmer from Rosehill had arrived at Dallas to sell his produce at the fairgrounds. During the evening hours, Wolford and his son had gone to downtown Dallas until about 10:30 p.m. They were walking down Main Street near the intersection of Bopp Street, to retrieve their wagon team at the fairground wagon yard,. Three men then approached Wolford and while one of the men held a pistol, a second man started to go through Wolford's pockets. Unknown to the robber, Woldford held a knife in his hand and Wolford was shot after he swung the knife at the robber's neck.

Nearby mounted officers quickly galloped their horses in the direction of the gunfire finding Wolford mortally wounded, and the robbers having fled from the scene. Frank Wolford died of his wound at 2 a.m. Friday morning.

Gene Jones was soon arrested and quickly provided a statement identifying Bubber Robertson as the shooter.

Robertson was arrested, tried and convicted for murder. On the day of the execution, Robertson was informed a message had been received from Governor Thomas Campbell that he refused to grant commutation.

Robertson stated, "I suppose it's all over. It but remains for me to meet death like a man. I am ready for the end. Tonight will be my last on earth." Robertson told reporters, "I wish to warn boys and girls of my race to shun evil and bad companion."

Robertson also asked to make a statement to the newspapers and it "be presented for the good of his race." Robertson gave the following statement:

I Julius B. Robertson wrote the young boys and girls of my race just after Mother's day. This is the first Mother's day I have ever heard of when I received a white carnation to wear in remembrance of my poor old mother, I hung my head in tears because it brought back my remembrance the lessons I learned at my mothers knee the rules of life and the dear sweet far reaching prayer that nearly every mother has taught her son and daughter. Yes boys and girls of my race before you go out into the world of false and real pleasure remember the advice given by our dear parents, live true to yourself, true to your mother, true to your vows and promise you had made but before all be and live true and honest before God and the law of the country.

Shun evil companions, bad companions, bad language disdain,
God's name hold in reverence, nor take in vain,
Be thoughtful and honest, kind hearted and true,
Look over to Jesus; He'll carry you through,
Ask the Savior to help you,
Comfort, strengthen and keep you,
He is willing to aid you,
He will carry you through,
Remember these words boys and girls of my race.
Good bye.
Julius B. Robertson

On the day of the execution, Mrs. Frank Wolford, their daughter and Wolford's brothers were all present to watch Robertson stand on the gallows. Once the witnesses were allowed inside the jail, the death march from the death cell to the gallows was twelve feet. From the gallows Robertson said his chief desire was to meet all people where sin and treachery are not known. He expressed the wish that God would care for his mother and sister, and that no ill will towards anyone.

At 11:30 a.m., the sheriff pulled the lever, springing the trap. After the body was cut down, the remains were released to People's Undertaking at 130 Pearl Street in Dallas to prepare the body for shipment to Paris, Texas, for burial. It was estimated that 3,000 people past through the undertakers parlor to view the remains.

The *Dallas Morning News*, dated Saturday, May 14, 1910, provided readers with a detailed article about the crime and execution.

John Robinson

Race/Gender: Black Male   **Offense:** Robbery & Murder   **Offense Date:** May 4, 1911
Weapon: Coupling Pin   **Execution:** January 10, 1913

John Robinson was executed on January 10, 1913, for the murder of Otto Kahlkhoff on the night of May 4, 1911. While walking home along with his wife, the German couple was attacked near the intersection of Chestnut and Dawson Street in southeast Dallas. Both Otto and his wife were seriously injured from being beat with a coupling pin. The couple were both robbed, and left on the ground for dead. Three days later, Otto Kahlkhoff died from head injuries, and Mrs. Kahlkhoff survived.

On June 2, 1911, John Robinson and his accomplice Will Flowers were both arrested and indicted for Robbery and Murder in the First Degree. Will Flowers was first placed on trial, and on December 6, 1911, he received a life sentence.

John Robinson went on trial next for his crimes on December 13, 1911. The jury returned a verdict of guilty of murder in the first degree and recommended the death sentence. Robinson's attorney appealed to the Court of Criminal Appeals, and the court affirmed the lower court decision of November 6, 1912. On November 29, 1912, Judge Seay set the execution date to take place on January 10, 1913.

On the day before the execution, the stress of being hanged sent Robinson into a rampage within his jail cell. On that day, Robinson attacked a trusty who had gone to clean Robinson's cell. Sheriff Ben Brandenburg hearing the attack rushed into the cell to handcuff the prisoner when Robinson broke a milk bottle, and cut the sheriff.

The following morning Robinson dressed himself in a black suit, black socks and a white shirt, but refused to put on his shoes. Seven men then entered the cell and held held Robinson down as they put his shoes on his feet. Sheriff Ben Brandenburg then approached and asked Robinson if he wished to make a final statement to the crowd of 1,500 people who had gathered outside the jail. From a second story window, Robinson declared he was innocent of murder and that another Negro was responsible. When he completed his statement, Sheriff Brandenburg led Robinson to the steel trap door. When asked if he wished to make a final statement, Robinson remained silent. At 12:50 o'clock, John Robinson, was hanged from the same rope used in the execution of Burrell Oates on November 29, 1912, at Waxahachie, Texas.

The *Dallas Morning News*, dated Saturday, January 11, 1913, provided their readers with details of the crime and execution.

Floyd Stanton

Race/Gender: Black Male **Offense:** Murder **Offense Date:** December 3, 1912
Weapon: Pistol **Execution:** August 1, 1913

Floyd Stanton was hanged for the murder of his ex-wife, Naomi Station. On December 3, 1912, at about 3:30 in the afternoon, while Naomi and Stanton argued, Stanton pulled his pistol and shot his ex-wife nine times. He was immediately arrested and he told authorities he killed his wife because she continued to "bleed" him for money. When Stanton refused to give Naomi any more money, she was to had said "either give me money or I will have another man see you about it."

On December 17, 1912, Floyd Stanton was tried and convicted of the murder. The case was appealed and on May 28, 1913, and the Court of Criminal Appeals affirmed the decision.

On the appointed day, Sheriff Ben Brandenburg led Stanton into the corridor so that he could address a crowd of African Americans who had gathered outside the jail in hopes of seeing the execution. Stanton said:

"Dear Friends, I am guilty. I'm ready and willing to pay for my crime. I want you all to be good. Don't follow in my footsteps. I want to meet you in heaven, for that's where I'm going. Good-bye to you all."

Stanton was then led to the trap door within the jail where 200 witnesses had gathered. At 11:40 a.m. Sheriff Brandenburg read the court's death warrant. Stanton afterwards stepped upon the trap door and said, "I'm glad to be brave because I know I am going to heaven."

The *Dallas Morning News*, dated Saturday, August 2, 1913, provided details of the murder and execution.

Ed Long

Alias: Will Long **Race/Gender:** Black & Mexican Mix Male **Age:** 29
Offense: Murder **Offense Date:** September 9, 1910 **Weapon:** Pistol
Execution: December 19, 1913

Thomas Henry Bennett was a special policeman who worked for the Texas & Pacific Railroad in Dallas. Officer Bennett worked at the rail yards near the fairgrounds to arrest burglars who were frequently breaking into the fright cars.

On the early morning hours of September 9, 1910, Officer Bennett saw two black men with a wagon being pulled by a grey mare, while a third person was opening a gate east of the fairgrounds at Dallas Avenue. As Officer Bennett ordered the men in the wagon to stop, the man opening the gate shot him.

The bullet struck Officer Bennett to the right side of the chest with the bullet lodging in his back. Before collapsing, Officer Bennett drew his revolver and fired five shots at the fleeing burglars. Officer Bennett died hours later and he was was buried in Mesquite, Texas.

Ed Long was arrested a year later for murder and remained in jail until Ed Christian was located and arrested the following year. The murder trial began on February 6, 1913. During the trial, Long took the witness stand and testified in his own defense. Long told the jury he was present during the shooting, but denied that he fired the fatal shot.

George Williams who had turned state's witness testified that Ed Long shot Officer Bennett while Ed Christian, and himself were burglarizing the boxcar. On the morning of February 8, the jury returned a verdict of guilty and assessed the death penalty.

Ed Christian was tried the following week and he also was found guilty with the jury assessing the death penalty. Both men appealed their cases and Long's case was affirmed separately which separated the men from being executed together.

On October 22, 1913, Ed Long was taken before Judge Robert B. Seay for sentencing. Long told the judge,

"I admit that my intent was burglary, but I did not fire the shot, and had nothing to do with the killing."

Long then read from the indictment, which stated, "with malice aforethought," and then said to hang him was unjustified. Judge Seay explained that anyone who had made an agreement to violate the law must be held responsible regardless of who fired the shot.

Judge Seay then said, "You must learn from this, that the man who chooses for himself the right kind of associates and tried to do right, even if he falls into trouble, will find good men who will stand by him and help him. But when he chooses the other kind of associates and such terrible ones as you admitted you associated with, then there will be no one who will stand by you and even your companions will desert you to save themselves. As ye have sowed, so shall ye reap. It is now my duty to pass sentence of death upon you, to be hanged between noon and sundown on Friday, the twenty-eight day of November."

As Judge Seay pronounced sentence on Long, a woman in the crowd alerted Deputy W. W. Murphy of a bulge under the prisoner's shirt. After Long was removed from the presence of the judge, he was quickly searched. It was then discovered that Long was carrying a slingshot type weapon which had been constructed from two pieces of steel from a jail cot with a thick piece of leather. It was believed that Long intended to use the weapon on the deputy as he was being escorted back to the holding cell.

Ed Christian's sentence was affirmed, but on January 16, 1914, he received a thirty-day respite. Following the respite, the governor commuted he sentence to life imprisonment. On March 13, 1914, Christian was removed from the Dallas County Jail and transported to the Texas State Penitentiary at Huntsville to begin serving his life long sentence.

On the day of the execution, Ed Long walked to the gallows declaring he was innocent and that it was one of his accomplices who fired the fatal shot. At 12:10 the trap was sprung and eight minutes later the body was pronounced dead.

The *Dallas Morning News*, dated Saturday, December 20, 1913, provided readers with details of the crime and execution.

Leonard Dodd

Race/Gender: White Male **Offense:** Rape **Offense Date:** June 25, 1917
Execution Date: May 24, 1918

Walter Stevenson

Race/Gender: White Male **Offense:** Rape **Offense Date:** June 25, 1917
Execution Date: May 24, 1918

On the night of June 25, 1917, both Leonard Dodd and Walter Stevenson were driving in a car when they came upon Florence Orcutt and her date who were parked along the side of the road. Dodd and Stevenson jumped the couple and beat Orcutt's male friend until he escaped from the car and ran off. The two men then carried Orcutt to their own car where they both raped the woman.

On the day of the execution, Dodd attempted to avoid the gallows by taking an overdose of pain pills. The attending physicians were able to stop Dodd's suicide attempt so he could be hanged.

On the gallows, Stevenson prayed for the safe return of all American soldiers, a victory for his country and for a death upon the battlefield, rather than one on the scaffold. To soldiers near the cell he talked freely, telling them of the privilege he would like to have. He said, "I'll die like an American Ace."

As the caps were being drawn, Dodd said, Good-bye, Steve."

"Good-bye, old boy," was the reply.

The Sheriff gave the signal, and the deputies stepped back and the trap was sprung. In eleven minutes both bodies were pronounced dead.

The *Dallas Morning News*, dated Saturday, May 25, 1918, provided their readers with details of the assault and execution.

Will Jones

Race/Gender: Black Male　　**Age:** 28　　**Offense:** Rape & Murder
Offense Date: July 16, 1918　　**Weapon:** Knife　　**Execution:** August 30, 1918

On the night of July 16, 1918, at about 9:30 p.m., Mrs. Annie Bell Wolford was home with her children while her husband was away at work. The twenty-three-year-old mother of two daughters lived near Dallas in the small suburb town of Rose Hill. On that night Will Jones entered the home and sexually assaulted Annie. Annie resisted and fought off her attacker throughout the home and out onto the porch until Jones pulled a long bladed pocket knife. With the knife, Jones stabbed Annie to the chest, face, arm, and slit her throat. Leaving her for dead, Jones afterwards ran home. The fighting had wakened both children who saw their mother being attacked, and ran to a neighbor's home for help.

When Constable Mack McCallum and two physicians arrived, Annie was still alive and she was able to provide a statement that her attacker was Will Jones. At 4 a.m. the next morning, Annie Wolford died from her wounds.

Jones was immediately arrested and lodged in the Dallas County Jail. When residents learned of the murder of Annie Wolford and arrest of Jones, a mob of 1,000 angry men attempted to beat down the rear door of the jail to get to him. On the other side of the door sheriff deputies who were armed with pistols and shotguns threatened that they would shoot anyone who entered. After the disturbance settled down, eight men were later arrested for assaulting the jail.

Six hours after Annie's death, Will Jones was indicted for criminal assault and murder with the trial set for the following Monday, July 22, 1918. On the day of the trial, the jury returned a verdict by 4 p.m. of guilty and assessed the death penalty. A motion for a new trial was presented two days later before Judge Charles A. Pippen who overruled the motion. Judge Pippen afterwards set the date of execution to take place on August 30, 1918.

On the appointed day, Jones walked to the gallows within the jail and told the fifty witnesses that he had committed a serious sin and that he was willing to pay the death penalty.

The *Dallas Morning News*, dated Saturday, August 31, 1918, provided their readers with details of the murder and execution.

Green Hunter

Alias: James Brown & Hunter Green　　**Age:** 26　　**Race/Gender:** Black Male
Offense: Rape　　**Offense Date:** May 28, 1920　　**Weapon:** Knife
Execution: July 10, 1920

On May 28, 1920, Green Hunter arrived at the home of Mrs. Hatie Carpenter who lived near Hale Station in Dallas asking her for a drink of water. When Hatie returned and handed Hunter the glass of water, he grabbed the fifty-six-year-old woman by the hair and placed a knife to her neck threatening to cut her throat if she cried out. After the assault had been reported, a sheriff's posse captured Green Hunter hours later and transported him quickly to the jail before a lynch mob could take action.

One week later on Friday, June 4, Hunter was tried and confessed to the assault. The jury then found him guilty and assessed the death penalty. As Hunter was escorted to the death cell, he remarked, "I was born on Friday and Friday always has been my hoodoo."

Two days prior to being executed, Hunter confessed to have criminally assaulting a twelve--year-old girl near Bryan, Texas, in 1912, when he was eighteen-years-old. Hunter claimed he committed the assault, and that Ben Perry who was convicted of the crime, and sentenced to a life term in the state penitentiary was innocent. Hunter claimed, "I expected some day to make a clean confession of this crime, and to stand punishment. But the opportunity never presented itself for me to do so. I made the attack on the girl when I found her in a field about a mile from her home. I make this full confession, knowing that I am about to die and must stand before the bar of judgment."

On the gallows, Hunter confessed that he had killed a Mexican in southwest Texas with an ax, and attacked another black man with a cotton hook in South Texas. Hunter said he did not know if he had killed that man or not.

Hunter made two last requests before his hanging, which was scheduled at 11 a.m. First that his last meal for breakfast consist of chicken and a large watermelon. The second request was for him to be furnished with a new suit of clothes to be hanged in and for his burial.

From the gallows, Sheriff Dan Harston asked Hunter, "Have you anything to say to these people out here?"

Hunter replied:

Yes, suh. Ah'm sorry it happened. Ah'm guilty of the crime, ah also caused Ben Perry to be sent to the penitentiary, 'n' ah'm guilty of killing a Mexican near Robstown. Ah'm proud to say since ah've been here in this jail every one's been nice to me 'n' some have looked on me like I may not ever had opportunity. Ah, I leave it to yo all now. If yo are ready suh. Ah'm ready – to meet my Savior.

At 11:06 a.m. the black hood was placed over his head, the noose adjusted about the neck and Sheriff Harston sprang the trap.

The *Dallas Morning News*, dated Saturday, July 10, 1920, provided readers with details of the assault and execution.

Fred Douglas

Race/Gender: Black Male   **Age:** 22   **Offense:** Robbery & Murder
Weapon: Iron level   **Offense Date:** July 5, 1920   **Execution:** August 27, 1920

Fred Douglas worked at the Texaco Oil station at the corner of Haskell and Ross Avenue in the city of Dallas. On July 5, 1910, Douglas stepped behind the station manager, Irving T. Williams and hit his employer in the back of the head with a five pound iron level after Williams had opened the safe to count the daily receipts.

Douglas then took the money from both the safe and register, totaling $225 and fled to Shreveport, Louisiana, where he was captured on July 9. Douglas confessed to the murder and explained that the robbery was the motive and that he did not like Williams anyhow. On July 16, at trial, Douglas testified and told the jury he killed Williams in self defense. The jury deliberated one hour before returning a verdict of guilty and sentenced Douglas to die on the gallows.

On July 20, 1920, Douglas stood before Judge C. A. Pippen for sentencing. Judge Pippen asked Douglas if he had anything to say before the sentence was handed down. Douglas replied, "I think I ought to have another trial."

Judge Pippen replied that he had previously overruled on this motion for a new trial and therefore ordered that Douglas be executed on August 27, 1920.

On the morning of the execution, Douglas was escorted to the same jail gallows that Green Hunter was hanged from the previous month. Douglas made a short speech to the 200 witnesses in which he said that he was ready to die. He thanked the jail officers and deputies for their kind treatment since he had been in the jail and said, "In my prayers I've seen my Lord and he is waiting for me. I want you all, white and black, to meet me in heaven. I have committed a crime and I have sinned, so I must die for it. A great number of people here are looking for me to say what the other boy said (referring to Green Hunter), but I'm not going to do it, for I didn't lead the life he had."

At 11:18 a.m., as Douglas was saying his last prayer, Sheriff Dan Harston sprang the trap.

The *Dallas Morning News*, dated Saturday, August 28, 1920, provided readers with the details of the crime and execution.

Delta County

County Seat - Cooper

James Fisher

Race/Gender: White Male **Age:** 27 **Offense:** Murder
Offense Date: July 5, 1891 **Weapon:** Pistol **Execution:** May 27, 1892

James Fisher was convicted of killing his brother-in-law, Austin Hardy at Cooper, Texas, on July 5, 1891. Austin Hardy had married James Fisher's sister Nancy. Fisher had convinced himself that Hardy was having sexual intercourse with Hardy's ten-year-old daughter Alma and told his sister of his beliefs. Nancy told her brother he was wrong and she did not want to discuss or hear anymore of his nonsense.

One day Fisher and Alma took a walk into the woods when Fisher told Alma he was aware that Hardy was having an intimate affair with her. When Alma replied he was wrong, Fisher began speaking with other people in town asking for their opinion as to what they think should be done with someone having sexual relations with their daughter.

Then on the night of July 4, Fisher stayed the night at his father's home and left the next morning taking his father's pistol. Hardy returned to his sister's home and learned that Hardy was working in the field. Fisher went out into the field and confronted Hardy and said, "Austin Hardy, you have been criminally intimate with your own daughter. If you don't own up to it, I will kill you."

When Austin refused to admit to the accusation, Fisher pulled out his father's pistol and shot him. Hardy was able to take the pistol away from Fisher, but was too weak from the bullet wound to use the weapon. Fisher afterwards returned to his father's home and told him what he had done.

At the trial, Alma told the jury that her father had never been intimate with her, but that her uncle James had. Alma testified that during a night while asleep in the same bed with her uncle James, her uncle had pulled up her nightshirt and touched her genitals with his hand and penis.

James Fisher was found guilty of murder in the first degree and sentenced to death. The case was appealed to the Texas Court of Appeals and affirmed on December 2, 1891.

The execution was public and took place in the courthouse yard. Fisher made no statement as he asked Sheriff Acker to make a statement in his behalf in which Fisher exonerating his father, who was thought by some to have been an accessory to the murder.

The *Galveston Daily News*, dated Saturday, May 28, 1892, provided its readers with the details of the crime and execution at Cooper, Texas.

Denton County
County Seat - Denton

George W. Brown Jr.

Race/Gender: White Male **Age:** 26 **Offense:** Murder
Offense Date: May 1, 1876 **Weapon:** Shotgun & .44 cal. Pistol **Execution:** November 21, 1879

Andrew J. Brown

Race/Gender: White Male **Age:** 24 **Offense:** Murder
Offense Date: May 1, 1876 **Weapon:** Shotgun & .44 cal. Pistol **Execution:** November 21, 1879

In Denton County, all three executions that took place were the result of a change of venue from Montague and Cooke counties. The Browns in the beginning helped organize a secret vigilante society they named "Law and Order League." The society's intentions in the beginning was to rid the county of all horse thieves and other criminals roaming in the area. But soon afterward, the Browns were the main leaders of the League, and became murderous criminals themselves and were credited with committing fourteen murders.

George Brown, Jr. was tried and convicted of the murder of Doc McClain. On May 1, 1876, George Brown, Sr., George Brown, Jr. and Jesse Brown were out looking for Doc McClain. McClain lived with a family whose last name was Johnson. The Browns suspected the Johnsons of stealing horses. George Brown, Sr. was heard to have said, "There is a bad set over at the Johnsons, and we are going over there to get away with them."

On that day, McClain was seen walking across a small prairie while looking for his horse. A few minutes later George Brown, Jr., Andrew Brown, Sampson Barras and John Barras, were all armed with shotguns, and hiding within a small ravine located about 250 yards from the road. As McClain approached the ravine, the four men rose from their hiding positions and shot him. George Brown, Jr. then ran up to McClain, fired his pistol at the body, and then ran back to the ravine.

When a coroner's inquest was held at the site of the murder, located on Farmer's Creek at the point on the creek known as Chestnut Ford Crossing, Jesse Brown went to John Southerland who had witnessed the shooting. He asked Southerland to go to the inquest and tell the people that he had seen three men from the Indian Nation on the day of the killing hunting for the deceased and that he expected they "got away" with the killing. When the body was examined, the body contained twelve to fourteen buckshot pellets to the chest and one bullet wound to the side. Doc McClain's body was buried at the creek where it was found.

On June 11, 1877, a change of venue was granted with the trial being sent to Denton County, and held on March 9, 1878. George Jr. was tried and found guilty and sentenced to death. George Sr. and Jesse Brown escaped the noose by being acquitted. Both George Jr. and Andrew received a thirty-year prison sentence for murder and were returned to Denton in September 1879 for sentencing.

Andrew Brown was indicted along with J. W. Bell, Albert Harris and his brother George Brown for the murder of Robert S. "Rat" Morrow. On March 11, 1879, Andrew Brown was tried for murder in Denton, Texas.

Robert Morrow and his family lived near the Browns when a dispute over cattle occurred between the two families. On the night of September 4, 1873, J. W. Bell opened the gate to Robert Morrow's pasture and released his mules. The next morning Andy Brown, George Brown, Jr., Alfred Harris and Stephen Sullivan were eating breakfast when Jesse Brown arrived and told them to hurry up eating their meal before "Rat" Morrow comes after his mules.

The men grabbed their shotguns and pistols and ran to a ravine running next to the road. Andy and Harris Brown took one side of the road, while Stephen Sullivan and Andrew Brown took the other. Soon Robert Morrow was seen riding towards them along with his six-year-old son on one side of him and a Mr. Koozier on the other. The men ambushed Morrow by firing their shotguns at him. After falling from his horse, a shotgun was placed under his neck and discharged. The gunfire spooked the horses Mr. Koozier and the child were riding into a gallop and both returned home unharmed. The murder of the Morrow family did not stop with the death of Robert. Robert's wife, swore vengeance against the Browns for the murder of her husband and sought to have the Browns indicted in spite of her life being threatened. To protect her two sons and herself, Elizabeth Morrow moved her family to St. Jo, Texas. On the night April 15, 1875, the house that she rented was surrounded. Between thirty-five to forty bullets were fired at the house. Three bullets hit Elizabeth Morrow to her leg, back and stomach and she died in agony an hour later.

Both George and Andrew Brown were tried and convicted of murder in the second degree for the murder of Elizabeth Morrow and sentenced to thirty years to the State Penitentiary at Huntsville. The brothers were later returned to Denton to be hanged together for their separate murder conviction. At the gallows, Sheriff R. H. Hopkins read both men their individual death warrants and the telegram from the governor refusing to commute their sentence to life imprisonment. Afterwards George Brown spoke for five minutes to the crowd stating that he was no more guilty than those still at large. Andrew Brown only comment that he wished to make was that he was innocent of the murder of Doc McClain. At 2:10 p.m. the legs and arms were tied, followed by the ropes adjusted around the necks and the black caps placed over their heads. At 2:18 p.m. the sheriff cut the rope, dropping both brothers to their death. George died in nine minutes with a broken neck, where as Andrew strangled to death for eleven minutes. Both George and Andrew Brown are buried at the Oakwood Cemetery in Denton. The tombstone bears the inscribed word, "EXECUTED."

The *Brenham Weekly Banner* dated Friday, November 28, 1879, wrote, "A crowd estimated at 7000 persons were present – next to a circus, a hanging draws the biggest crowd in Texas.

John Quincy Adams Crews

Alias: Jack Crews, J. Q. A. Crews **Race/Gender:** White Male **Offense:** Robbery & Four Murders
Offense Date: April 12, 1894 **Weapon:** Pistol & Rifle **Execution:** October 14, 1895

At ten years of age, John Quincy Adams Crews, known as "Jack" was a runaway, and had been taken in by Thomas and Anna Murrell. The Murrells lived on a large farm near Callisburg, in Cooke County, Texas, where they raised their four children, Lendon, Hal, Morgan and Jessie. In later years, Jack continued to work on the Murrell farm, married and lived in one of the farmhouses.

On about April 2, 1894, Jack had some type of dispute with Thomas Murrell's sons. Thomas heard of the dispute and attempted to intervene by riding out to Jack's home to speak with him about the troubles. After failing to settle the disagreement, Crews told Thomas he had enough of the Murrells. Crews decided to quit his employment and immediately moved out of the farmhouse.

Once Crews and his wife moved out of the house, she told him that Thomas Murrell had made an indecent proposal to her which she refused. She further described to him a previous incident where Thomas Murrell had kissed her on the cheek when she was in his cellar. Angered by Murrell's actions, and the dishonor of his wife, Crews decided he would rid the country of the Murrells.

On April 11, Crews left his home carrying a pistol and went to Gainesville where he borrowed a Winchester rifle from a friend saying

Hanging of John Quincy Adams Crews, Photograph, October 14, 1895; *Digital image, (http://texashistory.unt.edu/ark:/67531/metapth12613/ : accessed April 21, 2013), University of North Texas Libraries, The Portal to Texas History, http://texashistory.unt.edu; crediting Denton Public Library, Denton, Texas.*

he wanted to shoot some turkeys. The next morning, Crews waited inside Thomas Murrell's barn for Thomas to walk out to the barn to feed his horse. When Thomas approached, caring a basket of corn for his horse, Crews shot him twice.

Anna Murrell heard the rifle shots and ran in the direction of the barn. Jessie, who had also heard the shots, was running out of the house toward the barn when he heard his mother cry out, "don't Crews, don't" followed by two more shots fired in rapid succession.

Jessie ran to Walter Clement's house which was about 300 yards distance for help. Jessie and Walter Clements entered the barn and saw his mother dead and his father lying on the ground attempting to raise his head. Clements went to Thomas and said, "Tom, who did this?"

Thomas replied, "Crews, Crews, Crews."

Lying next to Thomas was the basket with the corn along with Thomas' leather pocket book. Jessie picked up the open pocket book when his father said, "Yes, Crews robbed me and got on old Joe, and is gone."

Thomas was then moved from the barn to the house where he died forty-five minutes later.

After murdering Thomas and Anna, Crews rode the stolen horse to Morgan Murrell's house about two miles away. Without warning, Crews shot and killed Morgan. Thomas, Anna, and Morgan were all laid to rest at the Callisburg Cemetery.

The sheriff organized a posse of men to patrol roads leading to the Red River in an effort to capture Crews. Posse member Henry Freeman who was armed with a shotgun, fired at Crews after Crews refused to throw down his rifle and surrender. Crews was to far away for the shotgun to have any effect. Crews then took aim and returned fire at Freeman, and killed his forth victim.

The next day, a deputy U.S. marshal picked up the manhunt, and arrested Crews while he was hiding in Thackerville, Oklahoma, just north of the Red River in Indian Territory. Crews was returned to Gainesville, where he was indicted for the murders of the Murrell family. The case was transferred to Denton County on a change of venue where Crews confessed to the murders. The verdict by the jury was that Crews was guilty of murder in the first degree and should hang.

On the morning of the execution, Crews told a newspaper man:

> I have just received the news that there is no more hope for me this side of Heaven, and if that is so and I have to go, it will save me many a trouble and hardship, still, we all want to put that off to the last. I don't think I will be knocked out of more than 60 years of my natural life. As far as I am concerned, I think I can make preparations to meet my God, but will say that all I can leave my poor, true, beloved wife, is the history of my life, which has been full of misfortunes from the cradle to the grave. I will say that contrary to what the people have got me down; I am no tough nor never have been.

The tombstone of Thomas and Anna Murrell as it appears today in the Callisburg Cemetery. Note the word MURDERED across the bottom.

On the gallows, Crews told the crowd of 10,000, "I am sorry that I killed Mrs. Murrell, but for the killing of Murrell, I have nothing to say."

After the body was cut down, Thomas Murrell asked for the straps that tied the arms and feet as souvenirs of the man who murdered his father.

The *Fort Worth Gazette*, dated Tuesday, October 15, 1895, provided a full account of the execution, but had a slightly different version of the crime.

DeWitt County
County Seat - Cuero

Conrad Schwartz

Race/Gender: White Male **Age:** 19 **Offense:** Robbery & Murder
Offense Date: June 7, 1904 **Weapon:** .45 cal. Pistol **Execution Date:** March 22, 1905

During the early morning of June 7, 1904, Yorktown railroad depot operator, W. A. Earle was discovered murdered, and the money from the ticket office cash drawer stolen. Earle worked for the San Antonio Aransas Railway when he was found lying on his back dead inside the ticket office from two gunshot wounds from a .45 caliber pistol to the left breast and shoulder.

It had rained the night before the murder and a search of the area by lawmen located foot tracks leading away from the depot to where the killer's horse was tied to a hitching post at the oil mill. The lawmen noted that the horse's right front hoof was split. The horse tracks were followed for three miles to the home of Henry Schwartz.

Lawmen discovered nineteen-year-old Conrad Schwartz asleep in bed and quickly placed him under arrest. In the home, the officers recovered both the stolen money and murder weapon inside a locked trunk. The pistol cylinder was checked and showed to have two recently fired chambers. Schwartz's boots were checked, and they matched the tracks found at the scene. In checking the horse in the pasture, they found it had a front hoof split.

Conrad Schwartz was tried and found guilty of murder in the first degree and sentenced to death. The case was appealed and on October 24, 1904, and the higher court affirmed the decision.

On January 29, 1905, in the Cuero jail, Schwartz made a full confession of the murder in the presence of his father, L. A. Horn, Sheriff Thomas M. Stell and Deputy R. L. Boykin. Schwartz said:

> I first went to bed at 10 o'clock. I left home between 10 and 11 o'clock p.m. I rode my black saddle horse to town and tied him at the oil tank west of the depot. Then walked between cars and platform up to the depot. I stood there for some time in the dark, but saw no one in or about the depot. Finally a buggy came up and Bettie Walton got out and went in the depot. I heard someone, suppose it was the operator, talking. I remained there until the east-bound Davy Crockett came, when I went back to where my horse was after the Davy Crockett had gone, and hacks had left.
>
> I came back and watched the operator wheeling baggage into the depot. I followed him into the depot, where he was writing, and demanded his money. He took what money he had in the drawer and put it on the table, at my request. I then told him to open the safe and he refused. He walked to his desk and I supposed he was after a weapon whereupon I shot him and he fell, and then I fired at him while he was down. I then took the money up from the table, mounted my horse and rode home. No one knew of my trip to town and no one witnessed the murder. I am in my nineteenth year, and am sorry for my deed. While I intended to rob the operator, I had no intention of killing him, and would not have done so had I not thought he was going to kill me. I have told the whole truth in this confession and ask the sympathy of the public to the extent of securing for me."

The *Dallas Morning News*, dated Thursday, March 23, 1905, provided readers with details of the crime and some information as to the events on the scaffold.

John Brown

Race/Gender: Black Male **Offense:** Rape **Offense Date:** 1907
Execution: March 27, 1908

John Brown was tried and convicted on July 3, 1907, for the rape of a black woman by the name of Hattie Kennedy. On February 1, 1908, Judge Wilson sentenced Brown to hang on March 18, but Governor Thomas Campbell respited the execution for two weeks.

On the day of the execution, Brown walked to the scaffold, stopped and rubbed his hands over the coffin that would contain his body. Brown said he approved of the coffin, as it was a good one. He then mounted the scaffold without showing any signs of fear. Rev. J. W. Cowan, pastor of the Methodist Church offered a prayer on Brown's behalf. Brown made a fifteen minute speech in which he asserted his innocence, and warned the black spectators to keep out of trouble and to further profess religion, as he had done and then sang two or three hymns in a clear voice.

At 3:13, the trap was sprung, breaking his neck. Thirteen minutes later county physician Lackey pronounced Brown dead, and the body was cut down and turned over to relatives for burial at Yoakum.

The *San Antonio Daily Express*, dated Saturday, March 28, 1908, provided a short article that the execution had taken place at Cuero, Texas.

Monk Gibson

Alias: Monk Hanks **Race/Gender:** Black Male **Age:** 19
Offense: Rape & Multiple Murders **Offense Date:** September 28, 1905
Weapon: Adz Grubbing Hoe, Crow Bar & Knife **Execution:** June 28, 1908

Monk Gibson was seventeen at the time of the murders and worked for the Conditt family as a field laborer plowing fields at their farm located about two miles from the town of Edna in Jackson County. The family consisted of Mr. F. J. Conditt, Mrs. Lora Conditt, their twelve-year-old daughter, Mildred Lee Conditt, four sons age ten, eight, four, and ten months.

On September 28, 1905, Mr. Conditt had left the farm house to work on his rice farm located about five miles from home while Monk Gibson was plowing the field near the house. At about 1:00 o'clock Gibson along with Felix Powell attacked the family. The two older Conditt boys were about a 150 yards away from the house repairing a fence when they were both murdered. Both of the children's heads were crushed with the use of a crowbar. The four-year old was killed after his neck was cut with a knife. Both Lora and Mildred Conditt necks were slashed after both had been sexually assaulted. The two murderers spared the infant's life only because the child could not be a witness.

Suspicion immediately fell on Monk because of his blood stained shirt and of the conflicting statements he had given. Monk claimed while he was plowing the filed, he heard screaming and looked up to see a man chasing after Mrs. Conditt and a second man standing in the doorway of the house. The men supposedly caught him and after making him walk through the victim's blood allowed him to run away. Monk said he had never seen either man before and described both as having very dark skin and having very thin mustaches and would be able to identify either man if captured. Monk later claimed two men had told him in town of their intent to kill the Conditt family, but he did not know their names. While in jail, Monk refused to confess or provide the name of his accomplice, even though he had received 100 lashes from the sheriff. Captain William J. McDonald of the Texas Rangers began hearing gossip within the African American community that there was an accomplice. Once the Captain gained the trust of those witnesses, he obtained several statements implicating Felix Powell in the murders. From those statements, Captain McDonald swore out warrants for Powell's arrest.

Sheriff Egg fearing he would be unable to protect Monk from a lynch mob as the mob was beginning to form in Bay City, ordered deputies Powers and Hayeses to take Monk by horseback during the night to the jail at Halletsville. The two deputies, after placing Monk on a horse, failed to handcuff or tie him to the horse, and he made a break to escape by having the horse leap over two barbed wire fences three miles out of town. The horse fell and became so entangled in the wire, that it died from the deep gash wounds. The two deputies pursued after Monk until both of their horses became entangled in the barbed wire as well.

When the mob learned that Monk was no longer in the jail, and had escaped from the officers, the mob made accusations that the lawmen had allowed him to escape and threatened the deputies. Sheriff Egg angered by the accusation that his deputies had allowed Monk to escape, took his pistol out from his holster and dared any man to meet him out in the middle of the street to settle the matter.

Monk Gibson hid out for nine days in the barn of George Bales until discovered in the morning by Walter Warren. Warren tied Monk up and sent his son to notify the Sheriff. While Warren marched Monk back towards town, Sheriff Egg, Deputy Powell and Texas Rangers arrived on horses and buggies. Monk hands and ankles were retied and Monk was hid under the buggy seat and transported back to Edna. Two companies of Texas State Militia were then ordered to surround the jail to halt any attempt of mob violence. The sheriff then questioned Monk as to who had brought him food. Monk then pulled out dry corn from his pants pockets. Monk told Sheriff Egg he had been hiding in the barn since his escape and would slip out at night to gather corn to eat or to kill a chicken which he ate raw. To confirm his story, a doctor was called to the jail and used a stomach pump to check Monk's stomach content. Monk's stomach contents only showed corn.

Felix Powell requested his trial be severed from Gibson Monk with a change of venue. The requests were granted and his case was transferred to Castro County. Felix Powell was found guilty of murder and hanged at Victoria on April 2, 1907, for his part in the murders. (See Castro County)

On June 28, 1908, Gibson Monk was hanged from the same scaffold that dropped Conrad Schwartz and John Brown to their deaths.

The *Shiner Gazette*, dated Thursday, July 2, 1908, provided their readers with the history of the crime and execution.

Donley County
County Seat - Clarendon

George R. Miller

Race/Gender: White male **Offense:** Robbery & Murder **Offense Date:** March 20, 1909
Weapon: .38 caliber Pistol **Execution:** June 3, 1910

George R. Miller was a lifetime resident of Childress, Texas, who in March of 1909 for unknown reasons decided to steal dynamite from the cement factory where he was employed. Miller then walked to his uncle's house and stole a .38 caliber pistol. Carrying the dynamite and pistol, Miller burglarized the home of his friend. Taking what he wanted, Miller then blew the house up.

Miller knowing it was a best for him to leave town, jumped a boxcar on the Fort Worth & Denver Railroad. In the same car were two young men hitching a ride. Miller pulled his pistol and shot one boy in the back, and the other escaped by jumping out of the moving car. Miller then rolled the lifeless body out the doorway, were it fell onto the sandy banks of the Red River.

When the train stopped at Memphis, Texas, the brakeman found Miller and put him off the train. As soon as the brakeman was out of sight, Miller climbed back into another boxcar as the train was pulling out. The boxcar he chose was also occupied with two more young men, Floyd Autry, and Fred Garrett. During the trip, the boys smoked cigarettes with Miller and Autry played a harmonica.

When the train slowed down near the town of Giles, Miller told both boys he had no money and that is why he was riding a freight car. Autry replied that he had a little bit of money and if they got caught, he would pay their fare. Miller pulled out his .38 caliber pistol and shot Autry in the head. Miller then shot at Garrett just as he leaped through the car door to escape being killed. Wounded, Garrett ran toward the front of the train and reported the shooting to a brakeman.

The brakeman returning to the boxcar with Garrett, found Miller was gone. Autry was found alive, but lying face down with his pockets turned inside out. The train proceeded on to Hedley, Texas, where a sheriff's deputy was notified. Autry was carried from the boxcar to a hotel in Clarendon where he died the following day.

Miller was caught the following day at Hedley when he walked to a train yard cook shack and asked for something to eat. Once arrested Miller admitted to the murder and said that robbery was the motive for the crime. Miller was tried for the first murder in Childress and sentenced to life imprisonment.

Several months later Miller pled guilty to the murder of Floyd Autry. The plea was accepted and Judge J. N. Browning sentenced Miller on April 24, 1910, to hang on June 3, 1910. Miller afterwards filed an appeal on the grounds that he did not know he would be sentenced to death by pleading guilty to murder in the first degree. The Court of Appeals reviewed the case and affirmed the sentence.

The gallows were built a half-mile north of Clarendon in the sand dunes. The frame of the gallows had been enclosed with wood planks to conceal the body from the view of the 1,500 spectators when Miller dropped through the trap. While awaiting the arrival of Miller, lemonade and soda pop were sold to the crowd which was listening to campaign speeches from politicians running for office.

Miller soon arrived and took his place on the gallows with Sheriff Jim Patman, Deputy George Bugee, and a Catholic priest. On the gallows, Miller said that, "It was a little too late to be crying over spilt milk." Miller said he hoped that all the children in the crowd would be good children. Once the lever was pulled which released the trap, the crowd began pulling away the planks to view the dangling corpse.

The *Galveston Daily News*, dated Saturday, June 3, 1910, provided their readers with details of the crime and the execution at Clarendon, Texas.

Galveston Daily News, Saturday, June 3, 1910

HANGING AT CLARENDON.

Clarendon, Tex., June 3. – George Miller was legally hanged here today for the murder of Floyd Autry of Fort Worth in a box car at a freight train on the Denver Railway, near Giles, in this county, on March 19, 1909, while they were riding together in the fright car Miller went quietly to his fate on the gallows. He read a short statement, praying all for forgiveness. Sheriff Patman pulled the lever. Six minutes and eleven seconds after which, Miller was pronounced dead. Fully one thousand people gathered about the gallows, but only saw the condemned man as he read his short statement, after which the gallows was screened from view, making the execution as private as possible.

G. R. Miller, standing with the black cap and noose around the neck just before the tarps were raised. Photographed by H. Mulkey, June 3, 1910. *Author's personal collection.*

Duval County
County Seat - San Diego

Refugio Gomez

Race/Gender: Hispanic Male **Age:** 28 **Offense:** Murder
Offense Date: May 15, 1882 **Weapon:** Pistol **Execution:** June 6, 1884

Refugio Gomez by his own account was a violent career criminal who was responsible for several murders and property crimes. Gomez was tried and convicted for a shooting death of his friend Estefino Dimas at a fiesta. At about 8 p.m. on the night of May 15, 1882, on a street leading into the plaza, Gomez during a drunken argument drew his pistol and shot Estefino four times.

Prior to the execution Gomez bragged to a reporter that he had killed eight men, five in Texas and three in Mexico. One of the men in Texas he said was Bernard Schwartz, a wealthy pawnbroker in San Antonio that had been stabbed to death inside his store. The murder was unsolved until Gomez gave his confession implicating himself.

On the appointed day, Gomez was led out from the jail and his legs shackles were removed at the stairway of the gallows. The death warrant was read in English and then translated in Spanish. At the completion of he reading, Gomez declined to make a final statement. At 12:20 the trap was sprang and twenty-five minutes later the body was cut down and lowered into a coffin.

The *Galveston Daily News*, dated Saturday, June 7, 1884, provided readers with details of the shooting and execution at San Diego, Texas.

Ellis County
County Seat - Waxahachie

Wyatt Banks

Race/Gender: Black male **Age:** 25 **Offense:** Accomplice to Murder in the First Degree.
Offense Date: May 28, 1882 **Weapon:** Iron Pipe **Execution:** April 23, 1883

Addison D. Wyser served as both a deputy sheriff and jailer for Robertson County. As a jailer, his duties included serving meals to the prisoners twice a day, and it wasn't long before the prisoners were aware of Deputy Wyser's work routine.

Fred Waite was a prisoner at the time who had been incarcerated for the theft of a drummer's valise at the Junction House in Hearne, Texas. Another inmate was Wyatt Banks who had been charged with horse theft and default on payment for a gambling fine. Daniel Compton was jailed on the charge of committing incest with his fifteen-year-old stepdaughter. Banks during his incarceration was healing from a gunshot wound he had received while attempting to escape from a jail contract labor farm.

On the morning of May 28, 1882, Deputy Wyser arrived after 8 a.m. with the prisoners' food. Fred Waite struck the officer from behind on the head with an iron pipe. After Deputy Wyser fell the ground, Waite struck him four more times to the head, disarmed him, and then released the other prisoners from their cells to make their escape. The thirty-eight-year-old lawman died that night and was buried in Franklin Cemetery.

On June 29, 1882, Dan Compton testified as state's witness in exchange for avoiding the hangman's noose. In exchange Compton received a sentence of life imprisonment. Both Fred Waite and Wyatt Banks were found guilty of murder in the first degree and sentenced to death. The sentence was appealed to the Texas Court of Appeals who affirmed the lower courts decision. Fred Waite was executed on March 23, 1883, in Robertson County.

On the gallows the sheriff allowed Wyatt Banks to rant for two and a half hours before 2,000 spectators. During that time he accused the judge, county attorney and his counsel of paying Governor John Ireland $1,000 to not commute his sentence. Banks said if there was a heaven, he would go there, but he did not want to go where his prosecutors went. He said none of them would prosper, and they would end up going to hell. At 4 p.m. the rope holding the trap in place was cut and Banks dropped.

The *Galveston Daily News*, dated Wednesday, April 25, 1883, provided details of the murder and execution at Waxahachie, Texas.

George Young

Race/Gender: Black Male **Age:** 31 **Offense:** Murder
Offense Date: April 2, 1885 **Weapon:** Pistol **Execution:** May 8, 1886

George Young was known to become violent towards his thirty-two-year-old common-law wife, Fannie Young (Harrison), when he drank alcohol. A week before the murder of Fannie, he was convicted of purposely setting fire to furniture in the house, and destroying several other pieces of furniture. For this offense, Young was fined, but because he had no money to pay the fine, he was ordered to work the fine off by cleaning the streets in the town of Palmer, Texas. Each time Young drank, he blamed Fannie for having him arrested and fined.

On April 2, 1885, at about 11 p.m., Fannie and her thirteen-year-old daughter Mattie Henderson where preparing supper, when Young said he was leaving to get coal from the depot. As Young was leaving, he asked for Fannie to leave the front door slightly open so that the inside light of the house would shine outside.

Young soon arrived at the home of a constable and reported that he was concerned that there were armed men outside his home. The constable told Young to return home and to send someone back if the men were still there. A short time later, a shot was fired from the partially open south kitchen window. The bullet hit Fannie Young in the head while she was standing at the dinner table eating bread and drinking milk. Mattie ran from the house screaming for help.

When authorities arrived, Fannie was found lying on the kitchen floor. She was still alive and was moved to a bedroom in the house. The officers determined that the shooter had taken his boots off and crept up to the window in his socks to fire the shot. The officers tracked the shooter through the mud and located the socks where they had been pulled off while running through the mud. The socks were later identified as those belonging to George Young.

While officers continued to search, Young returned to a window of the house and called for someone to bring him his coat, pencil and pocket book. Mattie went to the window when Young asked her, "Mattie, do you think I killed your mother?"

Mattie said, "I don't know, Pa, but it looks very like it, or you would come into the house."

Young told her, "Well, if you have got that in your head, good-bye."

On April 5, Fannie Young died from her wound. Five days after the murder, Deputy Sheriff Will McCue and his posse were searching for George Young when he was flushed out of the brush near Palmer. Young was ordered to stop, and when he failed to stop, he was fired upon. The next day Young was found hiding, while buried in cottonseed in a cotton house, and suffering from a bullet wound. He was treated and jailed at Palmer to await trial for murder at Waxahachie.

County Attorney F. M. Maxwell prosecuted the case and made the following opening statement to the jury:

> Gentlemen, in the back part of this courtroom sit a number of Negroes, who are watching this trial to see if you will punish a Negro for murdering his wife. If you don't convict this Negro, people will not bring them to trial hereafter, but will hang them on the spot where the crime is committed. If you turn this man loose, then it is impossible to convict a man in circumstantial evidence, for it is plainer than any case reported.
>
> Gentlemen of the jury, look at the defendant; there he sits; can you not see the demon in his eyes? Does not his countenance declare him a murderer?
>
> Gentlemen, the welfare and peace of society depend upon your convicting this man. If you turn him loose you encourage mob law.

At the conclusion of the trial, County Attorney M. B. Templeton made the following closing argument before the jury went into deliberation. "Gentlemen, I believe George Young is guilty of this atrocious murder. I am not opposed to capital punishment, and believing him guilty, I would have the nerve to hang him."

The jury did find George Young guilty and imposed the death sentence. The case was appealed and the decision was affirmed on December 9, 1885.

The scaffold was built on a vacant lot near the creek known as the "circus lot," and on the day of the execution 6,000 spectators gathered. At 1 p.m. Sheriff W. D. Rayburn and his deputies, who were accompanied by Sheriff William Smith of Dallas, and two black ministers, left the jail with Young.

At 1:14 p.m. all mounted the scaffold, and Sheriff Rayburn read the death warrant and the sentence by the court. When the sheriff finished, Young spoke for sixteen minutes, admonishing all young men to forsake their evil ways and turn to Jesus. He declared his innocence to the last, and said that he was not afraid to die. Young said he wished to meet Sheriff Rayburn and the jury that convicted him in heaven.

At 1:51 p.m. the trap was sprung and the doomed man fell seven feet, breaking his neck. After hanging fifteen minutes, the body was cut down and turned over to friends for interment.

The *Dallas Morning News*, dated Sunday, May 9, 1886, provided a full account of the crime and execution at Waxahachie, Texas.

Fred Sawyer

Race/Gender: Black Male **Offense:** Rape **Offense Date:** June 5, 1898
Execution: January 13, 1899

Fred Sawyer was arrested and convicted for the sexual assault upon Mrs. Fannie Fuller of Ellis, Texas. Fuller had been hired two days earlier as an employee for the Bardwell Hotel in Ennis. Fred Sawyer was working as an assistant to a drummer (salesman) when he checked into the hotel.

At about 11 p.m., Fannie had gone to her room to go to bed. While in her bed asleep with her eight-year-old son, Fred Sawyer quietly entered her room at about 3 in the morning, and woke the woman by putting his hand over her mouth to prevent her from screaming. Sawyer threatened the frightened woman that if she screamed out or if she woke her son, he would kill both her and the child.

Sawyer sexually assaulted the woman, and left the room near sunrise. Sawyer was seen outside the hotel unloading merchandise from travel trunks for display when the assault was reported. He was next seen walking away from the hotel towards the Houston & Texas Central Railway depot 250 yards away. There, Sawyer purchased a ticket to Dallas and boarded the train. A telegram was sent to the conductor on the train, and Fred Sawyer was held for the police after arriving in Dallas.

Sawyer asked the officer what crime he was being held for. When the officer replied rape, Sawyer said, "Damn them, they will have to prove it."

For fear of a lynch mob storming the Dallas jail, Sawyer was quietly transported to the Fort Worth jail for safekeeping.

Sawyer was tried on June 16 and two days later the jury rendered a verdict in twenty-nine minutes. The foreman read the following verdict: " We the jury find the defendant guilty as charged in the indictment and access the punishment of death by hanging." The case was appealed and on November 2, 1898, the higher court in Tyler affirmed the verdict.

The gallows were built twelve feet high ground with the intention of having an eight-foot drop. With only 125 tickets issued by the sheriff, people sat in nearby trees in an attempt to view the execution over the privacy fence surrounding the gallows.

From the gallows, Sawyer said:

I feel that I am now prepared to meet my God. All I would like to state is that the statement made in a paper here is the only statement I intend to make. I do not want to go into details in that business. I would rather leave it to your inference. Anybody that reads that statement can term as inference that will help them come to an exact conclusion. No law has been broken in that business; I did not break anybody's law. There was no assault committed there; I was a participant in the affair, but not an assaulter. I leave this statement with you; that is all I want to say.

At 12:51, Sheriff Stewart released the trap and attending physicians pronounced the Sawyer dead twelve minutes later. The remains were afterwards lowered down into a coffin to be shipped to Dallas for burial. The noose was the same rope used in the hanging of John Shaw in Johnson County two months earlier.

The *Ferris Wheel*. Dated Saturday, January 21, 1899, provided a short article on the crime and execution at Waxahachie, Texas.

Brozier Smith

Race/Gender: Black Male **Age:** 21 **Offense:** Murder
Offense Date: February 24, 1903 **Weapon:** .38 caliber Pistol **Execution:** March 25, 1904

Brozier Smith was tried and convicted for the shooting death of his wife. Upset that she had spent money to go to the opera with friends, Smith followed her home after leaving the show. At about 11 p.m., the couple argued about her wasteful spending when she was last heard to say, "if you are going to kill me, why, shoot me."

Brozier Smith fired his .38 caliber pistol, striking his wife three times and killing her instantly. Smith then left his wife on the bedroom floor and with blood on his hands walked to a nearby saloon to tell the other men what he done. When Smith left the bar, officers placed him under arrest. Tried and convicted, Brozier Smith date of execution was set for March 25, 1904 after the court of criminal appeals affirmed the lower courts decision.

At 11:25 in the morning Brozier Smith calmly mounted the scaffold steps unassisted, and asked for a cigar, which was given to him. Smith smoked the cigar as he listened to the religious service, and when his pastor, Rev. G.W. Hill, began the prayer, Smith sank down upon his knees and joined in the prayer. On being asked if he had anything to say Smith replied no, then pulled off his shoes and stepped upon the trap.

Deputies bound his arms and legs followed by the noose being adjusted around his neck. After the black cap was placed over his head, Smith told the officers and his friends present good-bye, and shook hands with them. Just before the trap was sprung Smith asked Rev. Hill to tell his mother good-bye for him.

Sheriff J. P. Minnick sprung the trap at 11:37 a.m. and Smith fell seven and a half feet to his death. The drop did not break Smith's neck causing him to die by strangulation. After hanging for ten minutes, county physician Simpson announced that Brozier Smith was dead and after hanging for nineteen minutes the body was taken down and delivered to his mother for burial.

A large crowd, estimated at 1,500, was present around the private enclosure outside of the gallows where only 200 people were permitted by the sheriff's invitation to witness the execution. The rope used belonged to ex-sheriff W. A. Steward of Cleburne. The rope is said to have been used in seventeen executions including Fred Sawyer in 1898 and John Shaw in 1899.

The *Southern Mercury* (Dallas) dated Thursday, March 31, 1904, provided readers with details of the murder and execution.

John Henry Young

Race/Gender: Black Male **Age:** 20 **Offense:** Murder
Offense Date: May 1, 1904 **Weapon:** Double Barrel Shotgun
Execution: March 31, 1905

John Henry Young was accused, tried and hanged for the murder of Albertus Moore. The motive for the murder was that Young was having a relationship with Moore's wife, Cora and according to Young she wanted to have her husband killed.

Cora Moore testified that on the day of the murder, she and her husband were fishing on Grove Creek. Just as Moore turned to ask Cora to hand him the bait, he was shot in the back of the head by a shotgun. Afterwards Young emerged from the bushes with the shotgun and pushed the body into the creek. Cora testified that Young afterwards reloaded the shotgun and threatened to kill her if she told anyone of the murder.

Seven days later, Moore's body was found floating in the creek between Palmer and Boyce, about eight miles from Waxahachie. Because of the advanced stage of decomposition, the body was buried in the soft mud at the banks of the stream. Both Cora Moore and Young were placed under arrest on suspicion of murder, but were released for lack of evidence. Cora later provided a statement about the murder and Young was again arrested and indicted in September. On November 10, 1904, Young pled guilty to the murder and he was sentenced to death. The case was appealed to the court of criminal appeals and the court affirmed the decision on January 25, 1905.

On the day of the execution, Young was dressed in black slacks, black frock coat and hat. After the hat had been removed and the black cap pulled over the head, and the noose adjusted, Young asked that the black cap be removed in order to speak to the witnesses. Young told the crowd that he was innocent and asked the crowd, "Do I look like a guilty man."

After the black cap was again drawn over the head, Young knelt down over the trap and prayed for ten minutes out loud for those people who had any connection to his trial, conviction and imprisonment. At 12:15 Sheriff Minnick sprang the trap and sixteen minutes later County Health Officer Simpson pronounced the Young dead. The fall of nine feet broke the neck and at 12:35 the body was cut down and released to friends who would transport the body to Mexia for burial.

Young left a written statement in which he wrote that the murdered man's wife, Cora Moore fired the fatal shot. Young wrote the murder was committed without his knowledge and that he was completely innocent.

The rope used to hang John Henry belonged to ex-sheriff W. A. Stewart of Johnson County. The rope had been used in eighteen previous executions. The first being the executions of John Shaw on November 25, 1898. Afterwards the rope was used twice more at Cleburne, three times at Waxahachie, and Waco, twice at Bonham, once at Hillsboro, Sherman, Franklin, Kaufman, Wichita Falls and three other places.

Albert Johnson

Race/Gender: Black Male **Age:** 19 **Offense:** Robbery & Murder
Weapon: Tree Limb **Offense:** July 3, 1905 **Execution:** March 30, 1906

J. H. Taylor was a sixty-six-year-old Confederate veteran who lived near Ovilla, Texas, and farmed for a living. On July 3, 1905, at about 8:30 at night, Taylor was found sitting in his buggy three miles southeast of Waxahachie on the Ennis road. Taylor had been struck three times to the head with a blunt object, and was unconscious.

Taylor was taken to Waxahachie where physicians dressed and sewed the wounds, but he never regained consciousness, and died at 6 a.m. the following morning. It was learned from family members that Taylor had $67 dollars on his person and robbery was believed to be the motive for the murder as there was only a $1 silver coin in his pocket. Following the death of Taylor, Sheriff J. P. Minnick and Deputy Henry Forbes located Albert Johnson making purchases in a dry goods store and placed him in jail for the offense of robbery and murder of Taylor.

Johnson's first trial on November 1, resulted in a mistrial after the jury deliberated for three days and could not agree on a verdict. On November 21, Johnson was retried. At both trials Johnson took the witness stand in his own defense. At the first trial, Johnson denied knowing who may have killed Taylor, but at the second trial, Johnson changed his testimony from saying he had not known Taylor to claiming he killed Taylor in self-defense. Johnson claimed Taylor had pulled a knife and threatened him. Johnson explained he had been working for a farmer three miles east of Waxahachie when Taylor rode up in his buggy and asked Johnson to ride with him to town. Johnson said just before they reached town, Taylor gave him some money. In the buggy were two bottles of whiskey and Johnson asked if he could have a drink. Once they reached Waxahachie, Taylor turned east towards Ennis. After some distance from town, Johnson said he got out of the buggy after Taylor threatened him with a knife. Johnson said he picked up a locust limb and hit Taylor above the eye. Johnson said he then reached in the buggy and took a bottle of whiskey, and left for Charley Miller's house where he was boarding. After closing arguments, the jury deliberated one hour to return with a verdict of guilty and sentenced Albert Johnson to death.

On the day of the execution, Johnson addressed the crowd confessing to the robbery and murder. Johnson told the crowd he had been drinking and killed Taylor for his money. The rope used belonged to ex-sheriff W. A. Stewart of Johnson County. Albert Johnson became the twenty-first person hanged by this rope.

The *Fort Worth Record*, dated Saturday, March 3, 1906, provided readers with a large article detailing the murder and execution.

Burrell Oates

Race/Gender: Black Male **Offense:** Robbery & Murder **Offense Date:** November 29, 1904
Weapon: Pistol **Execution:** November 29, 1912

On the night of November 29, 1904, two men entered Sol Aronoff's general store located at 236 South Harwood Street in Dallas. One of the men made a twenty-five cent tobacco purchase then drew a pistol on Aronoff with the demand to "hold up his hands." The store owner was pushed back towards the bedroom where his son Nathan was asleep. Sol Aronoff was then shot above the left breast, and fell dead across his bed. After a third bullet was fired, Mrs. Aronoff rushed to her husband and shot at the robbers who quickly fled.

Burrell Oates and Holly Vann were arrested the same afternoon along with a Frank McCue. In return for not being charged with robbery or murder, McCue turned state's witness. Holly Vann was tried and convicted in Dallas, but Burrell Oates received a change of venue to Ellis County. Frank McCue testified that he was riding with Vann and Oates in Vann's buggy when Vann suggested they rob the store.

Tried and convicted seven times, it took eight long years of court battles to hang Burrell Oates. In six of the seven cases, the jury assessed the penalty at death, and one trial was declared a mistrial after the jury could not reach a decision as to the penalty. The court of appeals further reversed three previous sentences of death, but on June 26, 1912, the conviction was affirmed.

Attorneys made a request to the court of appeals for a rehearing, which was refused on October 16, 1912. On October 21, Burrell Oates was sentenced to hang with the execution date set for November 29, 1912.

To ensure the execution would be a success, the sheriff requested the same rope used in the Grayson County executions as his "good luck rope." The rope had been used for the execution of Wood Maxey, Sellars Vines and Sam Jones.

On November 29, 1912, as Burrell Oates ascended the scaffold, he said to a white minister:

Burrell Oates from the *Fort Worth Record*, Saturday, November 30, 1912.

"Good-bye, God bliss you, I am ready to die." A moment later he added, "It's a drop here and a rise over there.

I am ready to die if it's God's will. God's will be done, not mine. For eight years I have fought as hard as I knew how against the injustice of this thing and I can't stave it off any longer. I am innocent. I was not concerned in any way in the killing of Mr. Aronoff. I've tried a few times since I have been in jail to dislike some people, but I just couldn't do it."

At 12:38 the trap was sprung, and Burrell Oates was pronounced dead twelve minutes later.

The *Fort Worth Record*, dated Saturday, November 30, 1912, provided their readers with a large article detailing the crime and execution.

Joe J. Larkins

Race/Gender: Black Male **Age:** 24 **Offense:** Murder
Offense Date: February 27, 1915 **Weapon:** Knife & Steel Car Axle
Execution: April 17, 1915

Twenty-one year old Jack Jones had been raised in Waxahachie, and worked for the W. B. Jackson Motor Car Company in Waxahachie, Texas. Jones had worked for the automotive company for several months as a collector during the day, and slept in one the garages which he had converted into a bedroom, since he doubled as the night watchman.

On the night of February 27, 1915, Jones was wakened by the sound of breaking glass coming from the garage office. When Jones went into the office to investigate the noise, he interrupted men who were in the process of emptying the cash register of its contents. Evidence showed that about 11:30 at night, Jones had fought with the burglars near the entrance of the garage office. As they attempted to take hold of Jones, he broke away and ran to his bedroom to call for the police. The telephone switchboard operator saw that the panel board lit up, but when answered, she only heard what sounded like groans in the background coming from the receiver.

The next morning at 8 a.m., employees discovered the office in disarray, with an estimated amount of $600 dollars missing from the register. Jack Jones' body was found lying on the bedroom floor in a pool of blood. He was under the bed sheets that had been pulled from the bed and thrown over his body. After the murderers had torn the telephone from the wall, Jones apparently made a desperate fight for his life. Jones died as a result of his neck being cut, and his skull crushed from the use of a steel car axle.

At 1 p.m. that afternoon, Sheriff H. S. Dearborn and County Attorney Whipple apprehended a suspect by the name of Joe Larkins. Larkins was taken away from the sheriff by a lynch mob and taken to a railroad crossing where several hundred people had gathered. A noose was placed around Larkin's neck and the other end of the rope thrown over a telephone cable. Larkins was hoisted a couple of times as he pleaded his innocence. On the third hoist, with the threat he would be left hanging, Larkins gave the names of two men whom he said were responsible.

District Judge Hawkins, and County Attorney Whipple convinced the crowd not to lynch the man by explaining he would call for a special grand jury to indict Larkins and pleaded for them to allow the law to take its course. The mob allowed Larkins to be driven to the jail at Waxahachie where a second lynch mob had organized to storm the jail. Sheriff's deputies removed Larkins from the jail and placed him in the fastest patrol car they had to take Larkins to the jail in Dallas for safekeeping. As the patrol car sped away, several shots were fired at the car's tires and when that failed, members of the mob attempted to ram the deputies' car off the road. The officers were able to outrun the mob and safely arrived in Dallas.

On April 17, 1915, after having been tried and convicted, Joe Larkins was transported a mile from the Waxahachie County Courthouse where the scaffold had been erected. From the gallows, Larkins admitted to the large crowd that he took part in the crime by holding the victim down while the other man beat him to death. When the trap was sprung, several in the crowd clapped their hands while other spectators pulled down the obstruction around the scaffold to view the hanging corpse.

Three months after the execution of Joe Larkins, the second suspect by the name of Johnny Johnson was arrested in Kaufman County and indicted for the murder of Jack Jones on July 14, 1915.

The *Galveston Daily News*, dated Sunday, April 18, 1915, reported on the execution.

El Paso County

County Seat - El Paso

William Craig

Race/Gender: White Male   **Offense Date:** January 19, 1851   **Weapon:** Bowie Knife
Execution: January 31, 1851

Marcus Butler

Race/Gender: White Male   **Offense Date:** January 19, 1851   **Weapon:** Bowie Knife
Execution: January 31, 1851

John Wade

Race/Gender: White Male   **Offense Date:** January 19, 1851   **Weapon:** Bowie Knife
Execution: January 31, 1851

Alexander Young

Race/Gender: White Male   **Offense Date:** January 19, 1851   **Weapon:** Bowie Knife
Execution: February 12, 1851

Edward C. Clark worked as a member of the U.S. Boundary Commission at Socorro, Texas, and was the son of Rhode Island Senator J. W. Clark.

On Wednesday, January 29, 1851, Clark had rented a house for the purpose of having a fandango that night. During the dance, Alexander Young led a gang of "ruffians" which consisted of John Wade, Marcus Butler, William Craig, Stephen Stanly, Charles Hughes, Charles Ripley, Thomas McCasky, Alexander McNiven, S. C. Jackson, and John Frazer to the house where they intended to cause trouble. Young entered into an adjoining apartment where gambling tables had been set up and started an argument. Clark, hearing the disturbance, entered the room. Young, Wade, Craig and Butler stabbed Clark eleven times to his back, chest, stomach and face with bowie knives while other members of the gang blocked the doors. When the women in the room attempted to flee, Young threatened to shoot anyone who interfered or moved.

Young then drew his pistol and fired a bullet at a flickering candle flame, with a second bullet destroying a clock. While this was happening, Clark was able to walk out and staggered to the home of Doctor Bigelow. While Doctor Bigelow attended to the dying man, Alexander McNevin busted through the door while holding a large bowie knife planning to finish Clark off. The doctor in defense quickly grabbed a double barrel shotgun and leveled it at McNevin. McNevin seeing both barrels pointed as him was sober enough to understand that taking a knife to a gunfight were poor odds against him.

The following morning, Socorro residents requested the aid of additional armed men from San Elizario, the county seat at the time, to assist in capturing the wanted murderers. A search party was organized, and all suspected houses where the men might be hiding were searched. All of the suspects were located except for Young who had escaped earlier in the morning. The prisoners were taken before Judge Berthold on the charge of aiding or abetting in the murder of Edward C. Clark. During the hearing, the prisoners refused counsel but instead cursed the court and made threats to all witnesses. When court adjourned for the night, the prisoners were confined in the jail under a heavily armed guard of six men.

The next morning, Friday, January 31, at 10 a.m. the court adjourned and proceeded with the trial. The jury returned a guilty verdict on the charge of aiding and abetting murder against William Craig, John Wade, and Marcus Butler. Judge Berthold sentenced the men to death and ordered that the men be hanged one hour after the adjournment of the court. The prisoners were afterwards escorted to the church in the plaza to meet with the priest for their last rites, but all refused the services of the priest.

At sunset, the condemned were marched to a cottonwood tree to be used for their execution. Forty armed guards along with spectators circled around an old cottonwood tree. When the nooses were prepared, the ropes were thrown over separate tree branches from the same tree. After Wade had hanged for a second, he was let down so that the noose could be readjusted. Wade said, "This is a hell of a way to hang a man by God!"

After they were dead, the bodies of the three men were cut down and carried to be kept in the jail until the next morning, when the remains would be buried in the same town cemetery as Edward Clark had been laid to rest.

Young is the mean time had all intentions of avoiding the same fate as his companions, and fled into Old Mexico. A reward of $400 dollars was offered for the arrest of Alexander Young. Ten days later Young was apprehended in Mexico and returned to Socorro to stand trial. On February 12, Young confessed in court to the murder, and the jury returned a verdict of guilty of murder in the first degree. Sentenced to death and to hang within the hour, Young was taken before the priest where Young gave his final confession and received the blessing from the priest. Young asked the priest if he would bury him as respectfully as the circumstances in his case would allow.

Young was taken to the same hanging tree where the noose adjusted around his neck. He requested to make a last statement and told those who were younger than him to take warning from his example "You can see what gambling, swearing, drinking, and ungovernable temper with the worst of evil associations, has brought for me." Young told everyone he had run away from home at the age of fourteen and would never see his home again or his mother whom he had not seen in six years.

The *Republic Newspaper*, dated April 10, 1851 (Washington D.C.) provided their readers with a large story of the murder and execution.

Bartolo Mendoza

Race/Gender: Hispanic Male **Age:** 35 **Offense:** Murder
Offense Date: 1869 **Weapon:** Revolver **Execution:** August 13, 1869

In 1869, the small dusty village of San Elizario, located seventeen and a half miles east of El Paso in the upper farming valley along the Rio Grande River was the county seat, of El Paso County.

On August 13, 1869, Bortolo Mendoza was executed in the county for the murder of his stepdaughter Merced Avalos. Merced was engaged to marry a man who Mendoza did not approve of and wanted the engagement ended. As Merced prepared for her wedding day, Mendoza asked her if she was dead set on marrying. Merced answered yes, and told him there was nothing to keeping her from doing so. Mendoza pulled out a pistol and shot Merced in the chest, killing her. Murder was nothing new for Mendoza as he was already wanted in Mexico for killing a man.

On the day of the scheduled execution, a jail guard approached Mendoza and said, "Bartolo, you will soon be face to face with God. Won't you please tell him to send us a little rain? A few more days of the terrible drought and all of our crops will be ruined."

Mendoza replied, "Stop worrying."

Father Antonio Borrajo of the Catholic Church walked with Mendoza to the gallows. Once at the top of the platform, Mendoza knelt before the priest and received his last rites. After Mendoza's legs and arms were bound and the noose tightened, Sheriff Caleb B. Miller released the trap, dropping Mendoza to his death. Minutes after Mendoza was pronounced dead, it started to rain.

The *Galveston Tri-weekly News*, Galveston, Texas, dated Friday, October 1, 1869 printed the below announcement.

Bartolo Mendoza, who was hanged in Texas a fortnight since the murder of his step-daughter, refused to eat beans on the morning of his execution, because "they always disagreed with him," and made a particular request for a purple shroud.

Joseph Brewster

Race/Gender: White Male **Offense:** Rape **Offense Date:** 1882
Execution: July 5, 1883

Joseph Brewster, U.S. soldier, was hanged in El Paso County for the rape of a woman in Fort Davis. On the gallows, Brewster nervously spoke for twenty minutes before 800 spectators. During his speech, Brewster who had been given a bottle of whiskey to calm his nerves took several large gulps of the alcohol until his spiritual adviser grabbed the bottle away from him. During Brewster's talk, he made no confession to the crime of rape for which he was convicted of and sentenced to hang.

Once Brewster's hands and legs were bound, the sheriff sprang the trap. The knot did not break the neck, and Brewster struggled while the rope strangled him. The rope, which had been improperly tied, gave way and Brewster fell into the trap. After the officers carried Brewster to the top of the platform, retied the rope, and readjusted the noose, the trap was sprung a second time.

The *Daily Freeman*, dated Friday, July 6, 1883, provided the following short article of the execution.

A CRIMINAL HANGED TWICE

The Rope Around Joseph Brewster's Neck Gives Way Under His Weight.

El Paso, Tex., July 5.

Joseph Brewster, a Canadian Frenchman, who committed a violent assault on Miss Davis, at Fort Davis a year ago, was hanged Thursday at Ysleta, the county seat of this county. He was a United States soldier. The execution was private, all officials, and reporters being admitted. Brewster when sentenced broke down and could scarcely walk.

He made no confession on the scaffold, but spoke for twenty minutes during which time he fortified himself with two huge drinks of whiskey. The knot was tied in a bungling manner, and after the fall, Brewster writhed and twitched horribly. The rope gave away and he fell into the trap. He was dragged from the hole, and replaced on the platform. The rope was readjusted, and he was rehung. As soon as life was extinct, the body was placed in a red-wood coffin, and given to the Catholic Priest who was in attendance.

Rosalio Castillo

Race/Gender: Hispanic Male **Offense:** Rape **Offense Date:** September 1891
Execution: November 26, 1892

Rosalio Castillo was tried and found guilty on October 25, 1891, for the rape of an eleven-year old Mexican girl named Luz Romero who he assaulted in September of 1891. The death sentence was appealed to the Texas Court of Criminal Appeals when the lower court's decision was affirmed on June 23, 1892.

On the afternoon of November 26, 1892, a spring wagon was driven to the front of the jail to transport Castillo to the scaffold. When the sheriff came for Castillo, he looked up and said, "I am ready and prepared to die."

On the platform the death warrant was read, together with the governor's proclamation. Both were interpreted in Spanish, and in reply to the question if he had anything to say, Castillo stepped forward and said: "God forgive all the officers executing my sentence, and those who so unjustly have accused me of the crime for which I am to die. I forgive all. God knows that I am innocent. I have been unjustly accused, but they will be rewarded by Him."

After the body was declared dead, the remains were lowered into a coffin and buried at Concordia Cemetery, El Paso's boot hill cemetery, where noted western gunfighters such as John Wesley Hardin and John Selman are buried.

Antonio Flores

Race/Gender: Hispanic Male **Offense:** Murder **Offense Date:** March 19, 1899
Weapon: Knife **Execution:** January 5, 1900

On March 19, 1899, Antonio Flores had just left mass at a small village north of El Paso known as Smeltertown. Smeltertown was located on top of a desert null just outside the edge of the Territory of New Mexico that overlooked the Rio Grande River, and Mexico. The residents of the settlement were mostly employees for the American Smelter and Refining Company.

Flores upon seeing the woman he loved, Ramona Vizcaya, approached her and pleaded for her to come with him, but the woman refused. Flores became enraged after her refusals and stabbed the woman repeatedly with a long knife as he yelled, "If I can not have you then no other man shall." Nearby witnesses could do nothing in time to stop the attack, but held Flores for the authorities.

Two days later Ramona died and Flores was tried for murder. Upon his conviction of murder, Flores was sentenced to hang on January 5, 1900, along with Geronimo Parra who was convicted of killing a Texas Ranger.

On the day of the execution, Flores was to hang first. When the officers came to the holding cells to remove the prisoners, both Flores and Parra attacked the lawmen with crude wire daggers they had made from their waste bucket handle. Flores yelled out, "You shall all go to hell with me," and with his wire dagger plugged the weapon into Ed Bryant repeatedly into his clothing.

While Parra was covered with pistols, Flores was subdued and his hands, feet and knees were then bound. Officers then placed Flores over the trap while Deputy Comstock read the death warrant. While the reading was taking place, Flores recognized several of the witnesses and said to them, "*Adios senores, adios.*"

Flores was afterwards asked if he had anything to say, and he replied, "I wish to be pardoned for what I have done. I want my body to be delivered to my family. That is all I have to say."

The sheriff asked if that is all he had to say, and Flores cried out, "I want to talk with my son."

Father Pinto of the Catholic Church told Flores, "Be still, your talk will be with God." Moments later the trap was sprung and dropped Flores to his death.

Geronimo Parra

Alias: Jose Nunez **Race/Gender:** Hispanic Male **Age:** 36
Offense: Murder **Offense Date:** April 17, 1890 **Weapon:** Rifle
Execution: January 5, 1900

On Thursday, April 17, 1890, Texas Ranger, Charley Fusselman was in El Paso attending court from Marfa where he was assigned. Ranger Fusselman was born, Charles Henry Vanvalkenburg Fusselman on July 16, 1866, at Greenbush, Wisconsin. At four-years-old, his family relocated to Nueces County, Texas. At twenty-one, Fusselman enlisted as a private in the Texas Rangers and assigned to Company D on May 25, 1888. On June 19, 1889, he was appointed and received a duel commission as a deputy U.S. marshal. Fusselman was later promoted to the rank of sergeant in November of that same year.

During the morning, Sgt. Fusselman was speaking with El Paso Deputy Sheriff Frank Simmons when rancher John Barnes rode into town to report to the deputy the theft of his horses, which had been stolen during the night. Barnes related to the deputy how he had left thirty head of horses and a calf to graze on a north mesa near his ranch on Mundy Springs. That morning when he returned to the mesa to check on his horses, Barnes discovered the livestock missing and followed the horse tracks to the east side of the Franklin

Mountains. While trailing his stolen horses, he came upon the remains of a two-year-old steer that had been butchered. The trail continued on towards Smuggler's Gap, where at the canyon entrance, Barnes came upon a Mexican bandit who appeared to be the rear look-out for the other cattle rustlers. Barnes said he was unarmed at the time and when he saw that the bandit reached down toward his sidearm, he retreated back to town.

City Police Officer George Harold who was a former Texas Ranger agreed to join in with Ranger Fusselman and Barnes to go back to Smuggler Gap to arrest the bandits and recapture the stolen horses. Soon after arriving at the mouth of the mountain canyon, the lawmen arrested a well-known cow thief by the name of Yisidro Pasos. Further up the canyon, the lawmen could see the stolen horses grazing, and it appeared to the lawmen that the bandits, in order for them to escape from the lawmen, had abandoned the livestock.

Ranger Fusselman rode out toward the horses with Officer Harold directly behind him. Barnes followed from the rear as he held the reins of the horse their prisoner was riding. Unknown to the lawmen, they rode the mounts right into the bandits' camp. Suddenly and without warning, the lawmen were fired upon. Ranger Fusselman called out to Harold and Barnes, "Boys, we are in for it, and lets stay with it."

Those were last words the ranger spoke, as he was hit twice to the head by rifle bullets and he was thrown from the saddle. Harold and Barnes turned their horses and spurred their mounts down the mountainside in a running gun battle back to El Paso to report the ambush and killing of Ranger Fusselman. The prisoner who had been captured at the mouth of the canyon had also made his escape during the gunfight.

A large posse of lawmen rode back to the site of the ambush and found the bandits had stripped everything of value from Fusselman's body, and left a couple of cows and most of the stolen horses in the canyon.

Geronimo Parra, a leader of the bandit gang was identified as the person who shot and killed Ranger Fusselman. Arrest warrants were sworn out for his arrest, but Parra had fled into the territory of New Mexico.

Charles Fusselman's body was buried on April 19 in El Paso's Concordia Cemetery. Ten days later, Fusselman's brother arrived in El Paso and had his casket exhumed and transported to the cemetery at Lagarto, Texas, for reburial.

Famed Captain John R. Hughes of the Texas Rangers was reassigned to Ysleta, Texas, located southeast of El Paso. Captain Hughes began searching for Geronimo Parra to apprehend him for the murder when he learned that Parra had been arrested and convicted at Las Cruces, New Mexico, for assault with intent to commit murder and burglary and sentenced to the New Mexico Territory Penitentiary in Santa Fe since February 26, 1894.

After failed attempts to extradite Parra back to El Paso to stand trial, Captain Hughes worked out an agreement with Dona Ana County Sheriff Patrick Garrett. Garrett promised the captain if he located and arrested a wanted fugitive by the name of Pat Agnew, Garrett in return would use his influence with Territory Governor Miguel Otero to allow Parra's released to Captain Hughs for extradition back to Texas.

Captain Hughes did locate Pat Agnew at a ranch in the Big Bend country and delivered him to Sheriff Garrett. Governor Otero did authorize the extradition and Sheriff Garrett and Captain Hughes traveled back from Santa Fe by train to El Paso. Parra stood trial for the murder of Ranger Charles Fusselman and after being convicted was sentenced to hang on January 5, 1900. Scheduled to hang on the same day was Antonio Flores for murder.

On the afternoon of the scheduled execution, several lawmen gathered at the jail to assist with the execution. Once the cell door was opened both Flores and Parra sprang from the cell wielding wire daggers they had made from their waste bucket handle and attacked the officers. Parra attacked Jim Hunter who was guarding the cell door, but retreated back to a corner of his cell after Texas Ranger Saunderson drew his pistol and covered Parra. Flores in the meantime was subdued and handcuffed, and carried to the trap door.

Sheriff James Boone told the officers, "Gentleman, we have had an unfortunate happening. This second prisoner may make an attack on the man who enters his cell. I cannot afford to have good citizens or my deputies murdered by this lawless man. I propose to do my duty. If it is necessary for me to kill this man, I must do it. I shall go in myself and take him out. If it takes a bullet to do the work, that bullet will be fired. I will give him fair warning through an interpreter that resistance means death."

Sheriff Boone drew his pistol and ordered Parra to hold his hands up. The cell door was thrown open and the officers quickly seized Parra, and his arms and legs were bound.

After the reading of the death warrant Sheriff Boone asked Parra if he had anything to say. Parra responded by saying:

> Gentleman, I tell you all good-bye. There are some whom I have offended. I trust that you will pardon me. I ask the pardon of all of the world. There are those who have offended me and I forgive them all. Gentleman, I am going to die, but I am going to die an innocent man. I deliver my soul and heart to God, in whose presence I am. He is the only God."
>
> Gentleman, good-bye again to all. May God help you all. We have many of us made mistakes and we are all of us sinners.

Parra kissed a rosary held out to him by the priest, and then calmly bent his head so the sheriff could adjust the cap more easily.

At 2:04 p.m., the trap was sprung with a drop of seven feet. When the body reached the end, the rope cut deep into the neck and almost severed the head from the body.

The *El Paso Herald* dated Friday, January 5, 1900, reported the dramatic events that occurred on the day the execution of Geronimo Parra and Antonio Flores who were both hanged from the second floor of the El Paso County Jail.

Erath County

County Seat - Stephenville

Thomas A. Wright

Alias: Little Tom **Race/Gender:** White Male **Offense:** Murder
Offense Date: December 18, 1897 **Weapon:** Double Barrel Shotgun
Execution: November 10, 1899

John A. Adams was the Constable for Precinct 2 in Erath County, which included the town of Dublin. The forty-nine-year-old lawman was known for his vigorous enforcement of the liquor ordinance in his precinct, and within the town of Dublin.

Tom Wright and Tom Blassingame were operating saloon in Dublin and because the constable was interfering in their operation, Wright wanted the lawman dead. In an attempt to elicit anyone to kill the constable, Wright offered as payment, $100, a Winchester rifle, and a horse with saddle and bridle.

Wright met with Gus Blassingame, and told him that two other persons would pay an additional $100 each if he would kill the constable. Blassingame declined, and swore out an affidavit before the justice of the peace who provided a copy of the sworn statement to Constable Adams. Adams went looking for Wright in town and upon finding him, cursed and threatened him. The constable told Wright that he would not harm an unarmed man, but that Wright "needed to fix himself."

Wright then went to several people in an attempt to procure a gun and after failing to do so, asked Frank Leslie to assist him. Leslie did so by going to a nearby neighbor and asking to borrow his shotgun for the purpose of going quail hunting. Once Leslie received the shotgun and shells, he tested the firing of the weapon. Afterwards, both Wright and he traveled back to Dublin where Wright with the shotgun hidden behind a stairwell while Leslie watched for the constable. Upon seeing Constable Adams approaching, Leslie whispered out to Wright, "Here he is now, come on Tom."

As the constable walked pass, Wright slipped behind the constable and shot him to the back of the head. With the constable lying dead, Wright waived the gun at the body and said, "There goes John Adams."

Both Tom Wright and Frank Leslie were arrested and jailed until the court convened. Leslie attempted to assist Wright with a self-defense claim by stating that Constable Adams attempted to draw his weapon first, but that Wright was faster. Both men were convicted with Wright receiving the death sentence. On the gallows, Wright again told the witnesses he shot and killed the constable in self-defense.

Constable Adams was an eighteen-year law enforcement veteran with a wife and two children and is buried at the Old Dublin Park Cemetery.

The *Houston Daily Post*, Saturday, dated November 11, 1899, provided readers with the details of the murder.

Robert Johnson

Alias: Bob Johnson **Race/Gender:** Black Male **Offense:** Robbery & Murder
Offense Date: November 25, 1904 **Weapon:** Spade Handle
Execution: July 20, 1906

Albert D. Berry, a twenty-two-year-old white man and Robert Johnson were traveling southward together from Stamford, Texas, in Jones County on the Texas Central Railway on November 25, 1904. The two men arrived in Dublin, Texas, late in the night and obtained permission to sleep in a seed house at the Dublin

Cotton Oil Company. After entering the house, Berry made a hole in the pile of cottonseed and laid down to go to sleep.

An hour later, Johnson got up from where was sleeping and picked up a spade handle and walked over to where his sleeping companion was. Johnson then struck Berry four times about the head with the tool, killing him. After robbing Berry's body of $3 and a suit of clothes he was carrying, Johnson hid the body in the cottonseed, where it was not found until December 8.

At the time of the discovery, the sheriff had no suspects as to who might have committed the murder until Johnson pawned the dead man's suit. Johnson was placed under arrest on December 16. Immediately after his arrest, Johnson confessed twice to the murder and robbery to both the sheriff and district attorney, but during his trials maintained his innocence and denied that he ever made such confessions.

On the gallows, Johnson asked to have his shoes removed. After doing so, he stepped onto the trap. As Sheriff Mack Creswell adjusted the noose, Johnson stood perfectly erect and said, "Goodbye, gentlemen, I appreciate what you have done for me. Tell Mr. Cook, I thank him too."

The *Galveston Daily News*, dated Saturday, July 1, 1906, provided readers with details of the crime and the execution at Stephenville, Texas.

Falls County
County Seat - Marlin

William Hinton

Race/Gender: White Male　　**Offense:** Murder　　**Offense Date:** December 27, 1859
Weapon: Firearm　　**Execution:** March 25, 1860

On the night of December 27, 1859, Pleasant Clark "P. C." Whitaker and his wife Rebecca were having an eggnog party at their home. When P. C. learned that Rebecca was tired and not feeling well, he asked for their guests to leave. Rebecca's brother who was drunk at the time, became insulted by the request. Hinton then removed a rifle from the wall of the cabin, and shot and killed his brother in-law.

Dennis Nelson

Age: 34　　**Race/Gender:** White Male　　**Offense:** Murder
Offense Date: February 18, 1869　　**Weapon:** Firearms
Execution: August 13, 1869

Franklin and Jane Wallace lived on a farm near Marlin, Texas, raising vegetables for a living. Problems later developed between Franklin Wallace and Dennis Nelson that developed from arguments into assaults. In January of 1869, Wallace was to have said, "I will kill Dennis Nelson, and no such man should live in the range where I do. I came to this country for killing damned rascals."

In early February, Nelson shot at and wounded Wallace. Both men were arrested, but because the county had no jail, the sheriff placed guards over both men until things settled down.

On February 18, 1869, Franklin and Jane Wallace left their farm riding a two-horse team and wagon filled with produce to be delivered to Marlin. After delivering the produce, the couple began the return trip home with Jane driving the team because of the wound still bothering Franklin. On the main road leading to their home, Dennis Nelson and Joseph Young waited for the approaching wagon as they sat on their mules in the middle of the road. When Jane stopped the wagon, Nelson armed with both a double barrel shotgun and pistol said, "Wallace, I have come to kill you."

Wallace answered with, "What are you going to kill me for? I did not do it, go home Nelson, and let me alone for I am wounded and sick."

Nelson and Young then dismounted from the mules. While Nelson approached Wallace, he continued to state he was going to kill him. Wallace asked, "What for."

Nelson said, "You have threatened my life."

Wallace replied, "I have not threatened your life, and you cannot find the man who will say so. I did not, and I will go with you to town or anywhere else and show you I did not."

Nelson drew his pistol and pointed the barrel at Wallace and was about to fire the weapon when Jane placed herself between the muzzle and her husband. Jane then begged Nelson not to kill her husband and for him to go home. Jane told Nelson that she would get on her knees and pray to him if he would spare Franklin's life.

Nelson said, "God Damn him, I intent to have him."

Nelson turned to Joseph Young and said, "Young, are you not going to do anything?"

Joseph Young drew his pistol and pointed the weapon at the head of Wallace. Jane told her husband to fall back into the bed of the wagon, which he did. Jane then covered Franklin over with her shawl. Nelson then walked to the opposite side of the wagon and pressed both barrels of his shotgun to the back of Franklin

Wallace and discharged both barrels. The blast of the gun frightened the horse team into a run. Nelson and Young then mounted their mules and chased after the fleeing wagon. Nelson then fired two more shots with his pistol at Jane or at the body of Franklin Wallace.

Dennis Nelson was charged with murder in the first degree and Joseph Young with aiding and abetting in the murder. Young was tried and found guilty of murder in the second degree and received a ten-year prison sentence. Nelson was found guilty of murder in the first degree and sentence to death. The case was appealed and the sentenced affirmed.

Clark Jones

Age: 24   **Race/Gender:** White Male   **Offense:** Murder
Offense Date: June 6, 1868   **Weapon:** Firearms
Execution: August 13, 1869

Clark Jones was convicted for his part in the murders of Jesse and Sam Howard, but Jones maintained he was innocent. Jones related to the crowd from the gallows how he and Veto Dodd had started hunting and knew nothing of Dodd's intentions to kill the Howards, although the Howards were a personal enemy of his. Jones told the spectators that both Jesse and Sam Howard were sitting next to the rear wheel of their wagon drawing a bucket of water on Gen. Harrison's plantation when Dodd shot and killed Jesse Howard first, then shot Sam to death. Jones said he was responsible only for killing a man in eastern Texas and for shooting another man in Falls County. Jones again denied having taken any part in the murder of the Howard brothers. Although Jones did not speak of the murder of a man named Theodore Rice, he had been charged for that murder as well.

The double execution of Clark Jones and Dennis Nelson was public and estimated to have been witnessed by 5,000 people. Nelson told the spectators that he felt justified for his crime, while Jones claimed he was innocent. The gallows were erected one mile from the town square.

The *Cleburne Chronicle*, dated Saturday, August 21, 1869, reported on the double execution.

Silas Wood

Alias: Convich Silas Wood   **Race/Gender:** Black Male   **Age:** 29
Offense: Murder   **Offense Date:** August 17, 1876   **Execution:** November 10, 1876

On August 17, 1876, Silas Wood murdered his wife, Kesia Wood. Tried and found guilty of the murder, Judge Saunders on September 25, 1876, sentenced Wood to hang on November 10, 1876.

The *Galveston Daily News*, dated Saturday, November 11, 1876, printed the following short article of the hanging.

ANOTHER EXECUTION.

Hanging of Silas Wood for the Crime of Murder at Marlin.

{Special Telegram to the Galveston News.}
An immense crowd was in town today to witness the hanging of Silas Wood for the murder of his wife, which occurred in this county about two months ago.

By one o'clock p. m. a vast multitude had collected around the walls of the jail-house to await the appearance of the prisoner. At two o'clock he was led by the sheriff to the gallows, which had been erected in the jail-house yard. He mounted the ladder with a firm step and, when the sheriff had bandaged his hands, he requested to see a colored minister, who came in and read a chapter from the Bible and prayed fervently for the felon's salvation.

The sheriff then adjusted the noose around his neck and asked him if he wished to say anything. Being answered in the negative, he adjusted the bandage over Wood's eyes and made ready to pull the fatal trigger. At seven minutes after two the trap was sprung and Silas Wood stepped off into thin air. The knot slipped to the back of his neck but the fall broke his neck. Eight minutes after two a slight twitching of the arms was discernible – nothing more. Twenty-one minutes after two the physicians pronounced him dead and he was cut down after hanging about five minutes longer.

Much credit is justly awarded to Sheriff Conely for the efficient manner in which he performed this painful duty. Wood made no confession, but there is no doubt of his guilt. All passed off quietly and everybody went home satisfied.

Wash Washington

Race/Gender: Black Male **Age:** 30 **Offense:** Murder
Offense Date: May 27, 1885 **Weapon:** Shotgun **Execution:** March 31, 1886

Wash Washington always maintained he had been persuaded by Ephe Durden to kill his half-brother Willis Durden. The motive behind the murder was that Willis had accused Ephe Durden of stealing his gun, and that Wash Washington was his accomplice.

On the night of May 27, 1885, Washington shot Durden down with a shotgun. When Durden began to holler for help, Washington ran up to Durden to finish him off, but, "his heart failed him," as Durden, cried out, "Oh Wash! Oh Wash! Please, Wash, don't shoot me anymore!"

Durden lived for twenty minutes, which was long enough to tell a neighbor, who after hearing his cries for help, had ran to his aid, that Wash Washington had murdered him.

Washington was arrested and indicted on July 9, 1885, on a charge of murder in the first degree. The two-day trial ended on July 31, after the jury deliberated for thirty minutes to return the verdict of guilty and assessed the death penalty. On February 20, 1886, Judge Eugene Williams sentenced Washington to hang on Wednesday, March 31, 1886.

On the scheduled date at 11:30 in the morning, a parade of thirty heavily armed special deputies escorted the wagon containing Sheriff Cyrus Whitaker, with Wash Washington seated behind his coffin to the gallows which had been erected outside of town. Washington with the assistance of Deputy J. T. Barlow ascended the gallows at 11:40 a.m. Sheriff Whitaker announced to the crowd estimated to have been between 3,000 to 5,000 that Washington wished to make a statement.

Washington dressed in a white shirt and new black suit walked to the edge of the platform. The large crowd stood in silence as Washington made the following statement:

> A great many of you have come out to see Wash Washington hung. I hope it will be a warning to you all never let anybody persuade you to do evil. Ephe Durden, who is not here is the man who is the cause of my being here today. I intend to tell the truth; no matter who hears me. Ephe Durden, a half-brother of the deceased, persuaded me to kill Willis. I made two attempts before the evening I killed him an told Ephe that evening that I would make one more attempt that night and if I did not get him I would never make another, until Ephe said, all right, if you get him my wife and I will be witnesses to prove you clear, and if you don't, I will kill him myself, and you and my wife will be witnesses to clear me.
>
> I went down to the slough where Willis had to pass, an when he came by I fired on him. Willis fell and hollered so that I ran to him and started to kick him, but he kept hollowing so that I became frightened and ran up to Ephe's house, near by, and told him of it. Ephe asked me why I did not shoot him again, and I told him I had lost the cap from the other barrel. He then asked me why I did not hit him in the head. I told him my heart failed me and I could not do it. I killed Willis Durden, and it is just that I should be hung.

Washington then thanked God and told the sheriff he was ready. After a prayer was offered, Washington asked that a collection be taken among the crowd for the purpose of paying the transporting cost for his remains to be buried at Hammond Station in Robertson County. A hat was passed around and a total of $22.50 was collected. Washington thanked everyone who contributed and said, good bye everybody.

At 12:20 p.m. the hands and feet were tied, and at 12:35 p.m. the noose was adjusted with the black cap drawn over the head. Sheriff Whitaker shook Washington's hands and told him good-bye. The sheriff then stepped aside and raised his hat as the signal. Deputy Sheriff Barlow then pulled the rope that released the trap. Five minutes after the drop of seven feet, the physician announced there was no longer a pulse. Eighteen minutes later, Washington was pronounced dead. The body was cut down and laid in the coffin and turned over to the undertaker for the transportation of the body for burial in Robinson County.

The *Fort Worth Daily Gazette*, Thursday, April 1, 1886, printed details of the crime and execution. The paper wrote, "It was a cruel, unprovoked murder, and the general sentiment fully sustained the penalty inflicted by the law.

Wesley Williams

Race/Gender: Black Male **Age:** 40 **Offense:** Murder
Offense Date: March 5, 1887 **Weapon:** Steel Yard Pea **Execution:** September 29, 1888

Wesley Williams and his wife Eliza had been married for twenty-three years, but separated two months before her death. Eliza had moved into town and when Williams demanded the money he had previously given her, Eliza told him to "go to hell," and said she would not give him one cent.

Angered by her response, Williams picked up a two-pound steel yard pea (a cast iron weight used on scales) and struck his wife twice to the head. Eliza Williams died two days later. Williams later claimed after Eliza had told him to "go to hell," that she had picked up a butcher knife and came at him. Williams claimed he only struck her to the head with the pea in self-defense.

Williams then escaped arrest by following a dry bed creek for forty miles, to a house near the Brazos River in Milan County. There he hid with an old black man for eight months until discovered by Deputy Sheriff John Barlow of Falls County who arrested him and returned Williams to Falls County. After being found guilty of murder, the case was appealed. On June 6, 1888, the court of criminal appeals affirmed the decision and Williams was sentenced to hang on September 29, 1888.

On the morning of the execution Williams dressed himself in a new black suit furnished by the sheriff and was visited by his son. Williams took this opportunity to advise his son to keep away from bad company and to let liquor and gambling alone. Both then knelt together in prayer, and when concluded all the prisoners in jail responded with "Amen."

At 10:25 a.m., Sheriff Cyrus Whittaker entered the jail with several deputies and read the death warrant to the condemned man. Williams requested afterwards for the sheriff to turn over his remains to Alee Hamilton so his body could be laid to rest next to his wife.

At 11 a.m., an open spring wagon pulled up to the courthouse gate containing a coffin. The prisoner knelt on his coffin as he mounted the wagon smoking a cigar, and made a short and silent prayer. The procession of deputies and the Marlin Rifles, then rode toward the gallows that had been erected a half-mile west of the courthouse. Once on the gallows, Sheriff Whittaker asked him if he had any statement to make. Williams told the crowd of 3,000 the gratitude he had towards Sheriff Whittaker for his kind treatment. In speaking of the tragedy, Williams claimed any other man would do the same thing, and that his and his wife's hot temper had brought him to where he was. He told the black people that he was going straight to heaven and that he would meet them all there on the other side of Jordan.

At the end of the ten-minute statement, the legs were tied and his hands pinioned behind his back. After the black cap was placed over his head, Williams moved forward and stood over the trap door while showing no signs of fear. The noose was placed around the neck and as Williams sang a hymn, the sheriff released the trap. The fall was seven feet and broke his neck, and the body was lowered into a coffin.

A reporter from The *Galveston Daily News*, interviewed Williams and printed the conversation in the Sunday, September 30, 1888, edition:

> *Williams said, we had been separated two months shortly before the death of my wife, but we made up and lived together again. My wife and I had a box of clothing in Hearne. She came to me for money to go and get it. I gave her $55. She said that she would be back that evening, and I sent a wagon to the depot after her, she had returned; but I couldn't find her.*

On the 5th day of March, I came up town in hopes of hearing from her. I found her on that night in the kitchen of a farmer who had hired her as a cook. I had some of her clothing and gave it to her. I asked her why she treated me as she did. She replied, "Who in the hell told you to come here?" I said I didn't come here to make a fuss, but you should have told me if you wanted to cook, and then I wouldn't be uneasy about you. Give me the money I gave you and I will go home and have no more to do with you. She said, "I'll see you in hell before I give you a cent." I said she shouldn't talk that way.

I was then sitting by a table where there was a butcher knife near to her. She picked up the knife and struck at me, hitting my breast and cutting through the vest and shirt, and just cutting the skin. I then reached down to the floor and picked up a two-pound steel yard pea and struck her on the head twice. I then went to Milam county until arrested eight months afterwards.

My wife and I were raised in the same place in South Carolina. She was a good looking woman. She proved unfaithful only after our arrival in Texas. Deacon Pinkney Jones was not a Christian.

Judge Williams acted fairly with me at my trial, but, with the exception of Georgia Holmes, all the other six or seven witnesses were prejudiced against me and swore to lies. One Negro man named Mingus Strayhan swore he met me on the bridge, but I had not seen the nigger.

Elder E. Jordan is my spiritual advisor. I have been a member of the African Methodist church fifteen years. My wife had been a member ten years. I have experienced true religion, and know that God has forgiven me for what I have done, and I am now willing to go. I am sure of going to heaven and be with the angels, no matter what hour I may be called.

I hope Sheriff Whittaker will make them bury me beside my wife in the Marlin colored people's graveyard. The sheriff and his officers have been very kind to me since I have been in jail. I want The News to send a paper about my death to Sheriff Wheeler, John Kiner, Smith Levinson and Snidey Vance, all at Newberry post office, South Carolina.

This was promised.

John Roan

Race/Gender: Black Male **Age:** 22 **Offense:** Rape
Offense Date: June 18, 1901 **Execution:** April 19, 1902

John Roan was accused of raping thirteen-year-old Maud Smith on June 18, 1901. At the time of the assault, the girl's mother was 300 yards away picking cotton while Maud was left at the farmhouse to milk the cows and do other chores around the home. Roan rode up on a small bay pony and carrying a shotgun. Maud attempted to escape, but was caught by Roan and carried back to a corn crib where he assaulted the girl.

Later that night Maud told her mother of the assault and she immediately sent her son to the neighbors' house to notify the sheriff. Maud provided a description to the sheriff of her attacker and for the first few days, the sheriff brought in several black men for Maud to identify. Each time, Maud notified the sheriff that none of the men was the criminal.

Two weeks later, Roan was brought into town by the sheriff and identified by Maud as the man who had sexually assaulted her. On July 5, 1901, Roan was tried for the crime before Judge Sam R. Scott. The two-day trial concluded after the jury deliberated for six hours and returned a verdict of guilty and assessed the punishment at death. After the case was appealed and affirmed, Judge Scott on February 28, 1902, set the date of Roan's execution to take place on March 28, 1902.

Governor Joseph Sayers granted a one-week respite which delayed the execution until April 8. Sheriff C. P. Carlton seeing the citizens were upset over the respite and sensing trouble, placed Roan in a wagon and drove him to Camp Equipage and hid in the woods until the Houston & Texas Central train arrived so he could be taken to Waco for safekeeping. On April 8, and two hours before the execution was to take place, Governor Sayers granted a second and final respite until April 19.

On the gallows on the day of the execution, Roan told the crowd at the scaffold that he was ready to go, but innocent of the crime. When the black cap was adjusted, the sheriff asked Roan if he had anything further to say. Roan replied, "Good-bye to all, I am not guilty of this crime."

The *Houston Daily Post*, dated Sunday, April 20, 1902, provided details to readers of the crime and execution.

Dan McCline

Race/Gender: Black Male **Age:** 26 **Offense:** Murder
Offense Date: September 6, 1910 **Weapon:** .45 caliber Pistol **Execution:** March 29, 1912

Rosa Tubbs was a twenty-five-year-old woman who was pregnant with her fourth child and lived with her sister and husband. Dan McCline also lived in the home with Rosa. During her pregnancy, McCline asked for her to marry him. Rosa accepted the proposal to marry him after she had recovered from her child birth. During the pregnancy, McCline fully supported Rosa Tubbs with her needs. After the birth of the child, Rosa declined to marry McCline and moved from her sister's house and obtained her own home. After Rosa moved out, McCline became obsessed that Rosa did not live up to her promise to marry.

On Monday night, September 5, 1910, McCline who still resided with Rosa Tubb's sister and husband, told her that if Rosa did not return home, he would kill her. Later the same night, McCline went to Rosa's home and called her outside. When Rosa met McCline at the fence, he told Rosa that she had not kept her promise to marry him.

Rosa replied, "I know I promised to marry you, but you told me my ways did not suit you, so it is best for us not to marry."

McCline asked what she intended to do about the money she owed him, which he said was $50.

The following morning, McCline hitched his horse to his wagon and rode out to the Case cotton farm and watched as Rosa Tubbs and the other laborers picked cotton all day. At dinner time, the pickers began leaving for their meal. McCline then asked out loud about her promise to marry him. Rosa again admitted she had promised to do so, but that she had decided not too. McCline again asked about the $50 she owed him. Rosa replied the amount was closer to $4.50 and made arrangements with her employer to repay McCline that amount.

As Rosa was stepping through a fence, McCline yelled out, "Didn't you promise to marry me? Ain't you going back up yonder with me?"

Rosa replied, "No, I ain't going back up yonder anymore."

McCline then exclaimed, "I am going to kill you," while pulling out his pistol.

Rosa Tubbs then took off running with her arms up in the air. McCline caught up to her and fired the pistol into her back. The barrel of the pistol being so close that the flame set her clothing on fire. As Rosa laid on the ground and attempting to lift her head, McCline reached down and placed the pistol behind her neck and fired a second shot. McCline then returned to his wagon and rode back to Rosa's sister's house. Once there, McCline said, "I have broken Rosa's neck and I am satisfied she is dead. I have killed her and I am sorry I done it, but I had it to do."

Tried and convicted the case was afterwards appealed and the sentence affirmed on November 19, 1911. Judge Richard L. Monroe sentenced Dan McCline on February 24, 1912 to hang on March 29, 1912.

On the day of the execution, McCline confessed from the gallows and said he was ready to meet his God. His last words were, "Farewell to the world and everybody."

The *Galveston Daily News*, dated Saturday, March 30, 1912, provided readers with details of the crime and the execution at Marlin, Texas.

Jose Flores

Race/Gender: Hispanic Male **Age:** 17
Offense Date: November 4, 1920
Execution: July 21, 1921
Offense: Murder
Weapon: Pistol

Israel Jordan

Race/Gender: Black Male
Offense Date: November 4, 1920
Offense: Murder
Execution: July 21, 1921
Weapon: Pistol

Deputy Oscar Sharp when not patrolling the county, also performed the duties as jailer in providing meals to the prisoners housed in the Falls County jail. In November of 1920, prisoners began making plans for a jail escape, and turned to Jordan Flores to initiate the plan as he held a position as a jail trusty.

On November 4, 1920, the inmates decided to assault or kill the deputy if need be in order to facilitate their escape. At noon, the forty-year-old deputy carried the lunches to the cell run around known as the bullpen where the inmates were housed. After unlocking the door, trusty Flores approached the deputy to retrieve the meals from him to distribute to the inmates. As the officer handed Flores the meals, the trusty jumped the officer where the two men wrestled to the ground.

Flores then jumped on top the officer and held him down by the neck, while Israel Jordan had his arms pinned down and Pete Sanchez held down his legs. Flores grabbed the deputy's pistol, and shot and killed the lawman. Pedro Sanchez removed the jail keys from the body, but the keys were taken away from him by another inmate who threw the keys out the door, and sounded the alarm of the attack.

Jordan confessed that he and Flores had killed the deputy, and stated that Pedro Sanchez had no involvement. Sanchez was tried and found guilty of the murder and sentenced to death along with Jordan and Flores. The case was appealed to the court of criminal appeals. The higher court affirmed the decision on Israel Jordan and Jose Flores, but reversed the sentence on Pedro Sanchez.

On the afternoon of the execution, Flores had to be carried to the gallows as he was in such mental despair that he was unable to walk. At 2 p.m., the trap was sprung and fifteen minutes later the body was lowered. After the noose was removed from around the neck it was discovered Flores was still alive. Flores' body was carried back to the trap and dropped a second time. After suspending for ten more minutes, the body was lowered to the floor.

Israel Jordan walked next to the gallows, and in his last statement he exonerated Pedro Sanchez of having any connection with the killing of Deputy Sharp.

The *Dallas Morning News*, dated Friday, July 22, 1921, provided readers with details of the murder and execution.

Fannin County
County Seat - Bonham

Andrew Jones

Race/Gender: White Male **Age:** 40s **Offense:** Robbery/Murder
Offense Date: April 1844 **Weapon:** Firearms **Execution:** June 8, 1844

Harvey White

Race/Gender: White Male **Age:** 40s **Offense Date:** April 1844
Offense: Robbery/Murder **Weapon:** Firearms **Execution:** June 8, 1844

L. Wray
Also spelled as Ray

Race/Gender: White Male **Age:** 30-35 **Offense Date:** April 1844
Offense: Robbery/Murder **Weapon:** Firearms **Execution:** June 8, 1844

Mitchell

Race/Gender: White Male **Age:** 40s **Offense Date:** April 1844
Offense: Robbery/Murder **Weapon:** Firearms **Execution:** June 8, 1844

In April of 1844, a small band of Indians camped about two miles from L. Wray's house in Fannin County. When it was discovered that the Indians (three men and two boys) had horses, saddles, and deer skins with them, Andrew Jones, Harvey White, L. Wray and two men only know as Mitchell and Read conspired to kill the Indians and take their possession.

As the band was being fired upon, one of the boys ran towards the attackers and cried for mercy. Reed seized the boys by the arms and held him up high as Mitchell stabbed the child to death. The other child escaped, as did one of the Indian man who had been wounded.

After the murders, Mitchell was arrested at home, Jones and Wright were tracked by a posse of twenty men and arrested near Fort Houston as the two slept drunk. Wray was arrested after his return home from Shreveport, where he had been selling off his portion of the stolen Indian property. Upon his arrest, Wray confessed and implicated the four other men, but there is no record of Read ever being charged or apprehended.

Wray gave the following confession.

"Andy jones, Harvey white and Read came to my house and proposed to go kill a party of Indians, who were encamped about two miles and a half above my house on South Sulphur. At first I objected, but they insisted. We went and I prevailed on them to return. Upon our return we heard of Mitchell, and Jones observed that if it was the name Mitchell that he knew, he was of the "right sort." Jones went to Mr. Meatch's to get some corn; on his route back he met with Mitchell, and they came to my house and commenced talking about killing the Indians.

Again I endeavored to persuade them not to kill them, but to no effect – they started I went with them. When we arrived at the camp, which consisted of three men, two boys of the Delaware tribe, Jones shot on the men, Read shot another, both were killed instantly; Mitchell snapped at one and bent his gun by a blow upon the Indian's head, who ran off. They told me to pursue him, which I did, and ran about eighty yards, and then shot at him. When Mitchell came up and asked me which way he went. I told him to wait until I had loaded my gun and I would show him; we pursued him some distance. On our return we came back where a little Indian boy lay dead. I asked Mitchell who killed him. He said he caught him and read stabbed him with his knife. One Indian man, wounded, made his escape – also a boy, uninjured. The property taken from the Indians was twelve horses, four guns, three brass kettles, some saddles, and about forty deer skins all of which was equally divided between us – five in number."

A jury of twelve men was selected and returned a guilty verdict against all except for Wray, as the jury was undecided since he had confessed. The jury deliberated until the next day until an unanimous decision was reached, being guilty. The four men were then sentenced to death with the execution to take place the following day.

The Globe (Washington DC) dated Thursday, October 17, 1844 had the following short article of the execution.

Four men have lately been lynched in Fannin County by the most sanguinary process. Their names were Andrew Jones, Harvey White, L. Wray, and Mitchell, all lately from Missouri, and all notorious for their rascality before they left. The cause was for barbarously murdering and robbery of three friendly Indians. Upwards of two hundred persons attended the trial and executions. Three others named Benjamin Jones, Jewland, and Harris, were arrested and convicted of theft, and were made to hang the others, and ordered to leave the country in ten days.

Jim Burke

Alias: Will Clark, Jim Thompson, Wilson
Offense: Rape
Weapon: Physical Force
Race/Gender: Black Male
Offense Date: August 1, 1892
Execution: April 28, 1893
Age: 20

Sam Massey

Alias: Sam Winn
Offense: Rape & Murder
Execution: April 28, 1893
Race/Gender: Black Male
Offense Date: February 28, 1892
Age: 32
Weapon: Club

Jim Burke who later claimed that his name was Will Clark, was found guilty of raping Mrs. M. E. Clements, a fifty-one-year-old white woman who lived in Lamar County. The Clements' farmhouse was located nine miles southwest of Paris and Mrs. Clements was home alone on August 1, 1892, when Jim Burke arrived asking her for bread and water. When Mrs. Clements replied she had none, Burke grabbed her by the neck and choked her until she could no longer resist, and he assaulted the woman. Burke's case was moved on a change of venue to Fannin County where he was tried and convicted of criminal assault on March 23, 1893.

The day before the execution, Burke wrote the following letter to be published:

My name is not Burke or Wilson. It is Will Clark. I was born in Smith County, Tex. Don't know how old I am. Have been stealing and burglarizing houses and cars for several years. Never killed anybody. I committed the deed on Mrs. Clements by choking her down and holding my hands over her mouth. I did so because I wanted to. I had only been in Lamar County about a week when arrested near a house something near four miles from Paris.

Sam Massey on February 28, 1892, went to the home of William Smith who was a tenant on the Fitch farm located two miles east of Sherman. On that day, Massey arrived at the home and used a hackberry club to beat William Smith, his wife Elizabeth, and their two young sons, ages nine and seven, for the purpose of raping Elizabeth.

While Elizabeth laid unconscious, Massey assaulted the woman, and she died as a result of the injuries to her head. The crime was not discovered until the following day when twelve-year-old Elli Smith returned home from her grandfather's house, and upon opening the door she saw her two brothers lying dead. William Smith survived, but was permanently deaf as a result of the beating.

At noon of the day of the execution, both men refused dinner, but Massey accepted wine instead. Massey told a reporter, "I am nor afraid to die. Whiskey has put me here. It will put many another man in the same place."

Both Massey and Burke were given a new black suit, white shirt, black low quartered shoes and black hat for the execution. After Massey dressed in his new suit he said, "I tell you, I am a dude negro."

After both were dressed, the sheriff read the death warrant to each man. Both were then transported a half mile east from the jail to the pasture where the gallows had been built. Waiting at the gallows was an eager crowd of between 10,000 to 13,000 men, women and children to witness the execution.

On the gallows, Massey confessed to the crime, and told the crowd to take warning from him. Massey took hold of the rope, and told the crowd that the other end of the rope awaited for them if they did not heed to his warning.

After both Massey and Burke arms and legs were bound, Massey said, "Good-bye all."

Burke said, "Good-bye Massey, good-bye, good people."

The trap was sprung, and both men fell seven feet. After seventeen minutes, both men were pronounced dead and cut down. The remains were then placed in coffins, and buried in the potter's field.

The *Fort Worth Gazette*, Dated Saturday, April 29, 1893, provided a large article describing the double execution to its readers.

Dan Walker

Race/Gender: Black Male **Age:** 31 **Offense:** Murder
Offense Date: July 4, 1896 **Weapon:** Pistol **Execution:** May 28, 1897

Dan Walker was hanged on May 28, 1897, for the murder of his wife, Alice. In 1890 Walker married Alice Golden, and for the next six years, Alice and Walker would separate several times. The couple's home was located six miles from Bonham, Texas, where Walker made a living as a farmer.

In July 18, 1895, Alice told her husband she was going into town to visit her mother. Three days later when Alice still had not returned home, Walker went into Bonham to find his wife and to inquire what the problem was. Walker discovered that Alice was living with her mother in the suburb of Bonham known as "Sauktown," and working as a cook for the Tom Hackley family. Upset that Alice had left him again, Walker went to the courthouse and filed for divorce.

Later the couple reconciled with the help of Alice's father and they remarried in 1896. Alice however remained at her mother's home, while Walker remained at the farm, except for weekends. On the night of July 3, Walker had gone into town to be with his wife. During the night, a man arrived at the house drunk wanted to see Alice, and was told to leave. Afterward both Walker and Alice prepared for bed.

At 11 p.m., Walker was waken to see Alice was dressing and preparing to leave the house. When inquiring as to where she was going, Alice replied that it was none of his business. Walker accused Alice of wanting to leave at such a late hour to see the man that had arrived at the house drunk earlier. After Walker dressed, he pulled out his pistol from under the bed, and placed the weapon in his pants pocket.

As Alice was about to leave out the front door, Walker pulled his pistol and fired two shots at her. One of the two bullets hit her in the back. Alice then ran out the door, and crawled under the house. Walker chased after Alice and fired two more shots at her, with one bullet hitting Alice in the heart, killing her instantly.

Walker then ran a mile and a half from town where he attempted suicide by shooting himself. After coming to, Walker returned to town and surrendered to the sheriff. He was tried and convicted of murder in the first degree and sentenced to death. On January 27, 1897, the court of appeals reviewed the case and affirmed the court decision.

In preparation for the execution, Sheriff J. J. Reddling had the gallows built on the jail yard with a privacy fence surrounding the structure. On the day of the execution at 1:20 p. m., Sheriff Reddling read the death warrant to Walker. When being led out of his cell, the wife of Rev. W. Nichols pinned a bouquet to Walker's coat lapel.

Once seated on the gallows, Walker sang *Dark was the Day and Cold the Ground*, and *Where Once Our Savior Lay*. After a prayer and a third song, the sheriff told Walker he could make any final statement he wanted. Walker then spoke for ten minutes saying he was prepared to die. At the conclusion, the sheriff bound

Walker's limbs. As the black cap was placed over the head, Walker said, "Goodbye." Sheriff Reddling then sprang the trap and Walker dropped through the opening. The fall did not break his neck, and Walker strangled for seventeen minutes before being pronounced dead. After the body was lowered into a coffin, the remains were then transported for burial at the county poor farm.

The *Houston Daily Post*, dated Saturday, May 28, 1897, printed a full account of the crime and execution at Bonham, Texas.

Neverson Morris

Race/Gender: Black Male   **Age:** 30   **Offense:** Double Murder
Offense Date: April 22, 1899   **Weapon:** Ax & Knife   **Execution:** March 23, 1900

Frank White

Race/Gender: Black Male   **Offense:** Robbery & Murder   **Offense Date:** October 23, 1898
Weapon: Razor Blade Knife   **Execution:** March 23, 1900

In either November or December of 1898, Georgia Morris had separated from her husband Neverson, and moved to the town of Honey Grove, Texas, where she rented a cabin. Georgia supported herself and her three-year-old daughter Alma by doing the washing for Will Robinson at the town barber shop twice a week. Because of a recent outbreak of measles, her washing job had been temporarily suspended. On April 21, 1899, Georgia sent a note to Robinson requesting for him to come to her home so they could talk about her return to the washing. In reply to the note, Robinson sent Harvey Wallace to deliver the message to Georgia for her to come to Frietz's store to talk because he was tending both the barber shop and saloon, and he was unable to leave town.

Harvey Wallace arrived at the home after 11 a.m. and knocked on the front door and announced his presence. When there was no answer, Wallace peered through a window into the dark room, and could see the figure of a man standing in the room.

The man called out, "What do you want with the woman."

Wallace replied he wished to see Georgia. The person yelled back that Georgia had gone to Bonham on the cannonball. Wallace returned to town and told Robinson what he had been told. Robinson said something was wrong because he had been at the depot, and Georgia did not get on the 6:45 train.

At 2 p.m. in the afternoon, Robinson went to Georgia Morris's home and knocked on the front door. After not receiving an answer, he crawled through an unlocked window. Because quilts had been placed over the windows, the room was completely dark. After lightening a match, Robinson could see a figure lying in the bed, and pulled the quilt back to discover the bodies of both Georgia and Alma. Robinson ran from the home back to town to report the murders to Constable Jules Baughan and Town Marshal Dan Brown.

Marshal Brown located Neverson Morris and placed him under arrest. In searching Morris's clothing, blood was found on his socks, underclothing and under his fingernails. The marshal told Morris he was being charged with the murder of his wife and daughter, and warned him that any statement he made would be used as evidence at his trial against him.

Morris at first denied committing the murders, but then made a comment about Will Robinson. Morris said, "I have been living in hell as long as I can, and just as well be dead."

Morris then gave a statement that he and Georgia had quarreled earlier in the evening. At 4 a.m. in the morning Morris said he had gone into town to eat a steak. Afterwards he returned to Georgia's home and used an ax to strike Georgia on the head and cut her throat. When Alma sat up, he struck his daughter in the head with the weapon. At first he stated he murdered his daughter because there would be no one to take care of her, but than said he killed her to keep her from "telling tales."

Morris was tried and sentenced to death, and the court of appeals affirmed the lower court's decision on November 1, 1899. On February 14, 1900, Judge Chambers sentenced Morris to hang on the same day as Frank White.

On October 23, 1898, Frank White attended an African American festival in the town of Honey Grove. During the festival he had seen B. Johnson with a large sum of money, and invited him to stay the night at his home. Johnson accepted the invite and while asleep, White used a razor blade knife to cut across Johnson's abdomen. Before dying, Johnson was able to give a dying declaration as to White's deed.

On the day of the execution, both men were transported by wagon to the gallows erected on the outskirts of town. The gallows was surrounded by wire and armed deputies to keep the crowd of 8,000 from closing in on the gallows. When the religious services were completed, the sheriff gave each man the opportunity to make any last statement they wished.

White stepped up first and told the crowd he was innocent and killed Johnson in self-defense. White said, "I am ready to go and I hold no ill will towards any one."

Morris then spoke for fifteen minutes in which he said he was guilty, and was receiving justice for his crime. Morris said he felt no anxiety over his soul's future, feeling that God had freely pardoned his sins. He related to the crowd how he dreamed last night of being in a beautiful garden surrounded by flowers with his wife and daughter.

The *Galveston Daily News*, dated March 24, 1900, provided their readers with details of the murders committed by both men and of the double execution.

Fayette County
County Seat - La Grange

James E. Jones

Race/Gender: Black Male **Offense:** Murder **Offense Date:** December 24, 1875
Weapon: Pistol **Execution:** July 6, 1878

James Jones became the first man legally executed in Fayette County. He was executed for the murder of a man that occurred at a dance at High Hill on Christmas Eve of 1875. On that night, Jones shot and killed the man during an argument over dancing space at the dance. Jones fled from the dance directly after the shooting and was not captured until two years later. At trial Jones pleaded innocent and denied being the shooter in hopes he would not still be recognized. After his conviction and prompting by his attorney, Jones admitted to being the shooter.

On the day of the execution, Jones was said to have climbed the scaffold with a light, firm tread, bowed to the crowd, and made a few remarks in a loud, clear voice. Jones cautioned the spectators to take warning by his fate and avoid bad company and to control their passions. He said his sentence was just, and he was ready and prepared to die. Jones said he was a stranger to the crowd, but with Christ he was acquainted; and he could see the chariots of heaven coming to carry his soul to glory. Jones further said he forgave all his enemies, blessed and bade adieu to the crowd.

After the body was lowered into a coffin, the remains were interred at the city cemetery.

The *Galveston Daily News*, dated Sunday, July 7, 1878, provided a full account of the execution at La Grange, Texas.

Clay Ford

Race/Gender: Black Male **Age:** 24 **Offense:** Robbery & Murder
Offense Date: November 28, 1898 **Weapon:** Blunt Object **Execution:** July 20, 1899

Clay Ford was a cotton picker from Holman who arrived at LaGrange, Texas, on Saturday, November 26, 1898, without any money. Throughout the weekend, Ford approached townsfolk asking to borrow money, as he was penniless.

On Monday morning, November 28, Ford was seen loitering around the home of seventy-five year old Matilda Winston. Mrs. Winston lived with her six-year-old granddaughter, Ora Winston, in a small house along the Missouri, Kansas and Texas Railroad tracks in the town.

Ford went to the woman, and asked Mrs. Winston if he could borrow money from her. Mrs. Winston went to her bed and removed a rag from between the mattresses that contained about $20. At about 8 p.m. that night the bodies of both Matilda and her granddaughter were found severely beaten from the use of a fish plate and presumed to be dead. Ora Winston survived, but Matilda died five days later.

Deputy Will Loessin learned of Clay Ford's earlier attempts of borrowing money, and heard that Ford was later seen in saloons and gambling houses Monday before leaving town on a mule. Early the next morning, lawmen located Ford sleeping near Homan and placed him under arrest. On his person was $15 and some change, and on his jacket were spots of blood. The shoes he wore furthermore matched the shoe tracks leading to and away from Mrs. Winston's home.

On December 10, 1898, Ford was tried and two days later he was found guilty of the robbery and murder of Matilda Winston. The case was appealed to the court of criminal appeals on April 26, 1899, and affirmed. On May 27, 1899, Judge Teichmueller sentenced Clay Ford to death and scheduled the execution to take place on July 20.

On the night on July 19, Ford bade his mother and wife goodbye. At daylight, after Ford ate his breakfast, he dressed in a new black suit that was provided for him. During the morning, Rev. G. W. Townsend, spiritual advisor, read from the bible and sang hymns. Rev. Townsend asked Ford to pray with him. Ford dropped to his knees and looking up from his cell said, "Oh Lord, you know that I am innocent. Poor old Matilda, who was a good woman on earth, is with you now, and she knows I did not kill her. When I leave this sinful earth today, take my soul in a chariot of fire to the throne and let me sit by the side of old Matilda."

Once the prayer was completed, Sheriff August Loessin told Ford that a great many people had come to see him hang, but that the hanging would be private and only witnessed by a few with invitation. Sheriff Loessin then allowed Ford to address the people who had gathered outside the jail doorway. To the crowd, Ford then spoke with a clear voice and said:

> Ladies, gentlemen, and friends: This morning seems very, very, very beautiful. This is the prettiest morning of my life. This is the last day that I can stand and look you in the face and see the friends I played with and associated with. I am very proud this morning to see you all here; very proud to look at and talk to everybody this morning. I am here, sentenced to be hanged at a certain hour of the day, and the crime that I am accused of is a very brutish crime, very hideous. There was never a thought that run through this body that in my heart I could commit a crime like that. I want all of you to hear that. But today I pay the death penalty on the gallows for it and I am proud of it. I am in no way guilty. I look the whole world in the face and tell them that I am not the guilty man. I am perfectly innocent of the crime, and my soul is going where all crosses, trials and tribulations are over. They will all be over in a few hours. They will all be done with. I will be there where I can hear all. I will be out of the way. I am going to a place this morning where there are no liars, no disputing, no swearing. The days that I used to walk out on the green, I had a very bright life that I could see. I can say this morning with clean heart, clean hands, that I never ended a person's life, never put to death. I only had fights and scraps, and though I played cards for amusement, I worked hard for a living. They have accused me of killing old lady Winston. I went there and talked with the old lady, and she talked, and I gave her some pecans, and she was telling me what happened through the past week. Now, today, that I am standing before everybody, I confess that I am innocent of this crime, though I was picked up and convicted before the LaGrange courts without a sign of evidence.
>
> The man who committed the crime is out today, I must pay the penalty. I am willing and ready to go, because I know the soul will not be lost. They can cheat me out of the breath, out of this outward man, but this inward man, they cannot cheat me out of it. God takes that in hand; God rules that. Today I will be with Old Lady Matilda. Today I am going. Today I will be in her company. I will talk with her. I forgive everybody, and everybody that did anything for me I thank them wit the greatest gratitude. Today my lips will be chilled in death. It must be. I have got to go.
>
> The angels and archangels and God himself are waiting at the gates. I will walk bravely like a man; the sooner the better for me. I am glad to know that every man under the sun and every woman has got to pay the same debt. This is a debt that no man can get around. This debt has got to be paid and the day is coming when I will meet everybody, all these people. I will meet them in the great getting up morning, when the heavens will be split, when God shall walk out on the four wings of the wind. I will be there this morning. Feel in no way weak. Do not dread dying. Thank you for your attention.

Upon finishing his public statement, Sheriff Loessin led Ford back to his cell and read to him the death warrant. At the completion, Ford was handed a pair of white gloves. Ford said, "Wallace, tell all the boys to come to my funeral. It takes place at 3 o'clock this afternoon."

While being led to the gallows located in the back of the jail, Ford told the jail prisoners goodbye. Once on the scaffold, Ford kissed his father, shook hands with newspapermen and officers, and then thanked Sheriff Loessin for the kind treatment he was given while in custody. Once Ford was placed over the trap and preparations made, Ford turned to Rev. Townsend and said, "I am not guilty."

Sheriff Loessin sprang the trap at 1:15 p.m. and thirteen minutes later Clay Ford was pronounced dead. Ora Winston and her mother witnessed the execution.

The *Houston Daily Post*, dated Friday, July 21, 1899, provided its readers with the details of the murder and execution at La Grange, Texas.

Note: A fish plate is a metal or wooden plate bolted to the sides of two abutting rails or beams, used especially in the laying of railroad track. The hemp rope used for the execution was the same rope used to execute John Shaw at Cleburne on November 25, 1898. The rope was twenty-feet in length and had been especially ordered for Shaw's execution at a cost of $12 dollars, ($310 dollars at today's value of money).

John Boyd

Race/Gender: Black Male　　**Offense:** Rape　　**Offense Date:** June 16, 1905
Execution: January 8, 1909

On Friday, June 16, 1905, Mrs. B. A. Barsh was returning home from working all day in the field when a black man later identified as John Boyd attacked her in her yard. The man sexually assaulted Mrs. Barsh and afterwards fled. Mrs. Barsh reported the crime to her nearest neighbors who immediately notified the sheriff. Lawmen searched for a suspect, and one week later located John Boyd in Schulenburg, Texas, and was arrested on Friday, June 23. The officers afterwards took Boyd before Mrs. Barsh who identified him as her attacker.

On December 9, 1906, John Boyd went on trial for the crime of rape. At trial, Mrs. Barsh identified Boyd sitting at the defense table as the man who had sexually assaulted her. The defense then made an unusual request to the court asking that Mrs. Barsh be removed from the courtroom. The defense then attempted to bring discredit to Mrs. Barsh and her testimony by having Boyd change from the clothes he was wearing in court with another black man who had similar facial appearance. The other man dressed as Boyd and then took the seat Boyd had sat in, while Boyd took a seat on the opposite side of his attorney. When Mrs. Barsh returned to the witness stand, she was asked to point out John Boyd. Without hesitation, Mrs. Barsh quickly pointed out Boyd as the man who had assaulted her. The jury returned a verdict of guilty against Boyd and assessed the death penalty.

The case was appealed to the court of criminal appeals and on May 23, 1906, the case was affirmed. Attorneys then filed an appeal with the United States Supreme Court. The court dismissed the appeal for lack of jurisdiction. With the final appeal dismissed, District Court Judge L. W. Moore sentenced Boyd to hang on January 8, 1909.

Three years after the crime, John Boyd stood on the gallows where Clay Ford was executed. Boyd declined to make a last statement or receive any prayers from spiritual advisors.

The *Schulenburg Sticker*, dated Thursday, January 14, 1909, provided their readers with details of the assault, trial and execution.

Fort Bend County

County Seat - Richmond

Carrol Fike

Race/Gender: White Male   **Offense:** Murder   **Offense Date:** 1858
Weapon: Firearm   **Execution:** August 26, 1859

In 1858 Anthony Hanks operated a small store in Fort Bend County at a location known as Walkers Station. One day in the fall, Anthony Hanks was shot and killed while working in the store. Suspicion of the murder fell on Carrol Fike who was arrested and lodged in jail at Richmond. After Fike's sister and her husband R. Carlos provided an alibi during testimony, the case against Fike was dropped. Later R. Carlos returned back to the court and told the judge his conscience had been bothering him to tell the truth. Carlos explained that he and his wife had perjured themselves during their testimony to clear Fike of the charges.

When Fike was questioned and realized that Carlos had turned him in, he confessed to the murder and claimed that both Carlos and his sister had prompted him to commit the act, and that they both had promised to provide him an alibi.

Archie Gibson

Race/Gender: Black Male   **Age:** 35   **Offense:** Murder
Offense Date: November 25, 1884   **Weapon:** Knife   **Execution:** May 29, 1885

After several failed attempts to persuade his wife, Priscilla to return home with him, Archie Gibson armed himself with a knife and declared he would be bringing his wife back or he would kill her. While Priscilla labored in a field picking cotton, Gibson arrived and demanded for her to return home with him. After Priscilla replied she had no intentions to do so, Gibson plunged his dagger five times in her chest. As the poor defenseless woman fell to the ground, Gibson slashed her throat. Gibson then attempted to commit suicide by cutting his own throat and falling unconscious over his dead wife.

Gibson survived his suicide attempt and was later tried and convicted. On April 3, 1885, as he was about to be sentenced to death by the court, Gibson made a unique statement to the court. Gibson said that ever since he was seven-years-old he had been impressed with the idea that he would die on the gallows. Gibson said he frequently told his mother he would hang one day. Gibson declared, "The Negro race is a bad one, and I don't mind being hanged, no more than taking a drink of water, cause I always knew it would end this way."

On the day of the execution, Gibson walked up to the foot of the gallows and addressed the crowd:

> I am glad to see you all here. It is an awful thing to see a man hang, but it teaches you a lesson. My neck will soon be broken, let it be a warning to you. Don't commit a crime like mine. Don't violate any law. If you have a wife you can't live with, pack your bundle and fly. Do not kill her. I am going to Jesus. I will not die, but drift away.

Gibson then ascended the steps of the gallows and walked directly to the trap. He then told the spectators, "Goodbye." As the black cap was pulled over his head, Gipson asked that the trap be sprung immediately. At 12:22 p.m. the trap was sprung with the fall breaking his neck. Physicians present pronounced him dead twenty-six minutes later.

A reporter from the *Fort Worth Daily Gazette*, dated Saturday, May 30, 1885, wrote:

> *Since the day of his sentence Archie repeatedly declared that after he was dead he was going to induce his ghost to haunt his kinspeople, because they went back on him. He solemnly declared that his ghost would*

hang around their doors until the end of their lives and he would scare them to death. The colored ministers of the vicinity have assiduously attended the murderer during the past month, and under their guidance Archie experienced religion to a beautifying degree and when asked by a reported whether he was not sorry he had killed his wife, Gibson replied, "Oh, I have made that all right with Jesus. He has pardoned me." He protested vigorously when Sheriff Blakely offered to execute him in private. He said he was prepared to die; he "could see the glorious chariots being lowered from heaven to take him up." He wanted to be hung publicly, where he could talk to the "assembled multitude," as he had something to say to them, and he wanted every one that could to come and see him "go to Jesus on the 29th." The sheriff gratified his wish to be executed publicly.

Emanuel Morris

Alias: Emanuel Henderson
Offense: Rape & Murder
Execution: October 28, 1898
Race/Gender: Black Male
Offense Date: January 1, 1898
Age: 40
Weapon: Iron Rod

Near the town of Richmond, Henry Ellis lived with Ophelia Williams along with her five-year-old daughter, Fannie, who was blind. On the night of December 31, 1897, Ophelia left Fannie in the care of Ellis while she attended a New Year's Eve ball. After Ophelia had left, Ellis decided to go to the home of another woman for dinner. Afterwards when returning home, Ellis came upon Emanuel Morris on the road. Morris told Ellis he had just left Ellis' house and had seen an unknown man running from there. Ellis asked Morris to return back with him to his house to investigate.

Upon entering the dark room, Ellis struck a match and lighted a lantern. After doing so, the body of Fannie was found dead lying on the bed. Ellis turned to Morris and said, "Morris, did you do that dirty trick."

Morris replied, "Well, Ellis, if you won't tell, I will tell you all about it."

When Ellis attempted to restrain him, Morris broke away and ran. The next morning Morris was arrested at his home and returned back to the scene while a physician examined the body. The physician said out loud that he concluded the girl had died from being hit twice to the head and the body showed evidence of being outraged.

Morris replied, "Doctor you are correct."

Morris told the doctor that Fannie had been sitting next to the fireplace when he struck the child the first time to the side of the head. From the blow, Fannie fell forward on her face. Morris said he then struck Fannie a second time to the back of the head with an iron rod, killing her. Afterwards Morris said he had attempted to sexually assault the body.

Morris at first claimed in his confession that Ellis had been present, and it was Ellis who struck the girl the second time. After killing her, he claimed that Ellis and he both attempted to rape the body. While Deputy J. P. Stuart was in the process of transporting Morris to the jail at Richmond, he told the lawman he had lied earlier as to Ellis' involvement. Morris claimed he said those things against Ellis to save his own neck.

At trial, the district attorney closed his argument for the State by telling the jury:

> It was the lust of this wretch that caused the crime. After he had raped the poor blind child, he murdered her in cold blood; and, if he is permitted to go free, then God help your children and the children of this country. I will tell you the motive. After he raped the child she told him, "I will tell mamma." He told her, "if you do, I will kill you," and she repeated, "I will tell Mamma," and gentlemen of the jury, he killed her.

Morris was found guilty and received the death penalty. The case was appealed and affirmed on June 8, 1898.

Pete Autre

Alias: Spelled as Autrey
Offense: Rape & Murder
Execution: October 28, 1898
Race/Gender: Black Male
Offense Date: November 2, 1897
Age: Unknown
Weapon: Double Barrel Shotgun

Charlotte Bookman was a divorced woman who had a relationship with Pete Autre. Charlotte let it be known to Autre that she intended to move from Sugarland to Richmond. Autre in response told her he would rather see her dead than to have her move to Richmond. On November 2, 1897, Autre borrowed a double barrel shotgun from a friend telling him he intended to use the weapon to go duck hunting. Later that night, a person matching Autre's physical appearance walked up to the front door of Charlotte's home and opened the door. As Charlotte sat in her favorite chair, she was shot with number five buckshot to the side of the head and died instantly.

Autre was apprehended at his home, and his shoes were taken back to the scene. The track and deformity in the soles matched exactly to his shoes. The borrowed shotgun was examined. One barrel showed to have been recently fired and replaced with a number seven shotgun shell where the other barrel contained a number five and had not been fired.

Autre was tried and found guilty of murder in the first degree with the punishment assessed at death. The case was appealed and on June 20, 1898 the court of appeals affirmed the decision.

On the afternoon of October 28, 1898, Morris was led from his cell to the gallows first. After the death warrant was read, Morris confessed to the crimes, and thanked the officers for their kind treatment towards him. At 1:42 p.m., the trigger to the trap was pulled and Morris dropped five and a half feet and strangled to death.

Pete Audrey was led from his cell to the awaiting gallows while Morris's body was still suspended and being monitored by physicians to pronounced the body dead. While this was occurring the sheriff read the death warrant out loud. Upon completion of the reading, Audrey confessed his crime and then left instruction as to which relative he wished to have his hat and shook hands with those of the scaffold. At 2:26 p.m., the trigger was pulled and the fall broke Audrey's neck.

The *Galveston Daily News* dated October 29, 1898 printed an article describing the crimes both men had committed and the execution at Richmond, Texas.

Charley Green

Race/Gender: Black Male
Weapon: Stick
Offense: Rape
Execution: May 23, 1903
Offense Date: October 23, 1902

On October 21, 1902, Charley Green was released from a convict farm and two days later entered a house near the community of Duke in Fort Bend County. Once inside the home, Green located the homeowner's pistol and hid it outside. Green re-entered the house with a stick and struck the sixty-five-year-old housekeeper on top of the head and knocked her down to the floor. After threatening her with death, he raped the woman.

After the assault Green left the house, grabbed the pistol he left outside and fled into the woods. Once the assault was reported, Sergeant Boykin from the convict farm began tracking the fugitive with the use of bloodhounds. As the sergeant was passing by a thicket where Green was concealed, Green rose up from the brush and fired at Boykin, wounding him. Green again escaped, but was later captured and jailed at Richmond.

On November 13, 1902, Charley Green was found guilty of criminal assault and the jury assessed the death penalty. The jury also convicted him of burglary and sentenced him to twenty-five years with an additional five years for assault with intent to kill. After his conviction, Green was taken to the state penitentiary at Huntsville to begin serving his sentence until a decision from the court of criminal appeals reviewed his case.

On the day of the execution, Green talked to a crowd that had gathered outside the jail window and told them he was a child of God and wanted to meet all good people in heaven. Green said that it pained him to see colored people so neglectful of their own race; that he noticed that whenever one of them got into trouble they deserted the person, and that white people were left to look out for him.

At 3:30 p.m., Sheriff E. A. Pearson led Green to the gallows where he then read the death warrant to him. When the sheriff finished reading the court document, he asked Green if he wished to make any statements. Green told the witnesses he was innocent of the crime and said people had conspired against him. When the sheriff asked Green if he was ready, he became nervous and begged for mercy.

At 4:02 p.m., Sheriff Pearson sprang the trap and eighteen minutes later the body was cut down and placed within a coffin.

The *Dallas Morning News*, dated Sunday, May 24, 1903, provided details of the crime and execution.

Tom Jones

Race/Gender: Black Male **Offense:** Robbery & Murder **Date of Offense:** March 19, 1908
Weapon: Garden Hoe **Execution:** June 20, 1908

Tom Jones was executed for the premeditated murder of Morris Lemon that he had committed for the purpose of taking Morris' horses. While visiting with Morris for an hour, Morris dozed off to sleep in his rocking chair. Jones then used the steel head of the hoe to strike Morris in the head, killing him. To conceal his crime and in hopes of making Morris Lemon's death appear accidental, Jones set fire to the cabin. The death was believed to have been an accident, until the horses Jones was attempting to sell were recognized as those belonging to Morris. When Jones was arrested, he immediately confessed to the murder to the sheriff and gave the same confession before the grand jury. Jones told the jury:

I, Tom Jones, do make the following statement to S. J. Styles, district attorney of Fort Bend County: I have been warned by the said S. J. Styles that I do not have to make any statement at all and that if I do it might be used against me on the trial of this cause, about which this statement is made. Fully understanding the above I make the following voluntary confession to the killing of Morris Lemon and to burning his house and to taking three horses.

On Wednesday night, the 19th day of March, 1908, about 6 o'clock, I went to old man Morris Lemon's house and talked to him for about an hour. The old man was sitting in a chair and commenced to nod. I went outside of the house and picked up the hoe with handle and walked back into the house and struck old man Morris Lemon with the iron part of the hoe somewhere back of the head as hard as I could hit him. He dropped to the floor and I then struck him the second lick in the front of the head.

He was not dead till I hit him the second lick, which killed him. I dropped the hoe in the house and gathered some shucks and corn stalks; took them inside of the house and set fire to them and burned the house down on the dead body so that the people would think he had burned up, to hide my crime. The reason that I killed Morris Lemon was that I wanted to get his horses and sell them and get some money. I took two of his mares and one colt, took them to Rosenberg, where I offered them for sale for $30. I went to his house that night for the purpose of killing the old man and taking his horses. I was by myself. After leaving Rosenberg the bay mare gave out and I left the bay mare and colt in Mr. Wallace's pasture. I got a job from Mr. Wallace.

The next Friday I got Mr. Wallace's wagon to move my things. I did not get my things and was arrested on the way back.

In hopes of receiving a life sentence, Jones further pled guilty to murder during the trial that lasted one day and received the sentence of death.

Jones had requested his hanging be public so that his execution would be an example to the younger generation of what his crime has brought him. In the presence of a crowd of 2,000, Jones asked that his race make a living by honest ways. Jones requested the crowd to take up a collection for him to pay for his remains to be shipped to his home at Oakwoods.

Tom Jones was hanged with the same rope used for the execution of Felix Powell. The rope afterwards was requested for the execution of Monk Gibson to be held in eight days in DeWitt County.

The *Galveston Daily News*, dated Sunday, June 21, 1908, provided their readers with the details of the crime, trial and execution.

Freestone County
County Seat - Fairfield

George Solomon

Alias: George Wortham **Race/Gender:** Black Male **Age:** 34
Offense: Double Murder **Offense Date:** June 1877 **Execution:** June 28, 1878

George Solomon was convicted and hanged at Fairfield, Texas, for the murder of his wife and her daughter. The murders were said to have been committed during a fit of jealousy.

The *Galveston Daily News, Saturday*, dated June 29, 1878, provided the following short article of the execution.

Fairfield, Freestone County
Execution of a Colored wife Murderer.

Fairfield, June 28, via Mexia, 28. – The execution of Geo. Solomon, colored, took place at Fairfield to-day for the murder of his wife and step-child, committed one year ago this month. The murderer was about 35 years of age, of short, stout build, and possessing altogether a repulsive appearance. It is supposed that this was not his first offense of the kind.

At 1:30 P.M. the sound of his chain being cut came from within the jail, and at 1:40 he was led up the steps to the gallows, which was built in the jail yard. He proceeded to the gallows with a firm and steady tread, showing no outward signs of trepidation or fear.

A hymn was then sung, entitled "Show pity, Lord, O Lord forgive," after which the Rev. Daniel Moody, colored, prayed and offered a few remarks, the text being from the fourth verse of the tenth chapter of Romans.

The prisoner was then given time to speak, and his remarks were to the effect that he was innocent, and also that he was prepared to die, and wished the jury and judge to feel that he had no malice toward them for the execution of their duty.

Sheriff Robinson addressed the assemblage, saying that this was one of the most solemn occasions of his life. He was evidently much affected. He then adjusted the rope, and at 2:25 the rope was cut, at 2:32 the physicians pronounced life extinct.

It is estimated that there were 2,000 persons present to witness the execution.

Allen Towles

Race/Gender: Black Male **Offense:** Murder **Offense Date:** December 21, 1879
Weapon: Pistol **Execution:** March 26, 1880

On the night of December 21, 1879, Allen Towles arrived home drunk and immediately woke up his wife who was asleep in bed. Towles was angry at his wife for not staying up to wait for him to return home. When they started to argue about Towles coming home drunk and awaking her, Towles pulled his pistol and shot her five times. The burning powder from the discharge of the pistol caught her clothing on fire.

Towels afterwards walked to a neighbor's cabin, crawled into their bed, and passed out where he was arrested the following morning. He admitted to killing his wife, but told the officers he should not be held accountable for her death because of his intoxicated state at the time. Towles was tried and on the fifth day, the jury found him guilty and assessed the death penalty. Towles decided not to appeal the decision of the court.

Friends of Towles tried to give him their bible, which he refused by saying, "If there is a hell, I may have to go there. I will be sure to meet my jury if I do."

Towles walked from his cell to the awaiting gallows that had been built inside the jail in 1861. Upon seeing a childhood friend, Towles asked that he be a father to his children; second, that he forswear drinking; and lastly, that he never touch cards; as those two things brought him to the scaffold.

To the twelve witnesses, Towles said, "Colored people, I have only this to say; Take care of my two children; see that I am buried by my wife, and bring the children occasionally to our graves. Farewell." Towels further maintained that he was too drunk to remember shooting his wife, and should not be hanged.

At 2:14 p.m., the trap was sprung and Towles dropped four and half feet with the fall breaking his neck.

A reporter for the *Galveston Weekly News*, interviewed Towles two weeks prior to the execution. The interview was included in the Thursday, April 1, 1880, edition:

I was born in Alabama and was raised in Georgia. Came to this country when I was seven years old. Lived in Grayson county till '65, when I ran away from my mother and went to Freestone county. I never did anything mean except kill my wife, and I have been wretched every since then. I had rather die twice over than to suffer in my mind as I do when I think of her and my two little orphan children. Me and my wife went to Fairfield, the day of the night I killed her, to buy some things for Christmas. After we bought them, I got drunk, and she went home. Towards night I went home and went to bed. That's all I remember until after I had killed her. The witnesses said I went to bed with her. After I had been asleep a little while, she woke me up and called my name, and I told her if she knew me I would kill her. She answered and said, "Why, Allen, do you suppose I don't know you?" As soon as she said that I shot her. I am willing and I know I ought to die. I hardly know what to think of a hereafter. I have been treated very kindly, with only one exception; since I have been here. Whenever a woman comes in jail, the jailer jokes and tells her not to come near me; that I kill women. I don't like to hear this; it grates on my feelings. Otherwise the jailor is as kind as he can be.

During his last interview, Towles further said he had killed an Irishman one night, by dirking him to the hilt in the breast seven times at Bryan in 1874. At Waco, in 1876, he had exchanged shots with a white man and did not know if he had killed him as he fled the city.

Floyd Thompson

Race/Gender: Black Male   **Offense:** Murder   **Offense Date:** May 24, 1914
Weapon: Firearm   **Execution:** January 7, 1916

James I. Casey was a white farmer who had sold a horse to Floyd Thompson. After Thompson had not paid the balance of $55 as promised, Casey went to Thompson's home on Sunday, May 24, 1914, to discuss the debt. During the confrontation, Thompson shot and killed him. After killing Casey, Thompson dragged the body to a pond of water where the body was dumped into the water.

Once the body was discovered, the sheriff organized a posse of 100 men who searched the brush and captured Thompson. On May 31, 1915, Thompson was tried and convicted of murder and his attorneys immediately filed an appeal. On October 20, 1915, the court of criminal appeals affirmed the lower court's decision, and Thompson's hanging was et for December 11.

On the afternoon of the appointed day, Thompson asked Sheriff George Burleson if he would allow for him to speak personally with the crowd who had gathered in front of the jail. When the sheriff permitted the request and Thompson was taken to the front of the jail, Thompson jerked away and attempted to escape. Officers then had to forcibly carry him back to his cell. When the hour of the execution had arrived, Sheriff Burleson and six deputies had to restrain and drag Thompson out of the cell to the gallows located in the jail. Thompson had to be held by officers over the trap until the sheriff sprang the trap at 3:45 p.m.

The *Corsicana Daily Sun*, dated Friday, January 7, 1916, reported on the execution.

Galveston County
County Seat - Galveston

Henry Forbes

Race/Gender: Black Male   **Offense:** Burglary & Escape   **Execution:** November 13, 1840
Offense Date: 1839

Henry Forbes was the first man convicted and legally hanged in Galveston, but not the first man hanged there. Twenty-one years earlier in November of 1819, Jean Lafitte ordered the execution of Captain George Brown to be hanged for disobeying his order. Lafitte warned his pirate ship captains not to attack any American vessels, as he feared severe reprisal from the United States for any such attack. On October 28, 1819, Captain Brown ignored the ordered and attempted to attack an unarmed American ship near the Sabine River.

Henry Forbes was arrested for burglary and jailed. He escaped, but recaptured. Forbes was tried and although he was found innocent of burglary, the jury found Forbes guilty of escape from custody and sentenced him to death. Either offense under the criminal code of the Republic of Texas was considered a capital offense with punishment by death.

The *Brazos Courier*, dated Tuesday, December 1, 1840, provided background on Forbes in which he claimed he was a free slave.

Charles Henniker

Race/Gender: White Male   **Offense:** Robbery & Murder   **Offense Date:** 1843
Weapon: Mallet   **Execution:** December 8, 1843

Charles Henniker was convicted and executed for the robbery and murder of Benjamin Tyson. On the day of the murder, Henniker struck his partner in the head with a mallet. Believing he had killed him, Henniker dropped the unconscious man into a well. Tyson came to and struggled to climb out from his intended watery grave. Henniker then beat Tyson about the head with the mallet and held him under the water until he drowned. Afterwards, Henniker stole everything of value from Tyson's home, and then set fire to the cabin.

Upon Henniker being sentencing, the judge ordered that Charles Henniker hang until "dead as the devil."

On the day of his execution, Henniker rode to the gallows while seated on top of his coffin. While smoking a pipe, Henniker threw his last dime to the crowd. Once on the gallows, Henniker rejected the white cap being placed over his head. The drop did not break the neck, and Henniker strangled to death.

The *Northern Standard*, dated Saturday, February 17, 1844, provided details of the execution.

Jesse Hamilton Shultz

Aliases: John Schultz, Jesse Hamiltonand James Baker   **Age:** 44   **Race/Gender:** White Male
Offense: Robbery & Murder   **Offense Date:** January 10, 1845   **Execution:** June 29, 1855

Jesse Schultz was born near the Wabash River in Indiana in May of 1811, but raised by his grandfather in Green County, Kentucky, after his parents died while he was very young. His grandfather soon moved to Tuscumbia, Alabama and later to Purdy, Tennessee.

In 1835 at the age of twenty-four, Jesse Shultz traveled to Natchez, Mississippi, where he heard Texas militia recruiters encouraging men to come to the aid of Texas by enlisting in the Texas Army to fight for Texas' independence from Mexico. Schultz volunteered and was assigned to company A, First Regiment Infantry and served until the fall of 1837 when he was honorably discharged.

During his service, no one suspected Schultz of murdering his commanding officer, Col. Henry Teal on May 5, 1837. Teal had insulted Schultz during an Indian campaign and Shultz vowed revenge. On the night of the murder, Schultz quietly approached his commanding officer's tent and could see the outline of the colonel sleeping. Just as the sky thundered from a bolt of lightening, Schulz fired his rifle at the sleeping figure. The rifle ball struck Col. Teal to the heart.

Schultz later confessed to murdering his cousin, named Green, in 1844. Schultz had traveled to De Soto County, Mississippi, and told his uncle of an excellent tract of land he received because of his service in the Texas Army. Schultz convinced his uncle to allow his cousin to join him and settle on the land with him. The uncle agreed and provided Schultz and his son with horses, equipment, a slave and money for their journey.

During the trip to Texas, the two men drank and gambled most of the money away and therefore had to sell the slave for a horse and buggy. After arriving in Gonzales, Texas, Shultz and Green engaged in an argument and Shultz killed Green.

The murders that Jesse Shultz was convicted of committing and sentenced to hang occurred on January 10, 1845. At Gonzales, Shultz met Simeon Bateman and they quickly became friends with Bateman inviting Schultz to stay at his ranch house. In January of 1845, Bateman and his friend James Matthew Jett decided they would ride to Galveston for the purpose of taking a streamer to New Orleans to purchase slaves. Bateman asked Schultz to accompany Jett and himself to Galveston so he could return their horses to the ranch.

Bateman was reportedly carrying $6,000 and Jett $1,000. At Virginia Point near Galveston Bay, Schultz murdered both men, taking their money and other valuables then escaping on the New Orleans steamer before the bodies were discovered. For ten years, Schultz remained free until he was recognized at Walterboro, South Carolina. Schultz was arrested for both murders and returned back to Texas to stand trial.

On June 9, 1855, Judge N. C. Munger sentenced Jesse Shultz. Schultz was told that a pardon was beyond all hope and that the only hope of forgiveness was in a repentant heart before meeting his God. Judge Munger told Schultz, it is ordered "that you be removed from this place to the county jail whence you came, there to be kept in close confinement until Friday the 29th day of June, 1855, in which day, between the hours of 10 a.m. and 4 p.m., you are to be removed to the place of execution by the sheriff of the county, and hung by the neck till you are dead, dead, dead, and may the Lord have mercy on your soul."

On the appointed day, Shultz sat on his coffin as he was being transported by a wagon to the beach where the gallows had been built. While being driven, Shultz attempted to escape by jumping from the wagon, but was recaptured and bound. Once Shultz stood on the gallows, he told the 500 witnesses there was no God, and then confessed to the murders of Teal, Bateman and Jett.

The *Texas Ranger*, dated Saturday, July 14, 1855, reported on the execution, calling Shultz a "cold—blooded, cowardly murderer."

Lucy (Dougherty)

Race/Gender: Black Female **Age:** 50 **Offense:** Murder
Offense Date: January 3, 1858 **Weapon:** Hatchet **Execution:** March 5, 1858

Lucy was a slave who had been sold to Joseph and Maria Dougherty of Galveston. Slaves often took the last name of their masters as their own. The Doughertys owned the Columbia House Hotel at Strand and 24th street where they put Lucy to work. Lucy was said to be rebellious towards her masters, and a week prior to committing the murder attempted to burn the hotel down. Lucy on other occasions attempted to flee from her owners, only to be captured and punished by being placed in stocks. Stocks are a medieval device where the person's hands and feet are placed through openings between two boards and locked.

At 10 a.m., Monday morning, January 3, 1858, Lucy was working in the kitchen with two German girls named Ann and Mary Kiese. Maria Dougherty entered the kitchen and told the girls to go out and attend to a baby who was crying. As the girls left, Lucy asked for them to close the kitchen door, leaving Maria alone with Lucy. When Maria could not be found three or four hours later, a search was initiated and the body of Maria Daugherty was found in the cistern.

The investigation determined that Lucy had struck Maria to the center of her forehead with a hatchet and a second blow to the temple. Both blows were considered fatal. The body was afterwards dragged from the kitchen to the pump house and dumped into the cistern. When questioned, Lucy admitted to the murder, and said she would do it over again.

On January 8, Lucy was indicted for the murder and tried ten days later on January 18, 1858. Upon Lucy being found guilty of murder, Judge Peter Gray sentenced her to death with the date of execution scheduled to take place on March 5, 1858. On the day of the execution, Lucy was taken to the second floor of the jail where the gallows had been constructed. In the presence of the twenty witnesses, Lucy prayed to God for forgiveness. After the cap and noose were adjusted, Sheriff J. H. Westerlage sprang the trap.

Jasper Rhodes

Race/Gender: Black Male **Age:** 34 **Offense:** Murder
Offense Date: October 21, 1884 **Weapon:** Pistol and Knife **Execution:** May 22, 1885

Jasper Rhodes was convicted of the murder of his twenty-seven-year-old wife, Mary May whom he had married in April of the same year. The murder occurred on the night of October 21, 1884. At about 7:30 p.m. that evening, Jasper Rhodes and his friend Sam Wilson, visited the residence of a Mr. Tiernan where Rhodes' wife was staying.

During Tiernan's absence the two gained access to the rear yard through a side gate. Rhodes, hiding in the background, had Wilson go to his wife and ask for her to come out in the yard, as he wanted to speak with her. Not suspecting anything, Mary May stepped out into the yard to hear what Wilson had to say. When Mary reached the shadow of the building, Rhodes instantly stepped out from hiding and confronted her. After a few heated words between them, Rhodes drew his pistol and shot Mary May in the head. To ensure he had killed her, Rhodes slashed her neck with a knife.

Sam Wilson was arrested the following day but Rhodes eluded capture for several days by hiding inside outhouses during the day and under the porches of houses at night. While hiding, Rhodes contemplated committing suicide and wrote a note which read:

I heard before committing suicide on myself that Sam Wilson called my wife out for me to kill her, but he is innocent of the act. Jealousy was the cause. Jasper Rhodes.

The letter was found when Rhodes was discovered hiding in a yard under an up-turned boat on Post Office Street. On January 21, 1885, Sam Wilson was acquitted of the murder, but the jury took less than ten minutes to find Jasper Rhodes guilty of murder and assessed the death penalty. The case was appealed and affirmed by the higher court.

On March 20, 1885, Judge Cook scheduled the execution to take place on May 22, 1885, and ordered the sheriff to keep the execution private. Therefore the sheriff had Rhodes executed in the attic of the jail. On the day prior to the execution, Sheriff William Owens allowed more than 1,200 people to walk through the jail and past Rhodes' cell so they could view or speak with the condemned prisoner on his last day just to satisfy their curiosity.

Rhodes told reporters that he had not premeditated the murder of his wife, but instead had gone to the home where she was at in order to pick up his clothes. That night, Sheriff Owens became suspicious that Jasper Rhodes was going to attempt to cheat the gallows somehow. The sheriff removed Rhodes from his cell and had him placed in another cell so that the cell could be searched. When nothing was found, Rhodes was told to remove his clothing and try on his new suit of burying clothes. The sheriff searched the pants Rhodes had been wearing and in the watch fob pocket he found a tobacco bag. The bag contained powdered glass, which Rhodes intended to swallow during the night.

At 7:30 a.m. the next morning, Rhodes was served ham and eggs for breakfast. At noon Rhodes was led from his cell where he embraced his father and kissed him goodbye for the last time. Rhodes ascended the ladder that led to the scaffold which had been prepared in the attic of the jail. A hole had been cut through the ceiling over the stairway leading to the second floor. Once Rhodes took his seat on the chair over the trap, Sheriff Owens read the following death warrant.

> *The State of Texas vs. Jasper Rhodes, indicted for murder in the first degree, convicted, appealed and affirmed. In appearing to the court that the mandate of the Court of Appeals in this case has been returned and filed in this court, wherein they say: "this cause came on to be heard on the transcript of the record of the court below, and the same being inspected because it is the opinion of this court that there was no error in the judgment, it is ordered, adjudged and decreed that the judgment of the court below be in all things affirmed, and this decision be certified below for observance, wherefore we command you to observe the order of our said Court of Appeals in this behalf, and in all things have it duly recognized obeyed and executed." And it further appearing by the records of this court that heretofore, to wit, on the 21st day of January, 1885, the defendant was convicted and adjudged guilty of murder of the first degree, and his punishment fixed at death, according to the verdict of the jury, which verdict and judgment have been, as hereinbefore recited, affirmed by the Court of Appeals and their mandate sent down to this court as aforesaid, now, on this day, to wit, the 20th day of March, A. D., 1885, the defendant Jasper Rhodes having been led to the bar of the court by the sheriff and ask what he had to say in bar of sentence, says nothing, it is ordered by the court, in close custody, until Friday, the 22nd day of May, 1885, when he shall take the defendant to the place to be provided for the purpose by the sheriff, and between the hours of 11 o'clock a. m. and sunset of said day, in presence of such person as are allowed and required by law to be present, and execute the judgment of this court according to the verdict of the jury, by hanging the defendant, Jasper Rhodes by the neck until he is dead. The sheriff of Galveston county is further ordered to execute this judgment within the walls of the jail of said county if practicable; and if not, then in a place in the jail yard to be prepared by him for the purpose and as privately as it can be done, avoiding publicity, except so far as the law and necessity required. The clerk is ordered to issue all necessary process in carrying out this order, and the sheriff shall make return thereof, as the law requires.*

Sheriff Owens then said, "Now I shall proceed to execute you, Rhodes. If you have anything to say, then say it now."

Rhodes stood up and shook hands with his two brothers and ministers. Rhodes told the forty witnesses, "I want my relatives and friends to leave off bad habits and stay away from bad places."

As Sheriff Owens was about to place the black cap over his head, Rhodes asked his brother, William Rhodes to remove his gold ring from his finger and for him to give the ring to their mother. Rhodes last words were, "Pray for me."

At 12: 14 p.m.the trap was sprung, and Rhodes fell eight feet, which broke his neck. A black flag was then waived from the window to the outside crowd signaling that the execution had just occurred. The body remained suspended for twenty-two minutes before being lowered into an awaiting coffin with a glass viewing plate. Deputies afterwards opened the main hallway of the jail to allow the thousands of people who had gathered outside to walk past the coffin and view the remains.

The *Fort Worth Gazette*, dated Saturday, May 23, 1885, printed a full account of the crime and execution.

Edmund Shelton

Race/Gender: Black Male **Offense:** Murder **Date of Offense:** October 14, 1907
Weapon: Colt .41 caliber Pistol **Execution:** May 14, 1909

Edmund Shelton was tried and convicted for the shooting death of Ephriam Bass on the night of October 14, 1907. The shooting took place in the alleyway off 13th Street, between avenues N and M in Galveston, Texas. Earlier in the day, Shelton told witnesses that when his woman was released from the hospital, Bass had better stay out of his private affairs and not interfere any longer with the woman or he would kill him.

Shelton while armed with a Colt .41 revolver went looking for Bass on the day of the murder. Shelton located him in an alleyway, and when Bass saw Shelton coming towards him, he yelled, "Don't shoot me!"

Shelton fired his pistol at Bass with the bullet striking him to the head. Bass fell to the ground next to the curb in the alleyway. As the man laid dying on the ground, Shelton walked up to Bass and fired three more bullets into the body. Deputy Sheriff William Thomas, who was riding into town from the circus, heard the pistol shots and galloped his horse in the direction of the gunfire. As the officer approached the scene, Deputy Thomas came upon Shelton walking away while carrying the pistol in his hand. After placing Shelton under arrest, the officer checked the pistol cylinder and saw that four bullets had been fired.

The trial was held on July 21, 1908, with the jury finding Edmund Shelton guilty of murder in the first degree and sentencing him to death. The execution was scheduled to take place May 14, and was almost delayed for the lack of wagon drivers who were willing to deliver the needed lumber for construction of the gallows. The black dray drivers refused to drive the wagons to the county jail where the gallows were to be built for fear they would be haunted by the ghost of Edmund Shelton.

At 1 p.m. in the afternoon on the day of the execution, Governor Thomas Campbell sent a telegram notifying the sheriff that he would not interfere with the execution, and to allow the law to takes its course. As Shelton was escorted to the gallows in the jail, a newspaper reporter asked Shelton if he had anything to say. Shelton replied, "Nothing, I have been treated fine by Mr. Thomas and the other white people, and I am not afraid to die. I am confident of my salvation. People of my own race put me where I am, but it's all right; I have made it right with God. I am not afraid to die; I'm glad of it."

Shelton then bid goodbye to Sheriff Thomas and his deputies. After the cap and noose were adjusted, Shelton prayed out loud saying, "Lord, I am coming, make way for my soul; Lord be merciful."

Shelton then called out for Deputy Doherty who made his way to the top of the platform. Deputy Doherty took Shelton by the hand and bid him farewell. Sheriff Thomas asked, "Are you ready?"

Shelton replied, "Yes, Mr. Thomas, let her go."

As the sheriff sprang the trap, Shelton was heard saying, "Lord, I'm coming." Eleven minutes later Edmond Shelton was pronounced dead by the attending physicians and they announced the neck had been broken.

The *Dallas Morning News*, dated Saturday, May 15, 1909, provided readers with details of the murder and execution.

Gonzales County
County Seat - Gonzales

Frank Hill

Race/Gender: White Male **Offense:** Murder **Offense Date:** 1856

The first legal hanging that ever occurred in Gonzales County took place in 1856, when Sheriff A. D. Harris executed a man by the name of Frank Hill for the murder of a shepherd named Ben Weed. Both parties were white men and the execution created a great sensation at the time.

Other reports have Frank Hill murdering a man named John Oliver.

Joshua Robert Bowen

Alias: Brown Bowen **Age:** 28 **Offense:** Murder
Offense Date: December 17, 1872 **Weapon:** Pistol **Execution:** May 17, 1878

Two of the most publicized executions in Texas took place in 1878. The execution of William "Bill" Longley on October 11, 1878, in Lee County, and that of Brown Bowen in Gonzales. A lot of Bowen's notoriety came from being the brother-in-law of Texas' most noted desperado and gunfighter, John Wesley Hardin.

Bowen was tried and convicted for the murder of Thomas Holderman. On December 17, 1872, Thomas Holderman, John Wesley Hardin and Bowen had been all drinking at the Billings' store in the town of Nopal in Gonzales County. Holderman was drunk to the point that he stumbled outside to a nearby tree to lay down in the shade where he passed out.

Thirteen-year-old Mac Billings was outside at the time when he observed Bowen walk up to the sleeping man and shoot Thomas behind the head with his pistol. The next day Bowen returned to the Billings' store when William Billings confronted Bowen as to why he had to shoot and kill Holderman in the presence of his son. Bowen replied that his finger was already on the trigger and it was then too late by the time he had seen Mac.

After the murder, Bowen was taken to Yorktown and a bond of $2,500 was set where he remained until February when he was transported back to Gonzales. In March, Bowen with outside assistance escaped by cutting a hole through the floor of the jail and fled to St. Rose County, Florida. In 1875, Bowen married and fathered a child.

Governor Edmund Davis after the escape posted a $500 dollar reward for Bowen's arrest, which finally occurred at Escambia, Florida, on September 17, 1877. He was returned to Texas to stand trial on October 18, 1877. After the conviction, Bowen continued to maintain his innocence by claiming that it was John Wesley Hardin who killed Thomas, and that Mac Billings had mistaken him for Hardin. The conviction was appealed to the Texas Court of Appeals who affirmed the decision in March of 1878. On April 10, 1878, Bowen stood before the court and was sentenced of death.

The gallows were constructed outside in the jail yard between the jail and the jailer's quarters. The gallows was described as being seventeen feet six inches from the top beam to the ground. The platform was ten feet six inches from the ground, giving a fall of seven feet.

Sheriff A. T. Bass almost became the victim of his own gallows. Sheriff Bass along with Bowen and sheriff's deputies were standing on the platform, Sheriff Bass was standing directly over the trap door when Reverend Seale accidently put his hand on the trigger, which released the trap. Sheriff Bass quickly grabbed the platform railing, saving him from falling through the opening. Once the sheriff had recovered from his near fall, the death warrant was read out loud to Bowen before the crowd.

Bowen did not address the crowd, but his statement of innocence was read by Reverend Seale:

Fellow Being: Here before you stands a poor, unfortunate man who is about to suffer the extreme penalty of the law for a crime of which he is innocent. I am but now in the fair prime of life; am but 28 years of age, having been marked by the world as a bad man, owing to the company, I have been seen in. But, God knows circumstances over which I had no control placed me in such company.

In my lonely cell, as I recall the early days of my childhood and think of the many prayers of a kind and devoted mother, who while on earth watched my early career. – but, alas! God took her away, and I was left to take care of my sisters, who I sent to school, my father having gone to Florida.

The country was divided into parties who were killing each other. What was I, a poor, unguided boy, with no mother to guide his erring way, to do? For self-protection I had to stay with my friends. These friends showed me no bad example, but at the same time where looked on not as the best of citizens, and of course the world included me in that number. I recollect in m early days having been with my father. When near Helena we came to a place where a man was taken out and hung by a mob for stealing a yearling. His name was Lewis. With what horror did I, a boy, look at such a crime! J. Tomlinson, A. Strickland and J. Strickland came after my father to help take that man out of jail and hang him. My father would not go. Oh, what a curse these mobs have been in Texas ever since, and what a bad effect it has had upon me and many others! Nothing more nor less than such ahs brought me to what I am today.

I have been tried and condemned for a crime, as I said before, of which I am not guilty. J. W. Hardin killed Thomas Holderman, for the only reason that he was afraid of him being a spy for J. Tomlison, J. Helms, and W. W. Davis. He told me himself these men had sent Thomas Holderman to watch him. I started from my father's to go to Billings's store to buy coffee. J. W. Hardin went with me there. After we got to Billings's, Birtsell and Holderman came in. Holderman and I were personal friends. Hardin walked up to Holderman and asked him to let him have his horse to run a race. Holderman told him he had just come from Harrisburg, and could not run his horse. From that a quarrel ensued. I went one time and took Holderman away from Hardin in fact, several times. Holderman stopped under a tree. Hardin and Gip Clemens went into the store and commenced drinking, after which Hardin called to me out of the store. When he got out I asked him what he wanted. He told me he was going to show me how to kill a man. I told him for God's sake not to do that for there was no harm at all in him, and he was my friend. After the deed was done I came in. Gip Clements asked him if that was done right. Hardin told him yes, it was equal to our Kansas trip. Hardin took me out and told me that if anything was said about it for me to go to Clement's house, but went to Holderman's and told him I killed his son, and on that I was arrested.

This, fellow-citizens, is the truth. I am not guilty of this terrible-crime. Young men, beware of bad company, for this is where bad company will end. My request is to see that my body is taken care of. I thank you now for your kindness and your Christian consolations to me while in a felon's cell.

Judge DeWitt will assist you to carry my body to my father's place. I have full confidence in him. He is a friend which will carry out his promise to a dying man, for which please accept the earnest thanks of the unfortunate Brown Bowen.

My heart felt thanks to Capt. Lee Hall, Lieut. Armstrong, and their faithful followers, for the kindness they have shown me. They are doing great good for the country. May they ever prosper. My prayers are with them.

Good bye, all; I do hope you will all pay attention to these my dying statements; there has been no attention paid to them during my life. Farewell, all.

Bowen then called for John Holderman to come to the scaffold and asked if he believed he had killed his brother. John replied that he did based from the evidence. Bowen replied, "then you believe a doggoned lie," and that his last words would be that he did not do it.

After the white cap had been put on, Bowen asked for a little time to send a message to his wife. Bowen again maintained his innocence, and for her to keep their child away from bad company. The cap was replaced, and his limbs were then tied. Bowen's last words before the crowd of 4,500 was, "Oh, Lord, receive my spirit."

The *Lampasas Dispatch*, dated Thursday, May 23, 1878, provided a full account of the execution and printed Bowen's last appeal to John Wesley Hardin.

On Friday, 17th of May, I have to pay the penalty of law for your crime. John, you know I am innocent of this deed. I ask you to clear my name for my children's sake. John, you know you have to appear before a God who knows all, and can you stand before that great tribunal and look on your God and say, "I did not kill Haldeman?" You know you will have to say, "I John Hardin, did it, and allowed Brown Bowen to be punished on this earth for it," which, if you do, will be another of the dreadful murders which you will have to answer for.

Isaiah Walker

Race/Gender: Black Male   **Offense:** Murder   **Offense Date:** February 1873
Weapon: Rifle   **Executed:** July 28, 1881

Isaiah Walker murdered his wife Rena in February of 1873, and eluded capture until 1881 when he was arrested in Palestine, Texas. Walker and Rena had been married about one year when he shot his wife.

Rena was staying at another house and had sworn out an affidavit that her husband, Isaiah Walker had whipped her. Walker claimed the reason he had whipped Rena was because he had caught her in bed with another man.

Walker who had been tried three days earlier for assault, hid and waited for his wife to approach the house where she was staying. Just after dark Rena arrived while in the company of other women. Walker came out from hiding and confronted his wife. Walker asked if she had "swore a lie for another man."

Rena replied, "No, I swore you whipped me, and you know you did. I am sorry I did, but I will help you pay the fine."

Walker replied, "I don't want your goddamn money, you are free, I suppose, to do as you please, and I am a slave. Are you ready to go?"

Rena asked, "Go where?"

Walker replied, "Go the hell goddamn you," and raised a breech loading rifle. Thinking the weapon was a stick, one of the women begged for him not to hit Rena with the stick when Walker fired the rifle, and the bullet struck his pregnant wife just above the heart.

Walker then ran back to where he had been hiding and picked up a bundle of clothes, and fled. Seven years later, Walker was tried for murder and found guilty. The case was appealed and the higher court affirmed the decision on March 18, 1881.

On the day of the execution, 2,000 people gathered to watch the execution. At 2:45 p.m. Walker stepped up upon the gallows. Rev. Gregory and Rev. Mens read the scriptures and sang, *The Sweet-By and-By*, aided by Rev. Mens. When the song was finished, Walker called Griffin Anderson, his father-in-law, and asked him about his health and that of the family. Walker then said, "Get all you have in your heart against me out of it as soon as you can, for God's sake, for I have nothing against you, I love you."

Anderson replied, "I have nothing against you, only you killed my daughter."

Walker then said he had gotten forgiveness, and he had no fear. He had done his duty, had a clear conscience and was not afraid to die. He had asked God to be with him today and he had done so.

After shaking hands, Deputy Anderson placed the noose around his neck and drew the black cap. Sheriff W. E James threw the lever which dropped Walker eight feet and broke his neck. After fourteen minutes Walker was declared dead and placed in a coffin.

The *Galveston Weekly News*, dated Thursday, August 4, 1881, wrote, " Sheriff W. E. Jones deserves much credit for the care and humanity he manifested to and for the doomed man. "

Will Blackwell

Race/Gender: Black Male   **Age:** 20   **Offense:** Robbery & Murder
Offense Date: July 12, 1890   **Weapon:** Pistol   **Execution:** March 6, 1891

Will Blackwell lived with and worked for John Rainey and his young brother Lump Rainey. On Saturday morning, July 12, 1890, the boys woke early and decided to eat their breakfast without starting a fire in the fireplace.

At 8 a.m., John Rainey, Gus Jones and Jack Kent arrived at the home and all decided to walk down to the nearby creek and do some fishing. Staying behind at the house was Blackwell and Lump. Once at the creek, John Rainey and Gus Jones undressed to swim and play in the water. Soon afterwards Lump rode up to the water hole on horseback and said he was going to look for horses in the pasture. Jones decided to join Lump, but once they were in the pasture, the two separated. Jones heading east and Lump riding west along the fence line. Less than ten minutes later, Jones heard a pistol shot and started riding in the direction, when he heard a second shot. Jones then saw Blackwell with a pistol in his hand as he spurred his horse and riding in a full gallop away from a body.

A few minutes later while John Rainey was redressing from his swim, he heard the sound of a horse running full speed. He looked up to see his sorrel stallion being ridden by Blackwell who then crossed the creek and continued riding. Moments later, Jones notified John that his brother Lump had been shot, and was dead. John rode to his brother's location and found Lump lying along the west pasture fence and gasping his last breath of air.

John then rode to get his weapon from the house to discover the house had been set on fire and was fully engulfed. Returning to his brother, John found Blackwell's hat, a bundle containing three pairs of pantaloons, a coat, vest, socks and cuff buttons next to the body. John then realized robbery had to have been the motive for his brother's death as most of the articles belonged to him and had been locked within a trunk and he possessed the only key, which was still in his pocket. The locked trunk had also contained, two watches, fifteen cents in silver and a $5 bill.

Lawmen searched for Blackwell and found the stolen stallion in the brush. Nearby, Blackwell was found hiding and was apprehended. The pistol he carried showed to have been recently fired and was the same caliber as the bullet removed from Lump's head. Blackwell denied committing the murder, or sitting fire to the house.

At trial the district attorney argued that Blackwell had broken into the trunk, stole the articles and set fire to the house to conceal his crime and rode off on John Rainey's horse. While riding away, Blackwell unexpectedly rode up on Lump and murdered him. Blackwell was found guilty of murder and the death penalty assessed. The case was appealed to the higher court who found no error and affirmed the decision.

The scaffold used was built in the jail on the second floor. In preparation for the execution, the rope and scaffold were tested with the use of a 160-pound anvil.

At 1:45 p.m., Blackwell was brought out from the cell wearing a new black frock suit with a white collar and mounted the scaffold unassisted. After a prayer by Reverend Wadkins, the condemned man offered a short prayer for himself.

At 1:54 p.m. the black cap was placed over his head and as the sheriff asked, "All ready?"

Blackwell responded by saying, "Goodbye." The trap was sprung and Blackwell fell nine and a half feet, with the fall breaking his neck. Fifteen minute later the rope was cut and the body lowered into a black coffin.

The *Gonzales Inquirer*, dated Thursday, March 12, 1891, wrote that Blackwell's father was tried in the same court years earlier for the murder of his wife and was sentenced to life in the penitentiary.

Jim Barber

Alias: James Andrew
Offense: Murder
Execution: October 7, 1898
Race/Gender: Black Male
Offense Date: March 20, 1897
Age: 28
Weapon: Pistol, Hatchet, & Knife

On October 7, 1898, Jim Barber stood upon the same gallows on which Will Blackwell stood on March 6, 1891. Dressed in a dark suit, white shirt and white tie, Jim Barber's last words to the fifty witnesses inside the jail were, "Goodbye, I hope to meet you all in heaven."

When the trap was pulled, the drop broke his neck. After hanging seventeen minutes, the body was cut down, and placed in a coffin. Afterwards, friends took possession of his remains which were buried in the

Gonzales public cemetery.

Barber was executed for the murder and mutilation of his wife Patsy on March 20, 1897. On that day, Barber who worked as a butcher by trade, arrived home in the early evening and placed meat on the kitchen table he had brought home for their dinner. Entering the bedroom, Barber saw that Patsy was dressed in her finest clothes and was preparing to leave for a dance. Barber told Patsy she was not permitted to go which resulted in an argument. Barber angrily left the house, only to return minutes later with a revolver that he had borrowed from a co-worker at the butcher shop.

After Barber entered the house, he bolted the door shut and shot Patsy three times. Neighbor girls who were outside playing heard the shots and ran to the front door to find the door had been locked. The girls then went to a window and they heard Patsy begging for mercy, and crying out to the girls to break out the window. Barber closed the curtain, and threatened the girls if they did not go away he would hurt them.

One of the girls ran next door to Mr. Moore's house and reported to him what they had heard and seen. Moore ran to the front door, and he to discovered the front door bolted. Peering through the window Moore observed Barber striking Patsy's body. Moore called out for Barber to stop and to come outside. Barber responded back that he would after he finished.

Minutes later, Barber emerged from the house and showed Moore a scratch on his neck. Barber said Patsy came at him with a knife and he had no choice but to defend himself. Barber then ran back to the butcher shop and told the co-worker the same story he had told Moore. Picking up a butcher knife, Barber threatened to commit suicide by cutting his neck. The co-worker told Barber that if what he told him was true, then he should surrender himself at the jail as he would go free for defending himself.

Barber took the advice and walked to the jail and told the sheriff he had just killed his wife. In responding to the scene, the sheriff found Patsy's body lying on the floor near a hatchet, pistol and knife. It was determined that Patsy had been shot twice, her neck cut, and her head crushed from several blows from a hatchet.

On the day of the execution, Jim Barber walked up the scaffold when it was announced that he desired to sing a song he had written entitled, *There Will be somebody to Miss Me When I'm Gone*. At the conclusions of the song, Barber bade those on the scaffold a goodbye, and then looking down to the audience below he said, "Goodbye to all of you, I hope to meet you in heaven."

From the crowd, the response was, "Goodbye Jim."

At 2:32 p.m., the trap was sprung and after hanging fifteen minutes, the body was lowered into an awaiting coffin.

The *Dallas Morning News*, dated Saturday, October 8, 1898, provided readers with a large article of the murder, history of previous executions, and printed the last statement by Jim Barber which read:

MY EXPLANATION

I was married to Miss Patty Price on March 17, 1888. We lived happily together and shared each other's joys until the year 1896, when she began to receive the attention of other people, then she treated me with contempt and was somewhat unkind to me. She would neglect her home affairs, go from home persuaded by other people. Her whereabouts I did not know at the time. I was kind to my wife, oh so kind. She wanted for nothing in the world. I made every effort possible in making every convenience for her, and every person in town knows these to be facts. One child, a female was the fruits of our marriage. She was persuaded to leave me and the child behind and go from home by parties I took to be my friends, to San Antonio, where she and a man lived as man and wife for some time. Then her health failed and she sent for me for assistance, acknowledging her wrongs and promising never to treat me unkind again. I loved her with love that seemed to lift me to the very gates of heaven, and sent her money to come home. After some delay she came. We agreed and went together. I forgave her and considered her as dear to me as ever. We lived very well for a while. Then confusion began to exist again and I made up my mind to leave town for comfort, but by being persuaded by her and others both white and blacks I decided not to go and resolved to try again to live with her. Had I ever mistreated her I, of course, would not have expected any better, but heaven knows I treated my wife like an angel and every one knows it who knows anything about us. They can't say anything else and speak the truth but that I treated her well, supported her and tried to make her happy and life a pleasure. When she wanted money or anything else she always got it by making her wishes known and Mr. Scheck can witness these facts if he will let the truth from his lips. It is known by several that I have been threatened often about my wife by black people and have risked my life several times unaware of danger. She has often told other people that she was not afraid of me. I never had any intention whatever to do what I have. Could have done so plenty of other times. When my wife was in company with other girls, hugged up by men where I could see it, the men would make sport of me and sing "sporting" songs, giving hints to me and at the same time armed for me. I wanted to shun trouble and tried every way possible to do so. She knew I loved her and that is why she treated me as she did. I never did object to her going in respectable company but I did not want her to keep the company of those she was keeping and why I did what I have is not because of her going with such people. I would never have done so had she not first assaulted me with a knife. I was not thinking of anything of the kind. I was preparing to go to a ball. Had my clothes on my bed making ready to dress when she cut me with a knife. I having no idea that anything of the kind was going to happen, and when I got into this trouble all the people who knew about how I had been treated kept their mouths and would not speak the truth. Why didn't they keep their mouths before and be ladies and gentlemen?

JAMES ANDREW Alias JAMES BARBER.

Albert Howard

Alias: Albert Black **Race/Gender:** Black Male **Age:** 20
Offense: Rape **Offense Date:** October 27, 1920 **Execution:** March 18, 1921

The last legal hanging in Gonzales County took place on March 18, 1921, when Albert Howard was executed for the rape of a elderly white woman. Howard and Joe C. Nathan had been arrested for theft and carrying a pistol when they escaped from jail. The pair made their way to a farmhouse near Harwood, and on Wednesday night, October 27, 1920, Theresa Kuntscick who lived alone was attacked. The poor woman was gagged and bound to her bedpost.

Five days later, both men were captured at a railroad camp on November 1, 1920. On January 15, 1921, both men were tried for rape. The jury deliberated for twenty-four hours and found both men guilty. Nathan was sentenced to ninety-nine years in the State Penitentiary, but Howard's punishment was assessed at death.

As Howard sat each day looking out through the window of his cell in the direction of the courthouse, he began counting down the hours he had left to live. In frustration, Howard cursed the clock and predicted the clock would prove his innocence claiming the clock would never keep correct time after his death. Supposedly the clock never did, leaving people with the belief that Howard had placed a curse on the clock.

At 3:20 p.m. on the afternoon on the appointed day, Howard was escorted to the gallows in the jail as he smoked his last cigar. Standing over the trap door, Howard said,

"Gentlemen, this is caused by running in bad company. I am not guilty, Joe Nathan is the guilty one, but the law has to take its course. Goodbye, everybody."

The *Galveston Daily News*, dated Sunday, March 20, 1921, provided their readers with details of the crime and execution.

Grayson County

County Seat - Sherman

William O. Blackmore

Race/Gender: White Male **Offense:** Robbery & Murder **Offense Date:** January 24, 1869
Execution: March 26, 1869

John Thompson

Race/Gender: White Male **Offense:** Robbery & Murder **Offense Date:** January 24, 1869
Execution: March 26, 1869

William Blackmore and John Thompson were both arrested on Saturday, February 13, 1869, for the murder of a man never fully identified. The victim was only known as Wilson and said to have been from Rolla, Missouri. Both men were tried and convicted in February 1869, and each accused the other as the person who was responsible for plotting the murder. Both were found guilty of murder and robbery and sentenced to hang.

Thompson made the following confession from the gallows, which the *Galveston Daily News*, dated Wednesday, April 14, 1869, printed:

I am to die today, and my sentence is just. I desire to live, for life is sweet; and I can't say I am afraid to die, but I am not willing to die. As I pass off before you, however, and join the uncounted company beyond the flood, I desire to administer a warning to the young men of my country, that they may turn to good account:

I have lived long enough to attest from my own experience that a man's circumstances are inexorable, and that they make him what he is. No man is independent of the company he keeps; he may vainly think so, but before he is aware of it, that company, be it good or bad, had molded him into its own image. Young men, these words, issuing from the trembling lips of a dying man, ate worthy of earnest attention!

While yet a boy, I mingled in bad company, an I can see now, too late to improve the lesson it brings however, that my mind and morals took on a bias, that like the hand of unyielding destiny has led me to this sad and solemn hour of my profitless history. I played at cards and soon was led into gambling. I took the social glass with my friends, but soon I detected the presence of a fondness for the exhilarating stimulant. It grew into a habit with me, and not unfrequently I was beastly or widely intoxicated. I was an habitual and persistent Sabbath breaker; and often without the knowledge or consent of my parents, would steal off from home to play at cards, or fish on Sundays. I have lived a wild and wicked life. While he was going on, I was with very wicked company, and did many things along with my comrades, I ought not have done.

After the war was concluded by a peace, I went back to my home in Missouri, but I was pursued and driven away from home; from political differences and private prejudices, I could not live there in peace. I then came to Texas – thinking I would make this State my home; but not long afterwards, I went back to Missouri, but I could not stay. Last fall I returned to Texas and felt almost desperate. I had been to your State but a short time when I aided in the commission of the crime for which I am presently to suffer and die. I am deeply sorry that I did it, but I can't undo it now. As to Mrs. Mallow, with whom I was boarding, she is a good woman, and entirely innocent of any connection whatever with our crime. I thought for a while that I was safe in the wickedness I had done — that no one would accuse me of doing the deed; but somehow the eye of God seemed to be upon me, and my sin has found me out. I do believe that a man's sins, sooner or later, blood hound-like, will scent him up and hunt him down. I have been running in sin a long time, but it has overtaken me at last.

And now young men, as I turn away from you to die, let me beseech you to avoid drinking, swearing, Sabbath breaking and gambling, the sins which first start me down the hill of crime, amid the shadows of whose base I must surrender the life I am unworthy to keep. I hope none of you feel bitter towards me when I am gone. To give up the life I have forfeited is the highest price I could pay for my sins; and as the promised flowers

of a coming spring shall presently bloom over my sleeping form, as the perfume-laden breezes are to sing my only lullaby, as I can't now brush the tears from the cheeks of the widow and orphans whom I have helped to deprive—the one of a husband and the other of a father, and as I would live better if my life could be spared—I pray you do not send your personal hatreds into the grave after me. My friends, a kind but long farewell!
John Thompson.

Julius Toettel

Race/Gender: White Male **Age:** 32 **Offense:** Murder
Offense Date: September 22, 1878 **Weapon:** Butcher Knife **Execution:** November 13, 1879

Julius Toettel was a thirty-two-year-old Frenchman who settled in Denison, Texas, after his discharge from the U.S. Army. Soon after his arrival, Toettel began running a nightly tab for whiskey in Joseph Brenner's saloon. When Brenner presented the bill to Toettel for payment, Toettel refused to pay the tab. Brenner in return told Toettel to leave his saloon, and to never return unless he was returning to pay his tab.

During the early night on January 15, 1879, Toettel returned to the saloon and was quickly told to leave the bar by Brenner. When Toettel refused to leave the saloon, Brenner physically threw Toettel out of the bar and out onto the street.

Angered by his treatment, Toettel returned to his room at the boarding house where he was staying to retrieve a butcher knife. Toettel told the landlord he needed a light in order to sharpen his butcher knife to "cut out a man's guts out." Not satisfied after his attempt to sharpen the blade, Toettel took the knife to the town butcher and asked him to sharpen it. After the butcher finished, Toettel told the butcher, "If there is a dead man found the next morning, tell the people that Toettel killed him."

At midnight, Toettel returned to the saloon and walked straight up to Brenner who was tending the bar. A struggle ensued between the two men and Toettel pushed away from Brenner and ran out of the bar. Brenner yelled out that he had been stabbed, and fell dead two minutes later. Julius Toettel was apprehended three days later in the Oklahoma Indian Territory and returned to Sherman to stand trial for murder.

On the scaffold, Sheriff William Everhart asked Toettel if he wished to make a statement. Toettel replied, "No, I'm ready."

As the black cap and noose were being adjusted, Toettel murmured, "God, have mercy, God, have mercy."

At 2:10 p.m. the trap was sprung and Toettel fell six feet. The drop did not break he neck and he strangled for eleven and half minutes before dying.

The *Brenham Weekly Banner*, dated Friday, November 21, 1879, wrote of the execution and concluded their story by printing, "Texas needs more hangings, they have a wholesome affect on those who would commit murder."

George Smith

Race/Gender: White Male **Age:** 30 **Offense:** Robbery & Murder
Offense Date: January 14, 1891 **Weapon:** .45 caliber Pistol **Execution:** July 8, 1892

It was believed that the man using the name of George Smith who had robbed the Risenberg's saloon, and killed the Bells town marshal was using an alias name. On the Wednesday at about 10 p.m. at night on January 14, 1891, George Smith entered Sam Riseneberg's saloon located inside the Pacific Hotel armed with a .45 caliber revolver.

Smith walked up to the bartender, and drawing a pistol ordered all the money to be placed on the bar counter. Smith then ordered another customer to remove all the valuables from the pockets of the other saloon customers. Smith, not knowing at the time that the bartender was James Isbell, the town marshal.

When the opportunity arose for Marshal Isbell to make his move for his own pistol, the marshal jerked up his revolver, and fired a shot at Smith. The bullet missed its mark, and Smith returned fire. The bullet struck the marshal to the right side of the face, and exited through the back of the neck. Smith fled from the saloon, but was overtaken and captured by a citizen by the name of John Martin who brought Smith back to the saloon.

Because of talk among the angry citizens of the town for a lynching, Sheriff R. Lee McAfee transported the prisoner by train to Sherman for protection. The popular marshal lived for three days before dying of his wound on the night on January 17, 1891.

Smith was tried and convicted of murder and sentenced to death. On the afternoon of the appointed day at 2:08 p.m., doctors injected a one-fourth gram of morphine into Smith's arm.

At 2:18 p.m. Sheriff McAfee arrived at the cell to read the death warrant to the condemned man and once he finished reading the court order, Smith was led to the iron trap. As the black cap was being placed over his head, Smith said, "A fellow can't breath much in this." When the knot of the noose was being drawn about his neck, Smith said, "That's pretty tight."

At 2:28 p.m. the trap was sprung and fifteen minutes later the body was lowered into a coffin and released to his friends for burial.

The *Sherman Daily Register*, dated Friday, July 8, 1892, provided their readers with details of the murder and execution.

John Z. Carlisle

Age: 44   **Offense:** Murder   **Offense Date:** April 28, 1892
Weapon: Shotgun   **Execution:** May 12, 1893

Charles Luttrell

Age: 44   **Offense:** Murder   **Offense Date:** April 28, 1892
Weapon: Shotgun   **Execution:** May 12, 1893

In the early morning hours between 1 and 2 a.m. on April 28, 1892, John Carlisle and Charles Luttrell were accused of quietly placing a ladder up against the home of William T. Sharman and Carlisle climbing the ladder and placing a shotgun up to the bedroom window. While Sharman was asleep in bed with his wife and their infant child, Carlisle fired the weapon, killing Sharman.

John Carlisle was charged with murder in the first degree and Charles Luttrell as an accomplice to the murder. The execution took place on the north side of the jail by throwing the noose over a convenient gas jet. The men stepped out of their cells carrying a banquet of flowers and walked directly to the trap door. The sheriff asked both men if they wished to make a final statement.

Charles Luttrell spoke first:

"I don't know that I have much I care to say, but I do desire now to state that there had been no ill-treatment on the part of Sheriff Hughes and his guards, who have treated me kindly, they have been humane in every particular. I feel that some of the evidence against me has been manufactured, but I have no malice in my heart. I forgive everyone as I feel I have been forgiven."

He then turned to Carlisle and took his hand and said, "John shall we meet in heaven."

Carlisle replied, "I feel that we shall."

Luttrell turning back towards the witnesses and said, "I feel that my loss on earth will be my gain in Heaven. Sheriff let me thank you and ask you not to forget the little request I have made."

John Carlisle briefly said, "I haven't much I care to say, except to thank the sheriff and the officers for their many kindnesses. We have been treated nicely. I have nothing more to say."

The flowers both held were then handed over to an officer with the request that the flowers be placed inside their coffins. The black caps were adjusted and promptly at 2:18 p.m. Sheriff Hughes pulled the trigger sending both men down seven feet. Both were pronounced dead twelve minutes later. The bodies were afterwards cut down and placed on stretchers. With the black cap covering the dead men's faces, hundreds of people were allowed to view the corpses. Once the crowd dispersed, the bodies were placed in coffins with the flowers laid across their chests and released to the undertaker.

The *San Saba County News*, dated Friday, May 19, 1893, provided readers with details of the double hanging at Sherman, Texas.

Sidney "Sid" Spears

Race/Gender: Black Male **Offense:** Murder **Offense Date:** July 2, 1899
Weapon: Razor Knife **Execution:** June 18, 1900

Sidney Spears was a barber by trade and married to Emma Spears, but had separated because of issues of infidelity. On the morning of July 2, 1899, Spears went to the home of George E. Cook in Sherman where Emma was employed. While Emma was cooking breakfast, Spears entered the kitchen through the open screen door and cut his wife's throat with a razor blade. Emma ran from the kitchen and into the yard where she collapsed and died. Spears walked calmly to the jail and surrendered to Sheriff A. D. Shrewsbury. The sheriff asked Spears if he had purposely killed his wife. Spears replied, "That was my intent."

Spears was tried on July 20, and told the jury that he and wife had separated and had reconciled their differences. Spears tried to convince the jury that the death of his wife was accidental and offered an explanation. Spears said after he had entered the kitchen where Emma was working, his wife attacked him with a stove hook. Spears claimed he only drew his razor blade knife to scare Emma back. Spears went on to say he had accidentally cut Emma's throat after she had rushed him, and they had struggled.

The prosecution delivered the theory to the jury that Sid Spears had continuously treated his wife cruelly. For this reason, Emma had left her husband and took refuge at her father's home. Spears later convinced Emma that he had changed, and she agreed to return home with him. Once she returned back to the house, Spears again subjected her to cruel treatment and she left Spears a second time. It was then that Spears decided to kill her.

The jury not believing the explanation presented by Spears convicted him of the murder and assessed the death penalty. The execution was ordered to be held on June 4, 1899, after 11 a.m. and before sunset.

On May 31, Governor Joseph Sayers granted a two-week respite after receiving a request to commute the death sentence to life imprisonment from Judge E. C. McLean. Governor Sayers reviewed the application for commutation and made the following reply on June 15:

After a most careful examination of all the papers submitted to me I have not been able to discover a single fact or circumstance that would tend to excuse in the least the act of the appellant. The killing was absolutely without justification and the extreme penalty of the law will be none too severe.
    JOSEPH D. SAYERS, Governor.

On June 18, 1900, at noon, Spears walked out of his cell as a string band of black musicians played at his request, *Home Sweet Home*. After stepping upon the trapdoor, Spears said, "May God save my enemies."

After a white silk handkerchief was bound over the eyes and black cap adjusted, the trap was sprung. After the body was declared dead and placed in a black coffin, the sheriff opened the jail doors to allow hundreds of people to enter and view the body.

The *Galveston Daily News*, dated Tuesday, June 19, 1900, provided details of the murder and execution to their readers.

Wood Maxey

Race/Gender: Black Male **Offense:** Murder **Offense Date:** October 16, 1910
Weapon: Single Shot Shotgun **Execution:** August 9, 1912

On Sunday night, October 16, 1910, Wood Maxey attended the black Methodist church and was baptized. On his way home, Maxey entered the Crystal Café on Travis Street in Sherman. Ernest Johnson, the cashier asked Maxey to remove his hat. Maxey refused and took exception to the request and attempted to strike Johnson with a ketchup bottle. Johnson drew a pistol and hit Maxey on the head and then threw Maxey out of the restaurant.

Johnson, not giving it any further thought about Maxey, was outside the restaurant enjoying the fall air as he was speaking with a friend about his up coming marriage. Maxey had returned to the restaurant to get even with Ernest, and crept up to the restaurant carrying a shotgun. While hiding behind a telephone pole, Maxey raised the shotgun and shot the cashier in the neck, killing him.

Maxey afterwards ran and hid inside of an outhouse near his home and that is where Sheriff Lee McAfee and Constable Ross Stark arrested him early the next morning. The lawmen quickly transported Maxey out of the city to another jail for fear a lynch mob would storm the jail and hang him. Ernest Johnson was buried the next day in Greenville.

Wood Maxey and Sellars Vines (Sellers) were both hanged from the jail gallows on the same day, for separate murders they had committed in Grayson County.

Sellars Vines

Race/Gender: Black Male   **Offense:** Murder   **Offense Date:** September 27, 1911
Weapon: Pistol   **Execution:** August 9, 1912

Wood Maxey and Sellars Vines (Sellers) were both hanged from the jail gallows on the same day, for separate murders they had committed in Grayson County.

Sellars Vines, whom after escaping from the Dallas County jail, arrived in Sherman, Texas, by way of hopping on a train. On the night of September 27, 1911, two railroad inspectors reported to Constable Frederick Thomas Mounger about a trespasser seen inside a boxcar. Constable Mounger at the time was working as the night watchman for the Houston & Texas Central Railroad when he was alerted about the trespasser.

Constable Mounger responded and started checking the dark cars with his flashlight, but did not find Vines. As he turned his back, a shot rang out. The bullet hit the constable under the left shoulder blade and exited under the right side of the abdomen and he later died. The next morning Vines was captured six miles south of Sherman by Sheriff Lee McAfee, Chief of Police Henry De Spain, and Patrolman Will Corder.

One week prior to being sentenced to death, Vines attempted to escape from the jail the night of June 29, 1912. As the jailer was locking up the prisoners for the night, Vines ran past the officer and down the stairs. Another jailer heard the commotion and saw Vines running across the jail yard toward the horse corral and fired. The bullet struck Vines to the side of the face, split his tongue, passed through the mouth tearing away a portion of the jaw.

On the morning of the execution, Sheriff Lee McAfee entered the cell and read the death warrants separately to both condemned men. At the completion of the reading of the warrants, the sheriff said, "Boys, which one of you want to go first?"

Maxey answered with, "Its makes no difference to me."

Vines then spoke up and said, "Take me last, I want to stay here as long as I can."

The rope used for this execution was the same rope in the execution of Sidney Spears twelve years earlier in Grayson County on June 18, 1900.

Sam Jones

Race/Gender: Black Male   **Offense:** Murder   **Offense Date:** August 16, 1912
Weapon: Ax   **Execution:** October 16, 1912

On August 16, 1912, at 10 a.m., Sam Jones proposed to his ex-wife, Eddie Jones to return back to him. When Eddie refused, jealousy and rage overwhelmed Jones and he attacked his ex-wife by first choking her until she was unconscious. Then taking an ax, he struck the unconscious victim in the head. Jones was immediately arrested, and the grand jury indicted him before 3 p.m. on the same day.

On September 14, 1912, Jones stood before Judge J. M. Pearson of the 59th District Court to waive his appeal and receive sentence.

Judge Pearson: You understand that it will be the duty of the court to sentence you to be hanged by the neck, in accordance with the verdict of the jury?

Jones: Yes, sir.

Judge: You are willing now to withdraw your motion and waive your right to appeal?

Jones: Yes, sir.

Judge: You are willing for sentence to be pronounced?

Jones: Yes. I want one thing – of course I don't know how you all have your business arranged, but I want to be hung on the sixteenth day of next month.

Judge: I don't know whether that would give you thirty days or not. I will give you a longer time if you want it.

Jones: That is as long as I want.

Judge: You want to be hung on the sixteenth? It will be impossible. The law requires 11 o'clock the earliest time for a legal execution. Sam, you stand arraigned before the court for the purpose of having sentenced passed on you for the charge of murder. You are charged by indictment with having on the sixteenth day of August 1912, in the county of Grayson and State of Texas, having murdered your former wife, Eddie Jones. The proof and your own statement go to show that the only provocation she gave you was the refusal to marry you. You enraged and choked her into a state of insensibility. When she was unable to protect herself, or do anything to avoid being killed, you then cruelly took an ax and finished your bloody job by striking her in the head with the ax. You have been indicted by the Grand Jury, the court has appointed counsel to defend you, and you have been defended and every legal objection has been raised that is legitimate under the circumstances. You have filed a motion for a new trial, which you state this morning in open court, your wish to withdraw the same. You ask that sentence be passed. Have you anything further to say why sentence should not be carried into execution.

Jones: Her life was as sweet to her as mine is to me. I propose to take what you give me.

Judge: You asked that sentence be placed at that time, and it is in compliance with the law. It is ordered by the court what you be taken by the sheriff to the jail and on Wednesday, October 16, 1912, that you be hanged on that day by the neck until you are dead, dead, dead, and may the Lord have mercy on your soul.

Jones continued smoking his cigar throughout the sentencing, and afterwards shook hands with everyone he passed while being escorted back to the jail.

On the appointed day, Sheriff Lee McAfee asked Jones if he wished to make a final statement. From the gallows, Sam Jones said:

I haven't much to say, I am just a Negro and those who know me know that I have always kept in a Negro's place. I am guilty of the crime charged against me, and am ready to die; I do not fear to die. I hope I am going up yonder (pointing upward), and if there is any body present that has anything against me I ask for their forgiveness, and if there is one such person present, I wish you would come and tell me good-by; I want to tell you that I having nothing against anybody. This is all I have to say.

He then turned to Sheriff McAfee, Jailer Elatherly, Jimmie Gee and Arthur Vaughan, the last two having watched him ever since he was placed in the death cell, and shaking hands with each, said as he did so, "You have surely been my friends; goodbye."

As 12:11 p.m., the trap was sprung, and four minutes later the body was pronounced dead and released to the undertaker.

The *Galveston Daily News*, dated Thursday, October 17, 1912, provided readers with details of the crime and execution.

Carl Oliver

Race/Gender: Black Male   **Offense:** Murder   **Offense Date:** June 26, 1910
Weapon: Shotgun   **Execution:** April 16, 1915

Carl Oliver was executed for the murder of Robert D. Stanley at Mount Vernon, in Franklin County.

Robert who was a white man was shot-gunned to death when he attempted to protect Oliver's wife from being beat. Oliver claimed he killed Stanley in self-defense after finding Stanley in his house with his wife. The case was transferred from Franklin County to Grayson County on a change of venue. Found guilty of murder, Oliver appealed to the Supreme Court on the grounds that a black man should have the same rights as a white man as it pertains to the unwritten law of defending a man's home and honor of his wife. The Supreme Court ruled that Oliver did have the same rights and returned the case back to Grayson County for sentencing.

On April 16, 1915, the execution took place in the county jail with the witnesses only being lawmen or those invited by the sheriff. After Oliver refused to make a final statement, Sheriff Lee Simmons released the trap at 12:02 p.m. The neck was broken and the body declared dead in six and a half minutes.

The *Dallas Morning News*, dated April 17, 1915, provided their readers with a small article of the execution.

Gregg County

County Seat - Longview

Amos Ben Hadley

Alias: L. V. F. Franklin, Thomas Fields **Age:** 23 **Race/Gender:** Mixed Male
Offense: Robbery & Murder **Offense Date:** December 18, 1877
Weapon: Wood Clubs & Knife **Execution:** August 30, 1878

Diomed Powell

Race/Gender: Black Male **Age:** 23 **Offense:** Robbery & Murder
Offense Date: December 18, 1877 **Weapon:** Wood Clubs & Knife
Execution: August 30, 1878

The only legal hanging to take place in Gregg County was the double execution of Amos Handley and Diomed Powell that took place one mile east of Longview on August 30, 1878.

On December 18, 1877, Hadley, Powell and Nathan Reed went to August Reineke's Billiards and Saloon located four miles west of Gladewater. As the three drank liquor, Powell invited Reineke to shoot a game of pool with him. Not suspecting anything, Reineke accepted the invite, and while playing, Hadley struck Reineke inthe back of the head with a tree limb. After being struck several more times, Hadley cut Reineke's throat with a cheese knife. The three murderers stole about $50 from the cash box and fled on horseback.

When the three were captured, Reed jumped at the opportunity to save his neck from the noose by confessing to the crime and agreeing to turn State's witness against Powell and Hadley.

While awaiting his execution, Amos Hadley had the following two letters dictated.

LETTER TO THE BOYS,
The crowd I belong to:

Dear Boys – Remember how I stood to you from 1866 till now. Remember the life we have lived and how truly I have stood by you. Have often staked my life for the benefit of you all. Have broke some of the best prisons in the United States to relieve you. If it could not be done without blood spilt, we feared no man or anything. As it is, I can blame you in one respect. We were under oath never to be implicated with a Negro; but I am satisfied if you know the consequences of the case it would be changed, for the world thinks I am the head of the Reineke murder. But, boys, you know if I had been head of it there never would have been a Negro implicated in it. It was King's money, and good talk that led Negroes into it. My drinking, whisky and the love of it was the cause of my being there. Now, I have to be hung Friday, and will say, well boys, I am still a man. I have remained a man with you all through life and will remain so to the grave. I am willing to confess to the Reineke murder, because I think when a man comes to die he should confess what he died for. But, boys, as the day is at hand, I have not much to say to you all, but what I say more will be continued in prayer to God. Repent, think over my past life and have revenge for it as we did for the murder of Tom Fields. That will do for that. Now take down this.

Hadley then dictated a second letter "to the people of Texas," as follows:

TO THE PEOPLE OF TEXAS.

I have lived in Texas off and on ten years; been in every state. I am known as Ben Hadley, and by other names. When I first came to Texas there was no law; only mob law. Boys was getting mobbed over the state; some had cards pinned on their backs marked thieves, and some marked Black Republicans. We thought we would study plans to stop some of it. We raised a large crowd and organized it. Then we commenced getting revenge. We thought as they was making laws we should do the same. I had a brother mobbed close to Fort

Griffin. After this seven of us got on the track of those who did it, and got seven of them. We thought we were justified in killing them. There were several rewards offered for us. They began to get pretty strict after us, and we commenced to rob stages. (Who was your leader? Won't say. Was Bass among the crowd? Yes. Another question proved he never saw Bass. [Rep.] We stayed in Mexico and California three years, and I and two more came back to Texas. No one knew me, and there was no charge against me. I am condemned to die, but all the blood I ever spilt I had a right to spill. The people who tried me are supposed to be honorable people, but the jury that convicted me did not do it honorably. Why do I say this? Because the man who testified against me said he made the first licks on Reineke, and the doctor who testified said the two last licks was the death of Reineke. I do not blame the man who testified against me at all, because any man put on the stand, to save his life, will put his part of the crime on another. I blame no man on earth for me losing my life only my lawyer, Flannagan. I don't want anybody to hang me except Sheriff Durham and Flannagan. The sheriff did all he could against me, and controlled my lawyer. I don't want the stain of my blood on anybody except them two, for the stain of blood is such that it will follow me to the grave. Brown Bowen was hung innocently. J. W. Hardin did that murder. Hardin killed him because he was a witness against him in another murder scrape. I was with them half an hour before the murder. No one but Hardin had anything against him. Those murders that people are putting on Bill Longley God is putting on mob law. He is not guilty of the third of them. I was with him the day before he killed Anderson. He had a good right to kill him, for Anderson made the first attempt. Cattle thieves murdered Alex Rogers near Cross Timbers in Clay county; he was caught by them and hung. There was a card on his back, " horse thief." It don't make any difference how you die, by gallows or anywhere, if God is with you. I lose my life, but not honorably. Give all up into the hands of God. People think they are doing a great thing in hanging, but it is a small thing in sight of God. If I have to go I don't care how soon, as I suffer death most of the time. Well, that is all.

Upon finishing both letters, a Rev. Booth, who had been listening attentively, knelt down suddenly near the cell door of Hadley's cage, and said:

Ben, you have shown in your statement a spirit of vengeance and viciousness that proves you have not profited by my prayers. I have been prone to think you were getting penitent, that there was some hope for you, but now I despair; I grieve to say it, but I mourn to see you of such bloody state of mind. Unless you change, it is no use for me to come again. I bid you good-bye, for it is a brazen mockery for me to come here any more.

Hadley: Mr. Booth, I have nothing to say 'bout it. I say all them things to the world; they are not my feelings.

Rev. Booth (with some excitement): You can't with my sanction send out such statements as your feelings. There is no hope for you now.

Hadley: I think there is hope, Mr. Booth.

Rev. Booth: No, no; there is no penitence; you justify your crime.

Hadley: Sorry you think that way, Mr. Booth.

Rev. Booth: No, sir; you will go from the gallows to hell.

Hadley: Don't say that. I have been trying to get shut of this confession a long time. I hope God will hear your prayer.

Rev. Booth: My prayers avail not for such a spirit as yours.

Hadley: When I came to Texas there was the worst mob law in the world here. Got we boys started and . . .

Rev. Booth: I am imploring you, as your friend and minister, to turn while yet . . .

Hadley: If I had not listened to your prayers so solid for me I would have killed myself in here, and they would not have the pleasure to hang me.

Rev. Booth: It is loss of time to pray for a hardened man, who wants vengeance for his race.

Hadley: When the world was discovered; but I am sorry to hear you talk that way, Mr. Booth.

Powell: Booth, it is dia way wid me; I nebber was arrested for crime before.

Rev. Booth: Are you penitent?

Powell: I was in the murder party, but sorry for it, and know it was wrong.
If Reineke had to be killed by me he would never have been killed.

Rev. Booth preached to them earnestly twenty minutes, and then started a prayer, whereupon Powell and Hadley suddenly got on their knees, during which difficult process their heavy chains clanked ominously. The minister then went away.

The prisoners groaned piteously during the fervent appeal, and when the prayer was over tears were in the eyes of the men. Powell would have nothing to say to me except that: "De old man preached mighty solid, talked mightly strong."

On the day of the execution, Sheriff Durham swore in eighty men as special deputies to assist in the escort and crowd control. At 1 p.m. the prisoners dressed in white shirts, black pants and straw hats left the jail and were transported by wagons to the double gallows which had been built one mile east of town, on the slope of a hill. As both sat upon their coffins smoking cigars, an immense crowd of 4,000 followed behind the parade of officers to the scene of the gallows.

At the gallows, Hadley was the only who gave a statement. In a trembling voice, Hadley reiterated his statement in his letters and again said he was prepared to meet death, pleaded for forgiveness from men and God, even as he forgave all men. He said he was raised by a good woman, Nancy Kidd of Mississippi, and deserted her care for bad company. He reiterated his assertion that King, a saloonkeeper at Gladewater, hired him to commit murder, and referred to Powell at his side as being innocent of the crime.

The *Galveston Daily News* dated Saturday, August 31, 1878, provided a full account of the execution and interviews with both men.

Grimes County

County Seat - Anderson

William H. Roe

Age: 31 **Race/Gender:** White Male **Offense:** Murder
Offense Date: April 7, 1886 **Weapon:** Poison **Execution:** May 26, 1888

The only execution to have occurred in Grimes County was the hanging of William Roe. William Roe was an ex-prison guard, and former Huntsville City Marshal who was convicted of the killing of his wife, Jennie, with the use of strychnine poison while the two lived in Walker County. The motive behind the murder was a $2,000 life insurance policy Roe had taken out on his wife.

On a change of venue, the trial was moved to Grimes County. After his conviction, Roe made the claim that he believed the poison that had been used to kill his wife was intended for him by his wife's brother. Roe went on to say that the black men who had testified at his trial had been hired by her brother to put the strychnine into the coffee. Roe said, "That day, I did not drink any coffee, but my wife, being nervous did, and thereby obtained the deadly draught."

Three days before his execution William Roe prepared a public statement, which read:

May 23, 1888
To Persecutor's and Friends:
I will state here the parties that have persecuted me. I forgive for they know not what they do. Any good citizen would have done as they under the circumstances and the excitement, and I hope and trust that God will forgive them and I hope to meet them in a better world. It is fearful to think I am to be separated from relatives and friends under the circumstances, but a party convicted of a charge whether guilty or innocent is compelled to submit to the law. I have this consolation, that God has heard my prayers and I have no fear of death. I leave amidst my friends two children. If it was so I could take them with me, I would be contented, but I am compelled to be separated from them. Under the protection of God, I leave them and I trust they will be taught his commandments that they may have right to the tree of life and may enter through the gates into the city, and I hope if they are raised here that they will not be looked on with disgrace. If I have done any one any harm I ask their forgiveness. I have not got a word to say against any officer that I have come in contact with since I have been arrested. Most of my confinement was in Houston and I never was better treated than by the officers of Harris county, especially the jailer, Charles Wichman.
Signed, William H. Roe.

On the afternoon of the day of the execution, Deputy W. S. Neblett read Roe the death warrant from his cell. At 3 p.m., Sheriff Garret Scott and deputies escorted Roe to the scaffold that had been erected one mile south of town. At the gallows, Rev. Pharrar, spiritual adviser for Roe read his statement in which Roe declared his innocence of murder to the 6,000 spectators.

At 3:29 p.m., the black cap was adjusted, the trap was sprung and the drop of seven feet broke Roe's neck. Twenty minutes later the body was given to relatives and friends who took the remains and laid Roe to rest in the cemetery in Anderson.

The *Fort Worth Daily Gazette*, dated Sunday, May 27, 1888, wrote, "Roe's execution terminates a remarkable case in the criminal history of Texas, and, if his dying declarations should prove true, will end in one of its most remarkable and regretted tragedies."

Guadalupe County
County Seat - Seguin

Ed Wilcox

Gender/Race: Black Male **Age:** 19 **Offense Date:** August 14, 1892
Offense: Rape **Execution:** January 11, 1895

On August 14, 1892, after spending the day visiting with neighbors, Mrs. S. Herrescrap left for home where she lived with her husband, five miles from the town of Sequin. At a secluded spot, Ed Wilcox grabbed Mrs. Herrescrap, threw her to the ground, ripped her clothing, and assaulted the woman.

After the assault and when she returned home, she reported the assault to her husband who notified the sheriff. Sheriff Adam Seidemann quickly organized a posse in search of the suspect, and a deputy located Wilcox the following day and lodged him in jail where he was held until his trial and execution.

Wilcox was tried at the November term of the district court and found guilty. The conviction was appealed to the court of criminal appeals on May 26, 1894, on the argument that Ed Wilcox was either fifteen or sixteen years of age at the time the crime was committed and therefore he should be exempt from the death penalty. Other testimony placed Wilcox between seventeen or eighteen. The court sided with the state's argument and declared Wilcox an adult.

On the day of the execution, Sheriff Seidemann allowed Wilcox to sit at the entrance of the jail to shake hands and say his last goodbyes to friends and relatives. At 10:45 a.m., the hack arrived in front of the jail. The sheriff and three deputies along with Wilcox rode in the hack while heavily armed deputies followed on horseback to the gallows that had been erected two miles northeast of Sequin on the poor farm.

Arriving at the gallows, Wilcox was allowed two hours for his religious exercise and speech. Wilcox was asked if he believed the execution justified. Wilcox replied he did, and turned to the officers and thanked them for their kindness. Once the preparation for the hanging was complete, Sheriff Seidemann released the trap at 1:04 p. m., dropping Wilcox eleven feet, and breaking his neck. After fifteen minutes, physicians Anderson and Williams pronounced Wilcox dead. Two minutes later Sheriff Seidemann ordered the body cut down and released to friends for burial.

The *San Antonio Daily Express*, dated Saturday, January 12, 1895, provided a full account of the crime and execution at Sequin, Texas.

Ellis Misher

Alias: Blackbird **Gender/Race:** Black Male **Age:** 21
Offense: Rape **Offense Date:** April 13, 1899 **Weapon:** Large Rock
Execution: January 12, 1900

On the spring morning of April 13, 1899, Rosa Macha walked along the railroad tracks on her way home from church. Ellis Misher who had been following the unsuspecting girl, caught up to her and attacked her with a large rock. Misher severely beat Rosa about her head and body. While unconscious, Misher assaulted Rosa and afterwards placed her across the railroad tracks so the next passing train could strike and kill Rosa to make his crime look like a terrible accident. Luckily, Rosa was found before an approaching train had arrived.

At the trial Misher denied he had committed the crime even though Rosa pointed him out in the courtroom during her testimony. Misher was found guilty of criminal assault and sentenced to death. On the gallows, Misher asked for whiskey, which was given to him. Rev. Sheffield, a black minister, talked to the condemned man and asked if he had made his peace with God. Misher replied yes, and repeated that he was not guilty and he was going to die for another man's crime.

After Sheriff William Duke finished reading the death warrant, he asked Misher if he wished to make a statement. Misher addressed the witnesses and said:

> Well, gentlemen and boys, I am up before you and I want to tell you that you should try to do better. I am here on account of another man's crime. This comes from being caught in bad company. I want to warn you all to keep out of bad company for that is what brought me to this.

Rev. David Abner, Jr. went up to him and asked: "Do you mean to say positively that you are not guilty of this crime?"

Misher answered, "Yes, I am not guilty."

When asked whether or not he had considered the matter of death, he said: "I'm alright on the matter of death. Been making arrangements ever since I came to Sequin, and am ready to die."

Moments before the trap was sprung, Misher asked Sheriff Duke, "Mr. Sheriff, tell my grandfather at Eagle Lake, I will meet him in heaven."

The *Weimer Mercury*, dated Saturday, January 27, 1900, provided their readers with an account of the crime and execution at Sequin, Texas.

Albert Varner

Race/Gender: Black Male **Offense:** Rape **Offense Date:** October 27, 1911
Execution: February 16, 1912

On October 27, 1911, Albert Varner was a prison convict who had escaped after serving five weeks of a forty-year sentence for burglary. On this date, Varner raped a farmer's wife in Colorado County and was captured days later. The citizens of Eagle Lake in the mean time had offered a $350 reward, as did Governor Oscar Colquitt adding $250 for the capture of the rapist.

After Varner's arrest, he confessed to the crime and later pleaded guilty on December 13, 1912, and received the death penalty. The gallows were erected on the poor farm two miles from Sequin with the execution being held privately. At 12:42 p.m. Sheriff Phil Medlin pulled the trap, which dropped Varner to his death. In thirteen minutes, the body of Albert Varner was declared dead and lowered into a coffin. The rope and black cap were reported to have been used in four previous executions.

The *Galveston Daily News*, dated Saturday, February 17, 1912, provided their readers with details of the assault and the execution at Sequin, Texas.

Will Hemphill

Race/Gender: Black Male **Offense:** Rape **Offense Date:** April 13, 1913
Execution: February 26, 1915

Will Hemphill was tried twice and convicted of raping a fifty-six-year-old German woman in 1913. Annie Dittmar was out looking for her horse and passed by Will Hemphill twice. Once she had gone out into the pasture, she saw the black man approaching her. Although frightened, but not wanting to show her fear, Annie offered Hemphill a $1.50 if he found her horse and returned the animal back to her home.

Hemphill replied he did not want money, but wanted sex from her. Annie replied, "Oh God, what do you want with an old woman like I am." Hemphill grabbed Annie by the neck and dragged her into the brush where she was assaulted.

Sheriff John Neighbors located Hemphill at Kingsbury and returned him back to Sequin to stand trial. Upon conviction, the jury assessed the death penalty and the sentenced was appealed. On November 12, 1913, the court of criminal appeals sent the case back to the district court for retrial based on the closing statements made by the prosecuting attorney to the jury. In closing, the district attorney urged the jury to convict the man to prevent mob law, and told them if Hemphill was released, he could not blame the people from taking the law into their own hands. The attorney continued by telling the jury it would be better to convict

Hemphill than to turn him loose to give him the opportunity to rape their wives, daughters and sisters in a week or two.

On the second trial, Hemphill was again convicted and the sentence was affirmed on October 21, 1914.

The *Dallas Morning News*, dated Saturday, February 27, 1915, reported the execution had taken place at Sequin, Texas.

Hardin County
County Seat - Kountze

James Franklin

Race/Gender: Black Male **Offense:** Murder **Offense Date:** October 21, 1917
Weapon: Knife **Execution:** August 16, 1918

James Franklin and his wife Willie lived at Silsbee in Hardin County, but their marriage was a troubled one. On October 1, 1916, while Franklin was away at work for the Santa Fe Railroad, Willie decided to take that opportunity to leave her husband. When Franklin returned home and discovered his wife gone, he immediately assumed Willie had left him for another man.

On October 5, Franklin went into Silsbee asking people if they knew of his wife's whereabouts. Franklin approached T. Bonner and asked if he knew where he could find her. Bonner replied he had no idea and why would he want to know.

Franklin replied, "That goddamn bitch is gone, and I asked everybody around Silsbee where she is at, and nobody knows. If I ever find her, I am going to kill her."

As Franklin continued to search for Willie while making threats of killing her, several townspeople warned Franklin if he continued to hunt for Willie while threatening to kill her, he would surely end up in the penitentiary.

Franklin replied, "I don't give a damn what they do with me, just so I find her."

Franklin did find Willie in Orange, Texas, and on October 18 he went there after her. On October 21, witnesses saw Franklin leaving the train at the Fletcher depot with a black woman. The couple was last seen walking towards Silsbee, five miles away. At noon, railroad workers saw Franklin walking alone towards town carrying a bundle of clothes and a pair of women's shoes tied together hanging across his shoulders under his coat.

A week later, the townspeople began talking about how Franklin had gone after his wife, and that Willie had not been seen since getting off the train. On November 1, a search was organized and on that day T. Bonner and Matt Wilson located the decomposed body of a shoeless woman about 200 yards from the railroad tracks and half way between Fletcher and Silsbee.

It was determined the body was that of Willie Franklin who had died as a result of her neck having been cut. Because the corpse was so badly decomposed, the body was buried at the location where it was found.

Franklin was arrested directly afterwards and tried for murder before Judge J. Llewellen. At trial, Franklin pleaded innocent to the charge and took the witness stand in his own defense. Franklin testified that his wife and he had left Orange, and stayed the night at Beaumont. On the morning of the 21st, they both boarded the train to return home, but he claimed during the train ride he had gone to the restroom to put on a collar when Willie jumped off the train at Fletcher with another man. Franklin said this was the last time that he had seen his wife.

The jury did not believe Franklin's testimony and sentenced him to death for the murder. The conviction was appealed to the Texas Court of Appeals who affirmed the lower courts decision of January 23, 1918. On August 16, 1918, James Franklin became the only person legally executed in Hardin County.

Harris County
County Seat - Houston

John Christopher Columbus Quick

Race/Gender: White Male **Offense:** Murder **Offense Date:** Unknown
Weapon: Firearm **Execution:** March 28, 1838

David Jones

Race/Gender: White Male **Offense:** Murder **Offense Date:** November 1837
Weapon: Firearm **Execution:** March 28, 1838

John Quick was tried on Friday, March 23, 1838, for the of the murder of M. W. Brigham. The jury deliberated for one hour before returning a verdict of guilty.

David Jones was tried for the murder of Mandred Woods which he committed in November of 1837. Jones was tried on Thursday, March 22, 1838. After only twenty minutes of deliberating, the jury returned its verdict of guilty of murder and both men were sentenced to be executed the following Wednesday, March 28th between the hours of 9 a.m. and 4 p.m.

On March 28, at 2 p.m., both Jones and Quick were hung in the presence of between 2,000 and 3,000 spectators. After the bodies were suspended for thirty-five minutes, the rope was cut. Both Quick and Jones' heads were cut off so that the brains could be removed and studied for scientific purposes.

Both Quick and Jones were said to have been veterans serving for the Republic of Texas with Jones fighting at the battle of San Jacinto.

The *Telegraph and Texas Register*, dated Saturday, March 31, 1838, reported on the execution of both men.

Johnson

Race/Gender: White Male **Offense:** Murder **Execution:** July, 1855

The *Texas Ranger Newspaper*, dated Saturday, July 14, 1855, provided the following article.

DISOBEDIENCE TO PARENTS.

Johnson, who was hung in Harrisburg, just before the execution confessed the murder of his wife, and while he admitted the possibility of having killed Collier, said he had no distinct recollection of it. He had been wild and reckless from his youth up, deserting his home at an early age, and wandering to and fro through the land, leading a vagabond life. Without education, and beyond the reach of moral or religious teachings, deficient in intellect, and of vicious and intemperate habits, he led a brief and disgraceful career, and died an ignominious death upon the scaffold.

The first downward step in Johnson's career, and that which in all probability hastened his ruin, was disobedience to his parents; for according to his own confession he deserted them early in life, and has been an outcast, and wanderer from his home ever since. His parents, we are informed, are still living in Alexandria, Virginia, and are respectable citizens, and, members of the Presbyterian Church. He has also several brothers and sisters living, none of whom, however, "visited him while in prison," or were present at his death scene.

John K. Hyde

Alias: John Carne
Offense Date: February 1853
Race/Gender: White Male
Execution: July 11, 1856
Offense: Murder

John Hyde was accused and tried of murdering Charles Butler in 1853 in Harrison County and was sentenced to death. Hyde was not tried for close to three years as he had hid out throughout the state and later fled to Arkansas. He was apprehended there and and returned to Houston to stand trial. During his freedom, Hyde killed Levi W. Young on September 14, 1853, in Bastrop County, and was further believed to have killed five other men during this time period.

On December 24, 1855, Hyde was tried for the murder of Charles Butler. The jury deliberated seven minutes before returning a verdict of guilty of murder in the first degree. Hyde immediately appealed the decision to the Supreme Court, which affirmed the judgment of the District Court. On June 16, 1856, Hyde stood before Judge Gray for sentencing. Judge Gray asked Hyde if there was any reason why sentence should not be passed upon him. Hyde admitted that he had killed Charles Butler, but knew nothing of the other men for which he had been accused of. He expressed that those accusations against him had created prejudice in his case. Judge Gray then ordered that Hyde be executed on July 11, 1856.

The *Galveston Weekly News*, dated Tuesday, July 22, 1856, provided a short article of the execution.

Jake Johnson

Race/Gender: Black Male
Offense: Robbery/Murder
Offense Date: November 30, 1869
Execution: August 5, 1870
Weapon: Iron bar

In Houston, B. W. Loveland operated a small store on Fannin Street where he lived alone in the back of the store. On the night of November 30, 1870, Loveland had been cutting a side of bacon when Jake Johnson entered the store on the pretense of buying molasses. As Loveland bent down to draw a bottle of molasses from a barrel, Johnson struck Loveland twice to the back of the head with an iron dray pin, killing him.

The following day, the store appeared to be closed all day, but a door was ajar. A woman along with children entered through the door and discovered Loveland lying dead beside the barrel.

Authorities soon learned that Jake Johnson was bragging about being involved in the murder. Houston Chief of Police, Captain Davis and Harris County Deputy Sheriff Keeland quickly located Johnson and placed him under arrest. Three other men, Jules Mitchel, John Jamison and Doc Wheeler were also arrested and charged with being accessories to the crime. However, Jules Mitchell turned witness and charges against him and Jamison were dropped. Doc Wheeler weathered away in jail with remorse. He stopped eating and died in jail on March 17.

Tried and found guilty of murder in the first degree on April 20, 1870, Johnson was sentenced to death.

On July 2, 1870, Jake Johnson learned the Supreme Court had affirmed the case and taken before the district court judge for sentencing. The judge asked if he had to say. Johnson replied that two witnesses testified falsely against him, and that he was not guilty of murdering Loveland. Johnson told the judge, "My last words at the execution will be that I had nothing to do with the killing of Mr. Loveland."

On July 27, 1870, Jake Johnson was interviewed by a newspaper reporter and received his confession to the robbery and murder.

Reporter: I have come to get your last confession, and will take down anything you have to say.
Johnson: I don't want to be bothered now. All the time I've got I must give to my God.
Reporter: Well, you are going to die, and you should make some confession, it might warn others not to do as you did.
Johnson: I've said all that I can say. Now I want to pray.
Reporter: I have come to see you with the best intentions and hope you will say something. Where

were you born?
Johnson: In South Carolina, Beanfort district. I used to belong to Pillor Johnson; I came out to Texas during the war.
Reporter: I have heard you said you did the murder. Tell us who killed Loveland?
Johnson: I did it. Doc Wheeler didn't do it. Doc Wheeler and John Jamison persuaded me. We three made it up together to kill Loveland. They appointed to meet me on Monday night (29th November, 1869, to kill Loveland: I didn't meet them that night, but I met them Tuesday night – the next night; they were playing cards when I came to them. (Here the murderer suddenly broke off, and learned his face on his hands and seemed lost in painful thought.)
Reporter: Who struck the lick?
Johnson: I did.
Reporter: How many licks were struck?
Johnson: Only two
Reporter: What was Loveland doing at the time?
Johnson: He was standing up when I struck him.
Reporter: What did he do or say when you struck him the first lick?
Johnson: He started to holler. After the first lick he fell. After Loveland was killed I divided the money with Doc Wheeler and Jules Mitchel.
Reporter: Did anyone else strike Loveland?
Johnson: No. The other men didn't strike him. Nobody struck him but me. Now I don't want to say any more.
Jailer: You ought to tell all about it.
Johnson: No. I want to think on God. I do hope and trust I am going to a better world. Oh, let me pray to the Lord. (To the jailor.) I want all my friends to come and pray with me. I will say something when I come to be executed.

At noon of the day of the execution, the sheriff A. B. Fall emerged from the jail with his prisoner and placed him in a hack. The sheriff then drove the hack to "Hangman's Grove'" located southwest of the city, under the pine trees near the cemetery, where the gallows had been erected. Present was a crowd of 1,000 spectators. Johnson firmly ascended the steps to the platform while being followed by the sheriff, a jailer and minister, Rev. Sandy Parker.

Johnson first asked if his brother was present among the crowd. Johnson then told the spectators that he had a dream in which John Jamison or Jules Mitchel had appeared and pressed him to confess. Johnson said he committed the murder and he has made peace with God. Johnson said Doc Wheeler pressed him to take part in the deed, but he had at first backed out; but was persuaded, and did the crime alone. On the night of the murder he had gone to Loveland's store pretending to buy molasses. As Loveland was measuring it, he (Jake) struck him. Johnson said he killed Loveland, and nobody else had anything to do with it but him.

Afterwards the money from the robbery was divided between Doc Wheeler, Jules Mitchel and himself. He asked that no one in the crowd grieve for him as he was going home. Johnson wished to meet all on Canaan's happy shore. Johnson continued his twenty-minute speech by warning all young men like him, and said he was not afraid of the rope, and thought he would never come to being hung. Johnson said he hoped no man would hurt a hair on Jules Mitchel's head.

At the conclusion, a hymn was sung, followed by Johnson knelling before the Rev. Sandy Parker and received a prayer. When the prayer was finished, Johnson told the crowd farewell and the black cap was drawn over the face.

Flake's Weekly Galveston Bulletin, dated August 10, 1870, provided their readers with details of the execution.

Henry Quarles

Race/Gender: Black Male **Age:** 25 **Offense:** Murder
Offense Date: June 7, 1879 **Weapon:** .32 caliber Pistol & Iron Bar
Execution: June 11, 1880

Henry Quarles was a Houston barber, who had been separated from his wife for several months. On Saturday morning, his wife Rosa arrived at his home and Quarles accused her of stealing $25 from him earlier in the week. Rosa denied taking the money, which led to a heated argument. Quarles then threw his wife to the floor and pulled out a .32 caliber pistol, which he had bought at a pawnshop the day before.

Rosa screamed, "For God's sake don't kill me!"

The first bullet fired missed his victim. A second bullet struck Rosa in the hand and crushed two fingers. Quarles then killed his wife by firing two more bullets into her head. Not satisfied with killing his wife, Quarles used a heavy iron bar to crush her skull.

Immediately after the murder, Quarles fled but was arrested about midnight. Quarles told the officers he was crazy when he committed the shooting and that he was, "mighty sorry."

On the day before his execution, Quarles gathered all of his personal belongings, which he desired to keep with him. He then drafted a document which read,

The State of Texas, Harris County, - Know all men by these presents that I have this day placed in the hands of Rev. J. J. Clemens the sum of eight dollars and seventy-five cents to be held in trust by him for the benefit of my daughter Anna R. Becca Quarles, who is now a resident of Houston, Texas and of the age of four years. The above sum of $8.75 to be delivered to my said daughter Anna, with all interest that may average thereon, which she arrives at the age of eighteen years. This he signed, and it was duly witnessed by Messrs. W. W. Glass and J. W. Stacey.

Quarles was then moved from the cell he had been occupying to the death watch cell on the lower tier located in the main body of the jail. The following afternoon Quarles was led from the cell to the gallows for the sentence to be carried out. The Texas Old Guard Artillery and the Houston Light Guard were both called out by the sheriff to preserve order among the 3,000 people who had gathered.

On the gallows, Sheriff Cornelius Noble asked Quarles if he desired to make a last statement. Quarles replied, "No, Mr. Noble. I have got nothing to say against you. I have nothing at all to say. I am ready."

In the final preparation, Quarles began praying and said,:

Lord have mercy, and God of love look down, tender loving heart. You know my mind, and know my soul. Lord my Father, Thou said, knock and it shall be opened; ask and ye shall receive. I am poor, and weak, and needful. I can do nothing without a helping hand above. Father, Lord, make peace between me and all mankind. I am gone, gone my last road, I want to go no further. Remember me as you did the dying thief upon the cross.

Quarles then turned to the sheriff and his deputies and thanked them for their kindness, and bid them all farewell.

At 1:57 p.m. the noose had been adjusted and the signal was given to release the trap. Quarles then fell seven and a half feet to his death. At 2:15 p.m., Quarles was pronounced dead and lowered into a coffin.

Later that same night, the jailer named Paris was awakened by a loud sound that resembled a gunshot and prisoners screaming in terror. Paris grabbed his pistol and ran to the cells. The black prisoners screamed at the jailer that the ghost of Henry Quarles had returned to his cell and was "raising hell in it." Upon investigation it was discovered that Quarles had left a bottle filled with molasses in the cell. The molasses had fermented and caused an explosion sending glass and molasses from the cell and out into the corridor.

The *Galveston Daily News*, dated Saturday, June 12, 1880, printed a full article of the murder, capture, trial, execution and his history. In conclusion the paper wrote, "Thus has the law been satisfied and the majesty of justice been recognized, and thus has one of the coldest, cruelest murders committed for years, been avenged."

John Cone

Race/Gender: Black Male **Age:** 27 **Offense:** Rape
Offense Date: January 16, 1882 **Weapon:** Iron Boot Jack **Execution:** July 6, 1883

Mr. and Mrs. E. M. Scott resided near the ten-mile tank on the Galveston, Harrisburg and San Antonio road. On January 16, 1882, Mrs. Scott was home alone when John Cone arrived around 11 a.m. After approaching the house, Cone asked Mrs. Scott for something to eat, and asked her what time it was. When Mrs. Scott turned her head to look at the clock, Cone stepped forward and grabbed her by the arm and throat.

Mrs. Scott attempted to fight off her attacker and screamed. Cone reached down to the floor and picked up an iron bootjack and struck the woman to the head with it. After assaulting her, Cone fled towards Bray's Bayou. Mr. Scott and his father-in-law after learning of the assault rode into Houston and reported the crime to the sheriff.

On Friday, January 20, the sheriff rode out to Cone's father's house and after locating Cone placed him under arrest and lodged him in the Harris County jail. When Mrs. Scott arrived at the jail, Cone was lined up in the jail corridor with thirteen other black men for Mrs. Scott to identify her attacker. Mrs. Scott immediately pointed out John Cone. The prisoners were then told to change their clothing several times, and each time Mrs. Scott correctly pointed out Cone.

On June 22, 1882, Cone was tried and convicted of rape and assessed the death penalty. The conviction was appealed, but affirmed by the criminal court of appeals. Cone was then sentenced to death on April 27, 1883, with the execution to take place on July 6.

On the morning of the execution, Cone awoke and asked for both a glass of tea and a glass of whiskey, which were given to him. The previous night, a search of the cell by a jailer discovered a bottle of laudanum hidden in a jar of molasses. It was presumed Cone was intending to commit suicide during the night by overdosing on the opium.

Cone, wearing a new black suit and white gloves, was then led out of his cell to the jail tower where the gallows had been erected. Cone took his position over the trap door and knelt down. While Sheriff Fant read the death warrant out loud, Rev. Halsey Werlein provided a prayer for the condemned man. After receiving water, Cone spoke to the 250 witnesses and said:

> I am arraigned on the gallows today and stand as one ready for death. I want all within sound of my voice to remember that they, on the 6th of July, saw a poor innocent man put to death in the name of the law. I have made my peace and know that I have only a few moments to live, and I am glad of it. I hope to meet you all in heaven. I have spoken fully and truly, and this is all I have to say.

At the conclusion, Cone returned to his seat and a hymn was sung. Cone again asked for water, and Deputy Glasscock brought it to him. At the end of the song, Cone's hands and feet were bound with cords. Cone then said out loud, "Isn't this a horrible sight, and don't it make you all sad? Let it be a lesson to you all."

While awaiting his the drop, Cone said, "I want all in the sound of my voice, both white and black, to take warning from my fearful fate."

He then took a swallow of water. Sheriff Fant asked Cone if he had anything more to say and he replied, "No."

At 12:17 p.m. the black cap was adjusted and a minute later the sheriff adjusted the noose around the neck. Sheriff Fant pulled the lever, that dropped John Cone nine feet. The drop did not break the neck and Cone strangled to death. After thirty minutes, the rope was cut and the body lowered. Because Cone's parents refused to take possession of the remains, the body was turned over to the undertaker to be buried.

A reporter from the *Fort Worth Daily Gazette* interviewed John Cone at the jail and printed the story in the Saturday edition, July 7, 1883:

> *I am not yet twenty-six years old, nor do I know exactly how old I am, but think I am near twenty-three or twenty-four years of age. I have parents living in the outer part of town. They have not been to see me for three or four weeks. I don't think that they or anybody are making any effort to get me pardoned or to procure my release by any means. I have an aunt who visited me the day before yesterday. Rev. Dr. Werlein has been to see me several times and we have talked about religion. I feel that I am a member of the church now. I was baptized*

in the Methodist Episcopal church when a boy. I did not live up to the rules of the church after it.

Since the time that the decision of the criminal court has affirmed by the court of appeals I have been trying to lead a better life and make peace with my God. I don't see any possible way of evading the terrible sentence that has been passed upon me. I suppose I have some desperate hopes of escape.

If the house were to fall or be blown away, or by some supernatural power the doors be thrown open, I might escape. These are accidents that my hope rests upon. I am not guilty of committing the deed or which I have been convicted. I did not have a fair trial. I was not near ten-miles tank when the deed was committed. My rest is very uncertain. Some nights I don't sleep at all, and I never sleep in the day time. During sleepless hours I sing sometimes, and walk up and down my cell and talk to myself and then pray. I would rather have it daylight than darkness. I feel more miserable at night than during the day. I pray three or four times a day; sometimes more and sometimes less. I pray just whenever I feel like it. I have no set hours of prayer. I can't write, but can read a little. The ministers have given me a prayer book, and Bible and catechism. I read them a little at times. No colored minister has visited me lately. Dr. Werlein comes down oftener than any one else and talks to me about my future. It is a comfort to have him come. He remains fifteen or twenty minutes when he comes. I don't think it is necessary that he should come any oftener than he does.

I believe I will go to heaven when I die. I believe so because I am innocent of the crime charged against me. I will say on the gallows that I am not guilty. I don't think that I will make any speech from the gallows. I don't know that my speech would be of benefit to anybody if I should say anything. I feel without heart during my waking hours at night, but when I think about my going to heaven, it consoles me some. The thought of dying is terrible. I shudder to think of being killed. My terror does not arise from what comes after death, but from undergoing the operation of having my life taken away from me.

Burke Mitchell

Race/Gender: Black Male **Age:** 36 **Offense:** Murder
Offense Date: June 4, 1888 **Weapon:** Knife & Shovel **Execution:** August 31, 1888

Mitchell and his wife Annie Mitchell had separated for some time, when on the morning of June 4, 1888, Burke confronted Annie because he wanted her to come back to him.

At about 9 a.m. that morning Annie was walking on the sidewalk along side of the First Baptist Church at Fannin and Rusk Street carrying a basket of clothes. Mitchell confronted Annie about moving back in with him. When Annie refused and told him she would no longer listen to his talk, Mitchell pulled out a long bladed knife and began stabbing Annie in the head and chest.

Annie took off running screaming, "He is killing me!"

Mitchell caught her by the arm, and slung Annie up against the wall of the church. After Annie collapsed on the ground, Mitchell knelt down on top of her prostrated form and continued stabbing her in the head and neck.

A man named Andress seeing the assault taking place ran up and struck Mitchell with his fist and pulled him off of Annie until he saw the bloody knife in his hand and backed away. Mitchell then grabbed a spade away from another man who had intended to use the shovel as a weapon to stop the attack.

Annie in the mean time had gotten up and was staggering out onto the street when Mitchell ran up behind her and struck her in the head with the spade. Mitchell continued striking her head until Roland White arrived on the scene and put his pistol up to Mitchell's head and threatened to shoot him if he raised the shovel once more.

The knife blade, which was three inches in length and one inch wide, had broken off near the knife handle with the blade lodging deep inside her body. The handle and broken blade Mitchell held in his hand was bent and curled from striking Annie so violently to the head. With the pistol pointed at his head, Mitchell was walked to the sheriff and jailed.

In asking why he had murdered his wife, Mitchell replied, "Because I was jealous of Dan Carvin and George Ridley. I asked her this morning if she would not come and again live with me, and her answers were so short they made me mad and I stabbed her."

When asked, "Don't you know you will hang for this?" Mitchell said, "Yes, but I am satisfied. I knew I would go to Huntsville as soon as I struck her with the knife, but she made me so damned mad I didn't care, and I felt like I might as well finish up the job and go up for something good, so I finished her."

On June 21, Mitchell was arraigned and through his attorney, William P. Hamblen, pleaded guilty to murder in the first degree. The jury returned a verdict of guilty and assessed the penalty at death. Judge Cook passed sentence upon Mitchell and set the day for his execution for Friday, August 31, 1886.

The scaffold was the same one used in in the execution of John Cone. The scaffold stood in the jail's tower room that was sixty by thirty, and twenty-feet high and allowed a drop of eight feet. The gallows itself was eight feet long by six feet wide, with the center trap door being a four feet square. Bolts held the trap door in place until released by a lever. Only those with passes were allowed into the tower to witness the event.

On the morning of the execution Sheriff George Ellis read the death warrant to the doomed man in his cell. Seven minutes later Mitchell who was dressed in a new black suit and wearing white gloves climbed the stairs leading to the tower. Sheriff Ellis asked Mitchell if he had anything to say. Mitchell walked over to the railing of the scaffold, and leaning over it, bid everyone goodbye in a low and trembling voice.

At 10:52 a.m., the noose was placed around his neck and the black cap over his head. Sheriff Ellis then pulled the trigger dropping Mitchell to his death. The fall broke the neck and after twenty-five minutes the body was cut down and turned over to his brother who would bury the remain twelve miles from town.

The *Galveston Daily News*, dated Saturday, September 1, 1888, edition provided readers with a full account of the execution at Houston, Texas.

William Caldwell

Race/Gender: Black Male **Age:** 26 **Offense:** Murder
Offense Date: August 1, 1888 **Weapon:** Shotgun **Execution:** July 31, 1891

The Jaybird-Woodpecker War, 1888-1890, was a Texas feud between two Democratic factions fighting for the control over Fort Bend County. The "Jaybirds," representing about ninety percent of the white population, sought to rid the county of the African American-dominated Republican government, which had gained control during Reconstruction. The "Woodpeckers," which numbered about forty people and also claimed to be Democrats, and were the officials and ex-officials who held office as a result of the African Americans voting on the Republican ticket.

J. M. Shamblin was a prominent Democratic leader and citizen of Fort Bend. On August 1, 1888, while at his home sitting and talking with his family, he was shot and killed by his employee, William Caldwell. The following morning a torn out piece of paper from a notebook was found posted at the front gate of the Shamblin home. The note read, "Let this be a warning to all damn democrats." The warning was directed towards Democrats who were influencing the African American community to vote on the Democratic ticket.

On August 20, 1888, Governor Lawrence Ross posted a $200 reward for any accomplices and accessories that murdered J. M. Shamblin and to deliver said persons to the Fort Bend County Sheriff. The Young Men's Democratic Club of Fort Bend also posted their own reward of $200 on September 1, 1888.

When Caldwell was arrested, the notebook he carried contained a torn out page, which fit exactly to the note posted on the gate when compared.

After the case was twice appealed to the Texas Court of Appeals, and once to the United States Supreme Court, William Caldwell was sentenced on June 22, 1891, to hang for the murder on July 31, 1891.

Prior to the execution Sheriff Ellis handed out 200 passes for admittance into the jail to witnesses the execution. The pass holders and several hundred other people had gathered outside the jail by 9 a.m. on the morning of the execution. One of the witnesses present was the victim's father to insure his son's death was revenged.

Rev. E. Lee of Mount Vernon, Caldwell's spiritual advisor met him in his cell. After several prayers, Rev. Lee administered the baptism rites and poured water from a glass over Caldwell's head. Minutes later, Caldwell's mother could be heard wailing as she approached the cell. Caldwell then asked his mother, "Why do you weep and cry, mother?"

She replied, "Are you prepared to meet me in heaven?"

Caldwell replied, "Yes."

Sheriff Ellis allowed the cell door to be open wide enough to allow her to kiss her son goodbye for the last time.

Caldwell said, "Mother, be prepared to meet me at the bar of God."

Caldwell's mother was then escorted out of the jail to allow Sheriff Ellis to read the death warrant. Sheriff Ellis then ordered the path cleared in the halls where people had gathered to either witness the doomed man march to the gallows or watch the execution itself.

Sheriff Ellis, deputies and two ministers, escorted William Caldwell up the steep steps of the gallows. On the platform Rev. Lee gave a prayer for the condemned man and offered him broken bread and wine to eat and drink, and followed by the singing of hymns. At the conclusion of the hymn, Sheriff Ellis signaled for William Caldwell to take his place over the trap.

Caldwell stepped upon the trap and said, "I have nothing to say except to bestow my blessings upon Revs. Lee and Edwards and you, kind sheriff and your deputies."

Jailer Anderson then bound Caldwell's elbows behind him. Caldwell then shook hands with the ministers and said, "God bless you. Meet me in paradise."

Turning to Jailer Anderson said, "Goodbye, Mr. Anderson. My heartfelt sympathy is bestowed upon you forever."

His hands and ankles were then tied. Once the noose and black cap were adjusted and pulled over his head, Jailer Anderson gave the signal to Sheriff Ellis that all was ready. At 11:14 a.m. the sheriff pulled the lever dropping William Caldwell seven and a half feet to his death. Doctors Rutherford and Duffau checked the pulse and would announce the pulse beat out loud until 11:17 when no pulse could be felt. At 11:21 the rope was cut and the body was carried on shoulders down the stairs where it was placed in a wooden coffin. Examinations of the neck showed it to be have been broken. County undertaker Ross took possession of the body until 4 p.m. when the remains were be buried in the potter's field.

The *Fort Worth Gazette*, dated Saturday, August 1, 1891, provided readers with a full history of the crime, trial and execution.

Henry McGee

Race/Gender: Black Male **Offense:** Murder **Offense Date:** March 14, 1891
Weapon: Colt .44 Pistol **Execution:** August 12, 1891

On March 14, 1891, Officer James E. Fenn of the Houston Police Department was shot and killed while answering a disturbance call at Bill Davis's dance hall. After he had arrived, Officer Fenn was talking to a friend named Joe Walker while standing behind the band. Officer Fenn then noticed a man who appeared to have a pistol in his hand. He approached the person and called out to him. The man turned and fired several shots at the officer with one bullet striking him in the stomach.

The suspect then threw the pistol to his friend and accomplice, Sam Ashwood. Witnesses said Ashwood then attempted to shoot Fenn himself, but the pistol misfired. When questioned by police, Ashwood identified the shooter as being Henry McGee. Ashwood claimed the shooting of the officer was in revenge because McGee had been previously arrested for being drunk and disorderly. McGee was last seen running toward the International and Great Northern bridge in the direction of the Fifth Ward.

The thirty-five-year-old officer was carried to Dr. Duffau's house and succumbed to his wounds at 1:30 in the morning, and before his wife and three children had arrived to see him. Two days after the murder, Chief Wichman received a tip that the suspect was hiding in a cabin in the First Ward. With the description of the cabin, the chief with a posse of officers conducted a raid and arrested, Henry McGee.

The trial took place during the week of April 21, 1891, and three days later the jury deliberated seventeen minutes before returning a verdict of guilty and assessed the death penalty.

On the morning of the execution, newspapermen rushed into the jail to speak with the condemned man once more. When asked how he was felling, McGee replied, "I feel I can't complain, can't grumble, I feel first rate."

"Are you ready for the terrible trial?"

McGee replied, "Whenever God is ready to do his will, I am ready."

McGee then said, "I hope everything you say about me after I am gone will be correct. I want to appear before my Maker with that report to make my showing."

At 11:10 a.m. Sheriff George Ellis gave the signal that all was ready. The prisoner was then escorted to the scaffold. Once reaching the top of the platform Jailer Anderson immediately began binding the prisoner's hands behind him. With this the prisoner said, "God bless everybody, goodbye, God bless you Sheriff Ellis. God bless you Mr. Bob Sation, you have been good to me, God bless you, and you Mr. Anderson, you have been so kind to me, God bless you forever. God bless you all, I can't blame anybody, I got myself into it."

Officers moved McGee over the trap door and started their preparation. The knot was adjusted, and black cap pulled over his head. After Jailer Anderson pinioned the knees, Sheriff Ellis pulled the lever that dropped Henry McGee.

The *Galveston Daily News*, dated Saturday, August 13, 1892, printed a large article providing its readers with the details of the execution.

Walter E. Shaw

Race/Gender: White Male **Age:** 37 **Offense:** Double Murder
Offense Date: March 31, 1892 **Weapon:** Razor Blade **Execution:** August 4, 1893

On Wednesday night, March 31, 1892, Walter Shaw who many believed to have been insane, murdered his sixty-year-old mother, Anna Shaw and her forty-five-year-old sister, Belle Johnson. Both women were found dead in their single story, five-bedroom house on Prairie Street on Houston's Eastside.

Once the police were called and entered the home, the officers observed signs of a struggle, which had taken place, from the furniture that had been knocked over. Mrs. Shaw's body was located under the dining room table with her throat cut by a razor blade. Mrs. Johnson who was dressed in her bathrobe was found lying on the floor at the doorway leading to the dinning room from one of the bedrooms. A handkerchief had been stuffed in the woman's mouth, and a razor had also slashed her neck.

The sheriff later learned from a witness that Walter Shaw had boarded the Santa Fe train for Galveston during the night. Sheriff Ellis quickly wired Galveston police asking for them to locate and arrest Shaw, and that he would be catching the first train to Galveston. Upon the sheriff's arrival, he learned that Shaw had been located drunk in a saloon and arrested.

When questioned by the sheriff, Shaw admitted committing the murders. Shaw was stripped of his clothing and closely examined. Upon checking his clothing and body, blood was found on Shaw's undershirt, underwear, and outer shirt. Upon examining his fingernails, traces of blood was found on the edges. Both of his hands had scratches with one finger having a deep laceration.

It was learned the motive for the murders was $42 dollars that his mother and aunt had earned working over two or three days. Shaw wanted the money, which was denied to him by both his mother and aunt. He then attempted to take the money by force, and as a result during the argument took his razor blade and slashed the throats of both women.

Shaw was tried and convicted for both murders, and upon appeal, the case was affirmed. Once convicted and sentenced to death, Shaw's lawyer petitioned Governor Jim Hogg to commute the sentence. Governor Hogg sent a written response the day before the execution. The reply read that the Governor would not interfere, and would allow the law to take its course. When Shaw was notified the morning of his execution of the written response, he replied "I am glad of it," and that his attorney was a damned fool who did not know what he was doing.

Prior to the execution, Shaw sold his body for $35 to doctors George A. Lankford and C. E. Lankford to conduct a scientific autopsy. The remains afterwards were to be buried in Glenwood Cemetery. The two doctors published their finding later and wrote they believed Walter Shaw was insane due to the fact that Shaw's brain was smaller both in size, and weighed less than the average person.

On the gallows, Walter Shaw told the audience, that he "had been kangarooed, but was willing to die."

The headlines of the *San Saba County News*, dated Friday, August 11, 1893, read, THE LAW IS SATISFIED.

Alexander Terrell

Race/Gender: Black Male **Age:** 35 **Offense:** Rape
Offense Date: December 22, 1896 **Execution:** April 2, 1897

Three days before Christmas of 1896, Alexander Terrell arrived at the Jackson home at 1 p.m. in the afternoon asking for water. Mrs. Mollie Jackson handed Terrell a drinking glass and instructed him to get the water from the cistern. Terrell then asked her for something to eat. When Mrs. Jackson returned from the kitchen and handed Terrell a plate of food, he grabbed the woman by the neck and forced her back into the house and into the bedroom where he assaulted her.

Terrell who had been arrested was taken before Judge Ed Calvin for trial on February 10, 1897. Standing before Judge Calvin the indictment was read to him on the charge of Criminal Assault.

Judge Calvin asked, "How do you plead to this charge. Guilty or not guilty?

"Guilty," Terrell replied.

"Did I understand you to say that your pleading guilty?"

"Yes."

"With what are you charged" asked Judge Calvin.

Terrell answered, "The rape of Mrs. Jackson."

A jury was selected and Alexander Terrell pled guilty in open court. During the two hour court hearing, Mrs. Jackson took the stand and pointed out Alexander Terrell as the man who had assaulted her, and had threatened to kill her husband with her husband's own rifle if she told.

The jury deliberated for four and half minutes when the verdict was handed back to the court clerk. Judge Calvin instructed Clerk Ellis to read the verdict. "We the jury find the defendant guilty of rape as charged in the indictment, and fix the punishment at death." Geo L. Porter, Forman.

In February of 1897, a reporter of the *Houston Post* questioned Terrell as to his crime and pending execution.

Reporter: Do you fear death?
Terrell: No sir, I hope to be saved. I don't see any use being afraid, it has got to come.
Reporter: What do you think will be your future? Do you expect to go to Heaven?
Terrell: Yes Sir, I am trying to get my soul right. I am going to talk to a preacher and I am studying the bible. I think I will go to Heaven.
Reporter: Are you guilty?
Terrell: No sir, I am not.
Reporter: Why did you plead guilty?
Terrell: I was told it was the best for me to, that it would save my life. I was afraid all the time I would be mobbed.
Reporter: Were you not identified?
Terrell: Yes sir, but people sometimes make mistakes. They are honest in it through.

At the end of the interview, Alex Terrell asked Jailer Anderson to deliver the following letter to Judge Cavin:

Sir; I write you, sir, in my case of death sentence, which I was sentenced to hang April 2, 1897. I want you, sir, to please spare me until May 2 or fifteen days anyway, if possible, as I want to write a history and make a full confession before life expires.

Your humble prisoner,
Alex Terrell.

On the morning of April 2, a new suit of burying clothes was brought to Alexander Terrell to begin his preparations for his hanging. As the time for the execution drew near, Rev. Kelly Hayes visited Terrell. Rev. Hayes asked for Terrell to answer questions about his trial and the crime he committed. Terrell answered, "When I pleaded guilty, I did so to save my life. The law is taking my life, when according to the law, I should have a penalty, rather than a death sentence. I did wrong and was entitled to some punishment, but they should have spared my life."

At 10:55 a.m. Sheriff Albert Erichson entered the condemned man's cell and said, "Alexander, stand up."

Terrell stood before the sheriff with his arms crossed behind his back, and the death warrant was read to him. The sheriff then left to allow those with invitations to begin admittance into the jail.

A reporter standing outside the cell asked, "Alexander, are you ready?"

Terrell replied: "I am ready. It is a debt we have all got to pay."

Terrell asked the reporter for another cigarette and as he smoked, the reporter again asked, "Do you realize what is awaiting you?"

"Yes, sir, I realize it."

"In the presence of these ministers of God you say you are ready. Do you think that God who gave His only begotten Son that sinners might be saved, will receive your soul?"

"Yes, sir, I does, and I am ready to go."

At 11:16 a.m. the march to the scaffold commenced. Sheriff Erichson asked, "Alex, have you anything to say?"

The condemned man turned to Rev. Kelley Hayes and asked him to speak for him. The preacher said:

I can say for him that I have been with him nearly all the time when he was convicted, and I believe that he is converted man. I have pointed out to him God, and he confessed what he did, repented and feels that God has pardoned him for his crimes. He requested baptism and got it. He requested the Lord's Supper be administered to him and he got it. He says his path is light and that he will go straight from earth into glory. He thanks the sheriff of Harris County, the jailers and the watchmen who have watched over him through night and day, and he says they have all treated him well. They can't help with what has got to be done today. According to the law the man must die and now he thanks everybody and bid's them a final farewell.

Terrell then said:

It's true, I committed it and have got to pay for it. I've got no reason to live here in the world, and I want the world to hear what I have to say. I ask mercy from God and know that he had prepared for me to meet my maker. It's an unjust law that's taking my life for that crime, but I have made up my mind to give up my life and there aren't anyone who will grieve after me. I shall look to the Lord to receive me and save me from my sins. He has washed away my sins and I am prepared to go over the river. I am ready, and have nothing more to say, so farewell, everybody.

Alex turned and extended his hand to assistant jailer Wilson and said, "Mr. Wilson I shake hands with you for the last time. You are a good man. Be good to yourself."

He turned to the jailer, Archie Anderson, "I shake hands with you. Mr. Anderson, take care of yourself."

Turning to the sheriff, he said: "Goodbye Mr. Erichson."

Sheriff Erickson replied, "Goodbye Alex."

As the hands and legs were being pinioned, Terrell was heard saying, "Lord this is the last of it. Jesus be with me." To the witnesses he said, "Goodbye, people. We have all got to die. It's all over, so farewell, everybody."

The *Houston Daily Post*, dated Saturday, April 3, 1897, printed a full account of Alex Terrell's last day on earth.

Pate E. Burton

Alias: Pink Hines **Race/Gender:** Black Male **Age:** 25
Offense: Robbery & Triple Murder **Offense Date:** July 18, 1898 **Weapon:** Ax & Hatchet
Execution: March 24, 1899

On the dreadful day of Monday, July 18, 1898, Pate Burton set out to kill the entire Meyers family who lived twenty-fives miles from Houston in the small town of Cypress. His motive was for the money be believed was in the house. Henry Meyers had participated in a barbecue and had hidden the proceeds of approximately $80 in a mattress. Pate Burton had worked for Meyers in the past and again on Sunday, July 17, and on Monday morning, July 18, and was aware of the money.

During the morning, Burton worked with Meyers pulling fodder (long hay) from the field until noon. The family had enjoyed a nice lunch and decided to take an afternoon nap on the front gallery of the home. Burton first attacked Henry Meyers and killed him with an ax. He then struck Emelie Meyers with the weapon and believing she was dead continued into the other rooms of the house to kill the rest of the family.

Burton struck the two-year-old girl as she laid in her cradle, and the child died two days later. Burton then struck ten-year-old Gotleib Meyers to the head. Gotleib woke from the blow and started kicking, screaming and hitting Burton, who then pulled a knife. One of Gotleib's fingers was almost severed as the boy fought to keep Burton away. Emelie Meyers started screaming from the front gallery on the house, diverting Burton's attention from the boy and toward her. Gotleib took the opportunity to escape by jumping through the window to run to a neighbor's home for help.

While Goteib ran for help, Burton broke everything in the home in search of the money. Not finding the money, he ran into a nearby field near the railroad tracks and jumped a fright train to Houston. After wanted posters with Burton's description had been posted, he was arrested two weeks later in Liberty County. At the time of the arrest, Burton carried the watch belonging to Henry Meyers which contained his engraved initials.

Pate Burton went on trial for the murders on October 17, 1898. To ensure correct courtroom identification, three more black men entered into the courtroom and sat at the defense table next to Burton. When Gotleib Meyers entered the courtroom and took the stand, without hesitation he immediately identified Pate Burton as the man who attacked him with the hatchet and knife.

Burton took the stand in his own defense and denied committing the murders or having worked for Henry Meyers. Three days later at 5:30 p.m., the prosecution rested its case, and the jury retired for deliberation. The jury deliberated for fifty minutes and returned a verdict of guilty and assessed the death penalty. The court of criminal appeals affirmed the decision on December 7. The mandate was returned on January 30, 1899, and Pate Burton was sentenced on February 16.

On the day of the execution, Burton was given whiskey and smoked a cigar during his walk to the scaffold. On the gallows Burton said:

> During my life I have not known God. I have prayed, but it seemed to me to be in vain. I am no infidel, but there was a prejudice in my heart and I wouldn't get rid of it. I have been treated as nice as possible while I have been a prisoner here. I don't believe you could have a better man for your sheriff than Mr. Archie Anderson. I don't know this, mind you, but it is my belief. The jailers have been mighty good to me, too. Mr. Harry Anderson and Mr. Trammel and Mr. Wilson have all been good to me. I never killed those people. I know I've got to die, but you're not killin a coward. I don't want to go," but it must be done, according to law." I say this, that I am not guilty, yes, but still I have to die just the same."

When someone shouted at him, asking if he was guilty, Burton turned around and said, "No, I am not guilty. Didn't I tell you I was not? Goodbye to all and everybody."

While standing on the trap as the black cap was being adjusted, Burton spoke out and said, "If any man sees me tremble, speak out."

A voice from the crowd yelled out, "I saw it."

Just as Burton responded with, "That's a damn lie," the trap was sprung at 1:47 p.m. dropping Burton to his death. After the body was cut down, the crowd rushed forward in a wild scramble to cut pieces of the hangman's rope to keep as souvenirs. The body was afterwards buried in the potter's field.

The *Houston Daily Post*, dated Saturday, March 25, 1899, provided readers with a large article detailing the murders, execution, and other killings that Burton said he had not committed.

Marcellus Thomas

Race/Gender: Black Male
Weapon: Shotgun
Offense: Murder
Executed: September 3, 1909
Offense Date: October 9, 1905

On the evening of October 9, 1905, John Blair and Ben Shrapshire left the town of Spring, Texas, riding north on horseback toward their homes near Wilburton. While riding, the men realized there was a rider behind them and they called out to find out who it was. The rider announced himself as being Marcellus Thomas. The two men heard differently and thought the rider said he was a Doctor Sellers. One of the men was to have called Thomas a lying son of a bitch and demanded that Thomas ride ahead of them.

Thomas rode ahead 400 to 500 yards to his house and armed himself with a shotgun, then waited along a road to ambush both Blair and Shrapshire. Blair had gotten off his horse and was shot in the abdomen. Shrapshire was shot in the right arm and knocked off his horse. Blair was forty-three years of age, married and father of ten children. He was also was a farmer and operated a store near Wilburton. He died just after midnight on the morning of October 11, 1905. Shrapshire's injuries appeared to be less severe, but he also died several days later at a Houston hospital.

Thomas was located and arrested the following day at an aunt's house in the small village of Westfield, nineteen miles north of Houston. Immediately, Thomas told the officers he had shot both men in self-defense, as he believed the men meant him harm. When asked to explain further, Thomas refused to provide any further statement.

On December 23, 1905, Thomas took the witness stand and testified he shot both Blair and Shrapshire in self-defense. Thomas claimed both men were riding together on the road. One man was armed with a gun while the other with a knife. Thomas testified that one of the two men was to have said, "there's that negro again."

One man dismounted and Thomas said after giving significant time for the men to leave, he emerged from his place of hiding and shot the person on the horse first, and then shot the man of foot next with his shotgun. The jury did not believe Thomas' version of events as there was no evidence either man was armed with any type of weapon. Thomas was found guilty of murder and the verdict was appealed, but was affirmed on April 25, 1906.

On August 2, 1909 Judge E. R. Campbell called for Marcellus Thomas to be brought before the court for sentencing. Judge Campbell asked Thomas, "Can you give me any reason why sentence should not be passed upon you?"

Thomas replied, "Yes sir, Judge, your honor, I pray to almighty God that you will ask the governor to grant me a pardon of fifteen days longer."

Why Thomas asked for the additional fifteen days was not asked by the judge. Judge Campbell then ordered the execution to take place on September 3, 1909. On the scheduled day of execution, Thomas was escorted to the same jail gallows that Alex Terrell and Pate Burton were executed on.

The *Palestine Daily Herald*, dated Friday, September 3, 1909, provided a short article about the crime and execution.

Louis Utley

Race/Gender: Black Male
Offense Date: April 14, 1915
Age: 20
Weapon: Winchester Rifle
Offense: Murder
Execution: February 1, 1916

Constable William Clint Harless at the time of his death was a popular twenty-four-year-old officer, and was believed to have been tallest lawman in Texas, standing six feet-six inches and weighing 350 pounds. Constable Harless had also been cross-commissioned as a Harris County deputy sheriff.

On the evening of April 14, 1915, Constable Harless rode his horse to the home of Levy Jackson to serve a Walker County arrest warrant on Louis Utley for a charge of burglary. When Constable Harless first arrived, Utley and Sam King were sitting outside on the steps of the home, while Levy Jackson was inside eating dinner.

Constable Harless rode up a few feet away from the front gate and said, "Good evening."

King answered back, "Good evening."

Constable Harless told King he wished to see Utley. King began backing off the steps towards the door, then turned and ran inside. Constable Harless yelled, "Come back here," while at the same time reaching for his pistol. From inside the house, a shot was fired through a window and the bullet struck the lawman in the neck.

G. A. Adams, a section foreman for the International & Great Northern Railway, saw the shooting take place, and ran to the wounded lawman. Constable Harless was conscious and asked Adams to help him stand up as he was choking on his own blood. Adams told the Constable he could not stand, but he would raise him up as it appeared to him that the constable was paralyzed.

The International & Great Northern Railway arranged for a train to transport the wounded lawman to the Baptist Sanitarium in Houston. X-rays revealed that the bullet had entered the neck on the left side, shattered the vertebrae and lodged to the right side. Doctors feared any operation would kill the officer and left the bullet in the neck. At 2:45 p.m. of April 15, 1915, Constable William Harless succumbed to his injury.

Spring Constable J. P. Gillespie, investigated the shooting, and examined the window through which Constable Harless was shot. Constable Gillespie observed that the window shade was up and only the curtain was over the window. The curtain and window both had evidence of powder burns. Officers from Hempstead and Harris County sheriff's deputies soon arrived from Houston by automobile to join in the search for the murderer. While the search was being conducted, guards were posted over the three bridges at Spring Creek leading from town to prevent any escape.

Utley made his escape by running north toward Conroe, and jumping on a train at Cleveland, but was arrested at Livingston. After Utley was transported back to Houston, he was indicted for murder in the first degree by the Harris County grand jury.

At trial Utley said he did not know the constable was a peace officer and that the constable never made that clear to him. Utley claimed he was told by the constable, "If you run, you —, I will shoot your head off."

Utley said, "So I ran away then and so I came into the house and asked him again what did he want? He said, 'I want to kill the _____,' and so I just picked up the gun and fired through the window. I thought he was going to kill me. I ran out of the kitchen to get to him and he had the gun tilted up and cocked it. He said, 'I could not make it fast enough to him.' and I said, Oh _____, don't shoot that way. I was hollering to him all the time and when I got the gun, he had done fired."

On the morning of the execution, Utley walked out to the gallows and after stepping on the trap door said, "Goodbye to all."

The *Galveston Daily News*, dated Wednesday, February 2, 1916, reported that the execution had taken place.

Henry Sampson

Race/Gender: Black Male **Offense:** Robbery & Murder **Offense Date:** May 4, 1915
Weapon: Metal Bar **Execution:** February 15, 1916

Located in the Fifth Ward of the city of Houston, Charles Bourgois operated a small grocery store. On the night of May 4, 1915, the fire department responded to a fire at the small store. After the fire was extinguished, Charles' body was found within the ruins of the store.

Eighteen-year-old Abram Shelton was later arrested and charged with the murder of Charles Bourgois after he had pawned property belonging to the victim. This arrest and confession led to the arrest of Henry Sampson. On July 30, 1915, Shelton was tried and found guilty for his part in the murder and received a life sentence with the eligibility of being paroled after serving five years. Shelton told reporters that he was relieved when the jury did not put his neck in the hangman's rope and instead received the life sentence.

On May 14, 1915, Henry Sampson signed a confession in which he wrote that he had hit Bourgois in the head with a iron bar killing him. After stealing the store's money box, he threw kerosene on the store and set the building on fire to conceal his crime. Though the confession, the officers recovered the money box, valuables from the store and the murder weapon.

On June 16, 1915, the jury returned after eight minutes of deliberation to read the verdict of guilty and assessed the punishment at death. On the morning of the execution, Sampson wearing a new black suit and tie was escorted to the window to address the crowd of 2,000 people who had gathered outside the Harris County jail. Sampson first sang to the audience *In the Sweet Bye and Bye*. Sampson then yelled out, "They're goin' to hang me, but not my soul. This is Sampson talkin' — do ya hear me. I'm on my way to heaven, to heaven this morning. All of you good people turn around and live for God — live for God!"

Sampson was then lead away from the window and escorted to the gallows. Once on the scaffold, Sampson began repeating, "Trust in Jesus, trust in Jesus," until the black cap was placed over his head. After the trap was sprung and the body cut down, Sampson's father told a reporter at the execution, 'I'm glad he died like a man."

Clarence Cooley

Alias: George Washington, Clarence Wise   **Race/Gender:** Black Male   **Age:** 21
Offense: Robbery & Double Murder   **Offense Date:** August 10, 1916
Weapon: .38 caliber Pistol & 16 gauge Shotgun   **Execution:** October 18, 1916

At 6:30 in the morning of August 10, 1916, Clarence Cooley left on foot from his sister's home in Houston, carrying a .38 caliber revolver. Cooley had walked fifteen miles when he came upon a farm house located about two and a half miles north of the town of Aldine.

Going up to the farmhouse, Cooley discovered the front door unlocked, and the house unoccupied as the residents were laboring several hundred yards away in the field. Cooley took this opportunity to enter the home and search for money and other valuables in the home.

The home belonged to thirty-three-year-old Johanne Hanson. As Cooley ate bread and salmon in the kitchen, he observed Hanson through the window returning home for lunch. Cooley shot at Hanson with Hanson's own shotgun, but missed. Cooley then pulled his revolver and shot Hanson in the chest.

Seventeen-year-old Louis Teten who was a neighbor and a farmhand for Hanson, heard the gunfire and went to the house to investigate. As Teten walked up to Hanson's body, Cooley shot him in the back of the head with the shotgun. After searching both bodies for any additional money, Cooley finished burglarizing the house, taking eight dollars, clothes and other valuables.

Cooley returned to Houston, but suspicion for the murders fell quickly on Cooley as he was known not to have money, and he had brought attention to himself by his spending. Cooley was arrested and clothing and other articles belonging to Hanson were found in his sister's house.

On August 14, 1916, Cooley provided a signed confession which read:

I looked out of the window and saw the older man coming toward the house, and I got out of the back window and went around to the corner of the house and hid there from the man. He came on up to the house and went in and made a fire in the stove and started to cooking. He put some potatoes in a stew pot and put them on a stove to cook. Hansen took a break from the cooking and stepped out on the front porch. While he was standing there or just as he stepped down on the step I cocked the gun and put the gun to my left shoulder and fired at him.

Cooley wrote he missed and Hansen being startled by the shotgun blast turned around and said, "What is the matter?"

Cooley wrote, "I shot him then with my pistol and he fell. When I shot at him both times I intended to kill him."

Cooley confessed to the murder of Teten and said, "The boy stopped at the pump and got a drink of water and then came on up near the body of the first man I had killed there, and he stopped and looked at the man on the ground and I shot him with the shotgun and he fell. I went a little nearer to him and he had turned over and I shot him with my pistol."

In Cooley's confession he also admitted to killing two other men over the past three months.

Cooley was tried for the murder of Johanne Hanson on August 31, 1916, and he pled guilty to the charge.

The trial took less than two days with the majority of the time spent selecting the jury. Once the jury was sworn and seated, the prosecution spent two hours presenting testimony and another fifty-five minutes in closing arguments as to why Cooley should receive the death penalty.

Defense for Cooley afterwards argued for seven minutes as to why Cooley should receive a sentence of life in the penitentiary. On the second day, the jury retired to the deliberation room and within three minutes the jury had selected a foreman and returned back to the courtroom to announce the verdict of guilty.

On September 15, 1916, Cooley was taken before Judge C. W. Robinson for sentencing. Judge Robinson was very short in his sentence of Cooley and very simply said, "Clarence Cooley, stand up! Have you anything to say why the sentence of the court should not now be pronounced on you?"

Cooley replied in a tremorous voice, "No sir."

Judge Robinson said, "The sentence of the court is that you be taken from here to the county jail, where you shall be confined until October 18, on which day you shall be hanged by the neck until you are dead. That's all."

On the day of the execution, Cooley was lead to a window in the jail to address the large crowd that had gathered outside the jail. Cooley said:

> Well, good people, I'm here to tell you I have been a murderer and a thief and a burglar and all that, but people, I have the grace of God in my heart. I'm going home to meet Jesus. I ain't scared to die. This is a sweet thing, to be with Jesus. I want to tell you young people not to walk in my footsteps. It will lead you to ruin. Don't worry about me. I'll be better off than you. I'm going home. They have treated me fine here. They gave me everything I wanted. They gave me the whole jailhouse. Oh, I've got the grace of God in my heart. Now I'm going to sing you a little song.
>
> My mother, she's gone to enter the golden gate.
> Never let it be said it's too late to enter the golden gate.
> My father, he, too, is gone to enter the golden gate.
> Never let it be said it's too late.

When Cooley finished his song, he was then led away to the gallows.

The *Galveston Daily News*, dated Thursday, October 18, 1916, provided readers with the details of the murders.

Harry L. Walker

Race/Gender: White Male   **Age:** 43   **Offense:** Robbery & Murder
Offense Date: April 26, 1919   **Weapon:** Pistol   **Execution:** May 10, 1921

On April 28, 1919, two farmers at Camp Logan located a fresh mound of dirt and curious as to why it was there, started kicking the dirt around. To their surprise, the farmers partially unearthed the remains of Henry Ottersky who had been buried in a shallow grave of about two feet.

The police were called and determined that the deceased had been shot two times and had been buried for at least two days. The officers determined the corpse to have one bullet wound to the back of the head and a second wound to the chest. The identity of the person was unknown at the time, although the body was well dressed. In checking the clothing for any means of identification, a bank book was found in the inside jacket pocket that had been overlooked by the murderer. The bank book read, "City National Bank of Corpus Christi, Henry Ottersky."

Harry Walker was arrested two weeks after the murder when he forged the signature of Henry Ottersky on two checks made payable to Ottersky. Walker then deposited the checks into his own account at Lumberman's National Bank.

On June 14, 1919, Harry Walker took the stand and testified at his trial for two hours. On the stand, Walker admitted he had killed Ottersky, but claimed he had killed him in self-defense. Walker related to the jury how Ottersky and he were to deliver a car in Houston, and during the trip they had stopped and bought beer, whiskey and food.

At Camp Logan, the two stopped and walked out to the woods to eat lunch and play cards. During the card game an argument occurred between Walker and Ottersky. Walker testified that Ottersky had lunged at him with a pistol in his hand. Walker said he was able jump on Ottersky and gain control of the weapon and shoot him four times.

Walker told the jury he left the scene afterwards to get a digging tool and returned with a spade to dig the grave. Walker said he had raffled through Ottersky's clothing in search of any identification to conceal the identity of the body should it be found. To throw off any further suspicion of Ottersky's disappearance, Walker shipped Ottersky's suitcase to Galveston under a fictitious name. Next, Walker wrote a forged letter as coming from Ottersky to his employer, B. F. Morris in San Antonio. The letter informed his employer that he was "Mexico bound."

The $45 to $50 dollars Ottersky had on his person, Walker said he had won during the card game. Two checks issued to Henry Ottersky in the amounts of $26.40 and $10 had been endorsed with the signatures of Henry Ottersky and Henry Walker and cashed at the Lumberman's National Bank on Saturday, April 26 after Ottersky was already dead and buried.

The jury deliberated and returned a verdict of guilty and assessed the death penalty. Franklin P. Davis, the foreman for the jury later told a *Houston Press* reporter, that the jury had deadlocked during the deliberation of the sentence. The jury was having difficulty in rendering a decision whether the penalty should be life in prison or death. The jury then decided to "draw lots" to decide the penalty and death won.

On April 5, 1921, District Court Judge C. W. Robinson read the following sentence to Harry Walker.:

In Criminal District Court, Harris County. Indictment returned in this court on May 22, 1919, charging you with the murder of your friend, Henry Ottersky. On Friday, June 13, 1919, you were arraigned and entered a plea of not guilty, and after the evidence was all introduced the jury was charged as to the law, and after the attorneys discussed the evidence as applied to the law the jury retired to consider the verdict and on the same day returned into this court with a verdict finding you guilty of murder and assessing your punishment at death. Therefore your attorneys filled a motion for a new trial, and on June 23, 1919, same was overruled by the judge of this court, whereupon your attorneys gave notice of appeal to the court of criminal appeals of this state. Thereafter, on April 28, 1920, that court affirmed the judgment of this court and thereafter overruled the first and second motions for rehearing. On April 2, 1921, the order of the court of criminal appeals was received by the court, commanding this court to proceed with the execution of its judgment.

Have you anything to say why the judgment of this court, as approved by the court of criminal appeals, should not be executed?

No, then, in accordance with the verdict of the jury and the judgment of this court, and the affirmance of the court of criminal appeals, it is the order, judgment and decree of this court that on May 10, 1921, the sheriff of this county shall between the hours of 11 o'clock and sunset, in the jail of Harris County, Texas, hang you by the neck until you are dead. And the clerk of this court is hereby order to issue the proper warrant commanding the sheriff of this county to execute the judgment and sentence rendered here in.

At 2:15 p.m. on the appointed day, Walker who was dressed wearing a black mohair suit, white shirt, black scarf, black shoes and black socks was led to the second floor gallows of the jail. Five minutes later, Sheriff Thomas Binford pulled the lever releasing the trap.

The *Galveston Daily News*, dated Wednesday, May 11, 1921, provided readers with the details of the execution.

Carl Parker

Race/Gender: White Male   **Offense:** Robbery & Murder   **Offense Date:** February 21, 1921
Weapon: Pistol   **Execution:** May 4, 1922

Mortie Conroy was a young cab driver in Houston attempting to make a living from the fares. On the morning of February 21, 1921, Conroy told his father that he had a prearranged fare to pickup and was taking a party of people to the Goose Creek Oil Field. The party being Carl Parker, Walter E. Ussery and Flora

Moore, who was nicked name the "Bobbed Hair Girl."

Parker told Ussery and Flora Moore he intended to kill the driver so he could steal the car. As scheduled, Conroy drove to a hotel on Congress Street and picked up his passengers. Carl Parker took the front seat while Walter Ussery and Flora Moore took the back seat. About three miles from Goose Creek, the bullet-riddled body of Mortie Conroy was found lying near the roadway the next morning. Conroy had been shot five times in the chest, with each bullet being fatal. The cab was later found abandoned in Fisher, Louisiana. Ussery and Moore were arrested days later, and Parker was located and arrested three weeks later at Salem, Illinois, and returned back to Houston on March 6.

When apprehended, Walter Ussery provided a confession and both Ussery and Moore turned state's witness. Flora Moore testified the three of them had become financially destitute and planned to rent a car and driver to carry them to Beaumont. Parker who was drunk on boot-legged corn whiskey turned toward Conroy and shot him several times. The body was removed from the car and thrown into a roadside ditch.

Carl Parker in his defense said he was not responsible for the murder, as he was temporarily insane from whiskey and drugs at the time. The jury felt otherwise and found Parker guilty of murder, and assessed the penalty at death. The case was affirmed by the court of appeals and Governor Pat Neff further refused to interfere after meeting with Parker's wife and daughter days before the execution.

On May 3, 1922, Parker was quoted as saying:

There is nothing new that I have to say. I have already told the people of Houston my side of the case and so far as I know there is nothing to add. It does seem hard that I should be held accountable for what happened while the rest of them are not bothered. The wine I drank was doped and I do not know and am not responsible for what happened after that. I would not complain if the others were here with me, but it does seem hard for them to go free while I have to shoulder all the blame.

On the morning of May 4, 1922, Parker said, "I am not showing any white feathers and I am not afraid to go."

At 11:11 a.m. as Carl Parker was removed from his death cell and marched to the gallows, his attorney, J. H. Letis rushed to the Federal Courthouse to make a last minute appeal before Judge J. C. Hutcheson to issue a writ of habeas corpus.

On the gallows, Parker told the witnesses, "God have mercy on those people; they don't know what they are doing."

After the sheriff adjusted the black cap he then patting Parker on the shoulder and said, "Goodbye, old-man, God bless you." The sheriff then tripped the lever, and Parker's body shot through the trap door. Once Parker was pronounced dead, the body was lowered into a coffin and turned over to the undertaker for shipping to West Virginia.

The Parker's attorney had arrived during this time and asked Judge Hutcheson to issue the writ on the grounds that women had purposely been excluded from the jury when Carl Parker was convicted. At 11:23 Judge Hutcheson requested Marshal Harvin to call Sheriff Bindford to delay the execution until he could hear the plea for the writ. When the call was received, the marshal was informed that the trap had been sprung at 11:16. Judge Hutcheson informed the lawyer, "I cannot issue a writ of habeas corpus for a dead man."

The *Galveston Daily News*, dated Friday, May 5, 1922, provided readers with details of the murder and execution.

Harrison County

County Seat - Marshall

Anthony Walker

Race/Gender: Black Male **Age:** 36 **Offense:** Murder
Offense Date: November 12, 1883 **Weapon:** Double Barrel Shotgun **Execution:** January 23, 1885

Anthony Walker was lured into murder by greed for land, money and the lust of a woman. Walker who was married with six children knew the Ten Commandments better than most, as he was a African American preacher.

Sometime in 1883, the wife of William Henry approached Walker with the offer of $50, and 150 acres in land if he would kill her husband. Mrs. Henry told Walker she wanted her husband dead as she did not want to lose her portion of the farm and family assets from a divorce. Walker told Mrs. Henry he considered William not only his neighbor, but also as a friend and refused. However, it wasn't long after that Mrs. Henry invited Walker into her bedroom to continue the conversation, and soon Walker agreed to the murder of Henry.

Not having a weapon of his own, Mrs. Henry furnished Walker with a double barrel shotgun, buckshot and with the information as to when her husband would be coming home from town. On the night of November 12, 1883, Walker hid along the road and waited for Henry's return home. Henry was with three other African American men when he arrived at the designated spot. Walker then stepped out from his place of hiding onto the road and fired both barrels into William Henry.

After several hours of agonizing pain, Henry died from his wounds. Walker was recognized by one of the three men and they immediately notified the sheriff of the murder. After Walker's arrest, he quickly confessed to the sheriff of the conspiracy. With this information, the sheriff obtained an arrest warrant for Mrs. Henry as well.

After being tried and found guilty, Walker stood before Judge Boory for final sentencing on December 23, 1884. In response to the judge's inquiry if he had anything to say as to why the sentence of the court should not be pronounced against him, Walker said:

May it please the court; I have nothing much to say. I am guilty of the offense charged in the law. I ought to and am willing to suffer for it. I am thirty-six years old. All my life I have tried to live a Christian life. I have been a preacher for eight or nine years trying to teach men how to live honest and virtuous, and obey the laws of God and man, but in all of that I fell. Let my fall be a lesson. The Good Book teaches us that we must confess ours sins, one to another. I confess mine, and I pray God's forgiveness, and I ask all men to forgive me for any harm I may have done to them. I have little more to say further than to ask the court to let the execution take place as soon as possible. I have nothing more to say.

Judge Boory answered with:

On the 12th day of November, 1883, some person lying in ambush shot the deceased, William Henry, in Harrison County, Texas, and inflicted upon him injuries from which in a few hours he died.

On the 28th day of November, 1883 the grand jury at Harrison county presented at the bar of this court a bill of indictment, in which they solemnly declared that you were the murderer.

On the 17th day of June 1884, a jury in Harrison county, composed of thoughtful, intelligent and conscientious men, after hearing all the evidence in your case, and after hearing the argument of the counsel for the state, and the argument of the counsel who so ably and zealously defended you, brought into this court a verdict by which they solemnly declared you to be guilty of murder in the first degree, and assessed your punishment at death.

Your faithful counsel manifesting the same zeal and energy which have characterized their conduct during their entire management of your cause, prepared and filed a motion for a new trial, and urged it before this court, in earnest argument, but the court deemed it its duty to refuse it, and they thereupon gave notice of appeal to the court of appeals. The record of your case was sent there, and that high tribunal, far removed from local prejudice, if there was any, after a patient, thoughtful and conscientious investigation of your cause, with naught before them save the silent record, came to the conclusion that in the trial resulting in your conviction no error had been committed, and solemnly affirmed the judgment of this court, and sent here their order commanding that the judgment of this court obey and execute.

A way back in the law of Moses it is declared that who shed man's blood by man shall his blood be shed and this dreadful declaration is about to be verified in your execution. You stand at the bar of this court to hear the awful sentence that you must die. The last source from which legal relief might have been hoped for has been appealed to unavailingly. In the face of your public confession that yours is the hand that fired the fatal shot which sent the soul of William Henry unwarned, and it may be, unprepared, to its final account, it is scarcely possible that you can hope for clemency from the governor of the state. It there be hope for you it is in the declaration of him who has mercifully declared through your sins be as scarlet, they shall be as white as snow.

It is difficult for one in the vigor of health and the middle of manhood to realize that his active limbs will soon be cold and pulseless in death. There lurks in the heart a sort of half hope that a doom so awful will, by some means, be averted. I warn you not to suffer yourself if to be deceived by any such delusion. Do not fail to realize that on the day fixed for your execution you will surely die. While I believe that you should die for the horrible crime you have committed, I assure you of my sympathy in your fearful situation. Your condition is the spectacle of human distress and the generous heart hath always sympathy for human suffering.

I counsel you most solemnly to devote the few days that remain to you to a preparation for death. Give yourself to reflection, to meditation, to prayer, and it may be that He who so loveth all, the least of His creatures, that he giveth to the thirsty worm its dew-drop, to the ant its crumb, and to the bee its flower, will not refuse mercy to any of his creatures, even though his hands be red with the blood of his fellow being.

It is the sentence of this court that on Friday, the 23d day of January, 1885, between the hours of 11 o'clock in the morning and sunset, that the sheriff of Harrison county, either in the jail of said county, or at some other place in said county to be by him selected, do hang you by the neck with a rope till you are dead, DEAD, DEAD, and may God have mercy on your soul.

On the day of the execution Sheriff S. R. Perry, with a large number of deputies, present, seated Walker on his coffin, and drove him to the scaffold that he had erected in a field northwest of the city. After Sheriff Perry finished the reading of the death warrant, Walker was asked if he had anything to say. Walker said:

My Friends—I trust that this little paper may touch your sympathies. If so, please purchase a copy, that I may leave to my wife and children a small pittance—the gift of kind friends and may God, in his mercy, bless you for the charity. Respectfully, Anthony Walker.

The mistake of my life have been many,
The sins if my heart have been more;
I scarce and see for my weeping,
But I'll knock at the open door.

I know that I am weak and sinful-
It comes to me more and more;
But when the dear savior shall bid me,
But enter the open door.

I'm lowest of those who love him;

I'm weakest of those who pray;
But I'll come to the feet of my Savior,
And he will not turn me away.

My mistakes his free grace will cover,
My sins He will all wash away,
And my feet, through they toiter and falter,
Shall walk through the gates that day.

If I must die, oh, let me die
In peace with all mankind;
But through all this I was led astray,
As many other here to-day.

So often has my mother dear
Warned me of sin to fear
But through all this I was led astray

My friends, all dear, I warn you here
Of dangers sure to come;
And when we part on this green earth;
I say to all, and mean it well,
To think of me, and say farewell.
Amen.

The *Fort Worth Daily Gazette*, dated Saturday, January 24, 1885, printed full details of the crime, interview, and execution.

D. L. Spearman

Race/Gender: Black Male **Age:** 34 **Offense:** Murder
Offense Date: June 18, 1894 **Weapon:** Firearm **Execution:** October 25, 1895

D. L. Spearman was sentenced to hang on October 25, 1895, for the murder of Horace Stephens. Stephens lived in Spearman's rental home which was located next to his own home. While Horace Stephens was away from home working for the Texas & Pacific Railroad, Spearman gave special attention to Mattie Stephens in her husband's absence.

On the morning of June 18, 1894, Spearman shot Horace in the back of the head and killed him. The body was afterwards dragged through a field and pushed into a creek. Eight days later two boys went to the same creek four miles north of town to swim when they spotted a hand sticking out of the water and notified the sheriff that a man had drowned. Chief Deputy Sheriff Sid Curtis responded and entered the creek and pulled the body out. Once the body was pulled to dry ground, the remains were identified as being Horace Stephens.

It was discovered the body had been anchored at the neck and knees with large rocks and tied with pieces of a plow line. Deputy Curtis afterwards traveled to the Stephens' farm and found both Spearman and Mattie Stephens plowing a field together and placed them both under arrest for murder.

The motive was believed to be Spearman wanted Mattie for himself. Tracks from a horse drawn buggy with a bolt protruding out from the wheel were found in the sand leaving the scene. A buggy at the Spearman home with the protruding bolt matched the track and this was some of the evidence introduced at Spearman's trial. Spearman was found guilty and the jury assessed the death penalty. The case was appealed to the court of criminal appeals, and the court affirmed the decision.

While awaiting execution in the Marshall jail, D. L. Spearman conspired with Ed Wilson, Charles Porter, Henry Jackson and a fourth inmate to escape from the jail by assaulting or killing the jailer if need be.

During the day, the prisoners had the freedom of the corridor run of the cellblock. They used this time, with a bent wire, to jimmy the lock to the door which secured the corridor from the rest of the jail. On December 12, 1894, the four prisoners armed themselves with an iron bar and sticks, and then climbed to the top of the cells to wait for the arrival of jailer. When the unsuspecting jailer entered, inmate Nathan Rodgers who was in jail for murder warned the officer of the pending assault waiting for him.

The jailer backed out of the cellblock and notified the sheriff. The sheriff immediately returned to the cell with several deputies, and ordered all four prisoners down from the top of the cells. The inmates at first defied the orders and swore they would rather die then surrender. After an hour of spraying cold water from fire hoses on the prisoners, the inmates dropped their weapons and climbed down to be shackled in leg irons and locked inside their cells.

On the day of execution, Spearman was transported to the gallows, that had been erected three miles northwest of town on a field that had been cleared. Once on the platform, a hymn and a prayer was offered by Rev. F. H. Wilkins. After the song was finished, Deputy A. S. Curtis read out loud the death warrant before the 7,000 to 8,000 spectators. The hands and feet of Spearman were afterwards tied. In asking Spearman if he wished to say anything, Spearman only said, "goodbye, goodbye."

After the noose and black cap were adjusted, Sheriff Harry Bell cut the rope at 2:20 p.m., which released the trap. When Spearman fell through the seven-foot drop, his neck was not broken because his feet reached the ground. Deputies quickly rushed under the gallows and dug a hole under Spearman's feet so that he would be suspended. Spearman strangled to death and was not pronounced dead by the county physicians for twenty-three minutes.

The *Fort Worth Gazette*, dated Saturday, October 26, 1895, provided readers with details of the murder, investigation, trial, and execution at Marshall, Texas.

Sam Collins

Alias: Sam Fite **Race/Gender:** Black Male **Age:** 31
Offense: Murder **Offense Date:** September 4, 1904 **Weapon:** Four-foot Long Gum Stick
Execution: May 19, 1905

Sam Collins was executed on the gallows three miles from Marshall on the county poor farm, for the murder of his mistress, Maria Jacobs. The death was investigated after Collins told his landlord that Maria had been sick and she died during the night. Collins asked for his assistance in purchasing a coffin, and the landlord quickly reported the death. When the body was viewed, it was estimated Maria had been dead for two days due to the early stages of decomposition. An examination of the body showed eight broken ribs, both arms broken, and the body covered in bruises.

Collins was arrested for murder, and three days later tried and found guilty. It was the district attorney's theory that Sam Collins had repeatedly abused and beat Maria Jacobs with a tree branch to the point he had killed her.

On March 16, 1905, Sam Collins stood before Judge R. B. Levy for sentencing. When the judge asked Collins if he had anything to say before the sentence of death be passed, Collins replied, "Please judge, let me live as long as possible."

Judge Levy replied that he had better use his time that he had left to make peace with his God and then sentenced Collins to be executed on May 19, 1905.

On the morning of May 19, 1905, the death warrant was read to Collins from his cell. Collins was then driven in a surrey while mounted armed deputies escorted him to the county farm where the gallows had been erected.

On the gallows, Collins waved his hands to those in front of him and said, "Goodbye."

Sheriff W. T. Munden cut the rope that held the trap door in place and the body shot down eight feet. The knot slipped around to the back of the head, but the neck had been broken. Twelve minute later, Collins was pronounced dead and turned over to his friends for burial.

The *Galveston Daily News*, dated Saturday, May 20, 1905, provided readers with details of the crime and the execution at Marshall, Texas.

Hays County

County Seat - San Marcos

Benignio Guerrero

Race/Gender: Hispanic Male **Offense:** Murder **Offense Date:** April 21, 1914
Weapon: .45 cal. Pistol **Execution:** April 9, 1915

On April 21, 1914, Benignio Guerrero told his sister-in-law, Isabel Morales, that if she did not run away with him, he would kill her. Guerrero also warned Isabel if she told anyone of the secrets they shared, then he would kill her for that as well. Isabel being fifteen-years-old ran home to her father, Nicholas Morales and told him of the threats Guerrero had made towards her life if she did not leave with him. Morales confronted Guerrero with this information, and Guerrero simply replied, "If you can prove it, go to the law."

Three hours later, Guerrero walked out into the field where Isabel was working. Without warning, Guerrero placed the barrel of a .45 caliber pistol up to Isabel's head and pulled the trigger. Guerrero afterwards walked home and went to bed as if nothing had happened until he was placed under arrest for her murder.

At trial, the district attorney told the jury the motive for the murder was Benignio Guerrero was afraid Isabel would divulge the secrets they shared to her parents. The jury did convict Guerrero on April 21, 1914, and assessed the punishment at death. The case was appealed to the court of criminal appeals who affirmed the decision on December 9, 1914. Judge Frank S. Roberts sentenced Guerrero on March 4, 1915, to hang by the neck until he was dead on Friday, April 9, 1915, between the hours of 11 a.m. and sunset.

On the day of the execution, Guerrero asked for a match to light his cigar while making the death march to the gallows. Guerrero puffed on the cigar while standing over the trap door until his hands were tied. Just before the black cap was about to be pulled over the head, Guerrero asked that the cigar remain within his mouth, and the sheriff granted the request.

From the gallows, Benignio Guerrero told the witnesses, *"Adios amigos."*

At 1:15 p.m. trap was sprung and thirteen minutes later Guerrero was pronounced dead. Benignio Guerrero was the only person ever legally executed in Hays County. The rope used in his execution was said to be the same rope used in eight other execution including the hanging of John Henry Brock on May 30, 1913, in Travis County.

The *Galveston Daily News*, dated Saturday, April 10, 1915, provided readers with a short article of the murder and the execution in San Marcos, Texas.

Henderson County
County Seat - Athens

Robert Giles

Race/Gender: Black Male **Offense:** Robbery & Murder **Offense Date:** December 14, 1886
Weapon: Ax **Execution:** October 14, 1887

Robert Giles and Albert Williams shared a cabin and worked beside one another splitting rails for the railroad. Each morning after breakfast, both men would walk into the woods and begin their work splitting ties late into the evening until dinner.

On December 14, 1886, John Williams who lived next door saw both Albert Williams and Giles walk into the woods to begin their usual work day. A short time later, Giles walked up to John Williams and commented that he had not yet ate his breakfast and was going out to where Albert was so he could get the house key to eat something.

Giles later returned to John Williams' home and reported that he found Albert dead at their tie camp on the Trinity bottom where they had been working. Williams followed Giles back into the woods and saw Albert's body partially burned from the campfire. The head, arms and shoulders were lying in the fire, and the left side of the skull had been crushed. Williams saw the shirt had been burned off the body, and the pants pockets had been turned inside out. Some distance from the body, a pool of coagulated blood was located where Albert Williams had been struck, and then dragged to the fire.

Suspicion fell on Giles for the murder with robbery being the motive. On Giles's person was $4 in silver and a $5 bill. The bill was recognized as being paid the previous day to Albert Williams. The murder weapon was soon located in a vacant house near the home where Albert Williams and Giles lived. The ax had blood on the handle and poll (hammer side) and the ax was identified as belonging to Giles. During the search of Giles' cabin, officers located the work pants Giles had been seen wearing earlier in the morning. Officers examining the pants found bloodstains on both pant legs.

Officers confronted Giles with the evidence, and Giles denied he committed the murder, but said he was present at the time. Giles gave a name to the officers who he said committed the murder, but that information later proved to be a lie.

At the trial, Robert Giles pled guilty to murder. Judge F. A. Williams instructed the jury that the defendant pled guilty to the charge of murder contained in the indictment which has been read to them, and their duty was to determine what degree of murder he was guilty of, and to assess the proper penalty.

District Attorney Faulk asked the jury to return a punishment of life imprisonment. The jury reached a verdict of murder in the first degree and assessed the death penalty. A motion for a second trial was granted with the court date scheduled to take place on February 24, 1887. Again Robert Giles pled guilty at his second trial, and the jury for the second time assessed the death sentence. Robert Giles afterwards appealed his case to the court of criminal appeals where the case was affirmed on April 13, 1887. The execution was then ordered to take place on October 14, 1887.

The execution was public, with spectators arriving three days early so they could pitch their tents to get the best view of the gallows that had been erected one mile east of town. At 1 p.m. Sheriff George Osborne and Deputy Sheriff McRae, emerged from the jail with Giles and escorted him to an open hack containing a coffin.

Arriving at the scaffold at 1:45 p.m., Giles stepped up on the gallows and addressed the witnesses. Giles told all to live better and build themselves up. He advised his young black friends not to play craps or gamble. Giles said he had quarreled with Williams and then killed him. At his conclusion, Deputy McRae adjusted the black cap and Sheriff Osborne sprang the trap.

A reporter for the *Galveston Daily News*, interviewed Giles the day before his execution and was printed in the Saturday, October 15, 1887, edition:

Albert Williams and myself were employed chopping ties near Malakoff, Tex. Early in the morning on the day of the killing we became involved in a quarrel, and he (Williams) began cursing me, calling me a son of a bitch and a damned bastard. I told him I would not take that from any man and started for him. Williams said, "Go away Giles and don't fool with me now." He then raised his ax as if to strike me. I caught his ax with my left hand and struck him on the head with my ax, killing him instantly. I left and returned next morning. I then discovered that his clothing had caught fire during the night from the fire we had built the day before to warm by. I then took money from his pants pocket. I did not kill for robbery. I have no ill will against anybody. I pray for the jury that sentenced me and I am ready to die.

Hidalgo County
County Seat - Edinburg

Casmero Livar

Alias: Also spelled as Leva, Liva, Lavar, and Leva   **Race/Gender:** Hispanic Male   **Offense:** Murder
Offense Date: December 10, 1887   **Weapon:** Pistol   **Execution:** December 7, 188

Casimero Livar was tried and convicted for the murder of Theodore Marx whose remains were not found until December 31, 1887. Prior to his murder, Marx operated a store at Agus Negra, and attempted to have Casimero Livar indicted for horse theft and the theft of a pistol. Livar afterwards set out to get even by taking Marx's life.

On December 10, 1887, Casimero Livar, his brother Francisco Livar, and Criscenscio DeLeon, Bonfaco DeLeon, and Ramon Ruiz had seen Marx go to the home of a woman he was seeing. When Marx left the home, the men waited at the gate Marx was to pass through. Casimero Livar then jumped Marx from the back and pinned his arms while his pistol was taken from him. Marx was led out into the brush where he was shot and killed with his own pistol. The next day the body was cut up, doused with kerosene, thrown into a pit and set on fire.

Casimero Livar was tried and sentenced to death for murder in the first degree on May 11, 1888. The court of appeals affirmed the decision of October 10, 1888. On the day of the execution, Livar sang a Mexican ballad from the gallows for the spectators who had gathered to see him hang. The ballad was composed by Casimero and told the story of his fate, and for others not to follow his path of crime.

The *Galveston Daily News*, dated Saturday, December 8, 1888, printed the following short article:

CASIMERO EXECUTED FOR THE CRIME OF MURDER.

His Neck Was Broken and Death Resulted in Fourteen Minutes.

Brownsville, Tex., December 7 – Casimero Lavar, the murderer of Theodore Marks, was hanged at Edinburg at 4:33 p.m. today. He met his fate gamely. His neck was broken, and he was pronounced dead in fourteen minutes. A large crowd witnessed this execution.

Abraham Ortiz

Gender/Race: Hispanic Male   **Offense:** Rape, Robbery & Murder   **Offense Date:** February, 1912
Weapon: Club   **Execution:** May 2, 1913

The second person to hang in Hidalgo County was Abraham Ortiz. Ortiz was executed in the county jail's hanging tower in Edinburg on May 2, 1913, for the crime of murder in the first degree and rape of a woman who's husband he had just murdered.

In February of 1912, Ortiz and Domingo Gonzales followed behind Martin Martinez and his wife Florencia Luis as the couple walked from the town of Hidalgo. Just as Martinez walked past the town cemetery, Ortiz picked up a heavy tree limb and hit Martinez in the back of the head. Ortiz continued to beat the unconscious man with the wood club until he was sure Martinez was dead while Florencia begged and cried for the men to stop. After robbing the body of $15, Ortiz raped Florencia.

Gonzales fled to Mexico to avoid arrest, but Ortiz was apprehended and tried on the separate charges of rape and murder. Ortiz was found guilty of both offenses and sentenced to death. The verdict was appealed, but affirmed on December 11, 1912. On the day of his execution, Ortiz last words from the gallows were, "There is no heaven and no hell."

The *Galveston Daily News*, dated Saturday, May 3, 1913, provided their readers with a short article of the crimes and execution.

Hill County
County Seat - Hillsboro

Tom Robinson

Race/Gender: Black Male   **Offense:** Rape   **Offense Date:** September 26, 1898
Execution: April 28, 1899

Tom Robinson was arrested, tried and convicted on the criminal assault upon twelve-year-old Mary "Nannie" Adams. Mary was working for Robinson picking cotton when he brutally beat and repeatedly raped the young girl. When found, Mary was in critical condition and partially paralyzed, and she never walked again.

Found guilty of rape, Robinson was sentenced to hang on April 28, 1899. On the scheduled day, Sheriff Bell went to Robinson's cell were he proceeded to read the death warrant to him. At 12:30 the sheriff and deputies led Robinson to the scaffold followed by his spiritual advisors. Sheriff Bell asked Robinson if ten minutes would be long enough for him to make his last statement.

Robinson replied, "Can't you give me twenty?"

Sheriff Bell said, "Yes, I'll give you twenty."

Robinson then said:

Good people, I am leaving you good and cheerful. I am leaving you innocent. Lord bless the people who swore falsely against me. May we meet in a better world. My friend here, (laying his hand on Sheriff Bell), has to do his duty by law and not by his will. Why does he believe I am guilty? Because the colored race got him to believe it, and his opinion can't be changed until changed by God. We will be in better shape when we meet again because he will see then I have told the truth. I would rather any man would do this than Mr. Bell, because when he learns I am innocent its going to hurt him to the heart. The Lord knows whether I have told the truth or not. Jesus knows. I pray thee, oh, Lord, be with my wife and child; stand by and befriend them. May we meet in bright glory, Bless the man my hand is on to-day," (laying his hand on Sheriff Bell). "As my body goes down may my soul go up to the presence of Jesus. Jesus knows I have told the truth. Oh, Lord, this is the way I know you intend for my body to leave this world. I am leaving with my body clean of this. Forgive each and everyone who has had anything to do against me. There is nothing in my heart against anybody. God go with me today. Grab my soul and raise it up above the clouds, they can't hurt the body. It is a burden to any man to see a man's soul pass as mine is. Jesus, go with me. Amen.

Robinson then called out to Deputy Sheriff J. A. Jones and bade him goodbye. Spiritual advisor, Adam Oliver said, "We are about to close these services, my brother. I hope to meet you in heaven. Are you going to meet me there?"

"Yes, Lord, I'll meet you," Robinson said.

"Before we close there is nothing more you want to say; nothing you want to confess?" Oliver asked.

"No, thank God. I have nothing to die for and have nothing to tell. I'm leaving with a pure soul," Robinson said.

Sheriff Bell then said, "Your time is short, Tom. If you've got anything on your heart you had better tell it."

"There is nothing on my heart. I am all right," Robinson said.

Robinson then told witnesses, "Come over and tell me goodbye. Don't be scared of me. I ain't going to hurt you."

Sheriff Bell replied, "Your time is up".

"Can't you give me any longer?" Robinson asked.

"Now Tom, If there is anything you have held back tell it. Don't die with a story on your lips," Sheriff Bell said.

"Well, Mr. Bell, God is my witness, I am innocent," Robinson said.

Sheriff Bell and his deputies at this point started tying his legs and arms. Robinson asked if he could take his shoes off and the request was granted. As Sheriff Bell started to adjust the cap, Robinson asked Sheriff Bell to tie a handkerchief over his eyes. The cap was lifted and the handkerchief was tied in place.

Robinson then asked, "Does anybody here want to bring me a cup of water?" The water was quickly brought up to him and the cap was slipped down over his face to allow him to drink. Once the cap was re-adjusted, Robinson began complaining to the sheriff that the rope was choking him as the noose was being tightened.

Robinson then said, "I'll tell you when I'm ready, Mr. Bell."

"I'll tell you when I'm, ready," said the sheriff.

"You are choking me, Mr. Bell."

Sheriff Bell replied, "All's ready, Tom. You're gone to eternity," as he sprang the trap.

The *Dallas Morning News*, dated Saturday, April 29, 1899, provided its readers with details of the crime and execution at Hillsboro, Texas.

Hood County
County Seat - Granbury

Nelson A. Mitchell

Alias: Cooney
Offense: Murder
Execution Date: October 9, 1875
Race/Gender: White Male
Offense Date: March 28, 1874
Age: 80
Weapon: Firearms

In 1868, Nelson "Cooney" Mitchell settled in Hood County to ranch and raise his five children. The ranch was on the Brazos River located about twelve miles south from Granbury, and became known as "Mitchell's Bend."

In the spring of 1872, Mitchell and his oldest son Bill were out looking for stray cattle when they came upon a family and their broken down wagon on Comanche Peak. The James Truitt family were out of food and had no money and must have been a poor sight for Mitchell.

Feeling sorry for the family, Mitchell took them in. He eventually sold fifty acres of land to the Truitts, and the Mitchell's helped the Truitts build a cabin and smokehouse. Mitchell at times also brought the Truitts meat to be smoked. Within two years, the Truitt family were on their feet and prospering. James Truitt became a preacher and started preaching the word of God at the Methodist Church. Soon thereafter, a feud would spring up between two families. The result of the feud would cause for blood to be spilled, men sent to prison, and one man hanged.

The feud was the result over the ownership of a strip of land near Mambrino, located about even miles outside of Granbury. At first the argument had the appearance of being kept peaceful as it was decided to allow the district court to settle the dispute. On March 28, 1874, the court heard the case and ruled in favor of the Truitts.

After court, the Mitchells left town for home, but stopped along side of the road, when they were passed by James, Sam, and Isaac Truitt who cheered for their court victory while throwing insults at the Mitchells as they galloped past. Unknown to the Truitt boys who later stopped to water their horses at Contrary Creek, they were being pursued by Cooney Mitchell along with Bill Mitchell, Mit Graves, Jim Shaw and J. W. Owenss.

At the creek, Cooney Mitchell was to have yelled, "Give' em hell, boys!" When the gun smoke cleared, both Sam and Ike were dead. James, who received a wound to the shoulder, was able to mount his horse and escape to the safety of his family.

Immediately after the shooting, Bill Mitchell fled to New Mexico Territory to avoid arrest. Everyone except for Mit Graves was charged with murder in the first degree. At the murder trials of Jim Shaw and J. W. Owens, both received a prison sentence. Cooney Nitchell testified before the jury that it was the Truitt boys who cursed at them while firing the first shots as they rode past. The jury did not believe the Mitchells and Nelson "Cooney" Mitchell was sentenced to hang.

While awaiting the day of his execution, Mitchell was being held in the log cabin jail in Granbury. Two nights before his scheduled execution, Mitchell had placed a long string out his cell window knowing that his youngest son, Jeff, was to sneak up during the night. That night Jeff Mitchell was shot and killed by a jail guard after he saw a figure crouching low near the jail. The next morning, the lifeless body of Jeff Mitchell was found. Upon examination, the body was found armed with a shotgun, two pistols, and a bottle of laudanum.

On October 9, Mitchell rode to his execution while sitting on his coffin in the bed of the wagon driven by Sheriff Andrew Wright. Once at the scene of the scheduled execution, Mitchell stood and addressed the crowd while the noose was placed around his neck. Mitchell spoke as to how he was proud of his son Jeff, and that there was not a drop of cowardice in the boy's blood. When Mitchell spotted Jim Truitt in the crowd of 5,000 spectators, he turned his attention to him.

"Jim, when you didn't have nothing but one pony, a wagon and starving, didn't I take you in and feed you?" Mitchell said, "Didn't I."

When you wanted to go preaching, didn't I buy you the first suit of clothes you ever had? Didn't I buy you a Bible? A good Bible, to start you out?" Mitchell continued.

Mitchell then called out to his son, Bill, moments before the wagon was driven from under him. Cooney yelled out, "Bill, wherever you are, take revenge against my murderers," referring to Jim Truitt.

Soon after the hanging, things calmed down and people went on with their lives. Jim Truitt moved to Timpson in Shelby County to become the pastor of the Methodist Church. In 1884 he married and in 1885 he was the editor for the *Timpson Times* newspaper.

But time is not always a healer as was the case for Bill Mitchell. On July 20, 1886, he walked through the of door James Truitt's house and shot Truitt in the head as he sat in the parlor. After serving two years at the penitentiary in Huntsville, Bill Mitchell escaped from the prison on July 14, 1914, and returned to New Mexico.

The *Cincinnati Daily Enquirer*, dated Friday, October 15, 1875, provided a full account of the execution and ended the article by writing:

> *He was pluck to the last, and died without the least exhibition of fear. The Mitchell -Truitt tragedy has created the utmost excitement in Hood County. The results may be summarized as follows: The killing of the two Truitts, of Jeff Mitchell while conveying poison to his father, the hanging of the old man, two men (Snow and Owens) in the Penitentiary for life, and William Mitchell and Mit Groves fugitives from justice, with the hand of every man against them and a price upon their heads.*

Houston County
County Seat - Crockett

Henry Y. Johnson

Race/Gender: Black Male **Age:** 40 **Offense:** Rape & Murder
Offense Date: December 27, 1883 **Weapon:** Knife **Execution:** November 14, 1885

Henry Johnson was tried and sentenced to death for the rape and murder of twenty-year-old Mollie Murcheson. On December 27, 1883, both Johnson and Newton "Newt" Owens forced Mollie into the brush seven miles east of Crockett. The crime was unknown until Newton Owens went into town and reported Mollie's abduction to the sheriff. Owens reported that he had been walking along the road with Mollie, when two white men came up to them and cursed him and ordered him to leave. Owens claimed he last saw Mollie as she went into the woods with the strangers, and later heard her scream.

When officers went to investigate, they found the dead body of Mollie Murchison about 150 yards from the road with her throat cut. While searching for evidence, tracks lead to a water hole where a bloody handkerchief was found. These facts and other circumstances led to Newton Owens being charged with her murder.

Owens was tried and convicted of the crime, but appealed the conviction. The court after careful review of the case reversed the decision. Owens was tried again and this time was sent to the penitentiary for twenty years.

Evidence introduced from both trials provided the circumstantial evidence needed to arrest and convict Henry Johnson. After Johnson was tried, and sentenced to death, he also appealed to the high court. The court of appeals found no error and affirmed the lower courts decision.

On the morning of the execution, Johnson dressed himself in a new black suit. After Sheriff E. F. Payne read Johnson the death warrant, the Crockett Rifles lined up outside the jail, and marched the prisoner the 100 yards to the gallows. From the gallows, Johnson told the crowd of 5,000 that his soul and body belonged to God. While maintaining his innocence, he quoted Scripture and said it was better to let ninety-nine guilty men escape than to punish one innocent man. Johnson told them that everyone must die, but he hoped that when they were called, they would be as ready as he was. Johnson said he was aware a good many of them expected for him to confess to the murder of Mollie Murcheson, but that he could not confess anything that he was not guilty of. Johnson said he wanted the crowd to know when someone in the future should say that Henry Johnson was hung for the murder of Mollie Murcheson, that it was a lie, and that if anyone who said that they attended his hanging for the murder of Mollie Murcheson it would be a lie as well because he was hanged by lying tongues.

At 12:30, the noose was adjusted and the cap placed on his head. The trap was sprung and the fall of eight feet failed to break the neck. After hanging for fifteen minutes, the body was cut down and given to relatives.

A reporter from the *Galveston Daily News*, interviewed Johnson in jail. During the interview, Johnson maintained he was innocent of any crime. When asked if he wanted the service of a minister, Johnson replied if anyone could save him from being hanged he would like to see him, but as far as saving his soul was concerned, he already knew where that was going, and did not want the prayers of any one.

A full account of the crime, and execution was printed in the Saturday, November 14, 1885, edition.

John Andrew Johnson

Alias: John Anderson Johnson **Race/Gender:** Black Male **Age:** 18
Offense: Rape **Offense Date:** June 14, 1888 **Weapon:** Physical Force
Execution: December 21, 1888

Miss Ollie Sims lived five miles north of Crockett, on her father's farm. While her father and brothers were working in the field, Ollie went to where her horse was staked and led it into the field. John Johnson who worked at the adjoining neighbors' farm as a field hand, came up behind Ollie and grabbed her by the throat and forced her down onto the ground and raped her. Another hand by the name of Coke Gunnels sat on a fence and watched as the assault took place.

After the assault, Johnson returned to the field and resumed his plowing. After the assault was reported, a neighbor located Johnson and rode up to him and Johnson said, "What, you want me?" Johnson then threw down the plow reins and ran to his employer's house and crawled under the their bed begging not to be handed over for fear of being lynched.

When a posse of men arrived, Johnson slipped out the back door and escaped. The following evening after the assault, Railroad section hands who were working close and were aware the posse was looking for a black suspect. Upon seeing Johnson acting suspicious along the woods line near the railroad tracks, the railroad workers on false pretense to speak with Johnson, offered him a job. Once close enough to Johnson, the workers grabbed Johnson and took him into town where he was turned over to officers.

The sheriff learned that a lynch mob was forming and that sledgehammers had been placed at various points around the jail and the mob intended to storm the jail at night to get at Johnson. The mob placed four men to watch the jail for any attempt by the sheriff to move Johnson, but nobody thought to watch the back door. By the time the mob realized that Sheriff Bayne had his deputies move Johnson from the jail, the officers had too much of a head start for the mob to intercept them. Johnson was taken to a train station and transported safely to the jail in Houston.

On October 18, 1888, the case was brought to trial. During the trial Ollie took the stand and gave her testimony of the assault and pointed out John Johnson seated in the courtroom as the man who raped her. A second witness for the state was a young black boy who told the court he had been a witness to Johnson's rape of Ollie and later confronted Johnson with what he had seen and Johnson bragged to him of committing the crime.

The jury deliberated only fifteen minutes and returned a verdict of guilty and assessed Johnson's punishment at death. The defense attorneys afterwards made the argument that Johnson was under the legal age to be executed, as he was only fifteen. This argument failed after several witnesses testified that Johnson was eighteen-years-old.

From the gallows, Johnson made no statement to the 4,000 witnesses. Johnson had told the sheriff he was innocent of the crime and claimed that Coke Gunnels committed the rape. It was Gunnels who testified as a state witness against him at his trial. Johnson said he did not fear death, but would prefer any other death than from the gallows.

The *Galveston Daily News*, dated Saturday, December 22, 1888, ended the editorial of the hanging with, "Thus ends the last chapter of this gloomy drama. May God be more merciful to John Andy Johnson than he was to that pure and beautiful girl."

Frank Jones

Race/Gender: Black male **Age:** 25 **Offense:** Murder
Offense Date: July 1900 **Weapon:** Ax **Execution:** November 1900

Jones murdered his wife Georgia in the farming community of Lovelady located fifteen miles from Crockett, in Houston County. He murdered his wife by striking her in the head with an ax after she had left him to be with another man.

Jones was arrested four days later, tried and convicted of the murder in the first degree. The gallows were built near downtown Crockett, and Jones was executed by public hanging.

Lee Russell

Race/Gender: Black Male
Weapon: Clubs
Offense: Rape & Murder
Execution: October 1, 1909
Offense Date: April 7, 1909

Lee Russell was one of four men charged with the murder of Molly Harris, whose body was found in a well. On the night of April 7, 1909, Molly was sleeping in bed when four men entered her bedroom. Breaking wood furniture, the men used the pieces of the wood to beat her to death.

After the murder the body was tied to wooden planks and dropped into a nearby well. The remains were not discovered until four days later when a cowboy rode to the well and observed the horses refused to drink the water. Upon investigating the horse's behavior, he discovered feet protruding above the water's surface and notified the sheriff.

Russell pled guilty to the murder, and on August 8, 1909, he was sentenced to hang by Judge Gardner on October 1, 1909. Of the other three defendants, two were under the legal age for execution and were sentenced to life in the penitentiary. The third and youngest of the four was found not guilty.

The execution was held in public, as the jail was too small to hold the gallows. More than 8,000 people gathered around the scaffold to watch the hanging as Russell declared his innocence and asked for all those present to meet him in heaven.

The *Galveston Daily News*, dated Saturday, October 2, 1909, provided readers with the details of the murder and execution.

Hunt County

County Seat - Greenville

Charley Little

Race/Gender: White Male **Offense:** Robbery & Murder **Offense Date:** November 12, 1897
Weapon: Iron Bar **Execution:** May 4, 1899

L. B. "Ben" Stonecypher was a cotton picker from Arkansas whose remains were found on the morning of November 13, 1897, in a burned down vacant house. An examination of the skull indicated it had been struck twice with a blunt object. An iron bar, believed to be the murder weapon, was found in a caved-in cistern. After a watch belonging to Stonecypher was traded to a storekeeper in Wolfe City, along with six dollars for another watch, Charley Little was identified and suspected of committing the murder.

After Little was arrested, he confessed to Sheriff R. M. Patton that he had killed Stonecypher in self-defense. Little claimed he and Stonecypher had stopped at a vacant house to play poker during the night. The winning pot in the card game had grown to a $1.60 when Little supposedly had caught Stonecypher cheating. During the argument, Stonecypher reached for his shotgun when Little struck him with an iron bar, killing him. To conceal the murder, Little set fire to the house.

On April 27, 1898, the jury heard evidence how Little had sold the victim's watch and had killed Stonecypher for the $109 Stonecypher was carrying. The jury listened to Little's testimony of the events leading to the murder and the claim of self-defense, but found him guilty of murder in the first degree and sentenced him to death.

The *Galveston Daily News*, dated Friday, May 5, 1899, provided readers with details of the murder, and details of Charley Little's last hours on earth before the execution at Greenville, Texas.

Bob McKinney

Race/Gender: Black Male **Offense:** Double Murder **Offense Date:** September 22, 1899
Weapon: Firearm **Execution:** April 16, 1900

Bob McKinney was tried and convicted on November 17, 1899, for the double slaying of Margaret Leslie and Simon Smith which occurred on September 22, 1899. Simon who was visiting Margaret at her home when they were both shot because of the jealousy McKinney had for Margaret.

Margaret was shot between the eyes, as she was rocking back and forth in her favorite chair. Smith who had been sitting behind Margaret, ran for the door when he was shot down and died the following day.

A month later, McKinney was tried for the murder of Margaret and found guilty. Although already condemned to death for murder, he was later tried for the murder of Smith.

On the morning of the execution, it was estimated that 8,000 spectators arrived at Greenville to witness the public execution, which took take place on the northeast corner of the jail yard. On the gallows, McKinney was asked if he wished to say anything. He then stepped to the edge of the platform and said:

> Well, ladies and gentlemen, one and all alike, my time to leave has come; I am satisfied. I am not sorry. It will soon be over. I want to warn you all not to do as I have done. I have nothing against anyone and hope no one has anything against me. I feel that God has forgiven me and everything is all right. I bid you all goodbye.

After a prayer, and the shaking of hands, the trap was sprung.

The *Dallas Morning News*, dated Tuesday, April 17, 1900, provided details to readers of the murders and execution at Greenville, Texas.

Henry Brown

Race/Gender: Black Male **Age:** 18 **Offense:** Murder
Offense Date: August 5, 1899 **Weapon:** Straight Razor **Execution:** May 7, 1900

On August 5, 1899, at around 4 p.m. in the afternoon, eighteen-year-old Henry Brown walked into Freeze's Barber Shop in Commerce, where he worked as a bootblack man (boot shiner). The shirt Brown wore was blood soaked and he threw down a barber's straight razor on a table and said, "There, Mr. Freeze, I'm done with that razor."

Freeze asked what he meant by that statement.

Brown said, "I have cut a Negro woman's throat from ear to ear. The girl had gone back on me and I had warned her if she did not do me right, that I would kill her."

Brown explained he had thrown his arm around Francis Milton's neck, drew her head back, cut her throat, and broke the blade on her neck bone in the process.

Town Marshal Musgrove was notified and when he arrived at the barber shop, Brown repeated the same story to him. In going to the home, the marshal found the eighteen-year-old girl dead, as Brown described. Brown's conviction and sentence was appealed, but the court affirmed the decision on January 24, 1900.

From the gallows, Brown addressed the crowd and said:

Friends, I am getting just what I deserve. I did wrong and ought to hang. My only regret is that I did not go with Bob McKinney. We had everything arranged then, but I am as well prepared as then. I can close my eyes and see the prettiest city I ever saw with a home and a crown there for us all. I want all to meet me there. I love everybody, even my enemies. I want this to be a warning to you young men. Leave whiskey, gambling and women. It is that which has brought me to this. Stay away from saloons.

As the black cap and noose were being adjusted he said, "Look here young boys, see what's going around my neck, be warned. Don't do as I have done. Lead pure lives and avoid this."

Moments before the trap was sprung he called out to the African Americans who were waiting to take the body to Commerce for burial and said, "Remember, Boys, I sho' want to be buried by the side of that girl," referring to Francis Milton.

The trap was sprung at 2:30 p.m. and fifteen minutes later the body was cut down and placed in a coffin.

The *Galveston Daily News*, dated Tuesday, May 8, 1900, provided readers with a full account of the murder and execution.

Will T. Manning

Race/Gender: White Male **Offense:** Murder **Offense Date:** December 29, 1904
Weapon: Poison **Execution:** July 7, 1905

Will Manning was executed for the poisoning and murder of his wife, Eva Manning. Manning had been having a sexual relationship with Eva's fourteen-year-old sister, Ida. He had decided to murder his wife in order to marry Ida McGuire.

On December 28, 1904, Eva gave birth to their first child. As Eva rested in bed from the childbirth, Manning began administering strychnine to his wife on the pretext that he was giving her medicine. Less than twenty-four hours later, Eva Manning was dead. The death at the time was not suspected of anything other than complications from childbirth.

The death did not become suspicious until March 27, 1905, when Manning traveled to Sherman, with a forged letter giving him permission to obtain a marriage license for Ida and himself. It was then that the relationship between Manning and Ida was discovered.

After Manning was arrested, he believed the charge was for forgery and he became angry with his father-in-law for having him arrested. Manning told the deputy he had already been intimate with his sister-in-law, but that he had taken good care to allow her to reach the age of consent before he let anyone know it, and stated further that when his father-in-law heard what he had to say, he would be glad to let him go on and marry the girl. Manning also stated that he had been criminally intimate with the girl while he was married.

After these statements were made the girl was interviewed and confessed that Manning had been intimate with her. She also said that on one occasion Manning told her that his wife would not live long and they would get married after her death.

The remains of Eva were exhumed and her stomach contents were tested for poison, and showed the presence of strychnine.

On April 10, 1905, a case was presented before the grand jury and indictments against Manning were returned for criminal assault and forgery. On April 15, the grand jury returned an indictment against Manning for the murder of his wife. The following day Manning was tried for criminal assault. The jury returned a verdict of guilty and sentenced him to life in the penitentiary.

Ten days later on April 25, Manning again stood trial, this time for the murder of his wife. The trial concluded on April 29 when the jury deliberated for five hours and returned a verdict of guilty of murder and assessed the death penalty.

Manning's attorney informed the court that he would file an appeal, but Manning told the judge he had no desire to appeal and was prepared for the court to pass sentence upon him. Judge R. L. Porter told Manning he would not accept his request until May 8, so that Manning would have time to decide his options. On that day, Manning was brought back before Judge Porter and reiterated his former request for immediate sentence.

The Judge, in passing sentence, said:

> The grand jury, at the present term of this court, has presented two indictments against you; one of which charges you with criminal assault upon Ida McGuire, a young girl, about fourteen-years-old, and the sister of your deceased wife. This other indictment charges you in this case with the terrible crime of murdering your own wife, Eva Manning, by the means of poison. Our lawmakers, in their wisdom and in view of the fact of the terrible state of depravity of one who might be guilty of such offense, have declared, after defining murder generality, that all murder committed by the means of poison shall be murder in the first degree.
>
> I gave your trial in this case the most careful attention and consideration that it was possible for me to do, You had a jury of twelve of the best men of this county to pass on your case, and they sat patiently and earnestly through the whole trial, listening to very word of testimony given by the witnesses, the argument of the counsel, and the charge of the Court. You were ably and most earnestly represented by your counsel, who left nothing undone that could possible avail you the least advantage on the trial of the case, and certainly no complaint can attach in him for the result of the trial.
>
> The testimony in this case satisfied the jury beyond reasonable doubt that on the 29th day of December, 1904, in Hunt County, Texas, you with your malice aforethought, deliberately and willfully murdered your young wife by administering to her strychnine as medicine. And at this point I will say that I can not conceive how a man could become so heartless and cruel as to take the life of a loving and confiding wife, and that, too, just about twenty-four hours after she had borne him her first child, and that while the innocent and helpless little creature lay unconscious at its mother's side. But the proof in this case establishes the fact beyond a reasonable doubt, that you took the life of your wife, Eva Manning, under just such circumstances, and doubtless with no motive except to satisfy your lusts.
>
> Man is created in the image of his Maker for a noble and useful purpose, and there is nothing in earth grander and superior to a good and noble man, one who tries to live right and just before God and man. But it is sad indeed to see or contemplate a man, who at one time in life was guideless and guiltless, and could become a peer ad example among the children of men, but who neglects and abuses his opportunities and turns his thoughts and energies to evil habits and vicious lusts, and destroys his good impulse and usefulness, and becomes a slave to vice and sin.

In passing upon your case, the jury has found you guilty of murder in the first degree, and finding nothing in the testimony to excuse, justify or extenuate the awful crime, they assessed your punishment at death.

Since your trial was concluded, I have reviewed carefully and most seriously the whole case in detail, and have satisfied my own conscience that you have received a fair and impartial trial, and it only remains now for me to pronounce the sentence of the court upon you, which is:

That you W. T. Manning, will be remanded to the jail of Hunt County, Texas, where you will be securely kept in close confinement until the 7th day of July, 1905, when you will be taken by the Sheriff of Hunt County, Texas, and between the hours of 10 a.m. and 4 p. m; he will hang you by the neck until you are dead. This is a sad ending and awful fate and I trust you will try to make peace with your God and fellow man before the end.

On the scheduled day, at 2:15 p.m., Will Manning was taken to the gallows and dropped seven feet, breaking his neck. The body was afterwards taken down and released to the undertaker for burial in the city cemetery.

The *Galveston Daily News*, dated Saturday, July 8, 1905, provided coverage detailing the murder, trial and execution.

Jack County
County Seat - Jacksboro

Ely Bly

Race/Gender: Black Male   **Age:** 28   **Offense:** Murder & Robbery
Offense Date: June 16, 1874   **Weapon:** Four-Foot Bar   **Execution:** August 7, 1874

Thomas Carmichael Jr. was a twenty-six-year-old man who made his living as a trader. Carmichael lived in Parker County and would travel to other nearby towns and forts to trade and sell various goods. On June 14, Carmichael was at Fort Griffin, eighty miles west of Jacksboro when he met Ely Bly. Bly had been earlier discharged from the army, and asked to ride with Thomas.

During the return trip, Carmichael made several stops selling his goods. After crossing Rock Creek, the men stopped and camped for the night. The next morning, two travelers found a body lying in a pool of water. Near the body was a heavy bar that had evidence of blood and hair and had evidently been used to crush the skull. About fifty yards away stood Carmichael's wagon and horses, except one horse was missing.

When the news of Carmichael being murdered reached town, Sheriff Lee Crutchfield of Jack County learned of a black man who had an unusual amount of money and had sold Carmichael's rifle. On the morning of the June 18, the sheriff learned the black man had gotten on the stage for Fort Worth. Sheriff Crutchfield took pursuit after the stagecoach and stopped the driver twelve miles out of town. Bly who was wearing Carmichael's pants, was placed under arrest. When searching Bly, the sheriff found that he was also carrying Carmichael's pistol and handbook.

Four days later, Bly was indicted for murder and on the June 28, found guilty of murder in the first degree. On July 4, Bly was taken before the court and he was sentenced to hang on August 7. Once sentenced, Bly was confined to the courthouse by being chained and shackled to a post. On the day prior to the execution, the scaffold was built outside one of the courthouse windows of the room Bly occupied.

The next day on the gallows, Bly told the crowd, "It's hard for a man to die when he has committed no crime. I am willing to die. I see I have to die, but I never killed Thomas Carmichael. I never killed Thomas Carmichael."

After the Bly was declared dead and lowered into a coffin, Carmichael's father stepped forward and made claim to the noose, which was given to him. He then paraded around town displaying the noose to all who wanted to see it.

Ely Bly was the only person legally hanged in Jack County and the *Herald & Torch Light*, dated Wednesday, September 9, 1874, provided a full account of the execution.

Jasper County
County Seat - Jasper

Claude Golden

Race/Gender: Black Male **Age:** 45 **Offense:** Rape
Offense Date: July 14, 1908 **Execution:** February 12, 1909

On the morning of July 14, 1908, fourteen-year-old Alma Belle Hopkins went out looking for her horse when she came upon Claude Golden. Golden told the girl he had seen the horse, and directed her toward the woods. Once shielded by the trees and brush from the road, Golden grabbed the girl. Alma fought off her attacker and screamed for help.

A young boy hearing the screams and seeing Alma being attacked ran to nearby houses to report the assault. Picking up a tree limb as a club, Golden beat Alma about the face and head in order to sexually assault her. Hearing the nearby neighbors running into the woods to come to her aid, Golden ran off.

Claude Golden and Mathew Fennels were both arrested two days later as suspects and transported to the jail in Galveston for safekeeping. Matthew Fennels was later charged with perjury, and the assault charge dropped. Alma identified Golden from photographs as her attacker, and other witnesses identified Claude Golden as the man they had seen going into the woods with Alma Hopkins.

On the gallows, Golden told the few witnesses that a doctor was the only one who could have testified that an outrage had been committed upon the girl, and that he was being hung on the testimony of a nurse. The papers considered this to a partial confession from Golden as he had always maintained he was innocent.

The *Galveston Daily News*, dated Saturday, February 13, 1909, provided readers with details of the assault and execution.

Jefferson County
County Seat - Beaumont

Jack Bunch

Alias: Jackson Bunch **Race/Gender:** Black Mix Male **Age:** 20
Offense: Murder **Offense Date:** May 25, 1856 **Weapon:** Shotgun & Pistol
Execution: November 21, 1856

Jack Bunch was executed for his participation in the ambush and murder of an Orange County deputy sheriff by the name of Samuel L. Deputy on May 25, 1856. Samuel Deputy by all accounts was an honest and hard working lawman who unfortunately worked for a sheriff who was not honest and who would rather use the authority of his office to protect his friends from the law.

Deputy Samuel Deputy arrested a man named Clark Ashworth, a free black man for the theft and butchering of a stolen hog. The deputy took Ashworth before Justice of the Peace A. N. Reading who then bound the charges over to the District Court for trial, and released Ashworth on a security bond promised by his cousin, Samuel Ashworth.

Infuriated by the arrest of his cousin, Ashworth immediately afterwards armed himself with a double barrel shotgun and confronted Samuel Deputy on the outskirts of Madison. Ashworth challenged the lawman to a gunfight. When the officer refused, Ashworth became verbally abusive toward the officer after not accepting the challenge. Samuel Deputy returned to town and obtained an arrest warrant from Judge Reading to arrest Samuel Ashworth for the criminal offense of "Using Offensive Language from Negroes."

Ashworth was arrested and brought before Judge Reading. The judge sentenced the defendant to receive thirty lashes to the bare back and remanded Ashworth over to the sheriff's custody to execute the sentence of the court. Sheriff Edward C. Glover who was friends with the Ashworth family reported back to the court that Ashworth had escaped custody before the sentence could be carried out. By the end of the day, the sheriff returned the warrant back to the court stating the defendant could not be found.

Ashworth now sought revenge against the lawman and went to his cousin, Henderson Ashworth who lived on Cow Bayou. There he obtained a couple of double barrel shotguns, a Colt pistol, a skiff, and old clothing to use as a disguise. Ashworth left the home with his other cousin, Jack Bunch and rowed the skiff out from Cow Bayou near the Sabine River to await Samuel Deputy returning home.

Ashworth and Bunch soon spotted Samuel Deputy rowing his boat toward his home. Accompanying the officer was A. C. Merriman, the Orange County Court Clerk. Once Samuel Deputy was within twenty-five yards, Bunch rowed his skiff out from their hiding spot. Samuel Ashworth then unloaded both shotguns and three rounds from his pistol at the deputy. Deputy fell out of the boat and was clinging to the side when Ashworth struck the officer to the top of the head with the breach of one of the shotguns. Merriman was able to escape unhurt and reported the ambush and murder.

The sheriff attempted to give the appearance of going after the murderers by organizing a posse of eight men, which were all friends of the sheriff. The posse had received information that the wanted men were hiding out in a cabin. The posse had got within a half mile of the cabin when the sheriff turned his posse away from the cabin and headed back towards town. The next day the sheriff wrote "Not Found" on the arrest warrant and returned the warrant back to the court.

Sam Ashworth and Jack Bunch remained hidden in the swamps for several days until crossing the Neches River. Bunch was later recognized and arrested in Montgomery County. On a change of venue to Beaumont in Jefferson County, Bunch was convicted of murder in the first degree and on November 12, 1856, and sentenced to death by Judge Maxey.

On November 21, 1856, Bunch was escorted to the scaffold on the courthouse lawn. Upon seeing the crowd, Bunch said, "Goddamn it, How do you all do?"

As Bunch ascended to the top of the ladder with the noose around his neck, he requested that his body not be given to doctors for study, but that he be decently buried. Upon reaching the top, the ladder was pulled out from under him, and Bunch strangled to death. Samuel Ashworth escaped captured after fleeing to the Indian Territory, and later joined the Confederate Army. Ashworth was reportedly killed at the Battle of Shiloh in April of 1862.

The *Springfield Republican*, (Springfield, MA), dated December 24, 1856, provided a short article of the execution.

Bill Madison

Race/Gender: Black Male **Age:** 24 **Offense:** Murder
Offense Date: April 6, 1884 **Weapon:** Firearm **Execution:** January 15, 1886

On April 6, 1884, Bill Madison had gone to speak with Elbert Smith, a logging contractor about wages. During the conversation, Smith began teasing Madison who was not in any mood for jokes. When Smith continued to tease him, Madison left walking away towards his home telling Smith not to leave, as he would be returning to blow his brains out. Smith yelled back to Madison that he had no intentions of leaving and would be right where he left him. Madison walked the quarter of a mile to his home and retrieved his weapon. Upon his return, he walked up to Smith and shot him to the face. Smith stood up, walked a few paces, and then fell dead face first to the ground.

Bill Madison was immediately arrested and tried. Upon conviction, the case was sent to the court of criminal appeals who affirmed the lower courts decision on June 20, 1885.

On the morning of the execution, Sheriff Thomas Langham took the following telegram from his pocket and read it to the prisoner:

Thomas H. Langham, Beaumont, Tex.: I decline to interfere with the judgment in Bill Madison's case.
   John Ireland, Governor.

Madison simply replied, "I knew you were going to read me that paper. I saw you get it yesterday and bring it over here to read to me. I knew what it was as soon as you pulled it out. I am prepared to die. I have made my peace with God, and an willing to go."

The gallows used for the hanging had been borrowed from Orange County and erected on the courthouse square. On the gallows, Madison turned to Sheriff Langham and said, "I am ready to die and leave this treacherous world."

Upon stepping over the trap, Madison uttered the words, "Look at me, this is where I stand." At 11:35 a.m. the sheriff drew the noose, and the last words from Madison were, "Draw it tighter."

The *Galveston Daily News*, dated Saturday, January 16, 1886, ended the full editorial of the crime and execution with, "The spectacle of to-day will have its effect on both white and colored citizens of this community, and it is thought will deter many others from committing like offenses."

Willie Jones

Alias: Anthony Hopkins **Race/Gender:** Black Male **Age:** 27
Offense: Murder **Offense Date:** May 3, 1899 **Weapon:** Razor Blade
Execution: March 9, 1900

Willie and Lou Jones had only been married a short time when Jones started abusing and beating his young wife. Two weeks prior to her murder, Jones used a rope to beat Lou, and afterwards she left Jones and rented a boarding room.

On the night of the murder, Jones gained entrance to the boarding house and into Lou's room. There he chased after Lou and with a razor knife cut a hand off, slit her throat, and cut her across the chest. Lou covered in blood and dying, ran from the boardinghouse to a nearby saloon, fell against a refrigerator and then fell to the floor dead.

At about the same time George Ligon was crossing near the intersection of Miller and Orleans streets on his way home, when he was startled by a man running past him and then the man sat down in the street. Seeing the man hands covered in blood while holding a razor, Ligon drew his pistol.

Jones stood up and said, "Mr. George, I have killed a woman. I know she is dead for I cut her throat and her body may be found on the public schoolyard. She went in that direction, but she is dead. I loved her and I killed her and I am ready to swing for it."

Ligon then accompanied Jones to the residence of Sheriff Langham and he was subsequently placed in jail.

At the preliminary hearing, Willie Jones made the following statement:

> Yes, I killed her. I had been looking for her for two days for that purpose. I used a razor which I had stolen from a switchman whose room I looked after. I carried it with the intention of cutting her throat the first time I met her, and I did. I learned of her where abouts that day and at about 11 o'clock that night I went to the house. The land lady met me at the door and asked what I wanted. I laughed and told her that I only wanted to talk with my wife for a few minutes. With this I pushed into the house. My wife was standing by the bed, a man was near her, and it was my intention to kill him, but he had escaped when I finished with my wife, I chased the woman around the room with my razor ready and when I caught her she grabbed the razor in her hand and I pulled it away, nearly cutting her hand off. I then knocked her down and drew the blade across one side of her throat and then the other. I know she was finished, but in getting up I slashed her over the heart. Discovering then that the man had escaped I left with the intention of finding and killing him, but I see, Mr. Ligon and decided to surrender.

Jones said he knew that he would either be hanged or sent to the penitentiary for life, but that he preferred hanging as the penitentiary meant hard work in the hot sun, which he was opposed to doing.

Willie Jones was quickly found guilty of murder and sentenced to death. The execution, which was public, drew a crowd of between 4,000 to 6,000 witnesses on the courthouse lawn. At 11:38 a.m. when the trap was sprung, the noose slipped causing the knot to rest directly behind the head. As a result the neck was not broken and Jones strangled to death. Ten minutes later the body was declared dead and lowered into a coffin to be shipped for burial at Waco.

The *Galveston Daily News*, dated Saturday, March 10, 1900, provided a full article detailing the murder and execution at Beaumont, Texas.

Will Murray

Alias: Michigan Kid **Race/Gender:** Black Male **Offense:** Murder
Weapon: Knife & Iron Slats **Offense Date:** September 22, 1903 **Execution:** April 25, 1904

On September 21, 1903, Will Murray argued with his girlfriend Josephine Baker, and made repeated threats that he would kill her. Murray and Josephine lived in a shanty on the river front near the Tram Lumber Mill in Beaumont.

Because of her fear from his threats, Josephine did not return home, but instead decided to stay with a friend whose shanty was in the rear of the Tram Lumber Mill on Cypress Street. When Josephine did not return home, Murray went to the friend's house at about 10 p.m. and knocked on the door. After receiving no answer, Murray broke down the door and pulled Josephine out from under the bed and then beat and stabbed his twenty-five-year-old girlfriend to death.

On October 16, 1903, Murray was arraigned and pled guilty to murder before Judge W. H. Pope of the 58th District Court. The jury deliberated seven minutes to return a verdict that Murray was guilty of murder in the first degree and received the death sentence. Afterwards the case was appealed to the court of criminal appeals who affirmed the decision.

On March 21, 1904, Murray was returned back before the court for final sentencing. When Judge Pope asked if Murray had anything to say, he asked that he be allowed to live for sixty days. Judge Pope then ordered the execution to take place on April 25, between 11 a.m. in the morning and sunset.

On the appointed day, Murray declined to speak before the 3000 spectators who had arrived to witness his execution.

The *Galveston Daily News*, dated Tuesday, April 26, 1904, provided details of the murder, execution and county's past history of executions.

Robert H. Burgess

Race/Gender: White Male **Offense:** Murder **Offense Date:** January 27, 1915
Weapon: Pistol **Execution:** April 29, 1916

In 1910, Robert Burgess married Nellie "May" Rigsby for the first time. Sometime in 1914, the couple divorced, but reunited and remarried in May of 1914. In November, Nellie separated from her husband and returned back to her parents' house located at 690 Alma Street in Beaumont.

On January 26, 1915, Burgess received May's petition for divorce and immediately left from Cross Plains for Beaumont. Driving all night Burgess arrived at May's parents' house early the next morning. Upon entering the back door, Burgess found Nellie washing dishes in the kitchen. Nellie's mother, Mrs. Wiley Rigsby heard Nellie begging not to be killed and rushed through the kitchen door at the very moment Burgess shot her daughter. Mrs. Rigsby witnessed Burgess shoot her twenty-eight-year-old daughter in the abdomen, hip and in the back as she laid on the floor.

Burgess then walked to the sheriff's office and surrendered to the jailer saying he had just shot his wife. Burgess then sat down and wrote out a telegram to his brother, W. M. Burgess at Hico, Texas, which read, "Shot May," Bob.

Robert Burgess was tried on April 27, 1915, and convicted of murder in the first degree on May 1, 1915. The court of appeals affirmed the decision of November 17, 1915.

On the morning of the execution, Robert Burgess attempted to cheat the gallows by taking poison. Doctors were called into the cell and they quickly took action to save the man, only to be hanged an hour later. Burgess said he had taken the poison in hopes that the sheriff would not have to perform the task. After Burgess was positioned over the trap he said, "Goodbye, everybody, God have mercy on my soul. Be good to my baby, all of you." At 12:37 p.m., the trap was sprung.

The *Galveston Daily News*, dated Sunday, April 30, 1916, printed a short article that the execution had occurred at Beaumont.

Johnson County
County Seat - Cleburne

Samuel Houston Myers, Jr.

Race/Gender: White Male **Age:** 21 **Offense:** Murder
Offense Date: February 21, 1877 **Weapon:** Firearm **Execution:** March 19, 1880

Sam Myers. Sr. moved to Johnson County, Texas, in 1851, with his wife and six children. In 1866, Myers married his third wife, Mary Ann Hunter after his two previous wives had each died. When Myers died in 1874, his will contained the stipulation that in the event of his death, should his widow remarried, then the 183 acres he owned were to be returned to his estate. Mary Ann did remarry, (Hester) and remained on the farm, and lived in the farm house, which caused resentment in the Myers family.

On February 21, 1877, Mary Hester was sitting at the dinner table with her family when a bullet fired through a window struck her to the right side of the head, killing her.

In trying to determine who had murdered Mary Ann, tracks found at the scene were followed and led to the home of James M. Bowden. Bowden had married one of Sam Myers' daughters, Mary "Mollie" Myers. Once arrested, Bowden confessed that Thomas Myers and he had planned the murder, and named Sam Myers, Jr. as the person who fired the weapon.

Thomas Myers pled innocent to the charge and spent three years in prison during the course of three trials until a jury declared he was not guilty and he was released.

Sam Myers, Jr. pled innocent, but was found guilty and sentenced to death. James Bowden was tried in Somervell County and sentenced to fifteen years in prison. Years later, it was rumored that Bowden had confessed that he was the person who had murdered Mary Hester.

The *Brenham Weekly Banner* dated, Friday, March 26, 1880, wrote that Myers made a speech before the 5,000 spectators in Cleburne, in which he declared he was innocent of the crime.

John Wilkins

Race/Gender: White Male **Age:** 22 **Offense:** Robbery & Murder
Offense Date: October 31, 1895 **Weapon:** Shotgun & Pistol **Execution:** June 26, 1896

In October of 1895, John Wilkins rode a gray mare into the town of Cleburne and was arrested on suspicion of horse theft. Wilkins rode the horse to the Alliance wagon yard in Cleburne, and told the wagon yard keeper that he was from Burleson, Texas, and wanted to sell the horse. The yard keeper, W. J. Clark, declined to buy the horse as he recognized the mare as being the same animal that C. E. Taylor had been riding two days prior.

Wilkins then took the horse to the town square and sold the horse at auction. The high bidder paid Wilkins for the horse, but became suspicious of the title Wilkins handed him and informed the sheriff. Wilkins told Sheriff W. A. Stewart he received the horse as payment for picking cotton for a man named Abbott. Sheriff Stewart was not convinced and decided to hold Wilkins in the jail because he believed the horse fit the description of a stolen horse from South Texas.

While the sheriff was walking Wilkins to the jail, Wilkins made a break to escape by bolting from the sheriff. Sheriff Stewart swung into the saddle of his horse and chased after him. Wilkins ran about a quarter of a mile south of the town with Sheriff Stewart closing in on him. Wilkins drew a pistol and fired four shots at the sheriff, and Sheriff Stewart fired back twice. One of the bullets Wilkins fired at the sheriff went through Sheriff Stewart's hat and a second bullet hit the saddle tree. After Wilkins fired his last bullet, he surrendered. This time Sheriff Stewart searched his prisoner and found Wilkins to be carrying three razors, a watch, and a pocketbook.

The following morning, on November 2, 1895, the body of forty-five-year-old Grince Taylor was found in his home near Grandview. Grince had last been seen alive riding his horse back toward his home at 9 p.m. on the night of October 31, 1895. Nearby neighbors riding home became suspicious that something was wrong when they saw all of the windows of his house covered over and the door nailed shut. Looking through the covering, Taylor's body could be seen lying on the floor in one of the rooms and Sheriff Stewart was notified.

An examination of the body showed Grince had been killed from a shotgun blast to the head, and a bullet wound to the neck and right shoulder. It was then discovered the that gray mare Grince owned was missing, and resembled the horse Wilkins had sold. The sheriff also learned a razor and watch belonging to the victim was missing from the home.

The trial of John Wilkins lasted three days and ended on January 6, 1896. During the trial, Wilkins took the stand in his own defense and testified he had bought the horse, razor and watch all for $20. The jury was not convinced by Wilkins' story, and after deliberating for three hours returned to announce the verdict. Forman N. T. McAlister announced, "We the jury, find the defendant guilty of murder in the first degree and assess his punishment at death."

The court of appeals reviewed the case and affirmed the lower court's decision on March 4, 1896. On April 22, 1896, John Wilkins stood before a judge who ordered that "John Wilkins shall on Friday, the 26th day of June, A. D., 1896, in Johnson County, Texas, be hung by the neck until he is dead and it is the order of the court that the execution shall take place at any time after 11 o'clock and before sunset."

Two days prior to the hanging, Wilkins was aware that the *Daily Enterprise* was in competition with the *Johnson County Review* for an exclusive interview and confession from him. Wilkins sent word to the editor, named Scurlock, of the *Daily Enterprise* that he had a statement of his life and career that he wished to sell. Although Wilkins had differences with the editor after Scurlock told Wilkins he, "Intended to roast him after he was hung," Scurlock immediately raced over to the jail and bargained the selling price of $2.50 for Wilkins to provide a seventeen page written confession.

The $2.50 was all paid in quarters per Wilkins' instructions. Wilkins then wrote, "Life of John Wilkins from 1885 to 1896. I was in Racine, Missouri, a free boy, and in 1886, I am in Johnson County jail, Cleburne, Tex., 17 pages."

Wilkins handed the paper back to Scurlock who became furious and demanded his money back. Wilkins replied, "I'll keep this to pay for the roasting you promised to give me."

Wilkins then gave Sheriff Stewart, deputies Long, Grimes, Pollard, City Marshal White and Deputy Marshal Goodwin each a quarter as keepsakes of him.

On the morning of his execution, John Wilkins wrote the following letter verbatim, misspellings and all, to his brother, James Wilkins, in Racine, Missouri.

Dear Brothers and Sisters: I will answer your most kind and welcome letter that come to hand some time ago and was glad to here from you. I have bin wating to here from the govner, but have not herd from him yet and he had not got but about five ours to say in, but Jim there is no show now for me but to die. But I would just as soon die as to go to the pen for Life Still as Long as there is Life there is hope. But I don't think there is any hopes for the govner to do anything now. But still I don't know but I will ask you not to truble about me any more than you can help for there it but one time to die and we all haf to Die sooner or Later.

Jim I have just now herd from the govner and he would not do nothing more me, so I am bound to die to day. I know it is sad for you all to think about and that hurts me worse than to die, but don't truble will soon be over for me. Jim, I will send you my pictures. I will send them to you and you can divide them to the rest of all. Jim, I have been robbed of my life, but it cant be helped now. I have not got but a few hours to Live. I am to be hanged at 1 o'clock to day Jim. I am standing it just Like I had to and hope you al will not truble about me for it is no use to grieve for me now, so I will close by telling you good by now, but hope we will meet in the world to come.

So I will close my last letter to all on earth, so good by to all from
John Wilkins.
To all, mother, sisters and Brothers, less meet where truble is all over. A kiss to all.

At 12:45 p.m. a closed carriage pulled by two white horses took a position at the jail gate entrance of the jail yard to transport Wilkins to the gallows. The condemned man wearing a white shirt, navy blue suit with a rose pinned to the lapel, patent leather pumps, and a crush hat was afterwards escorted out of the jail by flanking deputies Pollard and Churchwell to the waiting carriage. Once in the carriage, Wilkins was joined by Sheriff Stewart, and both deputies along with reverends Leach and Shaw for spiritual advise while he was being transported. To ensure no escape attempts would me made, the carriage was surrounded by heavily armed lawmen. Guarding the front was Constable Tom Coulter, Deputy U.S. Marshal Irvine, Bosque County Sheriff John Metcalf, and Hood County Sheriff Tom Hiner. On the right of the carriage were J. H. Keith, J. V. Leatherwood, John I. Rodgers, Wyatt Griffith, J. M. Henderson and Nat P. Cothran. On the left, A. C. White, Emmett Goodwin, Collin County Sheriff Molden, ex-sheriff John C. Brown, and W. E. Mahaney. Guarding the rear were Reagan Teague, Oran Pollard, D. B. Casey, High Blassengame, Henry Bennett and H. R. Rogers.

The gallows had been erected about 100 yards south of the jail in a depression on the west side of Buffalo Creek and surrounded with the barbed wire. After the carriage stopped inside the wire enclosure, a crowd of 10,000 to 15,000 people rushed forward and pushed the front row of people into the barbed wire. Wilkins exited the carriage and mounted the gallows with a firm step to an awaiting chair placed over the trap door.

At 1:19 Reverend F. E. Leach offered a prayer and afterwards Wilkins stood up to make a final statement. Wilkins said:

> Friends I haven't got much to say, except that I want to meet you all in heaven, and I want to bid you all good bye. My statement is in the hands of my attorney. I have no ill will against anybody, I thank the officers for their kind treatment. I have been treated as white as anybody could be treated under the circumstances and I have nothing against anybody.

Wilkins then retook his seat, and Reverend A. R. Shaw provided a second prayer. After the prayer, Wilkins stood and shook hands with the officers, newspaper reporters and lawmen standing on the gallows. At 1:26 p.m. Sheriff Stewart and Deputy Long secured Wilkins' ankles and wrists while the crowd stood silently watching. Just as the black cap was about to be placed over Wilkins' head, he located his attorney, W. H. Bledsoe, standing in the crowd. Johns called out to him and said, "Goodbye Will."

The attorney answered back, "Goodbye John."

At 1:30 p.m. Sheriff Stewart cut the rope, which released the trap. The fall did not break his neck and Wilkins strangled to death. Seventeen minutes later doctors J. H. Happel and E. B. Osborn announced that Wilkins had no pulse. After twenty minutes, the physicians pronounced Wilkins dead. The body was afterwards cut down and placed in a plain dark coffin.

John Wilkins did write a full confession, and it was published by both the *Johnson County Review* and the *Dallas Morning News*, dated June 27, 1896.

John B. Shaw

Alias: Stokes Shaw **Race/Gender:** White Male **Offense:** Murder
Offense Date: November 3, 1897 **Weapon:** Pistol & Rifle **Execution:** November 25, 1898

John Shaw worked as the manager for a small ranch located near the Thomas Perry Crane farm. Tom Crane worked as a farmer to support his wife and their three small children. Shaw became deeply infatuated with Crane's wife and attempted to persuade her to leave her husband. Mrs. Crane flatly refused, telling Shaw that she was a happily married woman. Shaw believed in his mind that if he got Thomas Crane out of the way, that Mrs. Crane would reconsider him.

On November 3, 1897, Shaw had Lee Wilson, who worked for him as a laborer, to go to the field where he knew Crane was plowing. Shaw directed Wilson to go to Crane on the pretense of needing his assistance to free a steer that was trapped in a nearby swamp. When Wilson asked Crane for his help, the farmer followed Wilson into the thicket where he was soon cornered by Shaw and Wilson.

When told of his impending death at the hands of Shaw, Crane promised Shaw if his life was spared he would leave the country for good and never return. Crane begged for his life while calling out the names of his children, and pleaded with Shaw not to kill the father of his children. When this had no influence on Shaw, Crane called out the name of Shaw's own mother and asked for him to think of what he was doing. Crane then attempted to escape with his life by spurring his horse to get away. Shaw took aim at Crane with his pistol and fired. The bullet hit the fleeing man in the back, knocking him off his horse.

Wilson and Shaw dragged Crane back and tormented the wounded man again with death by telling Crane that he "needed to pray, for his time on earth was short." Crane again made an attempt to escape on his horse. Wilson this time shot at Crane with his rifle. As Crane fell from his horse, his foot was caught in a stirrup, and he was dragged for several yards.

Shaw and Wilson ran up to Crane and shot him a third time in the back of the head. Shaw afterwards mutilated the face and skull with strikes from the butt of the rifle. Crane's body was left in the thicket, and immediately after committing the murder; Shaw went directly to the Crane farmhouse. There, Shaw told Mrs. Crane that her husband was wanted and that he had fled from the country, and that Thomas left her and the children in his care. Not believing what Shaw had told her, Mrs. Crane reported her husband missing to Sheriff W. A. Stewart. Mrs. Crane expressed her suspicion of Shaw because of his recent solicitation to her to leave her husband and she feared Shaw might be responsible.

Sheriff Stewart accompanied by trackers, searched for Thomas Crane for three days, finally discovering his mutilated body lying in the thicket. Wilson and Shaw were arrested and both charged with murder. Wilson requested to see the county attorney where he then provided a full account of the murder and agreed to testify as State's witness. In exchange for his testimony, Wilson received a life sentence in the penitentiary.

On January 10, 1898, Shaw was tried and found guilty and sentenced to death. After the court of appeals affirmed the decision, Shaw's date of execution was set by Judge J. M. Hall to take place on August 5, 1898. On August 3, the governor granted a reprieve in order to review the application for commutation. The governor afterwards refused the application and date of the execution was reset for August 12.

Three days prior to the scheduled execution, Shaw escaped from the jail as his guard slept. The governor quickly posted a $500 reward for Shaw's capture with the sheriff matching the same amount. Hundreds of bounty hunters and trackers with bloodhounds participated in the search for Shaw. Shaw was finally captured by Deputy Sheriff Walter Anthony near the town of Malakoff, Texas, on August 21, and returned to jail.

Texas law at the time permitted for an affidavit for lunacy to act as a stay of execution until a trial was held to determine if the person was sane or not. Shaw's sister filed such an affidavit and the lunacy trial took place on November 14. The trial lasted for three days with the verdict from the jury finding John Shaw sane.

On November 25, 1898, at 11:46 a.m., Shaw was hanged and within seventeen minutes he was declared dead.

The *Houston Daily Post*, dated Saturday, November 26, 1898, wrote, "Never has man died so reluctantly, fighting every inch of the ground, determined to live if possible. Never a murder more cold blooded to be revenged by the law."

John Renfro

Race/Gender: White Male **Age:** 29 **Offense:** Murder
Offense Date: February 3, 1899 **Weapon:** Pistol **Execution:** July 27, 1900

On February 3, 1899, John Renfro was at the Johnson County Courthouse in Cleburne to appear as the defendant on a charge of slander against a woman. As witnesses arrived at the courthouse, Renfro stood just inside the south courthouse entrance. The woman's father, Mr. M. M. Williams who was unarmed, arrived and entered through the courthouse door. Just after entering Mr. Williams was immediately met by Renfro who then drew his pistol and fired four or five bullets into the sixty-year-old man's abdomen without warning. Williams staggered several steps, then collapsed just outside the window of the county judge's office. Williams died about thirty minutes later.

Renfro was quickly arrested by Deputy Constable Onan Pollard and jailed. Although Renfro refused to give a statement as to the motive for the shooting, he gave a plea of self-defense as justification for the murder. Renfro claimed that Williams had tried to hit him with a rock. Renfro's attorney made a request to the court for a change of venue which Judge Hall quickly refused and tried Renfro in the same courthouse in which he committed the murder.

On July 9, 1900, after two previous respites by Governor Joseph D.. Sayers to review the evidence, the governor refused to interfere any longer with the sentence of the court. After a last claim at insanity, which failed, Renfro told reporters, "I want to be hanged and have this agony over with."

The gallows had been built behind the jail with an enclosure surrounding it. John Wilkins and John Shaw were previously hanged from the same gallows, and Renfro was hanged with the same rope that was used to execute Shaw. The Sheriff W. A. Stewart issued 100 tickets into the enclosure to witness the execution, and fifty to sixty spectators arrived. At 11:50 a.m. Renfro was escorted to the gallows and ascended the steps, and was met by Reverend Hendricks. After a prayer, Renfro told Reverend Hendricks, "I have made peace with God, and I am not afraid to die. I know I have to die sometime."

To the witnesses, Renfro said:

> Men and friends—you, of course, expect to hear me say something; I have nothing particular to say, but would not be true to myself if I did not say that a great injustice has been done to me. But I have forgiven every enemy and all who have had any hand in bringing me to this point. I have no malice toward any man; we all have to die sometime and my time is now. Of course life is dear to me as to any one, but I have resigned myself and will cheerfully meet the requirements of the law.

After his final statement and the preparations were complete, Sheriff Stewart sprang the trap as 12:12 p.m. The drop broke his neck and after being suspended for twelve minutes, County Physician J. D. Rucker pronounced Renfro dead. The body was then released to relatives who transported Renfro's remains to Benbrook in Tarrant County for burial.

The *Houston Daily Post*, dated Saturday, July 28, 1900, provided their readers with the details of the murder and execution at Bastrop.

Henry Fugett

Race/Gender: Black Male   **Offense:** Murder   **Offense Date:** June 3, 1903
Weapon: Butcher Knife   **Execution:** February 12, 1904

Henry and Laura Fugett had been married three or four years, when Laura Fugett separated from her husband. She told Fuggett she did not love him any longer and said she had been seeing another man.

On June 3, 1903, witnesses were alerted to the screaming by Laura's mother, Millie Hamilton, "He's killed her! He's killed her!"

Witnesses rushing into the house saw Henry Fugett straddled over Laura Fugett who was on her hands and knees while he plunged the butcher knife into her head and neck, which almost decapitated the woman. As the police were being called, Henry Fugett said, "There is no need for that, I will surrender myself."

Fugett had purchased the butcher knife earlier for fifteen-cents and stabbed Laura seventeen times. Fugett was arrested for murder and tried for the crime on June 19, 1903. After the case was affirmed, Henry Fugett wrote the following letter to Governor Lanham asking for him to commute his sentence:

> *Hon S. W. T. Lanham, Governor of Texas, it is a matter of very grave circumstances that I appeal to you for your assistance. Your honor, I have no doubt that you have heard of my trouble before now, as it has been published time after time. Providing you have no remembrance of it, I will try to put the facts before you as near as I can. On the 3d day of June, 1903, I was crazed with love and jealousy over my wife, and the more I thought of it, the crazier I got, until I lost my mind altogether. And after I had done that I went to her house and killed her by cutting her with a knife. I was so crazy that I didn't realize what I was or had done until after it was all over. I then went and gave up to the officers and told them what I had done. I was indicted by the Grand Jury and tried for murder on the 19th day of June. The jury found me guilty of murder in the first degree and assessed my punishment at death. Me being a Negro and a very poor one, I had to depend on the Court for counsel. Well they did all they could for me. They took an appeal on my case and it was affirmed on me. My day has been set for executing. Honorable Judge Poindexter passed my sentence on me the first day of January. He then set the*

day for me to hang on the 12th of February.

Now that I have been waiting for my lawyers to take action in the case, I have delayed writing you in regards to the matter. Your honor, this is the first trouble of any kind that I have ever been guilty of at all, and if I had had my right mind I wouldn't have done what I did for my own life, for I loved my wife and I loved her dearly. I am a Negro of good character and can say that I always went and carried myself in a Negro's place. I am a believer in the Lord and have been all my life.

Your honor, I can get some of the best men in Johnson County to swear to my being a good negro. They will all give me a good recommendation and all say that they don't want me to hang, and that they will do all they can to prevent me hanging. Your honor, I fully realize my condition, and I am at your mercy. I fully realize that I have violated the laws of the State and know that I deserve punishment. But by hanging me I would be punished for a few minutes only. I have always been used to hard labor, and I know that if you, your Honor, will have mercy on me and let me spend the rest of my days in the State Penitentiary, I will be a man at anything that they would desire me to do. And I think that the State would derive a profit from my labor. Your Honor, I am more than willing to sign an agreement not to ask for a pardon under any circumstances, and will never give the officials any trouble at all. Now, I will close my plea by praying to God that you, Your Honor, will give my case and plea your deepest thought and consideration. With the best wishes for the near future, I beg to remain your humble servant. Signed, Henry Fugett

Henry Fugett in Jail.
The *Weekly Enterprise*, Cleburne, Texas
February 11, 1904

The governor refused to interfere and on the morning of the execution, Sheriff H. F. Long went to Fugett's cell for the purpose of reading the death warrant to him. The death warrant read as follows:

THE STATE OF TEXAS

To the Sheriff of Johnson County, said State, Greeting:

Whereas, on the 20th day of June A. D. 1903, in the District Court of said County, Henry Fugett was duly and legally convicted of the crime of murder in the first degree, as fully appears by the judgment of said court, entered upon the minutes of said court as follows, to-wit:

THE STATE OF TEXAS

HENRY FUGETT, No. 9717   June 20, 1903,

On the 19th day of June, 1903, this case was called for trial and the State rendered by her County Attorney and the defendant Henry Fugett appeared in person, his counsel also being present, and the said defendant having been duly arraigned and having pled not guilty, both parties announced ready for trial and the defendant Henry Fugett in open court pleaded not guilty to the charge contained in the indictment herein, thereupon a jury, to-wit P. W. Huffhine and eleven others, was duly selected, impanelled and sworn, who having heard the indictment read and the defendant plea of not guilty thereto, and having heard the evidence submitted and having been duly charged by the court, retired in charge of the proper officer to consider of their verdict and afterwards, on this 20th day of June, 1903, were brought into open court by the proper officer, the defendant and his counsel being present, and in due form of law returned into open court the following verdict, which was received by the court and is here now entered upon the minutes of the court, to-wit:

"We the jury find the defendant guilty of murder in the first degree and assess his punishment at death. "P. W. Huffhine, Foreman."

It is therefore, considered and adjudged by the court that the defendant Henry Fugett is guilty of the offense of murder in the first degree as found by the jury and that he be punished as has been determined by the jury, that is with death, and that said defendant be remanded to jail to await the further order of the court herein.

And where as on the 1st day of January, A. D. 1904, the said court pronounced sentence upon the said Henry Fugett in accordance with said judgment, as fully appears by the said sentence entered upon the minutes of said court, as follows, to-wit:

THE STATE OF TEXAS Vs. HENRY FUGETT, NO. 9717.

This day this cause was again called, the State appeared by her County Attorney, and the defendant Henry Fugett was brought into open court in charge of the Sheriff for the purpose of having the sentence of the law pronounced in accordance with the verdict and the judgment herein rendered and entered against him on a day of a former term of this court, his counsel also being present. And thereupon the defendant, Henry Fugett was asked by the court whether he had anything to say why sentence should not be pronounced against him, and he answered nothing in bar there of; where upon the court proceeded in the presence of the said defendant Henry Fugett to pronounce sentence against him as follows: "It is the order of the court that the defendant Henry Fugett who has been adjudged to be guilty of murder in the first degree, and that the punishment has been assessed by the verdict of the jury at death, shall on the 12th day of February, 1904, in Johnson County, Texas be hung by the neck until he is dead and that the clerk of this court issued a death warrant in accordance with sentence, and direct and deliver the same to the Sheriff of said Johnson County, Texas, who shall execute the same in accordance with the law in such cases provided. And the said defendant remanded to jail to await the execution of this sentence.

These are therefore to command you to execute the aforesaid judgment on Friday, the 12th day of February, A. D. 1904, at any time after 11 o'clock and before sunset on said day, last stated, in the County of Johnson, said State, by hanging the said Henry Fugett by the neck until he is dead, and that in said execution you observe and obey the provisions of the law governing in such cases.

Herein fail not, and due return make hereof in accordance with law. Witness my signature and seal of office on this the 9th day of February, A. D. 1904.

Q. C. Templeton,
Clerk Dist. Court Johnson Co., Texas.

Henry Fugett's Baptism as published in the Weekly Enterprise, Cleburne, Texas, February 11, 1904.

The scaffold was built behind the jail with a privacy fence surrounding the gallows. At the gallows, Sheriff Long asked Fugett if he wished to make a statement to which Fugett replied, "No sir."

As the black cap was being placed over the head, Fugett stood still with a smile on his face. At 12:25 p.m., Sheriff Long cut the rope holding the trap door, as he said, "Goodbye Henry." The trap door opened and Henry Fugett was pronounced dead in six minutes by physicians who said the neck had been broken.

The *Weekly Enterprise*, Cleburne, dated Thursday, February 11, 1904, provided a large article giving a full account of the murder, testimony, photographs and execution.

Karnes County
County Seat - Karnes City

Joe B. Guiles

Alias: John D. May
Offense: Robbery & Murder
Execution Date: May 26, 1894
Race/Gender: White male
Offense Date: June 25, 1893
Age: 22
Weapon: Pistol

Joe B. Giles was originally from Dallas, Texas, and had served five years in prison for horse theft. Six months after his release from prison, Giles and four other men, who he might have been imprisoned with, conspired to rob the San Antonio and Aransas Pass train. The train was said to be carrying a large sum of money that was to be delivered to a Beeville bank.

On Wednesday afternoon June 25, 1893, the train had just left the Brickenridge station, (Falls City) forty-six miles south of San Antonio when Guiles jumped over the tender box, across the coals and into the engine cab. Guiles pulled out his six-shooters and pointed the pistols at the engineer, Mike Tearny, and fireman Frank Martin ordering them to slow down the train and then stop a quarter of a mile down the track, after they crossed the San Antonio River where his four partners were waiting.

Engineer Tearny threw the engine into reverse, and both Frank Martin and he jumped from the cab. Angered by their actions, Guiles opened fire on both men, hitting Frank Martin. The bullet struck Martin in the heart, and he fell back onto the tracks and was run over by the train. The conductor hearing the gunshots and suspecting something wrong quickly applied the air brakes from inside the coaches, which brought the train to a stop.

Guiles then jumped from the engine cab to escape and ran down the tracks toward the river. The engineer, conductor and express messenger detached the engine from the cars to use to the train as cover during a pursuing gun battle with the robber. Guiles ran into the brush and took cover behind a tree where the men opened fire on him. After several shots were fired pinning Guiles down behind the tree, he threw down his pistols and surrendered.

After Guiles was tied with rope cord, four horsemen were seen riding away from the river. Guiles was transported to Floresville where he was jailed. A posse of men searched for the other suspects at the scene of the robbery, but only recovered Guiles' horse, saddle and Winchester rifle. Guiles later told United Stated Marshal Richard Ware that he and his unnamed confederates had planned the robbery several weeks prior after hearing that the Pacific Express Company car would be carrying a large amount of money for a Beeville bank.

Guiles was tried and sentenced to hang. The gallows were built outside the new jail on the northeast corner of the public square with the intention of the execution being public. A wooden enclosure was later built around the scaffold after the Governor Jim Hogg sent a telegram ordering the execution to be private.

On May 26, 1894, Joe Guiles walked out of the jail at 3:45 p.m. and before stepping up on the scaffold, said, "Well boys, I hear there is a money bet that I will have to be assisted to the scaffold, now watch me."

Unassisted, Guiles mounted the scaffold and turned to address the crowd. "Well, gentlemen, I have but little to say. I am innocent of the crime I am charged with and I say it as my last words, that it was an accident." Turning to Mr. Martin, he said, "Mr. Martin, I killed your boy, but did it accidentally, I would not have harmed a hair on his head, and I hope God had mercy on his soul, and I hope I will meet him in heaven today. I am very thankful to Sheriff Swale and Campbell for their kind treatment of me, and I know my lawyers did all they could under the circumstances, and I am very thankful to them for it. Now, boys, I don't look excited, do I."

A person from the crowd yelled, "No, no!"

"Now, Mr. Martin, remember my last words are; I killed your boy accidentally, " Guiles said. "Gentlemen, goodbye."

The *Fort Worth Gazette*, dated Saturday, May 26, 1894, provided a full account of the crime, execution and Guiles' background.

Ramon Campos

Race/Gender: Mexican Male **Offense:** Double Murder **Offense Date:** May 26, 1906
Weapon: Razor Blade Knife & Pistol **Execution Date:** February 1, 1907

Ramon Campos fell in love with Juana McHaney and wanted to marry her. The problem was that Campos was already married, but he proposed to McHaney anyway and promised he would divorce his wife, so that they both could be together. Campos did divorce his wife, and upon doing so went to McHaney and asked for her hand in marriage. McHaney however changed her mind and refused to marry Campos.

On May 26, 1906, McHaney was driving a buggy with her twenty-year-old younger sister, and brother when they came upon Campos walking, and McHaney invited him to ride with them. Campos accepted the ride and climbed into the buggy sitting directly behind McHaney. During the ride, Campos again proposed marriage to McHaney and she again refused his proposal. Angered, Campos drew a razor blade knife from his pocket and cut her throat.

McHaney's younger sister started screaming and Campos drew a pistol. The girl then grabbed the barrel of the gun trying to gain control. As they both struggled over the pistol, they both fell from the buggy. Campos regained possession of the pistol, and shot at the girl as she was running away. The bullet hit her to the head, killing her instantly. McHaney's younger brother escaped unharmed. Campos was soon arrested, and confessed to both murders.

The *Palestine Daily Herald*, dated February 1, 1907, provided the history of the murders to their readers and little information as to the execution itself.

Kaufman County
County Seat - Kaufman

Bill Payne

Alias: Jack Moore **Race/Gender:** Black & Native American Mix Male **Age:** 23
Offense: Robbery & Murder **Offense Date:** May 17, 1876 **Weapon:** Wood Log
Execution: November 3, 1876

Eugene Catchings

Race/Gender: Black Male **Age:** 23 **Offense:** Robbery & Murder:
Offense Date: May 17, 1876 **Weapon:** Wood Log **Execution:** November 3, 1876

John Love was a sixty-five-year-old man who lived alone in a small hut next to the railroad tracks near Terrell. In the early morning hours of May 17, 1876, both Jack Moore and Eugene Catching stopped at Love's small hut and asked for directions. After leaving, Moore and Eugene Catchings discussed returning back to the old man's home during the night and killing him for any valuables he might have.

Catchings and Moore did return during a lightning storm and could see Love sitting. While Catchings engaged in casual conversation with Love, Moore crept up behind the old man with a wood log. Moore then struck Love in the back of the head knocking him down. After killing Love, the men ransacked the home and after finding no money or valuables, they set fire to the house.

Both men were arrested and tried. The jury deliberated five minutes before returning a verdict of guilty. It was estimated that 6,000 to 7,000 spectators witnessed the double execution.

Eugene Catchings from the gallows said:

As the day has been set for my hanging, I want to give you warning. I don't want anyone to follow my course. I can't say I am sorry for anything so much as for the murder of old man Love. When a young man starts out and follows drinking and card playing, he will come out just as I have. Whiskey will ruin any man. Whiskey and cards have been the ruin of many men. Drop it! Go no further. Quit now.

Question from the crowd: Do you think you will have forgiveness for your sins?

Catchings: No, I know I have not.

Question: What about the clothes of old man Loves?

Catchings: I took nothing from the house, except a piece of tobacco. I got no money; he had no money. I thought he had money, but he hand none. I did not do the killing—my partner did it.

Bill Payne said:

My life ought to be a warning to all. I have been raised well; and knew better than to do murder, but I did it. I hope the young men especially will take warning from my fate. There are worse men looking at me than I am—plenty of them, and I hope they will reform. I always believed there was a hell, and I still believe it. I know Mrs. Hartman as one of the best women who lives. I think she was a true Christian. She told me to mend my ways and quit my evil doings. I have prayed to God to forgive me. I believe I am prepared to meet him. I feel that I have done wrong, and am sorry for it. I know I am bound to die, and I know that no one can save me. Men and talk alike are useless to save me.

Subsequently he again got up and said he had given his body to Dr. Splawn, to be used for dissection, for the benefit of mankind. He then sat down, and was chained to Catchings who was cool and collected.

Eugene Catchings had given his body to Dr. Mulkey while Jack Moore donated his to Dr. Splawn for the benefit of medical science.

On November 11, 1876, the *Dallas Weekly Herald* printed a full account of the execution and interviews that was conducted with both men prior to their execution. The paper wrote:

> The confession of Eugene Catchings was printed and sold on the grounds. It corroborates in all vital points, the confession of Payne, and sold like hot cakes. Thus once more is the majesty of the law vindicated in the great State of Texas.

King Martin

Race/Gender: Black Male **Offense:** Rape **Offense Date:** July 5, 1899
Weapon: Knife **Execution:** March 16, 1900

King Martin was a farm laborer who worked for James Wilson on his farm located six miles southeast of Kaufman. On the evening of July 5, 1899, Wilson and his wife left their farm and their sixteen-year-old daughter, Lizzie Wilson, at home to take care of chores along with King Martin and Martin's wife.

Soon after the Wilsons were out of sight, Martin went up to the house complaining to Lizzie of an injury to his foot that had been caused by a hay rake. Martin told his wife to go to their cabin and make him a poultice for his injured foot. After Martin's wife had left, Martin pulled a knife and threatened to kill Lizzie if she screamed out, and then assaulted the girl. Martin threatened the girl before leaving that if she told anyone what he had done, he would kill her entire family. The next afternoon, Lizzie told her parents what Martin had done, and the authorities were immediately notified.

Both lawmen and a posse of citizens searched for King Martin who was located as he attempted to hide himself in high weeds, and was shot in a knee. Martin was then turned over to lawmen who transported him to the Dallas County jail for fear a mob would overrun the jail and take him out to be lynched.

On September 20, 1899, King Martin was tried by a jury that returned a verdict in ten minutes, finding him guilty of criminal assault and sentenced to death. While waiting for the date of his execution, Martin and six other inmates attempted to escape from the jail, but the plan was foiled when a trusty notified the sheriff. Sheriff Jim Keller quickly forced the prisoners back into their cells and in the process shot and wounded Martin in the side.

On February 11, 1900, Judge

King Martin standing in the center while handcuffed to flanking deputies on March 16, 1900.

James Elizer Dillard ordered Martin's date of execution to take place on March 16, 1900. A week before the execution, the gallows were erected on the poor farm near Kaufman with an eighteen-foot wall surrounding the gallows so only those invited could witness the event.

On the day of the execution, 1,500 people arrived at the execution site to discover the hanging was private and that only sixty-five passes were handed out. On the gallows, Martin sang his favorite song, *Amazing Grace*. Afterward Martin sang the song, he bade all of those present on the scaffold with a "goodbye," and thanked the officers for their kindness.

The *Dallas Morning News*, dated Saturday, March 17, 1900, printed the details of the assault and execution.

Henry Johnson

Race/Gender: Black Male
Offense: Rape
Offense Date: May 25, 1903
Execution: May 30, 1903

On May 25, 1903, at about 4:20 in the afternoon, Sheriff Bill Henderson was notified of the criminal assault upon Mrs. Jennie Whitworth, which had occurred at her home on the Munson farm. The sheriff immediately rode out to the farm with a posse to begin investigating and search for the suspect.

The sheriff learned that the suspect was a black man by the name of Henry Johnson who worked on the same farm and lived in a nearby cabin. The sheriff and posse began trailing Johnson who was spotted near the town of Kemp at about 9 p.m. that night. When Johnson attempted to escape, the posse shot at him with their shotguns. The shotguns were loaded with birdshot and the balls from the shot peppered Johnson's face, mouth, body, and several of his fingers were torn off. Once captured, Johnson immediately confessed to being guilty of the crime. Johnson told Sheriff Henderson he had gone to the Whitworth house asking for salt when he grabbed Mrs. Whitworth and committed the assault.

On May 29, 1903, Sheriff

Henry Johnson seated over the trapdoor moments before his execution.
Author's personal collection.

Moments after Henry Johnson dropped through the trapdoor.
Author's personal collection.

Henderson and the Terrell Rifles military company, armed with rifles and bayonets, carried Henry Johnson into the Kaufman County courtroom on a cot. The judge ordered that no one would be allowed in the courtroom other than witnesses called to testify. A jury of twelve men were selected and seated in eighteen minutes.

Johnson pled guilty to committing the criminal assault upon Mrs. Whitworth. Dr. Bishop testified that Mrs. Whitworth sustained lacerations to her throat, mouth and face from the attack. Because her injuries were so severe, the doctor testified Mrs. Whitworth was in no condition to testify. Sheriff Henderson and Deputy Stralee both testified that after Henry Johnson was captured, he confessed to committing the assault as well.

At 11:30 a.m. the jury retired to deliberate and returned four minutes later with the verdict of guilty as charged, and assessed the punishment at death. Johnson requested the court to waive the required thirty days for an appeal, and asked that he be executed immediately. Judge Dillard asked Johnson if he had anything to say why sentence should not be passed upon him. Johnson replied, "I wanted to see my people, but they had not come, and therefore I want to be hung."

Judge Dillard said, "Very well, it is the sentence of the court that you be taken by the sheriff and hanged by the neck until you are dead; that the execution take place tomorrow sometime between 10 o'clock and 4 o'clock, as he may select. There is nothing further to say. Mr. Sheriff take charge of him."

The entire court proceeding took one hour and fifteen minutes from the time to seat a jury, testimony, verdict and sentencing.

The *Fort Worth Star-Telegram*, dated Sunday, May 31, 1903, printed the following short article of the execution at Kaufman, Texas.

BLACK CAP FOR NEGRO JOHNSON

Brute Who Criminally Assaulted Mrs. Whitworth is Hanged.

MEETS DEATH QUIETLY

Confesses His Guilt and Urges Other Negroes to Take Warning

Dallas, Texas, May 30.—Before the biggest assemblage of people that Kaufman county ever had together, Henry Johnson, the Negro who committed criminal assault on Mrs. Charles Whitworth last Monday, was hanged this afternoon. The gallows was in plain view and thousands of people witnessed Sheriff Henderson adjust the noose and spring the trap.

The drop fell at four minutes after 1 o'clock. The Negro fell eight feet and his neck was broken by the fall.

Johnson was brought from the jail to the scaffold by the Terrell rifles and the sheriff's force. He was weak from his wounds, but was stoical as an Indian and did not display a trace of fear. Before the black cap was drawn, Johnson made a speech to those around. He again confessed his guilt and urged all Negroes to beware of his fate.

After the execution the throng quickly and quietly dispersed and Kaufman became as peaceful as it was before the beginning of the stirring scenes of this week.

Kinney County
County Seat - Brackettville

Camilio Gonzales

Race/Gender: Hispanic Male **Offense:** Robbery & Murder **Offense Date:** November 1, 1884
Weapon: Firearm **Execution:** April 16, 1886

Camilio Gonzales was tried and convicted for the robbery and murder of Peter Johnson at the small country store Johnson owned. On November 1, 1884, Camilio Gonzales and three other Mexican bandits gagged and tied up the store owner while the store was ransacked and $800 in cash stolen. Before the bandits left the store, Johnson was shot above the right eye and killed.

On April 16, 1886, Camilio Gonzales ascended the scaffold with a firm tread, took hold of the dangling rope and placed the noose around his neck, where a deputy promptly removed it. On the gallows, Camilio made a short speech protesting his innocence. He then turned toward the jail, and while waving his hand to the prisoners who were standing with their faces pressed up against the window said, "Goodbye, my companions, Goodbye."

Camilio's arms and legs were then bound. When the lever was sprung at 2:30 p.m., Camilio was laughing as he fell through the trap. The fall broke his neck and Camilio was pronounced dead in eight minutes.

Camilio had property in Mexico which consisted of ten head of cattle, twelve horses, a house, and three and one half days of water irrigation rights. He left everything he owned to a local prostitute by the name of Camella Elaeruza.

A reporter for the *Fort Worth Daily Gazette*, wrote the following description of Camilio in the Saturday, April 17, 1886, edition.

Camilio Gonzales was a wild beast caged. In a state of liberty he was an impartial and picturesque thief; in prison he was an ill-conditioned ruffian, with a curse for his keepers and a kick for all supernal and infernal. And yet it was a pity that so straight a man should die. Broad-shouldered and deep-chested, long armed and thin-flanked, powerful and graceful, he was a picture of human physical possibilities, the highest type of uneducated, but splendid brute force, an Adonis of the chaparral. Over his brawny breast fell a coal black silken beard, through the heavy mustache, behind sensual thick lips, sheen savagely glittering teeth, and on his bull neck the muscles rose in cords. His copper skin glowed with health, and the animal spirits in him found vent perpetually in some outbreak against his captors, his fellow prisoners or his fate. He was a product of the arrested development of his nation, a simple child of nature, a variegated scoundrel. The face, while very handsome, was Mexican in the extreme, only it had none of that nation's dreaminess. It was a quick and powerful face, the clear cut lines and high cheek bones showing its descent. Gonzales was a "Palado," that is, a mixture of Aztec, Castilian and Indian. Filtered down, condensed, extracted from countless generation, in him were all the vices of the nations whose diverse blood ran in his veins. He was a leader among his people, and known on both banks of the river for many miles.

He was as daring a rider as ever crossed a horse, a deadly shot, or unshaken nerve, or magnificent vitality, a gambler, a drinker, a cut-throat, a guitar player and singer of high tenor ballads. There died with him a restricted, but singular knowledge. For years the first in all local border criminalities, there passed out of life in his teeming brain secrets that grizzled sheriffs and tanned coastguards would have given their ears to know. Many a wild tale of midnight foray and the flash of the Winchester in the darkness. Many a jolly story of soft midnight and smuggled bales, many a legend of sodden upturned faces in the river, many a recital of delirious rides in the tearing chaparral with the law's sleuth-hounds on his trial. They all died with him. He was a predatory villain, and made his livelihood in Mexico and the United States impartially. That which he could steal was his, and what he couldn't steal no man could lift. With ribaldry and oaths he passed his long days. Thee dark-skinned women on the street wiped their eyes when they spoke of Camilio, and the men gravely discussed him, and hoped, in sibilant, Spanish, that the great God would be good to him, for he was only a poor man and would not mind the priests. That this noted smuggler, this prince of raiders, this chief of his desperate fellows, this wild-riding Ishmael should die like a sheep in the shambles, made their only sorrow. They had shared the goat's milk with him many a time, had seen him fly by in the night on an errand of crime or love, and had wondered at what hour in the day and in whose hands would be the Winchester that would curtail a life so full or motion. It is a hard thing for a Mexican to be thus broken up in his pre-arrangement of destiny, and his companions suffered with Camilio.

Lamar County

County Seat - Paris

Isham Scott

Alias: Sam Scott **Race/Gender:** Black Male **Offense:** Murder
Offense Date: January 10, 1881 **Weapon:** Shotgun **Execution:** January 5, 1883

Joe Spear was a butcher who lived in a one-room shack on the Greenwood road in Paris, Texas. It was rumored that Spear kept a large sum of money hidden inside his home. Isham Scott, Joe Bonner, and John Hancock heard the rumor and decided they would rob "Old Man Spear."

The men arrived at the home during the night of January 10, 1881, and chased chickens around the yard thinking Spear would come out of his house to investigate. When he did not, the men went up on the front porch and knocked on the door. Spear cracked the door open a couple of inches, when he was hit by a shotgun blast. The door had been chained and remained intact. The next morning, people passing by heard a moan coming from inside the house and stopping to investigate they found Joe Spear wounded. Because of the loss of blood and the severe wound, Spear died hours later.

The three suspects were arrested with Joe Bonner turning State's witness against John Hancock and Isham Scott. John Hancock was sentenced to life imprisonment and Isham Scott received the death penalty.

On the day of the execution, the talk among the citizens in town was that friends of Scott were going to make an attempt to rescue him from the gallows. The news alarmed Sheriff G. M. Crook who quickly swore-in fifty trusted men as special deputies to escort Scott to the gallows that had been erected a half-mile west of the town square. At the gallows, a crowd of 3,000 to 5,000 people waited for the parade of armed officers to arrive with their prisoner who arrived sitting on his coffin.

Isham Scott mounted the scaffold on his own and declared to all present that he was innocent, and blamed the murder on Joe Bonner and Gid Adams. Scott claimed he only held the horses while everyone else did the shooting. Scott told the crowd he was prepared to meet his God, and was not afraid to die. Scott then appealed to both races to "take warning from his doom." While his arms and legs were being secured, Scott told the sheriff he wanted to die "easy." At 3 p.m. the sheriff sprang the trap, and the fall of eight feet broke Scott's neck.

The *Waco Daily Examiner*, dated Saturday, January 6, 1883, provided their readers with details of the crime and execution at Paris, Texas.

Bill Bass

Race/Gender: Black Male **Age:** 25 **Offense:** Rape
Offense Date: 1882 **Execution:** October 31, 1884

Bill Bass who claimed he was innocent of raping a white woman was tried and convicted of the crime. Lon Williams was a paralytic who lived at the county poor farm where she was employed, and testified Bass raped her.

On the gallows, as the death warrant was being read, officers had to help Bass to stand upright as he was about to faint. After the reading, Bass gave a short statement claiming he was innocent. After the legs and arms were bound, the crowd of 1,200 spectators watched as Bass sobbed and cried until the trap was sprung.

The *Galveston Daily News*, dated Saturday, November 1, 1884, printed the following short article of the execution.

THE GALLOWS
Execution of Bill Bass, an Outrage Fiend at Paris.

(Special to The News)

Paris, October 31.—Bill Bass was hanged today in the jail-yard at 4:50. A large crowd was in the court-yard and streets to witness the hanging.

Bill Bass was a colored man, twenty five or thirty years old, and the crime for which he paid the penalty with his life today was outrage, committed two years ago, on a white girl, an inmate of the poor-house and who was paralyzed. His case was appealed to the court of appeals and affirmed and the time of the execution set for August 1. Governor Ireland gave him a respite for sixty days, and then a further respite until today.

He made a few remarks on the gallows and said he was innocent of the charge. After the rope was placed around his neck he broke down completely and cried.

The trap was sprung a few minutes before 5 o'clock, and Bill Bass was launched into eternity. This is the second hanging in Lamar County in the last two years.

Mannon Davis
Also Spelled – Manning

Race/Gender: White Male **Age:** 30 **Offense:** Murder
Weapon: Knife **Execution:** March 30, 1894 **Offense Date:** December 26, 1891

Mannon Davis was tried and convicted for the murder of his neighbor at Eagletown located on the Choctaw Nation in the Indian Territory.

On the morning of December 26, 1891, John Roden had been hunting and killing hogs while Mannon Davis was out looking for horses. At about noon, Davis stopped by John Roden's house as he was passing by. During their conversation Roden told Davis that when he was finished hunting hogs, he would send Davis some spare ribs and backbone.

That evening after eating supper, Roden started salting the hog meat when Davis appeared at the gate and hollered for Roden. Roden walked out to the gate and invited Davis inside his home. Immediately after entering the house, Davis told Roden he has had heard that Roden was "carrying a gun for him."

Roden replied that he had heard wrong for he had no gun for him. Davis pulled out a long bladed knife and stabbed Roden once to the eye, and eight times to the chest. Roden's wife who was pregnant, fell to her knees and pleaded to Davis not to kill her husband and the father of their unborn child. Davis responded by saying, "I know it sis, but I can't listen to you."

Moments after Roden died, his wife gave birth to their child.

Davis afterwards ran to his father's farm where he took a horse and fled to Arkansas. A month later, Deputy Sheriff Callie Dollarhide went to the cabin of Bob Alford to apprehend Henry Alford, who had escaped from the Arkansas State Penitentiary and was believed to be at the home. Once the posse of lawmen surrounded the cabin and announced their presence, Henry Alford and Mannon Davis both ran out the back door to escape when they were shot and captured. Soon after the arrest, Davis said he killed Roden because he had insulted his wife. The wound to Mannon Davis' left leg was severe enough that Davis had to be transported to the Federal Court in Paris, Texas by stretcher.

Davis was found guilty of murder and sentanced to be executed on March 30,1894, along with Eduardo Ray Gonzales and James Upkins. After the reading of the death warrants on the gallows, Davis declined to speak when given the opportunity and collapsed in such a state that Davis had to be supported on the trap by the officers.

Eduardo Ray Gonzales

Race/Gender: Hispanic Male   **Age:** 26   **Offense:** Murder
Offense Date: May 16, 1893   **Weapon:** .32 Caliber Rifle   **Execution:** March 30, 1894

John Daniels had arrived in the Choctaw Nation of Blue County (now Bryan County) Indian Territory in mid-April, 1893, to teach singing at the school located there. The students mostly consisted of young ladies, except for a Mexican pupil by the name of Eduardo Gonzales. A short time later, the female students informed their teacher that Gonzales made them feel very uncomfortable. The students demanded that Gonzales not be allowed to attend class any longer or they would all quit. Daniels informed Gonzales that he could no longer accept him as a student and not to return. Gonzales left the school swearing vengeance in return.

On May 16, 1893, as Daniels was standing teaching class with the front door open, a rifle was fired from outside. The bullet hit Daniels and lodged under the skin of his head. When the bullet was extracted, the projectile was recognized as being from a .32 caliber target rifle. Only one such rifle was known to be in the area, and it belonged to a nearby farmer.

Deputy Marshal Andy Fryar searched the outside of the schoolhouse and located a bullet casing in the yard along with bare foot tracks. The deputy noticed that right large toe in the track protruded outward, while the second toe was longer than the others. The tracks then changed from bare feet to shoe tracks with the hobnails leaving an impression in the soft mud. Those tracks were followed to the house where Gonzales lived as a boarder. The deputy examined the rifle and determined the weapon had recently been fired. The shoes Gonzales wore matched the tracks found at the scene, as did his right foot. Gonzales was placed under arrest and lodged in jail at Paris, where he was tried and convicted of murder.

Gonzales then contacted the Mexican Consulate and asked for him to intervene with the execution and request a petition to commute the sentence to imprisonment. When this failed, a signature petition was sent to President Grover Cleveland who refused to interfere.

Sentenced to hang on March 30, 1894, along with James Upkins and Mannon Davis, Gonzales declared his innocence from the gallows and said, "I die with no malice in my heart for anyone. I forgive all who have done me wrong. God bless all."

James Upkins

Race/Gender: Black Male   **Age:** 26   **Offense:** Rape
Offense Date: September 6, 1893   **Weapon:** .32 Caliber Rifle   **Execution:** March 30, 1894

James Upkins was born in Grayson County, Texas, in 1867, and raised in Denison. As an adult, Upkins worked in the Missouri, Kansas and Texas railway yards, until 1891. That year Upkins married and moved his wife and her two children to the town of Ardmore, Indian Territory, to work as a brick and mortar layer.

On September 6, 1893, James Upkins was alone in the house with his six-year-old stepdaughter, Mary Wood when he sexually abused the child. The crime was quickly investigated and Upkins was arrested and tried in Federal Court at Paris, Texas. On March 30, 1894, James Upkins was found guilty and sentenced to hang on the gallows for this crime.

On the day of the triple execution, at 11 a.m., Unites States Marshal Sheb Williams read the death warrant to the three prisoners condemned to hang. Afterwards the prisoners were led to the gallows, under a strong escort of deputy marshals. Reverend G. M. Fortune of the First Baptist Church and Elder G. H. Farris of the First Christian Church conducted the services. The choir sang *Jesus, Lover of My Soul* and *They, Never Say Good-by in Heaven*.

Upkins first stepped up to the edge of the gallows to address the crowd. He advised the people to profit from his example and to rely upon religion. He said, "Be of good cheer, all is well with me."

Once the trap was sprung, the necks of the men were broken by the fall. After hanging for twenty-seven minutes the bodies were cut down and placed in coffins. James Upkins was buried in an African American cemetery at Paris, Texas.

The *Fort Worth Gazette*, Saturday, dated March 31, 1894, provided a full account of the triple execution at Paris, Texas.

Tom Moore

Race/Gender: White Male   **Age:** 33   **Offense:** Murder
Offense Date: May 1, 1889   **Weapon:** Firearm   **Execution:** September 18, 1894

Tom Moore was tried in Federal Court at Paris for the Eastern District of Texas who had jurisdiction over crimes committed in the Indian Territory of Oklahoma. Both of the men's crimes were that of murder.

He was tried and convicted for the murder of a neighbor by the name of Charley Palmer. Moore believed Charley Palmer suspected him of murdering a man named Camp, and believed that Charley had been looking for Camp's body or evidence of the murder. For this reason, Tom Moore killed him.

Before he was executed Marshal Williams asked Tom Moore if he had anything to say. Moore replied he could tell him many things, but that it would do not do him any good now. Deputy Marshals D. E. Booker and D. J. Harper escorted Moore to the gallows who was almost in a state of collapse.

After thanking the Marshal and deputies for their kind treatment, he asked that he be given a decent burial. Tom Moore was buried in the potter's field.

The *Fort Worth Gazette*, dated Saturday, September 29, 1894, provided a full account of the crimes both men committed and of the execution.

Eugene Fulke
or Fulks

Alias: Eugene Davis   **Race/Gender:** White Male   **Age:** 18
Offense: Murder   **Offense Date:** February 23, 1894   **Weapon:** Club & Firearm
Execution: September 18, 1894

Eugene Fulke was convicted of murdering seventy-year-old John McGuire while robbing the man of his money and personal belongings. Before Judge David Bryant pronounced sentence upon Eugene Fulke, he asked Fulke if he had anything to say as to why sentencing should not be pronounced. Fulke replied he only had one request. "I want my execution to be set for noon so I can find a good warm dinner awaiting me at the place where I am going."

Judge Bryant responded, "You are likely going to a place where all dinners are warm."

Fulke retorted by telling Judge Bryant, "I will be there waiting to fan the flies off when you arrive."

Judge Bryant then ordered that Fulke be executed on September 18, 1894.

On the morning of the execution ministers arrived at the jail. The marshal asked Fulke if he desired to speak with for spiritual guidance. Fulke replied, "Well, if they have got any pardons or commutations to give out, I would like to see them. Other wise I will enjoy their society better outside. I'll get my pardon at the end of a three-quarter rope."

Deputy Marshal's Best Brown and George Oglesby escorted Fulke to the gallows after posing for photographs. Fulke then said he was "jobbed into this." Turning to Tom Moore who was being executed at the same time, Fulke said, "Tom old boy, I don't know what country we are going to meet in next, but if we get separated, you'll know my tracks, I'll be barefoot."

While the noose was being adjusted, Fulke looked up to the jail window and said, "Good bye Charlie, by God it's tough to die this way, but I reckon it's fair." After the black cap and knot were adjusted, Fulke said, "This damned thing is choking me, don't let it do that till I drop."

Fulkes had his body donated to Dr. S. S. Robinson for study.

The *Fort Worth Gazette*, dated Saturday, September 29, 1894, provided a full account of the crimes both men committed and of the execution.

Charles H. Key

Race/Gender: White Male   **Age:** 38   **Offense:** Robbery & Murder
Offense Date: July 2, 1894   **Weapon:** Ax   **Execution:** September 13, 1895

The county seat of Lamar County is located in Paris, which borders the Indian Territory which would later become the State of Oklahoma. Because local and state lawmen had no jurisdiction, the Indian Territory became a haven for outlaws and wanted criminals who fled from Texas lawmen in order to escape capture.

Charles Key was nothing more than a murderous conman who filled his victim's head with lies about work, money and adventure in order to lure him to his death so that he could rob him of his possessions. Smith L. McLaughlin was a twenty-two-year-old man who lived with his mother on a small farm, five miles from Gainesville, Texas.

In late June of 1894, Charles Key represented himself to Smith and his mother as being a wealthy rancher. Key sounded convincing with his claim of having a large heard of cattle near the town of Wright located southeast from Sherman, Texas. Smith had his own wagon and team, and Key proposed to Smith to come work for him, attending to his stock, at a $1.50 a day for the remainder of the summer. Smith accepted the job with excitement as this was his first time away from home. On July 1, Mrs. McLaughlin packed her son's travel trunk with quilts, a family album and his bible. After the trunk was placed in the bed of the wagon, she watched her son and Charles Key ride off together towards Sherman.

On July 2, Smith and Key turned north from Sherman towards Denison. Once they crossed the Red River into Indian Territory, Key and Smith bought hay for the team, which was thrown into the bed of the wagon. At about 10 p.m. that night the river toll-bridge keeper was awakened at his home by someone yelling from the bridge. The same person then came to his house demanding that the bridge keeper unlock and open the gate and allow him to cross. The bridge keeper who only opened the gate in cases of extreme emergency at night refused to answer his door. A short time later, another man led his horse under the bridge chains and crossed over the Red River and came upon Charles Key who was alone next to the wagon and team and said he was going to cross the river else where.

The next morning two bundles of quilts and comforters, both having blood and brain matter were found in the river. That afternoon Smith McLaughlin's body was found in the brush not far from where the two had camped. The United States Marshal from Denison was notified of the murder and traveled to the scene. While the Marshal began his investigation, Charles Key approached an auctioneer at a public sale in Denison and told the auctioneer he wished to put his wagon and team up for sale for any amount he could receive. The wagon and team sold for $55 and afterwards Key signed the bill of sale using the name C. H. Kerr. Once paid, Key took the trunk containing an album, clothing, and bible belonging to Smith to the train depot at Sherman. Key was immediately arrested by the City Marshal on suspicion of murder.

Key fabricated a story that Smith had been murdered by a rancher by the name of John Cox who had hired them to help move a cattle herd to his ranch in West Texas. Key was found guilty of the murder and sentenced to death. Forty people who had received tickets for admission were admitted into the jail yard of the federal prison to witness the execution.

As Marshal Williams read the death warrant, Key was given whiskey to calm his nerves. Key afterwards told the witnesses to lead religious lives, and asked all to read the bible and accept its teachings. Once the black cap and noose was adjusted, Executor Ogleby sprang the trap at 12:25 p.m. The neck was broken and in fifteen minutes the body was pronounced dead, cut down and buried in the pauper's graveyard.

The *Fort Worth Gazette*, on September 14, 1895, printed the following two letters that were written by Charles Key and given to a fellow inmate.

My Dear Elli: I know you would due eny thing in the world for me. But I am afred honey it is too late for you to due me eny good know, but God knows that I am not gilty of the Crime that I an Charged of but My Der Elle I du woosh I cud be with you always. I know you air the Best frind I have got on the face of the erth but my mother and farther My heart is Broken I cannot write any more so Good by I dreamt you come to the Bars and shok hands me Please keep this until after I leve heare I would like to talk to you if I had time I am as ever yours. Chas. H. Key.

Bonham Jail 16-6, 95 this is the public at Large I was arrested last July the 3 day, 94 on a charge of murder and I have bin in jail from that time up till date I was convicted April the 10, 95 for the murder of Sith McGlothlin this Charge I am not guilty of as John Cox cud not Bee found he is the man that murdered Smith McGlothlin if he was murdered as I did not see him murdered nor did I know of him Beeing murdered until I was rested I have got this to say that I am not guilty of the Charge end the time will come when the World wil know hoo did due it and it will not due me no good after I am gone.

I want to make this statement as I am going to tell the truth all the way thure this statement thare is something that I did wrong that was seling the wagon and teems and I aut to have bin punish for that Crime and not for a Crime that I am not guilty of and I know that God al mity will punish the 12 men that set on my jury that convicted me and the men that Soarn Liles ganst me know this porters Come to Die thare will have to give an count of all this that is if the Bible is true and I think it is and then the truth will be told all men that sead or heared of this due not take a poore mans Life away unless you know that he is guilty one Kom as you all will Laff as you see or here of me being hung.

I do not think you wil see or heare of it I am going sedle that part of it my selfth and I will save you the trouble of it and save the U S that fifty $50.00 dollars that she gives to spring the trap on me I have got this to say if I was giltey of the crime that I am charge of I wuld go up like a mand and bee hung and die as Brave as any man then I wud cal it Bravry. I am looking to bee taken Back to Paris at eny day Long to see that day for I am dien Little by Little and soner the beter fore me this is furst time that I ever was in jail, and it is the furst time I was of eny Crime I have charged of fiting and gambling but never did Commit eny grate Crime in all of my Life and I can say this with a true hart. I meant kind harted persons to due one thing that is if he or she will due it with a free Good will and I do not want eny one to have eny thing to due with it that is eny may be realated to me in any way shape or forme. Less it is my mother and farther and frank heffner and his famley my farther and mother lives in Midway Mississippi and frank heffner lives in South Prairie Stephens County Texas heare is what I want dun is Put this on my hed bord this:

I am not Guilty of this Crine that I am charge of, Chas H Key.

I never did Call on eny of my people to help before and I did dedBeat on them. I have an uncle that lives heare in this town Bonham that is a preacher but I doe not think there is any Christian in him. I think any true Christian would have come to seene me. Where he would have done eny thing for me or not that would have bin a Christian ack for him to come to see me any way I gess that Jug Brint is going to set my time to die. But I woll beat him to it. I have got my time set jest ahed of him and I intend to fulfill this my sefth and that will be one crime that I have carmited and I think it will bee a glores for me and let the world know of it so I here not got anything more to say.

I think the jailer for the kind treatment to me and the depertes Dock and Hoskins is as kind a harted man as ever was I gess he Cud not Bee Beat no where in the world I don't care what you heare about I know I tride him and I know he is as true as steell. I don't want no one to bee eny better to me and he has bin to me duering the time I have been in jail under him. I would like to as one more favor of oficers of this couty that is to please for my sake have this publish to the world. So goodbye. I am going to the happy hunting grond. Chas H. Key

P.S. Please send this to my loving mother and farther, R.C. Boutwell. Please let all of boys in jail Read this then please give this to Dock so fare you well.

The *Shiner Gazette*, dated September 19, 1895, provided details of the execution.

George Wheeler

Race/Gender: White Male **Age:** 37 **Offense:** Murder
Offense Date: August 1894 **Date of Execution:** September 4, 1896

George Wheeler was convicted for the murder of Robert McCabe in August of 1894, near Tishomingo, Indian Territory, Oklahoma. On the day of the execution, Wheeler told the marshal he did not want to be executed at the same time with the negro men (Lee Silas and Hickman Freeman) and he requested to be hanged separately. The marshal granted the request. At 11 a.m., Wheeler took the death march to the gallows where he met his spiritual advisor, Rev. George M. Fortune, a former pastor of the First Baptist Church. After prayers, Rev. Fortune said his goodbyes and departed from the gallows.

After the black cap and noose were adjusted, Deputy Marshal C. R. V. Hamilton pulled the lever that sprung the trap at 11:17. Eighteen minutes later the body was cut down and released to an undertaker.

The *Shiner Gazette*, dated Thursday, September 10, 1896, reported on the triple execution that had taken place at Paris, Texas.

Lee Silas

Race/Gender: Black Male **Offense:** Murder **Offense Date:** November 14, 1895
Execution Date: September 4, 1896

Hickman Freeman

Race/Gender: Black Male **Offense:** Murder **Offense Date:** November 14, 1895
Execution: September 4, 1896

Lee Silas and Hickman Freeman were tried and found guilty of the murders of "Jeff" Maddox, Edward T. Canady, Paul Applegate and a fourth person on a boat on the Red River. The fourth person's identity was not known until a month after the hangings. The fourth person was identified as being Hepborne Pierce of Sunrise, St. Tammany Parish in Louisiana. The murders were over a gambling quarrel.

At noon Silas and Freeman made their last walk. At 12:07, after both men declined to make a statement, their arms and legs were bound. Their spiritual advisor, the Rev. Connor, told the 100 witnesses both had requested for him to tell those present to take warning of their fate and to shun evil companions, to whom they attributed of the crimes they committed. Ten minutes later the noose was adjusted and the trap dropped. After both bodies were pronounced dead, the remains were delivered to an undertaker who prepared both for shipment to relatives at Goodland, Indian Territory, Oklahoma.

The *Shiner Gazette*, dated Thursday, September 10, 1896, reported on the triple execution that had taken place at Paris, Texas.

John Harris

Race/Gender: Black Male **Offense:** Murder **Offense Date:** October 18, 1902
Weapon: Pistol **Execution:** December 19, 1902

On October 18, 1902, John Harris was attending a black church festival on the outskirts of the town of Blossom when fighting broke out and Harris fired a pistol. Blossom City Marshal Benjamin J. Hill attempted to arrest Harris who turned the revolver at the marshal and fired three bullets at him. The first bullet struck Marshal Hill in the right ankle, a second bullet missed, but a third bullet struck the marshal in the stomach. Harris escaped into the night, and in his wake left three other men wounded, and Marshal Hill, who was fatally wounded and died at 2:30 in the morning. The twenty-eight-year-old lawman was laid to rest at the Knights of Pythias Cemetery at Blossom.

Harris was arrested the following day and a jury found him guilty and assessed the death penalty five days later. On October 28, Judge Denton sentenced Harris to be executed on December 5. While Harris was waiting for his execution, his brother Will Harris pled guilty to being an accessory to the murder and received a five-year sentence to the penitentiary.

The execution, which had been scheduled for December 5, was delayed after Governor Joseph Sayers granted a respite until December 19. On the December 18, Governor Sayers telegrammed Sheriff Sel Carpenter to "Immediately inform John Harris that his application for commutation of the death sentence imposed on him is denied."

On the gallows, Harris shouted over the walls of the scaffold to the crowd to take warning of his fate.

Harris said, "Whisky and gambling has brought me here and I hoped all boys, white and black, will shun those evils." After his arms and feet were tied he shouted, "I am going home to rest and I'm proud of it."

The black cap was adjusted and Sheriff Carpenter pulled the lever that sprang the release of the trap door. Sixteen minutes later the body was declared dead and turned over to his mother for burial at Blossom.

The *Dallas Morning News*, dated Saturday, December 20, 1902, provided their readers with details of the execution.

Will McIntosh

Race/Gender: Black Male **Offense:** Murder **Offense Date:** February 5, 1909
Weapon: .44 caliber Winchester rifle **Execution:** October 1, 1909

Will McIntosh was madly in love with Mary Boyd and asked for her hand in marriage. When Mary rejected McIntosh, he immediately assaulted and threatened to kill her. Mary took the threats seriously and complained to a Paris police officer who filed the complaint for an arrest warrant for McIntosh's arrest.

Once McIntosh heard that Mary had made a complaint to the police, he made several more threats to kill the woman or any officer who attempted to arrest him, as he was an excellent shot with a rifle. On the first of February, McIntosh broke into a Paris store at night where he stole a .44 caliber Winchester rifle.

On February 5, 1909, Constable Matthews and Deputy Constable William Robert Draper went to Mary Boyd's home at about 8 p.m. to ask where they could find McIntosh so they could serve the arrest warrant. While speaking with the woman, McIntosh appeared. In learning that the officers were there to arrest him, McIntosh grabbed the Winchester rifle from behind the back door. Deputy Draper ordered McIntosh to put the weapon away and not to shoot. McIntosh fired two shots from the rifle with the second bullet striking Deputy Draper in the stomach. The thirty - seven-year-old lawman died a few minutes later and was laid to rest at the Evergreen Cemetery in Paris.

McIntosh, who had fled after the shooting, was captured at Wister, Oklahoma and returned to Paris on February 9. On February 24, McIntosh was indicted for murder and tried and convicted on March 1. Two month's later on May 5, the Texas Court of Appeals affirmed the lower courts decision.

The *Galveston Daily News*, dated Saturday, October 2, 1909, wrote a short article informing the readers that the execution had taken place.

Virgil Sampson

Age: 24 **Race/Gender:** Black Male **Offense:** Rape
Offense Date: April 12, 1921 **Execution:** May 27, 1921

On April 12, 1921, fourteen-year-old Minnie White and her younger brother were walking alone from the community of Honey Grove in Fannin County towards their home when Minnie was attacked and sexually assaulted.

Prior to the assault, Virgil Sampson had been seen on the road and near the site of the attack. When arrested, both Minnie and her brother identified Sampson at the jail as the person who had assaulted them. Sampson further confessed to the sheriff and put his mark on the paper as his signature.

Fearing vigilante justice, a change of venue moved the case from Fannin County to Paris, in Lamar County. On April 20, 1921, five Rangers from Company B were also present to keep order during the trial. When a reporter asked Captain Ron Hickman if they were called in to protect the prisoner, Capt. Hickman responded by saying, "We're not here to protect the Negro, but to protect the law by order of the governor."

Dean Sampson, wife of the accused, testified that her husband was not responsible as he was home at the time. Minnie White then testified and pointed out Virgil Sampson three times to the jury as the man responsible for the attack. After Minnie's testimony it took the jury but a few moments to return with a verdict of guilty and the punishment assessed at death.

While awaiting execution, Sampson confessed to the sheriff that he was responsible for murdering Blanche Wadford and her three-year-old daughter which occurred on January 21, 1920. Sampson told authorities he had seen Blanche working in the field, and made advances on Blanche. After she had threatened to tell her husband, he shot her to death with a twelve-gauge shotgun. Fearing the child could identify him; he reloaded the single shotgun, and killed the little girl. When Luther Wadford arrived home and found the bodies he reported the murder of his wife and daughter to the sheriff. Wadford was arrested and charged for the double homicide and sat in jail for sixteen months. Wadford was only released after Sampson made his confession.

On May 27, at 11 a.m., Virgil Sampson was brought to the courthouse elevator and escorted to the County Judge's office. There, Sampson was led to climb through the window to the awaiting scaffold that stood on the northwest corner of the courthouse. A privacy fence had been erected to obstruct view from the awaiting spectators. Sampson then spoke from the gallows of the double murder he had committed near Paris, but did not speak of the sexual assault for which he was being executed. Fannin County deputies while bounding the prisoner's arms and legs had to evacuate from the platform quickly for fear of the scaffold collapsing after large popping cracks could be heard from the supporting beans. The trap was sprung and Sampson hanged for seventeen minutes before doctors pronounced him dead.

The *Galveston Daily News*, dated Saturday, May 28, 1921, provided readers with details of the crime and execution.

La Salle County
County Seat - Cotulla

Jose Maria Mendiola

Race/Gender: Hispanic Male   **Age:** 24   **Offense:** Murder
Offense Date: March 7, 1885   **Weapon:** Winchester Rifle   **Execution:** January 15, 1886

G. M. Hodges operated a store in the small town of Encinal, where he also served as the station agent for the International and Great Northern Railroad. On March 7, 1885, Jose Mendiola was working for Hodges in the store and sold his pistol to Hodges for $10. Mendiola later returned to Hodges and demanded the return of his weapon. Hodges reminded Mendiola that he had sold him the pistol and that the weapon was now his.

Mendiola walked into the store and loaded a Winchester rifle that Hodges kept in the store. When Hodges was outside visiting with a friend, Mendiola shot Hodges twice, once in the chest and once in the back. Hodges died instantly, and Mendiola ran into a store and hid behind the safe until Sheriff C. B. McKinney arrived and placed him under arrest.

On the gallows, Sheriff McKinney slowly read the death warrant out loud and pausing at the end of each sentence to allow for interpretation. At the passage that ended with, "To be hanged by the neck," Mendiola slightly shrugged his shoulders and said, *"Muy bien,"* (very well).

Father Koshiel of the Catholic Church turned in the spectators and said:

Citizens of Cotulla, this poor Mexican now standing by me will shortly be hanged for a heinous crime, of which he admits the commission. He would like to talk to you and is unable to speak English, so I do it for him. He begs pardon of all whom he has offended and especially asks the forgiveness of the relatives of the man whom he slew. He leaves this life without a grudge against any one, without a hard feeling against anyone, without a hard feeling against anyone on all this earth. To the sheriff and jailer, he returns thanks for many kindnesses. He asks your forgiveness as a penitent, humbly, and hopes to obtain mercy for himself from the Most High. He asks me to tell you, fathers and mothers who hear me, to so rise the children that are growing around you that they may take warning by a man who bids farewell to earth in his prime, and turn from evil courses, that they may avoid his doom by avoiding the paths in which he has trodden. He stands here a victim to his own passions. He says to you all, good-bye. He humbly asks the sympathy of all men.

When the trap was sprung, Mendiola dropped eight feet and was declared dead in four minutes. The body was placed in a pine coffin, covered by coarse black cloth, and taken to the church, where the last rites were performed. He was buried in Cotulla Cemetery at the county's expense.

The *San Antonio Daily Express*, dated Saturday, January 16, 1886, printed the following interview by a reporter with Jose Mendiola:

He was a long Mexican of cadaverous aspect, deeply sunken, large dark eyes and yellow skin. He was loose-jointed and of shambling aspect. He stood in his grated cell, and the odors which rose around him were sickening. The air was raw, all the windows were kept closed, and the living mass of human criminality cooped with him laughed and jested and swore while he replied to the interviewer. It was a rambling talk made in reply to numerous questions, but all the information he had was cheerfully furnished. He had been freely supplied with whiskey about the only thing he cared for, and as he drew his blanket shivering around his shoulders he sucked mildly at the stump of a very loud smelling cigar. His straight black hair fell in a shock over his eyes and his fingers had a nervous, shifty motion.

I was born," he said, "at Las Mores, Kinney county, Texas. I have no exact record of my birth, but I believe

I am 24 years old. I was reared in Southwestern Texas and have never lived anywhere else. I have never wanted to live anywhere else. I am not married, so have no wife and children to mourn for me. There are quite a crowd of us living in the neighborhood of Encinal, LaSalle County. My mother and father are both living. I have also one married sister. Some of my people will doubtless see me die to-day. They will see that I am not afraid. I have never been very much under home influences. I have led rather a wild life. I have drank some mescal, - not a great deal. I was never what you would call a drunkard. Yes, the man whom I killed was called Hodges. I had been working for him about eight months. He owed me $5 for trips I had made hauling provender for him. He would not pay me. You must not ask me much about the killing, because I know very little about it. I killed him. I recollect, but not much more. He took my pistol from me – a white handled pistol – and would not give it back. He swindled me, and I shot him. There was a man there – a school teacher – who was ready to kill me. There was also a saloon man who wanted to kill me. I shot the dead man to protect myself, and because he cheated me. What do I think of my sentence? There is no justice in it. If there were any justice in the man who tried me, they would not take my life on the thing they are building out there. Please understand that I am not afraid. All I want is whiskey, cigars and a black suit on clothes. These are the only request I leave – no – messages for a single soul of those I leave behind. I was reared Roman Catholic, but I am an Universalist – I believe in all churches getting a fair show. If I had my way, they should all have a fair show. No, I don't think I am a very religious man. I have been treated well since my incarceration. The jailer has done all he could for me, and Sheriff McKinney once saved my life – saved me from a mob. I have positively nothing to say against any of the peace officers with whom I have been thrown in contact. It has been supposed that I had an ulterior motive in the killing of Hodges; that other parties were concerned in it; that I was paid to do it. Such is not the case. I make the plain, unvarnished statement that I shot him because he swindled me – for no other reason in the world, and I do not think I ought to hang for it. Have I any hope of pardon? None in the world. I don't know anyone who would move a finger to save my life. With the exception of my immediate family, I die friendless. Do you hear that saw and hammer? Do you see them nailing the planks? That has been going on for a very long time. What is the use of asking a man how such sounds affect him? Every nail in that frame work is one step nearer my grave. I know that, and I have tried to shut out the sound, but I cannot do it. Only at night when the carpenters stop work, I get some rest. It is very cruel to hear them at work all day. I could stand it better if it were not for that. I can't say anything about my trial. All the proceeding were in English and I did not understand a word. When it was finished and the people got up to go, they told me I would be hung. The priest told me that. He has been to see me since; quite frequently of late. It took everything my father and other had to pay the expenses. I myself did not have much, but that little went too. It is cold and I have stood the suspense a long time. I shall soon be a dead man, but I say, I that speak to you say, that I am not afraid. Yes, I'll take a cigar. Thank you. I like to smoke.

A week before the execution, the *Fort Worth Daily Gazette* dated January 7, 1886, wrote, "No Cards of Regret. Mendiola appearance was that of a cowardly coyote more than a species of humanity. There will be no regrets expressed for him in this section when his neck is broken."

Lavaca County
County Seat - Hallettsville

Indian Pocket

Race/Gender: French & American Indian/Male **Age:** 22 **Offense:** Murder
Offense Date: February 14, 1878 **Weapon:** Pistol **Execution:** September 12, 1879

A half-blooded Sioux, Indian Pocket took his Canadian-French father's last name of Pocket, and he was only known as "Indian Pocket." On September 12, 1879, Indian Pocket was executed for the murder of an Englishman by the name of Leonard Hyde whom Pocket had shot and killed on February 14, 1878. Pocket had been drinking whiskey all day and making a nuisance of himself in town. While drunk, Pocket borrowed guns from the owner on the pretense that he had seen wild turkeys and therefore needed guns to hunt and kill them.

Hyde decided he would tag along for the hunt and Pocket turned on Hyde and told him, "God damn you, if you follow me, I'll kill you."

Pocket afterwards shot Hyde to the forehead and rode off. It was believed Pocket had probably fled to the Indian Territory, so the governor authorized a $500 reward for his capture. To the surprise of the lawmen, Pocket returned to Texas a year later, and was captured by Constable C. S. Hayes in Bosque County. Pocket told the constable "I killed a fellow down in Lavaca County, and I reckon they will stretch my neck for it when they get me down there."

On the morning of the execution Indian Pocket was given gifts of whiskey, beer, and champagne by well wishers until Sheriff J. W. Bennett ordered it stopped. The sheriff did allow Pocket to keep two bottles of beer and to drink a glass of champagne.

At 2 p.m. Pocket stepped out of the jail and into a hack with Sheriff Bennett, deputies Griffin, Richardson and Hargrove, and Rev. Bush. An immense crowd then followed the officers to a thicket half a mile west of town, where the gallows had been erected and where another 2,000 to 3,000 people had gathered around the ropes surrounding the scaffold, while other spectators sat in the treetops.

Pocket was then asked if he wished to make a last statement. Pocket turned to Rev. Bush and asked for him to speak on his behalf. Rev. Bush said that Pocket expressed the hope that he would be forgiven; that it was whiskey that caused him to do the deed for which a good man lost his life, and now it would take his own. Rev. Bush said Pocket believed his peace had been made above, yet warned all against the drinking of liquor, especially the young.

Pocket then wiped his eyes, and walked firmly to the trap, raised his head up to looked at the rope and cross beam above, and then to the crowd and said, "Good-bye, all." To this there were numerous responses of "Goodbye, Pocket," with one man saying, "May you go to a better world."

The noose was placed around the neck, and after the cap was adjusted, the signal was given to cut the rope, which held the trap in place with a hatchet.

After the body was declared dead, Pocket was placed into a black coffin, and transported by Sheriff Bennett to the African-American graveyard for burial.

The *Galveston Daily News*, dated Saturday, September 13, 1879, gave a full account of the execution and wrote, "It is a strange coincidence in the history of this matter that the deceased and his murderer were both under twenty-one years of age, friendly with one another up to the last moment, and both strangers in the land which has given to each of them a grave."

Zedolph Davis

Alias: Frenchy
Offense: Rape
Race/Gender: Black Male
Offense Date: April 24, 1892
Age: 21
Execution: April 28, 1893

In the early morning hours of April 24, 1892, Zedolph Davis kicked in the front door and pulled Lou Ballard out of her bed, dragged her outside and into the brush where he raped her. Mrs. Ballard recognized her attacker as the county convict who was contracted to work for a neighbor. The next morning, Davis attempted to escape officers and was shot in the arm and captured.

Davis was tried and convicted of the rape and his punishment was assessed at death. The case was appealed to the Criminal Court of Appeals where the decision was affirmed on November 16, 1892, after finding no error by the lower court.

On the appointed day of the execution, Sheriff Houchins walked Davis to the Catholic Church to give him the opportunity to make his last confession. That afternoon, Davis who was dressed in a black suit and wearing slippers, walked to the scaffold and took a chair. Once the reading of the death warrant was finished, Davis rose from his seat and bade all those present with a goodbye and shook hands with the sheriff and deputies. The trap was sprung and Davis dropped seven feet. Davis was declared dead in twelve minutes and afterwards was laid to rest at the county's poor farm.

The *Galveston Daily News*, Saturday, April 29, 1893, provided their readers with a full account of the execution that had taken place at Hallettsville, Texas.

Marguerito Reyna

Race/Gender: Hispanic Male
Offense Date: April, 1903
Age: 28
Execution: December 4, 1903
Offense: Rape

Marguerito Reyna was hanged in Hallettsville for the criminal assault of a child in Wilson County. Reyna had been living in a camp with the mother of the child on the farm where they both worked. The child's mother had gone to a water tank located 400 yards from their tent to get water she needed for preparing their dinner when Reyna sexually assaulted the girl. Upon her return to the tent, both she and the child were threatened with death if either one told anyone what he had done. Ten days after the assault, the child's mother reported the crime to authorities and Reyna was arrested.

On April 14, 1903, Reyna was indicted for the rape of seven-year-old Monica Arrendondo. The one-day trial was held on April 23, and after the child testified and pointed out Reyna as the person who had committed the assault, the jury deliberated only for a few minutes returning with a verdict of guilty, and assessing the death penalty. The case was appealed and affirmed by the Court of Criminal Appeals.

On the day of execution Reyna exhibited great boldness on the scaffold. When asked by Sheriff Noble if he had anything to say, Reyna replied that he was innocent of the crime for which he was about to be executed. Reyna said, "It was hard to die under the circumstances, but as it was ordered by the law it would have to be."

Reyna thanked the Sheriff, jailers, and all those who had attempted to have his sentence commuted. Reyna asked the sheriff that he be allowed to take off his shoes as he did not want to die with them on. Reyna requested both his shoes and hat be given to a Mexican boy who would come to the jail to visit him. Reyna afterwards bade those present goodbye, and shook hands with everybody

Father Vrann, of the Catholic Church, provided spiritual comfort on the scaffold. The execution was private, except for ministers, doctors, lawmen and newspaper men. To insure the privacy, a board fence thirty feet high enclosed the scaffold. When the trap was sprung, Reyna fell seven and one-half feet, which broke the neck. Attending physicians pronounced Reyna dead in thirteen minutes and cut down and placed his body in a coffin to be buried at the poor farm.

The *Shiner Gazette*, dated Wednesday, December 9, 1903, provided details of the assault and the execution at Hallettsville, Texas.

Lee County
County Seat - Giddings

Dan Puryear

Race/Gender: Black Male **Offense:** Rape & Murder **Offense Date:** November 14, 1874
Execution: November 21, 1874

Little information can be found as to the murder and execution of Dan Puryear. Some reports show he was lynched rather than executed.

The *Bastrop Advertiser*, dated Saturday, November 21, 1874, provided the following short article;

Miss Victoria, age 14, daughter of Mrs. Martha and the late Robt. Hogue, died, in Percent 3, Lee County. She was raped and murdered last week. The Negro Dan Puryear was arrested Saturday for the crime. He was found guilty and was hung. It is believed Puryear poisoned his former mistress who died some time ago.

William Preston Longley

Alias: Wild Bill **Race/Gender:** White Male **Age:** 27
Offense: Murder **Offense Date:** April 1, 1875 **Weapon:** Double Barrel Shotgun
Execution: October 11, 1878

William "Wild Bill" Preston Longley was born on October 16, 1851, at Mill Creek, in Austin County, Texas. He became one of the most noted gunmen in Texas and at seventeen-years-old, Longley killed his first man, being a black man. But it was the killing of Wilson Anderson, which led to his execution on October 11, 1878.

Wilson Anderson had killed William Longley's cousin, Cale Longley in Bastrop County, Texas. On April 1, 1875, William Longley rode his horse to the Anderson farm and found Wilson working in his cotton field. Without saying a word, Longley pulled his shotgun and dismounted from his horse. Longley then avenged his cousin's death by unloading both barrels into his boyhood friend.

On the day of his execution, October 11, 1878, it was estimated that 4,000 people had gathered about 600 yards northwest of the Giddings depot to watch the execution. At 1:30 p.m., Longley walked to the gallows with a cigar in his mouth. Once on the gallows, Longley drank a glass of whiskey and addressed the crowd by telling them:

> Well, I haven't got much to say. I have got to die; no man is willing to die such a death. I see a good many enemies around me, and only a mighty few friends. I hope to God you will forgive me. I believe that I will be forgiven for the sins I have committed. I hate to die, but I have learned this by taking the lives of men who loved life as well as I do. If I have any friends here, I hope they will do nothing to avenge my death. If they want to avenge my death, let them pray for me. I deserve this fate. It's a debt I owe for my wild, reckless life. When it's paid, it will be all over. I have nothing more to say.

Longley kissed the Sheriff and the Priest, then thanked everyone on the scaffold and told the crowd, "Goodbye, everybody."

As the black cap was being pulled over Longley's head, spectators from the crowd yelled, "Farewell Bill." Rumors had circulated by Longley's friends that any man who tried to put the noose around Longley's neck would be shot down. Sheriff Jim Brown did not flinch from his duties, and tightened the noose around Wild Bill's neck. Everything being ready to cut the rope, the sheriff asked, "Where's the hatchet?"

Longley, in a jocular way said, "What do you want with a hatchet, are you going to split my head open?"

At 2:37 p.m., the trap was sprung and Longley fell eight feet and suspended between Heaven and earth. The physicians present pronounced him dead in eleven minutes.

Longley had publicly boasted that he had killed thirty-two men. While receiving spiritual guidance, Longley confessed to Fathers Spillard and Querat of the Catholic Church that he had only killed eight men total, "six white and two colored."

Longley was buried at the Giddings Cemetery and rumors soon circulated that Longley had cheated his death by wearing a suit, which contained a steel harness concealed within it. A steel neck collar further prevented his neck from being snapped or to straggle. The rumor had become so widely known that it was published on Friday, June 13, 1879 in the *Brenham Weekly Banner*.

A Cock and Bull Story

Madame Rumor is responsible for the assertion that once notorious William P. Longley, known as Bill Longley, is yet present in the flesh on this mundane sphere and that although he was duly and appropriately hanged by legal process at Giddings something over a year ago, the hanging was only a seeming one, and that although actually hanged he was not killed.

The story goes that some of Longley's wealth relatives from California were in the vicinity of Giddings about the time of the hanging frolic was to come off. It is related that Longley was furnished with a suit of steel harness or armor extending from his heels to his neck, the latter being furnished with a steel collar so as to prevent the unpleasant sensation of strangulations. That when the attempt was first made to hang Longley he fell to the ground alighting on his feet and that when taken up for the second hanging the drop or was fall was very short and that he was not in the least injured. The ceremony of the hanging having been gone through with Longley's body was delivered to his friends for burial and it was to have been buried secretly to prevent the doctors obtaining it for a subject. Dame Rumor has it that Bill Longley is now in California alive and well and doing well. This rumor has been talked of in a confidential sort of a way for the past week or two coming to the knowledge of a Banner reported the story is repeated as told. The Banner is of the opinion that the story is manufactured out of the whole cloth, hence it is related under the caption of a "Cock and Bull Story."

The legend that William Longley faked his death was finally put to rest in 2001 when Longley's remains were exhumed by a team of forensic anthropologist from the Smithsonian National Museum of Natural History. Recovered artifacts included part of a celluloid flower that had been given to Longley on the day of his execution by his niece, and a religious metal he had received in jail. The absolute proof came from matching the DNA from the remains to that of Longley's great-great niece.

Brenham Weekly Banner, dated Friday, October 18, 1878, provided a full account of the execution.

James Taylor

Alias: Jack Taylor & Tom McBride **Race/Gender:** Black Male **Age:** 21
Offense: Rape & Triple Murder **Offense Date:** August 26, 1883 **Weapon:** Knife
Execution: December 21, 1883

James Taylor was executed for the rape and murder of Sarah Chappell and her two unborn babies. On August 26, 1883, Sarah was between four to six months pregnant and asked for Taylor to go pick green peas from the field for dinner. Taylor returned several hours later and when Sarah questioned him as to where the peas were, Taylor told her to get the vegetables herself.

Sarah took the empty bag, and walked out into the field and was soon followed by Taylor. While in the field, Taylor raped the woman. When Sara threatened to report the assault, Taylor decided to silence his victim by stabbing Sara twice to the chest and cutting her throat with a knife. The body was afterwards stripped of its clothing and dumped in a water tank. When the body was discovered a week later, it wasn't until the body was being removed from the tank when it was discovered that Sara had been pregnant with twins.

Taylor was arrested on suspicion of the murder and confessed. He then took the sheriff to the scene and grabbed a handful of blood soaked soil and said, "This is where I killed Sarah." Taylor further directed the sheriff where the sack containing Sarah's clothing had been hidden.

James Taylor was tried in the District Court on November 14, 1883, and was convicted of murder and the death penalty was assessed.

On the gallows, Taylor said he had been forgiven for his crime and that he was ready to die. Sheriff James Brown read the death warrant at 2:10 p.m., after which the prisoner was given an opportunity to talk to the 3,000 spectators who were present to witness the hanging. Taylor confessed he had killed Sarah Chappel without cause and was sorry for it. He then related while he was in jail, Sarah Chappel's spirit appeared to him with wings, descending and warning him to prepare for death. The spirit told him, "Death is coming and hell is moving. You will surely be hanged." Taylor said he had made peace with God, and then bade all goodbye.

Sheriff Brown adjusted the noose, placed the black cap in position, and sprung the trap at 2:25 p.m.. The fall of six feet broke the neck. After hanging thirteen minutes, the body was cut down and placed in a coffin.

The *Galveston Daily News*, dated Saturday, December 22, 1883, provided readers with Taylor's history, crime, and execution.

Oscar Hennegan

Race/Gender: Black Male **Age:** 21 **Offense:** Murder
Offense Date: September 14, 1895 **Weapon:** Shotgun **Execution:** December 17, 1895

Martha Bradley was a fourteen-year-old girl who had caught the eye of twenty-one year old Oscar Hennegan. Hennegan began seeing Martha and started bringing her small gifts for her affection, but when Martha's attention turned to another boy closer to her age, Hennegan asked Martha for her hand in marriage. When Martha's parents learned of the proposal, they quickly objected to any marriage as Martha was to young. Angered by the rejection, Hennegan decided he would kill Martha and the members of her family.

Hennegan went out into the field where Martha and her mother were working. He walked up to Martha's mother and asked if she would attend his hanging. Martha overheard this statement and told Hennegan he should not talk that way for fear something might happen to him.

On September 14, 1895, Hennegan armed himself with an old shotgun and went Martha's home. When approaching, Hennegan found Martha asleep on a pallet in the gallery. Hennegan crept up to Martha with the shotgun and placed the barrel up against her head and fired the weapon. The blast instantly killed Martha, and Hennegan then entered the house to kill the rest of her family. Upon seeing Martha's father, Hennegan pointed the shotgun and pulled the trigger, but the shotgun misfired which gave time for all the other family members to flee from the house. Police officer Black had arrived when Hennegan walked outside and surrendered. Hennegan told the officer, "I would have been perfectly satisfied if I had been able to have killed more of the girl's relatives, but the shotgun was no good and would not fire."

In November, Oscar Hennegan pled guilty to murder in the first degree, and was sentenced to death on December 17, 1895, by Judge Sinks.

On the morning of the execution, Sheriff James Scarbrough drove Hennegan in a buggy to a city water tank where Elder Matt Gaines of St. Paul Chapel baptized him. At 1 p.m., Sheriff Scarbrough drove Hennegan to a photo gallery to allow for him to have his photograph taken. Afterwards, the sheriff removed Hennegan's leg shackles and the two rode in the buggy to the scaffold while Hennegan puffed on a cigar and waved to the townspeople. Arriving at the gallows at 1:15, Hennegan stepped out of the buggy and walked directly up the steps of the platform and took a seat on a chair. He was then given a fresh cigar, and after lighting it, Hennegan stood up and addressed the crowd of 4,000 witnesses.

"I am here because of my disobedience. I hope you will not do as I have. Trust God. You have got to die and you don't know how soon, " Hennegan said. "I had a good mother, but did not obey her, an went in bad company. I did not trust God, who is more than the whole world, white and black. I forgive you all and ask to be forgiven and ask all to learn of God's word. Everybody quit your worldly ways. When you are in a passion remember me on the gallows. All of the troubles is in this world if you are serving God."

Recognizing a friend among the spectators, Hennegan told man, "If you do not change your ways, you will go to hell. Trust God, and he will make a better man of you. I am glad I am going home to glory."

The *Houston Daily Post*, dated Wednesday, December 18, 1895, provided its readers with a full account of the crime and execution at Giddings, Texas.

Jeff Mikel
Also spelled as Mikil

Race/Gender: Black Male **Offense:** Murder **Offense Date:** April 12, 1901
Weapon: Pistol & Grubbing Hoe **Execution:** December 13, 1902

Nancy Mikel was unhappy in her marriage, and for that reason decided to separate from her husband, Jeff Mikel. Angered by his wife leaving him, Mikel had made numerous threats that he would kill his wife if she did not return home to live with him.

Several months later on the afternoon of April 12, 1901, Mikel met with Nancy at a friend's house to speak with her. At first the conversation was pleasant until Mikel began making demands for Nancy to return home with him. When she refused and the two began to argue, Mikel pulled out his pistol and shot twice. The first bullet struck Nancy in the shoulder and the second bullet struck her just above the wrist. Mikel then grabbed a grubbing hole, and hit his wife in the head and that blow proved fatal.

Mikel then took out his pocket knife and slit his own throat in an attempt to commit suicide and fell unconscious across his wife's body. Physicians were called to the home and provided aid and saved his life.

Tried for murder, the jury assessed the penalty at death. The case was appealed to the Court of Criminal Appeals where the decision was affirmed on April 30, 1902.

On the afternoon of the execution, Mikel was led to the scaffold in the presence of 2,000 witnesses and warned his race to obey the law.

The *Houston Daily Post*, dated Sunday, December 14, 1902, provided their readers with details of the murder and execution.

Liberty County
County Seat - Liberty

George Walker

Race/Gender: Black Male **Offense:** Murder **Offense Date:** January 29, 1889
Weapon: Blunt Object **Execution:** April 5, 1889

Coret Laceur attended a debating society meeting that took place at the Liberty County Courthouse on the night of January 29, 1889. Coret, left the meeting early and he was last seen riding away on horseback. Coret failed to return home, but the next morning his horse was found, still saddled and bridled.

Three weeks later on February 18, the body of Coret Laceur was pulled out of the Trinity River two miles from town. An examination showed the back of the head had been crushed and the neck broken. Officers arrested George Walker and his son Robert. Robert Walker told the officers that his father had told him he intended to kill Coret and after Coret went missing, his father told him he had killed Coret.

George Walker was tried and convicted of murder and sentenced to death. On the day of the execution, the sheriff deputized eighty trusted men to insure no escape attempt was made, and to keep order among the 2,000 witnesses as George Walker was led to the gallows. Among the witnesses were Coret's father and brother. As Walker stood on the gallows, he asked for Coret's family to join him on the scaffold, which they did. Walker then asked for their forgiveness for the awful crime he had committed. Walker was told he would be forgiven if he gave a full confession. Walker stated that it was his son Robert, (Duce Bob), and son-in-law Charles Brown who were responsible for killing Coret.

The *Dallas Morning News*, dated April 6, 1889, provided their readers with details of the execution at Liberty, Texas.

Kit Robinson

Age: 21 **Race/Gender:** Black Male **Offense:** Robbery & Murder
Offense Date: June 1, 1895 **Weapon:** Iron Bar **Execution:** October 11, 1895

Kit Robinson was a career criminal, committing robbery and burglary of homes and businesses in order to support his gambling. In late May of 1895, John Johnson was carrying a large roll of money which he flashed in the presence of Kit Robinson. Robinson had previously burglarized Johnson's house of a gold watch, pistol and shotgun. Seeing the roll of money, Robinson knew he could find his victim working alone in one of the pump houses along the Houston East and West Texas Railway.

On June 1, 1895, Robinson crept up behind his unknowing victim and struck Johnson behind the head with an iron bar. After turning the pants pockets inside-out for the money, and taking Johnson's silver watch, Robinson piled wood over the body and set fire to it. He then waited for the murder to be discovered and for the Johnson family to be notified of the death so that he could burglarize the home a second time. A week later, Robinson was captured and confessed to Sheriff Mark DeBlanc of the murder, several other assaults, robberies, burglaries and arson. Robinson said:

> I wish to make a full confession of my crime. I went to Johnson's home about two weeks before the killing and robbed it, getting a six-shooter, shotgun, and a lady's gold watch. I afterwards made up my mind to kill and rob him, which I did by striking him with a piece of iron which I picked up by the side of the railroad track. I got a silver watch off the body. If he had any money I did not find it, as I got frightened and ran off before I had made a thorough search. I did not set fire to the body, but simply pulled the fire out of the furnace for the purpose of setting fire to the house with the body in it. No one else had anything to do with it or knew anything about it. I did it of my own

accord. My object in accusing Claiborne Jefferson was that I was told if I confessed and implicated others that it might be light on me. I now make this confession that Claiborne may be exonerated as he had nothing to do with it.

On October 11, 1895, Kit Robinson was hanged in the presence of 800 witnesses.

The *Galveston Daily News*, dated Saturday, October 12, 1895, provided a full account of Robinson's crimes, confessions, and execution at Liberty, Texas.

Abe Johnson

Race/Gender: Black Male **Age:** 57 **Offense:** Murder
Offense Date: April 16, 1921 **Weapon:** Knife **Execution:** September 22, 1922

Abe Johnson was executed for the murder of a co-worker at the Saner-Ragley Lumber Company. Johnson was the foreman of a repair crew for the tram railroad while W. L. Saxon was the foreman for the plant mill.

When the mill shutdown for repairs, Saxton sent an employee up to the tool shed to retrieve two additional shovels needed to mix concrete. Later Johnson appeared at the mill and told Saxton that he had five men and only three shovels and needed the tools returned for his crew. Saxton told Johnson to send the two men down without shovels to the mill, and he would put them to work. Johnson refused this, and pulled a knife. Johnson began walking towards Saxton as Saxton was backing away while keeping a distance of ten to twelve feet. Saxton then said, "Yonder comes the superintendent, let him settle it."

Before Superintendent R. M. Eagle could get to both foremen, Johnson had backed Saxton under the mill, where Saxton picked up a stick to defend himself. When Eagle reached the men's location, he had to pull Johnson away as he was about to stab Saxton a third time with the knife. Saxton died four days later from the wounds he received.

Johnson's first trial in Polk County ended in a hung jury. The trial judge then ordered the case transferred on a change of venue to Liberty County. The jury there on August 26, 1921, found Johnson guilty and assessed the death penalty. The case was appealed to the Court of Criminals Appeals where the court affirmed the decision on March 8, 1922.

The *San Antonio Express*, dated Sunday, September 24, 1922, informed their readers that the execution had taken place in Liberty, Texas.

Limestone County

Fred Robertson

Race/Gender: Black Male **Alias:** John Jackson **Age:** 22
Offense: Rape **Offense Date:** November 8, 1877 **Execution:** May 31, 1878

Fred Robertson was a twenty-two-year-old married black man that was convicted and sentenced to death for the crime of raping a white woman. On November 8, 1877, Robertson attacked a Mrs. Levi Whatley while she was working in the field. Robertson choked Mrs. Whatley with his hands until she was unconscious and then raped her. Afterwards Robertson threatened his victim that he would return and kill her if she told anyone, and told her his name was John Jackson.

Mrs. Whatley provided a description of her attacker and the clothing he wore to officers, who arrested Robertson at his home in Hornhill. Robertson confessed to the assault after explaining he had been drinking liquor since the previous night when he came upon Mrs. Whatley in the field.

The gallows were placed in the southeast corner of the jail yard, and stood twenty-five-feet high and in full view of the 3,000 to 4,000 spectators. On the day of the execution, Robertson gave the following statement:

> I am before you to day to suffer the penalty of the law for the crime of rape. I am guilty, and my punishment has been fixed at death by hanging. I feel that I had justice done me by the court and jury, and have no unkind feeling towards them. I am ready and willing to die, for I feel that I am going to a better world. I want you all to take warning by me and avoid a similar fate. I never before committed so heinous a crime, through I have been guilty of other small offenses. I am told that I will be the first man ever hanged legally in this county and I sincerely hope that I may be the last. I now if everybody knew the mental suffering that preceded such a death, I would be the last. I warn you all, and especially the young, against the use of whisky. It is the villain that robbed me of my life. Had it not been for liquor I would have been a free man to-day. The journey from the cradle to the grave is at most a short one, but you can make it long or short. I did not know how to appreciate life and liberty. Oh, that I could live over again and be a different man! But I am guilty of my crime, and have been forgiven by Him who rules the heavens. I am now about to be launched into that eternal world beyond, and bid you all, friends and enemies, a last farewell.

At the conclusion of his statement, Robertson in a rather calm, and clear voice said, "Goodbye all, be good."

The cap was drawn, and to the question, "Are you ready, Fred?" He replied "Yes," and the trap was sprung and the body fell. After fifteen minutes death was pronounced, and his body given to his wife and relatives.

The *Galveston Daily News*, dated Saturday, June 1, 1878, provided a full account of the execution and wrote, "Public opinion seemed satisfied."

Richard Burleson

Race/Gender: Black Male **Age:** 21 **Offense:** Robber & Murder
Offense Date: May 2, 1894 **Weapon:** Rock **Execution:** April 12, 1895

Richard Burleson was executed for the murder of seventy-year-old James Garrett McKinnon who lived seven miles southeast of Mexia. On May 2, 1894, James rode alone in a wagon into town to buy supplies. Once there, James purchased bran and coal oil and paid the store clerk with a $20 gold piece. In return James received $10 in currency, a $5 gold piece and .75 cents in silver. Richard Burleson who was sitting in the store and watching the transaction, was asked by the clerk to load the bran into James' wagon.

McKinnon was last seen alive two miles from Mexia on the Prairie Grove Road with Richard Burleson trailing behind from a distance. A mile further down the road, McKinnon was later found lying on the road unconscious with a skull fracture. At the scene was a blue jacket which was recognized as belonging to Burleson. The next morning, McKinnon died from his severe head injury cause by a large rock.

Officers suspecting Richard Burleson as the murderer rode out to his home, six miles west of Mexia in the Tehuacana Hills. When officers arrived, Burleson was placed under arrest for murder and searched. In his pockets was the exact amount of money the clerk had given to James. The pants Burleson had worn earlier in the day were found hidden in a barrel of meal that contained spots of blood. Burleson was tried and convicted and found guilty. The case was appealed to the Court of Criminal Appeals where the decision was affirmed.

The night before the execution, Burleson complained to a reporter, "I was taken up without an examination trial. If I had a trial, I should have been turned loose right away. They never did identify me, and the witness who swore about my clothes is damned badly mistaken. Anyways, I am innocent, and did not kill McKinnon nor know nothing about it. I have been treated very kindly by Mr. Gresham, the sheriff, and all the officers who have had me under their charge here in Corsicana and in Dallas."

The next morning Deputy Barron was in the process of taking Richard Burleson measurements for his coffin when doctors Brown and Cox arrived. The doctors offered Burleson $5 for his body after the execution. When the physician handed Burleson the money, he in turn handed the money to his half-brother who was also in jail on unrelated felony charges.

Just before 2 p.m., Sheriff Gresham and five deputies escorted Burleson to the gallows that had been erected behind the jail with an estimated crowd of 4,000 to 6,000 witnesses. On the platform Burleson declined to make a final statement. His hands and feet were then tied and the noose was placed around his neck. As the sheriff adjusted the noose, Burleson said, "That too tight, I don't want to be choked." The cap was adjusted and the trap released at 2:02 p.m. The fall of seven feet broke his neck, and Burleson was pronounced dead ten minutes later.

After the body was cut down, the physicians kept the body at Groesbeck, but sold the head to a dental student in Corsicana to conduct his own scientific examination of the teeth, throat, ears, and brain. After he completed his examination, the student kept the skull, but placed the flesh and brains in a sack which he given to a black man for disposal. The man was unaware of its contents until he reached the bridge on the north end of Beaton Street and accidentally spilled the contents on the ground. The man seeing what he was carrying immediately began yelling "Murder, Murder!"

This created great excitement among the black population, which swelled to over 1,000 people who had gathered as they believed a person of their own race had been brutally butchered. The officers and coroner were able to calm tension down after placing the remains in a box and releasing the remains to an undertaker for burial.

The *Fort Worth Gazette*, Saturday, dated April 13, 1895, provided details of the crime and hanging.

Hanging of Richard Burleson outside the Limestone County Courthouse at Groesbeck. *Author's personal collection.*

John Warren

Alias: Will Bryan
Offense: Robbery & Murder
Execution: August 15, 1902
Race/Gender: Black Male
Offense Date: November 1, 1901
Age: 35
Weapon: Ax & Knife

A store merchant by the name of Dock Stevens owned and operated a small store three miles west of Mexia. At about 9 p.m. on the night of November 1, 1901, John Warren arrived at the store and asked Stevens if he could stay. Feeling comfortable with his new acquaintance, Dock Stevens laid down on the floor of his store to rest and fell sleep. While sleeping, Warren took an ax and struck the sleeping man to the top of the head, and afterwards slit his neck with a knife. The $35 dollars kept in the cash drawer was then removed. Warren afterwards returned to his home at Marquez where he was arrested by the town marshal on suspicion of murder. Upon his arrest, Warren confessed to the robbery and murder and claimed the cash drawer only held $20. At his trial on January 31, 1902, Warren pled guilty.

On the day of the execution, John Warren provided the following statement and personal history to a reporter of the *State Herald*:

> My right name is John Warren. I was born and raised in Houston County, and about 36 years old and have been in the penitentiary once for being accused of killing a man, but was pardoned out and was not guilty. I had a wife, but she is dead. I have two children; I don't care anything about seeing them. I am guilty of the crime. I am going to die for and feel that I have been truly convicted as such the jury said I must die for committing the crime. I began making preparations to meet my God and about two before the judge set the time I felt that God had pardoned all my sins and now I am ready to die. I slept well last night. I have something I want to say to the good white people of Mexia, but will wait and say that on the scaffold, as I want all the people to hear it. I will say it slow and distinct so you can write it down, and I want you to write it just as I say. I have a good appetite. I sold my body for $5.00 to Mr. B. J. Williams and have eaten it all up but a nickel and am going to buy goobers with that and eat them before I die, all of them. Mr. Gresham and Mr. Nobles have been very good to me, just as good as they could be under the circumstances, and I love them for it.

The reporter asked why he had killed Dock Stevens. Warren replied he did not care to answer any further questions and ended the interview.

Sheriff Joe Gresham appeared at Warren's cell and read out loud the death warrant. At the conclusion, the sheriff said, "That's all John."

Warren replied, "That all right, I am satisfied."

At 1:30 p.m. while handcuffed and smoking a cigar, John Warren was escorted from his cell to the gallows where on the platform he talked, sang and prayed for thirty minutes. On the platform, Warren turned to jailer Nobles and asked, "Have I been a good prisoner or a bad one?"

Jailer Nobles replied, "You have been a good one, John."

Warren said, "I have a song composed by myself and I want to sing, and then I will offer up a prayer." Warren prayed out loud for the officers, and asked for God to save his soul. Warren asked Mr. A. C. Gresham to come up the scaffold as he wished to give to him a memento. Handing a nickel to Mr. Gresham, Warren said, "Now, Mr. Al, I want you to keep that all your life, God bless you."

After singing a song and a prayer offered by Rev. Swaney, Warren said, "That is all, I am ready now." In turning to the crowd of 2,000, Warren made a rambling talk with predictions. Warren said, "There will be another hanging here inside of a year and Mexia will furnish the man. Whiskey will be the cause of it. Mexia will be destroyed by a storm. May God bless you all. I am going now out of this world, but I hope to meet you all again, Goodbye to all."

Sheriff Gresham released the trap at 2:13 p.m. which dropped Warren seven and a half feet, the rope breaking the neck. At 2:21 p.m. John Warren was pronounced dead and the body was turned over to the undertaker who had paid Warren $5 for his body.

The *Houston Daily Post*, dated Saturday, August 16, 1902, provided their readers with details of the murder and the execution at Groesbeck, Texas.

Live Oak County
County Seat - George West

Vicente Losano
Also spelled as Bacente

Race/Gender: Hispanic Male   **Age:** 19   **Offense:** Robbery & Murder
Weapon: Ax   **Offense Date:** November 26, 1903   **Execution:** June 16, 1904

In October of 1903, Vicente Losano traveled from Mexico to Live Oak County, Texas, looking for employment picking cotton. Losano was hired and worked with another laborer by the name of Casamiro Sais who considered Losano his friend.

On the night of November 26, 1903, Casamiro proudly showed Losano that he had saved $18 of his pay. Later that evening, Casamiro and Losano walked a half-mile to another labor camp to borrow an ax so they could chop firewood. After receiving the ax, they promised the owner they would return his ax after they finished chopping wood. The next morning, the owner went to retrieve his ax and walked into Casamiro's and Losano's camp. There he found Casamiro dead with the body wrapped in cotton sacks. Losano could not be found, and Sheriff W. H. Lewis was notified of the murder. It was determined that Casamiro had been struck twice to the head with the ax.

In not finding Losano, Sheriff Lewis sent out a telegraph to all nearby counties with a description of Lozano and he offered a $100 reward for his capture. On December 7, 1903, Sheriff W. W. Shely of Starr County notified Sheriff Lewis that he had his man in custody. Sheriff Lewis traveled to Rio Grande City and met with Losano and learned that when Losano was arrested he was carrying Casamiro's shoes, hat, shirt and pants. Losano confessed to Sheriff Lewis of the murder and directed the sheriff to the well he had dropped the ax in. The ax was later recovered and was used as evidence at Losano's trial.

After Losano was convicted, he was returned back before the court for final sentencing. The judge asked Losano if he had anything to say before the sentence was pronounced. Losano replied he killed Casamero in his sleep because he was dreaming he was in a fight at the time.

On the day of the execution, Lozano was hanged privately in the presence of sixty witnesses in the jail. After the body was lowered into a coffin, the remains were buried in the potter's field.

The *San Antonio Express*, dated Friday, June 17, 1904, provided their readers with details of the crime and the execution at Oakville, Texas.

Ysidro Gonzales

Race/Gender: Hispanic Male   **Offense:** Murder   **Offense Date:** December 20, 1914
Weapon: Iron Rod   **Execution:** February 1, 1915

Federico Sanchez

Race/Gender: Hispanic Male   **Offense:** Murder   **Offense Date:** December 20, 1914
Weapon: Iron Rod   **Execution:** March 3, 1915

Deputy Harry Hinton was a three-year veteran of the Live Oak County Sheriff's office. The thirty-year-old deputy sheriff was married and fathered two children. On December 20, 1914, Deputy Hinton entered the cell corridor to bring inmates Ysidro Gonzales and Federico Gonzales their dinner. When Deputy Hinton bent over to place a food tray down, Gonzales struck the officer to the back of the head with an iron rod, and then choked him to death.

The following morning Deputy Harry Hinton's family became concerned when he had not returned home from work. When the jail was checked, it was discovered that three inmates had escaped, and Hinton had been murdered.

An angry mob first captured a third unnamed escapee, and rather than turn the prisoner over to authorities, they decided that he should pay for the murder of Harry. A rope was thrown over a tree limb, and a noose placed around his neck. The prisoner was pulled up, the rope was tied off around a tree, and then the body was riddled with bullets.

The sheriff's posse at a Mexican settlement near Oakville captured Federico Sanchez. On the pretense of returning Sanchez back to the jail at Oakville, the officers quickly drove Sanchez to the Bexar County jail in San Antonio for safekeeping. Gonzales was also spared from lynch justice after Judge Chambliss promised the mob that both men would receive a speedy trial. The promise was kept as Gonzales was tried for murder four days later on December 30. Gonzales was found guilty of murder and sentenced to death.

Federico Sanchez's trial then took place the following morning, and he too was declared guilty of murder. During the night, a Mexican mob of 150 men attempted to storm the jail in order to free Gonzales, but the attempt failed with the support of fifty American's who stood their ground, not allowing the jail to be overrun.

Jacinto Gonzales

Race/Gender: Hispanic Male **Age:** 17 **Offense Date:** 1915
Offense: Rape **Weapon:** Shotgun **Execution:** January 10, 1916

Jacinto Gonzales was tried and found guilty of sexually assaulting a ten-year-old school girl. Gonzales was to have threatened to kill the child as he assaulted her with a shotgun. Once Sheriff Charles Tullis was notified, he arrested Gonzales within twelve hours after the crime was committed and secured him at the Atascosa County jail for safe keeping from a lynch mob.

One week later the child testified from the witness stand and pointed at Jacinto Gonzales as the man who had assaulted her. Gonzales was found guilty and sentenced to hang on December 10, 1915, but acting Governor William P. Hobby granted a thirty-day stay to investigate Gonzales' claimed that he was not seventeen-years-old.

From the gallows, Gonzales declined to make a statement.

The *Dallas Morning News*, dated Tuesday, January 11, 1916, reported that the execution had taken placed.

Matagorda County
County Seat - Bay City

Diggs Perry

Race/Gender: Black Male **Offense:** Robbery & Murder **Offense Date:** September 1912
Weapon: Shotgun **Execution Date:** April 21, 1913

In September of 1912, Diggs Perry told Charles Brown that he was in desperate need for money and he would kill any man to get it. Perry and Brown believed that Jack Simmons possessed a large sum of money and they went to Simmons' home asking to borrow a shotgun to kill a bird. Simmons loaned his shotgun to Perry and later that day Brown and Perry returned with a dead pheasant. After Simmons had cleaned the bird and was in the process of salting the meat, Perry reloaded the shotgun and shot Simmons in the head and then pushed the body into the burning fireplace.

Perry searched Simmons' clothing and removed his wallet which contained $35. Perry handed Brown a $10 dollar bill. Both Perry and Brown were arrested and Brown turned state's witness in exchange for a life sentence in prison.

On January 18, 1913, Diggs Perry was tried and found guilty of murder. The case was appealed and remanded for a new trial. Perry was again found guilty and sentenced to hang. On April 21, 1913, Perry became the first and last person to be legally hanged in Matagorda County.

On the appointed day, the execution took place from inside a barn. On the gallows, Perry protested his innocence and said he had been falsely accused. Perry told all goodbye and stepped upon the trap door. The last thing Perry heard just moments before the trap was sprung, was the singing of a hymn by his friends.

The *Eagle Lake Headlight* dated Saturday, April 26, 1913, provided readers with details of the crime and execution.

Maverick County
County Seat - Eagle Pass

Richard H. Duncan

Alias: Dick Duncan **Race/Gender:** White Male **Age:** 28
Offense: Robbery & Quadruple Murder **Offense Date:** February 26, 1889
Weapon: Blunt object - Rifle Barrel **Execution Date:** September 18, 1891

On February 27, 1889, women washing clothes of the banks of the Rio Grande near Eagle Pass, Texas, discovered the floating body of a woman. The following day near the same location a second body of a woman was found. Four days later the bodies of a woman and a young man were found. All had been killed from a blunt object crushing their skulls. The bodies were in a bad stage of decomposition, but later matched the description of a widow by the name of Mary Ann Williamson, her daughters Levonia Holmes, Beulah Williamson and her son Ben Williamson. The family was to have lived on a small farm they owned near San Saba.

The investigation revealed that Richard Duncan had purchased the Williamson farm for $400 and he and his brother Tap Duncan had assisted the Williams family in loading the furniture in the wagon. The Williams were last seen alive traveling with their belonging by wagon with Richard and Tap Duncan escorting them. A few days later, Richard Duncan was at Eagle Pass attempting to sell the Williamson horses, wagon and property. When the bodies were identified by dental examination from a dentist, Richard and Tap Duncan were arrested, but Tap was later released. The examination of the teeth by Dr. A. E. Brown for the purpose of identification of human remains may have been the first known case to be used in the court as evidence. Duncan was tried for the murders and convicted. Duncan's execution was delayed through respite and appeals to the United States Supreme Court.

On September 18, 1891, Duncan embraced one of his guards saying to him in a whisper, "Years after I am dead they will find the real murderer," and was led into the corridor to the gallows. Duncan walked up the stairs to the top of the platform and he first addressed the crowd by saying, "Meet me in Heaven." To the minister, Duncan said, "I listened to the reading of the death warrant as coolly as a chapter in this prayer book." In turning to Sheriff Cooke, Duncan said, "I want you to forgive me. God has forgiven me. I have asked him to forgive, as I forgive my enemies. I feel that he has heard my prayer."

To those standing on the scaffold with him, Duncan said, "Goodbye, I hope to meet you in heaven, and feel that I am going there. I feel that I have committed no crime, and feel that I have been pardoned and washed whiter than snow."

He also told Sheriff Cooke, "I would be glad if I could talk to my friends a moment." The sheriff informed Duncan to take as much time as he needed. Duncan told the priest, "Father, I feel that I am prepared. I will meet you in heaven. I feel that is where I am going. I feel that the Lord has cleansed my sins as white as snow."

Duncan continued by saying, "If there are any friends who would like to shake hands with me come upon the gallows. I hope to meet you all in heaven." To the jailer, Duncan said, "I am hugging a dear friend."

Duncan told Sheriff Cooke, "I am ready anytime that you are, Mr. Cooke. Do you have to tie my hands that way? You could hang me without tying me as I would not resist at all. Thank God, I never have resisted any of you, and I have been in your power nearly three years. Where do you want me to stand, Mr. Cooke? I will stand anywhere you say."

As the hands were being tied, Duncan said, "It takes a long time. The rope will slip down below my knees if you don't watch it." When the noose was being adjusted, Duncan said, "Don't choke me, Mr. Cooke; slacken the rope just a little. I am ready, Mr. Cooke."

At 11:25 a.m. as the black cap was placed over the head, Duncan asked the sheriff if he would allow him to speak a word. Duncan said, "Tell me when you are going to drop, have mercy."

Sheriff Cooke asked, "Are you ready?"

When Duncan replied with "Yes, sir; I am ready," Sheriff Cooke sprang the trap, dropping Duncan eight feet into the trap.

After the execution, the body was released to the family, who transported the remains back to San Saba County where Duncan was buried at the Barnett Cemetery.

In the cell Duncan had left a letter addressed to Rev. Elliott which read:

I have lived a life of sin, but the sins that I did commit I was never accused of and now they take and murder me for some one else's black crime. I feel that I am going to a place where there are no false witnesses and every man is judged by his own deeds. I would be glad to have my statements taken and followed up and show the world that I am innocent and let my enemies think what they please.

The *Fort Worth Gazette*, dated September 19, 1891, provided readers with a full account of the murders and execution at Eagle Pass, Texas.

McLennan County

County Seat - Waco

Jake Wilson

Race/Gender: Black **Offense:** Murder **Execution:** August 1869

Little details can be found about the crime and circumstances in which Jake Wilson was executed for. *Flake's Weekly Galveston Bulletin*, Saturday, August 7, 1869 provided their readers with the following short article:

The Waco papers give full details of the execution of a negro, Jake Wilson, for killing John Colive. About twenty five hundred persons were present at the hanging. According to his story he has gone straight to glory.

Perry Davis

Race/Gender: Black Male **Offense:** Murder **Offense Date:** February 6, 1877
Weapon: Pistol **Execution:** August 30, 1877

On February 6, 1877, Perry Davis beat his wife and she afterwards fled to her father's home in east Waco. Davis, who was drunk, went after his wife, and the police were notified of the disturbance he was causing. Mounted police officer Alfred D. Neal responded and upon his arrival, Perry attempted to shoot the lawman, but his pistol misfired. As the officer was dismounting his horse and drawing his pistol, Davis shot the officer in the head and then fled from the scene.

Officer Neal never regained consciousness and was carried to his home. Surrounded by his wife and children, the officer died at 10 p.m. that night. Officer Neal who was a former Texas Ranger had been with the Waco Police Department for one year and was buried in the East Waco Cemetery.

When Perry Davis escaped, the governor posted a $100 reward. On February 23, 1877, Deputy Marshal Albert Bishop was alerted that Davis was in Leon County at Jewett, Texas, sixty-seven miles east of Waco. Deputy Bishop approached Perry and ordered that he surrender. As Perry was drawing a pistol, Deputy Bishop struck Perry in the head with the butt of his gun and disarmed him.

Perry was returned to Waco and was found guilty of Neal's death in June of 1877, and sentenced to death. On August 30, 1877, Perry Davis stood on the gallows and after a short prayer said, "My friends, I want you to sing, "On Jordan's Stormy Banks I Stand." At the conclusion of the song, Perry provided the following statement, "I am willing to go and I want for you to pray for me. I thank you all for helping to sing, *Jesus is my Word, Give me Jesus*. Friends, meet me on the other shore. I want you all to sing and then I want to pray, then I am ready to go."

Davis then asked for the Lord to come down and take his soul to Heaven. He then said, "I am prepared to go. The other shore is soon to be my home and I am satisfied and will be happy, Amen."

"Thank God," echoed from the crowd.

When the preparations were complete, and just before the trap was sprung, Davis told the crowd, "Goodbye."

The *Galveston Weekly News* dated September 3, 1877, provided details of the execution.

John Franklin Speer

Alias: John W. Speers
Offense: Murder
Execution: September 20, 1878
Race/Gender: White Male
Offense Date: July 13, 1875
Age: 26
Weapon: Shotgun

The farm of Parson Pledger was located next to John Speer's farm, which was separated by a wood fence. (Some reports listed Parsons as being Mr. Rev. J. S. Pledger). On July 13, 1875, Parson was plowing his field while a friend accompanied him. As Parson was turning his horse around to plow another furrow, he was shot in the back by a shotgun blast, which killed him. The friend notified the sheriff and identified Speer as the man he had seen shoot Parson's with the weapon at the end of the fence post. When arrested, Speer told the sheriff he had to kill Pledger, but refused to provide any further details why. It was believed by many that Speer had been hired to murder Parson.

Speer was tried twice and sentenced to death. On July 6, 1878, Judge Alexander sentenced Speer to hang on August 28. The day before the execution, Governor Richard Hubbard granted a respite until September 20. While waiting for his execution, Speer was asked to confess to the murder. Speer replied he would not confess to any man, as he would only confess his crimes to God.

On the gallows, which had been erected in the jail yard, Speer made no statement to the witnesses. After a prayer, Speer was moved over to the trap door where his legs and arms were bound. The black cap and noose was adjusted, and at 4:05 p.m., the wedge under the trap door was knocked away. The drop of three feet failed to break Speer's neck, and he strangled for twelve minutes until the attending physicians pronounced him dead. At 4:22 p.m., the rope was cut and the body was lowered into a coffin where the remains were released to friends and relatives to be buried at the Waco Cemetery. Seventy-five people including Parson's daughter and her four children witnessed the execution.

The *Waco Daily Examiner*, dated Saturday, September 21, 1878, provided a full account of the execution at Waco, Texas.

Lynesfield Burks
Also spelled as Lynchfield Burk, Burke.

Race/Gender: White Male
Offense Date: August 28, 1879
Age: 41
Execution: August 27, 1880
Offense: Rape

Lynesfield Burks was charged with the rape of nine-year-old Sarah McBee. Burks lived with Mary McBee and her daughter Sarah near Robinson, in McLennan County, Texas. The girl's mother was also charged as being an accessory to the rape, but the charge was later dropped after Sarah refused to testify against her mother.

The rape was first discovered after Sara had become ill, and her mother called for the doctor. After completing his examination of the child, the doctor notified the sheriff of her injuries. Once the sheriff completed his investigation, he arrested Burks and placed him in jail to await trial.

On January 6, 1880, Burks was found guilty at Waco for the rape of the child and sentenced to hang on July 29. Before the execution date, Governor Oran Robert granted a twenty-day respite, followed by a second respite for nine days.

On July 30, 1880, the *Galveston Daily News* printed the following confession:

> *J. Lynesfield Burks, now writes to clarify to the actual facts regarding the rape I am accused of committing on the person of Sarah McBee. Sarah McBee did, of her own accord, come at night and get into my bed, and intimated by words and actions that she wished me to have something to do with her. I allowed myself to fool with her with my hand; I discovered that she had propensities and passions almost as strongly developed as a grown person. While in my bed she continued to exert herself, and any injury she received was the result of such extortion on her part. She said, after a time, that my hand hurt her, and I took it away, and then I told her to go*

to her own pallet, as I did not wish to fool with her. She got up, went out doors, and was gone some minutes.

At that time I did not know that she was hurt to amount to anything, and some one else must have hurt her, who was not on the place, for she said nothing more about it then. She came back after some time, passing through my room into her mother's and asked her for some night clothes. Mrs. McBee asked her several times what she wanted with night clothes, and, receiving no satisfactory answer, got up, struck a light, and discovered blood on the girl's gown. I heard the conversation, and wondered myself what she wanted with night clothes. I got up and told the facts to Mrs. McBee as related above, and she then scolded the girl and said to her that she ought to be ashamed of herself. Sarah, then accused her mother of having visited my bed, and it struck Mrs. McBee so forcibly that she had nothing more to say. We believed at the time that her periodical sickness had come upon her, but upon examination her mother found she had been slightly injured. Having only known the girl's person with my hand, whatever injuries if any, I inflicted were made in that way. We remembered that the girl was in the habit of going down in the field every evening to pull grass for the claves, and concluded that we would tell that a man caught her in the filed that evening and hurt her. We thought this tale would look very reasonable and the mother, girl and myself agreed that we would tell it to the people, for we were ashamed to let them know we were living such a life. Not that we dreaded the law, but because the girl did not want the people to know that she was getting into bed with me, and the mother and myself did not want it known that we were living the life that we were. So we all thought that we would not give the true facts.

This was the first time I was ever guilty of living such a life with any woman, and I think I can honestly say, if I could live one hundred years longer I would never be guilty of living such a sinful life again with a woman. It is a great sin before God – one that I know I am guilty of; and I feel more guilty of it than I do of the one for which I am going to be murdered. Of the rape the court says I am guilty of committing on Sarah McBee I know I am not guilty, though I am condemned to die for it. Men may take my life and drink my blood, if nothing else will do, but I hope you will be the last district court to take an innocent man's blood as you are about to take mine. I pray to my God that my blood may be sufficient for all of you who have thirsted after it, so that you may never thirst after another innocent man's blood. O. sinful man, think of what you are about to take and which you can never give back again. O. man, think of what you have done, and turn to God and live. I hold no animosity against any man for taking my life, and would harm a hair on no man's head. I pray to my blessed God to forgive all of you for taking my life, and he will do it if you will let him. O, man, when this blood of mine becomes a bitter cup to you there is only one thing that can take it away from your soul, that is the blood of Jesus. O, come to the foot of the cross, and though your sins be as scarlet, they shall be made as white as snow. L. Burks.

At 3 p.m. Burks walked out to the same gallows used to hang Perry Davis and John Speer and took a seat. Burks was dressed in a new black coat and pants, white vest, gloves was then handed a glass of brandy and a cigar, which he smoked. After a prayer with Rev. B. A. Rodgers, Burks said that he had no remarks to make except to advise all to seek Christianity and meet him in heaven. At 4:10 p.m., the hands and feet were tied, the black cap was adjusted, and the lever pulled. After twenty minutes Burks was pronounced dead, cut down and buried at the old cemetery, on South First Street.

The *Galveston Daily News*, dated Saturday, August 28, 1880, printed a full account of the execution at Waco, Texas.

Conrad Jackson

Alias: Conyers Smith
Offense: Murder
Execution: July 16, 1888

Race/Gender: Black Male
Offense Date: July 16, 1887

Age: 20
Weapon: .32 Caliber Revolver

Exactly one year to the day of the murder of John Talley, Conrad Jackson stood on the gallows as his punishment. After Jackson killed his employers and fled ahead of a posse, Constable D. D. Pitman arrested Jackson as he rode into Fairfield. Jackson at first claimed he had killed John because other people wanted him dead and had asked for him to do it. Jackson later claimed that John had insulted his brother which made him angry and therefore decided to kill him.

The *Galveston Daily News*, dated Tuesday, July 17, 1888, printed the following short article of the execution.

CONRAD JACKSON HUNG.

IN THE JAIL-YARD AT WACO FOR KILLING MR. TALLEY.

He Ascended the Gallows Readily and Died Gamely – He Told the Story of His Crime and Admitted He Ought To Be Executed.

Waco, Tex., July 16. – At 2:05 o'clock this afternoon Conrad Jackson, a Negro, aged 20 years, was hanged in the jail yard under sentence of the court.

He confessed his crime in these words: "On the 18th day of last June I came to Waco and staid with my brother, Noble Jackson. Next day was the anniversary of freedom and we celebrated together. That afternoon I INVITED MY BROTHER to go home with me to Mr. Talley's farm. When we got there I rode into the yard and Noble was about to follow me, but Mr. Talley said, addressing me, "don't let that _____ _____ come into my yard. I got very mad and I could not get over it. I kept thinking and then I said I will kill him. On Saturday, July 16, 1887, I went into the field and talked friendly to Mr. Talley. I did not say anything about the name he had applied to my brother. As he took hold of his plow-handle to start, standing in the furrow behind him with a .32 caliber revolver, I shot him in the back of the head, and

HE FELL DEAD.

I took the horse he had been plowing and galloped away, but they caught me and it is right to hang me. In exactly one hour and a half I will be in heaven with my little sister. I want my body sent to Palestine to be buried in the Tennessee settlements, four miles from Palestine. My mother and sister are buried there."

His neck was broken. Radial pulsation ceased in eight minutes, and heart action ceased in eleven minutes. He was embalmed and sent to Palestine according to his requests. The colored Methodist defrayed the expenses. Witnesses to the execution, including those on the house tops, numbered over 1000. There were no disorder.

King Sims

Alias: King Simmons **Race/Gender:** Black Male **Age:** 20
Offense: Robbery & Murder **Offense Date:** May 11, 1891 **Weapon:** Ax
Execution: June 24, 1892

In May of 1891, King Sims received word from a prostitute, whom he knew very well, that she was confined in the Waco city jail for vagrancy. The prostitute asked Sims to pay her fine in order to bail her out of jail. Sims replied that he had no money, and therefore he was going to go out of the county to kill a man to get her the money she needed.

On May 11, 1891, Ed Brandon, a cotton picker was killed at his cottage near the town of Rosenthal, Texas. King Sims lived near by, and also worked on the adjoining plantation from the Brandon home. Sims was very familiar with the old man's habits, and was aware that Ed Brandon was the treasury for the Oak Grove Church and that the old man kept the church funds, as well as his own money inside his home.

While at Brandon's home, Sims struck the old man with an ax while he was washing his clothes in a tub. After committing the murder, the cabin was ransacked for the money and any other valuables. Because the victim lived alone, the murder was not detected until two days later. When Sims was arrested on suspicion of the murder, he was wearing a suit and other effects belonging to his victim.

On May 16, 1892, Sims was delivered before Judge L. W. Goodrich for sentencing after he had been convicted of the murder in the first degree. Judge Goodrich asked Sims if he had anything to say as to why the death sentence should not be pronounced upon him. Sims replied that he should be given confinement in the penitentiary for life. Judge Goodrich told Sims that was not within his power, and ordered the sheriff to hang King Sims in the jail yard on June 24, 1892.

On the night before the execution Sims began pacing his cell nervously and requested to speak to Sheriff Dan Ford. In a few moments Sheriff Ford entered the cell and asked, "What do you want, King?"

"I sent for you to talk it over." Sims replied, "but I want nobody else to hear. Yes Mr. Dan, I done it, sir. I kilt him."

"Well," said the sheriff, "tell me all about it."

"That's just what I sent for you fer. I went to Mr. Brandon's on Thursday, May 11, 1891. It was dinner time when I got there. I asked for something to eat and Mr. Brandon gave me a good dinner. After dinner I went to a gully and laid down under a bush. I waited there until dark. Then I went back to the yard and got the woodpile ax. With this in my hand I went back to the gully and with my barlow I cut the handle off so as to make a chop ax. After I got ready I went back to the door and entered. Mr. Brandon was rubbing his clothes in a tub. He heard me come in and he looked up mad.

"What you come back for?" he asked.

"All de money you got,' I said, says I, and he said, "Go away."

"He sorter turned round and then I hit him. I got $18.45 outen the trunk. I went back and he was on the floor breathing heard like. Then I hit him again. After I hit him again he died. Then I went out, stripped off and put coal oil on my bloody clothes. I set'em on afire by touching a match. Then I went in and put on Mr. Brandon's clothes. I got his best suit outen his trunk. I came to town that night and when I got here I met John Risber and I gin him $2.50 of the money I got offen the dead man. I had agreed with these man to help me, but they did not come. I mean by these men John Rishor, Tom Harrison and Frank Carter. Frank Carter was to rob the Waco Freight agent of the Missouri, Kansas and Texas that night and then we were all going to San Antonio together. "

"Is Mr. Brandon's your first murder?" the sheriff inquired.

"Yes sir. He is the first man I ever killed," the Sims replied. "But I have often robbed before. I growed up stealing. I have stole from cash drawers in stores mostly, but I never did get caught. I never did work much. I lived mostly by stealing. I want to tell it all. I want to leave the world right. My mother lives at Tyler, and I would like to be buried there. I once waited on Governor Hogg and I thought maybe he would save me, but now I have no hope. I know that I will never see the sunset tomorrow, but I hope Christ will save me from hell, I am sorry for all my sins."

The next morning, Sheriff Ford entered the cell and told Sims he had his death warrant which he would read to him. At the conclusion the sheriff left telling Sims he would be returning for him after his dinner at 2 p.m.. Just then the undertaker John Fall arrived and measured Sims for the coffin. Out loud the undertaker said, "Six feet and an inch allowed for stretching," then made an entry in his notebook and left.

Next came a clothier. "Well, Sims, old boy," the clothier said, "I come to give you a suit of clothes."

Sheriff Ford remarked, "Sims, you pick a good suit, I will pay for it. Tell the gentleman what sort of clothes you want."

"I want a sky blue suit of flannel," Sims said. "I was always stuck to get a blue suit; real blue, not binky blue."

"And your shirt," the sheriff asked. "What sort of shirt?"

"I want a shirt dyed with red speckles, Mr. Dan. I want a speckly shirt – percale. I want a shirt that will look well, done up pretty, with a collar on it, and I want a striped necktie – four-in hand."

At 1: 45 p.m. the condemned man descended the rear steps, and was led by the sheriff who held his arm. He mounted the scaffold steps then he turned to the crowd and said, "I am guilty and fully deserve the death penalty about to be inflicted. I am ready to go. I have made my peace with God. I hope none of you who see me will lead the life I have led and come to the death so near at hand for me. Think, my dear friends, a thousand times before you commit a wrong deed. Goodbye, all. Meet me in heaven."

He was then moved over the trap, where the sheriff and the deputies bound Sims hands and feet with rawhide strings. As the sheriff drew a black cap from his pocket, Sims cried out, "Goodbye, boys. I hope you will all live a better life than mine has been, Goodbye, all."

The sheriff placed the cap over the head of the prisoner, and pulled the trigger. After the body was cut down the crowd made a rush for the rope, which was cut into pieces and handed out as souvenirs. Home owners near the jail built platforms upon their roofs and sold space to eager spectators at $1 a person to give them a bird's eye view.

The *Galveston Daily News*, dated Saturday, June 25, 1892, provided its readers with a large article about the crime and execution at Waco, Texas.

Walter Ford

Age: 22   **Race/Gender:** Black Male   **Offense:** Murder
Offense Date: June 25, 1898   **Weapon:** .38 caliber pistol   **Execution:** October 27, 1899

Walter Ford said he was madly in love with seventeen-year-old Lucinda Moore and asked for Lucinda's hand in marriage. Lucinda quickly turned Ford's marriage proposal down saying she was too young to marry.

On June 25, 1898, Ford went to Lucinda's parents' home on South Fourth Street in Waco where she lived. Ford went to the home on the pretense of retrieving some of his personal items he had left there. Ford was to have gone into the room and told Lucinda he was there to pick up his razor and a pair of cuffs. Minutes later, Lucinda fled from the house while Ford chased after her with a pistol in his hand. In running in the direction of Waco Creek, Ford fired the pistol striking her in the back and neck. Ford caught Lucinda by her dress and dragged her to the ground. While begging for her life, Ford placed the barrel of the pistol to her head and fired a lethal shot.

Ford later made the claim once he entered the room he had asked Lucinda for his razor. Lucinda in response replied, "Yes, I'll give you a razor," and rushed at him with the sharp weapon and he drew his weapon in self-defense.

On October 24, 1898, Walter Ford was tried and found guilty of murder. Ford was first sentenced on June 9 with the execution scheduled for July 14, 1899, but Ford's attorney H. P. Jordan made a strong appeal to the governor asking that Ford receive commutation to life imprisonment. The governor declined the request, but granted a respite to deliver an affidavit for an insanity trial.

While waiting for his execution, Ford often spoke to Lucinda's spirit who reassured him of her love and forgiveness to him.

Sheriff Baker ordered the scaffold to be built in the jail yard at the corner of the new jail annex and the old county jail building so that the scaffold could be shielded from two sides, and out of view of the public. The other two sides of the scaffold were covered from view by canvas curtains. The same gallows had been used for the execution of King Sims in 1892 after which it was disassembled and stored in the courthouse loft.

On the gallows, Walter Ford said, "Hello, Mr. Sparks. Well this is my last hour on earth. I will meet you again in Heaven. I am getting along fine and am ready to go. I don't feel condemned, but the white folks say so, and I am ready. I hope to meet you all in heaven. This man here, he is all right, (Referring to his attorney H. P. Jordan). I feel fine. I will meet you 'all in heaven. That's all I got to say."

Ford then took the black cap and put it over his head himself. After the cap was adjusted and his arms and legs bound, Sheriff Baker asked if he was ready. Ford replied that he was, and the lever was pulled at 12:18 p.m.. Thirteen minutes later the body was pronounced dead and cut down to be placed in a coffin and shipped to Franklin in Robertson County for burial.

The *San Antonio Daily Light*, dated Saturday, October 28, 1899, provided readers with the details of the executions and crimes committed by three men who were all executed on January 27, 1899, in McLennan, Wilbarger and Travis County.

Will King

Age: 21
Weapon: Pistol
Race/Gender: Black Male
Offense Date: October 27, 1900
Offense: Murder
Execution: October 25, 1901

On the evening of October 27, 1900, at 7 p.m., Will King was at the Hannah Saloon on North 6th street in Waco, when he claimed someone had stolen a $10 bill from him. Angrily King announced that he was going to kill someone for the theft of his money.

King went home, grabbed his pistol and started walking back towards the saloon when he shot at a dog. King told Mrs. Josephine Nolan and her daughter who witnessed this action if either of them said a word to anyone, that he would kill them.

King then continued on when he walked up to W. M. Gillespie. With the pistol in his hand he said, "Goodbye, Mr. Gillespie, I am going to kill somebody and then to Hell."

As King walked away two men tried to stop King and convince him to go back home. King threatened both men to allow him to pass or he would kill them as well. Gillespie then telephoned the Waco police station to report a man with a gun at the Puss Hanaah's Chili Parlor. Officer William Davis Mitchell was ending his watch when the call came in, but since the disturbance was on his way home, Officer Mitchell volunteered to take the call.

King entered through the back of the saloon and told Will Cook, the bartender, that he, "Was going to kill all the white people or get his money."

King was informed that the police had been telephoned. King replied, "Let them come, I will murder them." About five minutes later, Mounted officer Mitchell arrived in front of the saloon. The officer had just begun to dismount from the right side of his horse when King fired twice at the officer. The officer staggered from being hit in the left arm and heart and attempted to remount his horse but could not.

Officer Mitchell then returned fire by shooting in the direction of King and then fell. Officer Mitchell fired two more random bullets, as King ran off. King was found hiding in a horse stable with a bullet wound to the knee. Witnesses believed that Officer Mitchell had shot King in the knee, but King claimed his bullet wound was from Will Cook who had shot him from behind the bar. A total of ten pistol shots had been fired during this shootout.

Officer Mitchell told Alderman Woodall, "Woodall, I am going to die, send and get my wife and children." Officer Mitchell's wife and children arrived, but he was unable to speak to them, and the thirty-six-year-old officer died.

Ten days later, King was indicted for the murder of Officer Mitchell. The jury found King guilty of the murder in the first degree and assessed the death penalty. The following day, King's attorney filed motions before the court for a new trial and to quash the indictment on grounds that the court had discriminated against his client as King was of black and that there was not one person of his race on the jury panel.

The court agreed with the motion, and King was re-indicted a second time during the same month. The jury again found King guilty of murder, but was deadlock in the punishment phase. Eleven for the death penalty and one for life imprisonment. Will King was tried a third time on January 24, 1901, and found guilty.

On the gallows, Sheriff Baker asked King if he wished to say anything. King stepped forward and said:

> I wish to say to the assembled congregation that this is an unjust hanging. I would say that at the judgment, they say I killed Officer Mitchell, but if I did, I didn't know it. All my friends and associates will tell you that I did not even know Mitchell. It is hard to stand the punishment, but I must do so. God forgive all who had anything to do with it."

> I wish to say further that Officer Mitchell did not shoot me in the leg, as many suppose, but the shot was fired by that brave man Will Cook, bar tender for Hanna. He shot from behind the bar and said he would have caught me if he could. I should not have had a verdict of murder in the first degree as the honorable citizens of McLennan County gave me. I have nothing against Cook for shooting me as he did. I hope to meet all of you in Heaven and I hope some of you who have been traveling the wrong road will take a new start today. I am going to say something which may

hurt some, but I ought to sat it. No honorable man will go into the jury box in this county, for the court that tried me is unjust.

The sparks boys stood by me although I did not have money. The important thing they kept me from hanging until my soul was saved. This was worth a million dollars to me. If I had thirty more cases on hand, I would have them to help me. I hope Sheriff Baker will overcome this and meet me in glory. I won't return any evil for evil, though some have drunk my blood.

At the conclusion of the statement, Sheriff Baker asked King if he was ready. King said, "Lord save me, knock it loose, Mr. Baker." Sheriff Baker then sprung the trap.

Will King was executed in the county jail yard and hanged by a rope that had become both dependable and infamous. The rope belonged to W. A. Stewart, ex-sheriff of Johnson County. King was the thirteenth victim hung by this rope and he was buried at the First Street Cemetery.

The Waco Times Herald, dated Saturday, October 26, 1901, provided readers with a large article detailing the events of the shooting, King's final hours alive, and the execution.

Anderson Norris

Race/Gender: Black Male   **Age:** 17   **Offense:** Murder
Offense Date: December 5, 1900   **Weapon:** Blunt Trauma   **Execution:** January 10, 1902

On December 5, 1900, at about 4 p.m., Mrs. Emma French, the wife of a young farmer named James French, was found dead on the gallery of their house. The woman died as a result of receiving several severe blows to the head from a target rifle. A piece of a target rifle was found in the dead woman's arms.

James French during the time of the murder was plowing his field when a neighbor notified him that his wife was found dead. On the way back to his home, his field hand, Anderson Norris, joined French. Soon thereafter the sheriff arrived and immediately placed Norris under arrest for suspicion of murder.

The sheriff found a snuffbox belonging to Norris at the scene, and Norris also had bloodstains on his clothes. The rifle used to bludgeon Emma to death had been purchased by Mr. French as an advancement of Norris' pay. However the agreement was that Norris was not to receive the rifle until the corn from the field had been gathered and brought in. It was believed by the lawmen that the rifle was the motive behind the murder. Officers believed that Norris had gone to the house asking Mrs. French for the rifle which she refused to release to Norris as she was aware of the agreement between her husband and him. It was their belief that Mrs. French and Norris had struggled over the rifle, and it angered him, so he beat the woman to death with the rifle.

After Norris' arrest, he was lodged in the jail at Corsicana. On December 10, the grand jury of Navarro County returned a true bill of murder against Anderson Norris. The case was called for trial in District Court on December 20, but was given a continuance because of the "presence of a mob."

In April 1901, the case was called to the Navarro County court for the second time. The court transferred the case to McLennan County, giving the reason that the defendant's life was in jeopardy in Navarro County and that the prejudice was so great in adjoining counties that it was necessary to transfer the case to an adjoining judicial district.

The case was taken up in the Fifty-Fourth District Court in McLennan County, before Judge S. R. Scott. At trial Norris claimed he was innocent of the murder as he was working in the field beside French when they both learned of the murder at the same time. Norris claimed the blood on his clothing was not human, but from a hog he had killed. On June 5, the jury reached a verdict fixing the penalty at death. The case was appealed to the Court of Criminal Appeals until October 30, when the judgment of the lower court was affirmed. The mandate was returned to the court and on December 9, lacking one day from being a year after the finding of the first indictment, the sentence was passed.

On the gallows, Norris pleaded his innocence and addressed James French who was standing next to the coffin in which Norris' body would be placed and said:

Mr. French, I know that you think that I killed your wife, but I did not. I hope that you will not hold any prejudice against me and I do not hold anything against you. They are going to hang me about your wife. I must pay the penalty of death, but I tell you as a friend that I never killed your wife. When I was in Navarro County, the night I was arrested, they found a snuffbox you said was mine, but it was not. You also said you saw me coming out of Ridgeway's yard; that you did not see me murder your wife, but saw me coming out of the yard. I want to say to you and to all others, be good, get into no trouble, suspicion has brought me to have my neck broke.

Mr. French, do you hold prejudice against me?

Mr. French replied, "As much as I ever did."

"Well," said Norris, "I hope you won't hold it any longer, as I did not murder your wife, I want you to strictly understand that."

Norris continued by saying:

I was at your house about two weeks, you know, well, you remember we killed three hogs with that target rifle at your house, and killed some more at another place, and you remember I got some blood on me from them hogs that they said was human blood; they examined it with a --- what was it? Oh, yes, a microscope ---and said that it was human blood. Well, then, you remember when we were in court, and Judge Cobb was on the bench, and you come in with a pistol to shoot me? Do you remember that? Well, Wiley Robinson said so, and he said your nerve failed and you couldn't shoot me. Here is one of my pictures, which I want you to keep (throwing one to him) and I hope it will do you good. You can look at the picture of Anderson Norris and remember that his flesh is killed, but his soul is not. When we get to heaven we'll get real justice and we won't be cheated out of any thing there. When you do meet me in heaven; this may hurt your feelings but I say it; then you'll forget all you hold against me here. It's miserable for me to stand and talk this way, and die for something I didn't do. There is one more thing; when you go back to Corsicana and see the people tell them they can hold prejudice against me, but they must die some day. I forgive them all.

At the close of the prayer his arms and legs were being bound. Norris said, "I am almost ready to go. You all saw Will King hung here and today January 10, you will see me, and you will see others. Don't get into trouble for it's easy to get into but hard to get out. You all know (calling out a name) well, he got into trouble and he's been in for eight years and ain't out yet. Well, I'm going home. I don't want anybody to pull the trigger but Mr. Baker.

Anderson Norris became the sixteenth person to hang from the infamous rope, owned by ex-sheriff Stewart of Johnson County, at Waco, Texas.

The *Waco Times-Herald*, January 11, 1902, provided a large article to readers detailing the history of the crime, trial, and execution.

Jesse Jones

Alias: Jesse Washington
Offense: Robbery & Murder
Execution: November 30, 1906

Race/Gender: Black Male
Offense Date: September 9, 1906

Age: 26
Weapon: Ax

Jesse Jones said he murdered his employer, Matthew Block, who operated a meat and merchant store for the money the store took in during the busy day. At the close of business, Block sat down in a chair to rest, when Jones hit him in the back of the head repeatedly with the butt of an ax, killing him. The next morning, Jones reported the murder to the police telling the officers he discovered the crime when he arrived to work. After Jones was arrested, he confessed to the murder, and disclosed the location of the $250 he had stolen, which was recovered.

On September 24, 1906, Jones was tried for the murder and after the case was affirmed by the Court of Appeals, he was sentenced to hang by Judge Scott on November 30, 1906. Sheriff George Tilley ordered the scaffold to be built on the yard of the county jail. Jones' favorite spiritual advisor was a black preacher who was in jail at the same time for assaulting and battering his wife. On the scaffold, Jones confessed his guilt.

At 12:35 p.m., Sheriff Tilley pulled the lever, dropping Jones seven feet to his death. The scaffold had been screened surrounding the trap with cotton bagging, but the crowd quickly tore it down to view the suspended body. Fifteen minutes later, the body was cut down and turned over to the undertaker for burial at the First Street Cemetery in Waco.

The *San Antonio Daily Light*, dated Friday, November 30, 1906, provided readers with details of the murder and the execution at Waco, Texas.

John Williams

Race/Gender: Black Male **Offense:** Murder **Offense Date:** July 13, 1915
Weapon: Firearm **Execution:** October 27, 1916

John Williams was convicted of the shooting death of a man named Allison Criner on the night of July 13, 1915. Williams' execution was first set to take place on July 28, 1916, but was delayed through respites by Governor James Ferguson. On September 25, District Court Judge R. L. Monroe reset the day of the execution, for the last time, to take place on October 27, 1916.

At 11:27 a.m., the trap was sprung and the body was pronounced dead seven minutes later. The remains were then carried to the cemetery at Mount Calm for burial. The rope reportedly had been used in previously executions at Dallas, Fort Worth, Waxahachie, Cleburne and Waco.

The *Fort Worth Star-Telegram*, dated Friday, October 27, 1916, provided a short article to readers of the execution at Waco.

Nat Hoffman

Race/Gender: White Male **Age:** 25 **Offense:** Rape & Murder
Offense Date: April, 1918 **Execution:** July 11, 1918

Camp MacArthur, which was named in honor of General Arthur MacArthur, father of General Douglas McArthur, opened in 1917 as a WWI training camp. The camp was located on the northwest side of Waco. Assigned to the camp was Private Nat Hoffman, who worked in supply for the 19th Field Artillery Division.

In April of 1918, Private Hoffman came across a boy and girl, both about eleven years-old, walking together in an isolated spot in the woods near the camp. Hoffman assaulted boy who ran away for help and reported what had happened to military police. Hoffman afterwards raped the girl. Police tracked Hoffman that evening and arrested him. Hoffman was court-martialed for his crimes and sentenced to hang.

The gallows were erected in the camp's stockyard. On the morning of the execution, Hoffman's only statement to the few witnesses who were permitted to be present was, "I deserved my fate."

At 5:45 a.m. the trap was released. The following the day, Hoffman's body was transported to his mother in Pittsburg, Pennsylvania.

The *Kansas City Star*, dated July 11, 1918, provided readers with a short article of the crime and execution.

Roy Mitchell

Race/Gender: Black Male **Offense:** Rape, Robbery, & Multiple Murders
Offense Date: January 19, 1923 **Weapon:** Ax, Shotgun, & Pistol **Execution:** July 30, 1923

For eleven months, Roy Mitchell terrorized McLennan County with rapes of women and the robbery and murder of his victims. When arrested on January 29, 1923, Sheriff Leslie Stegall searched Mitchell's home and found numerous articles of property belonging to several victims. Mitchell confessed to eight murders, but was only tried on six of the eight murders, and was found guilty. Mitchell confessed to and was also indicted on three criminal assaults (rape), two attempted rapes and two counts of attempted murder.

It was the murder of Ethel Denecamp on July 30, 1923, that Mitchell was sentenced to be executed for. On January 19, 1923, Ethel Denecamp and her male date had stopped the car to park where Mitchell waiting in hiding five miles southeast of Waco on the Springfield road. Mitchell first killed Ethel's date, W. E. Holt by shooting him three times with a shotgun. In the car was Holt's pistol that Mitchell used to murder Ethel with, and afterwards hid her body in a clump of bushes.

Mitchell was convicted for the following murders:
- On February 11, 1922, an ax wound to the head killed Mrs. W. H. Barker. Mrs. Barker was murdered along with her husband W. H Barker and her thirteen-year-old son, Homer Turk. All three persons were murdered at Concord, located northeast of Waco. Mitchel had gone to the home demanding money and immediately shot and killed Mr. Barker. He then killed both Homer and Mrs. Barker with strikes to the head with an ax. Mitchell was not charged with the murders of Homer or Mr. Barker.
- May 7, 1922, Mitchell hid in the garage of W. F. Driskell and killed him by a strike to the head with the ax as Driskell entered the garage.
- May 25, 1922, Harold Bolton was shot three times from the pistol belonging to W. F. Driskell that Mitchell stole from his home at the time of the murder. Harold was shot and killed on the Corsicana road, six miles from Waco.
- On November 20, 1922, Grady Skipworth was shot to death by a shotgun at Lover's Leap at Cameron Park on the outer edge of downtown Waco. Grady had parked his car with his date. Grady's date survived the attack by jumping over the cliff.
- July 30, 1923 both W. E. Holt and Ethel Denecamp both murdered.

On the morning of July 30, 1923, Mitchell wore his jail clothes and went to the gallows barefooted as he refused to put on the new suit the county had purchased for him. Mitchell who confessed several times to the murders and assaults on women, only said, "Goodbye, everybody."

At 11:02 a.m., Sheriff Leslie Stegall pulled the trap that sent the murderer and rapist to his death. After the body was lowered into a plain pine box, the remains were taken directly to the cemetery and buried.

The *Waco Times-Herald*, dated Monday, July 30, 1923, provided readers with a large article detailing all the crimes Mitchell committed and his execution.

Medina County
County Seat - Hondo

Henry Brown

Race/Gender: Black Male   **Age:** 46   **Offense:** Murder
Offense Date: July 25, 1902   **Weapon:** Shovel   **Execution:** November 30, 1906

Henry Brown was serving two separate life terms in the penitentiary when he killed another inmate by the name of Albert Taylor. Both men had differences with each other in the past, but their dislike escalated on July 25, 1902, with deadly consequences.

While working on a railroad gravel chain gang, Albert Taylor taunted Henry Brown by throwing a shovel full of gravel in the area Brown was working in. Brown warned Taylor not to be doing that. The second time Taylor threw the gravel into Brown's work area, Taylor threw down his shovel and both men began fighting. Once the fight ended, Brown walked back to his area and at the same time made threats directed at Taylor.

After everyone had calmed down and resumed working, Brown walked up behind Taylor and struck him several times in the back of the neck and head with his shovel, killing him.

One of the inmates yelled, "Bring a bucket of water and pour it on him."

Brown replied, "You can pour a barrel of water on that _____ _____ _____ and it won't do him any good," and struck the neck and head of Taylor again with the edge of the shovel.

At trial, Brown told the jury, "I had trouble with Albert Taylor that morning. He chased me around, striking at me with a shovel. Just before I killed him we were standing together unloading gravel from a car. He raised his shovel and said, 'I'll get you, you _____ _____.' Then I raised my shovel and struck him and killed him. I did not hit him on the back of the neck. I am telling the truth; got no reason not to, yes, I've killed some men before Taylor; that's what I'm in the penitentiary for. Well, I was sentenced eight years ago to the pen for life and after that I got another sentence for ninety-nine years."

The jury found Brown guilty of murder in the first degree and assessed his punishment at death. His case was appealed, and on May 23, 1906, the Court of Criminal Appeals affirmed the judgment.

On the gallows, Brown bid all those present with goodbye. At 11:20 a.m. the trap was sprung and fifteen minutes later Brown was pronounced dead.

The *Galveston Daily News*, December 1, 1906, provided their readers with details of the murder and the execution at Hondo, Texas.

Menard County
County Seat - Menard

Green Johnson

Race/Gender: Black Male **Offense:** Murder **Offense Date:** June 29, 1878
Execution: December 20, 1878

On December 20, 1878, Green Johnson was hanged for the murder of his wife. The fall did not break his neck and it took ten minutes for Johnson to strangle to death.

The *Galveston Daily News*, dated December 24, 1878, printed the following short article of the execution:

The Execution at Menardville
{Special Telegram to the News}

Mason, Dec. 23. – The following is condensed from to-morrow News extra.

Friday, Dec. 20, was a memorable day at Menardville, Menard county. At 1:45 the soul of Green Johnson, colored, was launched into eternity. Johnson was formerly a soldier stationed at Fort Kavett, and on the 29 day of June 1878, brutally murdered his wife in a fit of jealousy. The day was bitter cold and the attendance small. Everything passed off quietly. Johnson met his fate bravely and died in the hopes of entering a better world. His neck was not broken by the fall and he was dully ten minutes dying.

Midland County
County Seat - Midland

Lorenzo Porrez
Also spelled - Lorenza Parres, Perrez, Porez, and Pares

Race/Gender: Hispanic Male   **Age:** 20   **Offense:** Murder
Weapon: Knife   **Offense Date:** July 21, 1890   **Execution:** November 27, 1891

On the night of July 20, 1890, saddles were stolen from Sam Murray's ranch in Tom Green County, near Centralia Draw. After the theft of the saddles had been discovered, Murray followed tracks near the Bartlett Ranch where Will Lardrum lived. Murray asked Landrum to accompany him in pursuit of the thieves. The two cowboys first rode west toward the Hurd ranch and made arrangements for Hurd, and a ranch hand named McGruder to join the pursuit on soon as they could.

Having changed horses the two pressed on another twenty-five miles, when they came upon four Mexicans who had stopped at a windmill for dinner. Murray identified the saddles on the horses ridden by the Mexicans as his property, and identified Porrez as being one of the people in the party. Murray decided to leave and ride to the IX Ranch nearby for assistance. Not being successful in obtaining help, Murray returned back Landrum and they continued following the suspects until they found Murray's stolen quirt lying across the road.

At about 4 p.m. in the evening the Mexicans they were following charged Murray and Landrum from the rear firing their weapons. During the chase that ensued, the two cowboys separated and rode in different directions. Two Mexicans bandits chased after Murray while two others chased after Landrum. Murray was able to outrun those after him and to the safety of the IX Ranch, and reported what had occurred.

About an hour and a half later when returning to the scene, Landrum's horse, saddle, and his hat were found. The posse noticed blood within ten or fifteen feet on the road with drag marks in the sand and brush which led them to Murray's dead body. An examination of the body revealed two knife wounds in the chest. Four months later, Porrez and two other Mexican suspects were arrested and charged with murder.

On November 15, 1891, less than two weeks until the scheduled execution, Lorenzo Porrez acquired a dagger for the purpose of killing Sheriff W. D. Allison. One of the jail prisoners learned of the dagger and plot to attack the officer, and wrote a letter to the county attorney warning him of such.

Sheriff Allison with several deputies then confronted Porrez in his cell to surrender the weapon. Porrez backed into the corner of the cell, and made a motion that he was going to draw a weapon. The sheriff and deputies drew their pistols and pointed Winchester rifles at him with a warning not to make any further moves or he would be shot.

Porrez replied, "You are going to hang me up like a dog where all can see me, and I had just as soon die now as any time."

After two hours of keeping the officers at bay, one of Porrez's attorney arrived at the cell. The attorney promised that if the weapon was surrendered, he would attempt to have the governor commute his sentence. The weapon was then given up which was stout wire twisted into the shape of a dagger. Porrez was immediately placed in irons and remained wearing shackles until his execution.

At 2:15 p.m. in the afternoon on the day of the execution, the death warrant was read to Porrez by Sheriff G. A. Frazier of Pecos, who acted as interpreter.

At 3 p.m. Porrez ascended the scaffold, accompanied by the priest, Sheriff Frazier, Sheriff W. D. Allison and deputies. After, prayer, Porrez approached the banisters on the east side of the gallows that had been erected on the east side of the jail and said, "I am guilty of the crime for which I am about to suffer. If the people wished to punish me further than hanging, they are welcome to do so. I only asked that you forgive me for what I have done. Juan Benevides, who is to be tried at Colorado City, is not guilty of the murder, although he was along and followed Sam Murray for a distance, who escaped him."

At 3:15 p.m., the trap was sprung with the fall breaking the neck.

The *Fort Worth Gazette*, dated November 28, 1891, provided full details to their readers of the murder and execution.

Milam County
County Seat - Cameron

Charles McGill

Race/Gender: Black Male **Age:** 35 **Offense:** Murder
Offense Date: June 18, 1887 **Weapon:** Blunt Object **Execution:** January 25, 1889

On June 13, 1887, fifteen-year-old Willie Leonard left home, and was last seen alive five days later walking with Charles McGill. The next day, Leonard's body was found near the International and Great Northern Railroad tracks near Gause, Texas. It was determined that Leonard had been lying down to drink water from a creek when he was struck in the back of the head with a fishplate (splice bar or joint bar is a metal bar that is bolted to the ends of two rails to join them together in a track). When McGill was arrested, several articles belonging to Leonard were found in his possession. McGill was convicted of murder on November 30, 1889, and sentenced to death.

On January 25, 1889, the execution was private and held in jail. Charles McGill told the witnesses from the gallows that he was innocent and knew nothing of the murder. Once the black cap was adjusted, Sheriff Lewis at 1:25 p.m. pulled the lever dropping McGill eight feet. After suspending for fifteen minutes, McGill was pronounced dead and lowered into a coffin.

The *Fort Worth Daily Gazette*, dated Saturday, January 26, 1889, provided readers with details of the execution that had taken place at Cameron, Texas, which was the only execution in the history of the county.

Montague County
County Seat - Montague

Frank Smith

Race/Gender: Black Male **Offense:** Murder **Offense Date:** Unknown
Weapon: Unknown **Execution:** June 1875

Newspapers across the country reported on the execution of Frank Smith and focused primarily of Smith's bravery on the gallows and little history about the crime he committed.

From the gallows, Smith confessed to all present regarding the murder he committed and told his audience to avoid his errors. Smith offered a moving prayer to the witnesses present and asked for all to meet him in heaven, which brought tears to several of the witnesses. As the sheriff adjusted the noose around the neck, the spectators crowded around the gallows forcing the deputies to threaten the crowd with their pistols to back away while the crowd yelled out loud to, "Shoot the rope, liberate him, and Let him go."

Order was restored after Smith told the crowd to allow the law to takes its course and let him die like a man.

The *Galesville Independent* (Galesville, Wisconsin) dated June 17, 1875, carried the below news article which was duplicated and printed across the country:

> *A man was hanged in Montague County, Texas, the other day, who probably really found his way to heaven. He was a murderer; also a "damnnigger." His name was Frank Smith. Of course he prayed and exhorted on the gallows, but here begins the singularity of his case. His eloquence made such a sensation that the crowd, who were armed, rushed to the gallows, and demanded his release. But the doomed man, who was a Hercules in strength and stature, thus addressed them: "Stand back. This is no time for a row. I am guilty. Let the law take its course. I am a man, and I can die like a man." With which brave words the "noble savage" was "Launched into eternity," worthy at least of more sympathy than the philosophers of the Hangdog school, who believe the public safety to depend on periodical spasms if judicial strangulation.*

Charles Harris, Jr.

Race/Gender: White Male **Age:** 22 **Offense:** Murder
Weapon: Shotgun **Offense Date:** January 17, 1 878 **Execution:** August 29, 1879

Charles Harris, Sr. and his two sons, John and Charles lived on a small farm near the Red River in Montague County. During the winter of 1877, Charles Sr. warned his son Charles Jr. that he had better kill his brother John before John killed him. Charles Sr. at various times warned Charles not to come home for fear that John would kill him the next time he should see him. Charles Sr. told his son that John did not want him on his property any longer, as John believed that Charles was going to steal horses from him.

On another occasion, Charles Sr. gave Charles Jr. $1.50 with instructions that after he delivered a wagon load of cotton to the gin at Sherman, Texas, he was to buy arsenic. After purchasing the arsenic and returning home, Charles Jr. was told to pour the poison into a glass of milk in the morning, and for him to give the poison milk to John to drink. Charles Sr. explained that after John was dead, no one would suspect him of having been murdered. Once John was dead, he would sell all of John's property and he and Charles Jr. would use the money to travel elsewhere.

The plan failed after John refused the glass of milk and left the house. Charles Sr. advised his son he should leave and stay away for a while. Charles took his father's advice and left for Denton County where he married and returned back to Montague County four weeks later.

After arriving back in Montague County, Charles Jr. saw his father nearby. Charles Sr. immediately told Charles Jr. that if John saw him, he would kill him. Charles Sr. told Charles to go to the farmhouse and get his shotgun without being seen by John. It was decided that Charles Jr. should kill John that evening when John went out to feed his horses. It was planned that after Charles Jr. killed his brother, he would take a horse from a nearby neighbor's farm instead of one of John's horses as the theft might implicate him in the murder. Charles Jr. was told to hide out at Gainesville and wait for his father's arrival in two weeks. This would give him time to sell all of John's property.

Charles Jr. then waited until the following morning for his opportunity to ambush his brother. On the morning of January 17, 1878, John was killed with a shotgun as he was walking out to his horses. Charles Jr. then stole a horse from a nearby farm and fled to Denison, Texas, where he was captured and jailed for horse theft.

Sheriff L. N. Perkins had taken Charles Jr. to the town's blacksmith to be placed in irons when Charles Jr. handed the sheriff some papers. When the sheriff asked what the papers contained, Charles Jr. replied, "My confession as to how I killed John Harris."

Charles Jr. was warned that if the sheriff read the confession, then the confession would be used as evidence against him at his trial. Charles Jr. replied he would not have killed his brother had it not been for his father. A memorandum book that Charles Jr. possessed contained a letter he was writing to a newspaper and a second letter to his wife which read as follows:

Publish this in the paper, gentleman and ladies. I killed my brother, or tried, just because he talked the way he did, and I got a darling wife to mourn after me when I am gone. But shed not a tear o'er your husband's early bier, when he is gone. For she is all the world to me. I love my darling Josie better than I do my life, and I hope to meet her in heaven, if not in this world. I hope God will protect my wife and keep her from all harm. I hate to part from Josie, but it must be. Poetry by C. H.: I have a darling little wife, perhaps sisters thee, like wise my aged father, he shed his tears for me. Farewell to all on earth, but hope to meet you in heaven.
Charles Harris Jr.

Josie, this is true. If John and I meet, one of us must die, for his talk about me is too hard for me to take. And, Josie, I am going off, but I will send some money to St. Joe on the 4th day of July, for you to come, and, Josie you must come. I will tell you where to come first by letter, but I will back it to John Sims, and when you write to me, direct your letter to Franklin Pemberton. But I will write first, and tell you where I am at. So Josie, I will send you the money to St. Joe, and bring all of your things with you.

During the trial Sheriff Perkins testified as to the written confession and statements made by Charles, along with the memorandum book being submitted into evidence. On November 15, 1879, Charles Harris, Jr. was found guilty and sentenced to death. The case was appealed to the Court of Criminal Appeals and the sentence was affirmed. After the case was affirmed, Charles Jr. stood before the judge for sentencing. The judge announced that it was "therefore, considered and decreed by the court, that said Charles Harris on the 29th day of August, A. D. 1879, after eleven o'clock a. m. and before sunset of said day, to be hung by the neck till he is dead, as prescribed by law, and that the clerk of the court issue a warrant directed to the sheriff to execute this judgment and sentence in accordance with the law."

On the day of execution the sheriff escorted Charles Jr. out of the jail, wearing a blue navy coat and pants with a white vest to an awaiting wagon. With an escort of forty armed men, Charles Jr. was then driven to the gallows which had been erected three-quarters of a mile northeast of Montague near the cemetery. Once at the gallows, Harris climbed the structure with Rev. Crutchfield. Standing on the gallows, Deputy W. A. Morris first read the death warrant to Charles Harris, Jr.. Rev. Crutchfield then asked the crowd to join him in the singing of "Shall We Know Each Other There." At the conclusion of the singing, Harris addressed the crowd with:

Ladies and Gentlemen: I am here to pay the penalty of the law. I am sorry this crowd had to be called together to witness my execution. I do not believe they could be called around a better heart. I had a good mother, who taught me to be good, and I had no idea of coming to this. My aged father has been accused of being guilty of this crime. He is as innocent as the angels in heaven. He is an old man; I hope I shall meet him in heaven.

I hope to meet you all in heaven. I pray God that you will never be called again to witness such a scene as this. I am the first one ever executed in Montague County according to law, and I pray God there may never be another, and I pray God I may be the only one executed according to law in the whole world. There is not a man in the whole world around whose memory there clusters one particle of hate. I hope my fate will be a warning to all young men of this County. I ascend upon the scaffold high that others may take warning of me. My time has come, I must go, though it seems hard. I have been, and am now a friend of Montague County. I love everyone in the whole county. I love the prisoners in the jail: and here is the Sheriff, as good an officer as there is in the whole world. I hope to meet him in heaven. I love you all. I hate to go this way, but I must. May God watch over you all. Remember, you all must die. I am young: in the prime of life. I hate to go this way, but I must. May God watch over you all. Think of the dying man's words. I hope you may all think I am prepared. I hope to meet you all in heaven in a better world than this.

Rev. Crutchfield then asked the crowd to join Harris and him in the singing of "Sweet Bye and Bye." At the end of the song, Rev. Crutchfield kneeled as did thousands of the spectators in the prayer. The sheriff then allowed friends of Charles Harris, Jr. to ascend the gallows to shake hands with Charles Jr. and say their farewell wishes.

At 1 p.m. Charles Jr. took his place over the trap door. Deputy Sheriff R. A. Nix placed the rope of the right side and then moved the rope to the left side at the request of Charles Jr. The cap was placed over the head with the veil covering the face. Sheriff Perryman asked Charles Jr. which friend he wanted to cut the rope to the trap door. Charles replied that he thought the sheriff was his friend and for him to do it. After several times of asking Charles Jr. what other friend he would want to cut the rope, Charles Jr. finally said Deputy Nix. At 1:20 p.m. the rope was cut and twenty minutes later the body was pronounced dead by the attending physicians.

Charles Harris' last request was that he be buried next to his brother John on Framer's Creek.

Montgomery County
County Seat - Conroe

Warren Sheppard
Also spelled as Shepperd

Race/Gender: Black Male   **Offense:** Murder   **Offense Date:** March 22, 1878
Weapon: Double Barrel Shotgun, Tree Limb, & Pine Knot   **Execution:** November 12, 1880

Warren Sheppard who disliked and did not trust Levy Comer, walked up to him on March 22, 1878, while Comer was working chopping trees for Winkler's Mill. In the presence of the other lumbermen, Sheppard walked within range of Comer and said, "Let us compromise this matter."

After Comer agreed, Sheppard raised the shotgun and discharged both barrels of the weapon. Although Comer had been hit in the face and chin from the shotgun pellets, he ran from Sheppard who chased after him. After falling, Sheppard beat Comer about the back of the head with a tree limb and then used of a heavy pine knot to kill him. After the murder, Sheppard fled the scene.

A reward of $400 was soon posted for Sheppard's capture and two black men turned him in for the reward. While awaiting execution, Sheppard escaped from jail and went to the town's black blacksmith asking for him to cut the shackles off. The blacksmith quickly tied Sheppard's hands and secured him in a house to wait for a reward to be offered for the fugitive. When a $60 reward was posted, the blacksmith delivered Sheppard to the sheriff, and received the money.

On the day of the execution, 2,000 spectators gathered in an open field, one-quarter mile east of town where the gallows had been erected. Sheriff R. G. Ashe then escorted Sheppard to the foot of the gallows. Without any assistance, Sheppard climbed the ladder to the top of the platform and was met by other officers and black ministers. Sheppard addressed the below crowd looking up at him and said, "I have to leave this world, which I have entirely given up; I ask that everybody to pray for me, both white and black. Take warning from his fate; I cannot now help myself, but I feel that I have been saved. I done wrong, but I have been forgiven."

After the prayer Sheppard arose and asked if there were anyone in the crowd who would take his body after his death, and see that it was properly interred, and asked for that person to sing and pray over his grave. George Womack, answering for several others, said that he would see that his request was strictly complied with. Sheppard then bid farewell to the crowd, calling for mercy, and saying that he was prepared, but not willing, to die. He shook hands with those around him, and stated that he had nothing more to say.

Sheriff Ashe read the death warrant and afterwards adjusted the black cap. At 2:30 p.m. Deputy Sheriff Simonton sprang the trap, and Warren Shepperd fell eight feet, the fall breaking the neck.

A reporter from the *Galveston Weekly News*, interviewed Sheppard while awaiting his execution. The interview was printed in the Thursday, November 18, 1880, edition. Sheppard told the newsman that he regarded the negro as his enemy, and the white man as his friend. Even his wife, he said, had not visited him for several months. Sheppard spoke kindly of Sheriff Ashe, Deputy Simonton, Jailer Whitman, and Revs. Garrett Pugh and Padgett.

Morris County
County Seat - Daingerfield

Henry Graham

Alias: Harry Graham
Offense Date: December 16, 1892
Race/Gender: Black Male
Weapon: Pistol
Offense: Murder
Execution: June 9, 1893

On December 16, 1892, Morris County Constable F. M. Ledbetter received an arrest warrant from Titus County. The warrant was for the arrest of Henry "Harry" Graham on the charge of assault and attempted murder. Titus County lawmen had received information that Graham was at Omaha in Morris County.

The constable found Graham at the Omaha train depot, and when the constable attempted to execute the arrest, Graham fled to a woman's house outside of town. Constable Ledbetter and Deputy Sheriff Curlee pursued after the fugitive.

Once Graham was confronted in the home, the constable informed Graham he had an arrest warrant for his arrest from Titus County. Graham quickly drew a pistol and shot the constable in the neck then fled from the scene to Commerce, Texas, where he was captured.

The thirty-six-year-old lawman, F. M. Ledbetter, constable of Precinct 3, was married with five children. Constable Ledbetter was buried at Concord Missionary Baptist Cemetery at Omaha.

The *Fort Worth Gazette*, dated Saturday, June 10, 1893, printed the following short article;

HARRY GRAHAM KILLED.

**THE SLAYER OF OFFICER LED-
BETTER EXECUTED.**

**He Begged for More Time – Had to be Held on
the Trap – The History of
His Crimes.**

Daingerfield, Tex., June 9. – (Special.) – Harry Graham was hanged here today. He did not confess or deny the killing for which he was hung, but was asked the question several times. He talked a while, made a rambling talk with no sense to it, and begged for more time to the last, until made to sit down. He would not stand up and had to be held up on the trap and kept begging for more time.

The trap was sprung at 3:20 and he was not pronounced dead for twenty minutes. He had a clear fall of seven feet.

THE CRIME
for which he was convicted was the killing of F. M. Ledbetter, a constable, who was trying to arrest him. Graham was charged with assault and attempted to murder in Titus county. He came to this county and papers were sent here for his arrest. Ledbetter found him near the depot in Omaha attempted his arrest, but the Negro fled. He got a posse and gave chase, and he, by himself, came upon him in a Negro house a few miles from there. He went in and told Graham to consider himself under arrest, when the Negro shot him without warning, killing Ledbetter. He escaped, but was caught at Commerce. He was convicted of murder in the first degree and sentenced to be hanged on May 1, but was respited until today to give Governor Hogg a chance to investigate. The governor refused to commute his sentence and he paid the penalty of death for his crime.

Nacogdoches County
County Seat - Nacogdoches

Texas had its first legal hanging on February 8, 1834, when Samuel Looney, Barney Finch and John Saunders were all executed for the murder of Charles Luigi, his last name has also spelled as Luigt.

Commercial Advertiser, (New York, NY), dated Monday, May 12, 1834, printed the following short article:

EXECUTION. – A letter from Nacogdoches, in Texas, Feb. 9, to a gentleman in Washington, says – Since you left here, the murderers of the much lamented Mr. Charles Luigi have been discovered. They have been tried, convicted, and were hanged yesterday, 8th inst.

Their names were Samuel Looney, Barney Finch, and John Saunders. Looney was convicted for being an accessory to the murder before and after it; Finch for committing the act; and Saunders for allowing it to be done in his house, and not exposing it. Saunders was 82 years of age, and a most hardened villain. Neither of them made any confession, through it is thought that there are other accomplices in the affair. Charles S. Taylor, Esq. was the acting Alcalda, and has shown himself a man of perseverance, and much moral firmness; and the jurymen have done themselves and their country honor.

F. Marion Smith

Age: 69 **Offense:** Murder **Offense Date:** December 24, 1899
Weapon: Double Barrel Shotgun **Execution:** November 9, 1900

On the morning of December 24, 1899, Theodore Vawters asked his wife Elmina as he was leaving for the town of Appleby north of Nacogdoches, to release a certain sow and pigs out of the lot. After Elmina released the pigs, F. M. Smith arrived at the home and asked if she had turned the pigs out. When Elmina replied she had, Smith left and returned home. In the meantime, Elmina had gone out into her turnip patch to gather vegetables when Smith returned with a double barrel shotgun and shot his sister-in-law.

Smith afterwards walked the six miles to Nacogdoches to surrender himself and he was placed in jail. Elmina who was found still lying in the field, died at 3 p.m. that afternoon. Because of the threat of a lynch mob, Smith was transported to the penitentiary at Rusk for safekeeping.

On September 18, Smith was sentenced by Judge Tom Davis to hang on October 26, 1900. Because of a respite, the date of execution was reset for November 9. Smith who had served with Company D of the 14th Alabama in the Civil War had been wounded in battle, which included injuries to the head. After Smith was sentenced, Smith's attorney attempted to claim that he was insane due to the injuries he had received during the war.

On November 9, 1900, Smith spoke from the gallows, but did not speak about the crime he had committed. Smith told the witnesses that he had made peace with God, and had no ill feeling towards anyone.

The *San Antonio Express*, dated Saturday, November 10, 1900, provided readers with the details of the murder Marion Smith committed.

Jim Buchanan

Race/Gender: Black Male **Offense:** Rape & Triple Murder **Offense Date:** October 10, 1902
Weapon: Rifle & Blunt Object **Execution:** October 16, 1902

On October 10, 1902, Jim Buchanan went on a murder rampage on the Hicks family at their ranch home near Attoyac in Nacogdoches County. Buchanan shot and killed Duncan Hicks and his wife Nerva with a rifle. Buchanan then set his attention of the victim's daughter Ollie, raping the girl for several hours and then beating her to death with the rifle.

Immediately after the murder, Buchanan left the scene and bragged to another black family of the crime he had committed. After Buchanan left their house, they reported the murders to Sheriff John Spradley.

Sheriff Spradley located the murderer within a few hundred yards of the Hicks' farm and placed him under arrest. For fear of a lynch mob, Buchanan was taken to the jail in Shreveport, Louisiana, for safekeeping. While in jail, a *Shreveport Times* reporter interviewed Buchanan who told him, "I killed the old man first. I shot him. He never woke up. Then I shot the old woman. She woke up and I had to shoot her again. She fought me and I had to hit her on the head with the butt on the gun. Then the daughter came in and tried to run and I clubbed her to heath. I hit her a number of times and her brains were all over the floor. I did not outrage her."

Once the citizens of Shreveport learned of Buchanan's crimes, Sheriff Spradley again feared the mob would prevail as the citizens began organizing outside the jail. Sheriff Spradley quickly removed Buchanan and returned him back to Texas by train in hopes of securing him in the penitentiary. All along the train route, vigilante mobs were in waiting to remove the prisoner from the sheriff's custody. Sheriff Spradley wired Governor Joseph Sayers asking for assistance. In response, Governor Sayers ordered five companies of state militia to assist in the protection.

On October 17, 1902, the sheriff returned his prisoner back to Nacogdoches by train. Within minutes after arriving, the five companies of militia consisting of 200 men lined up and escorted the sheriff and his prisoner into the county courthouse. While the proceedings were just beginning inside the courthouse, men from the town cut both telegraph and telephone wires to ensure no further requests for additional aid could be communicated, and rails to the train tracks were removed to ensure that the prisoner would not be removed from town by train.

The prisoner was then taken before District Judge Davis where a jury panel was already seated. After the reading of the indictment by the district attorney, he asked Buchanan how did he plea?

Buchanan quickly answered guilty. The plea was accepted and the jury deliberated five minutes with a verdict of guilty of the first degree and accessed the death penalty. The judge first ordered the execution to take place in thirty days, but Buchanan asked that his execution not be delayed. After waiving his rights to a thirty day stay, the judge prepared the death warrant and ordered the execution to take place at 11:30 a.m. the same day. The gallows consisted of three poles tied together to form a tripod structure with a small platform and a trap door. This required that Frank Buchanan climb a ladder to reach the platform, and then have his legs, and arms bound and the noose placed around his neck. The body was left hanging until 5 p.m. so that other people arriving in town who missed the execution could witness the murderer and rapist hanging.

Photographer C. H. Casley later advertised pictures of Buchanan's hanging with an advertisement that read, "If you didn't see the NEGRO HUNG, come around and I'll show you how. If you want a photo, you can have one."

Within six days of Buchanan committing these crimes, and within four hours after his trial, 5,000 people witnessed the legal execution of James Buchanan. This execution became one of the quickest legal executions in Texas history.

The *Houston Daily Post*, dated Saturday, October 18, 1902, provided readers with large article detailing the crime and execution.

Dock Bailey
Also spelled as Doc

Race/Gender: Black Male **Offense:** Robbery & Murder **Offense Date:** September 4, 1907
Weapon: Pistol **Execution:** November 7, 1907

Dock Bailey was a professional gambler who had been making his living playing craps for the past five years. At his trial for the murder of Das Owens, Bailey testified he met Owens on Tuesday evening and proposed they play craps. Owens replied he could not play at that time, but would meet Bailey the following morning between his Uncle Jack Owens' house and Henry Day's place.

On Wednesday morning Bailey met Owens on the road and they scraped a place in the ground to throw the dice at $1 a throw. Bailey said at first he had lost $2 to Owens. Bailey claimed he won back his $2, plus an additional $30. As Owens was about to throw the dice, Bailey told Owens he was already down $20, plus the horse he rode in on. Bailey told Owens that his next throw would be $31.

An argument ensued over the amount, and Owens told Bailey he was a damned liar as the amount was only $20. Owens was to have told Bailey, "For a negro to talk that way to a white man was not right, and that he would kill him."

Owens picked up a tree limb and struck Bailey to the back of the neck and pulled a knife. As the two men struggled, Bailey pulled his pistol and fired twice into Das Owens' chest. Bailey said when he struck Owens to the top of the head with his pistol, a piece of the handle broke off.

To conceal the body, Bailey said he took a rope from the Jack Owens' corral, tied one end of the rope around Owens' neck and wrapped the other end around the saddle horn. Riding Owens' horse in a full gallop, Bailey dragged Owens, while still alive, for a 150 yards to the resting place where the remains were found.

When Owens failed to show up for the bridal party Wednesday night, a search party was organized, as Owens was to marry Maggie Wilkerson Thursday morning. The search party found Owens' body early Thursday morning. Bailey in the meantime rode to Rusk, Texas, where he sold the horse, saddle and bridle for $45 to the town liveryman who reported the sale to the sheriff.

As the train was about to leave the depot, Sheriff C. K. Norwood arrested Bailey and lodged him in jail on suspicion of horse stealing. After Bailey was charged with murder and robbery, he was placed in the penitentiary at Rusk for safe keeping because of the threat of vigilante mobs which had formed. After the arrest, Bailey confessed to killing Owens during a scuffle from an argument over a crap game.

At the trials closing arguments, the district attorney argued the motive behind the murder was robbery for the horse and tack Owens was riding. Owens was never known to gamble, and when the body was found the pants pockets had been turned inside out. The jury was out one hour before returning with a verdict of guilty of murder in the first degree and assessing the death penalty.

On November 7, 1907, at 2 p.m. the trap was sprung from under Dock Bailey dropping him to his death.

The *Galveston Daily News*, dated Friday, November 8, 1907, provided their readers with the history of the murder.

Navarro County
County Seat - Corsicana

Billy White

Alias:: Billy Riley
Offense Date: Unknown
Race/Gender: Black Male
Execution: January 22, 1875
Offense: Murder

There is not a lot of information currently available about the murder, or the circumstances in which Billy White killed another black man by the name of Thomas Thomason at Corsicana. White was arrested and tried for murder in the first degree and convicted. On the day of the execution, White confessed from the gallows of committing the murder in the presence of 6,000 spectators. This was the first recorded execution for the county.

The *San Francisco Bulletin* (San Francisco, California), dated February 13, 1875, printed the following short article about the execution:

> *When a man is hanged for murder, the belief of some is that if he professes religion he will go straight to heaven; but at the recent execution of Billy White in Texas no such pleasing confidence was manifested. The doomed man was obdurate, and the Rev. Clem Jones, a colored preacher, who officiated, told him that he would soon be in hell among the angels of Satan and all those who forget God. Then Mr. Jones offered a prayer just for the looks of it, and the wretched criminal was hanged.*

John E. Henry

Alias: John Henry Jonson
Offense: Murder
Execution: March 26, 1880
Race/Gender: Black Male
Offense Date: January 8, 1879
Age: 29
Weapon: Firearm

On the evening of January 7, 1879, John Henry and his friend Jim Young were attending an all black dance in Henderson County when Jim Young and Alonzo Whitman fought over the attention of a woman named Fanny Barrett.

The next morning Young and Alonzo again engaged in a fight where both men went at each other with weapons. Henry then ran into his house to grab his rifle. Coming out on to the porch, Henry raised the weapon and yelled out, "Clear the track, God damn it, I'll settle that fuss!"

Young jumped out of the way and Henry fired the weapon. Whitman turned and ran a few feet before falling dead. Henry then said, "I told you, God damn it, I would fix it," and walked away. After the murder, Henry fled, but was captured five days later by Deputy Sheriff Walker.

John Henry was tried and convicted of murder in the first degree. When the sentencing judge asked Henry if he had any last statement he wished to make before judgment be passed, Henry replied, "The killing was in self-defense, I don't care what you do with me so long as you leave breath in my body." The sentence of death was then passed upon him.

The gallows were built in the jail yard and in view from Henry's cell. Sheriff E. E. Dunn decided not to use the standard trap door, but the weights and pulley method where the condemned is "jerked to Jesus" when the rope is cut, dropping the weights then jerking the person upward breaking the neck.

On March 26, 1880, the execution was private except by invitation. Witnesses included five friends of Henry, Rev. Pardee, five justices of the peace, six physicians, twenty-one guards, and reporters.

After Sheriff Dunn concluded from the reading of the death warrant, he turned to John Henry and asked if he had anything to say. In response Henry said, "No, I have nothing to say. I am willing to take my portion, I am willing to go, and I've nothing to confess."

After the hands and feet were tied, Henry asked Sheriff Dunn to turn over any money he had left to Rev. Pardee to be given to his children. Sheriff Dunn replied he would and told Henry he could say anything he wished. Henry then made said, "I will make a few remarks to make you a warning. This is the only man I ever killed; never desired to kill anybody; I am sorry for my Maker that I did so; hope God will forgive me; I am willing to go; I have no hard feeling for anybody, for the keepers treated me very well. I hope to meet you all in Heaven. I have nothing more to tell."

The sheriff then adjusted the black cap and rope, and, stepping back, said: "Good bye, John." Deputy Sheriff Mallery cut the rope, and the prisoner was jerked up four feet, breaking his neck.

The *Galveston Weekly News*, dated, Thursday, April 1, 1880, printed the following interview a reporter had with John Henry two weeks before the execution.

I am in good health and feel pretty well, but I don't sleep much. I am 29 years of age. I lived in Matagorda county, this state, till I was 14 years old. My parents either died while I was an infant, or I was taken away from them; anyway I don't recalled my father or mother. I was never married, but had a wife once. I don't feel disposed to tell what I have done wrong besides killing Alonzo Whitman. I will say this much, however, I have always worn a good reputation till I killed Lon. I first fell out with Lon, in '74 at a ball. I walked out on the floor with a lady to dance, and he came between me and her. I told him then, never to cross my path or I'd kill him and he knowed I means what I said. I did not expect to kill him when I did, but the old passion sprung up in my heart when I say him and two or three other men fighting the rest who had almost been a father to me. The difficulty of the killing commenced on Thursday night before the day I killed him. I saw him at a colored lady's house that night and he tried to stab me. The next morning, when I saw him fighting my friend, I remembered him, and shot him dead in his tracks. I feel very sorry for what I have done. I believe in a God, and that if I keep on like I am I will be saved. Before I got in this trouble I didn't believe in religion, but now I do.

George Doren
Also spelled as Doran and Duran

Race/Gender: White Male   **Age:** 30   **Offense:** Murder
Offense Date: June 1, 1879   **Weapon:** Knife   **Execution:** August 20, 1880

George Doren was executed for the fatal stabbing of a man he worked with by the name of William Fitzsimons. Both men were of Irish decent and were employed by the Houston and Texas Central Railway as railroad section hands. When not working, Doren and Fitzsimmons competed for the affections of a local Corsicana prostitute by the name of Josey "Joe" Cash.

On the night of June 1, 1879, Doren spent most of the evening with Josey, but was told by Josey that he could not stay the night. When asked why, Josey said she expected Fitzsimmons to come and she preferred for him to stay the night with her instead of him. When Fitzsimmons entered Josey's bedroom, Doren pulled a large knife and cut Fitzsimmons across his abdomen. Fitzsimmons screamed out "Murder!" and ran out through the front door. Doren pursued after Fitzsimmons and stabbed him four more times to the bowels, lung, thigh, and back. Fourteen painful days later, Fitzsimmons died from his wounds.

The construction of the gallows used in the hanging of Doren was not the common trap door method, but instead employed the use of a weight and pulley. After the noose was adjusted around the neck, the rope holding a heavy weight is cut. As the weight falls, the victim is forcibly slung upwards several feet. It was believed if the force upward did not break the neck, the fall would. This method was often referred to in early publications as being "Jerked to Jesus."

At 2:50 p.m. on the day of the execution, the jail yard was cleared of all visitors except those allowed by law. Sheriff E. E. Dunn on the gallows said, "This is the saddest duty I ever had to perform, and God grant it may be the last of the kind ever required at my hands. I hold in my hands a warrant commanding me to hang George Doran until he is dead."

Sheriff Dunn then read the warrant and asked Doran if he wanted to say anything, to which Doran replied, "I forgive you all, you have been kind to me."

The *Galveston Daily News*, dated, Saturday, August 21, 1880, printed details of the witness testimony from the trial and execution at Corsicana, Texas.

Harrison Williams

Race/Gender: Black Male   **Age:** 28   **Offense:** Murder
Offense Date: June 26, 1883   **Weapon:** Club & Razor Blade   **Execution:** March 7, 1884

Harrison Williams beat his wife so often that it led the woman's sister, Ada Sallard to file a complaint on June 25, 1883, to the justice of the peace. When Williams learned of the complaint filed against him, Williams told several people that he was, "tired of having Negroes reporting him, and after he kill her, he would be willing to die."

When Ada had not been seen for a couple of days, a search party was organized on June 26, 1883. Ada's body was found near a road in the brush. The woman's head had been crushed from heavy blows from a club, and a handkerchief had been tied tightly around the neck. Williams was arrested the next day and denied that he had killed her. Williams was indicted on July 5, and tried the following month on August 10, 1883.

The jury found Williams guilty of murder of first degree and sentenced him to death. Counsel immediately made a motion for a new trial on August 13, which was denied. The decision was afterwards appealed to the Court of Criminal Appeals who affirmed the decision on November 21, 1883.

The scaffold was built in the jail yard with the weights and pulley method being utilized. The scaffold was purposely built in the yard to keep the execution private as required by law. Although held privately, the hanging was witnessed by hundreds of people sitting in the surrounding trees and rooftops of buildings.

On the gallows, Williams told all he was not ashamed to confess his crime as he had made peace with God and warned all to beware of letting their passion influence them, as it had him. That if it were to be done over again he would know better.

The sheriff then read the death warrant, and afterwards signaled that he was ready. At 2:40 p.m., the rope was cut, and Williams was sent six feet upwards in the air. The jerk and fall, however, failed to break his neck, and he died by strangulation. Twenty minutes later the body was cut down and turned over to his friend for burial.

A reporter from the *Fort Worth Daily Gazette*, interviewed Williams, and the newspaper printed the interview in the Saturday, March 8, 1884 edition. The reporter wrote:

He acknowledged having killed Ada Sallard, but denounced having allowed false witness and he should not have been convicted on circumstantial testimony. He said the brutal atrocities discovered on her body were made by other hands than his, and called on God to witness the truth of his assertions, He could not say how old he was, thought he was about twenty-eight years of age; was born a slave at Montgomery, Ala., and was owned by Dr. Griggs of that city; came to Texas about a dozen years ago, had worked hard since as a farm and plantation laborer, but had accumulated no property. Previous to the murder he had been a member of the African Methodist church, but just before the commission of the crime he had been expelled. Since realizing that he had to die, he had sought comfort in religion and believed he had found it. God had forgiven all his sins, and when the hangman should be through with his body, his spirit would go straight to Heaven and to his Savior; that he would be seated on a silver cloud, playing a golden harp and singing jubilee songs through all eternity. He said he would like to be executed publicly, so he could talk to all the people, but as the law commanded that executions should be private, he did not expect to be accorded the desired privilege. He said he was not going to weaken, but intended to die game, and to tell the same story on the gallows about the killing of Ada Sallard that he had always maintained in his prison life. So justly merited was Harrison Williams sentence of death regarded by the people of Corsicana and Navarro county that no effort was ever made or started to have the governor change it to a life term in the penitentiary. It was a case where capital punishment was regarded as a capital idea.

Lee Thomas

Alias: Henry Whitehead **Race/Gender:** White Male **Age:** 23
Offense: Robbery & Murder **Offense Date:** November 10, 1893 **Execution:** August 2, 1895

Lee Thomas was executed for the robbery and murder of J. M. Farley who disappeared on November 10, 1893. On December 9, 1893, hog hunters who were curious as to why a large number of buzzards were circling a ravine about 175 yards from Lee Thomas' house went to investigate and discovered the body of Farley.

The motive behind the murder was the robbery of Farley's horse and buggy, $40 and the excitement of the circus coming to town. Farley had gone to Lee Thomas on November 6, 1893, asking for work picking his cotton. On November 10, at about midnight, Lee Thomas arrived at his father-in-law's house where Thomas' wife was staying. Thomas told his wife that he had bought Farley's horse and buggy and he wanted to take her to Corsicana with him where he knew the circus would be setting up the following day. For the next month there was no suspicion of Farley's disappearance as Thomas had told everyone he had last seen Farley on the road to Kerens after he had bought the horse and buggy.

After the body was found partially buried in the ravine, Thomas was arrested on suspicion of murder. Thomas then confessed to killing and said he killed Farley during a fight over a poker game, in which he had won all of Farley's money. Thomas said he first tried to bury the body under the house, but found that it was too difficult, and therefore buried the body in the ravine.

On the day of the execution, Thomas was dressed in a black cutaway suit, and hanged in the presence of thirty witnesses. On the gallows, Thomas admonished those who were present to profit by his example. Thomas then forgave his enemies and blessed his friends. Thomas said he killed Farley because he had to, and that he felt innocent of the murder. After this statement, the sheriff then read the death warrant. At the conclusion, Thomas asked for a few moments to pray. Thomas knelled down and prayed out loud for nine minutes. Upon finishing his prayer, Thomas stood up and bade the officers and his friends once more goodbye.

As the black cap was about to be put over the head, Thomas turned his head and smiling said, "There is a larger crowd present than we had anticipated, isn't there Mr. Weaver?" At 2:44 p.m. the trap was sprung and the body was cut down at 3:08 p.m. and given to the care of the undertaker.

The *Dallas Morning News*, Saturday, August 3, 1895, provided readers with details of the murder and execution at Corsicana, Texas.

Thomas A. Morris

Race/Gender: White Male **Age:** 50 **Offense:** Robbery & Murder
Offense Date: June 1, 1900 **Weapon:** Ax **Execution:** January 31, 1902

Thomas Morris, a blacksmith by trade, was tried on April 21, 1901, for the murder of his friend, William G. Broome. On that day, the jury foreman announced Morris' verdict of guilty, and assessed his punishment at death.

The motive for the murder established by the district attorney was robbery. It was believed that on June 1, 1900, Broome and Morris had gone to a stock tank to go fishing. While at the tank, Morris struck Broome to the back of the head with an ax in order to steal his wagon and team. After the murder, Morris was suspected of attempting to conceal the body by weighing down the remains in the tank with a large sack of metal rivets. The body was later found when some boys wanting to cool off and have fun on a hot summer day, went to the tank to swim and they discovered the body and notified the sheriff.

On the morning of the execution, Morris told a deathwatch guard, "If you ever go into a thing with a friend, stand by him till the last hair drops."

Later a Rabbi Magill entered the cell corridor and found Morris praying. Unnoticed by Morris, Rabbi Magill heard him say, "O Lord, my Father, forgive me for this crime, which I have committed."

On the gallows, Morris was asked if he wished to make a statement and he said, "Without fear of God or man, I declare I am innocent of this crime. I do not think I had a fair trial, and I die for the crime of another. Mr. Robinson, I am ready."

Sheriff W. D. Robinson then adjusting the black cap, told Morris to nod his head when he was ready. Morris gave the signal and Sheriff Robinson pulled the lever releasing the trap.

The *Galveston Daily News*, dated Saturday, February 1, 1902, provided readers with details of the murder and execution at Corsicana, Texas.

Newton County
County Seat - Newton

Tom Wilson

Alias: T. W. Butler, & Tom Willison
Offense: Murder
Execution: October 22, 1909
Race/Gender: Black Male
Offense Date: September 10, 1909
Age: 28
Weapon: Shotgun

On the night of September 10, 1909, Newton County Attorney A. K. Nicks accompanied deputy sheriffs in a raid of a gambling house near the town of Burkeville. After the raid had been completed and the prisoners secured, Nicks leaned up against the outside door frame of the home when Tom Wilson walked up behind the attorney with a shotgun and fired a load of buckshot into his back. The load of buckshot broke ribs and tore into his lungs. An hour later, the twenty-seven-year-old attorney died from his injuries.

Three days later, Wilson was captured southeast of Newton. Wilson who had no involvement with the gambling house was asked why he shot and killed the attorney. Wilson replied, "I just wanted to kill a white man." On September 15, the grand jury convened and returned a indictment of murder. Three days later, on September 18, Wilson was tried. The jury was out only fifteen minutes when the verdict of guilty was returned with the punishment assessed at death. Tom Wilson became the only person legally hanged in Newton County.

On October 22, 1909, a crowd of spectators arrived at Newton expecting to witness the county's first execution. The spectators quickly learned that the attorney general had ordered the sheriff to conduct the execution in private and inside the jail.

The *Galveston Daily News*, dated Saturday, October 23, 1909, provided readers with the details of the murder and of Tom Wilson's past history.

Nueces County
County Seat - Corpus Christi

Andres Davila

Race/Gender: Hispanic Male **Offense:** Robbery & Murder **Offense Date:** May 9, 1874
Weapons: Firearms **Execution:** August 7, 1874

Hipolito Tapia

Race/Gender: Hispanic Male **Offense:** Robbery & Murder **Offense Date:** May 9, 1874
Weapons: Firearms **Execution:** August 7, 1874

Andres Davila and Hipolito Tapia were two from a gang of eleven bandits who set out to rob the only store in the town of Penascal, Texas, on Baffin Bay. Tapia had overheard an earlier conversation of a shipment of money and goods that were to be delivered to the store. The bandits set on robbing the store after the delivery arrived on May 9, 1874. When the bandits saw a ship out in the bay, they believed the ship had already delivered the shipment and was departing. Unknown to the bandits, the ship was just arriving.

When the store was attacked, four men were inside the store, the owner, John Morton, his brother Michael and two customers named F. M. Coakley and Herman Tilgner. Without warning, the heavily armed bandits surrounded the little store and entered. Coakley was immediately tied up and shot. Michael was shot four times to the head and John Morton was shot once in each arm and afterwards riddled with six more bullets. The bandits ransacked the store for its food, clothing, whiskey, and the store cash box that only contained $11 or $12. After the murderous robbery occurred, a posse trailed the outlaw gang and captured Davila and Tapia while they were asleep in their camp. Members of the posse tied ropes around their necks and threatened to hang them unless they confessed, which Tapia did.

Both Davila and Tapia were tried and found guilty of murder in the first degree and sentenced to death. On the day of the execution, both men were led to a makeshift scaffold that had been built from the second story balcony of the county's first courthouse. The paper reported that several hundred people were present to "satisfy their morbid curiosity," and for the chance to listen to any last statements.

Davila refused to say anything, but Tapia stepped up to the edge and said, "My friends, I am here today to die by hanging. I have killed no person nor helped to kill anyone. The people forced the party that was guilty to swear against me; but it is all right—goodbye." Tapia's last words were, "Pray for me, Father."

The *Semi-Weekly Wisconsin*, dated Wednesday, August 26, 1874, provided details of the double execution and marriage ceremony of Tapia to the mother of his children.

FROM ALTAR TO GALLOWS.

A strange ceremony, and one almost unknown in the annals of crime, was that of the marriage of Hypolito Tapia to his former mistress, while standing, as it were, with the rope around his neck. The woman, named Trinidad Bayestero, had long been living with Hypolito, and was the mother of several of his children. To have them legitimatized as far as possible, she induced Hypolito to consent to marriage, which he really did.

Hypolito, during the ceremony, preserved a calm, collected demeanor, and made all necessary responses in a clear, firm voice. Not so Trinidad, who barely preserved sufficient command of herself to go through the ceremony. Davila stood by, an interested but silent listener.

Pablo Parras

Race/Gender: Hispanic Male   **Offense:** Murder   **Offense Date:** December 2, 1870
Weapon: Knife   **Execution:** June 28, 1878

Pablo Parras was a Mexican bandit who was responsible for the murder of a Dr. Newman and the motive of the murder was believed to be robbery. It took eight years to arrest Parras and to bring him before the court for trial. On May 8, 1878, Parras was found guilty of the murder and the punishment was assessed at death.

On the afternoon of June 28, 1878, Parras was escorted to the gallows erected on the courthouse lawn by mounted state police officers and thirty members of the Star Rifles. After Parras reached the gallows, Sheriff Peter Beynon read the death warrant to the prisoner. Parras asked for whiskey, which was given to him, and he then protested his innocence.

In his last statement Parras asked that his father care for his children, and that they never be allowed to come to the United States. He said the governor of Texas pays for the conviction of Mexicans, and wants a letter written to the governor of Tamaulipas to that effect. Parras told the Mexican witnesses that Porfirio had sold out the Mexican republic and wants General Escobedo to know it. At the conclusion, Parras' last words were, *"Viva Mexico, Viva Mexicanos!"*

At 2 p.m. the trap was sprung which dropped Pablo Parras five and a half feet to his death. After hanging thirteen minutes the body was cut down and placed in a coffin.

The *Galveston Daily News*, dated Saturday, June 29, 1878, provided readers with details of the execution at Corpus Christi, Texas.

Antonio Garcia

Race/Gender: Hispanic Male   **Offense:** Murder   **Offense Date:** September 7, 1878
Weapon: Ax   **Execution:** July 11, 1879

Manuella Ariano and Augustine Anallo never married, but the two lived together for several years, and Anallo fathered several children. The couple lived and raised their children working as shepherds on R. Johnson's ranch near Corpus Christi. The family appeared happy until another shepherd named Antonio Garcia arrived and got the attention of Manuella. Soon thereafter, Garcia convinced Manuella to take the children and leave Anallo as he promised he could provide a better life for her.

Two months after his separation from Manuella, Augustine Anallo asked permission of Antonio Garcia that he be allowed to come to his home so that he could visit with his children. Garcia granted the request and further gave Anallo permission to stay overnight at his house. Anallo arrived on September 6, 1878, and visited with his children. He believed his differences with Garcia had been settled and therefore felt comfortable in staying overnight.

On September 7, after supper, Garcia asked Anallo to take a walk with him. A short time later, Garcia walked back to the house alone. Upon being asked where Anallo was, Garcia replied, "I struck him some blows with a club and left him out by the sheep pens."

When Johnson heard what Garcia had done, he directed his employees to go out and find Anallo. The group walked a short distance when Garcia told them, "If I have not already killed him, I have my knife with which I can finish him."

After the knife was taken away from Garcia, he walked about 300 yards to where the sheep pens were located and where Anallo was laying. Garcia walked up to the body, picked up Anallo's hand and felt for a pulse. After not finding a pulse, Garcia threw the hand down and said, "The devil has got him."

The group observed that the victim's skull had been crushed and found an ax with blood on the helve and handle. Johnson tied Garcia's hands together and asked for an explanation as too why he had committed the murder. Garcia replied that Johnson could choose to either shoot or hang him.

Antonio Garcia was tried and found guilty of murder in the first degree. After the Court of Criminal Appeals affirmed the decision of the lower court, Garcia was hanged on July 11, 1879.

The *Brenham Weekly Banner*, dated Friday, July 18, 1879, reported on the execution.

Special Note: *Some references have the trial and execution of Antonio Garcia taking place in Bosque County, which is incorrect.*

Andres Olivarez

Race/Gender: Hispanic Male **Offense:** Murder **Offense Date:** April 21, 1902
Weapon: Ax **Execution:** June 2, 1902

On April 21, 1902, the body of Eunice Hatch was found inside her farmhouse, which was a few miles from Corpus Christi. An examination revealed that Eunice died from an ax wound to her head, and her neck had been broken. Suspicion fell on Andres Olivarez who had been a guest at the Hatch home. After Olivarez had left the house, Eunice asked her husband Jim not to allow Olivarez back at their home as he made her feel uncomfortable the way he would look at her.

When Olivarez was arrested, blood splatter was discovered on his clothing, and shoe tracks found at the Hatch home matched to the shoes he was wearing. While the grand jury was in session, Olivares sent word to the sheriff that he wished to speak with him. When Sheriff Bluntzer arrived, Olivarez confessed to the murder and said he killed the woman, but did not know why. Olivarez later admitted his intent was to sexually assault the woman. The trial only lasted one day, with Olivarez being found guilty of murder in the first degree. The jury assessed the death penalty and the judge set the day of his execution to take place on June 2, 1902.

On the day of the execution, Olivares approached the gallows while smoking a cigar. Olivarez then threw the cigar down so that he could kiss the crucifix held by Rev. Claude Jaillette. Olivarez waved to the people in the crowd that he knew, and shouted out to greet them. Taking his place over the trap door, Olivarez yelled out, "Adios amigos!"

The *Houston Daily Post*, dated Wednesday, June 4, 1902, provided readers with the details of the murder and the execution at Corpus Christi, Texas

Apolonario Hernandez

Alias: Polo **Race/Gender:** Hispanic Male **Offense:** Murder
Offense Date: February 10, 1904 **Weapon:** .44 caliber Rifle **Execution:** December 23, 1904

Apolonario Hernandez was tried and executed for the murder of his wife. Hernandez had been an abusive husband who severely beat his wife. Because of his abusive ways, Hernandez's wife separated from him for two months before her death. In early February, Hernandez went to his wife while armed with a large knife and demanded that she return home. When she refused, Hernandez cussed and threatened his wife telling her that she would regret not returning home with him.

On February 9, 1904, Hernandez laid in a field with his .44 caliber carbine and waited for his wife to leave home and go into the field to work. When she emerged from the house, Hernandez shot her once in the chest and once in her back. Her father hearing the gunshots ran out into the field to find his daughter lying on the ground and asked her what was wrong.

"I am dying papa," she replied. In asking who did this to her, she replied "Polo."

Soon, Constable Lon Quinn arrived to help, and Mrs. Hernandez told the same to him before dying. Two days later Hernandez was apprehended in Alice, Texas, while still armed with the rifle.

On April 20, Hernandez was tried and convicted of murder. The case was then appealed and on June 25, 1904, the conviction was affirmed by the Court of Appeals. Judge Stanley Welch on November 21, 1904, sentenced Hernandez to be executed on December 23.

On the scaffold Hernandez shook hands with his spiritual advisers and officers and bade all with an "Adios." To the witnesses, he declined to make a final statement, but confessed privately of committing the murder to his advisor. After a prayer was given, the black cap was adjusted and Sheriff Wright sprang the trap.

The *Galveston Daily News*, dated Saturday, December 24, 1904, provided their readers with details of the murder and the execution at Corpus Christi, Texas.

Orange County
County Seat - Orange

Archie Washington

Race/Gender: Black Male **Age:** 21 **Offense:** Murder
Offense Date: April 4, 1891 **Weapon:** Pistol **Execution:** July 26, 1892

Archie Washington was tried and convicted twice for the murder of Clark Washington, a special police officer for the Orange City Police Department. After a city election campaign had ended, the candidates had already left the hall when Archie Washington boasted about having a handgun with him and dared anyone to try and take it away from him.

Clark told Washington, "If you don't quit making so much noise, I will arrest you and put you in jail."

Washington replied, "I guess you are a God dammed liar." As Clark grabbed Washington to arrest him, Washington jumped back a few feet and shot twice with a pistol. One bullet struck Clark to the abdomen and the second hit the left forearm. At the second shot Clark turned and ran, while Washington yelled, "Now die, you,_____die." Clark ran a short distance, staggered, ran into the hall at the door and fell mortally wounded upon the floor, dying twenty minutes later.

Archie Washington was tried and convicted of the murder and received a sentence of life in the penitentiary. Not satisfied with his verdict, Washington appealed his sentenced and was granted a new trial in October of 1891. The jury again found Washington guilty a second time, but assessed his penalty at death. Again an appeal was made to the Court of Appeals.

While waiting for the higher court to review his case, Archie Washington escaped custody on the morning of February 23, 1892. Although heavily shackled, Washington was able to enter the adjoining cell where a prisoner had previously sawed through a holding cage. The opening had been covered with an iron plate and secured in place with rivets. Washington sawed off the heads of bolts and entered into a corridor. Washington then pried two window iron bars apart, tied several blankets together as a rope, and climbed down twenty feet to make his escape to freedom. Five days later, on February 29, Sheriff J. A. Jones of Walker County in Huntsville recaptured Washington. After the Court of Appeals learned Washington had escaped from jail, the court refused to hear the case.

On July 26, Archie Washington became the first legal hanging in Orange County. At 2:30 p.m. Sheriff N. Burton announced that all was ready to start the march to the gallows. Washington answered, "I am ready," and the shackles were removed from his legs. Arriving on the platform, the noose and black cap were adjusted, and Washington said his goodbyes. At 2:47 p.m. the rope holding the trap in place was cut. The fall broke Washington's neck and twelve minutes later, the remains were placed in a coffin and then buried in the colored cemetery.

The *Dallas Morning News*, dated Wednesday, July 27, 1892, provided a full account of the murder and execution.

Prean Deon

Race/Gender: Black Male **Age:** 27 **Offense:** Murder
Offense Date: April 4, 1896 **Weapon:** Ax, Pistol & Knife **Execution:** July 9, 1897

Prean Deon was separated from his wife Margaret "Mag" Deon at the time when he brutally murdered her. Mag was a witness against her husband for attempting to burn her parents' home, and also a witness against Prean's mistress, Hannah Merritt, for malicious mischief.

On the late afternoon of April 6, 1896, Mag's body was found about four miles west of Orange, hidden in a clump of briers. It was determined that she had died as a result of her head being crushed and her throat cut.

When arrested, Prean first confessed to committing the murder, but later recanted his statement and attempted to implicate other people. In the confession, Deon stated he first hit his wife on top of the head with the ax and when the ax head flew off he then began beating her about the head with his pistol until the barrel bent. To ensure she was dead, he then cut her throat with a knife. Afterwards Hannah Merritt and he dragged the body into the brush, and then threw the pistol and ax head into the river. Both items were recovered and used as evidence as Deon's trial.

Hannah Merritt was placed on trial first and sentenced to a life term in the penitentiary. Satisfied in not receiving the death penalty, Hanna did not appeal the decision.

After being convicted of the murder and sentenced to death, Deon was jailed at Galveston for safe keeping for fear of an attack by a lynch mob. After the Court of Criminal Appeals affirmed the decision, Sheriff Jeff Bland picked up Deon from the jail without first searching him. Once the sheriff delivered Deon to the Houston jail, the jailer searched Deon and discovered that the prisoner was carrying a large knife, poison and string strong enough to make into a rope to commit suicide with.

The execution was public on the courthouse yard with 3,000 spectators. At Deon's request, the coffin in which he was to be buried was brought out and placed underneath the gallows. Deon knelt down on the platform to look through a crack in the floor to view the coffin. Deon stood up laughing and asked, "Is that the best you can do for me?"

Moments before the black cap was adjusted over his head Deon asked permission to say a few words and stepped to the center of the scaffold "I want to tell everybody I am here to die; will die in a few minutes and will rest with my wife. She rested in my arms night before last, and I will soon be by her side. I am ready to die. I want to say that everybody ought to be punished for what they have done. I am going to heaven and want to say goodbye to everybody."

He then called for Eli Boykin, the father of the murdered woman and shook hands with him and said,"I am going now and I am happy. I have treated you wrong and was a fool to be led away into this. The Lord has forgiven me and now I want to know if you will forgive me."

Deon then told the crowd, ""I want this to be a token to everybody not to be persuaded into anything wrong."

The trap was sprung at 1:03 p.m. and thirteen minutes later, the body was declared dead. Camille Deon, Prean's father took up a collection to raise money to have the remains transported by train to Lake Charles for interment.

The *Houston Daily Post*, Saturday, July 10, 1897, provided readers with a full account of the crime and execution at Orange, Texas.

Palo Pinto County
County Seat - Palo Pinto

John Dove

Alias: Albert Moore **Age:** 24 **Offense:** Rape
Offense Date: August 23, 1895 **Execution:** November 27, 1896

On the morning of August 23, 1895, near the Thurber mines, Mrs. Joe Meredith was at home with her two small children as she was recovering from the measles. At about 11 a.m. a stranger, later identified as John Dove, arrived at the farmhouse and asked for a drink of water which Mrs. Meredith provided. Dove then walked out into the watermelon patch, picked out a watermelon and sat down under the arbor of her home to eat the melon.

Once Dove finished the watermelon, he asked Mrs. Meredith for directions to the town of Gordon. While she was providing the directions, Dove grabbed hold of her and forced the woman back into her bedroom and onto the bed. After assaulting her, Dove fled from the home. The governor afterwards offered a $250 reward, and the wanted poster included a sketch of the wanted man

In January of 1896, Sheriff C. C. Dupree of Franklin County notified Sheriff O. L. York that the sketch on the wanted poster looked very similar to a prisoner he had in custody in his jail in Mount Vernon. Sheriff York traveled to Franklin County and returned with Dove. Once Dove was lodged in jail, Mrs. Meredith identified him as her attacker.

On March 14, 1896, Dove was tried before Judge J. S. Straughan, and the jury found him guilty of rape and assessed the punishment at death. The case was appealed to the higher court, which affirmed the decision on May 13, 1896. Judge Straughan sentenced Dove to hang on October 30, but the execution was delayed after the governor granted a respite until November 27.

On the day of the execution Dove had to be helped to his feet, but then he walked without assistance to the scaffold. After his hands were tied behind him, Sheriff O. L. York asked him if he desired to make any statement.

Dove replied, "No, I have not got a word to say."

The sheriff then adjusted the black cap over his head and face and at 3:03 p.m. the rope was severed, the trap fell, and Dove was dropped to his death.

The *Galveston Daily News*, dated Saturday, November 28, 1896, provided details of the crime and execution.

Parker County
County Seat - Weatherford

Joe Williams

Race/Gender: Black Male **Offense:** Robbery & Murder **Offense Date:** June 13, 1868
Weapon: Firearm **Execution:** December 18, 1868

On June 13, 1868, a peddler by the name of Thomas Bird was traveling by foot on his way to Weatherford when he stopped on the side of the road to rest. Nearby farmers heard a shot and went to investigate when they came upon Joe Williams who was in the process of robbing the body. Once discovered by witnesses, he then escaped by running into the brush.

After a $200 reward was posted, an acquaintance of Williams by the name of Jeff Eddleman knew Williams was fond of singing. Eddleman had a woman sit in her backyard to sing old slave songs while Eddleman hid out of view with his rifle. As the woman sang the tunes, a short time later Williams appeared to join in the singing. Eddleman then demanded Williams surrender. As Williams turned to run back into the brush, Eddleman fired his weapon with the bullet striking Williams to the right elbow. Williams escaped into the brush and stole a grey mare from a nearby farm.

On June 17, 1868, Williams was captured at the small settlement of Buchanan in Johnson County and returned to Weatherford to stand trial. Williams was found guilty of murder and on November 14, was sentenced to hang on December 18, 1868. On the day of his execution, Williams sat on his coffin in the bed of the wagon for his two mile journey to the gallows.

James B. Cason

Race/Gender: White Male **Age:** 35 **Offense Murder:** Robbery & Murder
Offense Date: January 31, 1907 **Weapon:** Pistol & Ax **Execution Date:** May 22, 1908

L. F. McLemore of Longview was on his way to the New Mexico Territory to resettle when he stopped at Weatherford for supplies. There he met James Cason who befriended him and decided to join McLemore in his travels. The two men were last seen leaving Weatherford in McLemore's wagon for Mineral Wells. Six miles south of Weatherford, the two men camped in a man named Eddleman's pasture on Rock Creek. McLemore would not be seen alive again.

On February 18, 1907, Eddleman's son went looking for cattle in the pasture when he observed buzzards flying in a circular pattern above a ravine. Thinking there might be a dead calf, the boy rode to the area to investigate when he discovered that the buzzards were not attracted to a calf, but were feeding on the human remains of L. F. McLemore. The body which had been buried in a shallow grave had been partially uncovered by wild animals. The boy quickly ran home and notified his father who alerted the sheriff.

On February 22, 1907, Cason sold McLemore's wagon and two horses for a $110, along with a silver headed souvenir cane for a nickel, which was identified as belonging to McLemore. McLemore was last scene alive with Cason, and after it was discovered Cason had sold the victim's property in Fort Worth, he was arrested for murder.

Cason told the sheriff that Charlie Boynton had ridden into camp and murdered McLemore. Cason explained that after eating supper together, Cason had left to feed the horses, when Boynton picked up Cason's gun and shot McLemore in the head, and fired a second shot into McLemore's chest. Boynton stripped the body and burned the clothes, and then took the body away. Returning, Boynton threw him down a wad of money, saying, "Here's your share." Boynton was also alleged to have told Cason to take the team and sell it, and if ever he told of the circumstances he would kill him.

The eight-day trial ended on April 3, 1907, with the jury not believing Cason's story a verdict of guilty was returned along with the death penalty. A reporter later asked Cason if he had anything to say. Cason replied, "I have not had justice. My trial in court here was like kangarooing a dog. They brought up all sorts of things against me which were sworn to by men who never saw me before in my life."

On December 4, 1907, the Court of Criminal Appeals affirmed the conviction. On April 4, 1908, District Court Judge J. W. Patterson had Cason brought before the court for sentencing. Judge Patterson asked Cason if he had anything to say before the sentence of death was pronounced upon him. Cason replied, "Nothing more than that I am not guilty, and I ask the court for all the time it can give me."

Judge Patterson then gave the sentence saying, " The sentence of the court is that you, J. B. Cason, shall be taken by the sheriff of Parker County on Friday, May 22, to the place of execution and hanged by the neck until you are dead. If you have any arrangements to make either concerning this world or the next, my advice to you is to make them, and may the Lord have mercy upon your soul. Remove the prisoner Mr. Sheriff."

On the day of the execution James Cason's only statement from the gallows was that he was an innocent man. The body was claimed by his brother and taken to Kaufman County for burial.

The *Brownwood Daily Bulletin*, dated Saturday, May 23, 1908, provided their readers with the history of the murder.

Polk County
County Seat - Livingston

Jim Hill

Alias: John Blair **Race/Gender:** Black Male **Age:** 26
Offense: Murder **Offense Date:** December 7, 1894 **Weapon:** Pistol
Execution: July 3, 1896

Guy Morris Hooker was a yard foreman for the Trinity & Sub-line Railroad and possibly had been deputized as a Polk County deputy sheriff. On December 7, 1894, Jim Hill set out to kill his girlfriend, Ella Mitchell, and William McLeod, after he became suspicious that the two were having an affair.

Taking his pistol, Hill located William McLeod and shot him in the head, but the bullet only grazed the scalp. At the same time Hill wounded another man named Pasley. The foreman of the railroad mill notified Hooker of the trouble and asked him to handle the situation. Hooker saw that Hill was with Doctor Herrington and called out for him to stop. Hill Seeing Hooker reached into his vest and pulled his pistol and shot him in the head.

Polk County Sheriff W. G. Standley then offered a $150 reward for Hill's capture. To the west of Polk County, Deputy Dan Taylor of Brazos County tracked Hill and attempted the arrest him alone, and the two struggled. Deputy Taylor had to pull his revolver and shot Hill in the hip. Hill was returned to Polk County and on November 28, 1895, tried for murder and found the guilty. The sentence was appealed to a higher court and affirmed on July 3, 1896.

It was estimated that 2,000 people gathered at the gallows to watch Jim Hill hang. At 2 p.m., Sheriff W. G. Standley with twenty deputies led Hill by the hand to the awaiting gallows. Hill had requested that Rev. J. T. McClure of the Methodist church, speak on his behalf. Rev. McClure told those present that Jim Hill had never been guilty of any crime before this. The crime he said was "attributed by his wrong doing from gambling, drinking, and keeping bad company, which he was then placed into evil associations."

After prayer by Rev. McClure, Hill's legs and arms were tied, and the black cap placed over his head. As soon as the rope had been properly adjusted, the sheriff said: "Jim, are you ready?"

He replied, "Let her go," and Sheriff Standley pulled the lever.

The *Galveston Daily News*, dated Saturday, July 4, 1896, provided details of the crime and execution at Livingston, Texas.

Jack Wilkerson

Race/Gender: White Male **Age:** 44 **Offense:** Murder
Offense Date: May 2, 1905 **Weapon:** Single Barrel Shotgun **Execution:** June 29, 1906

On May 4, 1905, the body of Lillie Wilkerson was found several hundred yards from her home on an unused road. An examination of the body showed Lillie had been dead for two days and she had been killed from a shotgun blast to the back of the head. Suspicion immediately fell on her husband, Jack Wilkerson. When officers arrived at his home, they learned he had fled. A sheriff's posse tracked Wilkerson into the brush not far from the murder scene and captured him the next morning.

After his arrest, the officers warned Wilkerson that any statement he made would be used at his trial. Wilkerson confessed and related how his wife was riding to her aunt's house several miles away. Wilkerson said he rode up behind her and shot Lillie to the back of the head to keep her from telling secrets which would send him to prison. Wilkerson did not divulge what those secrets were, but explained that Lillie and he had separated, and Lillie had threatened to expose those secrets.

On May 2, against the advise of his attorneys, Wilkerson pled guilty to murder in the first degree and he was sentenced before Judge L. B. Hightower on May 28. When Judge Hightower asked Wilkerson if he had anything to say before the sentencing by the court, Wilkerson replied he would rather die at the end of a rope than at Huntsville. Wilkerson asked Judge Hightower to schedule his execution at the earliest possible date. Judge Hightower granted the wish, and ordered Jack Wilkerson to hang by the neck until his body be dead on June 29, 1906.

On the afternoon of the scheduled execution, Wilkerson walked sixty yards from the jail to the scaffold that had been erected in the yard. On the gallows, Wilkerson was asked if he wished to make a final statement. Wilkerson then said he had been accused of other crimes and murders, but that such charges were false. He admitted to killing his wife, but said God and he only knew what the motive was. Wilkerson said that he had made peace with God and was ready to die.

The *Shiner Gazette*, dated Wednesday, July 4, 1906, provided readers with details of the crime and execution.

Willis Macklin

Race/Gender: Black Male **Offense:** Murder **Offense Date:** March 29, 1907
Weapon: Pistol & Shotgun **Execution:** July 2, 1908

Jack Darden was well liked and a well to do elderly farmer, estimated to be in his eighties. He allowed several families to live on his farm, including Willis Macklin. Macklin was married to Darden's great niece.

On the night of March 29, 1907, while Darden sat next to the fireplace eating peanuts and talking with Press Scott, a bullet was fired through an open window of Darden's cabin. The bullet struck Darden in the head, killing him. Press Scott watched as Macklin walked up to the window with the pistol in his hand to view the probate body laying on the floor. After leaving, Macklin walked past another house and shot and wounded John Swearingen and George Rich.

Prior to murdering Darden, Macklin had killed his mother-in-law, Ann Darden. A mob quickly organized with the idea to either capture or kill Macklin. Once the mob arrived at Macklin's cabin, the mob fired several bullets into the house. Macklin had loaded his shotgun with lead slugs and when Robert Johnson swung open the cabin door, Macklin fired his shotgun killing Johnson. Macklin picked up Johnson's shotgun and fired at the mob, who fled into the thickets. Although wounded to the leg, Macklin was able to escape.

A week later T. S. Spurlock was shot in the head and killed. Sheriff S. C. Chapman learned where Macklin was hiding in the brush and organized his posse. Sheriff Chapman's force was then joined by Sheriff Watts of Angelina County with his posse and bloodhounds. Macklin was pushed out of the thickets into an open field and shot at the lawmen who returned fire, hitting Macklin to the shoulder.

On December 13, 1907, Macklin was tried on three counts of murder and two attempted murders and found guilty of all charges. The case was appealed to the Court of Criminal Appeals which was affirmed on March 11, 1908.

On July 2, 1908, Macklin was lead to the scaffold dressed in a new black suit and executed in the presence of 2,000 spectators. The drop of six feet broke his neck, and Macklin was pronounced dead in seven minutes.

The *Schulenburg Sticker*, dated Thursday, July 9, 1909, provided their readers with a short article of the execution.

John W. Cannon

Race/Gender: Black Male **Offense:** Murder **Offense Date:** November 28, 1908
Weapon: Double Barrel Shotgun **Execution:** July 8, 1910

Warren Perryman was on his way home from work on the afternoon of November 28, 1908, but never made it. The next morning searchers concerned for Perryman's safety followed drag marks from the roadway through the woods for three-fourths of a mile where the body of Perryman was discovered partially buried in a ditch.

Perryman had been shot and killed with a shotgun. Afterwards, a rope had been tied to the feet and the body dragged by a horse to its resting location. John Cannon was suspected of the murder as revenge against Perryman who had testified as a witness against Cannon for stealing a cow.

At trial, Cannon testified on his own behalf the he had killed Warren Perryman in self defense, after Perryman told him he was going to kill Cannon and drew a pistol and fired a shot at him. Cannon said he then fired back twice with the use of a shotgun. The jury did not believe Cannon's account, and returned a verdict of guilty and assessed the death penalty. The case was carried to the Court of Criminal Appeals which affirmed the decision on May 18, 1910. Judge L. B. Hightower, Sr. on May 30 passed sentence on Cannon to hang until dead on July 8, 1910.

On July 8, 1910, Cannon warned the 2,500 witnesses of committing wrong doings and bade all goodbye. At 2 p.m. Sheriff S. C. Chapman pulled the lever that released the trap dropping John Cannon seven feet.

The *Galveston Daily News*, dated Saturday, July 9, 1910, provided their readers with details of the murder and the execution at Livingston, Texas.

Louis Johnson

Alias: Oleva Johnson   **Race/Gender:** Black Male   **Age:** 20
Offense: Rape   **Offense Rate:** October 7, 1911   **Execution:** January 30, 1912

At about 3 p.m. of October 7, 1911, a strange man arrived at the home of C. D. Peterson which was located about a half mile west from the town of Dayton. Mrs. Peterson was home alone as her husband had gone to Crosby to buy supplies. A black man went to the door and asked Mrs. Peterson for something to eat. Mrs. Peterson complied and handed him some food. While the stranger ate the food on the porch, he asked for a glass of water. Mrs. Peterson directed the man to get his water from the well.

The man afterwards gave Mrs. Peterson the impression he was leaving. As Mrs. Peterson walked up the stairs to the second story of the house, the stranger who had taken off his shoes, crept up behind and attacked her. Mrs. Peterson was then dragged from inside her house to the barn. Once in the barn, the man tore off her clothing and sexually assaulted the sixty-five-year-old woman. After the attacker fled, Mrs. Peterson crawled outside the barn, and was able to get the attention of a Southern Pacific Railroad foreman for help. The foreman ran to her aid, and afterwards pumped a handcar to Dayton to notify both the sheriff and town doctor of the assault.

The stranger was later identified as Louis Johnson, who claimed his birth name was Oleva Johnson. Johnson was tried and convicted at Livingston on December 19, 1911, for criminal assault. The jury found Johnson guilty of the crime, and assessed the death penalty.

On the gallows, Johnson protested his innocence of the crime for which he was to be hanged before the 1,000 witnesses. He declared before hanging that he was resigned to his fate and he had made peace with God. At 2:46 p.m. the trap was sprung and he was pronounced dead eleven minutes later.

The *Galveston Daily News*, dated Wednesday, January 31, 1912, provided readers with details of the assault and execution.

Presidio County

County Seat - Marfa

Juan Duran

Race/Gender: Hispanic Male **Offense:** Robbery & Murder **Offense Date:** November 1, 1882
Weapon: Blunt Object - Pistol **Execution:** December 14, 1883

On November 1, 1882, Guadalupe Lacon invited a Chinese man, who he learned was carrying a large sum of money, to stay the night at the bunkhouse on the Smith Ranch. After the man accepted the offer, Lacon went to Juan Duran with the idea of killing the foreigner for his money.

That night, both Duran and Lacon held the man down and pistol whipped him to death with his own pistol. The body afterwards was robbed of all valuables, then dragged outside the house to a nearby arroyo and buried in a shallow grave.

Days later, the ranch foreman followed a blood smear on the bunkhouse floor to drag marks on the ground leading away. The foreman followed the marks and came upon the partially buried remains of the man and informed the ranch owner of his finding. The foreman said he suspected Duran and Lacon as being responsible. Lacon had left directly after the murder and he could not be found, but Duran remained and was arrested. Upon his arrest, Duran was carrying a $5 gold piece and a pistol which he later admitted as belonging to the dead man. Duran gave the below confession and afterwards placed his mark as being his statement:

When I was coming up with the cows last Saturday, one week ago (I don't remember the exact day), at Smith's ranch, on the Pelegos, in Presidio County, Texas, the Chinaman was coming up at the same time. There was another Mexican at the ranch, taking care of the cows, named Guadalupe. When I got to the ranch, Guadalupe told me that the Chinaman had about three hundred dollars. Guadalupe then kept after me until about eight o'clock at night to kill the Chinaman. About nine o'clock we went to kill him. I held the Chinaman by the feet until the other man killed him. We killed him in the house. There was nobody else around. If there was, I did not see them. Guadalupe killed the Chinaman with a gun by striking him on the head. He struck him on each side of the head and on the top. He struck him about 5 or 6 times, I held that Chinaman all the time. He was shaved on the front and sides of the head, shaved all over, but had a long strand hanging down his back.

Guadalupe only abused me if I did not help to kill the Chinaman, and, rather than stand the abuse, I held the Chinaman while he killed him. I could have left if I had wanted to, and Guadalupe would not have done anything to me. I am over twenty-one years of age. After we killed the Chinaman we carried him to the arroyo, and dug a little hole and buried him. Guadalupe stripped all the clothes from him and carried them away with him when he left. We buried the Chinaman naked. The Chinaman's shirt was bloody. The Chinaman had three paper bills. Guadalupe took two and gave me one. We found five dollars in gold, also. I got that. Guadalupe took a pistol away from the Chinaman. In the scuffle the Chinaman grabbed his pistol. Then I caught the Chinaman and held him, and Guadalupe took the pistol. Guadalupe is a man about thirty years old. That is the pistol we took from the Chinaman – the pistol now in court."

His
"Juan + Duran."
Mark

The identity of the dead man could never be determined.

On May 12, 1883, the Court of Criminal Appeals affirmed their decision by closing their brief with the following:

After careful examination we find no error in the conviction. One ground of the defendant's motion for a new trial is that the punishment assessed is excessive. We cannot say that it is true, the deceased was a Chinaman, a foreigner and a heathen, and of a race of people for which civilized world has but little regard, but still he was a human being, and in the estimation of the law his life was precious, and as much entitled to protection, as that of the most exalted and best beloved citizen of our own State. We see no good reason why the defendant should not suffer the extreme penalty of the law, and the judgment of the court below is in all things affirmed.

The *Galveston Daily News*, dated Saturday, December 15, 1883, wrote that Duran "Took the doom coolly, considering it more of a holiday spree than anything else. "

Demeiro Fierro

Race/Gender: Hispanic Male   **Offense:** Robbery & Double Murder   **Offense Date:** July 23, 1889
Execution: November 1, 1889

In early June of 1889, William Nations and Jacob Simpson had left Alpine for the mineral hot springs in Mexico which were known to sooth or cure various ailments a person may have. Both men had stayed at the springs for almost a month when they crossed back into the United States, and camped along the banks of the Rio Grande River.

While camped, Demeiro Fierro and two other Mexican bandits killed both Nations and Simpson and robbed the victims of their money, guns, horses and tack. After the bodies were found, Governor Lawrence Ross offered a $200 reward for the arrest of the Killer or killers. Fierro was captured, but his two accomplices escaped into Mexico. The Mexican government was then asked for their assistance, but the government refused to cooperate by not allowing either man to be extradited back to the United States to stand trial.

The *Dallas Morning News*, dated Saturday, November 2, 1889, printed the following short article:

UNTO DEATH.
A Mexican, For Murdering Two Companions, Dies the Death.

Alpine, Tex., Nov. 1.- The execution of Demeiro Fierro for the murder of William Nations and Jacob Simpson, just on the Texas side of the Rio Grande, took place at Marfa today at 11:30 a.m.

It will be remembered that this was one of three Mexicans who brutally murdered the two above named a few months since, the other two escaping into Mexico and the authorities refusing to deliver them up.

The execution was public and was witnessed by a majority of the people both from this place and at Marfa, including many Mexicans, to whom it is hoped a lesson has been taught.

Rains County
County Seat - Emory

Henry W. Johnson

Race/Gender: White Male **Age:** 25 **Offense:** Robbery & Murder
Weapon: Hatchet **Offense Date:** April 27, 1890 **Execution:** June 8, 1891

Henry Johnson was described as a "fine specimen of physical manhood." He was described as a handsome man, having jet-black hair, dark piercing eyes, dark mustache, and a well-built physique. Johnson attracted and won the heart of Miss Nettie Ferguson, and the two were soon married.

During a dispute with a neighbor, Johnson was jailed after he could not pay the fine. William Shumate who was in his seventies, and a friend of Johnson's proposed paying his fine. In return for his release from jail, Johnson had to agree to work for Shumate on his farm. Shumate said he would supply Johnson with tools, horses, mules, wagons, and implements for the farming.

On April 27, 1890, Shumate asked Johnson to go to Emory to pick up an express package containing money for Schumate. Johnson believed the package contained $1,000 and killed Shumate with a hatchet as he was sleeping in front of the fireplace of his home. To Johnson surprise, the package only contained $10. Johnson then took a watch, smoking pipe and pocketknife from the body. With the assistance of his wife, they lifted the body onto a horse to carry it 400 yards from the cabin to be dumped into the thickets. Johnson afterwards filled one of Shumate's wagons with other belongings from his victim, and then drove the wagon towards the Indian Territory.

When Shumate disappeared, Joe Benton who lived nearby asked Sheriff Montgomery to investigate. The sheriff traveled to Shumate's home and noticed dry blood stains on the floor, and saw that the horses and wagon were missing. The sheriff organized a search party and located Shumate's body lying in the thickets and began trailing the murderer with the aid of William Shumate's son, Abe.

The men trailed the murderer to the community of Monkstown, located sixteen miles north of Honey Grove, and just below the Red River in Fannin County. Because of the recent heavy rains, and swelling of the river, Johnson was unable to cross, forcing him to find shelter at the Monkstown Inn. Abe Shumate and Sheriff Montgomery also arrived at the inn to rest and eat. When they went to the stable to unsaddle their horses the younger Shumate spotted his father's gray mule. While examining the animal, the sheriff noticed someone watching in the darkness and apprehended the man who turned out to be Henry Johnson. The next morning, the sheriff and his prisoner rode by horseback to Denison where they boarded a train back for Emory.

Johnson's trial was held on October 4, 1890. District Attorney Charlie Yolkham shocked the jury and courtroom spectators by saying that "Henry Johnson left the body of Shumate for the flies and hogs to eat his guts out."

Upon being found guilty and sentenced to death by Judge Terhune, Johnson made two requests of the judge. First that his execution be private from public view, and second, that he be held at the Greenville jail so that he could receive religious service from the Baptist ministers there.

The gallows were built on the west side of the jail with a black calico cloth draped down. On the day of the execution, 5,000 spectators arrived to watch Johnson take his place on the trap door. Once Johnson stood on the gallows, he disappointed the witnesses by not making a final statement. After the trap fell, and the body was cut down to be placed in the coffin, the spectators rushed forward to the gallows to take pieces of the rope, splinters from the gallows and calico cloth for souvenirs. The body was then removed and buried in the potter's field.

Nettie Johnson was later tried as an accessory for her part, but was acquitted.

The *Fort Worth Gazette*, dated Tuesday, June 9, 1891, wrote, "Johnson was hanged to expiate one of the foulest and cowardly murders it has been our misfortune to know of."

Red River County
County Seat - Clarksville

Note: A slave by the name of Peter Valentine was hanged on January 27, 1859, for murder in Red River County. Information on the crime and execution are not currently available.

Nelson
(slave)

Race/Gender: Black Male **Offense:** Murder **Execution:** June 9, 1848

The *Standard*, dated Saturday, dated June 10, 1848, was the only newspaper that reported on the execution below. It is unclear which county Nelson was hanged in.

The Negro Nelson, convicted of the murder of Luckey, was hanged on yesterday at about 1 o'clock.

He said he was prepared to die, but seemed much dissatisfied that the Boy Alec, and others whom he charged as engaged in the killing, were not also made to suffer punishment. Life remained with him, for perhaps ten minutes after being swung off. But he did not struggle much or appear to suffer much pain. He was a very smart, vicious, and very dangerous Negro.

Lovet Cady

Race/Gender: White Male **Age:** 50 **Offense:** Murder
Offense Date: September 1854 **Weapon:** Firearm **Execution:** June 29, 1855

In September of 1854, Lovet Cady shot and killed Samuel Sinclair near the town of Pine Bluff, which he claimed he did in self-defense of his own life. Cady claimed he had been beaten by and left for dead at Sinclair's direction.

On June 6, 1855, Cady was tried for murder and the jury retired only for ten minutes to return the verdict of guilty, and assessed the death penalty. The sentencing judge then pronounced his sentence upon Cady:

Lovet Cady, you are charged by the State with the crime of murder, you have been arraigned before a jury of your peers, and after argument of counsel and a careful and dispassionate examination of all the witnesses, you stand convicted according to the law and the evidence. It now becomes my painful duty to pronounce the sentence of the law against you for shedding innocent blood.

The crime of murder is one of awful malignity in the sight of God and of man, even when perpetrated on an enemy and under ordinary circumstances. How much more then in your case, when you have in cold blood and without apparent provocation taken the life of an unoffending man. If in the heat of sudden passion, which sometimes overcomes the wisest and the best, you had dealt the fatal blow, your guilt might have been somewhat extenuated; but you deliberately planed the murder, and as artfully sought to hid it after it was committed. You laid your plans in secret—you conspired against the life of Samuel Sinclair, your nearest neighbor, and you executed your hellish purpose under cover of your own roof. You ushered his soul into eternity by shooting a bullet through his body, whilst he stood, an unsuspecting victim, within the door of his won domicile enjoying, as he had a right to suppose, that security and that immunity from harm, which a man's house, or his castle, as the law regards it, seldom fails to afford in a Christian country. Your heart seemed steeped in depravity and totally bent upon mischief. You must therefore feel the justice of the sentence about to be pronounced on you, for although you are represented to be poor, and in your social position not high, you have had the highest privileges which the Law affords to any citizen. You have had the benefit of able counsel, who have faithfully performed their duty towards you – a jury of twelve impartial freemen, entertaining no prejudices against you but selected by yourself and sworn to do you justice.

By these you have been pronounced guilty of murder in the first degree, and under circumstances so cowardly and cruel as to leave no doubt upon my mind of your guilt. In granting you twenty-one days respite, I extend to you far more mercy than you showed to your victim. You gave him no time to take leave of wife, children, or friends or to make his peace with God.

To you, I grant all these privileges, and I earnestly recommend you to set about preparing for the awful moment, when you will have to meet your victim at a higher bar than this, and account to your God for the blood you have shed, which like Abel's cries to him from the ground. Lovet Cady, you have my deepest sympathies, not that you have to suffer the punishment of the law, for that is just, - but that you should have been depraved – so lost to virtue and every manly feeling of compassion, as to lift your hand to shed the blood of your brother.

I admonish you, therefore, as your fellow mortal, bound to account for all my acts, that you will humble your heart before God, and by deep repentance and humiliation, seek his pardon for your horrible crime. There is no pardon for you here, except in the Executive clemency, and it would be more than folly for you to indulge such a hope. God, however, is an all merciful, as well as an all powerful being, and able, though your sins be as scarlet, to make you white as snow.

My sentence is therefore, that on Friday, the 29th day of the present month, you be taken from the jail by the sheriff of the county, between the hours of 9 o'clock, A. M. and 4 o'clock P. M., and be hung by the neck, until you are dead, and may God have mercy upon your soul!

Cady then told the judge:

I confess that I killed Sam Sinclair. But I was compelled to do it to save my own life. I was shut up in my own house and was afraid to leave it. I had been assaulted, beaten and left for dead by the banditti crew, who finding they had not killed me, was determined to have my life anyhow. Three guns were kept loaded for three months to kill me, and for no other reason than that I kept an opposition house. I can prove this. My case had not been rightly managed. My case has not been understood or I would not now be under this sentence. Before God and this court this is true. I appeal to any one who has known me from my infancy, if I was ever inclined to injure any man unless compelled to do it. Before God and this court this is true.

The *Springfield Republican*, dated Thursday, August 2, 1855, provided a short article on the execution at Clarksville, Texas.

Andrew Jackson

Race/Gender: Black Male **Age:** 20 **Offense:** Murder
Offense Date: October 11, 1894 **Weapon:** Shotgun **Execution:** January 18, 1895

Henry Dyke had at one time considered himself best friends with Andrew Jackson. When Jackson was arrested for theft, Dyke paid the fine so that Jackson could be released. In return, Jackson was to work off his debt on Henry Dyke's farm.

When this debt was paid, Jackson wanted to leave, but Dyke reminded Jackson he still owed him for the clothes he had purchased for him. Jackson refused to pay this debt, so Dyke later went to Jackson's cabin to retrieve the clothes he had purchased to take back to the stores. Dyke recognized several items in the cabin that belonged to him and threatened to prosecute Jackson for the thefts unless he paid the money.

A few days later Jackson borrowed a shotgun from a neighbor saying he needed the weapon for squirrel hunting. Once Jackson had the weapon, he asked another neighbor to purchase ten cents worth of shotgun shells. On the night of October 11, 1894, Jackson put his plan into action by setting the corn cribs on fire outside of Dyke's home to lure him outside. When Dyke ran from his house, Andrew Jackson rose up from where he had been hiding and shot Dyke in the head and chest with the buckshot. Jackson afterwards fled to his father-in-law's home where his wife was and climbed in bed with her. Upon the approach of the posse, Jackson attempted to escape capture by running out the backdoor and hiding in a cotton patch. Jackson was quickly surrounded and captured. Upon arrest, Jackson confessed he had set fire to the corn cribs to draw Henry Dyke out of the house so that he could kill him.

Andrew Jackson was indicted by the grand jury on January 23, and tried on December 5. The jury deliberated twenty minutes before returning a verdict of guilty and assessed the death penalty. Judge McClelland afterwards set the execution to take place on January 18, 1895.

On the day of the execution at 1:22 p.m., Sheriff Seth Dinwiddie read the death warrant to Jackson in the corridor of the jail. At the conclusion of the reading, Jackson was lead out of the jail to an awaiting wagon where he was seated on his coffin. A parade of fifty armed special deputies surrounded the wagon as they traveled the half mile southeast of town where the scaffold had been erected. The caravan of officers and 6,000 followers arrived at the gallows at 2 p.m.

On the gallows, Sheriff Dinwiddle asked Jackson if he had any last words. Jackson requested that some of the black ministers pray for him. Revs. Williams and Hardeman ascended the scaffold and conducted religious services. Deputies Corley and Jap Dinwiddle and ex-sheriff Morse of Bowie afterwards tied the hands and feet and moved Jackson over the trap door. Once the noose and black cap had been adjusted, Sheriff Dinwiddle pulled the trigger at 2:19 p.m. dropping Andrew Jackson six feet to his death. At 2:28 p.m. doctors Cheatham and Dinwiddle pronounced Jackson dead and the body was cut down and released to Dr. J. B. Berry who had purchased it for $10 from Jackson several days prior to the execution.

The *Fort Worth Gazette*, dated Saturday, January 19, 1895, provided a full account of the crime and execution at Clarksville, Texas.

Henderson Pierson

Race/Gender: Black Male **Age:** 24 **Offense:** Double Murder
Weapon: Firearm **Offense Date:** August 20, 1899 **Execution:** February 2, 1900

Henderson Pierson and his wife and his mother-in-law lived on the S. E. Watson plantation twenty miles north of Davenport near the Red River.

On August 20, 1899, Pierson's wife and mother-in-law prepared to leave home to visit a neighbor, which Pierson protested against as he suspected his wife's infidelity with the neighbor. His wife insisted on leaving. Pierson followed both women outside and took his wife by the arm and led her back to the house. The woman again walked out the door with Pierson following them with a gun, which he laid down in the weeds without them noticing. Pierson ran up to his wife and demanded she return back to the house with him. An argument quickly ensued between the two with heated words being exchanged. Pierson broke away from the argument and ran to where he hid the rifle. Picking up the weapon, Pierson shot his mother-in-law in the side of the head, killing her. In the mean time, Pierson's wife turned to run in an attempt to escape. Pierson chased after her and placed the muzzle against her back and pulled the trigger, killing her.

Pierson was apprehended by nearby neighbors and turned over to authorities. On December 19, 1899, Pierson pleaded guilty to murdering his wife. On the second count of murder, Pierson pled not guilty. In taking the witness stand, Pierson told the jury he only intended to shoot his wife, but that his mother-in-law stepped in between them when he fired the weapon. The jury did not believe the excuse, and returned a second verdict of guilty of murder in the first degree and sentenced Pierson to death. Pierson did not appeal to the Court of Criminal Appeals or make a request to the governor for clemen-cy.

On February 2, 1900, Pierson dressed in a new black suit and pinned a bou-quet to his coat. At 1 o'clock, Sheriff Huffman read the death warrant. At the conclusion of the reading, Pierson turned to Rev. Wesley and said, "I will soon be going home." Pierson then took the ten-minute wagon ride east of town where the gallows had been erected.

Once upon the gallows, Rev. Wesley provided prayers and sang hymns. Pierson afterwards stepped forward and addressed the 5,000 spectators. "I have committed a great crime. My sentence was just. God has forgiven me. I am going home to Jesus."

As the last hymn was being sang, Pierson joined in with the singing from under the black hood when the trap was sprung.

The *Dallas Morning News*, dated February 3, 1900, provided their readers with details of the crime and execution.

John Reeves

Race/Gender: White Male **Offense:** Murder **Offense Date:** March 30, 1904
Weapon: Choked **Execution:** February 17, 1905

On April 1, 1904, John Reeves asked neighbors if they had seen his wife, Minnie as she was missing. Neighbors noticed that Reeves also had a scratch across his face, and asked him if he and Minnie had been involved in a fight. Reeves replied no, and said he had hit his face on low shingles inside his barn. Reeves told the neighbors he had gone fishing Wednesday evening, and returned home around 9:30 that night and Minnie was in bed asleep. When he woke up the next morning, Minnie was gone. Reeves chuckled, saying he at first thought Minnie was "fooling him" playing an April Fools joke. When nearby neighbors learned Minnie was missing, they quickly organized a search party to look for her.

Minnie's father, S. J. McCuistion after hearing his daughter was missing, arrived to join the search party and carried with him a five foot long metal rod with a pointed end. After not finding his daughter inside the house, McCuistion searched and probed the ground in the horse and cow stalls. Not finding any evidence of his missing daughter there, McCuistion walked out onto the freshly plowed onion field. While inspecting the field, McCuistion saw where clay had been unearthed. McCuistion knew the exposed clay came from a much deeper depth than what a plow could dig up, and he started prodding the ground with his rod.

McCuistion located soft ground where the metal rod pushed deep into the ground. When McCuistion inserted the rod a third time, he felt the rod hit something. The search party began digging and unearthed hair and a piece of a quilt. In exhuming the remains, the body had been wrapped in a quilt. Doctors arrived at the scene and observed finger size bruises surrounding the neck. The doctors determined Minnie had been strangled to death, and her neck was broken.

The following day, Sheriff Seth T. Dinwiddle placed Reeves under arrest for the murder of Minnie. Hearing the threat of mob violence, the sheriff quickly transported Reeves by train to Paris for safe keeping. During the train trip, Reeves confessed to the sheriff that he murdered Minnie. Reeves related that on the morning of her death, he had awakened from his sleep with his hands around her neck, and choked Minnie to death. Reeves said after killing Minnie, he left the body on the bed while he dug the grave. Leaving his wife dressed in her nightclothes, Reeves rolled the body in a quilt and buried her in the grave. Not wanting to bring any attention to the grave, Reeves hitched a horse to a farm implement and plowed the surrounding area to conceal the grave.

Reeves was tried and the jury assessed the punishment at death. The case was appealed and the Court of Criminal Appeals affirmed the decision of December 24, 1904. On January 2, 1905, Judge Ben Denton sentenced Reeves to hang on February 17. After Reeves was sentenced, a petition was circulated for signatures in support of asking Governor Samuel Lanham to commute the sentence to life in prison. The petition was never sent, as only four residents from Red River County were willing to sign it.

On the gallows, Reeves declined to make a final statement.

The *Galveston Daily News*, dated Saturday, February 18, 1905, provided readers with details of the murder and the execution at Clarksville, Texas.

Henry Ballard

Race/Gender: Black Male **Age:** 21 **Offense:** Murder
Offense Date: 1914 **Execution:** February 19, 1915

In late summer of 1914, after Henry Ballard escaped from a convict farm in Bowie County, he came upon a peddler whom he killed in order to take the man's clothing so he could discard his convict clothing. To conceal the murder, Ballard dragged the man to a cistern and dropped the body into the watery grave near Avery.

Upon capture, Ballard confessed to the murder, and on December 18, 1914, he pled guilty to murder and was sentenced to death.

From the gallows, Ballard only said he was ready to go. At 1:49 p.m. the trap was sprung and after fourteen minutes declared dead.

The *Galveston Daily News*, dated Saturday, February 20, 1915, reported that the execution had taken place at Clarksville.

Reeves County
County Seat - Pecos

Leon Cardenas Martinez Jr.

Race/Gender: Hispanic Male **Age:** 19 **Offense:** Murder
Offense Date: July 22, 1911 **Weapon.** .25 caliber Pistol & Knife **Execution:** May 11, 1914

Emma Brown was a single school teacher in her mid-twenties who lived with her sister. When needing supplies, Emma would purchase her items from Crenshaw's General Merchandise and Post Office located in Saragosa, a small ranch town near Pecos. The clerk at the store was seventeen-year-old Leon Martinez. Each time Emma purchased her supplies at the store, Martinez would make offensive and indecent comments to her.

On July 21, 1911, Martinez again approached Emma with an indecent proposal, which offended her. Upset and angry by what Martinez had said to her, Emma notified Mr. Crenshaw that she would be doing her business elsewhere as she had been insulted on several occasion by his clerk.

The following day, Martinez followed Emma as she was riding alone east on the Bartillo and Saragosa road in her buggy. That evening Emma's horse and buggy arrived at the front gate of the Coopers' home. The Coopers alerted Deputy Sheriff Pink Harbert of the horse and buggy as the buggy showed to have three bullet holes from a small caliber gun. Deputy Harbert immediately began a search and located Emma's body west of the road and about three miles east of Saragosa. Emma Brown had been shot in the back and had six knife stab wounds to the chest.

Deputy Harbert returned to the scene the next day and tracked a horse print with a left fore front of the hoof split. The horse track was followed to the Martinez home where the lawman learned from Martinez Sr. that his son Leon Jr. had been out riding the horse the previous day. Sheriff C. Brown was notified and directly afterwards located Leon Martinez in town and placed him under arrest. When arrested, Martinez was carrying the murder weapon, a .25 caliber handgun. At the jail, Martinez gave the following confession:

On July 22, 1911, about three miles from Saragosa, I met Miss Brown, who was riding in a buggy. I asked her to let me do what she had promised. She had promised to let me (have sex with her). When I asked her on the road on July 22, she said I would have to go somewhere else. I told her I just had to do something. She said, "what do you mean, you son of a bitch, I am going to have you arrested." I told her she did not need to have me arrested; all I wanted was for her to do what she had promised to do. She said she would kill me, and I put my hand on her hip. Then I commenced shooting and shot four shots with a 25-cliber semi-automatic pistol. Her horse ran away, and when I headed the horse, she stopped and got out of the buggy. When I got off my horse, the girl ran. She had a stick in her hand. I then stabbed her in the back with my knife. When she turned around she hit me with her fist, and I stabbed her four or five times in the breast. I got on my horse and loped away to Saragosa. I did not tell anyone until I was arrested. She was standing up when I left her. After eating supper at home, I went to Crenshaw's store and worked. On the morning of July 23, 1911, I met John Oates and Floyd Crenshaw in a buggy. Floyd told me that Miss Brown had been found dead; that she had been shot. I afterwards told Jim Mayfield about her being shot. Then I ate dinner and went to old Saragosa and from there I went to Mr. Honaker's place, where the body of Miss Brown had been brought. I looked through the window, but could not see the body. I stayed at Honaker's almost an hour, and then when Henry Everett and I went to a watermelon patch and ate a melon. I was coming out towards Saragosa when the officers arrested me. I had the gun that I did the shooting with, but the knife was at home in my other pants. Miss Brown did not pull any pistol at any time. When I told the officers about having killed Miss Brown, I did not tell them about her threatening to kill me, but I did tell Mr. Stuckler last night. This all happened in Reeves county, State of Texas. I was riding a dun mare, unshod, a little horse. The mare belonged to Crenshaw & Co. I killed Miss Brown about four o'clock in the afternoon. I had talked to Miss Brown at the store where I worked on the morning of July 22, and that was when she told me I could (have sex with her).

Signed, Leon Martinez.

On July 29, 1911, seven days after the murder, Leon Martinez was tried and convicted of murder. Judge Isaacks sentenced Martinez to hang on September 1, 1911, but the execution was delayed as Governor Colquitt granted a thirty day reprieve to investigate claims that Martinez was under fifteen-years of age.

Martinez spoke with newspaper reporters and claimed he was only fifteen-years-old, being born in 1896. Martinez told the reporters he knew nothing of Emma's murder, and only signed the earlier confession after he had been threatened with death. Martinez claimed that on the day of the murder he waited on Emma and loaded the supplies in her buggy. Martinez gave an alibi that he had been at work when Emma was murdered, and that he was only carrying the pistol to trade it.

After all appeals to the Court of Criminal Appeals and the United States Supreme Court were exhausted, Leon Martinez was executed on May 11, 1914.

The *Wichita Weekly Times*, dated Friday, May 15, 1914, provided a short article of the murder and execution.

Refugio County
County Seat - Refugio

Juan Flores

Alias: Juan Antonio Acosta, and Juan Juarez   **Race/Gender:** Hispanic Male
Offense: Robbery & Murder   **Offense Date:** June 8, 1874   **Weapon:** Firearms & Knives
Execution: June 26, 1875

Thaddeus Swift, his wife, Irene and their three children lived on their sheep ranch located three miles from Goliad on the Sous Creek. Irene at the time was eight months pregnant with their fourth child.

On Saturday, June 8, 1874, Thad sold sheep clippings and received the sum of $700 in silver. That night six Mexican bandits attacked and murdered the couple. The murders were not discovered until the following morning, when the three Swift children, the eldest being five-years-old walked the two miles to their Uncle Frank's house asking for breakfast. The child told his uncle she could not wake up Papa and Mama. Frank rushed to the house to discover Irene dead in the yard. She had been stabbed twenty-four times, her throat cut, and shot in the head. Upon entering the home, Frank discovered his brother dead. The head had almost been severed from his body, and Thad had been stabbed in the heart.

A posse was organized and tracked three of the murderers in the direction of Moharia, Mexico. In search of the suspects, the posse searched every ranch while trailing the murderers. Upon coming up on a hut fifteen miles from Goliad on Blanco Creek, posse member Dan Holland was shot and killed. The posse quickly surrounded the hut and waited for reinforcements. Soon a posse from Refugio and Goliad arrived. Soon thereafter three suspects surrendered and were placed in a wagon to be transported to the jail in Goliad. However, the three suspects were taken from the control of the sheriff and taken to a grove of trees. The men confessed to the murders and named Juan Flores as a fifth person involved. Afterwards the three prisoners were lynched and shot full of bullets.

Flores escaped into Mexico, but was later captured and turned over to the authorities at Brownsville. On the scaffold, Flores spoke through the interpreter who was Rev. E. A. Antoine, a Catholic priest. Flores told the 1,000 witnesses that he had served three years in the penitentiary at Huntsville, and he was the cause of the Swift murders. Flores said he had laid the plan out, and had two other men with him. Flores claimed one of the two was dead, but would not say how or when he was killed. The other person, Flores refused to provide the name of. Flores continued to say this was the only murder he had ever committed, and was sorry for what he had done. Before the trap was sprung, he asked the Swift family and their friends for forgiveness. Just before the trap was sprung, Flores said, "Goodbye, boys, I die like a man, and that is all that can be expected of me."

The *Galveston News* dated June 26, 1875, printed a full article of the execution at Rockport.

Juan Antonio Hernandez

Race/Gender: Hispanic Male   **Offense:** Double Murder   **Offense Date:** May, 1877
Execution: November 15, 1878

In mid-April of 1878, Juan Hernandez was tried and found guilty for the murders of two men, one named Welder and the other Maton. When the jury returned the verdict of guilty, Hernandez believed he was going to be executed immediately after the verdict. He stood up and took off his coat and pulled his shoes off and then handed them to a deputy asking him to return his clothes to his wife. The officer told Hernandez to put his coat and shoes back on as he was being transported to the jail in Galveston for safekeeping.

On November 15, 1878, Hernandez protested his innocence before the 1,000 witnesses who attended the Rockport execution.

The *Galveston Daily News*, dated Saturday, November 23, 1878, provided a short article reporting the execution.

Robertson County
County Seat - Franklin

Bill Walker

Alias: Richard Knight, Henry Walker   **Race/Gender:** Black Male   **Age:** 30
Offense: Murder   **Offense Date:** August 19, 1876   **Weapon:** Iron Grubbing Hoe
Execution: April 16, 1880

James Munroe was also known as Major Munroe, but was referred to as "Old Man Munroe" by the community. Monroe who raised and sold cattle was believed by many to keep large sums of money in his cabin. Earlier during the day of August 18, 1876, James sold some cattle to O. C. Morehead for his meat market. Morehead paid Munroe $20 with four $5 bills. One of the bills had a hole punched through it.

During the night Bill Walker and an accomplice entered Munroe's cabin with the intent of murdering the old man for his money. The next day, neighbors walking past the Munroe cabin on their way to milking stalls, heard a scuffling sound coming from inside the home and went to investigate. Munroe was found dressed in his night clothes and lying across his bed bleeding from a head wound. He was still breathing, but died before he could speak a word. The weapon used was an iron grubbing hoe.

Evidence of foot tracks, and the purchase of clothes paid for using a five dollar bill with a hole punched through it led to the arrest of Bill Walker. At the examining trial, Walker confessed before Judge Joiner who cautioned him that any confession he made would be used as evidence against him at his trial. Walker at first told the court that Green Patterson and he had intended to rob and kill old man Munroe for his money. In other statements provided, Walker named different accomplices. Walker was convicted twice and the Court of Appeals affirmed the lower courts decision.

On the day of the execution, the Calvert Guards and Salter Rifles surrounded the gallows to keep order among the 5,000 witnesses who had gathered at the scene. At 1:30 p.m., Bill Walker ascended the scaffold while being accompanied by Rev. A. M. Gregory, Dr. W. B. Morrow, Sheriff W. Q. Wyser, deputies Blood, Robertson and R. G. Scott. Rev. Gregory told the crowd Walker's requested for him to tell those present that, "bad company, gambling, and whiskey had brought him to his present unhappy end, and he wanted all present to beware of these vices."

After prayers and songs were finished, Sheriff Wyser told Walker if he had anything to say he could speak. Walker said, "My friends, I am here today, but I am not going to hell; I am going to fly straight to heaven; I want you all to come and go there too. I want all to go, both white and black. I want you to see how freely I die. Jesus was done worse than this, and I can stand it too. I will be home a long time before I would go. Farewell, farewell, farewell."

Sheriff Wyser and Deputy Scott then adjusted the black cap and Deputy Bland Roberson placed the noose around the neck. The drop was six feet and three inches, but failed to break the neck. After hanging sixteen minutes the body was taken down, and placed in a coffin.

A reported from the *Galveston Daily News*, interviewed Bill Walker and included the interview on the Saturday, April 17, 1880, edition:

> *My true name is Richard Knight. I have traveled under many different names. I first became reckless in Taylor county. I robbed a store in 1866. I lived in Trinity and Houston counties eighteen months; went from there to Rusk county, and there robbed another store. I was also arrested there for living in adultery with Jane Greenwood, the mother of my children, who now live in this county. I was in with the kuklux at one time. I robbed another house in Rusk county; broke jail in Henderson in 1873, and went to Shreveport, La.; remained there three months. I got in with some boys there and committed some robberies, and went from there to Harrison county, Texas, and was arrested for theft of cotton, but made my escape and came to Robertson county in January, 1875, and got in a fuss with a colored man named George Easterwood on the farm of Mr. Wash*

Hearne. I shot and killed Easterwood, but considered that I was justified in that. I was tried in the district court at Calvert, and convicted and sent to the penitentiary for ten years. I remained in the penitentiary only six months and was hired out to work on a farm in Milam county. On the way over there we camped in an old house near Capt. G. W. Lawdermilk's store, in Robinson county, and during the night I made my escape. This was December, 1875.

During the year of 1876, I twice robbed a store at Hammond station, in Robinson county. The first time I got two coats. The last time I got $100 in money. I then went to Palestine where I remained three months and returned to Robinson county. I went from there to Bryan and was myself robbed. I was jailed at Bryan for carrying a pistol. I only remained in jail thirteen days and then returned to Robinson. It was made up among several of us to rob old man Munroe. I also intended to kill a man I found living with my wife. I also intended to kill another colored fellow named Ben Avery, for telling my wife some tales on me which caused us to fall out. We intended to rob Munroe and then go straight to Louisiana."

Old man Munroe was killed mainly about a saddle owned by San Merrit, who had just broke jail in Limestone county. Merritt ran and left the saddle, and went to Leon county. When he came back and asked me to go in with him and rob the old man. He thought Munroe had plenty of money. I finally agreed, after being persuaded to go in with him. The agreement was not to kill or hurt him. Merrit went into the house and I remained at the gate with a shotgun. I meant to keep anybody outside from going into the house, but not hurt any one inside the house. Merrit came out and we divided the money. I went home and never heard of Merrit until I was arrested. When Merrit came out of the house he told me he had struck Munroe. After I was arrested I had Sam arrested, but when I was brought to Calvert and put in jail, Anshicha advised me not to tell on Merrit, but take it all on myself. I took his advice, and when I was carried to Bremond to testify against Merrit, I got up and stated that I killed Munroe myself. Anshicha told me that if I implicated Sam we would both be sent to Huntsville to serve out the ten years for which I was sentenced for killing George Easterwood. I do not think I ought to be hung, and would be satisfied with imprisonment in the penitentiary for life." The officers did not recognize Walker as the man who had been convicted for the killing of Easterwood and he was never recognized until after his conviction for the murder of Munroe.

Fred E. Waite

Alias: Fred Lightner
Offense: Murder
Execution: March 23, 1883

Race/Gender: White Male
Offense Date: May 28, 1882

Age: 27
Weapon: Iron Pipe

Deputy Addison D. Wyser was the brother of Robertson County Sheriff W. I. Wyser, and served as his brother's deputy and jailer. When working as a jailer, the prisoners became aware of Deputy Wyser's daily routine as to when he would deliver their meals.

Fred Waite was incarcerated for the theft of a drummer's valise from the Junction House at Hearne. Wyatt Banks was in jail for horse theft and default on payment of a gambling fine. Banks also was healing from a gunshot wound he had received while attempting to escape from a contract labor farm. Daniel Compton was arrested and jailed for committing incest with his fifteen-year-old stepdaughter.

On May 27, 1882, the prisoners conspired to attack, disarm, and kill the deputy to make their escape for freedom. The prisoners were housed in cells one and two, while the number three cell was empty. Inside this cell, the prisoners found a piece of iron pipe that could be used as a weapon. That night, Fred Waite stayed hidden in cell three and waited until morning for the arrival of Deputy Wyser to bring them their breakfast.

Just after 8 a.m. Deputy Wyser arrived and entered into the jail corridor with the breakfast, and locked down the prisoners in their cells. Once the prisoners were secured, Deputy Wyser entered and was walking past cell number three when Waite struck him from behind the head with the iron pipe. After he fell to the ground, Waite struck the officer four more times to the head, disarmed him of his weapon, and released the other prisoners from their cells and escaped. The thirty-eight-year-old lawman died that night and was buried at the cemetery in Franklin.

On June 29, 1882, Dan Compton testified as a state's witness in exchange for avoiding the hangman's noose, and received a life sentence to the penitentiary. Both Fred Waite and Wyatt Banks were found guilty of murder in the first degree and were sentenced to death. The sentence was appealed to the Court of Criminal Appeals who affirmed the lower courts decision.

On February 15, 1886, Judge W. E. Collard read to Waite the following sentence:

The sentence of the law which is death by hanging is hereby pronounced on the defendant that he may be by the Sheriff of Robertson County conveyed to the jail of said county and there be securely kept until Friday, the 23rd day of March 1883, at which time between sun up and sundown of said day, said Sheriff or proper officer shall hang the defendant, Fred E. Waite, by the neck until dead. This to take place on the court house yard.

On the appointed day, Waite's last meal consisted of hot chicken pot pie, old fashion lemon custard, sweet milk, two oranges, bananas, apples, hot biscuit and butter, champagne, and cigars. At 12:30 p.m., Waite dressed in a new navy blue suit was transported by a hack to the gallows that was built a half-mile south of town.

Two thousand spectators were gathered at the gallows. Waite refused any spiritual advisors, and requested that the sheriff take charge of his body. Waite had previously sold his body to doctors for $25, but after spending the money refused to honor the agreement. After a few remarks, Waite simply told the 2,000 spectators, "Good-bye boys."

After all the preparations were complete, a handkerchief was dropped to signal jailer Tom Raynhart to cut the rope. Waite fell seven feet with the drop breaking his neck. Eighteen minutes later he was declared death and placed in a coffin for burial.

One month later Wyatt Banks was hanged from the gallows in Ellis County.

The *Fort Worth Daily Gazette*, dated Saturday, March 24, 1883, printed a large article detailing the murder, jail escape, and execution at Franklin, Texas.

George Freeney

Race/Gender: Black Male   **Age:** 50   **Offense:** Murder
Offense Date: March 31, 1892   **Weapon:** Double Barrel Shotgun   **Execution:** November 25, 1892

George Freeney was tried and convicted for the murder of his twelve-year-old stepson John Robertson who he shot and killed with a shotgun. The boy was to have been gathering firewood when his stepfather found him sitting in a dugout breaking nuts. Seeing his stepson not doing his chores, he raised the shotgun and shot the boy in the back. When John failed to return home, his mother reported him missing, and a search failed to locate him.

About two weeks later a fresh grave was discovered in a graveyard near by. The grave was unearthed and the body of the boy was discovered about eighteen inches deep in the grave wrapped in an old shirt and bedspread. An inquest was held and the body was identified. Just prior to exhuming the body Freeny was questioned as to the whereabouts of the boy, and he denied knowledge. A search by officers located the dugout 200 yards from Freeny's house. The leaves were raked away, and fresh dirt was located where a hole about the length of the boy was found. In the hole was John's vest that contained blood and four pellet shot holes in the back.

At the examining trial George Freeny made a voluntary statement in which he told about the boy going after the wood and not returning. Freeny said he looked for the boy for a week and finally found him dead in the dugout. Freeny told his wife and they decided that it was best not to tell anyone or they might be accused of murdering John. The body was then temporarily buried in the dugout. A week later he and his wife exhumed the remains and reburied the body in the graveyard.

Freeney was unable to hire his own attorneys and therefore was appointed attorneys by the court. The attorneys worked out a plea agreement with the district attorney for George Freeney to plead guilty in exchange for life imprisonment. At the hearing, Freeny refused the bargain and pled innocent to the charge. Tried and found guilty, George Freeney was sentence to death, and decided not to appeal the verdict.

From the gallows built on the courthouse yard, Freeny told the crowd of 3,000 to bear witness to the execution of an innocent man. He said his sins were forgiven and that he was very soon going home to heaven. Freeney said he would meet them all at the bar of God, where a man could get justice; that he would leave this sinful world where justice could not be had.

After his speech Rev. G. H. Phair offered a prayer and sang a hymn. Deputy Sheriff White then adjusted the rope, drew the black cap, tied the hands and feet, and then pulled the trigger. The fall broke the neck and in fifteen minutes Freeney was pronounced dead.

Prior to his execution, George Freeney feared for the life of his eleven-year-old daughter Mary, and asked Sheriff J. W. White to take care of her. The sheriff's family raised Mary where she lived until she became an adult.

The *Galveston Daily News*, dated Saturday, November 26, 1892, provided details of the murder, trial and execution at Franklin, Texas.

Granville Jenkins

Race/Gender: Black Male **Age:** 24 **Offense:** Murder
Offense Date: May 14, 1898 **Weapon:** Shotgun **Execution:** March 30, 1899

On February 14, 1899, Granville Jenkins was sentenced to hang for the murder of Perry Odom who he shot to death on May 14, 1898. Jenkins claimed he had received word that Odom had made threats against his life and on the day of the murder waited out of view for Odom to ride up on his horse. When Odom arrived, Jenkins confronted him about what he had heard. Odom replied that he had not made such threats, and if he had he would not be telling persons of his intent. As Odom rode his horse past, Jenkins shot Odom in the back with a shotgun. After the murder, Jenkins fled to avoid capture.

On May 22, 1898, Sheriff T. B. Jones posted a $25 reward which read:

Granville Jenkins, he is 25 years old, about 5 feet 9 or 10 inch high, big mouth, thick lips, gun shot scar on right side of the neck, has served some time on county farm and has been whipped, probably scars from this on back. I will pay $25 reward for this man anywhere in Texas, or information leading to his arrest. I hold capias, T. B. Jones, Sheriff, Robertson County.

Jenkins was located at Eagle Lake where he was arrested and tried for murder on July 12, 1898. After the Court of Criminal Appeals affirmed the sentence, Judge W. G. Taliaferro sentenced Jenkins to hang on March 30, 1899.

Dressed in a new black suit, Jenkins stood on the gallows and read from the fourteenth chapter of John and asserted that he was "going straight to home to paradise, and would have everlasting home." Although he did not speak of the murder, Jenkins told the crowd his death was unjustified, and compared his execution to Christ. Jenkins said, "Be not afraid to die, the bravest man that ever ascended a scaffold is here now, ready to meet death."

The *Houston Daily Post*, dated Friday, March 31, 1899, provided its readers with an account of the crime and execution at Franklin, Texas.

Rusk County
County Seat - Henderson

Harris B. Robinson

Alias: Pad
Offense Date: April 2, 1868
Race/Gender:
Execution: June 11, 1869
Offense: Robbery & Murder

Willis H. Poe

Alias: Pad
Offense Date: April 2, 1868
Race/Gender:
Execution: June 11, 1869
Offense: Robbery & Murder

On April 1, 1868, Colonel William R. D. Ward of Marshall, Texas and Colonel Ely of Shreveport traveled together to Henderson for the purpose by buying cotton. The men carried $8,000 to $10,000 in gold and $3,000 to $4,000 in currency for this purpose. After staying the night at a hotel, in Henderson, the following day the two men hired a hack to complete the journey to Mount Enterprise.

At about 4 p.m., Colonel Ely was found sitting on the ground leaning against a tree calling out for help. Badly wounded from two gunshots to the back, before he died, Colonel Ely reported that he and Col. Ward had been attacked by two men from behind. Col. Ely said he held onto his horse bridle, but had seen Col. Ward fall from the hack when shot. As Col. Ward lay on the ground, two more shots were fired at him, but missed. The robbers then put the muzzle of their pistol to Col. Ely's face. The Colonel told them not to shoot him anymore, as they had already killed him.

A mile further down the road from where Colonel Ely was found, the body of Colonel Ward was found. He had also been shot to death. On the body was $1,543 in currency that the robbers had missed during the hasty search. Further away was the hack, and Col. Ward's satchel, which had carried the gold. The satchel was found broken open about 200 yards from the body.

The description Colonel Ely provided of the robbers and the horses the two men were seen riding lead to the suspicion of Willis Poe and Pad Robinson. A posse quickly organized and began tracking the outlaws. Robinson was located seven miles northeast of Greenvillein a house. Upon seeing he was about to be captured, he took a carving knife from the table and cut his throat. He also confessed to the murder and gave directions to where Poe had buried the money, near a house where Poe was arrested. In searching the location, the lawmen recovered $3,910 in gold.

Both Robinson and Poe were tried before Judge J. B. Williamson and were found guilty of murder in the first degree and sentenced to death. The verdict was appealed to the Supreme Court who affirmed the lower court verdict.

At noon on the day of the scheduled execution, both prisoners were escorted to the gallows, which had been erected outside the county fairgrounds. On the scaffold, Robinson and Poe were asked if they had anything to say. Robinson remained silent. Poe stepped forward and told the 6,000 spectators that he wanted to address his young friends. Poe warned those to never drink, and to take the advice of no one, about anything, that was not strictly right and honest; and to take his fate as a warning on these subjects.

Poe said, "I hope no one will think anything the less of my dear relatives on account of my fate." Poe then called out to Mr. Brooks, son-in-law to Colonel Ely. Poe told Mr. Brooks he had been forgiven for his crimes by his maker, by Maj. Turney, and most of the relatives of Col. Ward and wanted to receive forgiveness from him. Poe received his forgiveness from both Mr. Brooks and a Mr. Rains, another son-in-law.

When asked if he had anything else to say, Poe replied no, but asked that he be allowed ten minutes to pray. At the conclusion of the prayer, the traps were sprung. The drop broke Robinson's neck, but Poe strangled for several minutes before being pronounced dead.

The *Galveston Tri-Weekly News*, dated June 21, 1869 provided its readers with details of the execution and ended their story with "Thus ended the career of two young men raised in our midst. It was a terrible ending, but not without its lessons."

Tom Williams

Race/Gender: Black Male   **Age:** 21   **Offense:** Murder
Offense Date: September 22, 1880   **Weapon:** Pistol   **Execution:** September 23, 1881

J. A. Tinkle lived twelve miles from Henderson where he raised cotton on his farm. For several years, Tickle employed Tom Williams as a laborer. On September 22, 1880, at about 1 p.m., Williams called out to Tinkle to come outside to speak with him in regards to the fifty cents due to him for labor. As Tinkle stepped outside, Williams shot and killed Tinkle for the money he had inside the house. Williams was aware that Tinkle had recently sold his cotton crop for $400, and searched the farmhouse for the money until he found it.

Williams fled immediately after the murder and was captured by Sheriff W. T. Brewer and a posse of men at Nacogdoches. Williams stood trial and after his conviction he lost his appeal to a higher court.

At 12:40 on the day of the execution, Williams ascended the scaffold with his head bent low in the presence of the 3,000 witnesses who had gathered. Williams did not say anything except through his spiritual adviser, the Rev. Peter Evans. Rev. Evans said that Tom was ready to die, that he hoped that God would pardon his great crime.

The *Galveston Daily News*, dated Saturday, September 24, 1881, provided their readers with details of the execution at Henderson, Texas.

George Scott Jr.

Race/Gender: Black Male   **Age:** 28   **Offense:** Murder
Offense Date: July 27, 1890   **Weapon:** Shotgun & Ax   **Execution:** May 27, 1892

When George Scott, Sr. learned that his son Jr. had impregnated his half-sister, Scott Sr. told his son that he, "had better put her out of the way or when he returned back from church, he would put him out."

While alone on the farm with his sixteen-year-old sister, Scott Jr. shot his sister with a shotgun as she sat near the water well. Scott Jr. then took an ax and killed his sister by striking her to the head. Scott Jr. afterwards disposed of the body and ax by dropping both into the well. After Scott Jr. was arrested, he confessed to the murder and pled guilty in court. Before the sentence of death could be passed upon him, Scott Jr. escaped from jail and fled to Desoto Parish, Louisiana.

In February 1891, a jailer overlooked when locking the cells for the night that a prisoner had obstructed the door to his cell so that it would not lock. On the jailers return, the prisoner sprang upon the officer, gagged and tied him up. He afterwards released the other prisoners from their cells, one being George Scott, Jr. Scott Jr. hid from authorities for four months until his sister Lizzie Dannie provided his location to the sheriff in return for $20.

On the day of the execution, Scott Jr. was placed in a wagon and driven to the location of the gallows where 5,000 people congregated to witness the event.

At 2:06 p.m. and with a firm and steady step, Scott mounted the gallows. When the sheriff asked if he wished to say anything, Scott Jr. called for his sisters and requested for them to come forward. Scott said, "You all be good Christians and live right. I am going to leave you now."

Scott Jr. offered a prayer and when finished stepped upon the trap door. At 2:30 p.m. the cap was placed over his head and a minute later the trap was sprung. The neck was not broken by the fall and the body remained suspended for fifteen minutes before being lowered into an awaiting coffin.

The *Galveston Daily News*, dated Saturday, May 28, 1892, provided its readers an account of the murder, escape, and execution at Henderson, Texas.

Sabine County
County Seat - Hemphill

Robert Wright

Race/Gender: White Male   **Offense:** Murder   **Offense Date:** June 20, 1908
Weapon: Double Barrel Shotgun   **Execution:** December 17, 1909

Aaron Johnson lived on his farm near the small town of Geneva, located halfway between the towns of Hemphill and San Augustine. On the night of June 20, 1908, Johnson had just finished eating his dinner with his wife and child and moved from the dinner table to sit in his favorite chair. At about 8:30 that night while Aaron sat next to the open window taking in the summer night breeze, he was shot in the head from a double barrel shotgun. Since there was no nighttime phone operator available in Hemphill, Sheriff Nobel at San Augustine was notified. The sheriff in turn contacted the Texas Rangers who were already in the vicinity. The Rangers had been sent to Hemphill because of high race tension after several black men had murdered a white man by the name of Hugh Dean.

The next morning Ranger Frank A. Hamer and Oscar Latta arrived and learned that the suspicion of the murder had fallen on a black man by the name of Perry Price. The Rangers traveled to the Price home and upon arriving there, found that a lynch mob had Price surrounded in his cabin, and the mob immediately met the Rangers. Price, who was afraid to come out for fear of being lynched, was more than willing to be taken into the custody of the Texas Rangers for protection. The Rangers told the mob they were taking the prisoner so they could interrogate him for more information, but instead transported him to the jail in San Augustine for safe keeping.

Price confessed to the Rangers that he had been paid $5 by Robert Wright to kill Aaron Johnson. Wright was arrested the next day and both Price and Wright were transported by train to Beaumont for safekeeping. Unknown to the Rangers, while transporting both prisoners to Beaumont, a mob of 200 men removed the six suspected murderers from the jail at Hemphill to a grove of trees. While ropes were being thrown over tree limbs, the men were told they had seven minutes to pray to their God. At the end of seven minutes, the six were hanged from the trees.

On December 17, 1909, the county's first and only execution took place in the county jail at Hemphill. After Robert Wright declined to make a final statement from the gallows, Sheriff S. R. William sprung the trap at 2:24 p.m.

The *Galveston Daily News*, dated Saturday, December 18, 1909, provided readers with details of the murder.

San Augustine County
County Seat - San Augustine

Ben Lane

Race/Gender: White Male **Age:** 26 **Offense:** Murder
Offense Date: December 24, 1884 **Weapon:** Double Barrel Shotgun **Execution:** March 19, 1886

Sydney Ann Dykes was known by her neighbors as not being a very intelligent woman. Years prior to Dykes' death, Ben Lane told her that an arrest warrant had been issued for her arrest and presented a fictitious warrant. Lane gave Dykes the choice of either going to court and possibly be sentenced to prison or choose to live with him. The naive girl chose to stay with Lane instead.

Ben Lane during this time had been married for ten years and fathered five children. Lane also fathered a child with Dykes. Both women were repeatedly abused and forced to submit to the Mormon way of life, which neither woman wished to accept. Later, Dykes complained to the district attorney and Lane was indicted on five counts of cattle theft, hog-theft, attempted rape, and false imprisonment, along with other charges with Dykes being the principal witness for the state. Angered by her betrayal against him, Lane took a double barrel shotgun on Christmas Eve of 1884, and shot Dykes to death as she was cradling her baby in her arms.

At 11:40 a.m. on the day of the execution, Sheriff B. J. Lewis with a guard of twenty-five well-armed men placed Lane in a hack and drove him the 300 yards north of the courthouse square to where the gallows had been erected.

After arriving, Lane took his place on the platform and told the 2,500 to 4,000 witnesses that he killed the woman himself, but did it accidentally. He then warned all to take advantage of his example, and hoped he would be the last man on this earth to die as he did. Lane said he had made peace with God, and then asked all to join him in prayer. At the end of the prayer, he stood up and was pinioned at the hands and feet. After the noose placed around his neck, the sheriff drew the black cap. Lane objected to it being used and asked Sheriff Lewis not to put that on him. After placing the black cap over his head and the trap was sprung, he cried out, "God, have mercy on my soul!"

At high noon Lane was pronounced dead, and his body was lowered into a coffin, covered with plain black velvet, and then turned over to his brother-in-law for burial.

The *Galveston Daily News*, dated Tuesday, March 23, 1886, provided readers with detail of the hanging and history of the crime he committed.

John Hood Price

Race/Gender: Black Male **Age:** 43 **Offense:** Murder
Date of Offense: March 18, 1920 **Weapon:** Double Barrel Shotgun **Execution:** March 23, 1920

All in a span of five days after the murder of John Kennedy, John Hood Price was apprehended, tried, and executed. John Kennedy lived three miles northeast from San Augustine. On the night of March 18, 1920, as he sat next to the window reading a newspaper, Kennedy was hit from both charges of a double barrel shotgun. Kennedy's body was not discovered until the following day when a cook arrived to prepare his morning meal.

Price immediately became the primary suspect as a result of a dispute both men had on the previous day. Four days later a deputy sheriff located Price and arrested him in Alto. That afternoon the grand jury was assembled and Price was indicted. District Court Judge T. Adams who was sitting on the bench at Hemphill was notified and drove to San Augustine. A jury was empaneled, and by 9 p.m. that evening the jury declared Price guilty of murder and assessed the death penalty. Price waived his thirty-day right for a new trial or appeal, and was sentenced to hang the following day.

The next morning a scaffold was quickly assembled on the town square. At 11 a.m. that morning, John Price walked up on the scaffold and was publicly hanged in the presence of 2,000 witnesses.

The headlines of the *Brownwood Bulletin*, dated Tuesday, March 23, 1920, informed readers of the execution with the following headline:

PROMPT JUSTICE GIVEN EAST TEXAS NEGRO MURDERER.

LEGALY HANGED WITHIN TWELVE HOURS AFTER HIS CONVICTION.

San Jacinto County
County Seat - Coldspring

Alf Watson

Race/Gender: Black Male **Offense:** Murder **Offense Date:** August 15, 1893
Weapon: Pistol & Ax **Execution:** December 8, 1893

Elvira was at home by herself on August 15, 1893, when Alf Watson arrived. Elvira's sisters, ages twelve and eight were at a neighbor's house, when at about 12 p.m. the sisters heard Elvira screaming. The girls ran in the direction of their home where they recognized Alf Watson in their yard beating Elvira about the head with a pistol. Watson looked up to see both sisters standing in horror, and chased after them, but they were able to run back to the safety of their neighbors.

Watson afterwards returned to his own home two miles away. Officers soon arrived at the cabin and placed Watson under arrest. Although Watson had changed his clothing, the officers located the bloody clothes he had worn and those clothes were used as evidence at his trial.

At 2:30 in the afternoon of December 8, 1893, Alf Watson was hanged in the presence of 3,000 spectators. He had requested to be buried at the Snowfield graveyard, seven miles from Cold Springs, where his wife and children were buried.

The *Galveston Daily News*, dated Saturday, December 9, 1893, provided details of the execution at Cold Springs, Texas.

San Patricio County

County Seat - Sinton

Josefa Rodriguez

Alias: Chipita Rodriguez **Race/Gender:** Hispanic Female **Age:** 60s
Offense: Robbery & Murder **Offense Date:** August 23, 1863 **Weapon:** Ax
Execution: November 13, 1863

Josefa Rodriguez, better known historically as Chipita Rodriguez was believed for many years to have been the first woman executed in Texas. However, that historical distinction goes to Jane Elkins who was executed ten years earlier in Dallas.

Chipita was operating an inn in her home on the banks of the Arkansas River between Refugio and San Patricio. At her inn, Chipta provided meals and a cot on her porch for weary travelers. Chipita was running her inn with Juan Silvera, who is believed to have been her illegitimate son.

One of those travelers looking for a place to rest and receive a meal was John Savage. Savage who was a horse trader had earlier received $600 in gold coins from the sale of horses to the Confederate Army.

On August 25, 1863, the chopped up body of John Salvage was found floating in a burlap bag downstream from Chipita's home. The sheriff while investigating the murder located blood on the front porch of the inn and arrested Chipita. The motive to the murder was believed to have been the gold coins, but the coins were found on the riverbank.

Chipita and Juan Silvera were both indicted for murder on October 7, 1863, and tried before District Judge Benjamin F. Neal. The jury, which consisted of the sheriff who arrested her, and three members from the grand jury that indicted her, all recommended mercy to the court. Juan Silvera was convicted of second degree murder and sentenced to five years imprisonment. Judge Neal then sentenced Chipita to hang by the neck until her body was dead on Friday, November 13, 1863.

Because Chipita did not have a proper dress to be executed in, she was given a wedding dress for the occasion from a friend. Three months after Savage's murder, Chipita was taken to a mesquite tree by a wagon near the Nueces River and hanged. The body was cut down and buried near the tree in an unmarked grave.

Very few records exist today of the trial as the courthouse burned down in 1899. Today, it is believed that Chipita did not murder John Salvage, but that she went to her death protecting her son of the crime. In 1985, the Texas legislation absolved Josefa "Chipita" Rodriguez of the murder conviction.

Shelby County
County Seat - Center

Note: William Williams was hanged on May 8, 1844, for murder in Shelby County. Information on the crime and execution are not currently available.

Joe Rather

Race/Gender: Black Male **Age:** 29 **Offense:** Murder
Offense Date: January 6, 1887 **Weapon:** Firearm **Execution:** December 28, 1888

On the night of January 6, 1887, Joe and Nelley Rather attended a dance, and soon they were arguing with each other. After Rather threatened to kill his wife, he sent his wife home. Nelley returned to their cabin located near Shelbyville, and went to bed. Soon thereafter Joe arrived at home and picked up his shotgun and loaded it with squirrel shot. Joe entered the bedroom and shot Nelly in the head, instantly killing her. After killing Nelly, he returned back to the dance and told several people that he had killed his wife. No one attempted to apprehend him, and Joe fled to Tyler where he was arrested six weeks later, then later tried and convicted of murder.

On December 28, 1888, at 1:48 p.m., Joe Rather was hanged in the presence of 3,000 witnesses. From the gallows, Rather addressed the spectators warning them to stay away from wickedness, card playing, horse racing, and for black women not to attend festivals. He said had Nelly not attended the festival and had stayed away from men, he would not have killed her. Rather said whiskey contributed to him committing the crime and he hoped he would be the last person ever hanged in Shelby County. He ended his statement by saying his sins were forgiven and he was going to heaven where he hoped to meet all there.

The *Fort Worth Daily Gazette*, dated Sunday, December 30, 1888, provided readers with details of the murder and execution at Center, Texas.

Dick Garrett

Race/Gender: Black Male **Offense:** Murder **Offense Date:** November 17, 1906
Weapon: Pistol **Execution:** November 21, 1906

On the morning of November 17, 1906, officers attempted to arrest Dick Garrett for carrying and displaying a revolver in town. Garrett fled from the officers to the nearby offices of Hugh B. and C. B. Short. Garrett worked for both men and told them there were men out there trying to kill him. Both Hugh and his brother C. B. armed themselves with shotguns. When the town marshal arrived, he was refused entrance into the office and told to return with an affidavit. When the marshal left to obtain a warrant, Hugh Short told Garrett to take his horse which was hitched at the back of the building and for him to ride it over to Short's home.

Just after 2 p.m., officers learned Garrett had taken refuge at C. B. Short's home. Several citizens of the town were deputized to assist the marshal in executing the arrest. One of the town's most respected citizens was Dr. Mike M. Paul and he was one of the men deputized. After arriving at Short's home, the posse of lawmen entered the house with Doctor Paul taking the lead. Just as Doctor Paul entered the doorway, a bullet fired by Garrett struck him to the neck, and sent his body backwards and onto a chair. After a coroner's inquest, the body of Dr. Paul was buried at the Center Cemetery. Garrett who had surrendered was taken to jail under a heavy guard of officers, and three companies of militia to prevent any lynch mob from overtaking the jail.

On Wednesday morning at 9:30 a.m., November 23, 1906, a twelve man jury was empaneled for trial.

Garrett informed Judge S. M. Davis that he wished to plead guilty as charged in the indictment.

Judge Davis asked, "Do you understand, that in pleading guilty to the crime, the death sentence or a term of life imprisonment may be inflicted?"

Garrett: "Yes, I understand."

Judge Davis: "Are you doing this of your own free will and accord or have you been terrified or frightened into it?"

Garrett: "I am guilty of the charge and satisfied that something is to be done, and I want it done right away."

Judge Davis: "Then the plea is entered voluntarily?"

Garrett: "Yes."

An hour and a half later, the jury retired for deliberation, only to return seven minutes later with their verdict of guilty and assessed the death penalty. Dick Garrett afterwards waived all appeals, and two and a half hours later was hanged on the public square.

Garrett's attorney told Judge Davis that Garrett wished to file no motion for a new trial, and would waive the thirty days for appeal. Judge Davis asked Garrett if he understood his rights, and Garrett said, "Its got to be done, and I want it done right now so as my people can take me to Tenaha, and bury me and get back before dark."

Eight months later, on August 9, 1907, Judge C. B. Short was arrested while sitting on the bench hearing a civil case. Judge Short was informed he was charged as an accessory to the murder of Dr. Mike Paul, and his bond was set at $10,000.

The *Palestine Daily Herald*, dated Thursday, November 22, 1906, provided their readers with a short article of the execution at Center, Texas.

Smith County

County Seat - Tyler

Charles Scott

Race/Gender: Black Male **Age:** 40 **Offense:** Murder
Offense Date: July 12, 1892 **Weapon:** Double Barrel Shotgun **Execution:** April 15, 1893

In the winter of 1892, B. F. Curtis entered into a lease agreement with Charles Scott to lease a portion of his land. In exchange, Scott was to work the land and when the crop was sold, to pay Curtis a portion of the profits. During the summer, Curtis felt Scott was ignoring his crop and went to discuss the matter with him. Curtis told Scott if he was not going to work his field properly, than to allow him to do so, which Scott refused.

Two weeks later on July 11, 1892, Curtis became inpatient with the condition of Scott's field, and sent his son and field hands to work Scott's field. Scott seeing the men in his field, grabbed his pistol and ran everyone off, telling them that no man would work his crop. That afternoon, Curtis armed both of his sons with firearms and told them return to Scott's field and for them to guard over the field hands while they worked the land.

The following day, seventy-two-year old B. F. Curtis rode over to Scott's cabin to discuss the agreement and the condition of his crop. The discussion quickly became heated and led to an argument. As Curtis turned his horse to ride away, Scott grabbed his double barrel shotgun and shot Curtis to the side of the head. After falling from his horse, Scott jumped over a fence and unloaded the second charge into Curtis' forehead.

Charles Scott was arrested and indicted for murder in the first degree on September 6, and tried a month later on October 11. Scott was found guilty of murder in the first degree and the punishment was assessed at death. The case was appealed, but on December 1, the court affirmed the decision. Scott was first sentenced to be hanged on April 1, 1893, but Governor James Hogg granted a two week reprieve to review the trial evidence and the petition for commutation.

On the morning of the execution, Scott's brother visited him at his cell and said, "You are in a tight place." Scott replied, "Yes, but I will soon be free."

On the early afternoon of the execution, Scott spoke to the 5,000 witnesses from the gallows for thirty minutes, but refused to confess his crime. Scott said although many of his enemies were there to see him hang, their presence did not bother him. Scott blessed his wife, children and friends, and said he had no fear of dying as he would be with Jesus in a twinkling. Scott told the thousands of spectators that he had been educated in Smith County and studied both Greek and Latin.

While Sheriff John Regan of Cherokee County tied the hands and adjusted the cap, Scott thanked both the jailers and guards for their kindness and called them his friends. Sheriff John Smith then cut the rope dropping the only man to be legally executed in Smith County.

The *Fort Worth Gazette*, dated Sunday, April 16, 1893, provided readers with a full account of the murder committed.

Tarrant County

County Seat - Fort Worth

Solomon Bragg

Alias: Sol **Race/Gender:** Black Male **Offense:** Robbery & Murder
Offense Date: January 1872 **Execution:** May 8, 1874

Solomon Bragg was convicted of the murder of Matthew Green, a wagon freighter who was killed in January of 1872. In that year, Green was returning to Fort Worth from Parker County with a wagon and horse team when Bragg murdered him at Rock Creek, south of Fort Worth in Tarrant County. After killing Green and placing his body in a ravine, Bragg took his victim's wagon and team, which he was still in possession of when arrested.

On the scaffold, Bragg spoke from the gallows for thirty minutes. In his address to the crowd of 5,000, Bragg said he was innocent of killing Matthew Green, and that his partner Baz Moulden was the person responsible for firing the shot that killed Green. Bragg advised the young people in the crowd to remain at home and work for a living, and not to attempt to make a living as he had from gambling, horse racing and stealing. Bragg said he had been associated with several bad men, and said he had been shot five times and survived, only to be hanged. Bragg continued to say that although he was not afraid to die, and had made peace with God, that it should have been Baz Moulden who hung for murder and not him.

At the conclusion of his statement, Rev. Gough gave a brief prayer as officers adjusted the rope and hood. At 2:25 p.m. the rope, which held the trap in place, was cut with an ax. The fall did not break Bragg's neck and he strangled to death. Ten minutes later, Bragg was pronounced dead by Dr. Field, but remained suspended for thirty minutes.

Several weeks before the execution, Bragg had sold his body to a physician for $50 for medical study. The *Daily Phoenix*, (Columbus, S. C.) dated Saturday, May 30, 1874, wrote:

He confessed to a long career of crime in Texas, Arkansas, Colorado, California and Mexico, and asked all those present who had come to see his neck broken to be warned in time. A road of cheers and a "tiger" went up as the prisoner concluded, and before its echo had died away, Sol Braggs lifeless body was dangling from the end of the hangman's rope.

Isam Kapps
Name also spilled as Isham Capps

Race/Gender: Black Male **Age:** 30 **Offense:** Rape
Offense Date: February 25, 1880 **Execution:** May 7, 1880

Isam Kapps was a ten year Army calvary veteran who settled in Fort Worth after his military discharge. Although Kapps denied committing any previous rapes on white women, he was suspected of committing several in Fort Worth.

On February 25, 1880, Kapps knowing the work habits of C. C. Thornton, waited for Thornton to leave home for work. Once Thornton had left, Kapps enter the house through a window and immediately attacked Mrs. Thornton. Mrs. Thornton struggled and screamed for help while defending herself from Kapps whom she recognized. Kapps hearing another man rushing into the house to come to her aid, jumped out a window and hid. As Kapps hid outside, he heard Mrs. Thornton directing for the person to go where her husband worked and report the attack to him.

When Mrs. Thornton was alone again, Kapps reentered the house and again resumed his attack on Mrs.

Thornton. While attempting to assault his victim, Mr. Thornton ran into the room and chased after Kapps who escaped. The assault was immediately reported to Marshal S. M. Farmer and he was able to track Kapps back to his house, and afterwards located Kapps in town and placed him under arrest.

At trial, Mrs. Thornton testified about the assault and pointed to Isam Kapps as her attacker. The jury deliberated only fourteen minutes to find Kapps guilty, and assessed his punishment at death.

It was estimated that between 8,000 to 10,000 people gathered at the gallows located one mile from town to watch Tarrant County's second execution.

When Kapps stood over the trap, the father of the woman he raped had made the noose that was placed around his neck. At the close of the hymns, Kapps addressed the large crowd for ten minutes and confessed to the attempted rape, which sent a man by the name of Nathan House to the penitentiary, and a third attempted rape in which a man by the name of Ben Mosely was being held.

Kapps said, "I was a soldier in the union army for ten years, but bless God, I am now a soldier of the cross. I am another man now. I am perfectly satisfied and willing to die. O people, if you only had my feeling how happy you would be!" Kapps then bid all farewell. Moments just before the trap was strung, Kapps was heard saying, "O Jesus, I come this evening."

A reporter of the *Galveston Daily News*, interviewed Isam Kapps the day before the execution. The interview was printed in the Saturday, May 8, 1880, edition.

The reporter asked:

Reporter: Isam where were you born?
Kapps: I was born in Wayne county, North Carolina.
Reporter: How long have you been in Texas.
Kapps: I have been in this state since 1872.
Reporter: You of course were a slave.
Kapps: Yes, I belonged to Tarry Thoraton, of Wayne County, and was born his property, he being the owner of my mother at the time of my birth.
Reporter: What have you done, and where have you lived since the war?
Kapps: I have belonged to the United States Army for the past ten years, that is, up to the time of my coming to this county. I was a private in the tenth cavalry, and served in Kansas and the Indian Territory, having joined the army in Delaware. I was discharged from the army at Jacksboro while that was a post, and have my discharge at home.
Reporter: Have you a family
Kapps: I have only a wife, no children. I have been married one year and seven months, and was regularly married by a justice of the peace at Jacksboro.
Reporter: Now, Isam, it is rumored that you were forced to run away from Jacksboro for the commission or rape, or an attempted rape, at that place. Is there any truth in this rumor.
Kapps: Indeed it is not so. I was honorably discharged from the army at Jacksboro, and have my discharge at home, as I told you before.
Who told you this?
Reporter: Is it merely a rumor, Isam.
Kapps: Well, it is not so, anyways.
Reporter: Isam, you know you are to be executed tomorrow for committing the crime of rape upon the person of Mrs. Thornton. Now tell the plain, unvarnished truth about the matter.
Kapps: As God is my judge, I did not succeed in my attempt, but it was not my fault; I was just simply too drunk to commit the deed; I did try, but was unable to accomplish the act.
Reporter: Isam, you are accused of other rapes or attempted rapes. Are you guilty of them?
Kapps: This is the first place in which I ever attempted anything of the kind, and, thank God, it is the last; but I acknowledge it was I who made the attempt upon the person of the young girl who lived at Sturgeon's and it was I who was accused of attempting to rape Mr. Morris's little daughter. Now, in the Morris case I expected to find a white woman in the room instead of the little girl; and as soon as I saw it was the little girl, I left the house. This white woman formerly lived in this house, and I was intimate with her.

Reporter:	Why did you attempt these deeds.	
Kapps:	I can't tell, unless it was the whiskey I drank that caused it, anyhow I can't blame anybody or anything else except whiskey.	
Reporter:	Are you prepared to die.	
Kapps:	Yes; the preachers have been to see me, and prayed with me, and I feel that I have been fo given. I pray all the time, and one of the men reads the bible to me every day.	
Reporter:	Have you any feeling towards anybody in this matter.	
Kapps:	None at all, though I think my lawyers, if they had exerted themselves, might have got a lift time sentence, instead of the death penalty. But I have no hard feelings against anybody.	

Jim C. Garlington

Alias: Jim Darlington **Race/Gender:** White Male **Age:** 26
Offense: Robbery & Murder **Offense Date:** July 21, 1898 **Execution:** July 28, 1899

On the night of July 21, 1898, the southbound Gulf, Colorado and Santa Fe, No. 7 passenger train had just left the town of Saginaw, for Fort Worth when two masked men crawled over the coal and jumped into the engine cab with pistols drawn.

At about 10:15 p.m., the train came to an abrupt stop north of the Stockyards in Fort Worth. When the conductor got off the train with his lantern to investigate, several bullets were fired at him. Conductor Williams quickly jumped back onto the train where everyone remained for about an hour and half before getting back off.

This time, no more bullets were fired in his direction, and when checking the cab of the train, he discovered both the engineer and fireman were missing. Once the train was brought into town by another engineer, a second train was sent out to the scene to search for the two missing men. An hour and a half later, the second train returned back to town with the body of Fireman Watson Whitaker. Watson had been shot once to the chest and once below the right eye of the face. Engineer Joe Williams was found about one mile south of Saginaw. He too had been shot, but to the right leg just below the knee. Engineer Williams reported the robbers had thrown him from the cab. A few days later, Engineer Williams died from his wound.

The robbery was no surprise to lawmen or as to who was responsible. A week prior to the robbery, W. R. Petty warned the police department of the robbery plan, but the information was discounted. Petty who turned state's witness, identified the gang members who were all captured except for Charlie Ellis.

George Moore was captured in Ardmore, Indian Territory, on August 12 and received ninety-nine years in the penitentiary. Jim Garlington was captured near Corsicana on August 27, and sentenced to death. Dave W. Evans was captured on September 27, and sentenced to a four-year prison term for conspiracy to commit a robbery.

On the day of execution, Garlington dressed himself in a new black suit, black broad brimmed hat, and white gloves. Pinned to the lapel of his suit were white flowers. At 1:10 p.m. Sheriff Sterling Clark read Jim Garlington the death warrant while he sat smoking a cigar. After the reading of the warrant, Rev. A. W. McGaha of the First Baptist Church along with others sang, *It is Well with My Soul*, and *Jesus, Lover of My Soul*.

At the completion of the songs, Jim Garlington was escorted to the gallows by Sheriff Clark and jailers, only stopping along enough to shake hands. With a firm step, Garlington ascended the steps and immediately took his position over the trap door. Sheriff Clark then asked Garlington if he wished to make any statement. Garlington while facing the 200 spectators and said:

> Gentlemen, I have a desire to express to you my thanks especially for the kindness and consideration shown me since my incarceration. Also to those who signed petitions to Governor Sayers that my life might be spared till the Author of my being should call me home.
>
> As to those who secured my conviction, if they acted conscientiously and for what they believed to be for the best interest of society, and in accordance with their sworn duty, I thank them also; but if not in accordance with these motives, then I leave them to their consciences. As to the man who turned state's evidence, I have no wish to upbraid him, but will leave him to his God.

As to my case, you are all familiar with it, but there are some things that you do not know. I will say this, that I have said some things, which if it is necessary, will be revealed.

I wish to return my thanks to the officers here. Gentlemen, I will say to you that they have all tried to make it as pleasant as possible for me. Also to the attorneys, especially the one who has worked so hard for me. I wish him a successful life until we all stand together. When the mists shall roll away, and we shall all know each other better.

Rev. Mr. McGabe who has given me religious consolation too; but long before I saw him, however, I had gone to my Father and asked for forgiveness and while I stand here to pay the penalty for the crimes I have committed, I feel that I have been forgiven. And as to my family, I will say that I am the only member of my family who has been behind the bars, or stood in this place. I want to thank Sheriff Clark for the kindness to me and consideration. If Governor Sayers did this in the conscientiousness of his heart, and for the good of society as he believed it, then I thank him too; but if he did not, then I beg God to have mercy on him.

My thanks are to the people of Tarrant County—you have left it alone to the courts to consider my case and to name the penalty; you have remained in your homes —I thank you for that. You should observe the laws, for in them is the security of society. I now commit myself to Him, and say, It is Thy will, not mine, be done. I bid you farewell.

Garlington then turned to Sheriff Clark and told him goodby. The sheriff replied, "God bless you, Jim, and may He take you into His hands."

Garlington said, "Thank you, I believe he will."

Sheriff Clark was then assisted by Sheriff R. M. Patton of Greenville, ex-sheriff J. W. Moore of Wise County, Captain J. S. Luther of the State Penitentiary, and other deputies for the final preparations. After a handkerchief was used to bind over Garlington's eyes, he asked that the handkerchief be raised once more to make a final statement. Garlington then said, "Friends, I believe I'll soon be at rest. What I would like to say is this. I'd like to express my thanks to the prisoners here; and I would advise them. If they ever get out, that they should not obey the Evil Spirit anymore, but become good citizens and obey the laws."

The handkerchief was pulled back down over the eyes and the black cap over the head. The noose was then adjusted around the neck and the knot placed over the chest. The arms and knees were then bound with straps. At 1:49 p.m., Sheriff Clark released the lever with his foot, which sprang the trap door open. The fall of eight feet broke the neck and after eighteen minutes, life was declared extinct, and the body was lowered down. Once the noose was removed from around the neck, the remains were then placed in a coffin and carried downstairs to the main corridor of the jail. The jail doors were then opened to allow the public to enter and view the remains.

In thirty minutes, 1,075 people walked through the jail to view the corpse. Once the jail doors were closed to the public, the undertaker took charge of the remains so the coffin could be transported by the Houston & Texas Central Railroad to the family plot in Navarro County.

The *Houston Daily Post*, dated Saturday, July 29, 1899, provided readers with details of the crime and execution at Fort Worth, Texas.

Rufus Martin

Race/Gender: Black Male **Age:** 29 **Offense:** Robbery & Murder
Offense Date: October 28, 1903 **Weapon:** Pistol **Execution:** July 12, 1906

Charles Swackhammer was a young German cotton farmer whose farm was located west of Arlington. On October 28, 1903, Swackhammer drove his farm wagon to town to sell a bale of cotton. On his return home, Swackhammer stopped at Cobb's Store to leave fifty-five cents for Rufus Martin to pick up. Swackhammer had prearranged with Martin to pick up the money he owed him for his labor from the store on his trip home. Swackhammer was last seen alive driving his wagon away from the store with Rufus Martin riding in the bed.

At 7 p.m., the wagon team returned back to the gate of the Swackhammer farm. In the bed of the wagon was the body of Charles Swackhammer. Upon examination of the body, it was determined that Swackhammer had been shot three times. Rufus Martin being the prime suspect with robbery being the motive.

Martin was located at 1 a.m. by Fort Worth police officers and arrested. In Martin's possession was $33.45 and a Colt pistol and new holster. When the pistol was checked, the cylinder contained three empty bullet casings.

On December 19, 1903, Martin was convicted of the murder and sentenced to hang. Attorneys delayed the execution by filing appeals to the Texas Court of Criminal Appeals and next to the United States Supreme Court.

On July 12, 1906, Rufus Martin stood on the gallows and confessed that he was guilty of murder and told the crowd the following:

> I am not afraid to die, I'm glad to die, for I know that. I am going straight to Heaven and that when I reach the other side my Father will throw his arms around me and welcome me home. I'm a heap better off than most of you men down there, for I'm saved, and you all better get down on your knees and ask your almighty Father to forgive yours sins. Those of you that come here to profit by my example are all right, but you who came here just out of curiosity, are a lot worse off then me.
>
> I want to tell you that until a few days ago the devil had me. He laid his plans and got me in his tolls and that's why I'm here. I was bad, but I see where I was wrong and I know that I am all right now.
>
> In regards to the crime I am charged with, I am guilty of his blood, but now standing on the promises of God and know that my Savior has cleansed me from all unrighteousness and has wholly sanctified me. I am trusting in Jesus and although I didn't get full justice in the court of this world, I know I will get justice on the other side and that in a few minutes I shall be with my Savior. I want my example to be a lesson to all the boys in the city. Live right and keep out of the clutches of the devil.

The *Fort Worth Record*, Friday, July 13, 1906, provided their readers with a large article of the crime, execution, and past history of cases within Tarrant County.

Paul Fowler

Race/Gender: Black Male **Age:** 18 **Offense Date:** July 1, 1912
Weapon: Pistol **Execution:** August 7, 1913

Ernest Harrison

Race/Gender: Black Male **Age:** 18 **Offense Date:** July 1, 1912
Weapon: Pistol **Execution:** August 7, 1913

On July 1, 1912, both Paul Fowler and Ernest Harrison decided they would make some quick money by robbing someone. In looking for an easy victim, the two robbers saw a man whom they did not know walking alone on East Front Street and decided he would be a good target. As Robert Knetsch was walking on his way home, both Fowler and Harrison pulled their pistols, and demanded he hand over his money. Moment's later, two shots rang out. Both Fowler and Harrison shot Knetsch in the excitement and ran to Fowler's grandmother home to hide. Robert Knetsch died several hours later.

When police officers began investigating the murder, Fowler's grandmother informed them she did not believe her grandson had anything to do with the murder, but informed the detectives her grandson had arrived at her home late in the night with another man. The detectives searched for Fowler and arrested him the following day on suspicion of robbery and murder. When Fowler would not confess the crime, officers escorted his grandmother to the police department so that she could confront her grandson.

The grandmother said, "Paul Fowler, if you ever tol' de truf in your life, tell it now! It won't hurt yer bue er little while if de good Lord let's dese white folks break your neck. If yer tells de turf, I'll pray de Lord to forgive you for what yer done, if yer done it, and he may hear me dis once; but if you lies to dese white folks, dey'll fin' out erbout it some time erother, an din get yer'll neck broke an yer soul'll go ter hell."

Fowler then broke down crying and confessed everything to the officers.

The day before the execution, both men wrote a letter which they handed to the sheriff asking that it be given to Rev. L. R. Williams. The letter in read:

To Rev. L. R. Williams:
We want to say this to the younger boys and girls as advice. The crime we comitted is true, but just think why we did so. It is only on account of bad whiskey and other strong drinks, and is said to be one of the worst crime that has ever been committed in this county. But we have and still are praying for the Lord to forgive us of our sins and for myself. Paul feels as the Lord has forgave me, and Ernest says the same, and if we had done as our parents had taught us we would not be in this trouble, but we strayed away from our teachings, and boys, please stop and think what bad company and whiskey will do for you. So boys, we ask you sincerely to take this advice. We remain,

Paul Fowler and Earnest Harrison.
But Ernest did not shoot the shot that killed him, but I did and this happened on account of an accident, so God be with each and everyone of you until we meet again.

Fowler and Harrison had also asked the chief of detectives to take their individual photograph. The photographs were taken, and Fowler sent his picture to his sister, Ruby Doggott, who at the time was serving five years in prison for murder. Harrison sent his picture to Octavia Banks who was in prison for murdering her husband. Attached to the photograph, Harrison wrote, "Well, Octavia, I've got one more day for this old world, and I want you to meet me in the other."

The following day, Fowler walked to the gallows first. At 11:12, Fowler dropped through the trap door and was pronounced dead twelve minutes later by six physicians. Harrison was next led to the gallows, and he was dropped at 11:48. Both of the condemned were asked moments before the trap was sprung if they had anything to say. Fowler told the 100 witnesses said he was ready to die and had nothing further to say. Harrison thanked the officers for their kindness while he was in their custody, and said he too was ready.

The *Fort Worth Record*, dated Friday, August 8, 1913, provided readers with details of the crime, double executions and the history of the cities previous legal hangings.

Tommy Lee

Alias: Tom Lee Young **Race/Gender:** Black Male **Offense:** Murder
Offense Date: May 15, 1913 **Weapon:** Double Barrel Shotgun **Execution:** March 9, 1914

On the night of May 14, 1913, Tommy Lee entered Hiram McGar's Pool Hall located at 911 Jones Street in Fort Worth. Lee was then invited to join in a craps game with Pete Soles and Walter Moore. Lee who worked as a shoe shiner at the Congress Barbershop played the game until he lost all his money, being about $100. Broke and without any money, Lee blamed Soles and Moore for his loss, claiming both men had cheated him.

The following day at 2 p.m., Lee while armed with a breach loading, double barrel shotgun, went looking for both men to get even. Soles who was eating barbeque at a lunch stand located at 300 East Eighth Street was shot first. Lee then entered the McGar's Pool Hall where twenty men were either playing a game of pool or sitting at tables playing dominoes. Finding Moore in the crowd, Lee walked up to within eight feet of him. Lee then leveled the shotgun that had been loaded with turkey shot and fired. The shot struck Moore to the right side of the head, and he was dead within two minutes. Reloading the weapon and cocking both hammers, Lee covered the crowd with the shotgun as he backed out of the pool hall. Lee then hurried down the street while clutching the shotgun, and turned east towards Grove Street.

Policeman John A. Ogletree, a four-year veteran of the police force ran in the direction of the gunfire. Officer Ogletree who was running in the middle of street encountered Lee who was on the sidewalk at Eighth and Grove. Seeing Lee, Officer Ogletree ordered him to drop the shotgun. Lee then discharged both barrels striking Officer Ogletree in the hip, abdomen and chest and wounding two other young men at the same time. Officer Ogletree returned fire, but all four of his bullets missed. Officer Ogletree regained his balance and walked a few steps to collapse on the steps of a saloon. B. L. Pope who witnessed the shooting, ran to the fallen officer, and reloaded the pistol. Pope fired all six shots at Lee, but missed.

Police officers and civilians then chased Lee by foot and by vehicles as he ran toward the railroad yards. Lee continued toward the Rock Island Railroad Yard at Fourth Street and into a culvert under the railroad tracks. Seconds later, officers heard a muffled shot. As officers closed in, Lee was found severely wounded to the face. While Lee was running into the culvert, he slipped on the wet surface and accidentally discharged the weapon and shot himself to the lower portion of his face. When captured, Lee had two shotgun shells left. He was taken to University Hospital, and from there to the jail at Denton for safe keeping from lynch mobs.

When all the smoke cleared, Walter Moore who was an express wagon driver was dead, as well as thirty-six-year-old policeman John Ogletree. Pete Soles was wounded to the upper body. David Colton, an eighteen-year-old junk dealer received wounds to the back, chest arms and head. Lee Murdoch, was a seventeen-year-old schoolboy who was hit by several balls to the forehead, while other balls damaged his liver and right lung.

News of the shooting stirred several riots within the city, and the riots were only quelled after three companies of State National Guard assisted in regaining control of the city and restoring order. At 9 p.m. that night, a mob of 1,000 men formed at the jail demanding the sheriff release Tommy Lee to them for quick justice. At the same time, men began using a log battering ram to the back door of the jail and the sheriff warned that any man who entered would be shot. A brick was then thrown through the opening of the door and it hit Sheriff Rea to the head. Detective Tom Snow then fired a pistol shot in the air which caused those attempting to enter the jail to flee thinking they were about to be fired upon. A sixty-man state militia was afterwards dispatched to guard the jail.

Lee who was expected to die from his wounds, but survived and was able to later provide a statement. While incarcerated at the Denton County jail, Lee said, "I just don't remember shooting the policeman. I'm sorry I shot him. But that nigger Moore and Pete Soles, I just had to shoot. Them two robbed me of about $100 in a game of craps the day before and I started out to get even. I'm glad I got them."

Lee was tried for murder and sentenced to death. On the gallows. Lee bowed to the 150 witnesses who had gathered to watch the execution and said, "I am going like a game little man." When asked if he wished to make a final statement, Lee said:

> Just this, I was tried for killing Walter Moore, but I do not believe that it was for that, that jury said that I should die. I believe it was because I killed Mr. Ogletree. However, it was the Governor, the Board of Pardons and the citizens demand that I die. I will go down like a man. I would not have killed Mr. Ogletree if I had been at myself and I didn't know until I was in jail at Denton that I had killed him.

Lee, who had spent three years in the penitentiary for theft under the last name of Young, was dead in ten minutes after the trap was sprung.

The *Fort Worth Record*, dated Tuesday, March 10, 1914, provided their readers with details of the shooting and execution.

Clint Williams

Race/Gender: Black Male   **Age:** 19   **Offense Date:** December 11, 1914
Offense: Robbery/Murder   **Execution:** August 5, 1915

Oscar Scroggins, a white youth worked delivering messages on his motorcycle. Clint Williams a nineteen-year-old black male who expressed an interest in buying Scroggins' motorcycle. He told Scroggins he knew where a man named Keller, who lived seven miles from town, had buried $500 dollars. Williams proposed to Scroggins that he would split the money with him to buy the motorcycle.

Scroggins agreed and on their way out of town, Scroggins stopped at the gas station at Fifth and Commerce streets and told his friend Charley Ward of the agreement he had with Williams. Ward remarked, "He hasn't any money."

Williams overheard this statement and said, "Wait and see. I bet he (Scroggins) don't show up in the morning."

Seven miles from town on the E. R. Keller farm was an abandoned well. When Oscar and Williams arrived at the well, Williams shot Scroggins in the back with a gun he had stolen earlier in the day. Williams afterwards dumped Scroggins' body into a well.

When Scroggins failed to show up the following day, his mother notified the police who began investigating. Police found Williams in possession of the motorcycle and the stolen pistol. Williams confessed to the murder and directed the officers to the well. An autopsy showed Scroggins was alive when he was thrown into the well.

Tried and found guilty of murder, Williams appealed to the court of appeals contending that the evidence failed to show that he is seventeen and therefore the death penalty could not be sustained. The court believed the state's evidence showed that the Williams' family bible with the birth year for Clint Williams had been altered from being nineteen at the time of the murder to seventeen. The court affirmed the lower court decisions.

The night before the execution, Williams wrote the following unedited letter to his mother:

Dear Mother, I am still well. Hoping you don't know how I love you but we will meet again. I will no you and you will no me. So you must try and not to weary about me. I am so glad we will meet again and you no me and I no you. If I pray we will meet again. If we don't pray we won't so we must pray. So we will meet again. God will take care of you and me some day. This what we all get what don't mind their mothers. If had mind my mother I would not bin here today. All boys do not think before it is too late. Tell the boys what I am in by running around with bad boys. Mamma I want you to tell Miss May howdy for me and tell her I am praying night and day. Tell her I am praying to God to help her some day till we all meet again. Momma you done your best for me and no it. I no you love me and I love you. When I pray, I pray for you and my friends, God said come and go with him. He will give you best. Just think of that when you weary. I will close. From your dear son, Clint Williams. Be good, mamma till we meet again. Good by I am getting sleepy now.

The next morning, Chief Detective Blanton and Deputy Sheriff Fitch met Williams at his cell and escorted him to the gallows. With a cigar in his mouth, Williams told the Detective Blanton, "Take me right out after I am hanged, so if I'm not dead I can get loose." From the gallows, Williams addressed the witnesses and said, "Gentlemen, I thank you for what you have done for me. I am sorry for what I have done. I got into bad company, I have tried to make my peace with God.

Mrs. C. P. Lance, the mother of Scroggins approached and stood directly in front of the gallows and remained fixated on Williams up until the body was lowered and noose removed. Mrs. Lance afterwards stated, "The law has taken its course and the Negro was dealt with as he deserved. I am satisfied with the way the courts handled him."

The *Fort Worth Star-Telegram*, Dated August 5, 1915, provided their readers with a lengthy article of the crime and execution.

Charles A. Myers

Race/Gender: White Male **Age:** 60 **Offense:** Murder
Offense Date: January 20, 1915 **Weapon:** Firearm **Execution:** November 10, 1915

Charles Myers worked for the Texas & Pacific and International & Great Northern Railroad as a switchman. Myers later was fired from his job and blamed his termination and refusal for his reinstatement on Superintendent A. W. Montague.

Myers brood over his termination and believed Montague had blacklisted him from gaining employment with various railroads across the country. Without warning, on January 20, 1915, Myers shot and killed Montague as he walked onto the passenger platform of Union Depot.

Myers was quickly arrested and placed in the Fort Worth jail. When jail deputies learned that armed men were on their way to lynch Myers, the deputies quickly removed Myers and transported him to the jail in Dallas. A lynch mob did arrive and demanded that Myers be released to them. When the mob was told Myers was no longer an inmate in the jail, the mob was not convinced and entered. After thoroughly searching the jail to their satisfaction, the mob disbanded and left peacefully.

Twenty-four hours later, Myers was indicted by the grand jury and the case went to trial nine days later. The jury deliberated four and half hours before returning a verdict of guilty. The case was appealed to the Court of Criminal Appeals and affirmed on June 16.

After the verdict had been affirmed, Myers was taken before Judge James Swayne and when asked if he had anything to say before sentence was announced. Myers said, "I don't think I have had a fair trial. I feel, as though I had been railroaded, although, I have no complaint to make in regards to the lawyers who represented me. It was simply a case of capital versus poverty. I think I was more justified in killing Montague than the state of Texas is in hanging me. If I didn't think I was right, I wouldn't have done it."

Addressing the judge directly, Myers said, "You had that jury keyed up as a result of the way you roasted the jury in the Hays case to where they felt as through they had to give me the extreme penalty or they were like to get roasted too. If they hadn't been a bunch of muttheads, they wouldn't have done it, anyway."

Judge Swaney responded back, "I have nothing to say in regard to that. I feel that I have done my duty and my conscience is clear." The death sentenced was then pronounced.

The execution was delayed as attorneys filed for an insanity trial. The jury heard the arguments and declared Myers sane. Attorneys next petitioned the Court of Criminal Appeals. The higher court affirmed the decision and reset the date of execution for November 10.

Sheriff N. C. Mann after learning the governor had no intentions to interfere, requested to borrow the rope to be used for the execution from the Grayson County sheriff. When the rope arrived, the sheriff stretched the rope by using heavy sand bags.

At 11:30 a.m., Sheriff Mann walked to the gallows and stood on the platform as the priest led the slow march up the steps of the scaffold while chanting, "Have mercy on us, O Lord, Have mercy on us O' Lord."

Sheriff Mann asked Myers if he had anything to say. Myers replied yes and said:

"Speaking for the house, I wish to state that I thank all my friends and also my attorney. They have done everything they could or me they could do. I think that when I killed Montague I was justified in doing it and I still think so on this gallows. Now, any of my enemies that are sore at me, raise their hands. Can I see a hand? Furthermore, I wish to state that I will forgive all my enemies for what they have done, thanking the Lord for that. Is Mr. Power here? Is Mr. Nelson here? Is Walter Malone here?"

Mr. Power pushed his way to the scaffold. Myers told Mr. Powers, "I want to thank you people very kindly for what you have done for me and all my friends. I did get sore on my enemies, but will forgive my enemies for what I've done got in my hand here. I am going to forgive my enemies, every one of them, and am going to death with that in my hand."

Holding out a crucifix, Myers said, "There's all there is, Nace. Put it on me. Let me go through."

An officer started to pull the black cap over his face when Myers said, "Wait, Nace, before springing it, I want to make another talk . . . Gentlemen, I don't know how many enemies I have in this audience, but I wish to state before I go that if I have any friends I hope they will have better luck than I've had. I wish you all well, everybody, and my enemies I will do the same the other way. That's all."

Raising his hand to his lips, he kissed the crucifix. Sheriff Mann turned and while placing his foot on the trigger which would release the trap asked, "Ready, Mr. Myers."

The response was "Ready, let it go."

At 11:43, Sheriff Mann did just that. Myers fell through the trap and the weight of the 200-pound man along with the length of the drop caused for the rope to sever the head from the body. The next day the undertaker buried the remains of C. A. Myers at Mount Olivet Cemetery in Fort Worth. Not a single mourner was present.

The *Fort Worth Star-Telegram*, dated November 10, 1915, provided an article for readers of the crime and execution.

Rufus Coates

Race/Gender: White Male **Age:** 20 **Offense:** Murder
Offense Date: June 3, 1917 **Weapon:** Knife & Wood Club **Execution:** November 8, 1918

On the night of June 2, 1917, Rufus Coates went to the home of Zella Faulk. Coates asked his nineteen-year-old girlfriend to take a walk with him. Coates was said to be extremely jealous of Zella, and had asked for her hand in marriage, which she rejected. As they both walked though the woods, and into an old lamb pasture west of Oakwood Cemetery, Zella and Coates argued again over her rejection. Coates became enraged, picked up a tree limb, and struck Zella over the head. Believing he had killed her, Coates ran to a friend's house by the name of Clyde Tucker.

Coates told his friend, "Well I have done it. I have killed Zella." After Coates told Tucker what he had done, Coates led Tucker back to the scene to see the body. Upon returning, Coates discovered that Zella was not dead, but still breathing. Seeing that Zella was still alive, Tucker gave Coates his pocket knife and told him it would be best to finish her off. Coates then lifted her head back, and cut Zella's throat. The next morning, Coates and Tucker fled to Oklahoma City, and then to Portland, Oregon, where they were apprehended on July 10. Upon their arrest, Coates confessed that he alone cut Zella's throat.

On July 23, 1917, Coates and Tucker were extradited back to Texas. Coates then agreed to return back to the murder scene where he then rehearsed the killing for detectives. On August 11, Coates was found guilty of murder, and the jury assessed the death penalty. While the case was being appealed to the higher court, Coates entered the cell where Clyde Tucker was asleep, and slashed his throat with a knife used to cut potatoes in the jail's kitchen. Coates denied the attack, but Tucker reported that Coates was upset over the written statement Tucker had provided to detectives, and because Tucker had not yet been indicted for murder. On April 24, 1918, the Court of Criminal Appeals affirmed the lower courts decision, and Coates was scheduled to hang on July 5. The execution however was delayed by two respites from Governor William Hobby.

On the day of the execution, 1,500 people stood outside the jail in the rain to wait to see Coates coffin being removed. As Coates stood on the gallows, he joined in the singing of, *There is a Fountain Filed with Blood*. After the noose had been adjusted, Coates asked Sheriff N. C. Mann to come to his side and said, "Remember, there are no bad feelings. I'll meet you in the other side, there are some in Heaven I don't want to meet."

Moments before the sheriff pulled the lever to release the trap, Coates said out loud to the 200 witnesses present, "Goodby, everybody."

Rufus Coates is buried at Ash Creek Cemetery in Azle. Charges of murder against Clyde Tucker were later dismissed, but he continued to have several run-ins with the law for various theft and forgery charges.

The *Fort Worth Record*, dated Saturday, November 9, 1918, provided their readers with a large article of the murder, capture, trial and execution.

Taylor County
County Seat - Abilene

William H. Frizzell

Race/Gender: White Male **Age:** 27 **Offense:** Murder
Offense Date: January 24, 1891 **Weapon:** .38 caliber Pistol **Execution:** November 20, 1891

William Frizzell was tried and executed for the murder of his wife, Annie Frizzell. Frizzell had been divorced from his wife for several months, when on a January morning near Comanche, he went to his wife's tent where she made a living doing washing and sewing in the railroad camp. Frizzell asked Annie if they could reconcile and reunite with each other. Annie informed Frizzell she had no interest in doing so and was doing fine making her own living.

With her response, Frizzell replied, "If you won't live with me, you shan't live at all," and shot Annie with a .38 caliber pistol. Annie fled from the tent while being chased by Frizzell who shot her twice more in the back. After falling to her knees and raising her arms, Annie struggled to get back on her feet and said, "Mr. Frizzell for God's sake, do not shoot me anymore, for you have already killed me now."

Frizzell then shot Annie a fourth time with his last bullet. When the pistol was empty he said, "God damn you, I wish I had some more balls to put into you."

Since the shooting took place in the camp, the murder was witnessed by several workers who grabbed Frizzell and held him until the sheriff could be summoned. Annie was carried back into her tent and she died ten minutes later.

At the hearing, a request for a change of venue was granted, and the trial was moved to Abilene in Taylor County. On September 17, 1891, Frizzell was tried and found guilty of murder and sentenced to hang. Frizzell then petitioned Governor Jim Hogg asking for a thirty-day respite so that he could finish the novel he was writing detailing the history of his life. The Governor wrote back denying the request citing his reason for the respite was not a good enough reason, and that books of that character would cause more harm than good.

On the afternoon of the day of the execution, the death warrant was read to Frizzell by the sheriff. From the gallows Frizzell warned the 1,500 spectators to beware of his fate and to change their course of life. He said that he was going straight to Heaven and that he wanted all to meet him there, and that he was dying just as Jesus Christ. He wanted all to think of him as a brave man who died a brave death. He took occasion to tell all the newspapermen that he exacted one promise of them, and that they tell nothing but the truth.

Frizzell afterwards produced a small knife from his pocket that he said had been given to him by his wife. He requested that the knife be not taken from him or his pocket, or anything else that his pockets might contain, as he wanted everything to go to the grave with him. The noose was adjusted around his neck and his arms and feet were tied. The black cap was put over his head and he then requested that the hymn, *There's Never a Day to Sunny* to be sang. When the hymn was finished Frizzell said, "that's all," and the lever to the trap was pulled.

Prior to the execution, Frizzell sold his body to the local undertaker for the purpose of experimenting with the embalming process. The undertaker intended to place the body in an open receiving vault at the cemetery for advertising purposes.

The *Abilene Daily Reporter* wrote that William Frizzell, "Died with a cigar in his mouth, and Heaven in his eyes."

A reporter from the *Fort Worth Gazette*, interviewed Frizzell and the conversation was included in the Saturday, November 21, 1891 edition:

My name is William H. Frizzell. I was born at Leavenworth, Kansas., on January 29, 1864, and am now twenty-seven years of age.

I came to Texas the first time in 1869, but only remained until 1871 when I returned to Kansas, and afterwards returned to Texas in 1872 or 1873. I was married at Granbury, Tex., on February 9, 1890, to Miss Annie Brown, a daughter of Mrs. Mary Brown, a widow, by Rev. Mr. Hunt, a Baptist minister of Granbury. My wife was twenty-four years old when we were married and she was born in Missouri.

We lived together six or seven months, and a part of that time I might say happily, all of which time we lived in Hood county. I am a stone mason by trade, and I made a good living and I kept my family well supplied at all times. My mother-in-law and my wife's sister lived with me.

Men coming around my house first brought on my family troubles, as I thought that they were coming to see my wife. I at last separated from my wife on that account.

When the men first started to come around my house I tried to reason with my wife and get the thing stopped. I offered to do anything that I could, but when I saw that I could not cause the thing to be stopped, I left her and her people.

My sister-in-law was sixteen years old and lived with me. When I left I went to Dallas county, which was in September 1890, and I remained there for three or four months, when I returned to Hood county. My wife was still there, and I lived with her when I went back. My wife and her mother's family left Hood county about the last of December, 1890, and went from there to Comanche, Tex. I afterwards went to Comanche in January following. I had only been there one night, when I went to seem my wife the next morning. My object in going around to see her was to get her to make up and still live with me. When I called for her she and her mother's family were all together in the tent in which they were living near the depot in Comanche. When I saw her I told her that I wanted to talk to her and speak a few words with her. She replied that she had no talk for me. I then tried to reason the thing with her, and I told her that I had come down there to try and make up with her, which If I could not do I would have to quit for good. She then said that she had to go up in town on business. When I first went to the tent the old lady was the first one to speak after I had stated my business, saying:

"Mr. Frizzell, we have no use for you down here at all." I then asked her why not. My wife then started for town, coming towards me as she came out of the tent. She said she wanted to know how I expected to help myself if she would not live with me. She also said that she had heard that I had talked around about her. She then refused to talk with me and turned around and I then shot her with a Smith & Wesson 38-caliber revolver which I had owned for some time. I have carried a pistol all of my life, ever since I was able to carry one, and my father has whipped me several times for it. I had no intention of using it when I went down to the tent where they were living. I do not know for my life why I did use it after I did get there. I had never in all my life attempted to use a pistol on any one else before. I never was in nor before a court of any kind before in my life.

The Rev. J. C. Wingo, pastor of the First Baptist church of Abilene, is my spiritual adviser, I was raised in and brought up in the Baptist church. My father is now a Baptist minister and is pastor of a church near Glen Rose, Somervell county. He is seventy-one years old. I have five brothers and two sisters living. I am the youngest child. My brothers are farmers and are in very poor circumstances. Father is just able to make his living and that is all. When I first met my deceased wife and her family they were supposed to be making their living by taking in washing. This was in Hood county. At Comanche they claimed the same thing. My mother-in-law is fifty years old. I only knew my wife three weeks before we were married.

My mother died when I was only six years old. I have no fears as to my spiritual condition and am perfectly ready to die and I am glad to know the day and I am ready for it."

The same newspaper referred to the execution as being a "Master Peace."

Titus County
County Seat - Mount Pleasant

James C. Rowland

Race/Gender: White Male **Alias:** Sam Rowland **Age:** 26
Offense: Robbery & Murder **Offense Date:** October 10, 1871 **Weapon:** Pistol & Knife
Execution Date: May 3, 1872

In 1871, two German peddlers named Casper Abram and Cohn traveled together from town to town and door to door selling their wares. In October of 1871, the peddlers arrived at Mount Pleasant and met James Rowland who offered to board the peddlers for the night at an agreed price. When the weary salesmen paid Rowland, he had the opportunity to see that they were carrying a large roll of money. Rowland afterwards informed Jesse Reed of the salesmen staying at his home and suggested they rob the men for their money when they left.

On October 10, 1871, the two salesmen were sitting along the road resting when Rowland and Reed robbed them. During the robbery Cohn was killed and Casper Abram was left for dead after he had been shot and stabbed. Abram survived his wounds and testified at the trial.

The sheriff investigating the murder soon learned of a woman who had been washing clothes in the creek when the murder occurred. The woman said she recognized James Rowland as one of the two men. On October 20, 1871, Rowland was arrested and indicted for murder in the first degree. Reed was also indicted, but was never apprehended. At trial, the jury deliberated for five minutes and returned a verdict of guilty and assessed the death penalty.

On May 3, 1872, James C. Rowland became the only man ever legally hanged in Titus County and is buried in the Nevills Chapel Cemetery at Mount Pleasant.

Travis County
County Seat - Austin

Note: A slave name Lount was hanged on July 25, 1862, for robbery and murder. Information on the crime and execution is not currently available.

Tom Anderson

Race/Gender: Black Male **Offense:** Murder & Robbery **Execution:** 1863

The *Austin Daily Statesman* dated January 13, 1894, reported that the first person legally executed in Travis County was a black man by the name of Tom Anderson. Anderson was executed for the murder and robbery of an old German man who lived near the arsenal block not far from Waller Creek.

Meredith Haynes

Also spelled: Meredeth De Haynes **Race/Gender:** Black Male **Age:** 27
Offense: Murder **Offense Date:** September 14, 1871 **Execution:** December 15, 1871

Meredith Haynes was convicted on October 25, 1871, for the murder of John G. Billingsly and sentenced to hang for the murder.

Mary J. Haynes, the wife of Meredith Haynes, was also tried and convicted as a party to the murder. The jury assessed her punishment at seven years imprisonment.

The *Houston Union* dated Wednesday, December 20, 1871, wrote that a large crowd had been present at Austin, Texas to witness the execution.

George W. Barnes

Race/Gender: White Male **Age:** 24 **Offense:** Robbery & Murder
Offense Date: July 22, 1871 **Weapon:** Pistol **Execution:** April 14, 1873

Lawson Kimball

Race/Gender: White Male **Age:** 29 **Offense:** Robbery & Murder
Weapon: Pistol **Offense Date:** July 22, 1871 **Execution:** April 14, 1873

Joseph Philpot who was crippled, intended to purchase horses at Austin and resell the stock in Arkansas. Philpot was traveling in a two horse wagon filled with apples that he peddled during his trip to help pay for his expenses. Somewhere in North Texas, Philpot met and employed Lawson Kimball and George Barnes for the purpose of driving the horse herd back to his home.

After arriving in Austin, Philpot drove the wagon around town for two days selling apples and returned each night to camp under a large mesquite tree on Whitis Avenue. On the night of July 22, 1871, Lawson and Barnes told Philpot they were both going to Buaas Hall on Sixth Street to watch a play, knowing that Philpot would never leave the wagon and horse unattended. Lawson and Barnes had decided to kill Philpot for the $1,200 dollars he was carrying in his traveling trunk to buy the horses with.

To set up their alibi, Barnes and Lawson were the first to arrive at the hall to purchase their tickets for the play. Once inside the men made a disturbance to get the attention of the doorman. Then when the opportunity arrived for both to leave the hall unnoticed, Barnes and Lawson returned to the camp while Philpot was sleeping under the wagon, and shot him to death.

Quickly, the men removed money from Philpot's pants, and broke the trunk open to remove the rest of

Philpot's money. Since it was not unusual for a gunshot to be fired in Austin, no one went to investigate who or where the shot had came from. It wasn't until a dog in the camp would not stop barking that two men passing by stopped to investigate. The men discovered Philpot lying on a pallet under the wagon, dead with a gunshot wound to the head. In the meantime both Lawson and Barnes had already returned to the theater where word later arrived during the performance that a man had been murdered.

During the murder investigation both Lawson and Barnes were questioned by Austin police officers who noticed discrepancies in their stories. Two days later, police officers noticed the camp had been vacated. Both Lawson and Barnes were located separately and questioned again. This time Barnes and Lawson confessed to the murder and robbery and wished to turn state's witness against each other. In October of 1871, Lawson and Barnes were tried together and were both found guilty of murder in the first degree, and the jury assessed the death penalty.

On March 7, 1873, both George Barnes and Lawson Kimball were sentenced to hang on April 14, 1873. The scaffold had been erected on a sandy beach at the banks of the Colorado River near where the railroad bridge crosses. On the day of the execution, both Lawson and Barnes were seated handcuffed on their coffins in the bed of a wagon, while flanked with armed deputies to the ride to the river.

Kimball told the officers, "you are about to hang an innocent man."

Barnes was dressed in a spotted shirt, grey trousers, and a blue jacket. Kimball dressed in a striped shirt, yellowish pants and a dark jacket did a shuffle dance to the trap door, and asked for a tobacco chew as he stood on the trap door. Both men's arms were piniored at the elbows, and the black cap drawn over their heads. Deputy Sheriff Stokes then read the death warrant as both men stood motionless over the trap.

At 12:51 the trap was sprung and both men fell eight feet to their deaths. The neck of Barnes was broken, but the rope slipped on Kimball. Kimball was then pulled back up through the trap so that the rope could be readjusted. Seven minutes later, Kimball was dropped a second time which broke his neck. Both bodies were left suspended for thirty minutes, and then lowered to be examined by Dr. Carritte. The bodies were then placed in pine coffins and transported by a wagon to the graveyard for burial.

The *Democratic Daily Statesman*, dated Tuesday, April 15, 1873, reported on the double execution.

Taylor Ake

Alias: John Williams, Bunk Ake, and Banke **Race/Gender:** Black Male **Age:** 18
Offense: Rape **Offense Date:** July 28, 1878 **Execution:** August 22, 1879

Taylor Ake was accused of raping a thirteen-year-old German girl on July 28, 1878. On that date, Louisa Lumoscus left her sister's house to travel to her mother who lived five miles from Austin at Fort Prairie. As Louisa was riding her pony, she came riding up to a black man, later identified as Taylor Ake. The man took hold of the horse bridle and told Louisa to get down from her pony, and if she attempted to run off he threatened to shoot her.

Louisa told the man, he could have her horse if that is what he wanted. The man replied he had plenty of horses at home and led the horse to a tree. As the man tied the reins to the tree, Louisa jumped off the opposite side and took off running and screaming. Ake chased after her, grabbing Louisa and threatened to beat her with a stick if she did not stop yelling. Ake then took Louisa further into the woods where she was assaulted.

In November of 1879, Ake was tried in court for criminal assault. At trial Louisa identified Taylor Ake as the person who raped her, and he was convicted and sentenced to death. Ake claimed to be innocent, but admitted to committing a previous rape. Ake had been jailed three years earlier at the Travis County jail for assaulting another young girl. Those charges were dismissed after the family moved from the area and could not be located for trial.

On the morning of August 22, 1879, Ake addressed the following letter to Mr. Joe Ake, of Georgetown, Texas.

Austin, Texas, August 22, 1879
Mr. Joe Ake

Dear friends this is my last day on this earth. I thought I would write you a short letter. I have been in prison for over a year and I have been kindly treated by the jailors and the Sheriff. It is now about 10 o'clock and at 2 pm is my time to die. I warn you when you see my brothers to advise them and try to make them do right and not come to the gallows as I have.

You tried to bring me up right and you tried to make a good man out of me, but I would not take your advice and to-day I am to pay the penalty. Tell Mun Ake goodbye for me and tell him to try and be a good man and live right and do right. I have been bad and wicked and would not take your advice.

My first offense was committed in Georgetown and after that my crimes were many, robbing, killing and stealing. You know, I suppose what I am to hang for. You must tell all of my friends good bye for me, and tell them I hope to meet them in a better land. Good bye,

Your obedient servant
Taylor Ake

At 12:45 Sheriff Dennis Corwin, a sheriff's posse and six Texas Rangers escorted Ake to the gallows that had been erected on the banks of the creek near Preesler's Brewery. After arriving at the gallows, it was discovered the death warrant had been left at the jail. While a deputy returned to the jail to retrieve the document, the crowd of 4,000 asked the following questions.

Question - How do you feel in regard to your soul, Ake do you feel as though you are prepared to die? Ake nodded his head in the affirmative.

Q - Do you feel as though you are prepared to meet your savior?

Answer - Yes

Q - Do you feel that Christ is the Son of God and that you are prepared to meet your Savior?

A – Yes.

Q - (By a woman) Do you know Millie, who used to live in the mountains? Ake's face brightened up as he said yes.

Q - (From in the crowd) Are you willing to go, Ake?

A – Yes.

Another person called to him and asked if he knew him. Bunke said he did. The same person asked him if he bore in mind what he told him yesterday. Bunke said "yes."

A person from the crowd: "Do you remember, Bunke, what you told me on Pecan Street? Is it come plumb true?

A - No.

Q – Are you willing to die.

A - Yes.

Q – Bunke, are you guilty of the charge that they want to put you to death for?

A – No, sir.

Q – Do you know who did it?

A – Yes, I do.

Q – Can't you call his name?

A – Yes.

Q – Then call his name.

A – Why?

Q – I want to know his name.

A – If you were to hear his name you would not know him. He does not live in town. It is Ed Williams, but not the Ed Williams who lives in Austin.

The deputy then returned with the death warrant and was read by Sheriff Corwin. Ake afterwards shook hands with the preachers who moved off the gallows. He then told the officers goodby, and jailor Nichols commenced to adjust the black cap, when Ake asked that the cap to be removed as he had something to say.

Ake said: "Friends and everyone else. I have but a few minutes. I hope this will be a warning to all, young and old, black and white. See what has come to me from keeping bad company. I do not propose to say the charge against me in this case is true or not, but I am willing to die. Goodbye to all. I hope, if I never meet you any more this side of Judgment, I may meet you there. Goodbye, friends, white and black.

Ake asked that Sheriff Corwin, deputies Kirk or Moore to pull the lever. When the trap was sprung, Taylor Ake stood over the trap door singing, "John Brown's Soul Goes Marching Alone."

Daily Democratic Statesman, dated Saturday, August 23, 1879, printed a full account of the execution.

Ed Nichols

Race/Gender: Black Male **Age:** 19 **Offense:** Rape
Offense Date: March 30, 1893 **Execution:** January 21, 1894

On the evening of March 30, 1893, eleven-year-old Anna Straka was walking home from her uncle's house along Cedar Creek, sixteen miles southeast of Austin. Suddenly a large black man who spoke to her in English frightened the young girl. At the time, Anna did not speak or understand the English language. The black man then beat and raped the girl.

When later found by her father, it was not known if Anna would survive. Constable James Fowler tracked the attacker from the scene to his house where Ed Nichols was apprehended. Nichols was then taken before Anna who identified him as her attacker. Nichols was then taken to the jail and his clothing was examined for blood. Officers located bloodstains on his trousers and the opening of his undershorts.

Nichols at first said the blood had came from killing rabbits. Nichols later admitted to Sheriff Emmitt White that he had been lying, and then provided a short confession of the assault. Nichols would then go back and fourth through the media declaring his guilt or make claim of innocence of the crime by stating he had never confessed his guilt to anyone. Nichols was quoted as saying, "I am guilty of my sins before God and men, I have violated precept after precept, not only repeatedly, but intentionally, willfully. I cannot hope to be cleared by forces of law, and I give the above testimony to men and full account of myself to God. God be merciful to me, a sinner."

At trial, Anna Straka took the witness stand and testified as to the assault against her. During her testimony, Anna again pointed to Ed Nichols as her attacker. The jury found Nichols guilty and assessed the death penalty.

On the day of the execution, at 3:30 p.m., Nichols was marched from the cell to the scaffold. Nichols puffed on a cigar as he was being escorted by officers Thorp and Meredith, following by Rev. L. L. Campbell and four other black preachers.

On the scaffold Rev. L. L. Campbell read a statement prepared by Nichols declaring he was innocent of the crime. The statement read:

Ed Nichols sentenced to hang January 12, 1894 at Austin. I wish to say that I never thought of reaching this period in life. I am very thankful to the officials of the jail for the kind treatment at their hands. The few weeks respite from the hands of the governor were thankfully received. I feel grateful to the religious people for their visits and prayers. The sermons and scripture readings from Rev. L. L. Campbell of the Baptist Church here have been the means of my conversion and baptism. Sheriff White has been very accommodating to me indeed. I feel prepared to meet death. My soul is at peace with all mankind. Even those who testified against me have found favor in my sight. I am informed that rumors are out that I confessed the crime alleged. This is untrue. I have never confessed to anyone. If anyone has thought so they are mistaken. Many have talked with me about this matter, but I have never said I was guilty. My last words to you are that I am not guilty of the crime for which I am about to hang. God is my secret judge and ye are my witnesses. Farewell. Meet me in the better land where the father himself will execute and mete out justice to all.   *Ed Nichols.*

While Nichols was seated, Sheriff Emmitt White then read the death warrant. Nichols afterwards rose up from his chair, removed his hat and took his position over the trap door. While wearing black gloves, Nichols told both his spiritual advisors and the newspapermen goodbye as he shook hands with them. Officers Thorp, Meredith and Deputy Peck afterwards adjusted the noose around the neck and at the same time being bound with rope around his ankle, knees and hands.

At 3:58 p.m. Sheriff White sprang the trap and Nichols fell to his death. The fall did not break his neck and Nichols strangled to death until he was pronounced death fourteen minutes later. After the body was cut down, the body was turned over to undertakers Wood and Rosengreen who placed the body in a new walnut casket. Ed Nichols was then buried in the new potters field in the city.

The scaffold had been erected on the south side of the jail between the wall and cages. Sixty people that included the jury that sentenced Ed Nichols to death witnessed the execution.

The *Dallas Morning News*, dated Saturday, January 13, 1894, provided a full account of the crime, religious activities, and execution.

Eugene William Burt

Race/Gender: White Male **Offense:** Triple Murder
Offense Date: July 24, 1896
Weapon: Hatchet & Blunt Object **Execution:** May 27, 1898

Drawing of Eugene Burt, published in the *Houston Daily Post*, May 28, 1898.

Eugene Burt was such a habitual gambler he could not pay his debts or properly take care of his family. Because of his addiction, Burt was forging checks which he was arrested for and released from jail on bond. The sheriff further received a judgment ordering the forceful eviction for Eugene Burt, his wife Anna and their two daughters from the home where they resided, located at 207 E. 9th Street in Austin.

It is believed that on the night of July 24, 1896, Burt attempted to convince his wife to participate in some type of a fraud scheme. After she refused to participate, Burt killed her. Another theory was that Burt murdered his entire family for the life insurance policy.

Anna and the two children, Lucile, age two, and Eleanor, age four, were murdered by blows from a hatchet to their skulls. The bodies were then carried to the basement cistern and placed into the water. During the night Burt cleaned the home of any evidence, and boxed all the bloody garments, bonnets, bedding, pillows and hatchet. Burt then addressed the box under the fictitious name of A. Aimes of Austin to be delivered to J. C. Clark, Houston, Texas. Burt then boarded a train for Chicago where he was apprehended a month later, and returned back to Austin to stand trial for murder.

On November 25, Burt was tried, found guilty, and sentenced to death. The case was appealed to the Court of Criminal Appeals who affirmed the lower courts decision on December 26, 1897.

At 11 a.m. on the day of the execution, the jail doors were opened and officers allowed those persons with passes entry to view the execution. The 100 witnesses then made a mad dash up the stairs where the gallows were erected and climbed to the top of the low ceilings of the cells to have the best view. Deputy Corwin then escorted Burt from the cell to the gallows.

As Deputy Thorpe tied Burt's hands with ropes behind his back, Burt commented that the crowd was larger than he had expected. Burt's last words were, "Don't tie the rope so tight, please."

The black cap was drawn over his face at 11:18 a.m., and one minute later, Sheriff Emmitt White dropped the trap. The body fell eight feet, breaking the neck. After hanging for thirteen and a half minutes, the body was cut down and turned over to the undertaker. Burt had given specific instructions to the undertaker that he cover his body with the United States flag and permit no one to see his face, and to bury his remains in private.

On the morning of his execution Eugene Burt wrote a statement that he wished to be published only by the *Austin Daily Statesman* after his death. The *Statesman* did publish Burt's statement on May 28, 1898, which read:

Austin, Texas, May 27, 1898
To whom it May Interest:

Realizing that before noon of this day that I will be hung by the neck until I am dead, and that ere this is given to the public that I will be dead, I desire to say a very few words. A deliberate lie in the face of such a death is unpardonable either on earth, in hell or heaven. Where I go I soon shall know.

But now and forever I solemnly swear that my own hand did not kill my darling wife and sweet little Lucile and Elenor. I swear that I did no know that they were to be murdered. I swear that I was not an accessory or in any way connected with their murder. But I also solemnly swear that I knew before I left Austin who was guilty. And further, that in my rage no other idea save that of retribution ever possessed me.

Again, my firm belief is that ere another dies, who is now unknown to me, will acknowledge that he was the schemer and originated this plan of revenge on me, knowing that I would be accused, rather than taking my own life as satisfaction to him.

I solemnly swear that he who slew my loved ones is now dead and has been for many, many months, and that I was his slayer, and with my own eyes saw vengeance so full and complete, and that every bone and ligature of his carcass was absolutely destroyed.

Again, that no thought of allowing lawful justice was ever for a moment considered by me. And my desire for vengeance, the human fiend he made of me has never for a second regretted my action. I am glad of it. And in my haste and rage I destroyed everything that would have been of assistance to me in establishing my innocence, I have not a single regret. I never waver for a moment when my mind is made up.

I am unrelenting in the pursuance of any object and never let up until I finished. When I do a thing I considered every phase of the case and if called to account for my actions I am prepared to accept the situation with as little complaining as possible, face the new foe and have my banner of "satisfaction" unfurled to the breeze until it and I sink into everlasting oblivion.

This is all I have to say. One by one as you journey past the valley of death you will find that in this sworn death statement, that I have not lied.

Respectfully, W. E. Burt

Additional – Rumors have come to me hearing questioning the feasibility of some one else having written or composed the article that I was pleased to have published on last Sunday. I will say that no living human being ever knew one word or idea advanced which was contained in that article but myself. I requested the paper of Mr. Hughes of Friday morning and wrote said article Friday evening and night. Also sent word to the reported of my desire to see him and I delivered the manuscript to Asher Smoot on Sunday evening at 3:30. I never required assistance. If I cannot accomplish anything it must go undone. W. E. Burt.

P. S. – It is come to my knowledge that some parties were endeavoring to obtain facts of my life in order to write a history or novel. I sincerely trust not. I object, and, if possible after death, I would much multiply troubles and administer severe penalties on him who should attempt such a despicable thing, and would call fires upon him who buys.

W.E.B.

The *Houston Daily Post*, dated Saturday, May 28, 1898, provided readers with a large article detailing the murders, trial and execution.

Sam Watrous

Race/Gender: Black Male **Age:** 30 **Offense:** Rape, Robbery & Murder
Offense Date: June 2, 1899 **Weapon:** Shotgun, Pistol, Knife, & Rock **Execution:** October 27, 1899

Jim Davidson

Race/Gender: Black Male **Age:** 30 **Offense:** Rape, Robbery & Murder
Offense Date: June 2, 1899 **Weapon:** Shotgun, Pistol, Knife, & Rock **Execution:** November 24, 1899

On the evening of June 2, 1899, at about 8 p.m., a Swedish farmer by the name of George W. Engberg was preparing for bed when he was called to the door by a farm hand he employed. Upon opening the door, Engberg was shot in the head from a shotgun loaded with 00 buckshot. His wife, Emma, was also shot in the head by a second assassin from outside the open bedroom window. Both murderers entered the home, and both George and Emma made a desperate fight for their lives. The Engbergs were killed after their necks were cut with knives.

George Engberg was considered a wealthy farmer who lived two miles from Manor. Robbery was the motive behind the murders, as it was believed that both money and valuables were kept in the farmhouse. Rewards were offered by the local citizens and Governor Joseph Sayers totaling $1,200 for the arrest and capture of the murderers.

A month after the murders, Sheriff Emmitt White began putting the murder case together after Sam Watrous approached the sheriff and gave him a gold ring. Watrous told the sheriff he had obtained the ring from two boys, and he believed the ring belonged to the Engbergs. On July 7, Davidson was arrested at Manor on a charge of gambling. A week later, Davidson confessed to the sheriff that he and Watrous raped Mrs. Engberg and killed the couple. When tried, the jury deliberated ten minutes before returning a verdict of guilty and assessed the death penalty.

On the gallows, Watrous told the witnesses he was ready to go and that he had nothing to dread as he was going straight to heaven. Watrous afterwards thanked the officers and said he had been treated well by the jailers. At 11:15 a.m. the trap was sprung and physicians Wooten and Harper pronounced Watrous dead.

One month later, Davison stood on the same gallows and told the 100 witnesses, "I am before you today, only for a short while; I have to leave you soon. I am guilty of the crime I am accused of. I took part in it. It was a mighty horrible crime; but I am guilty. I hope the Lord has forgiven me; I believe He has and I will go to heaven. I stand here and say I took part in it, but I was led into it. Now my turn has come, God be with you all."

Davidson turned to Sheriff White and said he was ready, then kicked off his jail slippers to stand over the trap door in his socks. Davidson's ankles, knees, arms and wrists were then tied together with ropes. When the trap was sprung, the fall of seven feet and eight inches broke the neck. After thirteen minutes of being suspended, Davidson was pronounced dead and turned over to the undertaker.

The *San Antonio Daily Light* and *Fort Worth Morning Register* gave a full account of both the crime and executions.

Henry Simmons

Alias: Henry Williams
Offense: Rape & Murder
Executed: May 2, 1904
Race/Gender: Black Male
Offense Date: April 21, 1904
Age: 27
Weapon: Razor Blade

Henry Simmons was hanged for the rape and murder of eighteen-year-old Lula Sandberg which he committed on April 21, 1904. The murder occurred at the Walbarger Creek Bridge on the New Sweden Road, about a half-mile from the town of Manor, and thirteen miles east of Austin.

Lula was driving alone in a buggy near Wilbarger Creek Bridge at about 4 p.m. when she was stopped by Simmons who struck her over the head with a heavy walking cane. Simmons then beat the young girl with his fist and used a sash cord around her neck to prevent her from crying for help. The girl was then dragged out of the buggy and into the brush, about fifty yards where she was assaulted.

When Simmons heard the horse of Gustav Fritts, a cousin of Sandberg, being driven down the road, he became frightened, drew a razor and cut the girl's throat, and ran into the woods. In his haste, he left his coat behind and a leather case containing razors and a hair clipper. Simmons trade was that of a barber.

Sandberg's horse and buggy had been left in the road and when Fritts drove up, he recognized them as his cousin's. Seeing that the barbed wire fence had been torn down he became suspicious that something was wrong and told this to Eric Sandahl who drove up in a wagon. The two followed the drag marks in the ground and discovered the body. In the buggy, Simmons' broken wooden walking cane was found and identified as belonging to him.

Police who had been searching for Simmons were alerted four days later of a strange man hiding in a stable loft at 710 Colorado Street, being about a half a block from the police station. The police went to investigate and found their man who had been sleeping there and attempted to arrest him. Simmons tried to escape, but he ran in the direction of another officer who used the butt of a pistol to hit Simmons over the head and captured him.

On April 27, 1904, while in jail, and before a jury had been selected, Simmons had announced he wished to waive all rights, and be executed immediately. Simmons told an officer he'd rather be hanged, than to be burned at the stake. Simmons further confessed to three other murders, one which he said was a white ferryman in the Indian Territory. Simmons also became the prime suspect of a rape and murder of a New Braunfels woman who had also been killed with the use of a razor blade. Simmons never admitted or denied that murder.

On April 29, 1904, Governor Samuel Lanham dispatched three companies of state militia consisting of 500 guardsmen to escort Simmons from the Austin jail to the courthouse. A second detachment of twenty-five guardsmen with two Gatling guns was stationed within one block of the jail. Inside the courthouse were an additional 150 sheriff deputies. Simmons pled guilty to the charges read to him in court, and within three minutes, the jury returned a verdict of guilty and assessed the death penalty.

Simmons' attorney, Bouldin Rector, advised the court that Simmons was inclined to waive his thirty-day appeal, provided that Simmons would be given a few days to be baptized, visit with his wife, relatives, and make peace with God. The judge replied Simmons would be given that opportunity, and was returned back to his cell. Simmons then told a deputy, "I murdered and outraged that girl and for my crime ought to die and go to hell; I waived my rights under the law and want to be hung at once."

The deputy reported the statement to the court, and Simmons was returned back before the judge. Simmons told the court, he wished to be hung in three days. The court honored the request and ordered the execution to take place on Monday, May 2, 1904.

On the day of the execution while Simmons was ascending the scaffold, he told a *Times Herald* reporter, "I have no statement to make, I am glad and I am ready to die." Being pressed further to make a statement by the reporter to describe how he murdered the girl or if he committed rape, Williams refused to answer the questions, only stating that he was going to meet his Jesus and if his own mother were to rise from the dead and asked for him to make a statement, he would refuse her as well. Williams said that the white people are the black man's friend and advised all black people to live as good citizens and not bring disgrace on themselves as he has done. He also asked the white people not to be hard on his race on account of his crime, which he would now give his life in satisfaction of.

His arms and legs were then bound and as the black cap was being pulled over his head, Simmons said, "I have no grudge against anyone, and I am ready to die. Farewell to you all!" As Williams said, "goodbye" for the tenth time, Sheriff Matthews sprang the trap.

The ropes used to tie Simmons' hands and feet were then cut into pieces and thrown out to the crowd as souvenirs and they then pinned the pieces of hemp to their coat lapels and proudly walked the town streets showing them off.

The body was placed in a coffin and turned over to an undertaker for burial at Bethany Cemetery at the county's expense. Prior to the execution, Simmons left a letter with Rev. L. L. Campbell, pastor of the Third Baptist Church asking that the letter be published after his death. It was written on two sheets of Sheriff Matthews' letterhead. On the back of one sheet Simmons had drawn a coffin and a picture of himself in his cell. Under the drawing he had written, "I am here for only a few days, then I will be dead and gone to the world unknown where my life will be forgotten."

The letter dated April 27, read:

> *Henry Williams was born December 26, 1877, and has lived until 1904. Well, I thank the Lord that I have been here this long. I have had a hard time in this world, but now the time is all over with me. I have had plenty of friends, but I have lost all of them. Ever since I lost my dear mother I have been going crazy; lost my best friend.*
>
> *My dear people, I don't know what got in my mind to make me do this crime, but I can't help it now; if I*

could I would. I don't want nobody else to do as I have. It is a sin and a shame, but I do hope that the president and governor will colonize the Negro race to themselves; then this won't grow in the Negro race. That will be one great thing in this world.

Here is what I have to say. This is one of the best governors in the world, the Lord will bless him for what he had done for me. Every Negro in this world ought to love him; I do. This is the biggest trouble I was ever in in my life.

John Mallory (deputy sheriff) is one of my best friends. Bill Baylor is a good man, I have two girls in the world, one of them 4 years old, and the other 2 years old."

My first trouble was with white boys at the Robertson hill school. I did rock them every day for one season. At the Negro schoolhouse I had a fight every day. I used to set a pin on the seat for the teacher. That was plenty of fun. The teacher used to whip me for it.

I left town and went to he country and stayed on a farm one year. I cut a man all to pieces while shooting craps, I then went to Hunter's Bend. Had a fight there with John Gilbert, knocked him down with a rock. Then I came back to town and knocked an old letter carrier in the head. Then I went back to the country and cut a boy with a knife on March 7. Then I went to the Swede settlement and cut Jim Rafsed in the head and told him if he told I would kill him.

In the span of eleven days, Simmons was captured, convicted, and hanged from the day he committed the crimes.

The *Austin Statesman*, dated Tuesday, May 3, 1904, provided readers with a large article detailing the crimes, trial, Simmons' background and execution.

John Henry

Race/Gender: Black Male **Offense:** Murder **Offense Date:** September 2, 1911
Weapon: Razor Blade **Execution:** July 12, 1912

John Henry was tried and found guilty of the murder of his wife, Lula Henry. On September 2, 1911, John Henry walked up to his wife on Sixth Street in Austin, and slit her throat with a razor blade and then walked away. Henry surrendered two days later to officers and was tried for murder on November 2, 1911. Found guilty of murder, the case was appealed to the Court of Criminal Appeals who affirmed the lower court's decision on April 10, 1912. Henry's execution was then scheduled to take place on June 28, but Governor Oscar Colquitt granted a respite on June 24, until July 12.

On the day of the execution, John Henry spoke for forty minutes from the gallows and confessed to his crime. John Henry said:

If a man is in the fix as I am in and hasn't any money, his neck is gone. My dying wish is that the people shall say after I am gone, that Negro didn't have a fair trial; he was a good Negro. My mamma made me promise not to gamble, and I kept the promise; I always kept promises made to mamma. I acknowledge I did wrong, and I am sorry, but my conviction was due to false witness. There is Mr. Bright; I want to thank him for what he had done for me. He is the brightest young man I ever saw and he has worked long and untiringly for me. I'll be fooled if he is not right this minute at the telephone, sitting there, trying in some way to do something to stay this sentence. He is a deserving young man; I wish I could shake hand before I go. I've read in the paper where he is running for Count Attorney. I want all you gentlemen to vote for him. This minute, I am sure he is trying to save my neck.

As additional witnesses entered the jail, Henry said, "First of all, I hope this will be a lesson to every young man here, (waving toward the trap door). I am ready to die. I feel safe in the Lord, I feel as fine as any man here.

"The man who convicted me to drop here, (pointed at the trap door), was a false witness. If I had had a fair trial I wouldn't have been here now, gentlemen. I again declare and want it to be my dying words – a false witness convicted me to drop here.

"Goodbye, Mr. Matthews, you have been good to me, and I know you are doing your duty by dropping me here not because you think I am a bad nigger," as he shook Sheriff George Matthews' hand.

The *Austin Statesman*, dated Saturday, July 13, 1912, provided readers with details of the murder and execution.

John Henry Brock

Alias: Henry Brock **Race/Gender:** White Male **Age:** 45 **Offense:** Murder
Weapon: Pistol **Offense Date:** April 24, 1912 **Execution:** May 30, 1913

John Henry Brock, a former deputy sheriff and saloon owner in Austin, married Mary Josephine Williams in 1888. Brock fathered twelve children, and during this marriage he engaged in an extramarital affair with Mollie King for eight years. Mollie was a twenty-six-year-old woman who operated a beauty shop, and was the daughter of Constable Lern King.

For years, Mollie and Brock continued their affair, but Mollie began threatening John Brock's marriage by becoming more possessive and jealous over his time away from her.

In April of 1912, Brock was away from Austin when he telephoned Mollie asking for her to send him money so that he could return. Mollie did so, and after Brock returned to Austin, the couple had several arguments. It was then that Mollie told Brock that she had telephoned his wife. Mollie claimed to have told his wife that she had sent Brock money to return to Austin, and that he had been staying with her, and that was the reason he had not returned home. Brock told friends he feared that Mollie was going to go to his home, and that he would have to kill her.

A week prior to the murder, friends asked Brock how Mollie and his relationship was going. Brock was quoted as saying, "Mollie and I are having a hell of a time, and I'll have to get rid of that damn bitch, unless I kill her." The night before the murder, Brock was to have told Edgar East, a friend, "I'll kill that damn bitch before the sun rises."

On April 24, 1912, Brock stayed the night with Mollie King. The next morning, the couple was seen walking along an alley together in the area of town known as "Guy town," when a shot was heard. Witnesses then discovered Mollie lying dead in a yard with a bullet wound to the back of the neck. (Some accounts of her death read that she was stabbed to death). When Brock was arrested he had a cut to his face, which he claimed was caused by Mollie. Brock told the sheriff that Mollie became angry and cut his face with a knife. Brock said when he pushed Mollie off from him, his pistol accidentally discharged with the bullet striking and killing her. When the sheriff questioned Brock about the threats made towards Mollie, Brock denied making any such statements, but said if he had said such things, that it was while he was drunk, and was only joking without any intent of doing so.

John Henry Brock was tried for murder exactly one month after the death of Mollie King in the fifty-third district court. The jury heard testimony from witnesses of the threats Brock had been making toward Mollie King, saying he would have to "kill the damn bitch." The jury also learned that the bullet wound to the back of the neck contained powder burns indicating the barrel of the pistol was within a short distance of the skin. The jury did not believe Brock, and after one hour of deliberation found him guilty of murder and assessed the death penalty. The case was appealed to the Court of Criminal Appeals, and the case was affirmed.

On the morning of May 30, 1913, Brock issued a statement that read it was never his intent to kill Mollie King. At 3:30 p.m. 200 people gathered around the trap inside the Travis County jail to watch the execution. Sheriff George Matthews sprang the trap after Brock declined to make a statement.

The *Galveston Daily News*, dated Saturday, May 31, 1913, provided their readers with details of the murder and execution.

Harvey Hubert

Race/Gender: Black Male　　**Age:** 34　　**Offense:** Murder
Offense Date: October 31, 1916　　**Weapon:** Butcher Knife　　**Execution:** August 23, 1918

Harvey Hubert was twice convicted of murdering sixteen-year-old Randolph Clark on Halloween night, in 1916. Hubert allegedly stabbed Clark while the boy was trick-or-treating and Clark died an hour later. Hubert was quickly arrested and told the sheriff he had stabbed Clark because he had been annoyed earlier by a gang of Halloween frolickers who had thrown rocks at him.

Hubert was tried twice with the second trial taking place on March 2, 1917. Hubert was found guilty and the case was later affirmed by the Court of Appeals.

On August 23, 1918, Hubert mounting the scaffold, and while looking at the 100 witnesses, he recognized a white friend and told the witnesses of a quarrel he had with the man over a $20 debt. Hubert commented that he still owed the money and said, "So, you see, this is how I pay it."

The friend replied, "It's all right, Harvey, you have a receipt".

Hubert continued by telling the witnesses that he was prepared to die without fear and he bore no ill will toward anyone and had repented his sins. When the sheriff asked if he was through, Hubert replied, "Whenever you say. I just didn't want to waste a minute. I wanted to entertain the congregation as long as I was here."

Hubert then read passages from his bible and said, "I have the faith that will not shrink or quiver on the brink," (pointing to the trap). There is no sting in this for me. I will sleep with Jesus. He will receive me at the end of this rope, wherever the end of it is. Let there be no tears for me. Let's reason like men. I acknowledge to you men that I violated the laws of my God. I wish you had come oftener, Reverend. We could have talked together and we sure would have had a good time."

As the conclusion of his statement, the black cap was adjusted and Hubert could be heard saying, "Welcome death, welcome death." Once the body was pronounced dead, the remains were lowered into coffin and released to relatives for burial inBrenham.

The *Austin Statesman*, Friday, dated August 23, 1918, provided readers with details of the murder and execution.

Trinity County
County Seat - Groveton

Sam Jernigan

Race/Gender: Black Male **Offense:** Rape **Offense Date:** May 27, 1915
Execution: March 11, 1916

Sam Jernigan was tried and convicted for the rape of fourteen year-old Rosa Vondra who was working in a field alongside her father and mother about eight miles from the town of Groveton. On May 27, 1915 at about 1 p. m., Rosa left the field alone to walk the three miles home. While walking into the woods near the railroad tracks at Piney Creek, Rosa came upon a black man wearing blue overalls, black raggedy hat and carrying a bucket.

The man, later identified as Sam Jernigan, asked Rosa where she lived. Frightened, Rosa did not answer. The man told Rosa to come towards him and at that point, Rosa turned and ran in the direction of the field where her parents were working. The man chased after her, and dragged Rosa to the ground. Rosa was then pulled back into the woods and assaulted. As the man tried to muffle Rosa's screams with his hand, a man fishing on the creek shouted back in response to the screams. Jernigan fearing he was about to be caught, ran and jumped over the creek and continued running deep into the woods. Rosa than ran back to her mother in the field and reported the assault.

Witnesses reported seeing Sam Jernigan jumping off the train near the site of the attack carrying a syrup bucket to pick berries. Jernigan was arrested, but later escaped, only to be recaptured and jailed in Houston. Jernigan provided a verbal confession to a Houston police detective which was put into writing and read back to him. Jernigan then placed his mark upon the paper as being his signature that the written statement was true and correct.

On August 9, 1915, Sheriff Thornton was escorted by two companies from Company A, Third Infantry, The Houston Light Guard and First Texas Cavalry of the Texas National Guard on the train back to Groveton for trial. The soldiers after arriving pitched tents on the lawn surrounding the courthouse to provide security until after the trial.

At the trial, Rosa Vondra took the stand and while testifying of the assault, pointed out Sam Jernigan as the person who had assaulted her. The jury found Jernigan guilty of the criminal assault and assessed the punishment at death. The case was appealed to the Court of Criminal Appeals who affirmed the lower court's decision.

Sam Jernigan who had claimed he was innocent of the crime, confessed the truth to Deputy Sheriff R. F. Smith, but asked that the officer not tell the public until after his death.

The *Galveston Daily News*, dated Sunday, March 12, 1916, reported regarding the execution that occurred at Groveton, Texas.

Tyler County

County Seat - Woodville

James M. Wilson

Alias: Rhode Wilson **Race/Gender:** White Male **Offense:** Murder
Execution: June 2, 1854

James Wilson killed a slave by the name of Bill, and whom Anderson Barclay owned. Although Wilson was charged with murder in the first degree, killing a slave could be disastrous to the owner as the owner depended on his slaves for their labor in the field.

Wilson was found guilty of the murder and sentenced to death. A motion for a new trial was requested and denied. The judge further ordered that the date of execution by hanging take place on Friday, June 2, between the hours of 10 a.m. and 2 p.m. until James Wilson's body be dead.

Court minutes show the county treasurer was ordered to pay M. M. Willey $10 for the building of a coffin, H. W. Bendy $7.81 for the purchase of burial clothing, and Sheriff D. C. Enlow $30 for executing the death warrant.

Uvalde County
County Seat - Uvalde

Cruz Rodriguez

Race/Gender: Hispanic Male **Age:** 34 **Offense:** Murder
Offense Date: October 1885 **Weapon:** Winchester Rifle **Execution:** December 9, 1887

On December 9, 1887, Cruz Rodriguez became the only person legally hanged in Uvalde County. Pancho Garcia was a well respected rancher in Uvalde County and in 1885 Garcia discovered that one of his ranch hands by the name of Cruz Rodriguez had stolen several head of mules belonging to Garcia. Rodriguez had been employed for over a year and lived with his family up until the theft. After stealing the mules, Rodriguez had not been seen until October of 1885, when Rodriguez returned to the ranch and called for Garcia to come out to the gate. As Garcia's wife and daughter watched from the door, Rodriguez raised his Winchester rifle and shot Garcia to death.

A few days after the murder, a ranch hand by the name of Martin went to work early in the morning to prepare his wagon and horse team to haul lumber. After Martin had not returned home when expected, a search was initiated. Searchers located blood on the ground where Martin had been shot and followed a trail for fifteen miles where the drag marks came to an end at an old deserted well. When the search party looked in the well, they saw the mutilated body of Martin. A rope had been tide around the neck, and the body showed evidence of being dragged the distance by a horse. It was suspected Cruz Rodriguez had murdered Martin to keep him quiet as too what he knew about the stolen mules.

Cruz Rodriguez immediately crossed the Rio Grande back into Mexico to avoid arrest and prosecution of the murders. Sheriff Henry Baylor of Uvalde County convinced another Mexican man to have Rodriguez cross the Rio Brazos where he would have deputies hiding at Eagle Pass. Rodriguez did cross and upon doing so was immediately arrested and held in jail to stand trial for the murder of Pancho Garcia.

At the trial, Rodriguez admitted to be the murder, but told the jury that the court must prove his guilt first. The jury returned a verdict of guilty of murder in the first degree and assessed the death penalty. With the punishment of death assessed, Rodriguez was not tried for the murder of Martin.

On the day of the execution, Rodriguez said he had been a soldier and requested that he be executed by a firing squad. The request was denied. Rodriguez then refused the black cap and was hanged without it.

The *Galveston Daily News*, dated Saturday, December 10, 1887, printed the following short article on the execution:

HANGED AT UVALDE

Cruz Rodriguez Expiates His Crime Upon the Gallows.

Uvalde, Tex., December 9. – The drop fell at precisely three minutes past 2 o'clock, and Cruz Rodriguez fell eight feet. He died instantly, his neck being broken, and without a tremor or a word, only asking that the black cap be not put over his eyes.

Val Verde County
County Seat - Del Rio

Jose Maria Mendez

Race/Gender: Hispanic Male **Offense:** Robbery & Murder **Offense Date:** December 18, 1890
Weapon: Firearms **Execution:** December 10, 1891

On December 18, 1890, cattlemen riding to the Wilkins brothers' ranch store in Crockett County discovered the dead bodies of Frank Wilkins and his foreman, Si Walton in the store. Wilkins was found dead behind the store counter, while the body of Walton was found in the adjoining kitchen. Walton had been shot four times in the head at close range, while he sat at the kitchen table eating. The motive for the murders was robbery. From the stable, both horses and saddles were stolen. The Wilkins brothers quickly offered a $1,000 reward for the capture of the person or persons responsible for the murder of their brother and foreman.

Jose Maria Mendez was later arrested in Mexico, and extradited back to Texas to answer for the crime of murder. Tried and found guilty of murder, Jose Mendez was sentenced to hang by the neck until dead on December 10, 1891.

On the morning of the execution, Jose Mendez's fathered entered the cell to bid farewell to his son. At 11 a.m. the sheriff arrived and opened the prisoner's cell door, where Mendez stepped out to be escorted to the gallows. Once at the gallows, Mendez addressed the crowd with the following statement:

I am about to be executed for a crime of which I acknowledge I am guilty. I killed Frank Wilkins and I am sorry I did it, but he was a bad man to the Mexicans and I killed him in a heat of passion. May my death be an example to you all to not let your passions get the best of you. I am prepared and am willing to go. I am not afraid. The only regret I have is to leave my father and mother in so much trouble.

Mendez's picture was taken, but he requested that no one be allowed to have his picture other than his father, mother and the jailer, nor that his picture be printed in any newspaper. Mendez afterwards ascended the steps to the trapdoor and asked to smoke his last cigarette. When Mendez finish smoking, he stepped on the trap door and announced he was ready. After his feet and hands were tied, Mendez told all goodbye. After the noose was placed around the neck, Mendez commented how well the rope fit him. The black cap was then placed over his face which Mendez at first objected to, but finally consented. At 11:30 a.m. the trap was sprung dropping Mendez to his death, and nine minutes later the doctors pronounced him dead. Jose Mendez became the first and last person to be legally executed in Val Verde County.

El Regidor (San Antonio, Texas) dated Saturday, December 12, 1891, provide a short article on the hanging.

Van Zandt County
County Seat - Canton

Frank Wiley Dink

Race/Gender: Black Male **Offense:** Murder **Offense Date:** 1866
Weapon: Ax **Execution:** July 6, 1866

In the book, "Some History of Van Zandt County," published in the year 1919 by Wentworth Manning and Criswell Park, an article provides information on the first legal execution to have taken place in the county.

In the spring of 1866, a man by the last name of Houston lived near the town of Canton and was returning home from Wood County. Near the Sabine River, Houston decided to camp for the night. While preparing his dinner, Frank Wiley Dink appeared and Mr. Houston feed the Negro boy. The next morning, Houston's body was found in his camp, and it was determined he had been murdered in his sleep with an ax. Dink was trailed from the camp and quickly captured.

Dink was tried during the spring term of District Court and found guilty of murder of the first degree. The court ordered the sheriff to hang Dink between the hours of 10:00 a.m. and 2:00 p.m. on Friday, July 6, 1866.

D. C. White

Race/Gender: White Male **Offense:** Robbery & Murder **Offense Date:** February 20, 1877
Weapon: Double Barrel Shotgun **Execution:** February 2, 1882

A traveling peddler from Shreveport, Louisiana, by the name of George Conquest (or Cogner) made his living selling various goods out his wagon from town to town. Because of his poor health as a result of tuberculosis, Conquest hired D. C. White to drive his wagon and team. White and Conquest had reached Van Zandt County when it was decided to camp for the night. When Conquest's body was found with a shotgun wound to the back of the head, White quickly became a suspect in the murder as he was missing along with the wagon and horse team. Lawmen learned White had fled back into Louisiana, and the sheriff petitioned to the Governor for a warrant to arrest and extradite White back to Texas to stand trial.

It was believed that White was hiding at his sister's home near the town of Minden, Louisiana. Van Zandt Deputy A. D. Tanner had rode about eight miles outside of town to the fugitive's sister's home when he came across White riding a horse and he placed him under arrest. Deputy Tanner then transported his prisoner by stage to Shreveport and caught the train to Edgewood, outside of Canton.

On May 6, 1881, James S. Hogg who later became Governor of Texas prosecuted the case. At the end of the trial, a jury found White guilty of murder and assessed the death penalty. The case was appealed to the Court of Criminal Appeals who affirmed the lower courts decision.

The *Waco Daily Examiner*, dated Saturday, February 4, 1882, printed the following short article of the execution:

A Murderer Hanged at Canton — Celebrated.

Dallas, Feb 3. – The Herald's Willis Point special says: D. C. White was publicly hanged at Canton to-day for the murder of George Cogner, an Englishman of some means, on the night of February 3, 1877.

White died game, and contrary to expectations made no confession, but protested his innocence to the last. He was suspected of several murders prior to this, and in fact had been imprisoned in Louisiana for a murder, but was pardoned by Governor Warmouth.

Victoria County
County Seat - Victoria

Michael Campbell

Race/Gender: White Male **Offense:** Murder **Offense Date:** December 18, 1837
Weapon: Firearm **Execution:** April 28, 1838

Michael Campbell was a soldier who had enlisted in the Texas army on November 20, 1835, and served in an artillery unit until June 20, 1836. It is likely that Campbell fought during the battle of San Jacinto on April 21, 1836.

After his enlistment, Campbell appeared in Texanna on the Lavaca River in Jackson County with Millard M. Parkinson. On December 18, 1837, Campbell shot and killed the town blacksmith by the name of Stanford Lindsey during an argument. The case was first tried in Jackson County, but after several of the jurors were found to be under the influence of alcohol, the case was transferred to Victoria County.

On April 26, 1838, a grand jury indicted both Campbell and Parkinson for the murder of Lindsey. Two days later, the murder trial began before Judge James W. Robinson, and Campbell was found guilty of murder the same day. Judge Robinson then handed the death warrant to Sheriff Malcolm Johnson ordering that Michael Campbell be hanged by the neck until dead before sundown. Sheriff Johnson took the condemned man out to "Diamond Hill" to a large tree where he hanged Michael Campbell from a tree limb.

Millard Parkinson not wanting to take a chance of having a rope tied around his neck, worked out a plea with the prosecutor where the murder charge was reduced to manslaughter.

Will Asbeck

Race/Gender: White Male **Age:** 42 **Offense:** Murder
Offense Date: December 3, 1912 **Weapon:** Shotgun **Execution:** June 28, 1913

Will Asbeck married Susie Power, and the couple lived at the small town of Edna, northeast of Victoria where the couple raised their four children. From all witness accounts, the marriage was a happy one. It was never understood why Will Asbeck decided on the night on December 3, 1912, to murder his wife.

The Asbecks had rented out rooms to boarders. The family along with the boarders all played dominoes together, except for Will who said he had no desire to play and walked to the bedroom. From there, Will called out for someone to bring him writing paper. His daughter Mauldine got up from the table and took the paper to her father. Minutes afterwards Will called out for an envelope to be brought to him. Again Mauldine got up from her table and took the envelope to her father. After receiving the envelope, Will called for Susie to come into the bedroom. After Susie entered, she was heard screaming, "Oh, my God, come help!" This was followed by two quick blasts from a shotgun and she was shot in the right leg.

James Power was immediately notified that his sister had been shot, and he rushed to the home. There he found his sister conscious and lying on her bed. Susie told her brother she was dying and that Will had shot her. Susie explained that she saw Will with the gun, and screamed no, but Will told her it was too late. Susie Asbeck was transported to the Leuschaer Hospital at Victoria by train to have her right knee amputated. She arrived at the hospital at 10:30 p.m. and died at 4:14 a.m. the next morning. After Susie died, the nurse started to dress the body in preparation for burial when she discovered a handwritten letter in the clothing. The note written by Will Asbeck was addressed to his sister. The letter read:

My dear sister. I have come home. I did not come to see you or go to see my mother as I could not face her under the circumstances of the crime I am now about to commit. I hope that you and God Almighty will forgive me for the deed that I will commit. I am going to kill Susie and then myself, and if you ever see me any more, we will only meet in Heaven.

After his arrest, Asbeck was asked why he had killed his wife. Asbeck only replied, "God knows."

On December 17, 1912, Will Asbeck went on trial and pled not guilty. The following day at 3 p.m., the jury deliberated thirty minutes before returning with a verdict of guilty. The sentence was appealed and affirmed by the Court of Criminal Appeals.

The scaffold was built on the south side of the jail adjoining the courthouse. From the gallows, Will Asbeck thanked the Victoria officers for the kindness shown him during his incarceration, and after shaking hands with the officers said he was ready to suffer his punishment. At 1:40 p.m. the trap was sprung and seven minutes later Asbeck was pronounced dead. The remains were afterwards taken to the undertaker to prepare the body for shipment to Edna so Will Asbeck could be buried next to his wife. The rope used in the hanging had been used in nine previous executions.

The *Daily Advocate*, dated Saturday, June 28, 1913, provided readers with details of the shooting, execution and Will Asbeck's past history.

Walker County
County Seat - Huntsville

English A. Carter

Alias: L. B. Jones, and Doc Carter **Race/Gender:** White Male **Age:** 22 **Offense:** Murder
Offense Date: July 24, 1879 **Weapon:** Shotgun **Execution:** July 2, 1880

On the night of July 24, 1879, English Carter arrived at the home of W. K. Spaulding. Spaulding and his wife lived on their farm near the town of Dodge, located ten miles east of Huntsville. It was around 10 p.m., and Carter laid down his shotgun beside a tree stump at the front gate. He entered the home and visited with Spalding, his wife and her sister, Mrs. Conkling. After visiting for an hour, Carter asked Spaulding not to subpoena him as a witness to an upcoming trial because he did not wish to testify. Carter afterwards bade all good night as he was leaving.

At the door he turned and asked Spaulding if he would not mind walking him out to the gate so that he could keep his dogs away. Once at the gate, Carter told Spaulding goodnight and walked through the gate. When Spaulding turned his back to go back inside his home, Carter said, "Damn you, I've got you now." He raised the shotgun and fired the buckshot into Spaulding's back. Spaulding fell, but tried to raise back up when Carter fired a second time, and ran to his horse.

Carter was later captured in Grayson County and confessed to the slaying. He claimed a man who had a grudge against Spaulding had hired him. For his services, he was paid ten dollars, a pistol, and a horse. Carter was tried for murder and sentenced to hang.

When Carter learned the rope which he was to be executed with had been used to hang a black man, he demanded that he be executed with a new rope, which was granted.

Because Huntsville had no jail at the time, Carter was confined in the penitentiary. On the day of the execution at 1 p.m., Sheriff J. Harrison arrived at the prison with twenty armed special deputies to keep order. Carter was escorted behind the walls of the prison where the gallows had been erected. At 1:40 Sheriff Harrison read the death warrant out loud to Carter, while standing in the presence of 4,000 spectators.

After the reading Sheriff Harrison asked Carter if he had anything to say. Carter stepped forward and said:

> Gentleman and friends, standing all around here, friends of all nations, if I have any here. I have made all the confession I intend making or can make as regards my killing of W. K. Spaulding. I don't know what to say. I have said all I had to say. Furthermore I wish to speak regarding my ill-treatment since my trial by deputy sheriff J. M. Parrish, who has treated me cruelly and bad as any dog, but I have forgiven him. I am leaving this entire world with hope and trust to enter a better, thank God. I hope Mr. Parrish will lead a better, life in the future, and I hope his brothers will. I am alone in this world – no one to say 'aye' for me. Friends, I tell you bad company brought me here to-day, and you keep out of bad company. It was making association when I came to this country that I didn't have where I was raised. When I came here, I determined to lead an honest life and work hard, but bad company brought me here today. I had no showing on trial. It was not fair. I have forgiven everybody, and hope for mercy. Good by to all.

At 1:57 p.m. the black cap was adjusted and Sheriff Harrison released the trap. The drop of nine feet broke the neck, and at 2:20 the attending physicians pronounced the body of English Carter to be dead. Six minutes later the body was lowered into a coffin and transported to the prison graveyard.

Brenham Weekly Banner, dated Thursday, July 8, 1880, wrote, "The hanging gives entire satisfaction, and the people feel that the majesty of the law has been fully vindicated."

Hamp Wade

Alias: Hamp Banks
Offense Date: November 15, 1886
Race/Gender: Black Male
Weapon: Pistol & Pea
Offense: Murder
Execution: October 15, 1887

"Smutty My Darling," or just "Smutty" as he was known was said to be an ex-convict who mysteriously disappeared from his home six miles north of Huntsville.

When rumors of his murder where heard by Sheriff W. D. Adair, he placed Nelson Jones, Jones' wife, their daughter and Hamp Wade under arrest on suspicion of murder. Once jailed, Jones' wife and daughter confessed that Jones and Wade had murdered Smutty.

The women explained that Smutty and Jones had disagreements with one another, and Nelson Jones shot and slightly wounded Smutty. Hamp Wade afterwards struck Smutty with a pea and killed him. A search of the horse stalls by Sheriff Adair and District Attorney Campbell lead to the discovery of Smutty's remains.

During the examining trial, Wade confessed to the murder. The confession was used as evidence against him and lead to his conviction. At the examining trial, Wade said:

> I went to Henry Hood's on the night of the killing to see Smutty about a small amount he was owing me. Asked him for it and he told me he would get a dollar and pay me that. He had a gun at the time, and I asked him what he was doing with it. He said: "Cousin, --'s in me." I asked him what – was doing in him, and he said that every time the wounds Jones made on him at the time he shot him hurt him, that – got in him and he had Jones to kill. I asked him if he and Jones had not made friends. He said: "Yes, Cousin, but by – I laid out six months once in order to get a man. I cut a sheriff all to pieces once and they never did get me." He told me to go to Jones' house and tell him he had better be prepared; he was going to kill him that day or night. Said he wanted Jones' wife, as she was good-looking; would run off with her; could get any woman he wanted. I went down to Jones' that evening and told him what Smutty had said. "Are you going to let the man kill me?" "I said, "I will do what I can to save your life." Jones had a stick and a pea hanging up on his gallery. I asked him what he was going to do with that pea. He said he was bound to have some kind of weapon that Smutty was going to kill him. Said he had his gun, but wanted something else. I told Jones I would take the pea, and took it, carrying it to church.
>
> Smutty and I and, all left church together for Jones' house. Smutty had his gun loaded four fingers that night, but left it at Mary Seamore's. Don't know how he came to leave it. We went to Jones' house, Smutty and I stopping at the bars and the women going in. I tried to get Smutty to go in also, but he said, "Damn Jones, he wasn't going in his house." I said, "Haven't you and Jones made friends?" He said, "Go to hell cousin." I said, "don't cuss me, pet." He said, go to hell, you son of a bitch." I said, don't cuss me for _ _ _." He said, "You are a _ _ _ _." Then I struck him the pea on side of the head. Was at the time on my horse. When I struck him he fell. The blow broke the piece from the rod of iron holding it, leaving the latter in my hand, which I afterwards carried to the house and threw in the fire. After a while he was getting up, when I got off my horse and he and I got into a scramble. Smutty and I both hollered. At this time Jones came running up with his gun. Smutty saw Jones and jerked loose from me and started to run. Jones started to shoot him and I told him not to. I said let him go. Jones said, "No, no; it will not do to let that man go," and ran up and struck him over the head twice with his own gun. I asked Jones what he was going to do now. He said to stay there until he could go to the house and get his horse. We put him on the horse and carried him to the stable and buried him, Jones having selected that place that day.
>
> After we buried him I told Jones that if it came up and they put me in jail and kept me there too long, I would tell about it. Jones said not to tell anything, that it would break his neck. Jones said if it ever came up he would take all the responsibility on himself. Smutty and I were good friends. There was no stick used, only the gun and pea. Smutty was not armed. There was only two of us into it – Nelson Jones and myself.

Nelson Jones pled guilty to murder in the second degree and was given five years in prison. After Hamp Wade was convicted of murder, the case was appealed to Judge N. G. Kittrell on the basis the name of the victim was never known as anything other than "Smutty My Darling." Judge Kittrell ruled that the alleged name of the deceased is an unprecedented one and was immaterial and over ruled the motion.

On the scheduled day, Wade told the crowd of 2,000 from the gallows, "My sins have been forgiven and I am going straight to heaven." Sheriff T. A. Jones sprung the trap at 2:14 p.m.. The drop of twelve feet broke the neck, and in thirteen minutes life was pronounced extinct.

The *Fort Worth Daily Gazette*, dated Sunday, October 16, 1887, printed a full account of the murder and trial.

Alfred White

Alias: Alf **Race/Gender:** Black Male **Age:** 45-50 **Offense:** Murder
Offense Date: 1891 **Weapon:** Shotgun **Execution:** June 11, 1892

On the night of the murder, Deputy McKiblin was in a town saloon when he heard the report from a shotgun blast nearby. Stepping out from the front door, he and Dr. Watson discovered the shot had come from Rufus Bashful's house, and ran to the home. Arriving there, Bashful was found sitting in a chair while shouting, "Murder!"

Deputy McKiblin and the doctor carried Rufus to his bed so the doctor could examine him. Doctor Watson counted eleven wounds to the left side of the body and arm and told Bashful he was bound to die.

Bashful replied, "Oh, yes, doctor, they have killed me."

Deputy McKiblin asked who murdered him, and Rufus said, "Alfred White, Bob Cotton and Mr. Mason knew something about it." When asked if he saw them, Rufus replied yes, that he saw them by the fence in his yard when he was shot.

Alfred White was arrested and lodged in jail for the murder. White was tried and found guilty of murder on October 10, 1891. Attorneys quickly filed an appealed to the Court of Criminal Appeals. After review of the case, the court affirmed the decision on February 17, 1892. On March 29, 1892, Judge N. G. Kittrell sentenced Alfred White to hang on June 11, 1892.

The gallows were erected on a vacant lot just east of the depot. On the day of the execution, White who had maintained his innocence confessed to the crime and told the 8,000 witnesses he fired the fatal shot that killed Bashful.

At 2:23 p.m., Sheriff T. A. Jones pulled the lever which dropped Alfred White nine feet to his death.

The *Galveston Daily News*, dated Sunday, June 12, 1892, provided its readers with a full account of the murder and execution at Huntsville, Texas.

Alfred McDonald

Race/Gender: Black Male **Age:** 21 **Offense:** Double Murder
Offense Date: January 5, 1893 **Weapon:** Pistol **Execution:** November 17, 1893

Alfred McDonald was tried and convicted of the murder of his father and stepmother at their cabin, six miles from Huntsville. On the night of January 5, 1893, a friend of Alfred McDonald had come by the cabin so that the two of them could go into town to attend a party. McDonald told the friend to wait outside as he was going inside to ask his father if he could borrow his horse so he could ride into town. McDonald told the friend should his father tell him no, that he "would fix him."

A few minutes later, the friend heard pistol shots being fired from in the home. McDonald exited the house and said, "Some white men had come to the house and killed my father and stepmother. We should go and give the alarm."

The following day, McDonald was arrested on suspicion of committing both murders, and after his arrest, he confessed. Tried and found guilty, Judge Smither asked McDonald if he had any statement he wished to make as to why sentence should not be passed. McDonald replied that he had not received a fair trial, and that the case had not been proven against him.

On the gallows, Alfred McDonald claimed he was innocent of both murders, and had only made a confession for fear of the lynch mob. McDonald told the witnesses:

> Of the crime that I am charged with I am as innocent as the angels in heaven, still I am to hang for it. Men have told everything but the right thing about me. I was not at the house when the killing occurred. I have left a written statement which will be published. I am going to heaven and want to meet all of you there, even those who have persecuted me wrongfully. Sheriff Turner has treated me as well as a man could in my position.

At 2:54 p.m. Sheriff Turner sprung the trap that dropped McDonald nine feet to his death.

The *Shiner Gazette*, dated Thursday, November 23, 1893, provided readers with a short article of the execution that took place at Huntsville, Texas.

Rip Johnson

Race/Gender: Black Male **Age:** 19 **Offense:** Robbery & Murder
Offense Date: June, 1902 **Weapon:** Club & Pistol **Execution Date:** May 14, 1903

The only possible motive for Rip Johnson to kill his friend Mose Washington was for the pistol, watch, and the $5.85 he was carrying. In June of 1902, Both Mose Washington and Rip Johnson were walking together in the direction of Rip Johnson's home when they stopped to sit on a log along the road to rest. Johnson for no reason other than robbery, picked up a log and beat his friend until he was unconscious. Johnson afterwards removed Washington's pistol, dragged the unconscious man into a ditch, and shot Washington to make sure he was dead.

Rip Johnson was later arrested for the murder and he immediately confessed to the murder and gave the following statement:

> Me and Mose Washington were going to Huntsville from Oakhurst, and after we had walked a few miles we sat down on a log close to the road, and while Mose was sitting there, I hit him with a club on the arm, knocking him down, and I kept beating him with the club for several licks. I then dragged his body to the gully and took Moses' pistol and shot him three times. I then hid some clothes he had in a bundle and his watch and hid them in the woods near where I killed him. I went on to Phelps and bought some groceries and then went home, which is only a short distance from where Moses' body was found. I got $5.85 out of his pockets and I hid his pistol in a corner of the fence back of my house.

On the gallows, Rip Johnson declined to make a statement to the 2,000 witnesses who had gathered. His only request was that he be allowed to take off his shoes, which was permitted. After removing them, Johnson walked to the trap, dropped his hands to his side and stood motionless while his hands and feet were tied. While Sheriff W. M. Brooks adjusted the noose, Johnson whispered, "Be sure and send my things to my mother." At 2:15p.m., the trigger was pulled and Johnson was pronounced dead in eighteen minutes.

The *Galveston Daily News*, dated Friday, May 15, 1903, provided their readers with details of the murder and the execution at Huntsville, Texas.

John Wynne

Race/Gender: Black Male **Offense:** Murder **Offense Date:** October 18, 1908
Weapon: Shotgun **Execution:** June 24, 1910

John Wynne was a farmer who lived sixteen miles west of Huntsville with his wife and their eighteen-year-old son, Jim Wynne. On the night of October 18, 1908, at about 9:30 p.m., Wynne's wife had gone to bed.

While the woman was asleep, John Wynne placed a shotgun that was loaded with number four shot, up to his wife's stomach and fired the weapon. The woman lived until noon the following day, and had told the sheriff she did not know who had shot her.

Both John Wynne and his son were arrested for murder. John was tried on April 11, 1909, and found guilty of murder. The case was appealed, but affirmed on November 17, 1909.

On June 24, 1910, moments before the sheriff released the trap, John Wynne declared his innocence to the 2,000 witnesses of murdering his wife.

The *Galveston Daily News*, dated Saturday, June 25, 1910, provided their readers with a short article of the crime and execution.

Washington County
County Seat - Brenham

Henry Miller

Race/Gender: Black Male **Offense:** Murder **Offense Date:** April 1871
Execution: July 28, 1871

On June 30, 1871, Henry Miller was tried in Brenham, and found guilty by an all black jury for the murder of George De Hays. The jury further assessed Miller's punishment at death. The jury also found Andrew Robinson guilty of being an accessory to murder and sentenced him to life imprisonment. Four thousand people reportedly witnessed the execution.

On the day of the execution, Miller made the following statement from the gallows.

"The white people are hung too, sometimes, but they could read and know more than the black people, and it was not so hard for them to do right. God Bless poor old Missus, it would break her heart to see me this way."

The *Union*, (Houston), dated Monday, July 31, 1871, reported on the execution.

James Cooper

Race/Gender: Black Male **Offense:** Murder **Offense Date:** January 24, 1875
Weapon: Poison **Execution:** April 30, 1875

Griffin Williams

Race/Gender: Black Male **Offense:** Rape **Offense Date:** January 24, 1875
Execution: April 30, 1875.

James Cooper murdered an old German shoemaker and Griffin Williams raped a seven-year-old white girl who died two weeks before Williams was executed.

On the night of January 24, 1875, Cooper went to the home of a German shoemaker by the name of John Bier on the pretense of picking up his pair of boots he had left with the shoemaker for repairs. When Cooper returned, the shoemaker presented the boots along with the amount owed. Cooper who had brought with him a bottle of whiskey, laced with poison, invited the old man to take a drink. Immediately after swallowing the alcohol, Bier cried out for help, and Cooper fled. Bier lived long enough to tell a neighbor who had poisoned him.

Cooper was arrested and tried for murder. After being found guilty, he made a full confession. On March 16, 1875, Cooper was brought before Judge I. B. McFarland for sentencing who said:

> James Cooper, stand up! You have been convicted of murder in the first degree by a jury of your own choosing, and have had able counsel to defend you. The evidence shows that you deliberately took the life of a human being who thought you his friend. It now remains with me to pass the final sentence of the law upon you. What have you to say?

When Cooper replied nothing, Judge McFarland continued:

> The sentence of this court is, that you be remanded into custody of the sheriff of Washington County, and be removed from the bar of this court to the jail of said county, and there be securely kept until Friday, April 23, 1875, when, between the hours of 10 a.m. and 4 p.m., that you be taken by the sheriff of said Washington county to the place of execution, and then and there be hanged by the neck until dead, dead, dead, and may God have mercy on your soul.

Cooper with his head bowed said, "I hope so."

The *Galveston Daily News*, dated Saturday, May 1, 1875, reported both men declined to make a final statement, but simply said farewell to the 5,000 witnesses.

Lee Hughes

Race/Gender: Black Male   **Age:** 24   **Offense:** Murder
Offense Date: January 31, 1891   **Weapon:** Ax   **Execution:** October 30, 1891

Lee Hughes was hanged for the murder of his wife, Charlotte Hughes, whom he killed with an ax. On the morning of January 31, 1891, while the woman was leaning over the fireplace preparing their breakfast, Lee Hughes struck his wife with such force from the ax that she was almost decapitated.

Hughes was tried and convicted of murder in the first degree on March 21, and sentenced to death. The case was appealed to the Court of Appeals, which affirmed the lower courts decision. On September 23, 1891, Hughes was taken before Judge Beauregard Bryan for sentencing. Judge Bryan asked Hughes if he had anything to say as to why the sentence should not be passed upon him.

Hughes quickly leaped upon his chair and said, "Yes sir, I don't think it right dat I should suffer for somfin' I never done, and I didn't do it Jedge."

Judge Bryan then ordered the execution to take place on October 30, 1891, between the hours of 11 a.m. and sunset in the county jail or some other private place in Washington County.

Because the jail was too small and inadequate to have a scaffold built, Sheriff D. E. Teague announced on October 8, in the local paper that he had decided to make the execution public without the use of a privacy fence surrounding the gallows. The *Brenham Weekly Banner* gave great attention to the building of the gallows and announced the best locations for the public to view the execution. The paper wrote that the execution of Hughes was expected to bring a larger crowd to town than the approaching circus.

The gallows was built the week prior to the execution. The location being approximately one mile east of Brenham, on a empty lot south of the Central Railroad trestle. The gallows was constructed with four by four scantling, and ten feet square. The dreaded thirteen steps led to the top of the platform, which measured nine feet above ground. The cross beam stood seven feet and six inches above the platform in the center. A three-foot trap door was in the center. The door of the trap was fastened with a pair of stout hinges from underneath with a five-eights grass rope that ran through a hole with the trap door resting on the knot. The rope traveled to a wood block and tied to the opposite side of a banister. Once the condemned man was placed in position over the trap door, the executioner cut the rope that ran across the block. The cut rope then released the trap door, and the condemned would fall eight feet through the opening.

At 2:50 p.m. guards cleared the way through the sea of people for the two-horse hack, carrying Hughes so it could be driven up to the scaffold. At 3 p.m., Sheriff D. E. Teague led the way up the platform and called for Hughes to come up. Hughes then ascended the gallows with a firm step as deputies Sallus and Boyd escorted him. Sheriff Teague read the judgment, the history of the trial, conviction, and concluded with the reading of the death warrant.

At its conclusion Hughes faced toward the east and addressed the crowd, saying:

Friends I want to bid you all good-bye. Here is an innocent man going to be hanged, and I don't want any one to grieve after me. I am not afraid to die. The Lord wants all his soldiers to be brave, and I go to meet him in glory. I have been fed with the word of God, and I want to feed you all, for I want you to go and live with Jesus." Hughes then called out to a person named Thompson and said, "hanging ain't no disgrace, and while I am going to die Jesus will save the soul.

Hughes afterwards turned towards the officers, physicians, reporters, and told them goodbye while shaking their hands. His arms were then pinioned behind him, feet tied together, the black cap adjusted, the noose slipped over his head, and at 3:08 p.m. Sheriff Teague picked up the hatchet. Sheriff Teague asked Hughes if he was ready and at the reply of yes, the sharp tool cut the rope that held the trap door in place. The trap opened and Lee Hughes shot through, falling a distance of eight feet. The fall broke his neck and twenty minutes later the body was cut down and placed in a coffin.

As the execution was taking place, a Central train approached on the opposite side of the gallows. The train engineer seeing that an execution was taking place, brought the train to a stop so passengers could witness the execution.

The *Brenham Weekly Banner*, dated Thursday, November 5, 1891, provided its readers with details of the murder and execution.

Brady Rutherford

Race/Gender: Black Male **Age:** 18 **Offense:** Robbery & Murder
Offense Date: January 29, 1896 **Weapon:** Metal Gas Pipe **Execution:** May 20, 1896

John Rutherford

Race/Gender: Black Male **Age:** 30 **Offense:** Robbery & Murder
Offense Date: January 29, 1896 **Weapon:** Metal Gas Pipe **Execution:** May 20, 1896

Joseph Goodson

Alias: Joe **Race/Gender:** Black Male **Age:** 31 **Offense:** Robbery & Murder
Offense Date: January 29, 1896 **Weapon:** Metal Gas Pipe **Execution:** May 20, 1896

On the evening of January 29, 1896, Thomas B. Dwyer, Sr. failed to arrive home for dinner, which alarmed his wife. Accompanied by two men, both his wife and daughter walked to his office and entered from a side entrance off of St. Charles Street. Upon entering the office of the wealthiest man in town, they saw the safe door was opened with papers and other contents from the safe scattered on the floor. From the safe, drag marks in the dust covered floor could be seen going toward the opening of a large underground cistern.

Near the steps of the cistern, Thomas Dwyer's false teeth, and eyeglasses were found along with bloodstains. A barrel of lime and two metal window shutters was removed from the top of the cistern and Thomas Dwyer was not seen. After several attempts to snag the body with grappling hooks, Anderson Helm entered the cistern and swam to the bottom of the watery grave. Anderson located the body and he tied a rope around the body and pulled the corpse up to the surface.

A man named Ellis Prosper had arrived from Pensacola, Florida, to Texas in 1894. Sometime in September of 1895, Prosper moved to Brenham and began working for Dwyer plastering the walls of his office building. When Prosper was arrested on suspicion of murder, the watch belonging to Thomas Dwyer was found in his possession. Immediately, Prosper confessed to the murder and named his accomplices to the sheriff, and county attorney in the presence of the newspaper men.

Prosper told the Sheriff two weeks prior to the murder, Joe Goodwin came to him with the idea of killing Dwyer and "getting a roll." At 4 p.m. on the afternoon of January 29, 1896, Thomas Dwyer had left his office located at the corner of Main and St. Charles Street to go the post office. At about 5 p.m., Prosper related how Joe Goodwin, Brady Rutherford, and John Rutherford were standing near Thomas Dwyer's office and asked them what they were doing. Joe Goodwin then said, "We are going to get a roll; you wait here and see. You thought we were joking about what I was telling you, but we wasn't."

The four men then hid behind a partition between the office and an old hardware store and waited for Dwyer's return. A few minutes later, Dwyer returned and opened the safe in his office. Joe Rutherford then hit the man with a three-foot metal pipe. Dwyer was struck several more times and while holding up his left arm to deflect a blow his arm was broken.

Joe Rutherford then jammed the front door shut with a bar as John and Brady Rutherford dragged Thomas Dwyer by his feet towards the cistern. After picking up the body to be placed in the cistern, Dwyer came to and began resisting his attackers. The seventy-six-year-old man was then dropped into the sixteen-foot deep cistern. Two large iron window shutters and a barrel of lime were placed over the cistern opening to muffle his screams for help and to prevent Thomas Dwyer from escaping. The four men then returned to the safe where John Rutherford removed a pocketbook containing $800. Joe Goodwin removed $9 in change from a drawer; Brady Rutherford took $30 in silver and some paper money. Ellis Prosper obtained $8.40 in silver and Thomas's watch.

Sheriff D. E. Teague arrested all of the suspects, but fearing a mob would storm the jail and lynch the four suspects, the sheriff transported the prisoners to Kennedy where they boarded the Santa Fe southbound train to Galveston. The sheriff lodged his prisoners in the Galveston jail for safe keeping.

Ellis Prosper avoided the gallows after testifying against the other three defendants and was sentenced to imprisonment for life. At each trial, and on the gallows, each of the three defendants claimed to be innocent. The trials were held on March 23 for John Rutherford, March 24 for Brady Rutherford and lastly, March 27 for Joseph Goodson. The verdict for each defendant was guilty and the punishment assessed at death.

On the day of the triple execution, it was estimated 15,000 people were in attendance. Each of the condemned men briefly spoke to the crowd.

John Rutherford was the first person to speak and said told all he was innocent and on his way to bright glory and bid them adieu.

Joe Goodson spoke next and said he was before them all for his last speech. Goodson said he was innocent but willing to die. "When I fail, my spirit will rise in the heavenly concave and ascend to the blessed redeemer."

Brady Rutherford, the youngest of the three stepped forward and protested his innocence. He said, "Well, I am here before you, but I am going to bright glory, where I hope to meet you all. Goodbye."

At 2:10 p.m. Sheriff Teague asked the men if they were ready. When they replied they were, the sheriff released the traps.

The *Houston Daily Post*, Thursday, May 21, 1896, provided a full account of the crime and triple execution at Brenham, Texas.

Charles Kugadt

Race/Gender: White Male   **Age:** 35   **Offense:** Murder
Weapon: Unknown   **Offense Date:** October 9, 1896   **Execution Date:** October 20, 1898

Charles Kugadt was convicted of killing his elderly sister, Johanna Kugadt, for the money she had saved so that she could travel back to Germany. In 1893, Johanna had left California for Texas so she could live with Charles at his home located about three miles from the town of Washington. In August of 1896, Johanna informed her brother she had decided to return to her hometown of Bremen, Germany, by steamship. Johanna learned that the steamer *Halle* was scheduled to leave Galveston for Germany on October 14, 1898, and asked her brother to drive her to Galveston to catch the ship.

In the early morning hours of October 9, 1896, Charles loaded Johanna's travel trunk and a large wooden box containing her possessions into the bed of his wagon. The Kugadts were seen that morning traveling towards Brenham, but by 1 p.m. Charles Kugadt was seen traveling alone towards Washington with only the trunk in the bed of the wagon.

On Thursday evening of October 22, Lem Harris was hunting hogs on the Jackson Creek bottom. Near the creek and about 500 yards from the Washington and Brenham road, Harris discovered burned human remains. He also observed with the skeleton a piece of a dress, corset, hat pins and hairpins, along with wagon tracks near by.

As soon as news spread of human remains being found at Jackson Creek, Charles Kugadt boarded a train for San Francisco. From there Kugadt traveled on to Napa, California, under the alias name of John Frey. The governor of Texas offered a $300 reward for Kugadt's arrest and conviction. Kugadt was located, and after his arrest was extradited back to Texas.

Kugadt told Sheriff D. E. Teague that he and Joanna had stopped for lunch about three miles from Brenham. After lunch, he was picking up fodder left over by the horses when Joanna attempted to climb into the wagon by stepping on the front wheel. Just as she stepped on the wheel, the horses gave a sudden start causing Joanna to fall to the ground and the rear wheel rolled over her head and jaw. Kugadt said when he ran to Johanna, she told him in German that she was badly hurt and could not travel any further.

After putting her in the wagon and driving a short distance, he saw that Johanna was dead. Kugadt said he became frightened as to what he should do next, so he carried the wooden box to the creek bottom and set it on fire. Because he did not have any tools to dig a grave with, Kugadt placed Johanna's body in the fire. Kugadt afterwards returned home and threw her travel trunk in a gully near his home and set fire to it. Once learning Johanna's remains had been found, Kugadt said he shaved his beard and boarded a train for California to avoid being arrested.

Tried and convicted to hang, the night before the appointed execution, Kugadt was visited by his wife. Upon seeing her, Kugadt reached through the bars, and when he took hold of his wife's hands said, "This is our wedding anniversary. Nineteen years ago today we stood at the bridal altar and I promised not only to love her, but pledged her my best efforts."

The next morning Charles Kugadt told the sheriff he had no final statement to make and simply bid those present to witness his hanging with a goodbye. Ten minutes later, the body was pronounced dead.

The *Dallas Morning News*, dated, Friday, October 21, 1898, provided readers with details of the murder, and execution..

Charlie McClennan

Race/Gender: Black Male **Age:** 25 **Offense:** Murder
Offense Date: October 24, 1910 **Weapon:** Shotgun **Execution:** April 13, 1912

On the night of October 24, 1910, on an unusually dark night, Ed. C Hughes and his younger brother, Herbert Hughes, were riding in a buggy from Chappell Hill to Witman at about 9 p.m. After they had ridden eight miles out of Chappell Hill, the brothers came upon an obstruction in the bend of the road and stopped. Several black men then surrounded the buggy. Ed yelled, "Get out of the way and let us pass."

Someone from the crowd yelled back, "We won't do anything of the kind," and at the same time approached the buggy.

After the person approached, Ed Hughes recognized the man and said, "Is that you Johnson McClellan?"

In response the man replied, "you know damned well it is."

As Hubert Hughes was getting out of the buggy he asked, "Is that your brother Charlie over there with a shotgun?"

Johnson answered, "it's none of up business who it is." The crowd then opened fire with pistols and shotguns on the Hughes brothers. When the smoke cleared from a dozen pistols and shotguns being fired, Ed Hughes called out to his brother who was still in the buggy holding the team together and said, "They've killed me."

Herbert had his pistol by his side and laying near by was Johnnie McClellan who was dead with a pistol in his hand. The other men had already fled and left Ed alone with his brother. Herbert Hughes was later buried at the Prairie Lea Cemetery at Brenham.

On March 31, 1911, the jury deliberated for twenty minutes to return a verdict of guilty against Charlie McClennan and assessed his penalty at death.

On the day appointed day, the execution was conducted privately inside the jail. On the gallows, McLennan declined to make a final statement. At 1:58 p.m., Sheriff D. E. Teague sprung the trap.

The *Galveston Daily News*, dated Sunday, April 14, 1912, provided their readers with details of the murder and execution.

Webb County
County Seat - Laredo

Cresencio Uvalte

Race/Gender: Hispanic Male **Age:** 30 **Offense:** Murder
Weapon: Tree Limb & Drowning **Execution:** November 28, 1879

Cresencio Uvalte was a Mexican national who arrived in the United States with his newly wed wife, Martina. Soon after establishing their home, men began arriving to visit Martina while Uvalte was away herding sheep. When Uvalte learned of her male visitors, he and Martina began fighting over his suspicion of her infidelity. In response, Martina told Uvalte she wanted a separation.

The following day Martina went to a spring to either retrieve a bucket of water or was washing clothes in the stream. Uvalte came up behind Martina and struck her to the back with a tree limb, using such force that the blow knocked her into the spring. Uvalte then held his wife down under water until Martina drowned. He then pulled the body out of the water and up on the bank, where he mutilated the body with a large knife.

On October 21, 1879, the jury that listened to the testimony was out one hour before returning a verdict of guilty and assessed his punishment at death.

In preparation for the execution, Sheriff Dario Gonzales ordered for the scaffold to be built in a secluded corner of the courthouse. On the day of the execution, Deputy Sheriff Bruni escorted the condemned man from the jail up the stairs into the courthouse. Deputy Bruni read the death warrant, and at the conclusion asked Uvalte if he had anything to say. In response, Uvalte spoke in Spanish in a firm voice to the 300 spectators and said, "Good Sirs, I am going to bid you all good-bye; this has been my misfortune; I ask that you all recommend me to God, and send my picture to my parents. Nothing more. Adios."

At precisely 2 p.m. the trap was sprung, and the drop of nine feet broke the neck. Seven minutes later the body was lowered down and placed in a coffin to be buried at the Catholic cemetery.

The *Galveston Daily News*, dated Saturday, November 28, 1879, printed the following interview Uvalte had with a reporter:

In 1877, I married Martina Morales, at Canyon Salias, state of Nueva Leon, Mexico. She was then fifteen years old. I went into debt to my employer to establish myself in housekeeping. My mother-in-law gave me bad advice, and I finally ran away to this country and engaged to herd sheep for Don Roxado Garcia. My wife followed me, and, on the advice of friends, I went to live with her again. I was often away for a long time, and when I came back she did not treat me well. I knew other men had been to see her. I gave her money and did all I could for her, but she would not live with me. I was next day down at a pool of water, washing my clothes, when she came for water, and I took a stick to punish her for acting so bad. I hit her harder than I wanted to, and she fell into the spring. I held her down until she was drowned, and pulled her up under some tress on the grass. Her friends came soon to look for her, and I hid in the bushes. They threatened to kill me, and that made me mad. When they had gone, I came out and took my knife and cut her to pieces. I wanted to sever every joint, but they came and scared me off. I was soon captured, and plead guilty, but they sentenced me to be hanged. The sheriff has been very good to me. My wife did wrong to me, but I did wrong to kill her.

Christino Aldava

Race/Gender: Hispanic Male **Age:** 25 **Offense:** Double Murder
Offense Date: May 7, 1884 **Weapon:** Pistol **Execution:** August 14, 1885

Christino Aldava left Mexico to visit his brother in the United States. Soon after arriving at his home, Christino engaged in a relationship with his brother's wife, and convinced her to return to Mexico with him.

The woman did so, and remained with Aldava for three years. During the third year however, Gavino's wife returned to him asking for his forgiveness and pleaded for him to take her back. Gavino did so, but Aldava reappeared and again asked that she return back with him to Mexico. The woman replied she would never leave her husband again as long as he was alive.

On the night of May 7, 1884, Christino Aldava attended a Mexican dance at Encinal, Texas. After leaving the dance, Aldava rode to his brother's house and called for Gavino to come outside so they could talk. As soon as Gavino stepped out from the front doorway, Aldava shot him down and left in the darkness. While Gavino's wife and her half brother Francisco Saldania were attending to Gavino's wound, Aldava returned and kicked the front door open. Aldava entered the room with his pistol drawn and placed the muzzle of the barrel to Francisco's head. As Francisco dropped to his knees and pleaded for his life, Aldava fired three bullets into Francisco's body, killing him. Gavino lived for several days before he succumbed to his wound.

The next morning, Christino Aldava was laboring in his field as if nothing had happened when found by the lawmen and arrested. Aldava was incarcerated at the Webb County jail where he remained until his trial. At the trial, Christino Aldava was found guilty of both counts of murder in the first degree.

Christino Aldava was executed on August 14, 1885, along with Caledonio Chivarria in a double-hanging. *(See Caledonio Chivarria for additional details.)*

Caledonio Chivarria

Race/Gender: Hispanic Male **Age:** 23 **Offense:** Robbery & Triple Murder
Offense Date: May 5, 1879 **Weapon:** Winchester Rifle **Execution:** August 14, 1885

On the night of May 5, 1879, Guadalupe Trevino, her daughter Marta Torrez.who had her six-month-old son, were being driven on a cart by her husband Antonio. The family was traveling from Rio Grande City, Texas, to the town of Laredo located to the north. At nightfall, the family camped out under the stars.

As the morning sun made its first light in the eastern sky, the family was awakened by a rifle shot. When Antonio and Guadalupe sat up to the sound, they were both shot and killed. Marta Torrez was wounded in the shoulder and left for dead. Some reports have her child as being shot and killed as well. The shooter then appeared from the brush and began rifling through the cart looking for anything of value to steal. Marta did recognize the murderer, but took a mental imagine of the man who had slaughtered her family. Two days after the murder, Marta Torrez crawled four miles away to a farmhouse to obtain help.

Nineteen-year-old Caledonio Chivarria mostly worked as a sheepherder. On May 5, Chivarria decided to steal a horse from his employer and ride back to his native country of Mexico. The stolen horse was tracked near the Rio Grande to a clump of brush that was about 100 yards from the murder site. Four years later, Chivarria returned to Laredo and was immediately placed under arrest by the Sheriff for stealing the horse. The Sheriff remembering the massacre and the horse tracks near the murder scene, went to Marta Torres and inquired if she could still identify the murderer. When Marta replied that she could, she accompanied the Sheriff to the jail. There in the presence of ten other Mexican men, Marta Torres identified Caledonio Chivarria as the man who murdered her family. Chivarria was charged with the murders, tried and found guilty.

At 6 a.m. on August 14, 1885, the Mexican side of the Rio Grande River was lined with men, women, and children who were waiting for the first ferry boat to take them across the river to Laredo so that could attend the double execution.

By 8 a.m. the streets of Laredo near the jail were so packed with people, that police officers were sent to clear the streets so that wagons and carriages could pass. At 3 p.m. a crowd of 3,000 to 4,000 people stood in the 100-degree temperature and attempted to find relief by standing in the shadow of telephone poles.

The Laredo jail was secured by a twelve-foot wall which surrounded the building and jail yard. The scaffold was built in the jail yard, with the platform rising six feet above the wall. At 3:30 Father Souchon entered the cell of the condemned men to provide their last spiritual rites. Afterwards Officers escorted both Christino Aldava and Caledonio Chivarria to the scaffold. Without any assistance, both men climbed the ladder to the top platform and removed their hats. Aldava stepped forward and for twenty-five minutes read a prepared ten-page statement detailing his life's history and the crime for which he was sentenced to die. Chivarria during this time stood behind Aldava smoking a cigar, only to turn away to spit. When Aldava finished his statement, he then took his seat on the chair directly under the noose.

Chivarria stepped forward and addressed the crowd in both English and Spanish, making his plea of innocence. When Chivarria completed his statement, both men were furnished with a glass of wine as the death warrant was read. At 4:42 p.m., the hangman stepped to the front of the scaffold. Both Aldava and Chivarria reached for their ropes and self adjusted the noose around their own necks. Their arms were then tied and the black cap pulled over their heads.

In the crowd, Aldava had recognized a friend and requested that he take charge of his body. After the final preparations were concluded, the hangman descended from the platform to take a position directly under the platform where a rope was secured. Both Aldava and Chivarria began shouting to the crowd, "Good-bye! Good-bye! Good-bye!"

A deputy sheriff then signaled the hangman who then pulled downward on the rope. The pull of the rope released two bolts that held the trap door in place. Both men shot downward and remained suspended until 5:10 p.m. when physicians pronounced both men dead and they were then lowered into their coffins.

The *Fort Worth Daily Gazette*, dated Saturday, August 15, 1885, printed a full account of the crimes both men committed and of the double execution. Note that the newspaper article identified the victims as being the Rangel family.

James Barney Compton

Alias: J. B.   **Race/Gender:** White Male   **Age:** 32   **Offense:** Robbery & Murder
Offense Date: December 21, 1911   **Weapon:** Gas Iron Pipe & Knife   **Execution:** March 15, 1912

On the night of December 21, 1912, Lonnie Franks and James "J. B." Compton entered the jewelry store of G. J. Levytansky, the town's wealthiest jeweler, and a friendly, well-respected man. After the two men entered the store, Franks asked Levytansky if he would look at his watch and help him set the time. Franks then handed Levytansky his watch to distract the jeweler, as Compton walked behind him. Levytansky was then struck to the back of the head with an eighteen-inch-long gas pipe. When Levytansky dropped the watch, the face of the crystal broke upon hitting the floor.

Compton and Franks quickly turned down the store's lights and dragged Levytansky to a corner of the store. Compton then hit Levytansky a second time to the side of the head and stabbed the jeweler three or four times in the chest with a long pearl handled knife. Both men then opened the safe and removed a metal box containing $35,000 to $40,000 worth of diamonds, and approximately $400 in paper and silver currency.

After leaving the store, Compton and Franks returned to the Burley Hotel where Compton was registered to divide the diamonds and cash. Compton kept the $91 in American currency for himself and gave Franks the $370 in Mexican currency along with the mixture of Mexican silver coins. Once satisfied with the division of stolen goods, Compton and Franks left the hotel to hide the stolen gems.

While walking to the post office, Compton broke the blade of the murder weapon between two bricks of a building wall and threw the handle into a clump of bushes. Franks walked to the Laredo Post Office and mailed a package containing the stolen diamonds under the fictitious name of S. A. Austin in McKinney, Texas. Compton had wrapped his share of diamonds in tissue paper and decided to keep his stolen diamonds close to him by burying the gems in the rail yard of the International & Great Northern Railway.

The next morning, concerned friends entered the store through the unlocked rear door to find Levytansky's body. Friends and Laredo town citizens posted a $2,500 reward for the arrest and conviction of the parties responsible for his death.

Compton told Franks he was in desperate need of money so he could marry his girlfriend, and stayed in Laredo. Franks not wanting to take any chances of getting caught boarded the next train for San Antonio. Four days later on December 26, while walking around the San Antonio Plaza, Sheriff John Tobin and Deputy Sheriff James Galbreath arrested Franks on suspicion of the Levytansky murder. Days later Franks confessed to the murder and robbery and implicated Compton as his accomplice. Franks told the sheriff it was Compton's idea and Compton who had planned the robbery. Franks said although he knew the jeweler would be killed, he personally did not take part in the murder.

Compton who had maintained his innocence, had been arrested twice on suspicion of the murder, but was released each time due to lack of evidence. After Franks implicated Compton in the crime, he was arrested a third time, and this time confessed after learning of Franks' confession

After Franks implicated Compton in the Levytansky murder, he was arrested a third time, but this time confessed after learning of Franks' confession. Compton claimed it was Franks who initiated the robbery plans and that he only received $20 in cash and nine diamonds, while Franks kept everything else for himself. Compton did admit to the sheriff that he had struck and stabbed Levytansky to death. Compton then directed the sheriff to the location of his share of the diamonds, metal pipe, knife blade and knife handle. The package of diamonds mailed by Franks was also recovered by the postmaster at McKinney and mailed back to the Webb County Sheriff.

On January 17, 1912, Lonnie A. Franks, twenty-one-years-old, and thirty-one-year-old James Compton were tried and found guilty of murder in the first degree. The jury recommended that Franks serve the rest of his life in prison while Compton should hang for his crimes. Compton had applied to Governor Oscar Colquitt asking for his sentence to be commuted, but received word on March 11, that the Governor refused to interfere by replying, "Let the law take its course."

On the gallows, Sheriff Amador Sanchez asked Compton if he wished to make a final statement. Compton replied yes and said:

> There are some I wanted to see who are not here. I wanted to ask their forgiveness for anything I have done and want to forgive them. I have been converted, repented and have full faith in the Lord. If you all will read the first verse of the fourteenth chapter of St. John you will see where I get my strength." Then turning to City Marshal Brennan, who was standing near him, Compton said, "Mr. Brennan, I want to forgive you for what you have done and I want you to forgive me, too. I regret that District Attorney Valls is not here, for I want to forgive him for what he told the jury. I attributed my strength at this time to the fact that the Lord is with me, I want to ask all present to have more faith in the Lord and you will all be better now.

At 11:10, the trap was sprung, and five minutes later the body was pronounced dead.

The *Galveston Daily News*, dated Saturday, March 16, 1912, provided its readers with a large article detailing the crime and the execution at Laredo, Texas.

Wharton County
County Seat - Wharton

Jack Fields

Rack/Gender: Black Male **Offense:** Arson, Robbery & Double Homicide
Offense Date: December 24, 1891 **Weapon:** Clubs **Execution:** December 3, 1892

On Christmas Eve of 1891, Jack Fields and Eph George learned that Henry Kirby kept a large sum of money in his house. Henry and his wife, who was at the time six months pregnant, lived twelve miles south of Wharton. Just before midnight on a cold December night, Jack Fields, Eph George and two other men arrived at the couple's home. Armed with clubs, the men quietly entered the house and located the couple asleep in their bed where they beat them to death.

After committing the murders, the men searched the house for money and took anything of value. To conceal the crimes of murder and robbery, the house was set on fire. The fire did not completely destroy the house, and the bodies were discovered when the neighbors arrived to come to the aid of the Kirbys.

On May 7, 1892, Jack Fields was tried on the charge of murder, robbery and arson and found guilty. The case was appealed to the Court of Criminal Appeals who found no error in the trial, and affirmed the decision on June 1, 1892.

On the afternoon of the execution, Jack Fields was led from the main entrance of the jail to the scaffold in the jail yard. After reaching the platform Fields protested his innocence to the witnesses, and declared, "I have made peace with God and I will go straight to the bosom of Jesus."

After Fields finished his statement, Sheriff Hamilton Dickson adjusted the noose and cap and pulled the pin, which dropped the trap. The body dropped eight feet, and the rope completely severed the head from the shoulders.

The *Galveston Daily News*, dated Sunday, December 3, 1892, described the scene of the execution within the large bold typed headline:

JERKED HIS HEAD OFF.

**Horrible Scene at Jack Field's
Execution at Wharton.**

Jim Williamson

Race/Gender: White Male **Age:** 27 **Offense:** Murder
Offense Date: May 19, 1895 **Weapon:** Firearm **Execution:** June 25, 1897

Frank Martin

Race/Gender: White Male **Age:** 38 **Offense:** Murder
Offense Date: May 19, 1895 **Weapon:** Firearm **Execution:** June 25, 1897

E. C. Crocker lived on a farm outside Wharton with his wife Nancy Jane and their ten-year-old son, Wesley Crocker. Crocker had been involved in a land dispute with a man named Day, who Crocker eventually killed with a shotgun. At Crocker's trial, Frank Martin testified as a witness against him, and this caused resentment between the two men.

On Sunday, May 19, 1895, Gus Colburn and Jim Williamson, who had been friends of Day were riding across the prairie, when they spotted E. C. Crocker driving a yoke of oxen toward his cabin that was a mile away. Williams rode his horse behind a tree, and dismounted with his rifle. When Crocker was about twenty yards away, Williams fired two shots at him and missed. Crocker returned several shots directed at Williams, and Crocker then ran into a one-room cabin owned by Emmitt Colburn.

Colburn was alone in his home and had witnessed the running battle taking place, but offered no assistance to Crocker as he rushed inside. Jim Williams and Gus Colburn surrounded the cabin and began shooting into the dwelling. Emmitt Colburn first attempted to get Crocker to leave his cabin, but he refused.

Soon Williams and Gus Colburn were joined by John Rickard, Frank Martin and Jim Martin. All three were told about the shooting incident, and Frank Martin announced, "Lets go and kill him."

With the cabin surrounded by the cowboys, Frank Martin yelled out to Emmitt Colburn that it would be to his best health, if he left his home while he still could. Emmitt fled from his home immediately.

Nancy Jane Crocker learned her husband was in trouble and quickly arrived with her son Wesley and they rushed into the cabin carrying two shotguns and a pistol for her husband. At one point Wesley attempted to leave the house, but when bullets were fired at him, he ran back inside.

At about nightfall, Nancy ran from the house. Both Frank Martin and Jim Williams attempted to stop Nancy by firing shots at her. Nancy had ran three to four hundred yard distance when Jim Williams rode after her on his horse, and shot her down. Thinking that Nancy was lying dead on the prairie, Williams returned his attention back to firing on the cabin..

The cowboys fired their guns well into the night at any sound they heard coming from inside the house. Not being able to see inside the house, it was decided to set the cabin on fire. An old blanket hanging on the fence was removed and torn into strips to make balls which they saturated in coal oil. Once soaked, a ball was lit, and Frank Martin was slightly wounded when he ran up to the cabin to throw the fireball into the house. The second time the lit balls were thrown inside, Frank Martin saw Crocker hiding on top of a roof joist, and shot him in the stomach. Crocker fell from the joist, and crashed through the bed below. While he was crawling on the floor, Williams shot Crocker in the head from a cat hole in the door.

With Crocker dead, the door was forced open, and Crocker was shot several more times. Wesley was afterwards pulled out from under the bed his father had through, and John Rickard shot and killed him with a shotgun.

With the Crocker family dead, it was decided to get a wagon to move the bodies somewhere else. Once the wagon team was ready, the men first went to retrieve Nancy's body. When approaching her, Nancy said, "Oh, Frank Martin, I know you!" Nancy asked for water and was told, "Die, your hour has come."

Frank Martin then shot her in the head with his shotgun. The three bodies were all loaded onto the wagon and driven to a dense thicket seven miles away. The bodies were pulled off the wagon and laid out on the prairie where they remained for ten days until discovered. When found, the bodies were in such a terrible state of decomposition that unmarked graves were dug next to the corpses and they were pushed into the graves, and buried.

After John Richard was arrested for murder, he confessed and gave statements implicating everyone's involvement after he was promised immunity. Three weeks later, Sheriff Rabb A. Rich arrested Frank Martin. Martin openly confessed to the murders to the sheriff, even though the sheriff warned Martin he should remain silent or he would have to testify at his trial as to what he told him. Jim Williams was convicted and hanged on June 25, 1897, for the murder of E. C. Crocker. Frank Martin was convicted and sentenced to hang on June 10, 1898, for the murder of Nancy Crocker. The other murderers received a life prison sentence.

Frank Martin was a native Texan and described as a distinguished and handsome man, standing six-foot-four, brown hair with a long beard. On the gallows, Martin declined to make a statement, but had earlier admitted to taking part in the death of Mrs. Crocker. Because of his height, a hole two feet deep was dug out under the scaffold to insure Martin's feet did not touch the ground.

After the body was pronounced dead, the remains were lowered into an awaiting coffin and placed on a train to be shipped to Emory, Texas, to be laid to rest next to his wife.

Jim Williamson told a reporter, "My father is wrongfully accused; he was twenty-five miles away when the killing took place." He then said:

> I see there is no hope for me now. I will not lie about it. I am not totally innocent in the crime of the killing, but I was forced to take part in what I did, Crocker had assaulted me two or three times and it is true I did first assault him out on the prairie the evening of the killing. Other parties persuaded me to take part in the murder. They told me I was a coward if I did not kill Crocker. Now the strange part about it is I am accused of the killing of Crocker when he was killed by some one else, though I do not say I am innocent.

The gallows from which Jim Williamson was executed was erected on the lawn of the jail with a ten-foot privacy wall surrounding the structure. Citizens climbed rooftops of houses, barns and trees in order to watch the execution take place. At 9 a.m. Williamson was lead out of cell while being flanked by a deputy on each side and escorted to the gallows. Williamson was so frightened that he had to be injected twice with strychnine in order for him to mount the scaffold. The execution was quickly done as it appeared that Williamson was about to faint and had no statement to make.

When Williamson was dropped through the trap door, the only movement being the twitching of one hand. After hanging only three minutes, the rope was cut and the body lowered. As the body was being carried to the coffin, Williamson took a deep breath, and the physicians were called back and they declared that Williamson was still alive. A second rope was obtained, and Williamson was carried to the top of the scaffold and a new noose placed around his neck. Deputies then supported Williamson to stand upright until the trap was dropped. Williamson then fell through the trap door and remained hanging for twenty-two minutes. The physicians for the second time declare Williamson dead, and the body was again lowered and laid to rest in the coffin.

The *Shiner Gazette* dated June 15, 1898 and the *Houston Daily Post* dated June 26, 1898, printed large articles of the crime and executions of Frank Martin and Jim Williamson.

Jim King

Race/Gender: Black Male **Age:** 19 **Offense:** Murder
Offense Date: April 24, 1898 **Weapon:** Winchester Rifle **Execution:** December 2, 1898

Jim King and Lucinda Wade at first seemed to be a happy couple who had been living together for four years. However, in April of 1898, Lucinda informed King she wanted to end their relationship and separate.

On Sunday, April 24, 1898, Lucinda was walking home after attending Sunday school when King stopped her. While holding his rifle, King told Lucinda that he intended to kill her. After Lucinda knelt to the ground to beg for her life, King shot and killed her. King later told a deputy sheriff that the mere thought of Lucinda belonging to another man was more than he could bear, and it was then that he decided to kill her.

King was tried for murder and found guilty. Once convicted, he did not appeal the sentence, and on October 29, 1898, he was scheduled to hang on December 2, 1898.

On November 29, 1898, King told a reporter, "I did not kill Lucinda near the church, it was back of our house. I did not drag her from the tree; she was not on her knees when I shot. I heartily repent my hasty action and am sorry for it. I desire Rev. Cook to publicly thank my keepers, Messers. Holly and Earnest Anderson and Sheriff Davis, for their kind treatment during m stay here."

On the day of the execution, the fall of six feet did not break King's neck, and Jim King strangled to death. The gallows used was the same one used in the double execution of Frank Martin and Jim Williamson on June 25, 1897.

The *Houston Daily Post*, dated Saturday, December 3, 1898, provided a short article with the history of the crime and execution.

Sam Washington & Gus Thomas standing in the center wearing white gloves.
Courtesy of the Wharton County Museum, Wharton, Texas.

Sam Washington

Race/Gender: Black Male **Age:** 35 **Offense:** Murder
Offense Date: August 17, 1909 **Weapon:** Pistol **Execution:** February 26, 1910

Gus Thomas

Race/Gender: Black Male **Age:** 25 **Offense:** Murder
Offense Date: June 20, 1909 **Weapon:** Shotgun **Execution:** February 26, 1910

Sam Washington and Gus Thomas were both convicted and hanged from the same scaffold for the murder of women.

Sam Washington

On August 17, 1909, Lillie Fisher was leaving Sam Washington and had gone to the home to load her property from an agreed separation settlement onto her wagon. Just as Lillie was about to leave, Sam Washington who had been hiding and watching suddenly appeared and shot Lillie down. Washington then stood over her and emptied the remaining bullets from his pistol into her body.

Gus Thomas

On June 20, 1909, Gus Thomas chased down a young girl by the name of Ollie Cash with a shotgun after she had offended him at a party. She allegedly had said that Gus Thomas had once been a county convict. Angered by her remark, Thomas took down a shotgun from the wall rack and shot her. As Ollie pleaded for her life, Thomas reloaded the shotgun as he stood over her and then fired a second shot into her head.

On February 26, 1910, at 12:45 Sheriff Elo Koehi led both men out of the jail to the gallows. While smoking a cigar, Thomas first removed his shoes and talked from the scaffold for three minutes. Thomas told the large crowd of 8,000 that he was ready to die, and blamed his temper for the murder, and advised the young people to control their own tempers.

Washington addressed the witnesses by saying, "I am guilty and am going down for my money. I took up a woman, gave her all my love and money and preferred death than to see her leave me."

At 1:15 p.m. Sheriff Koehi released the trap dropping both men to their deaths. After suspending for twenty-five minutes, Dr. Andrews ordered the bodies cut down and placed in coffins. Washington's remains were released to his uncle to be carried back to Esperanza, Texas, where his mother lived. Thomas' remains were transported to his mother at Egypt, Texas.

The *Galveston Daily News*, dated Sunday, February 27, 1910, provided their readers with details of the crime and execution.

Cornelius Jackson

Race/Gender: Black Male   **Offense:** Robbery & Murder   **Offense Date:** January 2, 1915
Execution: July 3, 1915

Asu Ray was described as a friendly elderly man who operated a small store in the town of Peach Creek, located twelve miles north of Wharton. On January 2, 1915, Nathan Hughes, Alton Owens, Cornelius Jackson and Jackson's fifteen-year-old son murdered Ray during the robbery of his store. The murderers' loot consisted of canned goods, bushels of pecans, and a bucket of candy.

When the sheriff investigated the murder, he found an overcoat that had been left behind in the store. The coat was identified as belonging to Jackson's son and he was arrested and jailed on suspicion of murder. The boy confessed that he was forced to go with his father, and he named the other two men involved.

On May 10, the three men were indicted by the grand jury for murder. Jackson's son was not indicted, as he was believed to have been forced to go. During the week of May 17, all three men were tried separately. Alton Owens and Nathan Hughes were each found guilty of being an accessory to murder and received life sentences in the penitentiary. On May 22, 1915, the jury deliberated fifteen minutes to return a verdict of guilty on Cornelius Jackson for murder and sentenced him to death.

At Wharton, Cornelius Jackson stood on the gallows and spoke to the large crowd who attended execution. Jackson said he had long since made his peace with his God and encouraged those present to arrange their earthly affairs as he had done.

The *Victoria Daily Advocate*, Saturday, July 3, 1915, reported the execution.

Wilbarger County
County Seat - Vernon

George E. Morrison

Race/Gender: White Male **Offense:** Murder **Offense Date:** October 10, 1897
Weapon: Poison **Execution:** October 27, 1899

George Morrison was a Methodist preacher accused of murdering his wife of seventeen years by poisoning her with strychnine on October 1, 1897. Two hours prior to her murder, Morrison preached a sermon warning, "The wages of sin is death."

Morrison had learned of the considerable wealth possessed by Anna Whittelesey whom he had a relationship with in his early years at college in Illinois. Anna Whittelesey now lived in Topeka, Kansas, and Morrison began corresponding with Whittelesey professing his love for her, and traveled to her home on one occasion to visit.

Morrison told Whittelesey that he had quit preaching and became a successful cattleman, owning a large ranch in the Texas Panhandle. Morrison proposed marriage to Whittelesey, but the problem was, George Morrison was married. To end his wife's life, Morrison used strychnine after they had returned home from a church service where Morrison gave a wages of sin sermon and his wife sang in the choir. After poisoning her and seeing his wife convulsing in pain, Morrison waited until she died to send for the doctor.

The surroundings of her death were suspicious and while Morrison was at his fiancé's home in Kansas, he was arrested for the murder. Released seventy-two hours later, Morrison took the opportunity to flee the area. In the meantime the body of Mrs. Morrison was exhumed and an autopsy was performed. Test results showed the contents of the stomach contained the presence of poison. Morrison was located again in San Francisco where he was arrested and extradited back to Texas to stand trial for murder.

On a change of venue, Morrison's trial was held at Vernon in September of 1898. The star witness for the prosecution was Anna Whittelesey who testified for the state. Morrison was convicted and sentenced to death. While in jail, Morrison and two other inmates planned an escape and attacked a jailer, but the escape failed. Because of this attack on the jailer and the attempted escape, Governor Charles Culberson refused to interfere with the execution or to commute Morrison's sentence. While incarcerated, Morrison preached religious jail services for the inmates up until his execution.

On the gallows, George Morrison dressed in his new black suit said:

> I suppose there are many persons present here today to hear what I have to say. I also suppose there are many of you who were present when I made my talk on the day of my sentence. I have nothing more to say today than what I said then. I have no fault to find with the court or anyone for the circumstances under which I have been placed.
>
> I know that it is impossible for us in this world to discern between the guilty and the innocent, but the Bible tells us that there is a time when this discernment will take place. In the ninth chapter of Hebrews, twenty-seventh verse, we have the language: 'And it is appointed unto men once to die, and after this the judgment.'
>
> I believe the word of God; I believe every word to be the truth and I believe it to be inspired. A man asked me this morning if I had any hope for the hereafter. I have lived in the faith and the hope of my mother who is now on the other shore; I have lived according to the teachings of God's word, and I believe I am individually prepared to die. I believe that when life leaves this body it will pass at once into the presence of my friends and loved ones, who now await my coming on the other shore. I expect to meet my mother and other relatives and my own dear wife, for whose murder I stand charged.
>
> It is impossible for me to explain the circumstances, for I have tried to do that already. I know

that I have done a great many things that were wrong, all of us do, and for this I have received sufficient punishment. That package of strychnine was never opened while in my possession to my knowledge. I have done everything in my power to explain the circumstances in the case, but I couldn't do it to the satisfaction of the court and I can not make the explanation that you would want.

It has been said by a jury of twelve men that I must be hanged and this man standing here (placing his hand on Sheriff Williams' shoulder) had been ordered to execute the sentence. As I take him by the hand I say to him and to you that I have not a thing against him. He simply obeys the law, as each and everyone of you would do were you an officer or in his place.

I believe there were people in the trial who held the bitterest of feeling against me. Now, whether or not these feelings had anything to do with their testimony in the case in the way of making it stronger or putting it in stronger language I know not; that is a matter which they will answer for and not me. I will answer for my own actions and I praise God that I am ready. I am not afraid to die, nor am I afraid to stand before the judgment bar of God.

I say to you candidly that during the trial of the case there were times when I had the bitterest of feeling for those who testified against me, but I say to you now as I stand here before you to pay the dearest penalty a man can pay, that I have no hard feeling for them or for anyone. Now, I thought at the time Mr. Berry made his speech that he said very hard things about me and I believe that those things were calculated to make the jury harder on me, but I have forgiven all of this now and I have no bitter feeling toward him.

Now, I have made a statement in writing which is in the hands of the *Dallas News* representative. I suppose it will be published in the papers. All I ask is that I get fair treatment. Of course I know that if I had not been a minister of the gospel, the papers all over the Unities States would not have said so much about my case. A professed Christian man and a minister of the gospel is, of course, expected not to do these things and when they are accused of murder.

I don't know how the Panhandle people are now, in regard to the matter. I suppose they are still prejudged against me, as they always have been. They loved my wife and as did I love her. I lived with her seventeen years and I loved her as true as any man can love a woman. In that greater day of God's judgment we will know all about these things.

My dear friends, it is not all of life to live nor all of death to die, and after this life comes the spiritual life. Be true to your married one, be true to your wife and family and then there awaits for you a crown of eternal life. I want every one of you to try and bear me in your memory. Not at my worst, not as I stand here before you now, but at my best until God's time comes. He will reward us for the good things we do while here.

May God bless you as I say goodbye to you. I have no fears whatever of going. I believe when life leaves this body, the gates of Heaven will be standing wide open and I will have a glorious welcome. Now I am in the hands of your sheriff, but there is one thing I want to say, and that is I want to thank each and every one in the town of Vernon who has shown one particle of sympathy for my darling sister who has come here and done everything in her power for me. I commit her to the care and keeping of the ladies of this town, and may God reward you and her. Now I am done.

Rev. A. J. Tant led in the singing, *Jesus, Jesus, Blessed Jesus*. Morrison then told Sheriff Williams, "I am not afraid of the hereafter. I have made my peace with God and I am as sure of life everlasting as I was ever of anything. I know nothing of death in this way and it is the physical pain I dread. If I appear nervous to you it is for that reason alone."

Morrison then removed his overcoat and stepped upon the trap and stood still as his arms and legs were being tied and the noose adjusted. As Morrison could be heard praying to himself, Rev. Tant sang, *Jesus, Lover of My Soul*.

At 12:55 p.m. the sheriff pulled the lever dropping George Morrison to his death. Thirteen minutes later, Morrison's body was pronounced dead.

The *Salt Lake City Daily Tribune*, dated Saturday, October 28, 1899, printed the details of the crime and the execution at Vernon, Texas.

Williamson County
County Seat - Georgetown

Irvine Murray

Race/Gender: Black Male   **Age:** 38-40   **Offense:** Murder
Offense Date: December 10, 1885   **Weapon:** Ax & Razor   **Execution:** September 10, 1886

Irvine Murray suspected his wife, Mollie, of being unfaithful, and decided on the night of December 10, 1885, to kill her. In doing so, he killed her in the presence of his eleven-year-old stepson who testified at the trial. The stepson described to the jury how Murray used an ax to crush his mother's skull, and then cut her throat with a razor.

Irvine Murray was tried and found guilty of murder in the first degree, and appealed the case. The Court of Criminal Appeals affirmed the lower court's decision and he was sentence at the July term of court to die on September 10, 1886.

On the appointed day, Irvine Murray dressed in a new suit of clothes and was led out of the jail to an awaiting carriage. The gallows had been erected a mile from the town of Georgetown on a small prairie near the Gabriel River. Once on the scaffold, Murray told the 6,000 witnesses, "Few people have gone up on such a place with a clear conscience as I have."

Rev. J. C. Williams then began singing, *And Am I Born to Die, to Lay This Body Down*, with Murray joining in. At the end of the song, Rev. Williams told Murray goodbye and stepped to the side.

Murray walked forward onto the trap. Murray's arms were tied at the elbows and his legs at his ankles. Sheriff John Olive then pulled the black cap over Murray's face and told him goodbye. At 1:43 p.m., Sheriff Olive cut the rope that held the trap with an ax. The trap fell and Murray dropped seven and a half feet, breaking his neck. After twelve minutes, doctors W. T. Jones, W. W. Walton and J. H. Denson pronounced Murray dead. Five minutes later the rope was cut and the body was lowered into a coffin and transported for burial.

The *Fort Worth Daily Gazette*, dated Saturday, September 11, 1886, provided readers with the history of the crime, trial and execution at Georgetown, Texas.

Albert Rolly

Race/Gender: Black Male   **Age:** 20   **Offense:** Murder
Offense Date: May 8, 1895   **Weapon:** Pistol & Rock   **Execution:** March 20, 1896

Mat Mootry

Race/Gender: Black Male   **Age:** 20   **Offense:** Murder
Offense Date: May 8, 1895   **Weapon:** Pistol & Rock   **Execution:** March 27, 1896

On the night of May 1, 1895, Andrew Prickryl, a Bohemian immigrant, held a dance on his farm and had invited the other Bohemian farmers to attend. During the dance, Ike Creighton, his half-brother, Albert Rolly and Mat Mootry all arrived uninvited and Prickryl asked the men to leave. Other than throwing words of insult, the men left the dance without causing any further disturbance.

Then, on the evening of May 8, 1895, Albert Rolly and Mat Mootry were at the home of Tim "Quack" Creighton pitching horseshoes when Ike Creighton rode up on horseback. Creighton informed Rolly and Mootry that he had seen Andrew Prickryl with his cousin Henry fishing a mile away on Brushy Creek.

Mat Mootry and Albert Rolly then went to the creek with their pistols drawn and confronted Andrew

Prickryl. Mootry demanded an answer as to why they were not good enough to attend his dance. Prickryl who was on his knees pleading not to be killed was then shot. Seeing his cousin murdered, Henry immediately took off running. Rolly took pursuit after him, and shot Henry in the back, and left him for dead.

Rolly returned to Mootry who was still standing over Andrew Prickryl. Rolly informed Mootry he had killed Henry, and that Mootry needed to insure that Prickryl was dead. Mootry then picked up a large rock and brought it down on Andrew Prickryl's skull. Henry, who was not dead, crawled back to his home and told his family of the murder.

Ike Creighton, Albert Rolly and Mat Mootry were all arrested and charged with murder. At the trial, Henry identified Mootry as the person who killed Andrew Prickryl, and Rolly as the person who shot him. Ike Creighton who had turned state's witness testified saying when the three of them arrived at the creek, he turned around and went home. Rolly testified that it was Creighton who committed the murder, and it was Mootry who refused to go down to the creek. The jury not believing Rolly's testimony found both Mootry and Rolly guilty.

On February 17, 1896, Mat Mootry and Albert Rolly were both sentenced to death. Upon sentencing, Rolly again told the judge that Mootry was innocent, as did Mootry in his own behalf. Rolly further told the judge he believed his death sentence was unfair because Henry Prickryl recovered from his wound.

On March 7, Sheriff Henry Purl announced that the execution of Mat Mootry and Albert Rolly would be public. The sheriff explained that the ceiling in the Williamson County jail in Georgetown was too low for the proper distance of a drop. The sheriff further did not want the execution held within the jail yard in view or sound of his family. Elected sheriffs and their families typically had a residence within the jail building as was the case in Georgetown. The gallows were built one mile from town near the banks of the San Gabriel River.

On March 17, Governor Charles Culberson granted a one-week respite for Mootry, but not for Albert Rolly as he had admitted to his guilt.

On March 20, Albert Rolly stood on the gallows. Rolly confessed to the spectators that Ike Creighton had spoken the truth while testifying, and Mat Mootry was guilty of murdering Andrew Prickryl. Rolly said he was afraid of Mat Mootry and therefore had lied for him.

On March 27, Mootry spoke for fifteen minutes at which time he confessed his crime for the first time. Mootry advised the witnesses to lead Christian lives, and attributed his downfall to gambling and horse racing. After this he called out to numerous acquaintances in the crowd and bade them all goodbye. Mootry said he hoped that his children might be educated, a blessing he did not enjoy himself.

The *Houston Daily Post*, dated Saturday, March 21 and 28, 1896, gave accounts of both executions.

John Ransom

Race/Gender: Black Male **Age:** 29 **Offense:** Robbery & Murder
Offense Date: August 31, 1901 **Weapon:** Ax **Execution:** April 3, 1903

On August 31, 1901, John Ransom murdered his employer Wesley Rucker, at Circleville with an ax. The motive for the murder was robbery as Ransom was aware that Rucker was carrying $65 on his person. After the murder, and taking the money, Ransom fled to Austin. Upon his arrest, Ranson confessed to the murder.

Ranson was convicted of murder in the first degree and the jury assessed the punishment as death. On February 9, 1903, Judge R. I. Penn sentenced Ransom to death and ordered the execution to take place on April 3, 1903.

On the afternoon of the execution, Sheriff Sampson Connell approached the cell and read John Ransom the death warrant that he carried. At 1:30 p.m., Ransom was driven one mile in a hack to the fairgrounds near the river where the scaffold had been built. An inmate by the name of Lon Crayton, who had been sentenced to five years in the penitentiary for forgery, accompanied Ransom at his request.

On the gallows, prayers were given and songs were sung. Sheriff Connell asked Ransom if he desired to make a statement. Both Ransom and Lon Crayton stepped forward to the edge of the platform. Crayton said, "John Ransom was born in Lee County about twenty-nine years ago. He traveled a good deal and in his travels he came to Circleville where he got into trouble. He never did deny doing that crime. But he has been praying for two days in that dark cell and told me that Jesus had pardoned all his sins."

At 2:15 p.m., Sheriff Connell pulled out the peg that released the trap. The fall of nine feet broke the neck, and immediately afterwards, persons on and around the scaffold platform had to be moved away for fear that the scaffold was about to collapse.

The *Georgetown Commercial*, dated Friday, April 10, 1903, provided readers with details of the crime and execution.

Preston Tankersley

Race/Gender: Black Male **Age:** 31 **Offense:** Murder
Offense Date: August 6, 1904 **Weapon:** Pistol **Execution:** September 1, 1905

Preston Tankersley and his wife Lou had been married for nine years, and lived about three miles from Georgetown with their seven children. During the marriage Tankersley at times would become jealous of his wife and threatened Lou that if she were ever unfaithful, he would kill her.

On the morning of August 6, 1904, Preston Tankersley arrived home and again accused Lou of being unfaithful. Tankersley beat his wife with a bed slat. During the assault, Lou broke away from Tankersley and fled out of the house and into the yard. Tankersley grabbed his pistol and chased after his wife, shooting her twice in the left breast. Several men witnessed the shooting and did nothing to go to the woman's aid or to apprehend Tankersley other than to take his weapon away from him. After the men disarmed Tankersley, he was allowed to simply walk away.

A young boy ran to town and to Dr. Pettus's office asking for him to come to the aid of the wounded woman. Upon Doctor Pettus's arrival, he found Lou alive and breathing. In his examination, the doctor determined there was nothing he could do for her, and returned back to town to notify the sheriff. Lou Tankersley died a few hours later.

A sheriff's posse was organized and hunted for Tankersley who was able to elude capture. Sheriff Sampson Connell afterwards posted a $25 reward for Preston Tankersley's capture. Five days later, Will Palm found the murderer hiding in his watermelon patch. Tankersley after his capture, told the sheriff he had been surviving by eating the fruit since committing the murder.

Preston Tankersley was tried and found guilty of murder in the first degree and sentenced to death. On the morning of the execution, Tankersley was dressed in a new black suit with new shoes. While waiting in his cell, Tankersley told ex-ranger, Sergeant W. J. L. Sullivan that "I am ready to die and believe my sins had been forgiven."

Sheriff Connell then read Tankersley the death warrant. Afterwards, Tankersley was escorted outside the jail to an awaiting carriage. While walking to the carriage, Tankersley shook hands with men and women who stood in line to see the condemned man, and told them he wished to see them all in Heaven. The crowd of 200 or 300 spectators then followed the carriage in their wagons, buggies, horseback and by bicycle to the poor farm where the gallows had been erected.

On the gallows, Tankersley said:

> My name is Preston Tankersley, I am thirty-one years of age and was born in 1874. I tried to educate my children, a girl six-years-old and a boy eight. I worked all day and taught them to read and write. I loved my wife until she treated me wrong and I murdered her on August 6, 1904. Before my wife did wrong, I thought I had the best wife on earth. In a few minutes after I killed her I was sorry I did not keep my temper. But the Lord had forgiven me. I thank all the men who tried to save my life. I am ready to go and want all my friends to come and tell me goodbye. Govern your temper friends. I did not kill my wife because I was jealous but because of my temper and she treated me wrong. Mr. A. T. Irvine will tell you all that I worked for him on the farm and I tried to do right. I worked for months for my wife and children and never went to town and saved my money for them. I always taught my children to do right. I want to tell my people as I stand here in the hour of death to not lose your temper, let whiskey alone and don't gamble.

After telling his white friends thanks for attempting to have his sentenced commuted, said, "I will now sing you a song," and sang *Bear Me Away on Your Snowy Wings to My Immortal Home*. The sheriff then allowed all those present who wished to bid Preston Tankersley goodbye to come forward to do so.

Once Tankersley told all goodbye, both his arms and legs were tied, the black cap placed over his head, the rope put around his neck, and the noose adjusted. Sheriff Connell then released the trap. At the end of twelve minute, physicians pronounced Preston Tankersley dead. The body was then lowered into a coffin with the remains being released to relatives.

The rope used to hang Preston Tankersley was the same rope used to hang John Ransom three years earlier.

The *Georgetown Commercial*, dated Friday, September 8, 1905, provided readers with the history of murder, executions and past executions within the counties history.

Thomas J. Young

Alias: Jack Wade & Jack Hailey   **Race/Gender:** White Male
Age: 40   **Offense:** Rape & Murder
Offense Date: May 11, 1905   **Execution:** March 30, 1906

Thomas J. Young

Thomas Young was regarded as one of the cruelest men to have ever been executed in early Texas history. Thomas Young had served time in prison for horse theft and after his release, used different aliases to marry women while already legally married.

Young and his third wife took in his fifteen-year-old niece Alma Reese with the permission of her mother as Alma, and her stepfather did not get along. Immediately afterwards, Thomas Young beat and sexually abused his niece. When Alma told Young's wife that he had raped her, Thomas Young became enraged and tied the poor girl to a wagon wheel and merciless beat her with a club to the head, tearing the scalp. Young not satisfied with clubbing Alma, tortured the helpless girl by whipping her with either a blacksnake whip or chains for hours. Afterwards Young threw salt and acid upon her open wounds.

When reports of the girl's abuse reached town, men immediately responded to the scene to go to Alma's aid. Seeing riders quickly approaching, Young attempted to escape, but was captured. Alma was immediately taken to town for medical treatment where she gave a full account to authorities of her torture and sexual abuse at the hands of her uncle. Alma Reese died in agony the following day.

Tried in July of 1905, Thomas Young was found guilty of murder in the first degree. After the case was affirmed by the Court of Appeals, Judge Victor Brooks sentenced Young to hang on March 30, 1906.

The gallows built was the same scaffold used to hang Preston Tankersley and was erected one mile from town at the county poor farm. Two hours before the execution, Young confessed to his attorney J. F. Taulbee that he had murdered a man fifteen years earlier on the Colorado River, although another man was being accused of the crime. Thomas Young never admitted to torturing and killing Alma, except to tell Sheriff Connell that he had, "confessed to God and need not confess to man."

At the conclusion of Sheriff Connell's reading the death warrant, Tom Young stood up and said, "Yes sir, come, and let's finish this thing."

Young was handcuffed with a short chain held by a deputy. Young followed behind the sheriff while flanked by two deputies to the wagon waiting outside the jail. Young then shook hands with the sheriff's young son, Sampson Connell, telling the boy, "Goodbye Sampson. Be a good boy and meet me in Heaven."

Mounted deputies included the Austin chief of police, ex-Texas Ranger Sergeant Sullivan and town marshal of Taylor who escorted the wagon. Hundreds of people followed behind the prisoner's wagon in buggies, wagons, and horseback as the wagon passed in a parade fashion, past the citizens that lined the streets. Holding a bouquet of flowers, Young waved the flowers to women as he passed to get their attention.

During the ride, Young sang and hummed the song, *Happy Land, Happy Land*.

Upon view of the gallows at the poor farm, Young said, "That is no unpleasant sight to me."

After arriving, it was discovered that the black cap had been left behind at the jail. While waiting for the deputy to return from the jail with the cap, the Sheriff told Young, "Tom, that's a nice suit of clothes you've got on."

Tom replied, "I'll have a better one in Heaven. Young was asked if he was converted. In replying, Young said, "What's keeping me up now, but that? God is helping me bear my burden. The judge said hang me by the neck till dead, but God says I shall not die. He's stronger than the judge."

With the deputy returned with the black cap, the sheriff and his prisoner ascended from the wagon. While Thomas Young walked up to the gallows, a small choir began singing *I'm coming to the Cross*. On the gallows, Young told the 8,000 witnesses present, "I have no statement to make. My last request is that we sing a song before I go and that all my friends will meet me in heaven. Trust in Jesus Christ and he will save you. I'm happier now than ever before in my life."

After saying goodbye and shaking hands with everyone on the scaffold, the arms and legs were tied and the black cap pulled over the head. Alma Reese's mother, Mrs. Lena Hinton was present for the execution and stood at the foot of the gallows. At 2:07 p.m., Sheriff Connell pulled the lever to the trap. When the trap was sprung, Young fell a distance of nine feet, breaking his neck. Eighteen minutes later, the body was lowered and placed in a coffin. The remains were then transported to Austin to be buried next to his mother who had died the previous year.

Thomas Young wrote the following letter addressed to his father, S. P. Young:

Georgetown, Texas, March 29, 1906.
Mr. S. P. Young.

Dear Father: This morning while sitting alone thinking of you, I thought I would write you a few lines to let you know how I am getting along. I am well, yes, indeed. I am feeling better than ever in my life before because this morning Jesus Christ is on my side, and I know that the best of all and now I can tell the truth. I don't mine dieing because I am going to heaven to rest and I wont after to be tryed anymore but will be tryed before the justes bare of God and I am so glad I can meet my lord in pease. I am going to ask you all to meet me in heaven because I am goeing there for I know I have made sure my escape from and I am one of the happiest men on earth because I am free from sin now. Papa these is some of my last words on earth and I am goe to ask you to please treasure them in your heart and stamp them in membry as the appe of thire eye that you will not forget them Father som goe to ask your to read luke the 23 and 43 for my sake for I know it will do you good, and papa I want you to be sure and share this latter to all the rest of the family and beg them to turn on the lord side and work for the Master all of you all loves so when death comes unto you all you can say as I have said come death come death I will gladly goe with thee Papa I am sorry indeed of only one thing and that is you all are not here this morning so I could get to talk to you all before I depart this matral life and enter into a land of rest where I can be glad and rest from my laber so papa I want to be berried right side of mama if it could be possible and again I want you all to try and get my body down here from Waco and berry it right beside my grave so at the resurrection morning we can all get up to geather and pull of martilety and put on emartilety and sond to geather and face the judgment of hour God together and father my last plea to you is to start form this day on and work for the Master because he can do you good in the dieing in hour so I am go to ask you to give up your heart to the lord and beg the rest of the family to do likewise because it good yes it truly good to have the lord Jesus on your side in the dieing hour and papa I am goeing to ask you to please raise my two boys up rite and teach them to be lovers of the lord Jesus that they may be saved and tell Lolle to raise her children up right and keep them in the Sunday school tell my boys again to be good boys and don't get in bad company so I want you all to keep my saying and do as I have as you all to do so that's about all. I will close by saying meet me in heaven because I am goeing there,

Yours truly as ever,
J. T. Young

P.S. – Ah loven to all my friends in that country tell them I said howdy and goodbye.

The *Bartlett Tribune*, dated Friday, April 6, 1906, provided readers with a large article detailing the crime, trial, and execution.

Wilson County
County Seat - Floresville

Maximo Martinez

Gender/Race: Hispanic Male   **Age:** 36   **Offense:** Rape & Triple Murder
Offense Date: June 5, 1897   **Weapon:** Butcher Knife & Axe   **Execution:** July 30, 1897

Eighteen-year-old Juanita Acosta who lived with her elderly grandparents nine miles south of Floresville, made her living washing clothes. Nearby, thirty-six-year-old Maximo Martinez had been employed as a ranch hand at the Jim McDonald Ranch. Martinez was married and had fathered two children, but he fell in love for the young and beautiful Mexican girl. Soon after Martinez and his wife separated. Martinez asked Juanita if she would marry him if he divorced his wife. Juanita replied she would.

On a Sunday in May, of 1897, Martinez took clothes to Juanita to be washed. He then asked Juanita if she would meet with him outside at 11 p.m. the following Sunday so they could talk. Juanita said she would. Martinez arrived at the given time and waited, but Juanita never arrived. The following day, Martinez asked Juanita why she did not show up, and Juanita answered she did not have the time, but promised to meet Martinez the following Sunday night at the same given time. Like the time before, Martinez anxiously waited for Juanita's arrival, but she failed to appear for the second time. The following Saturday, on June 5, Martinez went and picked up the washed clothes that he had previously left. Martinez asked Juanita if she would come out that night to talk. For the third time, Juanita promised Martinez she would be there, this time, for sure.

When Juanita failed to come out, Martinez walked up to Juanita's grandfather's house, and entered. Locating Juanita's bedroom, Martinez entered and woke her up from her sleep. Martinez told Juanita he had been waiting for her to come outside. Juanita told Martinez to leave her room, and that she would come outside in a few minutes after she had dressed. After waiting several minutes, Martinez reentered the house and he discovered Juanita in bed asleep. Martinez again woke her up a second time telling Juanita to come outside, as he wanted to talk to her about their marriage plans. Martinez asked Juanita if she was coming outside, and she replied, "No."

Martinez asked, "are you fooling around with me."

Juanita said, "I have fooled, and made fools out of better men than you." Juanita went on to say it did not matter to her one way or another if she got married or not.

Martinez asked, "Are you making fun of me?"

Juanita then told Martinez that he was nothing but a "low down whelp."

Angered by the way Juanita had made a "fool out of him," Martinez pulled a butcher knife and stabbed the girl in the back. As Juanita cried out, Martinez told her, "your nothing but a flirt, and your worse than what you called me."

As Juanita attempted to escape, Martinez stabbed Juanita a second time to the chest. Juanita's screams woke up her fifty-one-year-old grandmother, Dolores Corrillo. As the woman entered the room, Martinez killed her with an ax that he had carried inside the house. Martinez then used the ax to kill Juanita's eighty-one-year-old grandfather, Plutarco Corrillo.

Afterwards, Martinez returned to Juanita's room and sexually assaulted her before stabbing her two more times. Before leaving, Martinez wrapped the girl's body up in a quilt and carried her outside and placed the corpse on the ground. Martinez then saddled his horse, and rode towards Mexico.

Lawmen from both Wilson and Karnes counties had pursued after Martinez for five days at a distance of 150 miles, when they located his saddled horse and clothing. On June 10, at the Osborn Ranch located between San Diego and Fort Ewell, a young boy asked the arriving lawmen if they were hunting the man he had just seen. The boy then pointed to a large cactus patch where he had last seen a man hiding.

With their rifles drawn, the posse surrounded the cactus patch and found Martinez lying low between the cactus and mesquite bushes. Wilson County deputy, Juan Garza leveled his Winchester rifle on Martinez's head and ordered for him to "throw up his hands."

Martinez walked out shoeless and immediately said, " I killed all three people because I loved the girl, but she rejected me."

While incarcerated in jail, Martinez openly gave jail house interviews to reporters. Martinez denied he had raped Juanita, but told the newspapermen he had killed the elderly couple after they had been awakened by Juanita's screams. Martinez said he further did not want any witnesses and therefore killed the elderly couple with an ax.

On June 23, 1897, at 11 p.m., the jury announced they had come to a decision as to their verdict. Forman S. A. Burris announced, "We, the jury, find the defendant guilty as charged, and assess his punishment at death."

Judge N. Kennon asked Martinez if he had anything to say before passing sentence. Martinez replied that he wished to make two requests. The first request was that he be allowed to see his wife. Second, that a brass band play at his execution while he was being hanged.

Judge Kennon then ordered that his execution take place on July 30. In preparation for the execution, the citizens of Floresville began taking up a collection to raise the $25 needed to pay for the brass band.

On July 30, 1897, Martinez, dressed in a black suit was escorted outside the Wilson County jail to the fifteen-foot high gallows. In the presence of 5,000 spectators, Martinez was allowed to sing and dance from the gallows. The song Martinez sang for the crowd was a love song he had written for the girl he loved and murdered. The song was recorded on a phonograph with part of the proceeds from sales to be given to his wife. At the end of the song, Martinez was told to be prepared.

Martinez took off his hat and used it to waved to his friends while shouting, "Adios amigos," while he danced for the last time. The drop of seven and half feet almost severed Martinez's head from his body.

The *San Antonio Light*, dated, Friday, July 30, 1897, provided readers with a full account of the crime and execution at Floresville, Texas.

Refugio Juareque

Race/Gender: Hispanic Male **Age:** 23 **Offense:** Rape
Offense Date: July 2, 1908 **Weapon:** Physical Force & Knife **Execution Date:** June 11, 1909

On December 17, 1908, Refugio Juareque was tried and convicted for the rape of fifteen-year-old Alvina Olenik on July 2, 1908. Just before dark, Alvina was walking home from the Sutherland Springs post office (twenty-one miles east of San Antonio) when Juareque grabbed her and a struggle ensued. Juareque dragged the girl from the road and into the brush where he raped her. Afterwards, Juareque beat, stomped on her face, and stabbed the girl to the left breast with a knife. Leaving the knife stuck in her breast, Juareque left believing he had killed the girl, but she survived

On the day of the execution, Juareque changed from his jail clothes to his new suit in preparation of his execution. Once dressed, and the reading of the death warrant concluded, Juareque was lead to the scaffold.

On the gallows, Juareque claimed he was innocent of the crime, and asked that his brother be permitted to shake hands with him which the sheriff permitted. Afterwards, as Sheriff William Wright was about to place the black cap over the head, Juareque stabbed the sheriff in the chest with a sharpened spoon handle just above his heart. Juareque fought with the officers to escape, and yelled for his brother to come to his assistance, which he did not.

Once Juareque was restrained, Constable Trainer turned to Sheriff Wright and seeing blood said, "Well, you are stabbed, go to the doctor."

Sheriff Wright replied, "I'm not hurt, he struck me with his fist." The sheriff quickly weakened and could not speak any louder than a whisper.

Juareque was placed over the trap, and after the noose was adjusted, Milam Wright, brother of the sheriff sprung the trap. Just as the trap was released, Juareque threw his shoulders back and fell over the trap opening. For ten minutes, the condemned man wrestled with the officers on the platform to remove him from the opening. After Juareque was stood back up and the trap reset, the trap was sprung a second time. The fall did not break the neck and Juareque strangled to death.

After the execution, officers searched the cell Juareque had occupied. In the old pair of pants he had been wearing, a second spoon knife was found.

The *Dallas Morning News*, dated Saturday, June 12, 1909, provided readers with details of the assault and the execution at Floresville, Texas.

Wise County
County Seat - Decatur

George Henry

Alias: Grant Carter **Race/Gender:** Black Male **Offense:** Murder
Offense Date: February 23, 1897 **Weapon:** Wood Log **Execution:** February 18, 1898

Wise County's only legal execution was the result of a change of venue from Denton County. Wise County had experienced other executions during the Civil War when five men in 1862, were hanged for treason against the Confederate States of America. Those five hanging were the result of a "citizens court," similar to the forty hanged in October of 1862, at Gainesville, Texas, in Cooke County.

On February 23, 1897, thirty-five-year-old Floyd Coberly had only worked as a jailer a week before his death. Because of his inexperience, Coberly may not have been completely familiar with the locking mechanism of the jail cells, and therefore assumed all of the jail cells were properly locked once he had pulled the lever down that bolted the cells shut.

Sadly, the circumstances of Floyd Coberly's death are familiar to other jailers who died in the line of duty in Texas. Jailers who were murdered by inmates with failed escape attempts, such as Wyatt Banks, Jose Flores and Israel Jordan who later stood on the gallows.

On February 23, 1897, at 11 a.m., Jailer Coberly had gone upstairs to the second tier of cells that housed the black prisoners to retrieve the dishes from the inmates. Coberly ordered the inmates back into their cells and told them to shut the cell doors.

All of the inmates complied; however, George Henry had discovered earlier that if the cell door was slightly ajar, the bolt did not lock the door when the lever was pulled. Retrieving a wood log from the stove as a weapon, he waited until the moment when the jailer would bend over to pick up the dishes. When Coberly did as Henry had hoped, he struck the officer to the back of the head, killing him. Henry then removed the jailer's keys and pistol from his holster. After Henry released inmates Will Miller and Arthur Gilmore, the three escaped through a jail office window. Trusty Guy Stokes then sounded the alarm of the escape and notified the jail physician of the injured jailer. Floyd never regained consciousness and died three and a half hours later.

By 5:30 that afternoon, all three escapees were recaptured. The sheriff fearing a lynch mob would assault the jail had George Henry immediately transported to the more secure jail at Fort Worth. On a change of venue, the murder trial was moved from Denton to Wise County where on November 11, 1897; Henry was tried and found guilty of murder in the first degree.

On the day afternoon of the scheduled day, George Henry was neatly dressed in a new black suit and driven to the gallows a half-mile south of town. When asked if he wished to say anything Henry replied no, except he wished to pray with his spiritual adviser. As both men knelt together, Henry prayed out loud and was heard saying, "Oh Jesus, for forty-nine days I have prayed and served thee and have been baptized with water. Receive my soul at last and if any sin be in me, remove it." Henry then bid goodbye to the preacher and said he was ready. The rope was then cut and Henry fell eight and a half feet, which broke hisneck.

The *Galveston Daily News*, dated Saturday, February 19, 1896, provided readers with a full account of the murder and execution at Decatur, Texas.

Young County

County Seat - Graham

Jack Post

Race/Gender: White Male **Age:** 29 **Offense:** Robbery & Murder
Offense Date: October 1879 **Weapon:** Firearm & Blunt Object **Execution:** October 28, 1881

In October of 1879, Mrs. G. B. McDermet (McDormott) returned to her farm located sixteen miles southwest of Graham, after visiting relatives to discover Lee Smith was living in her house, and her husband was missing. Smith told Mrs. McDermet he was renting the house from Jack Post after her husband has sold the farm to Post.

Mrs. McDermet who immediately believed her husband had been murdered, filed a complaint, and Jack Post, his brother Nelson and Lee Smith were all arrested. Lee Smith was later released as there was no indication he had anything to do with the missing man. Two weeks later, skeletal remains were found in a ravine two miles from the home of McDermet. An examination inquest suspected the remains had been in the ravine a month as the flesh had been eaten off by hogs. Those remains were identified by the beard, shirt and knife as being those of G. B. McDermet.

The theory of the murder was that Jack and Nelson Post broke into the house while McDermet was asleep. Dragging McDermet out of the house with a rope, the two men shot their victim seven times and hit him in the back of the skull with either an ax or some other blunt object. Motive for the murder was robbery as the Post brothers had taken over the farm, house and livestock.

On the day of the execution, a wagon pulled up in front of the jail to take Post to the gallows. As Post stepped into the wagon he saw his coffin there, and remarked, "I guess this is my box," and sat down upon it.

At the gallows, Post said that it would do him no good to plead his innocence; but that they were going to hang the wrong man. He said it was a horrible death, but many a good man had died that way, but that he could not shoulder that crime, nor would he lie to help anybody. He expressed a hope that his poor old mother and sister would be cared for, and then commended his soul to God, and told the sheriff to do his work.

When the trap was sprung, the rope slipped, and placed the knot of the noose to the front. Post was hoisted up to the platform, the rope was readjusted, and he was dropped a second time. After hanging nearly forty minutes, the body was cut down and placed in the coffin.

The *Galveston Daily News*, dated Saturday, October 29, 1881, provided a full account of the crime and execution at Graham, Texas.

Unknown County
"Holt"

Race/Gender: Unknown   **Offense Date:** Unknown   **Offense:** Unknown
Execution: November 1875

The *Camden Democrat* (Camden, New Jersey), dated Saturday, November 20, 1875, provided their readers of an interesting article of a person named "Holt" who was hanged four times on the same day in Texas.

Holt, a condemned Texas murderer, was found to have hanged himself in his cell when the time came for his execution. He was revived and taken to the scaffold, whereupon the bungling work of the sheriff justified Holt's sound judgment in having tried to do the hanging himself. The rope broke twice, so that altogether he was in effect hanged four times. And to the last he declared that he was innocent.

Texas Hangings in Alphabetical Order

	Name	Execution Date	Crime	County
1.	Ake, Taylor	August 22, 1879	Rape	Travis
2.	Aldava, Christino	August 14, 1885	Murder	Webb
3.	Anderson, Tom	1863	Robbery	Travis
4.	Apolinar, Clemente	February 23, 1923	Murder	Bexar
5.	Armstrong, John	April 26, 1907	Murder	Colorado
6.	Asbeck, William	June 28, 1913	Murder	Victoria
7.	Autre, Pete	October 28, 1898	Murder	Fort Bend
8.	Bailey, Dock	November 7, 1907	Murder/Robbery	Nacogdoches
9.	Ballard, Bob	November 22, 1901	Murder/Robbery	Brazos
10.	Ballard, Henry	February 19, 1915	Murder	Red River
11.	Ballew, Stephen	May 24, 1872	Murder/Robbery	Collin
12.	Baltimore, Chas	December 11, 1917	Murder/Mutiny	Bexar County – Fort Sam Houston
13.	Banks, Chillers	April 13, 1888	Murder	Chambers
14.	Banks, Wyatt	April 23, 1883	Murder	Ellis
15.	Barber, Jim	October 7, 1898	Murder	Gonzales
16.	Barnes, George	April 14, 1873	Murder/Robbery	Travis
17.	Bass, Bill	January 31, 1885	Rape	Lamar
18.	Bates, Henry	December 8, 1905	Robbery	Colorado
19.	Blackmore, William	March 26, 1869	Murder/Robbery	Grayson
20.	Blackwell, Will	March 6, 1891	Murder/Robbery	Gonzales
21.	Bly, Ely	August 7, 1874	Murder	Jack
22.	Boone, William D.	September 24, 1918	Murder/Mutiny	Bexar County – Fort Sam Houston
23.	Bowen, Brown	May 17, 1878	Murder	Gonzales
24.	Boyd, John	January 8, 1909	Rape	Fayette
25.	Brackenridge, Willim	December 11, 1917	Murder/Mutiny	Bexar County – Fort Sam Houston
26.	Bradley, Ezekiel	May 2, 1879	Murder	Brazos
27.	Bragg, Solomon	May 1, 1874	Murder/Robbery	Tarrant
28.	Brewster, Joseph	July 5, 1883	Rape	El Paso
29.	Brock, John Henry	May 30, 1913	Murder	Travis
30.	Brown Jr., George	November 21, 1879	Murder	Denton
31.	Brown, Alexander	July 28, 1893	Murder	Bastrop
32.	Brown, Andrew	November 21, 1879	Murder	Denton
33.	Brown, Austin	May 25, 1894	Murder	Bexar
34.	Brown, Henry	May 7, 1900	Murder	Hunt
35.	Brown, Henry	November 30, 1906	Murder	Medina
36.	Brown, John	March 27, 1908	Rape	DeWitt
37.	Brown, Larnon	December 11, 1917	Murder/Mutiny	Bexar County – Fort Sam Houston
38.	Buchanan, Jim	October 16, 1902	Murder/Rape	Nacogdoches
39.	Buenrostro, Jose	May 19, 1916	Murder	Cameron
40.	Bunch, Jackson	November 21, 1856	Murder	Jefferson
41.	Burgess, Robert	April 29, 1916	Murder	Jefferson
42.	Burke, Jim	April 28, 1893	Rape	Fannin
43.	Burks, Lynesfield	August 27, 1880	Rape	McLennan
44.	Burleson, Richard	April 12, 1895	Murder/Robbery	Limestone
45.	Burt, Eugene	May 27, 1898	Murder	Travis
46.	Burton, Pate	March 24, 1899	Murder/Robbery	Harris

Texas Hangings in Alphabetical Order

	Name	Execution Date	Crime	County
47.	Butler, Marcus	January 31, 1851	Aiding in Murder	El Paso
48.	Cady, Lovet	June 29, 1855	Murder	Red River
49.	Caldwell, Shack	August 18, 1882	Murder	Collin
50.	Caldwell, William	July 31, 1891	Murder	Harris
51.	Campbell, Michael	April 28, 1838	Murder	Victoria
52.	Campos, Ramon	February 1, 1907	Murder	Karnes
53.	Cannon, John	July 8, 1910	Murder	Polk
54.	Carlisle, John	May 12, 1893	Murder	Grayson
55.	Carter, English	July 2, 1880	Murder	Walker
56.	Cason, James	May 22, 1908	Murder/Robbery	Parker
57.	Castillo, Rosalie	November 25, 1892	Rape	El Paso
58.	Catchings, Eugene	November 3, 1876	Murder	Kaufman
59.	Chapa, Melquiades	May 19, 1916	Murder	Cameron
60.	Chappell, Andrew	March 18, 1896	Murder	Austin
61.	Chivarria, Caledonio	August 14, 1885	Murder/Robbery	Webb
62.	Clark, Oscar	June 20, 1871	Murder	Cooke
63.	Clayton, Joseph	July, 1834	Murder	Austin
64.	Coates, Rufus	November 8, 1918	Murder	Tarrant
65.	Collier, Babe	September 17, 1918	Murder/Mutiny	Bexar County – Fort Sam Houston
66.	Collins, Sam	May 19, 1905	Murder	Harrison
67.	Compton, J. B.	March 15, 1912	Murder/Robbery	Webb
68.	Cone, John	July 6, 1883	Rape	Harris
69.	Cook, Tobe	June 10, 1892	Murder/Rape	Bastrop
70.	Cooley, Clarence	October 18, 1916	Murder/Robbery	Harris
71.	Cooper, James	April 30, 1875	Murder	Washington
72.	Cordova Jr., Jose	July 7, 1879	Murder/Robbery	Bexar
73.	Crews, J. Q. A.	January 14, 1895	Murder/Robbery	Denton
74.	Curry, William	Janaury 31, 1851	Aiding in Murder	El Paso
75.	Davidson, Jim	November 24, 1899	Murder/Rape/Robbery	Travis
76.	Davila, Andres	August 7, 1874	Murder/Robbery	Nueces
77.	Craig, Augustus	March 14, 1901	Murder	Austin
78.	Davis, Bill	November 6, 1879	Murder	Caldwell
79.	Davis, Ira B.	December 11, 1917	Murder/Mutiny	Bexar County – Fort Sam Houston
80.	Davis, Mannon	March 30, 1894	Murder	Lamar
81.	Davis, Perry	August 30, 1877	Murder	McLennan
82.	Davis, Zedolph	April 28, 1893	Rape	Lavaca
83.	Deon, Prean	July 9, 1897	Murder	Orange
84.	Dink, Frank	July 6, 1866	Murder	Van Zandt
85.	Divins, James	December 11, 1917	Murder/Mutiny	Bexar County – Fort Sam Houston
86.	Dodd, Leonard	May 24, 1918	Rape	Dallas
87.	Doren, George	August 20, 1880	Murder	Navarro
88.	Dougherty, Lucy (slave)	March 5, 1858	Murder	Galveston
89.	Douglas, Fred	August 27, 1920	Murder/Robbery	Dallas
90.	Dove, John	November 27, 1896	Rape	Palo Pinto
91.	Duncan, Richard	September 18, 1891	Murder/Robbery	Maverick
92.	Duran, Juan	December 14, 1883	Murder/Robbery	Presidio
93.	Elkins, Jane Elkins	May 27, 1853	Murder	Dallas
94.	Felder, John	January 9, 1891	Murder	Cherokee

Name	Execution Date	Crime	County
95. Felder, Wade	January 9, 1891	Murder	Cherokee
96. Fields, Jack	December 3, 1892	Murder/Robbery	Wharton
97. Fierro, Demeiro	November 1, 1889	Murder	Presidio
98. Fike, Carrol	August 26, 1859	Murder	Fort Bend
99. Finch, Barney	February 8, 1834	Murder	Nacogdoches
100. Fisher, James	May 27, 1892	Murder	Delta
101. Flores, Antonio	January 6, 1900	Murder	El Paso
102. Flores, Jose	July 21, 1921	Murder	Falls
103. Flores, Juan	June 26, 1875	Murder	Refugio
104. Flores, Lino	January 5, 1854	Murder	Bexar
105. Forbes, Henry	November 13, 1840	Burglary/Escape	Galveston
106. Ford, Clay	July 20, 1899	Murder/Robbery	Fayette
107. Ford, Walter	October 27, 1899	Murder	McLennan
108. Fowler, Paul	August 7, 1913	Murder/Robbery	Tarrant
109. Franklin, James	August 16, 1918	Murder	Hardin
110. Freeman, Hickman	September 4, 1896	Murder/Robbery	Lamar
111. Freeny, George	November 25, 1892	Murder	Robertson
112. Frizzell, William	November 20, 1891	Murder	Taylor
113. Fugett, Henry	February 12, 1904	Murder	Johnson
114. Fulke, Eugene	September 28, 1894	Murder	Lamar
115. Gaitan, Quirius	June 9, 1882	Murder	Cameron
116. Garcia, Antonio	July 11, 1879	Murder	Nueces
117. Garcia, Vincente	June 22, 1866	Murder	Cameron
118. Garlington, James	July 28, 1899	Murder/Robbery	Tarrant
119. Garrett, Dick	November 21, 1906	Murder	Shelby
120. Garza, Florencio	June 22, 1866	Murder	Cameron
121. Gibson, Archie	May 29, 1885	Murder	Fort Bend
122. Gibson, Monk	June 28, 1908	Murder/Rape	DeWitt
123. Giles, Robert	January 14, 1887	Murder/Robbery	Henderson
124. Golden, Claude	February 12, 1909	Rape	Jasper
125. Gomez, Refugio	June 6, 1884	Murder	Duval
126. Gonzales, Camillio	April 16, 1886	Murder/Robbery	Kinney
127. Gonzales, Eduardo Ray	March 30, 1894	Murder	Lamar
128. Gonzales, Jacinto	January 10, 1916	Rape	Live Oak
129. Gonzales, Ysidro	February 1, 1915	Murder	Live Oak
130. Goodson, Joseph	May 20, 1896	Murder/Robbery	Washington
131. Grace, George	January 6, 1922	Rape	Bexar
132. Graham, Harry	June 9, 1893	Murder	Morris
133. Green, Charley	May 23, 1903	Rape	Fort Bend
134. Green, Johnnie	February 25, 1909	Murder/Robbery	Bastrop
135. Grinder, Jesse	November 30, 1846	Murder	Fannin
136. Guerra, Bartolo	January 22, 1871	Murder	Bee
137. Guerrero, Benigno	April 9, 1915	Murder	Hays
138. Guiles, Joe	May 24, 1894	Murder/Robbery	Karnes
139. Hadley, Amos	August 30, 1878	Murder/Robbery	Gregg
140. Hainline, Jacob	August 8, 1879	Murder/Robbery	Bexar
141. Harkey, George	June 30, 1903	Murder	Camp
142. Harris Jr., Charley	August 29, 1879	Murder	Montague

Texas Hangings in Alphabetical Order

Name	Execution Date	Crime	County
143. Harris, Caesar	March 16, 1899	Murder	Brazoria
144. Harris, John	December 19, 1902	Murder	Lamar
145. Harrison, Ernest	August 7, 1913	Murder/Robbery	Tarrant
146. Hawkins, Thomas C.	December 11, 1917	Murder/Mutiny	Bexar County – Fort Sam Houston
147. Haynes, Meredith	December 15, 1871	Murder	Travis
148. Hemphill, Will	February 26, 1915	Rape	Guadalupe
149. Hemple, E.	April 30, 1864	Murder	Colorado
150. Henderson, Henry	July 8, 1910	Murder/Robbery	Cherokee
151. Hennegan, Oscar	December 17, 1895	Murder	Lee
152. Henniker, Charles	December 8, 1843	Murder/Robbery	Galveston
153. Henry, George	February 18, 1898	Murder	Wise
154. Henry, John	March 26, 1880	Murder	Navarro
155. Henry, John	July 12, 1912	Murder	Travis
156. Hernandez, Apolonario	December 23, 1904	Murder	Nueces
157. Hernandez, Juan	November 15, 1878	Murder	Refugio
158. Hill, Frank	May 18, 1855	Murder	Gonzales
159. Hill, Jim	July 3, 1896	Murder	Polk
160. Hinton, William	March 25, 1860	Murder	Falls
161. Hoffman, Nat	July 11, 1918	Rape	McLennan
162. Holden, Fletcher	June 6, 1890	Murder/Robbery	Cass
163. Holden, Henry	June 6, 1890	Murder/Robbery	Cass
164. Holland, Frank	February 23, 1893	Murder/Robbery	Brazoria
165. Holt,	November 1875	Unknown	
166. Hornsby, George	April 14, 1922	Murder/Robbery	Bell
167. Howard, Albert	March 18, 1921	Rape/Robbery	Gonzales
168. Howard, Sam	June 18, 1880	Murder	Bastrop
169. Hubert, Harvey	August 23, 1918	Murder	Travis
170. Hughes, Harvey	April 7, 1923	Murder/Robbery	Brewster
171. Hughes, Lee	January 30, 1891	Murder	Washington
172. Hunter, Green	July 10, 1920	Rape	Dallas
173. Hyde, John	July 11, 1856	Murder	Harris
174. Jackson, Andrew	January 18, 1895	Murder	Red River
175. Jackson, Conrad	July 16, 1888	Murder	McLennan
176. Jackson, Cornelius	July 2, 1915	Murder/Robbery	Wharton
177. Jackson, Smith	December 14, 1878	Murder	Bastrop
178. Jenkins, Edward	August 17, 1874	Murder	Bexar
179. Jenkins, Granville	March 30, 1899	Murder	Robertson
180. Jernigan, Sam	March 11, 1916	Rape	Trinity
181. Johnson, Abe	September 22, 1922	Murder	Liberty
182. Johnson, Albert	March 30, 1906	Murder/Robbery	Ellis
183. Johnson, Frank	December 11, 1917	Murder/Mutiny	Bexar County – Fort Sam Houston
184. Johnson, Green	December 20, 1878	Murder	Menard
185. Johnson, Henry	November 14, 1885	Murder/Rape	Houston
186. Johnson, Henry	May 30, 1903	Rape	Kaufman
187. Johnson, Henry	June 8, 1891	Murder/Robbery	Rains
188. Johnson, Jake	August 5, 1870	Murder/Robbery	Harris
189. Johnson, John	December 21, 1888	Rape	Houston
190. Johnson, Lee	September 26, 1913	Murder	Bexar

Name	Execution Date	Crime	County
191. Johnson, Louis	January 30, 1912	Rape	Polk
192. Johnson, Rip	May 14, 1903	Murder	Walker
193. Johnson, Robert	July 20, 1906	Murder	Erath
194. Johnson, Sol	July 20, 1923	Murder/Robbery	Bowie
195. Johnson,	July, 1855	Murder	Harris
196. Jones, Andrew	June 8, 1844	Murder/Robbery	Fannin
197. Jones, Clark	August 13, 1869	Murder	Falls
198. Jones, David	March 28, 1838	Murder	Harris
199. Jones, Frank	November, 1900	Murder	Houston
200. Jones, James	May 13, 1887	Murder	Bowie
201. Jones, James	July 6, 1878	Murder	Fayette
202. Jones, Jesse	November 30, 1906	Murder	McLennan
203. Jones, Pryor	December 14, 1878	Murder	Bastrop
204. Jones, Ray	March 9, 1923	Rape	Colorado
205. Jones, Sam	October 16, 1912	Murder	Grayson
206. Jones, Tom	June 20, 1908	Murder/Robbery	Fort Bend
207. Jones, Wesley	August 11, 1876	Rape	Dallas
208. Jones, Will	August 30, 1918	Murder	Dallas
209. Jones, Willie	March 9, 1900	Murder	Jefferson
210. Jordan, Isreal	July 21, 1921	Murder	Falls
211. Juareque, Refugio	June 11, 1909	Rape	Wilson
212. Kapps, Isam	May 7, 1880	Rape	Tarrant
213. Key, Charles	September 13, 1895	Murder/Robbery	Lamar
214. Kimball, Lawson	April 14, 1873	Murder/Robbery	Travis
215. King, George	July 2, 1895	Murder/Robbery	Cherokee
216. King, Jim	December 2, 1898	Murder	Wharton
217. King, Will	October 25, 1901	Murder	McLennan
218. Kinny, George	May 28, 1904	Rape	Anderson
219. Kugadt, Charles	October 20, 1898	Murder	Washington
220. Lane, Ben	March 19, 1886	Murder	San Augustine
221. Larkins, Joe	April 17, 1915	Murder	Ellis
222. Lee, Nathan	August 31, 1923	Murder	Brazoria
223. Lee, Silas	September 4, 1896	Murder/Robbery	Lamar
224. Lee, Tommy	March 9, 1914	Murder	Tarrant
225. Leeper, Jim	September 29, 1891	Murder/Robbery	Coryell
226. Leva, Casimero	December 7, 1888	Murder	Hidalgo
227. Lewis, Joe	March 27, 1891	Murder	Bell
228. Little, Charley	May 4, 1899	Murder/Robbery	Hunt
229. Long, Ed	December 19, 1913	Murder	Dallas
230. Longley, William	October 11, 1878	Murder	Lee
231. Looney, Samuel	February 8, 1834	Murder	Nacogdoches
232. Losano, Vicente	June 16, 1904	Murder	Live Oak
233. Lount (slave)	July 25, 1862	Murder/Robbery	Travis
234. Luttrell, Charles	May 12, 1893	Murder	Grayson
235. Macklin, Willis	July 2, 1909	Murder	Polk
236. MacWhorter, Pat	December 11, 1917	Murder/Mutiny	Bexar County – Fort Sam Houston
237. Madison, Bill	January 15, 1886	Murder	Jefferson
238. Malone, Joe	September 2, 1898	Murder/Rape	Dallas

Texas Hangings in Alphabetical Order

Name	Execution Date	Crime	County
239. Manning, Will	July 7, 1905	Murder	Hunt
240. Martin, Frank	June 10, 1898	Murder	Wharton
241. Martin, King	March 16, 1900	Rape	Kaufman
242. Martin, Rufus	July 12, 1906	Murder/Robbery	Tarrant
243. Martinez Jr., Leon Cardenas	May 11, 1914	Murder	Reeves
244. Martinez, Maximo	July 30, 1897	Murder/Rape	Wilson
245. Massey, Sam	April 28, 1893	Rape	Fannin
246. Maxey, Wood	August 9, 1912	Murder	Grayson
247. Mays, H. L.	October 12, 1906	Murder	Bexar
248. McClennan, Charlie	April 13, 1912	Murder	Washington
249. McCline, Dan	March 29, 1912	Murder	Falls
250. McCoy, James	August 23, 1889	Murder	Bexar
251. McDonald, Alfred	November 17, 1893	Murder	Walker
252. McDonald, Thomas	September 17, 1918	Murder/Mutiny	Bexar County – Fort Sam Houston
253. McGee, Henry	August 12, 1892	Murder	Harris
254. McGill, Charles	January 25, 1889	Murder	Milam
255. Mcintosh, Will	October 1, 1909	Murder	Lamar
256. McKee, Alamo	October 25, 1895	Murder/Robbery	Cass
257. McKinney, Bob	April 16, 1900	Murder	Hunt
258. Mendez, Jose	December 10, 1891	Murder	Val Verde
259. Mendiola, Jose	January 15, 1886	Murder	La Salle
260. Mendoza, Bartolo	August 13, 1869	Murder	El Paso
261. Mikel, Jeff	December 13, 1902	Murder	Lee
262. Miles, Tom	June 6, 1890	Murder/Robbery	Cass
263. Miller, G. R.	June 3, 1910	Murder/Robbery	Donley
264. Miller, Henry	July 28, 1893	Murder	Dallas
265. Miller, Henry	July 28, 1871	Murder	Washington
266. Misher, Ellis	January 12, 1900	Rape	Guadalupe
267. Mitchell	June 8, 1844	Murder/Robbery	Fannin
268. Mitchell, Burke	August 31, 1888	Murder	Harris
269. Mitchell, Frank	August 1, 1908	Murder	Burleson
270. Mitchell, Nelson	January 9, 1875	Murder	Hood
271. Mitchell, Roy	July 30, 1923	Murder/Rape/Robbery	McLennan
272. Moore, Jesse	December 11, 1917	Murder/Mutiny	Bexar County – Fort Sam Houston
273. Moore, Tom	September 28, 1894	Murder	Lamar
274. Mootry, Mat	March 27, 1896	Murder	Williamson
275. Morris, Emanuel	October 28, 1898	Murder/Rape	Fort Bend
276. Morris, James	November 25, 1904	Murder	Colorado
277. Morris, Neverson	March 23, 1900	Murder	Fannin
278. Morris, Thomas	January 31, 1902	Murder/Robbery	Navarro
279. Morrison, George	October 27, 1899	Murder	Wilbarger
280. Moss, Enoch	September 3, 1900	Murder	Bastrop
281. Murphy, Jace	January 9, 1891	Murder	Caldwell
282. Murray, Irvine	September 10, 1886	Murder	Williamson
283. Murray, Will	April 25, 1904	Murder	Jefferson
284. Myers, Charles	November 10, 1915	Murder	Tarrant
285. Myers, Sam	March 19, 1880	Murder	Johnson
286. Nelson (slave)	June 10, 1848	Murder	Red River

Name	Execution Date	Crime	County
287. Nelson, Dennis	August 13, 1869	Murder	Falls
288. Nesbit, William	December 11, 1917	Murder/Mutiny	Bexar County – Fort Sam Houston
289. Nichols, Ed	January 12, 1894	Rape	Travis
290. Noftsinger Lucius	April 30, 1880	Murder	Cooke
291. Norris, Anderson	January 10, 1902	Murder	McLennan
292. O'Conner, W. J.	March 9, 1857	Murder	Calhoun
293. Oates, Burrell	November 29, 1912	Murder/Robbery	Ellis
294. Olivarez, Andres	June 2, 1902	Murder	Nueces
295. Oliver, Carl	April 16, 1915	Murder	Grayson
296. Ortiz, Abraham	May 2, 1913	Murder/Rape	Hidalgo
297. Para, Geronimo	January 6, 1900	Murder	El Paso
298. Parker, Carl	May 4, 1922	Murder	Harris
299. Parks, Cal	July 15, 1892	Murder/Rape	Burleson
300. Parras, Pablo	June 28, 1878	Murder	Nueces
301. Payne, Bill	November 3, 1876	Murder	Kaufman
302. Pearl, John	October 22, 1901	Murder/Robbery	Coleman
303. Perez, Lorenzo	November 27, 1891	Murder	Midland
304. Perry, Diggs	April 21, 1913	Murder/Robbery	Matagorda
305. Phillips (slave)	January 5, 1855	Murder	Cass
306. Pierson, Henderson	February 2, 1900	Murder	Red River
307. Pitman, William	June 8, 1860	Murder	Cooke
308. Pocket, Indian	September 12, 1879	Murder	Lavaca
309. Poe, Willis	June 11, 1869	Murder	Rusk
310. Post, Jack	January 28, 1881	Murder/Robbery	Young
311. Powell, Diomed	August 30, 1878	Murder/Robbery	Gregg
312. Powell, Ed	September 29, 1891	Murder/Robbery	Coryell
313. Powell, Felix	April 2, 1907	Murder/Rape	Castro
314. Price, John	March 23, 1920	Murder	San Augustine
315. Puryear, Dan	November 21, 1874	Murder/Rape	Lee
316. Quarles, Henry	June 11, 1880	Murder	Harris
317. Quick, John	March 28, 1838	Murder	Harris
318. Quiroz, Francisco	January 5, 1854	Murder	Bexar
319. Ransom, John	April 3, 1903	Murder/Robbery	Williamson
320. Rather, Joe	December 28, 1888	Murder	Shelby
321. Reeves, John	February 17, 1905	Murder	Red River
322. Renfro, John	July 27, 1900	Murder	Johnson
323. Reyna, Marguerito	December 4, 1903	Rape	Lavaca
324. Rhodes, Jasper	May 22, 1885	Murder	Galveston
325. Roan, John	April 19, 1902	Rape	Falls
326. Robertson, Fred	May 31, 1878	Rape	Limestone
327. Robertson, Julius	May 14, 1910	Murder/Robbery	Dallas
328. Robertson, Kit	October 11, 1895	Murder/Robbery	Liberty
329. Robinson, Harris	June 11, 1869	Murder	Rusk
330. Robinson, James	September 17, 1918	Murder/Mutiny	Bexar County – Fort Sam Houston
331. Robinson, John	January 10, 1913	Murder/Robbery	Dallas
332. Robinson, Tom	April 28, 1899	Rape	Hill
333. Rocha, Juan	August 2, 1901	Murder	Bexar
334. Rodgers, Robert	June 11, 1866	Murder	Cameron

Name	Execution Date	Crime	County
335. Rodriguez, Cruz	December 9, 1887	Murder	Uvarde
336. Rodriguez, Josefa	November 13, 1863	Murder/Robbery	San Patricio
337. Roe, William	May 26, 1888	Murder	Grimes
338. Rolly, Albert	March 20, 1896	Murder	Williamson
339. Rowland, James	May 3, 1872	Murder/Robbery	Titus
340. Russell, Lee	October 1, 1909	Murder/Rape	Houston
341. Rutherford, Brady	May 20, 1896	Murder/Robbery	Washington
342. Rutherford, John	May 20, 1896	Murder/Robbery	Washington
343. Sampson, Henry	February 15, 1916	Murder/Robbery	Harris
344. Sampson, Virgil	May 27, 1921	Rape	Lamar
345. Sanchez, Federico	March 3, 1915	Murder	Live Oak
346. Saucedo, Vincente	September 19, 1902	Rape	Bexar
347. Saunders, John	February 8, 1834	Murder	Nacogdoches
348. Sawyer, Fred	January 13, 1899	Rape	Ellis
349. Schultz, Jesse "John"	June 29, 1855	Murder/Robbery	Galveston
350. Schwartz, Conrad	March 22, 1905	Murder/Robbery	DeWitt
351. Scott, Charles	April 15, 1893	Murder	Smith
352. Scott, George	May 27, 1892	Murder	Rusk
353. Scott, Isham	January 5, 1883	Murder	Lamar
354. Shaw, John	November 25, 1898	Murder	Johnson
355. Shaw, Walter	August 4, 1893	Murder	Harris
356. Shelby, Arthur	January 15, 1873	Murder	Burnet
357. Shelby, Ben	January 15, 1873	Murder	Burnet
358. Shelton, Edmund	May 14, 1909	Murder	Galveston
359. Sheppard, Warren	November 12, 1880	Murder	Montgomery
360. Shutt, J. E.	May 29, 1903	Murder	Bowie
361. Simmons, Henry	May 2, 1904	Murder/Rape	Travis
362. Sims, King	June 24, 1892	Murder	McLennan
363. Singleton, John	April 27, 1877	Murder/Robbery	Bee
364. Slaughter, Howard	December 28, 1850	Murder	Cameron
365. Smith, Brozier	March 25, 1904	Murder	Ellis
366. Smith, F. M.	November 9, 1900	Murder	Nacogdoches
367. Smith, Frank	June 1875	Murder	Montague
368. Smith, George	July 8, 1892	Murder/Robbery	Grayson
369. Smith, Joseph	September 17, 1918	Murder/Mutiny	Bexar County – Fort Sam Houston
370. Smith, William	January 15, 1873	Murder	Burnet
371. Snodgrass, Charles	December 11, 1917	Murder/Mutiny	Bexar County – Fort Sam Houston
372. Solomon, George	June 28, 1878	Murder	Freestone
373. Spearman, D. L.	October 25, 1895	Murder	Harrison
374. Spears, Sidney	June 18, 1900	Murder	Grayson
375. Speer, John	September 20, 1878	Murder	McLennan
376. Stanley, James	October 20, 1883	Murder/Robbery	Colorado
377. Stanton, Floyd	August 1, 1913	Murder	Dallas
378. Stepp, Ezell	November 17, 1922	Murder	Collin
379. Stevenson, Walter	May 24, 1918	Rape	Dallas
380. Strawther, Clem	March 18, 1896	Murder	Austin
381. Swaid. A.	April 30, 1860	Murder	Galveston
382. Swan, Elisha	March 31, 1899	Murder	Bastrop

Name	Execution Date	Crime	County
383. Tankersley, Presley	September 1, 1905	Murder	Williamson
384. Tapia, Hipolito	August 7, 1874	Murder/Robbery	Nueces
385. Taylor, James	December 21, 1883	Murder	Lee
386. Terrell, Alexander	April 2, 1897	Rape	Harris
387. Thomas, Charles	August 11, 1882	Murder	Anderson
388. Thomas, Gus	February 26, 1910	Murder	Wharton
389. Thomas, Lee	August 2, 1895	Murder/Robbery	Navarro
390. Thomas, Marcellus	September 3, 1909	Murder	Harris
391. Thompson, Adam	July 1, 1881	Murder/Robbery	Dallas
392. Thompson, Floyd	January 7, 1916	Murder	Freestone
393. Thompson, John	March 26, 1869	Murder/Robbery	Grayson
394. Thompson, Miles	February 17, 1882	Rape/Murder	Austin
395. Toettel, Julius	November 13, 1879	Murder	Grayson
396. Torrez, Porfirio	August 14, 1914	Murder	Atascosa
397. Towles, Allen	March 26, 1880	Murder	Freestone
398. Turner, George H.	December 22, 1905	Murder/Robbery	Bexar
399. Upkins, James	March 30, 1894	Rape	Lamar
400. Utley, Louis	February 1, 1916	Murder	Harris
401. Uvalte, Cresencio	November 28, 1879	Murder	Webb
402. Valentine (slave), Peter	January 27, 1859	Murder	Red River
403. Vann, Holly	May 12, 1905	Murder/Robbery	Dallas
404. Vargas, Alberto	January 4, 1907	Murder	Callahan
405. Varner, Albert	February 16, 1912	Rape	Guadalupe
406. Vela, Juan	June 22, 1866	Murder	Cameron
407. Vines, Sellars	August 9, 1912	Murder	Grayson
408. Wade, Hamp	October 15, 1887	Murder	Walker
409. Wade, John	January 31, 1951	Aiding in Murder	El Paso
410. Waggoner, Perry	July 6, 1900	Murder	Cherokee
411. Waite, Fred	March 23, 1883	Murder	Robertson
412. Walker, Anthony	January 23, 1885	Murder	Harrison
413. Walker, Bill	April 16, 1880	Murder	Robertson
414. Walker, Dan	May 28, 1897	Murder	Fannin
415. Walker, George	April 5, 1889	Murder	Liberty
416. Walker, Harry	May 10, 1921	Murder/Robbery	Harris
417. Walker, Isaiah	July 28, 1881	Murder	Gonzales
418. Ward, Charles	August 21, 1882	Rape	Bexar
419. Warren, John	August 15, 1902	Murder/Robbery	Limestone
420. Washington, A. B.	February 14, 1907	Murder	Bastrop
421. Washington, Archie	July 26, 1892	Murder	Orange
422. Washington, Sam	February 26, 1910	Murder	Wharton
423. Washington, Wash	March 31, 1886	Murder	Falls
424. Washington, William	October 19, 1888	Murder/Rape/Robbery	Colorado
425. Watrous, Sam	October 27, 1899	Murder/Rape/Robbery	Travis
426. Watson, Alf	December 8, 1893	Murder	San Jacinto
427. Wheatley, James	December 11, 1917	Murder/Mutiny	Bexar County – Fort Sam Houston
428. Wheeler, George	September 4, 1896	Murder	Lamar
429. White, Alfred	June 11, 1892	Murder	Walker
430. White, Billy	January 22, 1875	Murder	Navarro

Texas Hangings in Alphabetical Order

Name	Execution Date	Crime	County
431. White, D. C.	February 2, 1882	Murder/Robbery	Van Zandt
432. White, Frank	March 23, 1900	Murder/Robbery	Fannin
433. White, Harvey	June 8, 1844	Murder/Robbery	Fannin
434. Wilcox, Ed	January 11, 1895	Rape	Guadalupe
435. Wilkerson, Buck	October 14, 1892	Murder	Bell
436. Wilkerson, Jack	June 29, 1906	Murder	Polk
437. Wilkins, John	June 26, 1896	Murder/Robbery	Johnson
438. Williams Griffin	April 30, 1875	Rape	Washington
439. Williams, Clint	August 5, 1915	Murder	Tarrant
440. Williams, Harrison	March 7, 1884	Murder	Navarro
441. Williams, James	July 31, 1908	Murder/Robbery	Bexar
442. Williams, Joe	December 18, 1868	Murder/Robbery	Parker
443. Williams, John	October 27, 1916	Murder	McLennan
444. Williams, Tom	September 23, 1881	Murder	Rusk
445. Williams, Wesley	September 29, 1888	Murder	Falls
446. Williams, William	May 8, 1844	Murder	Shelby
447. Williamson, Jim	June 25, 1897	Murder	Wharton
448. Wilson, Henry	December 14, 1914	Robbery	Calhoun
449. Wilson, Jake	August, 1869	Murder	McLennan
450. Wilson, James	June 2, 1843	Murder	Tyler
451. Wilson, Tom	October 22, 1909	Murder	Newton
452. Wood, Silas	November 10, 1876	Murder	Falls
453. Woods, Ball	January 15, 1873	Murder	Burnet
454. Woolridge, Albert	December 15, 1922	Murder	Colorado
455. Wray, L.	June 8, 1844	Murder/Robbery	Fannin
456. Wright, Albert D.	September 17, 1918	Murder/Mutiny	Bexar County – Fort Sam Houston
457. Wright, Allen	August 27, 1880	Murder	Dallas
458. Wright, Robert	December 17, 1909	Murder	Sabine
459. Wright, Tom	November 10, 1899	Murder	Erath
460. Wynne, John	June 24, 1910	Murder	Walker
461. Young, Alexander	February 12, 1851	Murder	El Paso
462. Young, George	May 8, 1886	Murder	Ellis
463. Young, John Henry	March 31, 1905	Murder	Ellis
464. Young, Risley W.	December 11, 1917	Murder/Mutiny	Bexar County – Fort Sam Houston
465. Young, Thomas	March 30, 1906	Murder	Williamson

Texas Hangings in Chronological Order

	Name	Execution Date	County
1.	Samuel Looney	February 8, 1834	Nacogdoches
2.	Barney Finch	February 8, 1834	Nacogdoches
3.	John Saunders	February 8, 1834	Nacogdoches
4.	Joseph Clayton	July, 1834	Austin
5.	John Quick	March 28, 1838	Harris
6.	David Jones	March 28, 1838	Harris
7.	Michael Campbell	April 28, 1838	Victoria
8.	Henry Forbes	November 13, 1840	Galveston
9.	Charles Henniker	December 8, 1843	Galveston
10.	William Williams	May 8, 1844	Shelby
11.	Andrew Jones	June 8, 1844	Fannin
12.	Harvey White	June 8, 1844	Fannin
13.	L. Wray	June 8, 1844	Fannin
14.	Mitchell	June 8, 1844	Fannin
15.	Jesse Grinder (slave)	November 30, 1846	Fannin
16.	Nelson (slave)	June 10, 1848	Red River ?
17.	Howard Slaughter	December 28, 1850	Cameron
18.	Unknown Mexican	December 28, 1850	Cameron
19.	Unknown Mexican	December 28, 1850	Cameron
20.	William Craig	January 31, 1851	El Paso
21.	Marcus Butler	January 31, 1851	El Paso
22.	John Wade	January 31, 1851	El Paso
23.	Alexander Young	February 12, 1851	El Paso
24.	Jane Elkins	May 27, 1853	Dallas
25.	Francisco Quiroz	January 5, 1854	Bexar
26.	Lino Flores	January 5, 1854	Bexar
27.	James Wilson	June 2, 1854	Tyler
28.	Phillips (slave)	January 5, 1855	Cass
29.	Jesse "John" Schultz	June 29, 1855	Galveston
30.	Lovet Cady	June 29, 1855	Red River
31.	Frank Hill	May 18, 1855	Gonzales
32.	Johnson	July, 1855	Harris
33.	John Hyde	July 11, 1856	Harris
34.	Jackson Bunch	November 21, 1856	Jefferson
35.	W. J. O'Conner	March 9, 1857	Calhoun
36.	Lucy Dougherty (slave)	March 5, 1858	Galveston
37.	Peter Valentine (slave)	January 27, 1859	Red River
38.	Carrol Fike	August 26, 1859	Fort Bend
39.	William Hinton	March 25, 1860	Falls
40.	A. Swaid	April 30, 1860	Galveston
41.	William Pitman	June 8, 1860	Cooke
42.	Lount (slave)	July 25, 1862	Travis
43.	Tom Anderson	1863	Travis
44.	Josefa "Chipita" Rodriguez	November 13, 1863	San Patricio
45.	E. Hemple	April 30, 1864	Colorado
46.	Robert Rodgers	June 11, 1866	Cameron
47.	Vincente Garcia	June 22, 1866	Cameron

Texas Hangings in Chronological Order

Name	Execution Date	County
48. Juan Vela	June 22, 1866	Cameron
49. Florencio Garza	June 22, 1866	Cameron
50. Frank Dink	July 6, 1866	Van Zandt
51. Joe Williams	December 18, 1868	Parker
52. William Blackmore	March 26, 1869	Grayson
53. John Thompson	March 26, 1869	Grayson
54. Willis Poe	June 11, 1869	Rusk
55. Harris Robinson	June 11, 1869	Rusk
56. Jake Wilson	August, 1869	McLennan
57. Bartolo Mendoza	August 13, 1869	El Paso
58. Clark Jones	August 13, 1869	Falls
59. Dennis Nelson	August 13, 1869	Falls
60. Jake Johnson	August 5, 1870	Harris
61. Bartolo Guerra	January 22, 1871	Bee
62. Oscar Clark	June 20, 1871	Cooke
63. Henry Miller	July 28, 1871	Washington
64. Meredith Haynes	December 15, 1871	Travis
65. James Rowland	May 3, 1872	Titus
66. Stephen Ballew	May 24, 1872	Collin
67. Arthur Shelby	January 15, 1873	Burnet
68. Ben Shelby	January 15, 1873	Burnet
69. William Smith	January 15, 1873	Burnet
70. Ball Woods	January 15, 1873	Burnet
71. George Barnes	April 14, 1873	Travis
72. Lawson Kimball	April 14, 1873	Travis
73. Solomon Bragg	May 1, 1874	Tarrant
74. Andres Davila	August 7, 1874	Nueces
75. Hipolito Tapia	August 7, 1874	Nueces
76. Ely Bly	August 7, 1874	Jack
77. Edward Jenkins	August 17, 1874	Bexar
78. Dan Puryear	November 21, 1874	Lee
79. Billy White	January 22, 1875	Navarro
80. James Cooper	April 30, 1875	Washington
81. Griffin Williams	April 30, 1875	Washington
82. Frank Smith	June 1875	Montague
83. Nelson Mitchell	October 9, 1875	Hood
84. Juan Flores	June 26, 1875	Refugio
85. Holt	November 1875	Unknown
86. Wesley Jones	August 11, 1876	Dallas
87. Bill Payne	November 3, 1876	Kaufman
88. Eugene Catchings	November 3, 1876	Kaufman
89. Salas Wood	November 10, 1876	Falls
90. John Singleton	April 27, 1877	Bee
91. Perry Davis	August 30, 1877	McLennan
92. Brown Bowen	May 17, 1878	Gonzales
93. Fred Robertson	May 31, 1878	Limestone
94. Pablo Parras	June 28, 1878	Nueces
95. George Solomon	June 28, 1878	Freestone
96. James Jones	July 6, 1878	Fayette

Name	Execution Date	County
97. Amos Hadley	August 30, 1878	Gregg
98. Diomed Powell	August 30, 1878	Gregg
99. John Speer	September 20, 1878	McLennan
100. William Longley	October 11, 1878	Lee
101. Juan Hernandez	November 15, 1878	Refugio
102. Smith Jackson	December 14, 1878	Bastrop
103. Pryor Jones	December 14, 1878	Bastrop
104. Green Johnson	December 20, 1878	Menard
105. Ezekiel Bradley	May 2, 1879	Brazos
106. Jose Cordova Jr.	July 7, 1879	Bexar
107. Antonio Garcia	July 11, 1879	Nueces
108. Jacob Hainline	August 8, 1879	Bexar
109. Ake Taylor	August 22, 1879	Travis
110. Charley Harris Jr.	August 29, 1879	Montague
111. Indian Pocket	September 12, 1879	Lavaca
112. Bill Davis	November 6, 1879	Caldwell
113. Julius Toettel	November 13, 1879	Grayson
114. George Brown Jr.	November 21, 1879	Denton
115. Andrew Brown	November 21, 1879	Denton
116. Cresencio Uvalte	November 28, 1879	Webb
117. Sam Myers	March 19, 1880	Johnson
118. John Henry	March 26, 1880	Navarro
119. Allen Towles	March 26, 1880	Freestone
120. Bill Walker	April 16, 1880	Robertson
121. Lucius Noftsinger	April 30, 1880	Cooke
122. Isam Kapps	May 7, 1880	Tarrant
123. Henry Quarles	June 11, 1880	Harris
124. Sam Howard	June 18, 1880	Bastrop
125. English Carter	July 2, 1880	Walker
126. George Doren	August 20, 1880	Navarro
127. Allen Wright	August 27, 1880	Dallas
128. Lynesfield Burks	August 27, 1880	McLennan
129. Warren Sheppard	November 12, 1880	Montgomery
130. Jack Post	January 28, 1881	Young
131. Adam Thompson	July 1, 1881	Dallas
132. Isaiah Walker	July 28, 1881	Gonzales
133. Tom Williams	September 23, 1881	Rusk
134. D. C. White	February 2, 1882	Van Zandt
135. Miles Thompson	February 17, 1882	Austin
136. Quirius Gaitan	June 9, 1882	Cameron
137. Charles Thomas	August 11, 1882	Anderson
138. Shack Caldwell	August 18, 1882	Collin
139. Charles Ward	August 21, 1882	Bexar
140. Isham Scott	January 5, 1883	Lamar
141. Fred Waite	March 23, 1883	Robertson
142. Wyatt Banks	April 23, 1883	Ellis
143. Joseph Brewster	July 5, 1883	El Paso
144. John Cone	July 6, 1883	Harris
145. James Stanley	October 20, 1883	Colorado

Texas Hangings in Chronological Order

Name	Execution Date	County
146. Juan Duran	December 14, 1883	Presidio
147. James Taylor	December 21, 1883	Lee
148. Harrison Williams	March 7, 1884	Navarro
149. Refugio Gomez	June 6, 1884	Duval
150. Anthony Walker	January 23, 1885	Harrison
151. Bill Bass	January 31, 1885	Lamar
152. Jasper Rhodes	May 22, 1885	Galveston
153. Archie Gibson	May 29, 1885	Fort Bend
154. Christino Aldava	August 14, 1885	Webb
155. Caledonio Chivarria	August 14, 1885	Webb
156. Henry Johnson	November 14, 1885	Houston
157. Bill Madison	January 15, 1886	Jefferson
158. Jose Mendiola	January 15, 1886	La Salle
159. Ben Lane	March 19, 1886	San Augustine
160. Wash Washington	March 31, 1886	Falls
161. Camillio Gonzales	April 16, 1886	Kinney
162. George Young	May 8, 1886	Ellis
163. Irvine Murray	September 10, 1886	Williamson
164. Robert Giles	January 14, 1887	Henderson
165. James Jones	May 13, 1887	Bowie
166. Hamp Wade	October 15, 1887	Walker
167. Cruz Rodriguez	December 9, 1887	Uvalde
168. Chillers Banks	April 13, 1888	Chambers
169. William Roe	May 26, 1888	Grimes
170. Conrad Jackson	July 16, 1888	McLennan
171. Burke Mitchell	August 31, 1888	Harris
172. Wesley Williams	September 29, 1888	Falls
173. William Washington	October 20, 1888	Colorado
174. Casimero Leva	December 7, 1888	Hidalgo
175. John Johnson	December 21, 1888	Houston
176. Joe Rather	December 28, 1888	Shelby
177. Charles McGill	January 25, 1889	Milam
178. George Walker	April 5, 1889	Liberty
179. James McCoy	August 23, 1889	Bexar
180. Demeiro Fierro	November 1, 1889	Presidio
181. Fletcher Holden	June 6, 1890	Cass
182. Henry Holden	June 6, 1890	Cass
183. Tom Miles	June 6, 1890	Cass
184. Jace Murphy	October 9, 1891	Caldwell
185. John Felder	October 9, 1891	Cherokee
186. Wade Felder	January 9, 1891	Cherokee
187. Will Blackwell	March 6, 1891	Gonzales
188. Joe Lewis	March 27, 1891	Bell
189. Henry Johnson	June 8, 1891	Rains
190. William Caldwell	July 31, 1891	Harris
191. Richard Duncan	September 18, 1891	Maverick
192. Jim Leeper	September 29, 1891	Coryell
193. Ed Powell	September 29, 1891	Coryell
194. Lee Hughes	October 30, 1891	Washington

Name	Execution Date	County
195. William Frizzell	November 20, 1891	Taylor
196. Lorenzo Perez	November 27, 1891	Midland
197. Jose Mendez	December 10, 1891	Val Verde
198. George Scott	May 27, 1892	Rusk
199. James Fisher	May 27, 1892	Delta
200. Tobe Cook	June 10, 1892	Bastrop
201. Alfred White	June 11, 1892	Walker
202. King Sims	June 24, 1892	McLennan
203. George Smith	July 8, 1892	Grayson
204. Cal Parks	July 15, 1892	Burleson
205. Archie Washington	July 26, 1892	Orange
206. Henry McGee	August 12, 1892	Harris
207. Buck Wilkerson	October 14, 1892	Bell
208. Rosalie Castillo	November 25, 1892	El Paso
209. George Freeny	November 25, 1892	Robertson
210. Jack Fields	December 3, 1892	Wharton
211. Frank Holland	February 23, 1893	Brazoria
212. Charles Scott	April 15, 1893	Smith
213. Jim Burke	April 28, 1893	Fannin
214. Sam Massey	April 28, 1893	Fannin
215. Zedolph Davis	April 28, 1893	Lavaca
216. John Carlisle	May 12, 1893	Grayson
217. Charles Luttrell	May 12, 1893	Grayson
218. Harry Graham	June 9, 1893	Morris
219. Alexander Brown	July 28, 1893	Bastrop
220. Henry Miller	July 28, 1893	Dallas
221. Walter Shaw	August 4, 1893	Harris
222. Alfred McDonald	November 17, 1893	Walker
223. Alf Watson	December 8, 1893	San Jacinto
224. Ed Nichols	January 12, 1894	Travis
225. Mannon Davis	March 30, 1894	Lamar
226. Eduardo Ray Gonzales	March 30, 1894	Lamar
227. James Upkins	March 30, 1894	Lamar
228. Joe Guiles	May 24, 1894	Karnes
229. Austin Brown	May 25, 1894	Bexar
230. Tom Moore	September 28, 1894	Lamar
231. Eugene Fulke	September 28, 1894	Lamar
232. Ed Wilcox	January 11, 1895	Guadalupe
233. J. Q. A. Crews	January 14, 1895	Denton
234. Andrew Jackson	January 18, 1895	Red River
235. Richard Burleson	April 12, 1895	Limestone
236. George King	July 2, 1895	Cherokee
237. Lee Thomas	August 2, 1895	Navarro
238. Charles Key	September 13, 1895	Lamar
239. Kit Robertson	October 11, 1895	Liberty
240. Alamo McKee	October 25, 1895	Cass
241. D. L. Spearman	October 25, 1895	Harrison
242. Oscar Hennegan	December 17, 1895	Lee
243. Andrew Chappell	March 18, 1896	Austin

Texas Hangings in Chronological Order

Name	Execution Date	County
244. Clem Strawther	March 18, 1896	Austin
245. Albert Rolly	March 20, 1896	Williamson
246. Mat Mootry	March 27, 1896	Williamson
247. Brady Rutherford	May 20, 1896	Washington
248. John Rutherford	May 20, 1896	Washington
249. Joseph Goodson	May 20, 1896	Washington
250. John Wilkins	June 26, 1896	Johnson
251. Jim Hill	July 3, 1896	Polk
252. George Wheeler	September 4, 1896	Lamar
253. Hickman Freeman	September 4, 1896	Lamar
254. Silas Lee	September 4, 1896	Lamar
255. John Dove	November 27, 1896	Palo Pinto
256. Alexander Terrell	April 2, 1897	Harris
257. Dan Walker	May 28, 1897	Fannin
258. Jim Williamson	June 25, 1897	Wharton
259. Prean Deon	July 9, 1897	Orange
260. Maximo Martinez	July 30, 1897	Wilson
261. George Henry	February 18, 1898	Wise
262. Eugene Burt	May 27, 1898	Travis
263. Frank Martin	June 10, 1898	Wharton
264. Joe Malone	September 2, 1898	Dallas
265. Jim Barber	October 7, 1898	Gonzales
266. Charles Kugadt	October 20, 1898	Washington
267. Emanuel Morris	October 28, 1898	Fort Bend
268. Pete Autre	October 28, 1898	Fort Bend
269. John Shaw	November 25, 1898	Johnson
270. Jim King	December 2, 1898	Wharton
271. Fred Sawyer	January 13, 1899	Ellis
272. Caesar Harris	March 16, 1899	Brazoria
273. Pate Burton	March 24, 1899	Harris
274. Granville Jenkins	March 30, 1899	Robertson
275. Elisha Swan	March 31, 1899	Bastrop
276. Tom Robinson	April 28, 1899	Hill
277. Charley Little	May 4, 1899	Hunt
278. Clay Ford	July 20, 1899	Fayette
279. James Garlington	July 28, 1899	Tarrant
280. Walter Ford	October 27, 1899	McLennan
281. George Morrison	October 27, 1899	Wilbarger
282. Sam Watrous	October 27, 1899	Travis
283. Tom Wright	November 10, 1899	Erath
284. Jim Davidson	November 24, 1899	Travis
285. Antonio Flores	January 6, 1900	El Paso
286. Geronimo Para	January 6, 1900	El Paso
287. Ellis Misher	January 12, 1900	Guadalupe
288. Henderson Pierson	February 2, 1900	Red River
289. Willie Jones	March 9, 1900	Jefferson
290. King Martin	March 16, 1900	Kaufman
291. Neverson Morris	March 23, 1900	Fannin
292. Frank White	March 23, 1900	Fannin

Name	Execution Date	County
293. Bob McKinney	April 16, 1900	Hunt
294. Henry Brown	May 7, 1900	Hunt
295. Sidney Spears	June 18, 1900	Grayson
296. Perry Waggoner	July 6, 1900	Cherokee
297. John Renfro	July 27, 1900	Johnson
298. Enoch Moss	September 3, 1900	Bastrop
299. Frank Jones	November, 1900	Houston
300. F. M. Smith	November 9, 1900	Nacogdoches
301. Augustus Davis	March 14, 1901	Austin
302. Juan Rocha	August 2, 1901	Bexar
303. John Pearl	October 22, 1901	Coleman
304. Will King	October 25, 1901	McLennan
305. Bob Ballard	November 22, 1901	Brazos
306. Anderson Norris	January 10, 1902	McLennan
307. Thomas Morris	January 31, 1902	Navarro
308. John Roan	April 19, 1902	Falls
309. Andres Olivares	June 2, 1902	Nueces
310. John Warren	August 15, 1902	Limestone
311. Vincente Saucedo	September 19, 1902	Bexar
312. Jim Buchanan	October 16, 1902	Nacogdoches
313. Jeff Mikel	December 13, 1902	Lee
314. John Harris	December 19, 1902	Lamar
315. John Ransom	April 3, 1903	Williamson
316. Rip Johnson	May 14, 1903	Walker
317. Charley Green	May 23, 1903	Fort Bend
318. J. E. Shutt	May 29, 1903	Bowie
319. Henry Johnson	May 30, 1903	Kaufman
320. George Harkey	June 30, 1903	Camp
321. Marguerito Reyna	December 4, 1903	Lavaca
322. Henry Fugett	February 12, 1904	Johnson
323. Brozier Smith	March 25, 1904	Ellis
324. Will Murray	April 25, 1904	Jefferson
325. Henry Simmons	May 2, 1904	Travis
326. George Kinny	May 28, 1904	Anderson
327. Vicente Losano	June 16, 1904	Live Oak
328. James Morris	November 25, 1904	Colorado
329. Apolonario Hernandez	December 23, 1904	Nueces
330. John Henry Reeves	February 17, 1905	Red River
331. Conrad Schwartz	March 22, 1905	DeWitt
332. John Henry Young	March 31, 1905	Ellis
333. Holly Vann	May 12, 1905	Dallas
334. Sam Collins	May 19, 1905	Harrison
335. Will Manning	July 7, 1905	Hunt
336. Presley Tankersley	September 1, 1905	Williamson
337. Henry Bates	December 08, 1905	Colorado
338. George Turner	December 22, 1905	Bexar
339. Thomas Young	March 30, 1906	Williamson
340. Albert Johnson	March 30, 1906	Ellis
341. Jack Wilkerson	June 29, 1906	Polk

Name	Execution Date	County
342. Rufus Martin	July 12, 1906	Tarrant
343. Robert Johnson	July 20, 1906	Erath
344. H. L. Mays	October 12, 1906	Bexar
345. Dick Garrett	November 21, 1906	Shelby
346. Henry Brown	November 30, 1906	Medina
347. Jesse Jones	November 30, 1906	McLennon
348. Alberto Vargas	January 4, 1907	Callahan
349. Ramon Campos	February 1, 1907	Karnes
350. A. B. Washington	February 14, 1907	Bastrop
351. Felix Powell	April 2, 1907	Castro
352. John Armstrong	April 26, 1907	Colorado
353. Dock Bailey	November 7, 1907	Nacogdoches
354. John Brown	March 27, 1908	DeWitt
355. James Cason	May 22, 1908	Parker
356. Tom Jones	June 20, 1908	Fort Bend
357. Monk Gibson	June 28, 1908	DeWitt
358. James Williams	July 31, 1908	Bexar
359. Frank Mitchell	August 1, 1908	Burleson
360. John Boyd	January 8, 1909	Fayette
361. Claude Golden	February 12, 1909	Jasper
362. Johnnie Green	February 25, 1909	Bastrop
363. Edmund Shelton	May 14, 1909	Galveston
364. Refugio Juareque	June 11, 1909	Wilson
365. Willis Macklin	July 2, 1909	Polk
366. Marcellus Thomas	September 3, 1909	Harris
367. Lee Russell	October 1, 1909	Houston
368. Will Mcintosh	October 1, 1909	Lamar
369. Tom Wilson	October 22, 1909	Newton
370. Robert Wright	December 17, 1909	Sabine
371. Gus Thomas	February 26, 1910	Wharton
372. Sam Washington	February 26, 1910	Wharton
373. Julius B. Robertson	May 14, 1910	Dallas
374. G. R. Miller	June 3, 1910	Donley
375. John Wynne	June 24, 1910	Walker
376. John Cannon	July 8, 1910	Polk
377. Henry Henderson	July 8, 1910	Cherokee
378. Louis Johnson	January 30, 1912	Polk
379. Albert Varner	February 16, 1912	Guadalupe
380. James Barney Compton	March 15, 1912	Webb
381. Dan McCline	March 29, 1912	Falls
382. Charlie McClennan	April 13, 1912	Washington
383. John Henry	July 12, 1912	Travis
384. Wood Maxey	August 9, 1912	Grayson
385. Sellars Vines	August 9, 1912	Grayson
386. Sam Jones	October 16, 1912	Grayson
387. Burrell Oates	November 29, 1912	Ellis
388. John Robinson	January 10, 1913	Dallas
389. Diggs Perry	April 21, 1913	Matagordo

Name	Execution Date	County
390. Abraham Ortiz	May 2, 1913	Hidalgo
391. John Henry Brock	May 30, 1913	Travis
392. William Asbeck	June 28, 1913	Victoria
393. Floyd Stanton	August 1, 1913	Dallas
394. Ernest Harrison	August 7, 1913	Tarrant
395. Paul Fowler	August 7, 1913	Tarrant
396. Lee Johnson	September 26, 1913	Bexar
397. Ed Long	December 19, 1913	Dallas
398. Tommy Lee	March 9, 1914	Tarrant
399. Leon Martinez Jr.	May 11, 1914	Reeves
400. Porfirio Torrez	August 14, 1914	Atascosa
401. Henry Wilson	December 14, 1914	Calhoun
402. Ysidro Gonzales	February 1, 1915	Live Oak
403. Henry Ballard	February 19, 1915	Red River
404. Will Hemphill	February 26, 1915	Guadalupe
405. Federico Sanchez	March 3, 1915	Live Oak
406. Benigno Guerrero	April 9, 1915	Hays
407. Carl Oliver	April 16, 1915	Grayson
408. Joe Larkins	April 17, 1915	Ellis
409. Cornelius Jackson	July 2, 1915	Wharton
410. Clint Williams	August 5, 1915	Tarrant
411. Charles Myers	November 10, 1915	Tarrant
412. Floyd Thompson	January 7, 1916	Freestone
413. Jacinto Gonzales	January 10, 1916	Live Oak
414. Louis Utley	February 1, 1916	Harris
415. Henry Sampson	February 15, 1916	Harris
416. Sam Jernigan	March 11, 1916	Trinity
417. Robert Burgess	April 29, 1916	Jefferson
418. Melquiades Chapa	May 19, 1916	Cameron
419. Jose Buenrostro	May 19, 1916	Cameron
420. John Williams	October 27, 1916	McLennan
421. Clarence Cooley	October 18, 1916	Harris
422. William Nesbit	December 11, 1917	Bexar
423. Larnon Brown	December 11, 1917	Bexar
424. Corp. Baltimore	December 11, 1917	Bexar
425. William Brackenridge	December 11, 1917	Bexar
426. Thomas James Wheatley	December 11, 1917	Bexar
427. Jesse Moore	December 11, 1917	Bexar
428. Charles Hawkins	December 11, 1917	Bexar
429. Carlos Snodgrass	December 11, 1917	Bexar
430. Ira Davis	December 11, 1917	Bexar
431. James Divins	December 11, 1917	Bexar
432. Frank Johnson	December 11, 1917	Bexar
433. Risley Young	December 11, 1917	Bexar
434. Pat MacWhorter	December 11, 1917	Bexar
435. Walter Stevenson	May 24, 1918	Dallas
436. Leonard Dodd	May 24, 1918	Dallas
437. Nat Hoffman	July 11, 1918	McLennan

Name	Execution Date	County
438. James Franklin	August 16, 1918	Hardin
439. Harvey Hubert	August 23, 1918	Travis
440. Will Jones	August 30, 1918	Dallas
441. Babe Collier	September 17, 1918	Bexar
442. Thomas McDonald	September 17, 1918	Bexar
443. Joseph Smith	September 17, 1918	Bexar
444. James Robinson	September 17, 1918	Bexar
445. Albert Wright	September 17, 1918	Bexar
446. William Boone	September 24, 1918	Bexar
447. Rufus Coates	November 8, 1918	Tarrant
448. John Price	March 23, 1920	San Augustine
449. Fred Douglas	August 27, 1920	Dallas
450. Harry Walker	May 10, 1921	Harris
451. Virgil Sampson	May 27, 1921	Lamar
452. Green Hunter	July 10, 1920	Dallas
453. Albert Howard	March 18, 1921	Gonzales
454. Isreal Jordan	July 21, 1921	Falls
455. Jose Flores	July 21, 1921	Falls
456. George Grace	January 6, 1922	Bexar
457. George Hornsby	April 14, 1922	Bell
458. Carl Parker	May 4, 1922	Harris
459. Abe Johnson	September 22, 1922	Liberty
460. Ezell Stepp	November 17, 1922	Collin
461. Albert Woolridge	December 15, 1922	Colorado
462. Clemente Apolinar	February 23, 1923	Bexar
463. Ray Jones	March 9, 1923	Colorado
464. Harvey Hughes	April 7, 1923	Brewster
465. Sol Johnson	July 20, 1923	Bowie
466. Roy Mitchell	July 30, 1923	McLennan
467. Nathan Lee	August 31, 1923	Brazoria

Sources

Books

Alexander, Bob, Winchester Warriors, *Texas Rangers of Company D, 1874 – 1900*, UNT Press, 2009.

Boggs, Johnny D., *Great Murder Trials of the Old West*. Republic of Texas Press, 2003

Bowman, Bob and Doris, *Death by Rope*. Best of the East Texas Publishers, 2009.

Caldwell, Clifford R. & Delord, Ron, *Texas Lawmen 1835 – 1899*. The History Press, 2011.

Cases Argued and Adjudged in the Court of Criminal Appeals of the State of Texas, Volume 3. F. H. Thomas and Company, 1878.

Cases Argued and Adjudged in the Court of Criminal Appeals of the State of Texas, Volume 4. F. H. Thomas and Company, 1879.

Cases Argued and Adjudged in the Court of Criminal Appeals of the State of Texas, Volume 6. F. H. Thomas and Company, 1879.

Cases Argued and Adjudged in the Court of Criminal Appeals of the State of Texas, Volume 7. F. H. Thomas and Company, 1880.

Cases Argued and Adjudged in the Court of Criminal Appeals of the State of Texas, Volume 11. The Gilbert Book Company, St. Louis, Mo. 1882.

Cases Argued and Decided in the Supreme Court of the State of Texas, Volume 35. The Gilbert Book Company, St. Louis, Mo. 1882.

Cases Argued and Decided in the Supreme Court of Criminal Appeals of the State of Texas, Volume 14. R. W. Swindrells, Printer and Stereotyper, 1884.

Cases Argued and Adjudged in the Court of Criminal Appeals of the State of Texas, Volume 23, Hutching Printing House, Austin, Texas, 1887.

Cases Argued and Adjudged in the Court of Criminal Appeals of the State of Texas, Vol. 47. T. H. Floof & Company, Publishers, Chicago, Ill. 1908.

Cases Argued and Adjudged in the Court of Criminal Appeals of the State of Texas, Vol. 49. T. H. Floof & Company, Publishers, Chicago, Ill. 1908.

Cases Argued and Adjudged in the Court of Criminal Appeals of the State of Texas, Vol. 53. T. H. Floof & Company, Publishers, Chicago, Ill. 1908.

Cases Argued and Adjudged in the Court of Criminal Appeals of the State of Texas, Vol. 64. T. H. Floof & Company, Publishers, Chicago, Ill. 1912.

Cases Argued and Adjudged in the Court of Criminal Appeals of the State of Texas, Oct., Nov., Dec., 1914, Vol. 75. Von Boeckmann – Jones, Publishers, Austin, Texas, 1916.

Cases Argued and Adjudged in the Court of Criminal Appeals of the State of Texas, Vol. 91. Feb, March, April, May, 1922. E. W. Stephens Publishing Co., Columbia, Missouri.

Davis, Joe Tom, *Historic Towns of Texas*, Eakin Press, Austin, Texas 1966.

Yadon, Laurence J. and Anderson, Dan, *Ten Deadly Texans*, Pelican Publishing Company, 2009.

Gammel, Hans Peter Mareus Neilsen. *The Laws of Texas, 1822 – 1897*, Volume 1, book, 1898.

Jackson, Alexander M., *Cases Argued and Adjudged in the Court of Appeals of the State of Texas*, Volume 5, Gilbert book Co, 1879.

Jackson, Alexander M., Cases Argued and Adjudged in the Court of Appeals of the State of Texas, Volume 6, Gilbert book Co, 1879.

Marohn, Richard C, *The Last Gunfighter – John Wesly Hardin*, The Early West, Creative Publishing Company, 1995.

McCombs, David G., *Galveston, a History*. University of Texas Press. 1986

Metz, Leon Claire, *The Encyclopedia of Lawmen, Outlaws, and Gunfighters*. Checkmark Books, 2003.

Metz, Leon C. *Pat Garrett, The Story of a Western Lawman*. University of Oklahoma Press, 1973.

Nash, Jay Robert, *Encyclopedia of Western Lawmen and Outlaws*. Da Capo Press, 1992.

O'Neal, Bill, *Encyclopedia of Western Gunfighters*, University of Oklahoma Press, 1979.

Parsons, Chuck, *Captain John R. Hughes, Lone Star Ranger*, University of North Texas Press, 2011.

Radison, Gary. *Last Words Dying in the Old West*. Eakin Press, 2002.

Reports of Cases Argued and Decided in the Supreme Court of the State of Texas, Vol. 32. E. M. Wheelock. Richard, Belo and Company. 1871

Stein Bill, *Capital Punishment in Colorado County History*. Vol.1, Number 5, June 1990.

Stephens, Robert W. *Bullets and Buckshot in Texas*. 2002.

The Southwestern Reporter, Volume 11, West Publishing Company, 1889

The Southwestern Reporter, Volume 15, West Publishing Company, 1891

The Southwestern Reporter, Volume 18, West Publishing Company, 1892

The Southwestern Reporter, Volume 19, West Publishing Company, 1892

The Southwestern Reporter, Volume 26, West Publishing Company, 1894

The Southwestern Reporter, Volume 31, West Publishing Company, 1895

The Southwestern Reporter, Volume 25, West Publishing Company, 1896

The Southwestern Reporter, Volume 45, West Publishing Company, 1898

The Southwestern Reporter, Volume 46, West Publishing Company, 1898

The Southwestern Reporter, Volume 47, West Publishing Company, 1899

The Southwestern Reporter, Volume 53, West Publishing Company, 1900

The Southwestern Reporter, Volume 96, West Publishing Company, 1906

The Southwestern Reporter, Volume 120, West Publishing Company, 1909

The Southwestern Reporter, Volume 141, West Publishing Company, 1912

The Southwestern Reporter, Volume 160, West Publishing Company, 1914

The Southwestern Reporter, Volume 200, West Publishing Company, 1918

The Southwestern Reporter, Volume 230, West Publishing Company, 1921

Texas Courts of Criminal Appeals, 36th Texas Criminal Reports.

Texas Courts of Criminal Appeals, Volume 38, Texas Criminal Reports.

Texas Criminal Reports. Cases Argued and Adjudged, Vol. 25. Published by the State of Texas, Austin, Texas, 1888.

Texas Criminal Reports. Cases Argued and Adjudged, Vol. 36. Published by the State of Texas, 1897.

Texas Criminal Reports: Cases Argued and Adjudged, Vol. 47. Gammel-Statesman Publishing company, 1902.

Texas Criminal Reports: Cases Argued and Adjudged, Vol. 43. Gammel-Statesman Publishing company, 1903.

Texas Criminal Reports: Cases Argued and Adjudged, Vol. 16. Ben C. Jones & Company, 1906.

Texas Criminal Reports: Cases Argued and Adjudged, Vol. 47. T. H. Flood & Company, Publishers, Chicago, Ill. 1908.

Texas Criminal Reports: Cases Argued and Adjudged, Vol. 50. T. H. Flood & Company, Publishers, Chicago, Ill. 1908.

Tise, Sammy, *Texas County Sheriffs*, Oakwood Printing, Albuquerque, N. M. 1989.

CLEAT, *The Ultimate Sacrifice: Trials and Triumphs of the Texas Peace Officer*. Walsworth Printing Company, 2000.

To Serve and Protect. A Tribute to American Law Enforcement. Turner Publishing Company, 1995.

Internet Resources

The Handbook of Texas Online
Famous Court Trials of Montague County by Marvin F. London
Genealogybank
National Law Enforcement Memorial

Newspaper Achieves
The Portal to Texas History, University of North Texas
Roots.web. Murder of the Crocker Family, Elo Shilling
Texas Escapes

Newspapers

Abilene Daily Reporter, March 20, 1891
Abilene Daily Reporter, July 7, 1912
Abilene Semi Weekly, September 1, 1911
Abilene Semi Weekly, September 17, 1912
Arlington Journal, June 4, 1903
Arlington Journal, September 24, 1903
Arlington Journal, October 29, 1903
Atlanta Constitution, (Ga.) February 18, 1905
Austin Daily Statesman, January 13, 1894
Austin Daily Statesman, November 24, 1899
Austin Statesman, May 3, 1904
Austin Statesman, July 13, 1912
Austin Statesman, August 23, 1918
Austin City Tribune, November 24, 1899
The Bartlett Tribune, April 6, 1906
The Bartlett Tribune, March 25, 1921
The Bartlett Tribune, April 15, 1921
The Bartlett Tribune, December 23, 1921
The Bartlett Tribune, March 10, 1922
The Bartlett Tribune, March 24, 1922
The Bartlett Tribune, April 7, 1922
The Bartlett Tribune, April 21, 1922
Bastrop Advertisor, November 21, 1874
Bastrop Advertisor, June 11, 1892
Bastrop Advertisor, February 20, 1909
Bastrop Advertisor, February 27, 1909
The Belton Independent, August 28, 1858
Belton Journal, April 13, 1922
Boston Post, (Boston, MA), December 25, 1856
The Brand, October 6, 1905
The Brazos Courier, December 1, 1840
Breckenridge American, July 10, 1920
Breckenridge American, August 27, 1920
Breckenridge Daily American, May 4, 1922
Brenham Weekly Banner, April 26, 1878
Brenham Weekly Banner, June 7, 1878
Brenham Weekly Banner, July 12, 1878
Brenham Weekly Banner, July 18, 1879
Brenham Weekly Banner, August 15, 1879

Brenham Weekly Banner, September 27, 1878
Brenham Weekly Banner, October 18, 1878
Brenham Weekly Banner, December 20, 1878
Brenham Weekly Banner, June 13, 1879
Brenham Weekly Banner, July 11, 1879
Brenham Weekly Banner, August 29, 1879
Brenham Weekly Banner, September 19, 1879
Brenham Weekly Banner, November 14, 1879
Brenham Weekly Banner, November 21, 1879
Brenham Weekly Banner, November 28, 1879
Brenham Weekly Banner, March 26, 1880
Brenham Weekly Banner, April 2, 1880
Brenham Weekly Banner, June 24, 1880
Brenham Weekly Banner, July 1, 1880
Brenham Weekly Banner, July 8, 1880
Brenham Weekly Banner, August 26, 1880
Brenham Weekly Banner, September 2, 1880
Brenham Weekly Banner, February 9, 1882
Brenham Weekly Banner, June 5, 1884
Brenham Weekly Banner, June 12, 1884
Brenham Weekly Banner, January 3, 1888
Brenham Weekly Banner, September 24, 1891
Brenham Weekly Banner, October 8, 1891
Brenham Weekly Banner, October 29, 1891
Brenham Weekly Banner, November 5, 1891
The Brownsville Daily Herald, August 10, 1897
The Brownsville Daily Herald, February 18, 1898
The Brownsville Daily Herald, April 5, 1901
The Brownsville Daily Herald, April 26, 1901
The Brownsville Daily Herald, November 23, 1906
The Brownsville Daily Herald, February 15, 1916
The Brownsville Daily Herald, May 19, 1916
The Brownsville Daily Herald, July 18, 1923
Brownwood Bulletin, March 23, 1920
The Central Texian, (Anderson, TX), June 20, 1856
The Central Texian, June 27, 1856
Cincinnati Daily Times, (Cincinnati, OH), August 20, 1874
Cincinnati Daily Enquirer, October 15, 1875
Civilian and Gazette Weekly, (Galveston, TX), January 5, 1858

Civilian and Gazette Weekly, January 19, 1858
Cleburne Chronicle, August 21, 1869
The Colorado Citizen, July 2, 1859
Commercial Advertiser, (New York, NY), May 12, 1834
The Corsicana Daily Sun, Janaury 7, 1916
The Corsicana Daily Sun, August 30, 1918
The Corsicana Daily Sun, August 27, 1920
Corsicana Semi Weekly Light, June 17, 1919
Corsicana Semi Weekly Light, July 31, 1923
The Daily Advocate, (Victoria, TX), April 2, 1907
The Daily Advocate, January 3, 1912
The Daily Advocate, January 27, 1912
The Daily Advocate, March 16, 1912
The Daily Advocate, March 30, 1912
The Daily Advocate, June 28, 1913
The Daily Advocate, August 8, 1913
The Daily Advocate, February 3, 1915
Daily Bulletin, (Brownwood), December 7, 1907
Daily Bulletin, May 23, 1908
Daily Confederation, (Montgomery, Al), September 8, 1859
The Daily Courier Gazette (McKinney) November 17, 1922
Daily Democrat, (Ft. Worth), August 28, 1880
Daily Democrat, July 2, 1881
Daily Democratic Statesman, August 23, 1879
The Daily Enterprise, (Cleburne, TX), June 29, 1896
The Daily Express, (San Antonio) April 20, 1902
The Daily Express, August 1, 1908
The Daily Express, February 27, 1910
The Daily Gazette, (Colorado Spring, Co.) October 20, 1883
The Daily Herald, Brownville, August 10, 1893
The Daily Herald, Brownville, June 29, 1893
The Daily Herald, Brownville, June 28, 1897
The Daily Freeman (Waukesha, WI), July 6, 1883
The Daily Phoenix, (Columbus, S.C.), May 30, 1874
Daily Register Gazette, (Rockford, IL), December 30, 1914
The Daily Tribune (Salt Lake City, Utah), October 28, 1899
Dallas Morning News, May 9, 1886
Dallas Morning News, October 21, 1888
Dallas Morning News, April 6, 1889
Dallas Morning News, August 24, 1889
Dallas Morning News, November 2, 1889
Dallas Morning News, June 1, 1890
Dallas Morning News, June 7, 1890
Dallas Morning News, March 7, 1891
Dallas Morning News, August 3, 1901
Dallas Morning News, September 19, 1891
Dallas Morning News, December 11, 1891
Dallas Morning News, February 24, 1892
Dallas Morning News, July 16, 1892
Dallas Morning News, July 27, 1892
Dallas Morning News, October 15, 1892
Dallas Morning News, August 5, 1893
Dallas Morning News, January 13, 1894
Dallas Morning News, September 29, 1894
Dallas Morning News, January 12, 1895
Dallas Morning News, June 27, 1896
Dallas Morning News, May 29, 1897
Dallas Morning News, May 23, 1898
Dallas Morning News, September 3, 1898
Dallas Morning News, October 8, 1898
Dallas Morning News, October 21, 1898
Dallas Morning News, March 25, 1899
Dallas Morning News, March 31, 1899
Dallas Morning News, April 29, 1899
Dallas Morning News, May 28, 1899
Dallas Morning News, July 8, 1899
Dallas Morning News, July 21, 1899
Dallas Morning News, August 2, 1899
Dallas Morning News, August 4, 1899
Dallas Morning News, November 10, 1899
Dallas Morning News, February 12, 1900
Dallas Morning News, March 10, 1900
Dallas Morning News, March 17, 1900
Dallas Morning News, March 24, 1900
Dallas Morning News, April 17, 1900
Dallas Morning News, June 12, 1900
Dallas Morning News, October 22, 1901
Dallas Morning News, November 23, 1901
Dallas Morning News, September 12, 1902
Dallas Morning News, December 20, 1902
Dallas Morning News, May 24, 1903
Dallas Morning News, August 13, 1903
Dallas Morning News, January 24, 1904
Dallas Morning News, April 26, 1904
Dallas Morning News, March 23, 1905
Dallas Morning News, May 13, 1905
Dallas Morning News, October 13, 1906
Dallas Morning News, November 22, 1906
Dallas Morning News, May 15, 1909
Dallas Morning News, June 12, 1909
Dallas Morning News, May 14, 1910
Dallas Morning News, September 12, 1910
Dallas Morning News, January 10, 1913
Dallas Morning News, January 11, 1913

Dallas Morning News, February 9, 1913
Dallas Morning News, February 27, 1913
Dallas Morning News, May 16, 1913
Dallas Morning News, August 2, 1913
Dallas Morning News, October 23, 1913
Dallas Morning News, December 20, 1913
Dallas Morning News, January 11, 1916
Dallas Morning News, December 12, 1917
Dallas Morning News, May 25, 1918
Dallas Morning News, August 30, 1918
Dallas Morning News, September 18, 1918
Dallas Morning News, June 4, 1920
Dallas Morning News, July 10, 1920
Dallas Morning News, July 21, 1920
Dallas Morning News, August 20, 1920
Dallas Morning News, April 26, 1921
Dallas Morning News, July 22, 1921
Dallas Morning News, March 17, 2002
Dallas Weekly Herald, May 9, 1874
Dallas Weekly Herald, November 11, 1876
Democratic Daily Statesman, April 15, 1873
The Democrat (McKinney, TX), May 18, 1893
The Democrat, (McKinney) November 7, 1889
Denton County News, February 25, 1897
Denton County News, March 31, 1904
Denton County News, May 6, 1904
Denton Record Chronicle, March 23, 1920
Denton Record Chronicle, March 5, 2003
The Desert News, (Salt Lake City, Utah), March 28, 1883
Eagle Lake Headlight, April 26, 1913
Eagle Lake Headlight, March 17, 1923
The Evening News, (Ada, Oklahoma), August 10, 1912
The Evening Light (San Antonio), August 12, 1882
El Paso Daily Herald, January 5, 1900
El Paso Daily Herald, January 6, 1900
El Paso Herald, May 30, 1913
El Paso Herald, May 19, 1916
El Regidor (San Antonio, TX), December 12, 1891
The Ferris Wheel, July 17, 1897
The Ferris Wheel, January 21, 1899
The Ferris Wheel, February 11, 1899
Flake's Semi-Weekly Galveston Bulletin, November 1, 1871
Fort Worth Daily Gazette, January 6, 1883
Fort Worth Daily Gazette, March 24, 1883
Fort Worth Daily Gazette, July 7, 1883
Fort Worth Daily Gazette, March 8, 1884
Fort Worth Daily Gazette, October 20, 1884

Fort Worth Daily Gazette, January 24, 1885
Fort Worth Daily Gazette, May 22, 1885
Fort Worth Daily Gazette, May 23, 1885
Fort Worth Daily Gazette, May 30, 1885
Fort Worth Daily Gazette, August 15, 1885
Fort Worth Daily Gazette, January 7, 1886
Fort Worth Daily Gazette, March 24, 1886
Fort Worth Daily Gazette, April 1, 1886
Fort Worth Daily Gazette, April 17, 1886
Fort Worth Daily Gazette, September 11, 1886
Fort Worth Daily Gazette, April 12, 1887
Fort Worth Daily Gazette, April 25, 1887
Fort Worth Daily Gazette, February 26, 1887
Fort Worth Daily Gazette, May 14, 1887
Fort Worth Daily Gazette, August 26, 1887
Fort Worth Daily Gazette, October 16, 1887
Fort Worth Daily Gazette, May 26, 1888
Fort Worth Daily Gazette, May 27, 1888
Fort Worth Daily Gazette, December 1, 1888
Fort Worth Daily Gazette, December 7, 1888
Fort Worth Daily Gazette, December 30, 1888
Fort Worth Daily Gazette, January 26, 1889
Fort Worth Daily Gazette, August 24, 1889
Fort Worth Daily Gazette, June 7, 1890
Fort Worth Democrat, August 13, 1876
Fort Worth Democrat, August 28, 1880
Fort Worth Gazette, April 25, 1891
Fort Worth Gazette, June 9, 1891
Fort Worth Gazette, June 23, 1891
Fort Worth Gazette, July 23, 1891
Fort Worth Gazette, September 19, 1891
Fort Worth Gazette, September 24, 1891
Fort Worth Gazette, September 30, 1891
Fort Worth Gazette, October 10, 1891
Fort Worth Gazette, October 15, 1891
Fort Worth Gazette, November 16, 1891
Fort Worth Gazette, November 21, 1891
Fort Worth Gazette, November 28, 1891
Fort Worth Gazette, May 19, 1891
Fort Worth Gazette, August 1, 1891
Fort Worth Gazette, April 13, 1893
Fort Worth Gazette, April 19, 1893
Fort Worth Gazette, April 28, 1893
Fort Worth Gazette, June 10, 1893
Fort Worth Gazette, July 29, 1893
Fort Worth Gazette, March 31, 1894
Fort Worth Gazette, May 26, 1894

Fort Worth Gazette, September 29, 1894
Fort Worth Gazette, December 13, 1894
Fort Worth Gazette, January 13, 1895
Fort Worth Gazette, April 13, 1895
Fort Worth Gazette, May 16, 1895
Fort Worth Gazette, August 3, 1895
Fort Worth Gazette, September 14, 1895
Fort Worth Gazette, October 14, 1895
Fort Worth Gazette, October 26, 1895
Fort Worth Gazette, March 27, 1896
Fort Worth Morning Register, July 29, 1899
Fort Worth Morning Register, October 28, 1899
Fort Worth Morning Register, November 25, 1899
Fort Worth Morning Register, July 10, 1900
Fort Worth Record, April 1, 1905
Fort Worth Record, March 31, 1906
Fort Worth Record, July 13, 1906
Fort Worth Record, May 15, 1909
Fort Worth Record, August 10, 1912
Fort Worth Record, November 30, 1912
Fort Worth Record, August 7, 1913
Fort Worth Record, August 8, 1913
Fort Worth Record, March 10, 1914
Fort Worth Record, May 25, 1918
Fort Worth Record, November 9, 1918
Fort Worth Record, July 9, 1920
Fort Worth Star-Telegram, May 31, 1903
Fort Worth Star-Telegram, December 5, 1903
Fort Worth Star-Telegram, May 16, 1913
Fort Worth Star-Telegram, May 18, 1913
Fort Worth Star-Telegram, May 23, 1913
Fort Worth Star-Telegram, January 10, 1916
Fort Worth Star-Telegram, October 27, 1916
Fort Worth Star-Telegram, July 9, 1920
Fort Worth Star-Telegram, July 11, 1920
The Galveston Daily News, August 18, 1869
Galveston Daily News, July 29, 1871
Galveston Daily News, January 28, 1873
Galveston Daily News, April 25, 1873
Galveston Daily News, April 7, 1874
Galveston Daily News, June 10, 1874
Galveston Daily News, June 12, 1874
Galveston Daily News, June 18, 1874
Galveston Daily News, August 22, 1874
Galveston Daily News, March 18, 1875
Galveston Daily News, May 1, 1875
Galveston Daily News, June 27, 1875

Galveston Daily News, July 4, 1875
Galveston Daily News, August 12, 1876
Galveston Daily News, November 4, 1876
Galveston Daily News, November 11, 1876
Galveston Daily News, January 19, 1877
Galveston Daily News, May 5, 1877
Galveston Daily News, June 1, 1878
Galveston Daily News, June 28, 1878
Galveston Daily News, July 7, 1878
Galveston Daily News, August 31, 1878
Galveston Daily News, September 24, 1878
Galveston Daily News, November 23, 1878
Galveston Daily News, December 15, 1878
Galveston Daily News, December 24, 1878
Galveston Daily News, May 3, 1879
Galveston Daily News, July 8, 1879
Galveston Daily News, August 8, 1879
Galveston Daily News, August 23, 1879
Galveston Daily News, September 13, 1879
Galveston Daily News, November 7, 1879
Galveston Daily News, November 14, 1879
Galveston Daily News, November 22, 1879
Galveston Daily News, November 29, 1879
Galveston Daily News, April 17, 1880
Galveston Daily News, May 1, 1880
Galveston Daily News, May 8, 1880
Galveston Daily News, June 10, 1880
Galveston Daily News, June 12, 1880
Galveston Daily News, June 17, 1880
Galveston Daily News, July 3, 1880
Galveston Daily News, July 30, 1880
Galveston Daily News, August 21, 1880
Galveston Daily News, August 28, 1880
Galveston Daily News, July 2, 1881
Galveston Daily News, September 24, 1881
Galveston Daily News, August 12, 1882
Galveston Daily News, June 11, 1882
Galveston Daily News, August 22, 1882
Galveston Daily News, January 6, 1883
Galveston Daily News, April 25, 1883
Galveston Daily News, July 7, 1883
Galveston Daily News, December 15, 1883
Galveston Daily News, December 22, 1883
Galveston Daily News, June 7, 1884
Galveston Daily News, November 1, 1884
Galveston Daily News, May 15, 1885
Galveston Daily News, May 23, 1885

Galveston Daily News, May 30, 1885
Galveston Daily News, November 14, 1885
Galveston Daily News, January 16, 1886
Galveston Daily News, March 23, 1886
Galveston Daily News, April 1, 1886
Galveston Daily News, January 22, 1887
Galveston Daily News, June 22, 1887
Galveston Daily News, June 23, 1887
Galveston Daily News, October 15, 1887
Galveston Daily News, April 14, 1888
Galveston Daily News, June 5, 1888
Galveston Daily News, July 17, 1888
Galveston Daily News, September 1, 1888
Galveston Daily News, September 30, 1888
Galveston Daily News, December 7, 1888
Galveston Daily News, December 8, 1888
Galveston Daily News, December 22, 1888
Galveston Daily News, January 10, 1891
Galveston Daily News, January 25, 1891
Galveston Daily News, March 28, 1891
Galveston Daily News, August 1, 1891
Galveston Daily News, August 13, 1891
Galveston Daily News, September 30, 1891
Galveston Daily News, October 10, 1891
Galveston Daily News, May 28, 1892
Galveston Daily News, June 12, 1892
Galveston Daily News, June 25, 1892
Galveston Daily News, November 26, 1892
Galveston Daily News, December 3, 1892
Galveston Daily News, April 16, 1893
Galveston Daily News, April 29, 1893
Galveston Daily News, February 24, 1893
Galveston Daily News, August 20, 1893
Galveston Daily News, November 18, 1893
Galveston Daily News, March 31, 1894
Galveston Daily News, January 19, 1895
Galveston Daily News, April 13, 1895
Galveston Daily News, April 16, 1895
Galveston Daily News, July 3, 1895
Galveston Daily News, August 3, 1895
Galveston Daily News, October 12, 1895
Galveston Daily News, October 26, 1895
Galveston Daily News, December 18, 1895
Galveston Daily News, March 19, 1896
Galveston Daily News, July 4, 1896
Galveston Daily News, February 19, 1898
Galveston Daily News, September 3, 1898

Galveston Daily News, September 27, 1898
Galveston Daily News, October 29, 1898
Galveston Daily News, December 3, 1898
Galveston Daily News, April 7, 1899
Galveston Daily News, May 5, 1899
Galveston Daily News, October 28, 1899
Galveston Daily News, March 10, 1900
Galveston Daily News, March 24, 1900
Galveston Daily News, May 8, 1900
Galveston Daily News, June 19, 1900
Galveston Daily News, August 3, 1901
Galveston Daily News, February 1, 1902
Galveston Daily News, April 20, 1902
Galveston Daily News, August 16, 1902
Galveston Daily News, September 20, 1902
Galveston Daily News, May 15, 1903
Galveston Daily News, May 27, 1903
Galveston Daily News, May 30, 1903
Galveston Daily News, July 1, 1903
Galveston Daily News, April 26, 1904
Galveston Daily News, June 17, 1904
Galveston Daily News, December 24, 1904
Galveston Daily News, February 18, 1905
Galveston Daily News, November 26, 1904
Galveston Daily News, March 17, 1905
Galveston Daily News, April 1, 1905
Galveston Daily News, May 20, 1905
Galveston Daily News, June 17, 1905
Galveston Daily News, July 8, 1905
Galveston Daily News, November 22, 1905
Galveston Daily News, December 9, 1905
Galveston Daily News, December 23, 1905
Galveston Daily News, June 30, 1906
Galveston Daily News, July 21, 1906
Galveston Daily News, December 1, 1906
Galveston Daily News, January 5, 1907
Galveston Daily News, April 27, 1907
Galveston Daily News, September 8, 1907
Galveston Daily News, October 5, 1907
Galveston Daily News, November 8, 1907
Galveston Daily News, June 21, 1908
Galveston Daily News, June 22, 1908
Galveston Daily News, June 23, 1908
Galveston Daily News, July 21, 1908
Galveston Daily News, August 1, 1908
Galveston Daily News, August 2, 1908
Galveston Daily News, February 13, 1909

Galveston Daily News, February 20, 1909
Galveston Daily News, May 15, 1909
Galveston Daily News, June 12, 1909
Galveston Daily News, August 3, 1909
Galveston Daily News, October 2, 1909
Galveston Daily News, October 23, 1909
Galveston Daily News, December 18, 1909
Galveston Daily News, February 27, 1910
Galveston Daily News, June 4, 1910
Galveston Daily News, June 25, 1910
Galveston Daily News, July 9, 1910
Galveston Daily News, October 8, 1911
Galveston Daily News, January 31, 1912
Galveston Daily News, February 17, 1912
Galveston Daily News, March 16, 1912
Galveston Daily News, March 30, 1912
Galveston Daily News, May 25, 1912
Galveston Daily News, July 13, 1912
Galveston Daily News, October 17, 1912
Galveston Daily News, December 18, 1912
Galveston Daily News, May 3, 1913
Galveston Daily News, May 31, 1913
Galveston Daily News, August 2, 1913
Galveston Daily News, August 8, 1913
Galveston Daily News, August 15, 1914
Galveston Daily News, February 20, 1915
Galveston Daily News, March 1, 1915
Galveston Daily News, March 4, 1915
Galveston Daily News, April 10, 1915
Galveston Daily News, April 18, 1915
Galveston Daily News, May 15, 1915
Galveston Daily News, July 15, 1915
Galveston Daily News, August 10, 1915
Galveston Daily News, February 2, 1916
Galveston Daily News, March 12, 1916
Galveston Daily News, April 29, 1916
Galveston Daily News, April 30, 1916
Galveston Daily News, September 16, 1916
Galveston Daily News, October 19, 1916
Galveston Daily News, March 3, 1917
Galveston Daily News, April 29, 1919
Galveston Daily News, June 15, 1919
Galveston Daily News, March 24, 1920
Galveston Daily News, January 24, 1921
Galveston Daily News, March 20, 1921
Galveston Daily News, April 21, 1921
Galveston Daily News, May 11, 1921

Galveston Daily News, May 28, 1921
Galveston Daily News, May 3, 1922
Galveston Daily News, May 5, 1922
Galveston Daily News, July 21, 1923
Galveston Daily News, July 31, 1923
Galveston Daily News, September 1, 1923
Galveston Standard, June 3, 1872
Galveston Weekly News, December 25, 1855
Galveston Weekly News, July 15, 1856
Galveston Weekly News, July 22, 1856
Galveston Weekly News, March 5, 1877
Galveston Weekly News, September 3, 1877
Galveston Weekly News, April 1, 1880
Galveston Weekly News, September 30, 1880
Galveston Weekly News, November 18, 1880
Galveston Weekly News, August 4, 1881
Gazette-Telegraph, June 26, 1897
Georgetown Commercial, April 10, 1903
Georgetown Commercial, September 8, 1905
Gonzales Enquirer, May 18, 1878
Gonzales Enquirer, July 30, 1881
Gonzales Enquirer, March 12, 1891
Gonzales Enquirer, October 6, 1898
Greenville Morning Herald, May 13, 1910
Greenville Morning Herald, October 19, 1910
The Herald and Torch Light, (Hagerstown, Md), Sept. 9, 1874
Houston Daily Post, July 29, 1893
Houston Daily Post, March 31, 1894
Houston Daily Post, December 18, 1895
Houston Daily Post, January 19, 1896
Houston Daily Post, January 31, 1896
Houston Daily Post, February 1, 1896
Houston Daily Post, March 21, 1896
Houston Daily Post, March 25, 1896
Houston Daily Post, March 28, 1896
Houston Daily Post, May 21, 1896
Houston Daily Post, October 4, 1896
Houston Daily Post, November 27, 1896
Houston Daily Post, February 11, 1897
Houston Daily Post, February 23, 1897
Houston Daily Post, February 24, 1897
Houston Daily Post, March 1, 1897
Houston Daily Post, March 7, 1897
Houston Daily Post, April 3, 1897
Houston Daily Post, May 8, 1897
Houston Daily Post, June 13, 1897
Houston Daily Post, June 15, 1897

Houston Daily Post, June 18, 1897
Houston Daily Post, June 25, 1897
Houston Daily Post, June 26, 1897
Houston Daily Post, July 10, 1897
Houston Daily Post, May 28, 1898
Houston Daily Post, June 8, 1898
Houston Daily Post, October 21, 1898
Houston Daily Post, November 18, 1898
Houston Daily Post, November 26, 1898
Houston Daily Post, December 3, 1898
Houston Daily Post, March 17, 1899
Houston Daily Post, March 20, 1899
Houston Daily Post, March 24, 1899
Houston Daily Post, March 25, 1899
Houston Daily Post, April 1, 1899
Houston Daily Post, April 29, 1899
Houston Daily Post, June 16, 1899
Houston Daily Post, June 20, 1899
Houston Daily Post, July 7, 1899
Houston Daily Post, July 19, 1899
Houston Daily Post, July 21, 1899
Houston Daily Post, July 29, 1899
Houston Daily Post, August 31, 1899
Houston Daily Post, November 11, 1899
Houston Daily Post, November 25, 1899
Houston Daily Post, January 7, 1900
Houston Daily Post, July 22, 1900
Houston Daily Post, July 28, 1900
Houston Daily Post, April 2, 1901
Houston Daily Post, June 6, 1901
Houston Daily Post, August 2, 1901
Houston Daily Post, October 23, 1901
Houston Daily Post, October 26, 1901
Houston Daily Post, January 11, 1902
Houston Daily Post, February 1, 1902
Houston Daily Post, August 16, 1902
Houston Daily Post, May 27, 1902
Houston Daily Post, June 4, 1902
Houston Daily Post, October 18, 1902
Houston Daily Post, December 14, 1902
Houston Chronicle, January 14, 2001
Houston Telegraph, June 22, 1871
The Jackson Sentinel, (Maquoketa, Iowa), January 9, 1873
The Jimplecute, December 3, 1904
The Jimplecute, November 17, 1906
The Jimplecute, November 24, 1906
The Jimplecute, December 1, 1906

The Jimplecute, April 3, 1908
Johnson County Review, July 3, 1896
Johnson County Review, August 3, 1900
Kansas City Star, (Kansas, MO), December 22, 1888
The Knox County News, (Knox, TX), March 12, 1909
Laredo Times, October 17, 1892
Laredo Times, January 7, 1912
Ledger and Texan (San Antonio), June 30, 1860
The Lampasas Dispatch, May 23, 1878
Macon Telegraph, (Macon, Ga.), November 14, 1880
Mississippi Free Trader, (Natchez, MS), March 5, 1851
National Aegis, (Worchester, MA), August 21, 1850
New York Herald, (New York, NY), March 27, 1880
New York Herald, August 9, 1879
New York Herald, May 1, 1880
New York Times, January 23, 1858
New York Times, April 25, 1873
New York Times, July 8, 1879
New York Times, August 22, 1879
New York Times, March 27, 1880
New York Times, April 30, 1904
The Northern Standard, February 17, 1844
The Orange Daily Tribune, (Orange, TX) May 30, 1903
Palestine Daily Herald, February 13, 1904
Palestine Daily Herald, May 3, 1904
Palestine Daily Herald, April 23, 1904
Palestine Daily Herald, April 26, 1904
Palestine Daily Herald. April 30, 1904
Palestine Daily Herald, May 25, 1904
Palestine Daily Herald, May 28, 1904
Palestine Daily Herald, November 28, 1904
Palestine Daily Herald, December 2, 1904
Palestine Daily Herald, December 22, 1904
Palestine Daily Herald, January 26, 1905
Palestine Daily Herald, May 20, 1905
Palestine Daily Herald, July 8, 1905
Palestine Daily Herald, September 2, 1905
Palestine Daily Herald, October 2, 1905
Palestine Daily Herald, October 9, 1905
Palestine Daily Herald, October 10, 1905
Palestine Daily Herald, October 11, 1905
Palestine Daily Herald, October 18, 1905
Palestine Daily Herald, December 11, 1905
Palestine Daily Herald, December 15, 1905
Palestine Daily Herald, December 27, 1905
Palestine Daily Herald, March 30, 1906
Palestine Daily Herald, July 13, 1906

Palestine Daily Herald, November 22, 1906
Palestine Daily Herald, November 30, 1906
Palestine Daily Herald, December 7, 1906
Palestine Daily Herald, December 13, 1906
Palestine Daily Herald, January 18, 1907
Palestine Daily Herald, February 1, 1907
The Paris News, May 27, 1951
The Paris News, May 24, 1979
The Paris News, September 18, 1998
The Paris News, September 21, 1998
The Paris News, February 24, 2000
Plain Dealer, (Cleveland, OH), August 30, 1879
Port Arthur Daily News, May 10, 1921
Union, (Houston, TX), December 20, 1870
Union, July 31, 1971
The Reformer, (Austin, TX), July 8, 1871
The Richmond Democrat, (Richmond, TX), October 6, 1888
Richmond Whig, (Richmond, VA), June 5, 1855
San Angelo Press, November 22, 1906
San Antonio Daily Express, January 16, 1886
San Antonio Daily Express, January 12, 1895
San Antonio Daily Express, October 8, 1898
San Antonio Daily Express, April 29, 1899
San Antonio Daily Express, October 28, 1899
San Antonio Daily Express, March 28, 1908
San Antonio Daily Light, October 27, 1888
San Antonio Daily Light, March 18, 1896
San Antonio Daily Light, July 30, 1897
San Antonio Daily Light, July 26, 1899
San Antonio Daily Light, October 27, 1899
San Antonio Daily Light, December 18, 1904
San Antonio Daily Light, November 30, 1906
San Antonio Daily Light, April 3, 1908
San Antonio Daily Light, May 23, 1908
San Antonio Daily Light, June 23, 1908
San Antonio Daily Light, February 6, 1909
San Antonio Daily Light, March 26, 1913
San Antonio Daily Light, August 19, 1913
San Antonio Daily Light, August 22, 1913
San Antonio Daily Light, September 26, 1913
San Antonio Daily Light, September 24, 1922
San Antonio Sunday Light, April 2, 1899
San Antonio Evening News, February 26, 1920
San Antonio Evening News, February 23, 1923
San Antonio Express, November 10, 1900
San Antonio Express, April 9, 1902
San Antonio Express, September 18, 1902

San Antonio Express, September 20, 1902
San Antonio Express, November 17, 1904
San Antonio Express, January 3, 1912
San Antonio Express, February 23, 1923
San Antonio Express, April 8, 1923
San Antonio Gazette, April 2, 1907
San Antonio Gazette, July 10, 1907
San Antonio Light, July 31, 1908
San Antonio Light, June 12, 1909
San Antonio Light, January 6, 1922
The San Saba County News, May 15, 1893
The San Saba County News, May 19, 1893
The San Saba Weekly News, September 25, 1891
The San Saba Weekly News, April 8, 1892
The San Saba Weekly News, August 11, 1893
The San Saba Weekly News, September 25, 1893
The Schulenburg Sticker, (Schulenburg, TX) January 14, 1909
The Schulenburg Sticker, July 9, 1908
The Schulenburg Sticker, March 17, 1916
Shenango Valley (Greenville, Pa), October 26, 1888
Sherman Daily Democrat, May 4, 1922
Sherman Daily Register, July 8, 1892
Sherman Daily Register, September 3, 1900
Shiner Gazette, August 3, 1893
Shiner Gazette, November 23, 1893
Shiner Gazette, May 31, 1894
Shiner Gazette, August 23, 1894
Shiner Gazette, July 11, 1895
Shiner Gazette, September 19, 1895
Shiner Gazette, October 31, 1895
Shiner Gazette, September 10, 1896
Shiner Gazette, June 1, 1898
Shiner Gazette, June 12, 1898
Shiner Gazette, June 15, 1898
Shiner Gazette, October 12, 1898
Shiner Gazette, November 30, 1898
Shiner Gazette, November 8, 1899
Shiner Gazette, January 17, 1900
Shiner Gazette, April 7, 1901
Shiner Gazette, August 7, 1901
Shiner Gazette, November 27, 1901
Shiner Gazette, April 15, 1903
Shiner Gazette, May 20, 1903
Shiner Gazette, June 3, 1903
Shiner Gazette, December 9, 1903
Shiner Gazette, October 4, 1905
Shiner Gazette, October 11, 1905

Shiner Gazette, July 4, 1906
Shiner Gazette, October 24, 1906
Shiner Gazette, December 12, 1906
Shiner Gazette, December 19, 1906
Shiner Gazette, February 6, 1907
Shiner Gazette, February 20, 1907
Shiner Gazette, April 9, 1907
Shiner Gazette, July 2, 1908
Shiner Gazette, February 25, 1909
Shiner Gazette, October 22, 1902
Shiner Gazette, May 4, 1904
Simi Weekly Wisconsin, (Milwaukee, Wisc.), Aug. 26, 1874
The Southern Mercury, (Dallas, TX), March 31, 1904
The Southern Mercury, April 28, 1904
The Southern Mercury, May 5, 1904
The Southern Mercury, June 2, 1904
St. Louis Republic, (St. Louis, Mo.), December 22, 1888
St. Louis Republic, February 19, 1889
St. Louis Republic, April 6, 1889
Springfield Republican, (Springfield, MA), August 2, 1855
Springfield Republican, December 24, 1856
The Standard, (Clarksville, TX), June 9, 1848
The Standard, February 17, 1855
The Standard, June 9, 1855
The State Herald, (Mexia, TX), August 22, 1902
Telegraph and Texas Register, (Houston, TX) March 24, 1838
Telegraph and Texas Register, March 31, 1838
The Terrell Times Star, March 23, 1900
The Texas Almanac, January 10, 1863
The Texas Ranger, June 16, 1855
The Texas Ranger, July 14, 1855
Texas State Gazette, October 7, 1854
Times Picayune, (New Orleans, LA), June 1, 1866
Times Picayune, November 26, 1898
Tulsa World, (Tulsa, OK), September 18, 1918
Tulsa World, September 25, 1918
The Victoria Advocate, December 28, 1986
The Victoria Daily Advocate, December 15, 1914
The Victoria Daily Advocate, May 22, 1915

The Victoria Daily Advocate, July 3, 1915
The Victoria Daily Advocate, August 12, 1916
The Victoria Daily Advocate, August 14, 1916
The Waco Daily Examiner, September 20, 1878
The Waco Daily Examiner, September 21, 1878
The Waco Daily Examiner, February 4, 1882
The Waco Daily Examiner, February 18, 1882
The Waco Daily Examiner, August 19, 1882
The Waco Daily Examiner, January 6, 1883
The Waco Daily Examiner, July 6, 1883
The Waco Daily Examiner, July 7, 1883
The Waco Daily Examiner, March 21, 1885
The Waco Daily Examiner, May 23, 1885
The Waco Daily Examiner, January 16, 1886
The Waco Daily Examiner, April 17, 1886
The Waco Evening News, July 16, 1888
The Waco Evening News, May 16, 1892
The Waco Evening News, April 5, 1893
The Waco Evening News, August 5, 1893
The Waco Evening News, January 13, 1894
The Waco Times-Herald, January 25, 1901
The Waco Times-Herald, October 26, 1901
The Waco Times-Herald, January 11, 1902
The Waco Times-Herald, July 30, 1923
The Weekly Enterprise, (Cleburne, TX), February 11, 1904
Weekly Houston Telegraph, May 4, 1838
Weimar Mercury, January 20, 1900
Weimar Mercury, January 27, 1900
Weimar Mercury, October 21, 1905
Weimar Mercury, February 20, 1907
Weimar Mercury, May 4, 1907
Weimar Mercury, November 11, 1910
Wichita Daily News, April 4, 1908
Wichita Daily Times, August 11, 1912
Wichita Weekly Times, May 15, 1914
Williamson County Sun, September 16, 1886
Williamson County Sun, August 11, 1904
Williamson County Sun, September 2, 1905
Williamson County Sun, April 5, 1906

About the Author

West Gilbreath is a career law enforcement officer with more than thirty years of experience. West first began his career with the Dona Ana County Sheriff's Department, Las Cruces, New Mexico as a deputy patrolman. In 2001, West retired as the lieutenant, and commander over the Criminal Investigations Division. He and wife Sabrina moved to North Texas to start second careers, and they reside near Denton.

West joined the University of North Texas Police Department in Denton, and is the captain over the Criminal Investigations of that law enforcement agency and has been crossed commissioned a Special Deputy U.S. Marshal.

West is a graduate of the New Mexico State Law Enforcement Academy, Santa Fe, the F.B.I. National Academy at Quantico, Virginia, and the National Forensic Academy, University of Tennessee, at Knoxville. He holds a Texas Master Peace Officer license and is a Police Instructor.

When not researching lawmen and outlaws of the Old West, West is an avid law enforcement badge collector who collects New Mexico and Texas sheriff badges and other law enforcement and Old West memorabilia.

His first book, *Death on the Gallows*, published by High Lonesome Press, detailed the men and women executed by hanging in New Mexico from 1847 – 1923.

www.ingramcontent.com/pod-product-compliance
Lightning Source LLC
Chambersburg PA
CBHW080833230426
43665CB00021B/2833